# Policies and Persons

## A CASEBOOK IN BUSINESS ETHICS

# Policies and Persons

## A CASEBOOK IN BUSINESS ETHICS

SECOND EDITION

**John B. Matthews**
Graduate School of Business Administration
Harvard University

**Kenneth E. Goodpaster**
Graduate School of Business
University of St. Thomas

**Laura L. Nash**
Graduate School of Management
Boston University

## McGraw-Hill, Inc.

New York   St. Louis   San Francisco   Auckland
Bogotá   Caracas   Hamburg   Lisbon
London   Madrid   Mexico   Milan   Montreal
New Delhi   Paris   San Juan   São Paulo
Singapore   Sydney   Tokyo   Toronto

## POLICIES AND PERSONS

A Casebook in Business Ethics

2 3 4 5 6 7 8 9 0  **DOH  DOH**  9 5 4 3 2 1

ISBN 0-07-040999-4

This book was set in Times Roman by University Graphics, Inc.
The editors were Cynthia Ward, Judith R. Cornwell, and
David A. Damstra; the production supervisor was Louise Karam.
The cover was designed by Carla Bauer.
New drawings were done by J&R Services, Inc.
R. R. Donnelley & Sons Company was printer and binder.

**Library of Congress Cataloging-in-Publication Data**

Matthews, John Bowers.
    Policies and persons: a casebook in business ethics / John B.
    Matthews, Kenneth E. Goodpaster, Laura L. Nash. — 2nd ed.
        p.      cm.
    Includes bibliographical references.
    ISBN 0-07-040999-4
    1. Business ethics—Case studies.      I. Goodpaster, Kenneth E.,
(date).      II. Nash, Laura L.      III. Title.
HF5387.M385        1991
174′.4—dc20                                                    90-6534

**John B. Matthews** is the Joseph C. Wilson Professor of Business Administration at the Harvard Business School, where he has taught since 1949. He holds an A.B. and an honorary LL.D. from Bowdoin College, and received his M.B.A. and D.C.S. degrees from the Harvard Business School. Professor Matthews has taught a course entitled "Ethical Aspects of Corporate Policy" in the school's Advanced Management Program and the Program for Management Development, and teaches "Managerial Decision Making and Ethical Values: An Introduction" in the first-year M.B.A. program. He has also taught in a number of executive programs and is currently serving as Faculty Chairman of the Advanced Management Programme at Oxford University's Templeton College. He has served as a consultant to a number of companies and presently serves on the boards of directors of Ampco-Pittsburgh Corporation, Guest Services Inc., and Johnson Partners. Professor Matthews has written a number of books in addition to this volume.

**Kenneth E. Goodpaster** holds the David and Barbara Koch Chair in Business Ethics at the University of St. Thomas in St. Paul, Minnesota. He received his Ph.D. in philosophy at the University of Michigan and holds an A.M. in philosophy from that school and an A.B. in mathematics from the University of Notre Dame. Professor Goodpaster taught graduate and undergraduate philosophy at Notre Dame before joining the faculty of the Harvard Business School in 1980, where he taught both M.B.A. candidates and business executives until 1990. His research in applied philosophy, focusing on the dynamic relationships among three levels of ethical analysis—the person, the organization, and the capitalist system—has led to course development, journal publications, and other recent books in addition to this text.

**Laura L. Nash** is Adjunct Associate Professor at Boston University School of Management, and Research Coordinator at the Institute for the Study of Economic Culture. She earned her Ph.D. in classics under a Danforth Fellowship at Harvard University. Professor Nash has taught at Brown, Brandeis, and Harvard University's Graduate School of Business Administration in addition to her consulting work with many of the nation's top corporations. She has also served as consultant to the Business Roundtable's Task Force on Business Ethics and to The Conference Board. In addition to this text and journal publications, Professor Nash has authored *Good Intentions Aside: Money and Morality in Business* (Cambridge, MA: Harvard Business School Press, 1990).

*for Margaret, Harriet, and Tom*

# CONTENTS

## PART 2

# Corporate Values: Looking Inward    71

How to develop a comprehensive ethics policy for a global
enterprise, even when local ethical norms may differ.

Some of the challenges faced in the implementation of a global
business conduct policy.

# Appendixes

A brief introduction to some of the major concepts of moral
philosophy and suggestions as to how they may be used in
analyzing cases.

A brief discussion of case (A) is presented so that students who are
new to the case method of instruction may familiarize themselves
with an approach to case analysis.

A bibliography of anthologies, books, and articles relevant to
business ethics and moral philosophy.

Our goal in this book is to provide a learning tool of extraordinary flexibility, containing high-quality case research on topics useful to both today's managers and students of management. The approximately 60 cases are grouped into four categories: (1) Personal Values, (2) Corporate Values: Looking Inward, (3) Corporate Values: Looking Outward, and (4) Corporate Values: International Business. Thus, they are organized to take the reader from individual decisions made on a personal level to corporate policies decided on the global scale.

The topics of the cases were chosen sometimes for their timeliness or fertility, and sometimes simply "because they were there" and reflected important realities of the business environment. We do not claim that they exhaust the field of business ethics, but we do believe that they illustrate the main types of issues encountered in management practice. New to this edition are twenty cases and background notes, covering such issues as industrial espionage, insider trading, hostile takeover, regulatory conflict, sexual harassment, responsible marketing strategies, environmental problems, investment in South Africa, intellectual property ownership, and other ethical concerns in global business policies.

We and the other contributors to this collection developed most of the cases over a ten-year period (1980–1990) in the field rather than in the library. Some are short, only a page or two. Others are fairly lengthy. Still others are divided into parts to provide "sequenced" learning opportunities. The shades of gray that are realistic in ethical decision making often require attention to depth and detail in a case. We have been guided by our sense of how much information was needed to achieve learning objectives, not by any predetermined standards of length or format.

The cases have been tested in the classroom at the Harvard Business School (both in the M.B.A. program and in programs for middle- and upper-level managers) and, in the first edition, found acceptance in academic programs in colleges and universities throughout the United States. Sometimes they were supplemented by other readings, role-played, or used for written assignments and examinations. For the most part, however, they have been used just as they are, to stimulate vigorous dialogue and self-discovery.

We have chosen not to accompany the cases with text. There is a very good reason for this decision. It has been our experience that as the field of business ethics has evolved, the number of different types of persons with an interest in the field has increased. Academics schooled in business administration have undertaken studies in ethics; philosophers and humanists have pursued studies in business management; and managers have undertaken both. As a result, business ethics courses have proliferated in schools of business, departments of philosophy, colleges of arts and letters, and corporate in-house education programs. It would be difficult to make accurate assumptions about the kinds of discourse with which educators in these various fields would feel comfortable. The permutations of this basic problem convinced us in the end that the case studies were the principal items of value that we wished to convey.

New to this edition is an Introduction that provides some background on the case method for the student. It defines the method, gives a brief history, describes the roles of student and teacher, elaborates the goals of the method, and shows how the method applies in the field of ethics. The student who has read this Introduction will be well versed in the rationale of the case method and will have a clear idea of what is expected of him or her.

Given the diversity in background and interests of those using the book, we believe the items in the Appendix are important: "Some Avenues for Ethical Analysis in General Management" is a brief introductory note on philosophical ethics, and "Illustrative Case Analysis for Consolidated Foods Corporation" gives students who are new to the case method an approach to case analysis. The Selected Bibliography directs readers to further readings relevant to business ethics and to moral philosophy.

An Instructor's Manual accompanies this text. In addition to teaching notes for each of the cases, it includes follow-up cases, sample syllabi for shorter and longer courses, and a summary matrix indicating topics or themes in each of the cases.

It is our hope that this book can be used not only in advanced undergraduate and graduate courses in schools of business but also in departments of philosophy and religious studies, in other humanities programs, and in corporate management education. It is also our hope that the cases are themselves important and interesting enough to merit a more general readership both inside and outside the academy. There are, frankly, many thoughtful people who underestimate the complexity of the decisions—economic and ethical—that confront business executives.

## ACKNOWLEDGMENTS

This book of cases draws heavily upon two types of sources. First are the companies, other organizations, and people that furnished information for the cases. Second are the people who made possible the processes by which the cases were gathered and gave support and encouragement to the processes and to us. We wish here to acknowledge, with deep gratitude, those many contributions.

Each situation in this book is taken from the "real world." Though the names of many companies and people have been disguised, the fact of disguises has, in no way, we believe, lessened the reality of the case situations. We are grateful to the companies and individuals—disguised or not—who contributed time, information, and thought to the cases. We cannot thank each individually, but a modest measure of our gratitude may be conveyed by acknowledging that, without those contributions, there would be no casebook.

Most of the cases in this book are Harvard Business School cases. But friends from other schools and organizations have added to the quality of the book and reduced our burden by giving us permission to use cases prepared by them. We are grateful to the following for permissions: Louis Banks (Massachusetts Institute of Technology) for a condensed version of his case on the Firestone 500 radial tire, and John Hennessey (formerly of Dartmouth College) for "Viking Air Compressor, Inc." To acknowledge new contributors, we wish to thank the National Wildlife Federation Corporate Conservation Council for its gracious permission to use its case entitled "Du Pont Freon Products Division," and the Council on Foundations for "Dayton Hudson Corporation: Conscience and Control."

Colleagues and friends at the Harvard Business School have been similarly helpful. We thank David Bell and Norman Berg for the American Cyanamid and Environmental Pressures cases, and Eliza Collins and Timothy Blodgett for the *Harvard Business Review* article on sexual harassment. We also thank Bart van Dissel and Thomas Piper for the Martha McCaskey and Poletown Dilemma cases, and Richard Vietor, who collaborated on the Du Pont Freon case with the National Wildlife Federation. Samuel Hayes has allowed us to use the Mebel Doran & Company case, and Joseph L. Badaracco, Jr., the IBM-Fujitsu case. In terms of case preparation we would indeed be remiss were we not to acknowledge our debt to Randel S. Carlock, Joanne Ciulla, Dekkers Davidson, Anne Delehunt, John Keller, Robert G. Kennedy, Sharon Kleefield, Michael Lovdal, Robert Massie, Richard Post, Forest Reinhardt, and David Whiteside, who wrote or contributed to the writing of several of the cases. Finally, the short cases on sexual harassment were written by three students: James Garvey, Ina-Lee Block, and Cherri Thomas.

Many others at the Harvard Business School have helped to make this book possible. Directors of the division of research have made time and funds available for case-writing purposes. Joanne Segal, director of the publishing division, has assisted and encouraged us, as has Audrey Barrett, permissions editor, publishing division. In the preface to the first edition of this book we made special mention of Kenneth Andrews, now an emeritus professor. At that time we called him a friend, mentor, critic, and encourager to each and all of us, and he continues to be all those things and more. J. Ronald Fox and Malcolm Salter, area chairmen, have our gratitude. Last, but by no means least, we thank former dean Lawrence Fouraker and John McArthur, the current dean, both of whom have continued the Harvard Business School's commitments to socially and ethically responsible corporations and managers.

Manuscripts require typing, editing, retyping, proofreading, and a variety of things both substantive and procedural. Many people have helped in many ways in these regards. Meredith Carder, a good friend and secretary without peer, has managed these processes with consummate grace, skill, and concern. Others who have helped have been Kathleen Chaudry, Rose Giacobbe, Leonie Morales, and Judith Pilgram.

We dedicated the first edition of this book to our spouses Margaret, Harriet, and Tom. We owed them much then. We owe them much now. They have our thanks, our respect, and our love.

John B. Matthews
Kenneth E. Goodpaster
Laura L. Nash

# Policies and Persons

A CASEBOOK
IN BUSINESS
ETHICS

# Introduction: The Case Method

James Russell Lowell once remarked: "One thorn of experience is worth a whole wilderness of warning."[1] Countless other aphorisms throughout the ages have made the same point: There is no substitute for experience. We can't learn to ski or drive a car by reading a book. We can't picture the scenery of a trip by looking at a map. We can't possibly imagine the fragrance of a flower by simply knowing its chemical composition. Nor can we arrive at an answer to a real-life ethical dilemma by standing back and reciting theoretical principles: We must put ourselves into the actual situation in order to decide what action is appropriate or desirable. That is the idea behind the case method. In the words of one discerning commentator, Charles I. Gragg:

> . . . a case typically is a record of a business situation that *actually* has been faced by business executives, together with surrounding facts, opinions, and prejudices upon which executive decisions had to depend. These real and particularized cases are presented to students for considered analysis, open discussion, and final decision as to the type of action that should be taken.[2]

The key word in this quote is "students." Cases, by themselves, are inanimate. Studies of the sort presented in this book must come to life in the classroom in order to be vehicles of learning. The case method is built around the student; it is a *learner-centered* educational tool. Many students find it takes a while to get used to this idea. They are accustomed to absorbing what a teacher tells them. For most of their academic life, they have been passive receivers of the accumulated wisdom and experience of those teaching them. The case method, however, requires the students to be

---

[1]James Russell Lowell, "Shakespeare Once More," *Among My Books,* (Boston: Fields, Osgood & Co., 1870). Quoted in C. Roland Christensen, "Teaching with Cases at the Harvard Business School," in *Teaching and the Case Method* (Cambridge, MA: Harvard Business School Publishing Division, 1987), p. 41.

[2]Charles I. Gragg, "Because Wisdom Can't Be Told," *Harvard Alumni Bulletin,* October 19, 1940. Reprinted in John B. Matthews, Kenneth E. Goodpaster, and Laura L. Nash, *Policies and Persons* (New York: McGraw-Hill, 1985), p. 485.

active participants in the learning process; if they are not, the method cannot succeed. As Gragg notes: "The outstanding virtue of the case system is that it is suited to inspiring activity, under realistic conditions, on the part of the students; it takes them out of the role of passive absorbers and makes them partners in the joint process of learning and furthering learning."[3]

It is important to note that the cases presented in this book have no "ideal solutions," even though most of them require decisions. There are no "answer keys" hidden in the Instructor's Manual. The value of the cases lies in the reconstructions they afford of moral dilemmas in business. Readers are invited to internalize the situations, struggle with the problems, and make decisions. They are called upon not simply to pass external judgments of right and wrong, good and bad, virtue and vice, but rather to place themselves in the middle of the practical and moral concerns that bombard the manager every day. Essentially, it is a process of learning by doing.

This style of open-ended participatory learning is nothing new. In ancient Greece, Socrates engaged his pupils in active discussions meant to elicit from them judgments and insights. Talmudic scholars practice the method to this day. But use of the case method in business study, at least by these comparisons, is relatively recent.

## HISTORY OF THE CASE METHOD

The case method was first introduced in the classroom at the Harvard Law School in the 1870s by its dean, Christopher Columbus Langdell (an apt name for an explorer in teaching methods). Langdell intended to replace textbooks with casebooks throughout the whole law curriculum. His point was that a student of law could dissect cases and develop hypotheses and test principles, as any natural scientist might. Moreover, studying cases and sorting out the principles on which judges have made

their decisions provided far more relevant training for being a lawyer than just receiving the distilled wisdom of the day and learning legal theory.

When the Harvard Business School opened in 1908, its dean, Edwin F. Gay, decided to use the case method as a means to link business students with the realities of the business world they would soon encounter. The school's statement of purpose called for giving "each individual student a practical and professional training suitable to the particular business he plans to enter." As C. Roland Christensen notes, the times and the setting were "hospitable to Dean Gay's dream." Converging were:

> . . . a vocation [business administration] struggling to take small steps toward formalizing its practice to meet the needs of an increasingly complicated industrial society; an absence of interest on the part of traditional academia in meeting these needs; a great university willing to experiment; and a new school committed to creating new ways of educating young people "for the oldest of the arts," to use [Harvard] President Lowell's words, "and the newest of the professions."[4]

At first the cases used at the Harvard Business School were just about anything teachers could get their hands on: legal documents, business reports, business problems they were familiar with. The instructors soon began to prefer using the problems as a basis of classroom discussions, and asked business acquaintances to write up cases and lead the discussions. Gradually the development of cases became more systematic as business schools sent people out to research and write up business cases. Today the generation of cases is a field of its own, resulting in complex educational tools based on intensive research. These sophisticated analyses are more appropriate to some

---

[3]Gragg, "Because Wisdom Can't Be Told," in *Policies and Persons* (1985), p. 488.

[4]C. Roland Christensen, "Teaching with Cases at the Harvard Business School," in *Teaching and the Case Method* (Cambridge, MA: Harvard Business School Publishing Division, 1987), p. 23.

business courses than to others, however. A course involving technical purchasing may require a case that includes internal company data, external industry data, and a great deal of supporting technical and economic material, whereas a business ethics case can be "as simple" as who should be promoted between two equally experienced and qualified candidates. The facts may be "simple" and the laws regarding discrimination "clear," but the issues and decisions are often apt to be far less so.

The case method is now widely recognized as the most "practical" and "professional" way of educating future business managers. Though use of the case method may be widespread, the success of the method rests on how well teachers and students fulfill their respective roles.

## THE ROLE OF TEACHERS AND STUDENTS

Perhaps the most important requirement of the instructor is willingness to learn, to be a student as well as a teacher. As Gragg puts it: "Not all the teaching should be done by the teacher. Not all the learning should be done by the students."[5] Teachers have the responsibility of assigning cases for discussion, provoking reasoned argument, guiding the discussion to cover important points, keeping the proceedings under control, and evaluating the students' individual contributions with an open mind.

For the most part the instructor sparks the students' participation by asking pointed questions, by clarifying the students' positions and identifying unstated assumptions, and, most important, by requiring the students to take the part of the decision maker and formulate a plan of action. It is tempting for instructors to reveal what they know and to point out what they consider the right way to go in the discussion of the case, thus saving time and effort. But this approach does not contribute to the students' ability to develop judgment and insight. Neither the teacher who comes up with the "right

answer" nor the teacher who tries to force a consensus within the classroom serves the case method well.[6] The teacher with patience, restraint, and open-mindedness does.

The fact that the teacher gives up center stage to the students in the classroom discussion does not mean that his or her role is unimportant. In fact, teaching by the case method is an art, requiring both craftsmanship and imagination. Professor Kenneth Andrews gives a clear idea of what is expected of the teacher:

> The instructor provides the impromptu service which any group discussion requires. He keeps the proceedings orderly. He should be able to ask questions which invite advance in group thinking and at the same time reveal the relevance of the talk that has gone before. He needs the ability to weave together the threads of individual contribution into a pattern which not only he but his class can perceive. He needs the sense of timing which tells him that a discussion is not moving fast enough to make good use of available time or is racing away from the comprehension of half the class. He knows what to do on such occasions. He exercises control over an essentially "undirected" activity, but at the same time he keeps out of the way, lest he prevent the class from making discoveries new also to him. Since unpredictable developments always distinguish real learning, he examines his class rather than his subject.[7]

The students have significant responsibilities of their own in the case method approach. As we noted previously, the student who is introduced to this method has to shed the role of "passive absorber." Students can no longer look to teachers for answers but instead must rely on their own problem-solving powers to identify possible solutions to particular cases. Perhaps the best way to convey what is ex-

---

[5]Charles I. Gragg, "Teachers Must Also Learn," *Harvard Educational Review,* **10** (1940), p. 30. Reprinted in Christensen, *Teaching and the Case Method.*

[6]Gragg, "Because Wisdom Can't Be Told," in *Policies and Persons* (1985), p. 488.
[7]Kenneth R. Andrews, "The Role of the Instructor in the Case Method," in Malcolm P. McNair, ed., *The Case Method at the Harvard Business School* (New York: McGraw-Hill, 1954), pp. 98–99. Quoted in Christensen, "Teaching with Cases at the Harvard Business School," p. 31.

pected of the student is to listen to the thoughts of one young woman who looked back on her experience with the case method:

> I entered the battle of the case method unarmed. The routines and tools that had allowed me to survive years of schooling no longer helped me; my own study habits were useless— counterproductive, in fact. For example, I had always been a diligent student, priding myself on completing the assignments I was given.... As a student in a case class, though, my assignments were open-ended: prepare the case and develop recommendations. I was supposed to decide how to approach the material, but it was hard to know how much to do, hard to know where to stop.... I had always been an outliner, finding that outlining helped me see the structure of the material. But cases by their very nature could not be outlined. They were not books, logically organized by the author to facilitate my understanding....
>
> Like a "real" manager in a "real" business situation, it was now my job to impose a meaningful framework on the unruliness of case facts. I had to search for the key nuggets of data, distinguishing central facts from peripheral ones. I had to sort out the conflicting explanations and alternatives presented to me, and arrive at a reasonable recommendation for action.
>
> I understand the importance of these skills in the real world. But that understanding didn't make the skills any easier to develop.... I rarely could walk into class secure in the knowledge that I had "cracked" the case. The uncertainty was frightening.[8]

This experience tells us a lot about the student's role. First, it is necessary to be willing to give up old study habits that are counterproductive. Second, the student must spend time with the case and locate the "facts" that are particularly relevant. Central facts must be separated from peripheral ones; conflicting explanations must be sorted out. Then the student must pull the information together in such a way that a possible plan of action emerges.

Preparation is vital to the case method but so too is what goes on inside the classroom. Students have to participate in the discussion. They must be prepared to present their recommendations in the case and defend them against criticism from other classmates. They also must be willing to accept criticism when warranted and to learn from others.

Students frequently experience anxiety or discouragement in their first encounters with the case method—the "frightening" uncertainty referred to by the student quoted above. It is a challenge to think actively, to make independent judgments, to defend these against others. Gragg finds students typically pass through three phases as they adjust to the case method. In the first stage they feel discouraged, unsure of their own contributions, and convinced of the superiority of their classmates' arguments. Gradually they learn that they can draw on one another's ideas in working out solutions—what Gragg calls "the pleasure of group pooling of intellectual efforts." In the final stage they recognize that no one, not even the instructor, knows the "best" answer, and that their own ideas are equally valid.[9]

## GOALS OF THE CASE METHOD

In describing what constitutes a "good case," Professor Paul Lawrence provides a glimpse of some of the goals of the case method. He calls a good case one that brings "a chunk of reality into the classroom." It presents "stubborn facts that must be faced in real-life situations." It also serves as "an anchor on academic flights of speculation."[10]

[8]Robin Hacke, *The Case Method: A Student Perspective,* unpublished working paper, Harvard Business School, 1986. Quoted in Christensen, "Teaching with Cases at the Harvard Business School," pp. 29–30.

[9]Gragg, "Because Wisdom Can't Be Told," in *Policies and Persons* (1985), pp. 489–490.
[10]Paul Lawrence, "The Preparation of Case Material," in Kenneth R. Andrews, ed., *The Case Method of Teaching Human Relations and Administration* (Cambridge, MA: Harvard University Press, 1953), p. 215. Quoted in Christensen, "Teaching with Cases at the Harvard Business School," p. 26.

Perhaps the primary goal of the case method is to develop in the student the qualities of understanding, independent thinking, judgment, and communication that are needed in the business world. That goal is accomplished by facing the stubborn facts embedded in the chunk of reality. It is not accomplished by repeating theoretical principles or taking off on flights of speculation; students must deal with the "as is," not the "might be."[11] The discussion of a business case should lead the student into an understanding of how to analyze and act on a specific situation. It is not intended to give rise to generalizations or codification of principles, as discussion of a legal case does. Over time, the study of a number of cases might enable a student to derive some generalizations, but these should be used with care and be tested frequently against the facts of a case.

The point is that the case method enables a student to see problems and analyze them; it is a matter of knowing *how* more than knowing *that*. The student who has not studied cases in school but has only absorbed textbook answers enters the business world unprepared for its unpredictability and caprice. This state of mind is captured in a limerick:

> A student of business with tact
> Absorbed many answers he lacked.
> But acquiring a job,
> He said with a sob,
> "How *does* one fit answer to fact?"[12]

Another goal of the case method is twofold: to develop the student's confidence in his or her own ability and judgment, but at the same time to instill humility through learning to give credence to another's point of view. These, too, are qualities needed in the business arena.

A specific goal of the case method when it is applied to problems of ethics is the develop-

ment of ethical insight—a basic understanding of what is right and what is wrong in our behavior. Although cases in ethics do not necessarily serve as a source for generalizations, they can be used to *test* our generalizations and our moral framework. Business ethics cases cannot be resolved easily. They require the decision maker to have a moral understanding, a judgment of what is right and wrong, in order to reach a conclusion. This moral framework is not something that can be taught, but it does not hurt to supplement cases with investigations of ethical theory. Let us turn now to a closer look at the case method as it applies to business ethics.

## THE CASE METHOD APPLIED TO ETHICS

The times are well suited for the study of business ethics. Perhaps never before in history have organizations or institutions played a more significant role in the lives and livelihoods of individuals. Private and public institutions have enveloped, if not replaced, individual persons as the focus of power and responsibility. The challenge of business ethics is to apply moral understanding to this personal and organizational reality. Interest in business ethics has grown dramatically over the past two decades. Business managers, academicians, and the general public have come to appreciate the importance of the relationship between economic excellence and ethical judgment. Several explanations have been offered as to *why* there is renewed interest in ethics: the aftereffects of Watergate, the environmental movement, concern over employees' rights, increased numbers of working women, affirmative action programs, new challenges in health and safety, insider trading scandals, competitions and comparison with European and Asian business practices. All of these have had an impact.

Many concerns addressed today under the rubric "business ethics" were dealt with in earlier decades under different names: business and society, social responsibility, human rela-

[11]Christensen, "Teaching with Cases at the Harvard Business School," p. 30.
[12]Quoted by Gragg, "Because Wisdom Can't Be Told," in *Policies and Persons* (1985), p. 489.

tions in organizations, business-government relations, international business. So there has been continuity in the study of ethics, under whatever name. What is new today is the application of principles from the humanities—from philosophy, theology, and literature—rather than just the social sciences.

Since certain terms—specifically, "ethics," "morality," "social responsibility," and "values"—come up frequently in the field of business ethics and cause confusion, it might be helpful to stipulate what we mean by such expressions. "Ethics" most often refers to a domain of inquiry, a discipline, in which matters of right and wrong, good and evil, are examined. "Morality" is what the discipline of ethics is *about:* The term refers to a pattern of thought and action in an individual, group, or society. "Social responsibility" can be misleading if it is used synonymously with "business ethics." Its domain is more limited: the relationships between business organizations and their external constituencies (consumers, government agencies, international competitors, the general public). "Social responsibility" does not deal with internal constituencies (employees, boards of directors, managers) or ethical issues not specifically tied to constituencies. "Values" are states of affairs (in the mind or in the world) to which human beings aspire, individually or collectively, from *some point of view* (political, economic, religious, scientific, artistic).

The cases used in this book are true stories of managerial decision making in value-laden situations. They are the stuff of the moral life in business. Some present situations that may seem impossible to resolve; in that eventuality they can at least serve the purpose of showing how such dilemmas might be *avoided* through better management. We have divided the cases into four parts to provide a manageable grouping.

Part 1, Personal Values, contains studies of business situations in which individual managers at various levels within various kinds and sizes of companies are faced with difficult personal decisions. Each must confront his or her own conscience and values in the context of sig-

nificant pressures, and each must make a decision that affirms certain values over others.

Part 2, Corporate Values: Looking Inward, focuses on business organizations as entities, even though individuals in the end are and must be the decision makers. In these cases, the values (stated or unstated) of corporations are tested in the internal policy arena of directors, managers, and employees.

Part 3, Corporate Values: Looking Outward, continues the focus on organizational values but does so by exploring the external policy arena of customers, suppliers, competitors, and communities.

Part 4, Corporate Values: International Business, widens the stage to global proportions. Here the ethical challenges include real or presumed conflicts of morality across countries and cultures. Such conflicts often increase the difficulty of the decisions confronting companies and their managers.

Progressively, then, the focus of the case groupings expands from individuals to organizations to whole societies, yet never totally leaves one level behind in considering the next.

## LIMITATIONS OF THE CASE METHOD

So far we have been extolling the case method as a learning strategy. But to be fair we should note that there are certain limitations to the system. No matter how true to life the situations are, they are not decided in a real-life setting. The student decision makers are subject to no risks from amateurish or unreasoned actions, nor can their conclusions be tested by subsequent developments in the business situation. As Gragg comments, "It is too much to expect that anything except experience can be exactly like experience."[13]

Another confine is that a case can never present *all* the facts in a situation. Certain facts must of necessity be selected by the case writer, who generally has a particular purpose in mind. Some "facts" are personal reports of events,

[13]Gragg, "Because Wisdom Can't Be Told," in *Policies and Persons* (1985), p. 491.

which introduce evaluation and possible bias. Some cases use press reports as a source of information, but the media sometimes have axes to grind in their accounts of corporate action (or inaction).

The student should be aware of these shortcomings, but not let them interfere with the joy of discovery that comes through the case method. Perhaps the best conclusion to this Introduction is to let some students speak for themselves:

> I learned something about myself; I really uncovered a blind spot in the way I deal with others.

• • •

> I didn't realize there were so many different ways of dealing with this "situation," and there are lots of "situations" in every case. I'm going to get away from "single track" thinking.

• • •

> I went into class with one point of view; it came under attack! In the old days I would have dropped my idea immediately, but I stuck in there, gave ground where I saw I was weak, and came away having convinced most of my section that our plan was right. I can do it![14]

[14]Quoted in Christensen, "Teaching with Cases at the Harvard Business School," p. 36.

## PART ONE

# Personal Values

Individuals bring personal values to their jobs and to the real or perceived problems of moral choice that confront them. Moral choices must be made because of tensions within individuals, between individuals, or between individuals and what they believe to be the values that drive their organizations. The series of case situations in Part 1 involve such moral decisions for people at different levels in organizations or at different stages of their careers. Those who study and discuss these cases have an opportunity to think about how the people involved in the case situations might or should solve the problems that they encounter—and also, we hope, to think introspectively and perhaps share with other discussants the ethical standards that they intend to bring to their professional work.

"Answers" to these case problems will not often come easily, nor will they be susceptible of proof as problems are in, say, geometry. But decisions must be made, for decisions are an inescapable part of life in a business career.

"Peter Green's First Day" is a short case. On his first day on the job, Peter Green is told to do something that the company's training program has not prepared him for, something that his moral standards would clearly define as wrong. The decision seems an easy one, but is it? And after Mr. Green makes his decision—whatever it may be—what should he do next?

The next case, "Dilemma of an Accountant," is more difficult; issues of right and wrong appear cloudier from the start. Daniel Potter thinks he knows what is right but seems less certain than Peter Green did. A number of issues confront him and his superiors. Matters of judgment are involved, both for Mr. Potter and for his more experienced superiors. What is at stake for Daniel as he responds to his situation, and what trade-offs may be involved? Does one "go along" in order to "get along"?

Going along and getting along are also on the mind of Martha McCaskey in the next case. Not only is Martha faced with a personal choice about how she will behave in the gray area between industrial espionage and competitor analysis; she must also consider the implications of her actions for the value system in her company.

"Ethical Quagmire" complements the Martha McCaskey case as it explores the pressures on middle managers to make ethical compromises. More than the McCaskey case, however, this one gives us a sense of the incremental character of compromise as Kevin Stoddard sinks gradually and by degrees into questionable behavior. Now in graduate school, Kevin looks back with a different perspective on his years at the management consulting firm described in the case.

The cases called "Jordan Chemicals, Inc. (A)" and "(B)" involve the president of a company. He has uncovered what he believes to be dishonesty among employees. The company is small and is suffering from an industry recession, and the amount of money involved is not insignificant. The problem may go beyond the company because outside parties are presumably at least tangentially involved. Mr. Royce, Jordan's president, faces a decision that involves a number of related and potentially conflicting pressures.

"Witness for the Corporation" also involves dishonesty among employees—but at the highest levels and with serious consequences for an electric utility and its public. This case affords a rare opportunity to examine in microcosm and in a business context some of the dynamics of character and cover-up that we saw two decades ago in Watergate.

"International Drilling Corporation" is a "whistle-blowing" situation. A middle-level executive learns, over a period of time, that some of the practices of his company are at worst illegal, and at least unethical according to his values. The basic questions that confront him have to do with whether, when, and how he should do something about those practices.

Part 1 closes with "Viking Air Compressor, Inc." George Ames has been given a mission having to do with Viking's corporate responsibility activities. As he works at it, he discovers that the mission and the contribution expected from him are less than clear. As the case ends, Mr. Ames finds himself being chastised by the president of the company, John Larsen. At issue are seeming value differences between him and Mr. Larsen, questions as to what the phrase "corporate responsibility" means, and the personal question of how he should react to Mr. Larsen's tirade. The case is useful in and of itself and also serves as a link to Part 2.

# Peter Green's First Day

Peter Green came home to his wife and new baby a dejected man. What a contrast to the morning, when he had left the apartment full of enthusiasm to tackle his first customer in his new job at Scott Carpets. And what a customer! Peabody Rug was the largest carpet retailer in the area and accounted for 15% of the entire volume of Peter's territory. When Peabody introduced a Scott product, other retailers were quick to follow with orders. So when Bob Franklin, the owner of Peabody Rug, had called District Manager John Murphy expressing interest in "Carpet Supreme," Scott's newest commercial-duty home carpet, Peter knew that a $15,000–$20,000 order was a real probability, and no small show for his first sale. And it was important to do well at the start, for John Murphy had made no bones about his scorn for the new breed of salespeople at Scott Carpet.

Murphy was of the old school: in the business since his graduation from a local high school, he had fought his way through the stiffest retail competition in the nation to be District Manager of the area at age fifty-eight. Murphy knew his textiles, and he knew his competitors' textiles. He knew his customers, and he knew how well his competitors knew his customers. Formerly, when Scott Carpet had needed to fill sales positions, it had generally raided the competition for experienced personnel, put them on a straight commission, and introduced a Scott product, other retailers were quick to follow with orders. So when Bob Murphy had been promoted eight years ago to the position of District Manager, he had passed on his sales territory to Harvey Katchorian, a sixty-year-old mill rep and son of an immigrant who had also spent his life in the carpet trade. Harvey had had no trouble keeping up his sales and had retired from the company the previous spring after forty-five years of successful service in the industry. Peter, in commercial-duty home carpet, knew that a $15,000–$20,000 order was a real probability, his original legacy to Harvey was being passed on to the best salesperson.

Peter was one of the new force of salespeople from Scott's Sales Management Program. In 1976 top management had created a training program to compensate for the industry's dearth of younger salespeople with long-term management potential. Peter, a college graduate, had entered Scott's five-month training program immediately after college and was the first graduate of the program to be assigned to John Murphy's district. Murphy had made it known to top management from the start that he did not think the training program could compensate for on-the-job experience, and he was clearly withholding optimism about Peter's prospects as a salesperson despite Peter's fine performance during the training program.

Peter had been surprised, therefore, when Murphy volunteered to accompany him on his first week of sales "to ease your transition into the territory." As they entered the office at Peabody Rug, Murphy had even seemed friendly and said reassuringly, "I think you'll get along with Bob. He's a great guy—knows the business and has been a good friend of mine for years."

Everything went smoothly. Bob liked the new line and appeared ready to place a large order with Peter the following week, but he indicated that he would require some "help on the freight costs" before committing himself definitely. Peter was puzzled and unfamiliar with the procedure, but Murphy quickly stepped in and assured Bob that Peter would be able to work something out.

After the meeting, on their way back to Scott Carpets' district office, Peter asked Murphy about freight costs. Murphy sarcastically explained the procedure: Because of its large volume, Peabody regularly "asked for a little help to cover shipping costs," and got it from all or most suppliers. Bob Franklin was simply issued a credit for defective merchandise. By claiming he had received second-quality goods, Bob was entitled to a 10%–25% discount. The discount on defective merchandise had been calculated by the company to equal roughly the cost of shipping the 500-lb. rolls back to the mill, and so it just about covered Bob's own freight costs. The practice had been going on so long that Bob demanded "freight assistance" as a matter of course before placing a large order. Obviously, the merchandise was not defective, but by making an official claim, the sales rep-

resentative could set in gear the defective-merchandise compensation system. Murphy reiterated, as if to a two-year-old, the importance of a Peabody account to any sales rep, and shrugged off the freight assistance as part of doing business with such an influential firm.

Peter stared at Murphy. "Basically, what you're asking me to do, Mr. Murphy, is to lie to the front office."

Murphy angrily replied, "Look, do you want to make it here or not? If you do, you ought to know you need Peabody's business. I don't know what kind of fancy think they taught you at college, but where I come from you don't call your boss a liar."

From the time he was a child, Peter Green had been taught not to lie or steal. He believed these principles were absolute and that one should support one's beliefs at whatever personal cost. But during college the only even remote test of his principles was his strict adherence to the honor system in taking exams.

As he reviewed the conversation with Murphy, it seemed to Peter that there was no way to avoid losing the Peabody account, which would look bad on his own record as well as Murphy's—not to mention the loss in commissions for them both. He felt badly about getting into a tiff with Murphy on his first day out in the territory, and knew Murphy would feel betrayed if one of his salespeople purposely lost a major account.

The only out he could see, aside from quitting, was to play down the whole episode. Murphy had not actually *ordered* Peter to submit a claim for damaged goods (was he covering himself legally?), so Peter could technically ignore the conversation and simply not authorize a discount. He knew very well, however, that such a course was only superficially passive, and that in Murphy's opinion he would have lost the account on purpose. As Peter sipped halfheartedly at a martini, he thought bitterly to himself, "Boy, they sure didn't prepare me for this in Management Training. And I don't even know if this kind of thing goes on in the rest of Murphy's district, let alone in Scott's eleven other districts."

# Dilemma of an Accountant

In 1976 Senator Lee Metcalf (D-Mont.) released a report on the public accounting industry which rocked the profession. Despite a decade of revisions in rules and regulations (variously established by the Securities and Exchange Commission, Accounting Principles Board, and Financial Accounting Standards Board), public accounting firms were still perceived by many on Capitol Hill as biased in favor of their clients, incapable of or unwilling to police themselves, and at times participants in coverups of client affairs. Senator Metcalf even went so far as to suggest nationalizing the industry in light of these activities.

Just prior to the Metcalf report, Daniel Potter began working as a staff accountant for Baker Greenleaf, one of the Big Eight accounting firms. In preparation for his CPA examination, Dan had rigorously studied the code of ethics of the American Institute of Certified Public Accountants (AICPA), and had thoroughly familiarized himself with his profession's guidelines for morality. He was aware of

ethical situations which might pose practical problems, such as maintaining independence from the client or bearing the responsibility for reporting a client's unlawful or unreasonably misleading activities, and he knew the channels through which a CPA was expected to resolve unethical business policies. Dan had taken the guidelines very seriously: they were not only an integral part of the auditing exam, they also expressed to him the fundamental dignity and calling of the profession—namely, to help sustain the system of checks and balances on which capitalism has been based. Daniel Potter firmly believed that every independent auditor was obligated to maintain professional integrity, if what he believed to be the best economic system in the world was to survive.

Thus, when Senator Metcalf's report was released, Dan was very interested in discussing it with numerous partners in the firm. They responded thoughtfully to the study and were concerned with the possible ramifications of Senator Metcalf's assessment. Dan's discussions at this time and his subsequent experiences during his first year and a half at Baker Greenleaf confirmed his initial impressions that the firm deserved its reputation for excellence in the field.

Dan's own career had been positive. After graduating in Economics from an Ivy League school, he had been accepted into Acorn Business School's accountant training program, and was sponsored by Baker Greenleaf. His enthusiasm and abilities had been clear from the start, and he was rapidly promoted through the ranks and enlisted to help recruit undergraduates to work for the firm. In describing his own professional ethos, Dan endorsed the Protestant work ethic on which he had been raised, and combined this belief with a strong faith in his own worth and responsibility. A strong adherent to the assumptions behind the profession's standards and prepared to defend them as a part of his own self-interest, he backed up his reasoning with an unquestioning belief in loyalty to one's employer and to the clients who helped support his employer. He liked the clear-cut hierarchy of authority and promotion schedule on which Baker Greenleaf was organized, and once had likened his loyalty to his superior to the absolute loyalty which St. Paul advised the slave to have towards his earthly master "out of fear of God" (Colossians 3:22). Thus, when he encountered the first situation where both his boss and his client seemed to be departing from the rules of the profession, Dan's moral dilemma was deep-seated and difficult to solve.

The new assignment began as a welcome challenge. A long-standing and important account which Baker had always shared with another Big Eight accounting firm needed a special audit, and Baker had reason to expect that a satisfactory performance might secure it the account exclusively. Baker put its best people on the job, and Dan was elated to be included on the special assignment team; success could lead to an important one-year promotion.

Oliver Freeman, the project senior, assigned Dan to audit a wholly-owned real estate subsidiary (Sub) which had given Baker a lot of headaches in the past. "I want you to solve the problems we're having with this Sub, and come out with a clean opinion (i.e., confirmation that the client's statements are presented fairly) in one month. I leave it to you to do what you think is necessary."

For the first time Dan was allotted a subordinate, Gene Doherty, to help him. Gene had worked with the project senior several times before on the same client's account, and he was not wholly enthusiastic about Oliver's supervision. "Oliver is completely inflexible about running things his own way—most of the staff accountants hate him. He contributes a 7:00 A.M. to 9:00 P.M. day every day, and expects everyone else to do the same. You've *really* got to put out, on his terms, to get an excellent evaluation from him." Oliver was indeed a strict authoritarian. Several times over the next month Dan and Oliver had petty disagreements over interpretive issues, but when Dan began to realize just how stubborn Oliver was, he regularly deferred to his superior's opinion.

Three days before the audit was due, Dan completed his files and submitted them to Oliver for review. He had uncovered quite a few problems but managed to solve all except one: one of the Sub's largest real estate properties was valued on the balance sheet at $2 million, and Dan's own estimate of its value was no more than $100,000. The property was a run-down structure in an undesirable neighborhood, and had been unoccupied for several years. Dan discussed his proposal to write down the property by $1,900,000 with the Sub's managers, but since they felt there was a good prospect of renting the property shortly, they refused to write down its value. Discussion with the client had broken off at this point, and Dan had to resolve the disagreement on his own. His courses of action were ambiguous, and depended on how he defined the income statement: according to AICPA regulations on materiality, any difference in opinion between the client and the public accountant which affected the income statement by more than 3%

was considered material and had to be disclosed in the CPA's opinion. The $1,900,000 write-down would have a 7% impact on the Sub's net income, but less than 1% on the client's consolidated net income. Dan eventually decided that since the report on the Sub would be issued separately (although for the client's internal use only), the write-down did indeed represent a material difference in opinion.

The report which he submitted to Oliver Freeman contained a recommendation that it be filed with a subject-to-opinion proviso, which indicated that all the financial statements were reasonable subject to the $1.9 million adjustment disclosed in the accompanying opinion. After Freeman reviewed Dan's files, he fired back a list of "To Do's," which was the normal procedure at Baker Greenleaf. Included in the list was the following note:

1  Take out the pages in the files where you estimate the value of the real estate property at $100,000.
2  Express an opinion that the real estate properties are correctly evaluated by the Sub.
3  Remove your "subject-to-opinion" designation and substitute a "clean opinion."

Dan immediately wrote back on the list of "To Do's" that he would not alter his assessment since it clearly violated his own reading of accounting regulations. That afternoon Oliver and Dan met behind closed doors.

Oliver first pointed out his own views to Dan:

1  He (Oliver) wanted no problems on this audit. With six years of experience he knew better than Dan how to handle the situation.
2  Dan was responsible for a "clean opinion."
3  Any neglect of his duties would be viewed as an act of irresponsibility.
4  The problem was not material to the Client

(consolidated) and the Sub's opinion would only be used "in house."
5  No one read or cared about these financial statements anyway.

The exchange became more heated as Dan reasserted his own interpretation of the write-down, which was that it was a material difference to the Sub and a matter of importance from the standpoint of both professional integrity and legality. He posited a situation where Baker issued a clean opinion which the client subsequently used to show prospective buyers of the property in question. Shortly thereafter the buyer might discover the real value of the property and sue for damages. Baker, Oliver, and Dan would be liable. Both men agreed that such a scenario was highly improbable, but Dan continued to question the ethics of issuing a clean opinion. He fully understood the importance of this particular audit and expressed his loyalty to Baker Greenleaf and to Oliver, but nevertheless believed that, in asking him to issue knowingly a false evaluation, Freeman was transgressing the bounds of conventional loyalty. Ultimately a false audit might not benefit Baker Greenleaf or Dan.

Freeman told Dan he was making a mountain out of a molehill and was jeopardizing the client's account and hence Baker Greenleaf's welfare. Freeman also reminded Dan that his own welfare patently depended on the personal evaluation which he would receive on this project. Dan hotly replied that he would not be threatened, and as he left the room, he asked, "What would Senator Metcalf think?"

A few days later Dan learned that Freeman had pulled Dan's analysis from the files and substituted a clean opinion. He also issued a negative evaluation of Daniel Potter's performance on this audit. Dan knew that he had the right to report the incident to his partner counselor or to the personnel department, but was not terribly satisfied with either approach. He would have preferred to take the issue to an independent review board within the company, but Baker Greenleaf had no such board. However, the negative evaluation would stand, Oliver's arrogance with his junior staff would remain unquestioned, and the files would remain with Dan's name on them unless he raised the incident with someone.

He was not at all sure what he should do. He knew that Oliver's six years with Baker Greenleaf counted for a lot, and he felt a tremendous obligation to trust his superior's judgment and perspective. He also was aware that Oliver was inclined to stick to his own opinions. As Dan weighed the alternative, the vision of Senator Metcalf calling for nationalization continued to haunt him.

# Martha McCaskey

Martha McCaskey[1] felt both elated and uneasy after her late Friday meeting with Tom Malone and Bud Hackert, two of the top managers in Praxis Associates' Industry Analysis division. Malone, the division's de facto COO, had said that upon successful completion of the Silicon 6 study, for which McCaskey was project leader, she would be promoted to group manager. The promotion would mean both a substantial increase in pay and a reprieve from the tedious field work typical of Praxis' consulting projects. Completing the Silicon 6 project, however, meant a second session with Phil Devon, the one person who could provide her with the information required by Praxis' client. Now, McCaskey reflected, finishing the project would likely mean following the course of action proposed by Hackert and seconded by Malone to pay Devon off.

Praxis' client, a semiconductor manufacturer based in California, was trying to identify the cost structure and manufacturing technologies of a new chip produced by one of its competitors. McCaskey and the others felt certain that Phil Devon, a semiconductor industry consultant who had worked in the competitor's West Coast operation some 12 years earlier, could provide the detailed information on manufacturing costs and processes required by their client (see Exhibit 1 for a summary of the required information). Her first interview with Devon had caused McCaskey to have serious doubts both about the propriety of asking for such information and about Devon's motivation in so eagerly offering to help her.

Malone suggested that she prepare an action plan over the weekend. Ty Richardson, head of the Industry Analysis division, would be in town on Monday to meet with Malone and the two group managers, Bud Hackert and Bill Davies. McCaskey could present her plan for completing the Silicon 6 project at that meeting. Malone said all of them would be ex-

[1]The circumstances described in this case are reported entirely from Martha McCaskey's point of view and do not necessarily reflect the perceptions of others involved. All names, places, and companies have been disguised.

tremely interested in hearing her ideas. Silicon 6 was turning out to be a very important project. The client currently accounted for 15–20% of the division's revenues. In a meeting earlier that day, the marketing manager representing the client had offered to double the fee for the Silicon 6 project. He had also promised that there would be 10 more projects for the division to do that would be just as lucrative, if they could come through on Silicon 6.

By Saturday afternoon, McCaskey had worked up several approaches to completing the Silicon 6 project. With the additional funds now available from the client, she could simply have Devon provide analyses of several alternatives for manufacturing state-of-the-art chips, including the one used at the competitor's Silicon 6 plant. The extra analyses would be expensive and time-consuming, but Devon most likely would not suspect what she was after. Another option was to hand the project over to Chuck Kaufmann, another senior associate. Chuck handled many of the division's projects which required getting information that a competitor, if asked, would consider proprietary.

McCaskey felt, however, that no matter which option she chose, completing the Silicon 6 project would compromise her values. Where do you draw the line on proprietary information, she wondered. Was she about to engage in what one of her friends at another consulting firm referred to as "gentleman's industrial espionage"? McCaskey reflected on how well things had gone since she joined the Industry Analysis division. Until the Silicon 6 project, she felt that she had always been able to maintain a high degree of integrity in her work. Now, McCaskey wondered, would the next step to success mean playing the game the way everyone else did?

## PRAXIS ASSOCIATES

Praxis was a medium-sized consulting firm based in Chicago with offices in New York, Los Angeles, and San Francisco. Founded in 1962 by three professors who taught accounting in Chicago area universities, the firm had grown to nearly 350 employees by 1986. Over this period, Praxis had expanded its practice into four divisions: Management Control and Systems (which had been the original practice of the firm), Financial Services, General Management, and Industry Analysis. These expansions had taken place within a policy of conservative, controlled growth to ensure that the firm maintained a high level of quality of services and an informal, "thinktank" atmosphere. Throughout its history, Praxis had enjoyed a reputation for high technical and professional standards.

Industry Analysis was the newest and smallest of Praxis' four divisions. It had been created in 1982 in response to increasing demand for industry and competitive analysis by clients of Praxis' Financial Services and General Management divisions. Industry and competitive analysis involved an examination of the competitive forces in industries, and identifying and developing ways in which firms could create and sustain competitive advantage through a distinctive competitive strategy.

Unlike the other three divisions, the Industry Analysis division was a separate, autonomous unit operating exclusively out of San Francisco. The other divisions were headquartered in Chicago, with branch operations in New York and Los Angeles. The Industry Analysis division had been located in San Francisco for two reasons. The first was that much of Praxis' demand for competitive analysis came from clients based in California, and particularly in Silicon Valley. The second reason was that Ty Richardson, the person hired to start the division, was well connected in Northern California and had made staying in San Francisco part of his terms for accepting the job. Richardson reported directly to Praxis' executive committee. Richardson had also insisted on hiring all his own people. Unlike the rest of Praxis' divisions, which were staffed primarily by people who were developed internally, the Industry Analysis division was staffed entirely with outsiders.

## THE INDUSTRY ANALYSIS GROUP

By 1986, the Industry Analysis Group consisted of 15 professionals, 12 analysts (called associates), and 6 clerical staff. In addition to Richardson, who was a senior vice president, the division had one vice president, who served as Richardson's chief of operations, and two group managers. The remaining 11 professionals formed two groups of senior associates which reported to the two group managers (see Exhibit 2).

The two groups of senior associates were distinctly different. The senior associates who reported to Bud Hackert were referred to as the "old guard." Several years earlier, they had all worked for Richardson when he had run his own consulting firm in Los Angeles. In contrast to the old guard, the senior associates reporting to Bill Davies all had MBAs from well-known schools. Consequently, the "new guard" had significantly higher starting salaries. Another difference between the two groups was that the new guard tended to spend their time equally between individual and team projects. The old guard worked strictly on individual projects.

Senior associates and group managers received their project assignments from Tom Malone, Richardson's chief of operations. For the most part, however, roles and reporting relationships among the professional staff were loosely defined. Senior associates often discussed the status of their projects directly with Malone or Richardson rather than with the group managers. Both group managers and senior associates served as project leaders. On team projects, it was not unusual for the group manager to be part of a team on which a senior associate was project leader. The assignment of associates to projects, determined by a process of informal bargaining among associates and project leaders, served to further blur the distinction between senior associates and group managers.

Malone and the two group managers also had previously worked with Richardson. Hackert and Richardson met when Richardson, who

had a Ph.D. in business administration, left academia to join the Los Angeles branch of a well-known consulting firm. Richardson left shortly thereafter to start his own firm in Los Angeles, consulting to high-tech industries. Malone had managed Richardson's Los Angeles operation.

Clients and employees alike described Richardson as an exceptional salesman. Very sharp in all his dealings, he had a folksy way with people that was both disarming and charismatic. Richardson was also a highly driven person who rarely slept more than four hours a night. He had taken major risks with personal finances, making and losing several fortunes by the time he was 35. Some of these ventures had involved Hackert, who had not made it in his previous employer's up-or-out system, and had gone to work for a major Los Angeles real estate developer. By age 40, the demands of both being an entrepreneur and running his own consulting business had played havoc with Richardson's personal life. At his wife's insistence, Richardson switched careers and moved to San Francisco, where his wife started her own business and he accepted a high-level job with a major international consulting firm. Within the year, though, Richardson had grown restless. When Praxis agreed to let Richardson run his own show in San Francisco, he left the consulting firm, taking Bill Davies and several of the new guard with him.

## MARTHA McCASKEY

Martha McCaskey, 29 years old and single, had been with Praxis for 18 months. She joined the firm in 1985, shortly after completing her MBA at Harvard. Prior to the MBA, McCaskey had worked at a major consumer electronics firm for three years, after graduating from CalTech with a degree in electrical engineering. In the summer between her two MBA years, McCaskey worked as a consultant to a young biomedical firm in Massachusetts that specialized in self-administered diagnostic tests. While there, she developed product strategy and implementation plans for a supplement to one of the product lines, and assisted in preparation of the firm's second equity offering. McCaskey thoroughly enjoyed the project orientation of the summer work experience and her role as consultant. The firm indicated a strong interest in hiring her upon completion of the MBA. McCaskey, however, had decided to pursue a career in consulting. In addition, she had grown up in the Bay area, and wanted to return there if possible.

Praxis was one of several consulting firms with whom McCaskey interviewed. Her first interview at the San Francisco branch was with Tom Malone, the division's vice president. Malone told her that the Industry Analysis division was a wonderful place to work, especially emphasizing the collegial, thinktank environment. He said that, as Praxis' newest division, they were experiencing tremendous growth. He also said they were just beginning to get involved in some very exciting projects. The interview ended before McCaskey could push him on specifics, but she wasn't sure that such questions would have been appropriate. Malone had impressed her as very dynamic and engaging. Instead of interrogating her, as she expected, she later commented that he had made her feel "pretty darn good."

The rest of her interviews were similar. Although she grilled the other people she met, they all told her what a terrific place it was. McCaskey was surprised that many of the senior associates, and even the two group managers, did not seem as sharp as she had expected. In one of the interviews, McCaskey was also surprised to see Jeff McCollum, a former classmate she had known slightly at CalTech.

Upon returning to Boston, McCaskey had a message from Ty Richardson, who had called to say he would be in town the following night and was wondering if she could meet him. Over dinner at one of Boston's most expensive restaurants, Richardson told her he was quite impressed with what he had heard about her. They were looking for people like her to help the business grow, and to handle the exciting

new projects they were getting. He also said that, for the right people, the Industry Analysis division offered rapid advancement, more so than she would likely find at the other firms she was talking with.

The next day Richardson called McCaskey with a generous offer. Later that afternoon she received a call from Jeff McCollum, who once again told her what a great place it was to work, that Richardson often would take everybody out for drinks Friday afternoon when he was around. In fact, he laughed, there had been a golf outing the day before McCaskey's interview, and everyone had still been a little hung over when she arrived. McCaskey called Richardson early the next week to accept the offer.

## WORKING IN THE INDUSTRY ANALYSIS DIVISION

McCaskey's first day at work started with a visit from Malone. He explained that the division was experiencing a bit of a crunch just then, and they needed her help on a competitive analysis study. In fact, she would have to do the project by herself. It was unusual to give a new person their own project, Malone continued, but he had arranged for Davies to provide back-up support if she needed it. McCaskey reflected on her first project:

> It was relatively easy and I was lucky, it was a nice industry to interview in. Some industries are tough to interview because they tend to be very close-mouthed. Some industries are easier. The consumer electronics industry, for example, is pretty easy. Other industries, like the electronic chemicals area, can be really tough. People making chips are very secretive.

Although it was her first assignment, McCaskey gave the client presentation and wrote a formal report detailing her analysis and recommendations. A few days later, Richardson dropped in on a working lunch among Davies's group to compliment McCaskey on her handling of the project. He went so far as to say that both he and Malone felt that her analysis was the best they had yet seen by anyone in the division.

Two weeks later McCaskey was assigned to a major project involving a competitive analysis for a company that made printed circuit boards. As with her first assignment, she was to work alone on the study, consulting Davies if and when she needed help. It was during this period that Malone began suggesting that she talk with two members of the old guard, Dan Rendall and Chuck Kaufmann, about sources of information. The project involved gathering some fairly detailed information about a number of competitors, including one Japanese and two European firms. The old guard handled many of the projects that involved gathering sensitive information on target firms, i.e., the client's competitors. This was always information that was not publicly available, information that a target firm would consider proprietary. It appeared to McCaskey that Dan Rendall and Chuck Kaufmann were the real producers in this group, often taking on projects when other members of the old guard had difficulty obtaining sensitive information.

Rendall was the recognized leader of the old guard. He could often be seen coming and going from Richardson's office on the infrequent occasions that Richardson was in town. Recently, Richardson had been spending about 80% of his time on the road. When McCaskey approached Rendall, however, she felt him to be difficult and uncooperative. McCaskey found subsequent attempts to talk with Rendall equally unproductive. Chuck Kaufmann was out of town on assignment for two weeks and thus unable to meet with McCaskey.

Given her difficulty in following through on Malone's recommendation to work with the old guard, McCaskey developed her own approach to the printed circuit board project. The project turned out to be extremely difficult. Over a period of six months, McCaskey conducted nearly 300 telephone interviews, attended trade shows in the U.S., Japan, and Europe, and personally interviewed consultants, distributors, and industry representatives in all

three countries. Toward the end, McCaskey remembered working seven days a week, ten to fifteen hours a day. Her European contacts finally came through with all the necessary information just three days before the client presentation. Despite the results that her efforts produced, McCaskey felt that Richardson and Malone disapproved of how she handled the project, that it could have been completed with less time and effort:

> The presentation went really well. Toward the end, I began to relax and feel really good. I was presenting to a bunch of guys who had been in the business for thirty years. There were a few minor follow-up questions but mostly a lot of compliments. I was really looking forward to taking a break. I had been with the company at this point for nine months, and never taken a day of vacation, and I was exhausted. And then, Richardson got up and promised the client a written report in two weeks.
>
> Davies was very good about it. We got in the car to go back to the airport, and he asked me wasn't I planning to take a vacation in the near future? But it went right by Richardson. Davies didn't press it, of course. Even though he had an MBA from Stanford, he was a really laid-back California type. That sometimes made for problems when you needed direction on projects or firm policy.
>
> The next day, I was a basket case. I should have called in sick, I really should have. I managed to dictate about one page. Richardson came by at the end of the day and said, well, what's the hold-up? I was so mad I got the report done in ten days.

The rate at which McCaskey wrote the report was held up by Malone as a new standard for Industry Analysis projects.

McCaskey's handling of the written report on her next project led to an even tighter standard for the division's projects. Hoping to avoid a similar bind on the project, McCaskey planned to write the report before the client presentation. Malone had told her she would not have any other responsibilities while on the project because the deadline was so tight. Two weeks later, however, Richardson asked her to join a major project involving the rest of Davies's group.

> He kind of shuffled into my office and said something like: Damn, you know, ah, gee Martha, we really admire you. I'd really like to have you on this team. We're a little behind schedule and we could really use your expertise. I've also asked Chuck Kaufmann to join the team and I'd like the two of you to work on a particularly challenging piece of the project.

Despite the dual assignment, McCaskey managed to complete the report on her original project before the client presentation. That also became a standard within the division.

In mid-1986, several senior associates left the firm. Bill Whiting and Cory Williamson took jobs with competing firms. Doug Forrest was planning to take a job with one of Praxis' clients. Jeff McCollum left complaining that he was burned out and planned to take several months off to travel before looking for work. Over the previous six months there also had been high turnover among the associates. It had become a running joke that Tuesday's edition of the *Wall Street Journal,* which carried the job advertisements, should be included in the set of industry journals that were circulated around the office.

While some of the turnover could be attributed to the increasing workload and performance expectations, a number of people had also been upset over the previous year's bonuses. Richardson and Malone had met with each senior associate prior to Christmas and explained that the division was going through a growth phase, and wasn't the cash generator everybody seemed to think it was. Each person was then given the same bonus and told how valuable they were to the firm, regardless of the time they had been with the firm or what they had accomplished. But, as McCaskey recalled, what really got to people was when Richardson and Malone showed up at the New Year's office party in a pair of brand-new Mercedes.

Chuck Kaufmann had gone to see Malone about the personnel situation. He warned Malone that unless something was done to improve things, several more people would leave. Malone responded that he could put an ad in the paper and get ten new people any time he wanted. Chuck had been shocked. For McCaskey, however, Malone's response was not surprising. In the lighter moments of working on team projects, conversation among members of the new guard had naturally drifted to views on Richardson and Malone, and what made them so successful:

> Malone was good-looking, married with two kids. He usually drove a Ferrari instead of the Mercedes. He was very aggressive. You could hear this man all over the building when he was on the phone. We decided he was just really driven by money. That's all there was . . . he'd go whip someone and tell them to get work out by the end of the month so we could bill for it. And have no qualms about doing it, all right, 'cause he's counting his bucks. He was also a very smart man. If you spent a couple of hours with him in the car or on a plane explaining a business to him, he'd have it. The man had amazing retention.
>
> Both he and Richardson were great salesmen. Malone could be an incredible bullshitter. At times, though, you wondered how much credibility you could put in these people. They kept saying they wanted you to be part of the management team. But then they'd turn around and wouldn't even tell us where or when they would go on a client call, so you really couldn't make a contribution.

Chuck's shock at Malone's response to the personnel question was also typical. McCaskey had worked with Chuck on a number of team projects and found him to be different from most of the old guard. He was working on his MBA in the evening program at Berkeley and really seemed to enjoy being with the new guard. McCaskey knew that Chuck also had a reputation for working on what were referred to as the "sleaze" projects in the office, projects that involved questionable practices in contacting and interviewing people who could provide very detailed information about target companies. Even so, McCaskey felt that he did this work mainly out of a sense of loyalty to Richardson and Malone.

Chuck was always torn between doing the job and feeling: These guys need me to help them run their business, because I'm going to be a group manager someday and they really need me. He was torn between that and trying to be, not diplomatic, but objective about his situation, saying: They're paying me less than anybody else but look what these guys are asking me to do.

He wanted to do good in the eyes of people he looked up to, whether it's Richardson and Malone, or peers like Dan or myself, because he has that personal attachment and can't step back and say: They're screwing me to the wall. He just could not make that distinction.

Chuck had been fun to work with, though. McCaskey had observed that many of their team projects had required increasingly detailed information about a client's competitors. These projects had given rise to discussions among McCaskey and her colleagues about what constituted proprietary information and what, if anything, they should do if they found they had to obtain such information. While there was some discussion about the appropriateness of such projects, McCaskey recalled a particular conversation that characterized how the issue was typically handled:

We were on a quick coffee break and Linda Shepherd said she really needed to get psyched up for her next call. Linda was a member of the new guard whom I liked and respected. She had an MBA from Berkeley and had been there about a year longer than I had. We became good friends soon after I arrived and ended up working together a lot on team projects.

I said, "Yeah, I know what you mean. I tried to get some discounting information from a marketing manager this morning and all he would give me was list price. As usual, I started out with general questions but as soon as I tried to get specific he was all over me. Like pulling teeth. Invariably, they slap it back at you. What

information do you have? You know, and you don't want to give away the plot because then he'd know what you're doing."

Chuck's advice was pretty funny. He said that he was working on a project that was so slimy he had to take a shower every time he got off the phone, and maybe that's what we ought to do, too.

As was the norm on most of the division's projects, McCaskey usually identified herself as a representative of a newly formed trade journal for the particular industry she was interviewing in. To McCaskey, that was not nearly as dishonest as visiting a target company on the pretense of interviewing for a job, as a friend of hers who worked for another consulting firm had done.

All in all, McCaskey felt that she had been given the freedom to do her work with integrity and quality. It was also clear that her performance was recognized by Richardson. Of the senior associates, Richardson spent the most time with Dan Rendall, McCaskey, or Chuck. While Dan often could be seen in Richardson's office, Richardson seemed to make a point of dropping in on Chuck and McCaskey. For McCaskey, these visits always seemed to be more social than work-related. Richardson's comments at a recent consumer electronics marketing research association convention were a typical example of how these meetings went:

We had gone to the dinner but decided not to hang around for the speeches. Instead, he asked me if I'd like to have a nightcap. I said sure. So we went to a bar, and he spent the evening giving me all these warm fuzzies; about how he really enjoyed having me with the company, how I was an important member of the management team of the company, how everything was wonderful with me there, and that he hoped that I would be with them for a long time. And on and on.

At the end of 1986, McCaskey received a substantial increase in pay. She also received a $10,000 bonus. Most of the other senior associates had received much smaller bonuses, in many cases equivalent to what they had received the previous year.

## THE SILICON 6 PROJECT

In January 1987, both Richardson and Malone met with McCaskey to talk about a new assignment. The project was for one of Praxis' oldest clients in the high-tech electronics field. Since its inception, the Industry Analysis division had done a lot of work for this client. The project involved a new type of computer chip being produced by one of the client's prime competitors, a company that had also once been one of Praxis' major clients. The project had originally been assigned to Lee Rogoff, a senior associate who reported to Hackert. The client was interested in detailed information about manufacturing processes and costs for the new computer chip. Although he had made numerous calls to the target company's clients and distributors, Lee had been unable to obtain any of the required information.

Normally, Dan Rendall would have been asked to take over the project if it had previously been handled by a member of the old guard. Instead, Malone explained, they had decided to approach McCaskey because of her background in electrical engineering. McCaskey had in fact done some coursework on chip design at CalTech. Malone also told her they had been impressed with her creativity and success in obtaining difficult, detailed information on previous projects. Malone added that there was one constraint on the project. The client had insisted that Praxis not contact the target company to avoid potential allegations of price fixing.

The project was code-named Silicon 6 after the plant at which the chip was produced, the sixth building of an industrial cluster in Silicon Valley. McCaskey began by contacting the Silicon 6 plant's equipment manufacturers. They were unusually close-mouthed. She was unable to get them even to say what equipment the plant had ordered, never mind its operating characteristics. McCaskey also contacted raw materials suppliers to semiconductor manufac-

turers. Again, she was unsuccessful in obtaining any information. She held meetings nearly every day with Malone, standard operating procedure for problem projects. For McCaskey, the meetings soon began to have a monotonous quality to them:

> How's it going? Well, OK. Let's retrench. Did you try this tack? Did you try that tack? Did you try this customer base? Did you try this group of calls?

Malone was especially interested in whether she was having any luck identifying exemployees. On several of the projects McCaskey had worked on, particularly those requiring detailed data, the best source of information had been ex-employees of target companies. McCaskey had generally found these people quite willing to talk, sometimes out of vengeance, but also at times because there was a sympathetic, willing listener available. People love to talk about their "expertise," she often thought. Industry consultants had been another good source of detailed information. It was not unusual for the Industry Analysis division to hire consultants for $1,000 or $2,000 a day on specific projects.

McCaskey felt that some of the senior associates had been rather creative in their use of this practice. Several months earlier, Chuck had confided to her that he had hired an ex-employee as a "consultant" to provide him with a list of software contracts for a target company. He said that this was something that Dan Rendall had done regularly on his projects. In one case, Dan had paid an ex-employee of a target company a "consulting" fee of $2,000 for a business plan and spreadsheets of a target company's upcoming new product introduction. Bud Hackert was there when Chuck had asked Dan if such information wasn't proprietary. Hackert had a reputation as a tough, no-nonsense manager who prided himself on running a tight shop and on his ability to get the job done, no matter what it took. Hackert said that if someone was willing to talk about it then it wasn't proprietary.

McCaskey had mentioned the incident to

*malone*

Linda Shepherd. They both agreed that Dan's behavior, and Hackert's response, only confirmed what they had suspected all along about the old guard; they routinely paid ex-employees of target companies to obtain highly sensitive information for Praxis' clients. Linda ended the conversation with a comment that, given such behavior, the old guard wouldn't last long when the division really took off and headquarters became more interested in the San Francisco operation.

Many consulting firms had formal, written policies regarding the solicitation and performance of contracts. For example, some firms required that employees identify themselves as working for the firm before beginning an interview. The Industry Analysis division did not have any written, formal policies as such. Richardson occasionally had given lunchtime talks concerning the division's policies, but, as McCaskey recalled, these tended to be quite vague and general. For example, for McCaskey, the bottom line in Richardson's "ethics" talk was quite simply, we don't do anything unethical. Besides, McCaskey knew from her friends at highly reputable firms that people occasionally broke the rules even when formal, written policies existed. After her discussion with Linda, McCaskey considered raising the old guard's use of ex-employees with Richardson but he was out of the office for a couple of weeks. By the time he returned, she was in the middle of several large projects and had all but forgotten about it.

McCaskey's only lead on the Silicon 6 project occurred through a seemingly random set of events. Working through a list of academics involved in semiconductor research, she found a professor at a small East Coast engineering school who actively consulted with several European manufacturers of semiconductors. When she called him, McCaskey found that he could not provide her with any of the information on the list. Malone had suggested, however, that she fly out and interview him because he might have some gossip on the new chip. The interview served to clarify McCaskey's understanding of the manufacturing processes involved but, as she had suspected, did not provide her with any new information. He did suggest, however, that she get in touch with Phil Devon, a consultant in southern California. He did not know Devon personally but knew that Devon recently had been involved in the design and start-up of a plant for one of the European firms.

Upon returning to San Francisco, McCaskey called Devon to set up an interview. During the call she learned that he had been a vice president at the target company some 12 years earlier. When she told Malone about Devon, he was ecstatic. He congratulated her on once again coming through for the division, letting her know that both he and Richardson felt she was the one person they could always count on when the chips were down.

McCaskey met with Devon the following Friday. He was in his mid-forties, very distinguished looking, and relaxed in his manner. McCaskey's first impression of Devon was that he was both professional and fatherly. Even before getting into the interview, she began to have qualms about asking for detailed information on the Silicon 6 plant. Feeling uneasy, McCaskey opened the interview by saying that she represented an international concern that was interested in building a semiconductor manufacturing plant in the U.S. Devon responded by saying that he couldn't understand why anybody would want to build another plant given the current global overcapacity for semiconductor production. He added, however, that he was willing to help her in whatever way he could.

McCaskey then suggested that they talk about the cost structure for a plant that would be employing state-of-the-art technology. Devon responded that he would need more information to work with if he was going to be of help to her. He explained that there were several new technologies available or under development, and it would make a difference which one they chose. It briefly crossed McCaskey's mind that this was an opportunity to talk about the Silicon 6 plant. Instead, she suggested that they might try to cover each of the options. Devon responded that it would involve an awful lot of work, and that it would be helpful if she could narrow things down. He then asked what kind of chips they intended to produce and whether there would be several products or just a single line. He added that, if he knew whom she was representing, it would help him to determine what type of facility they might be interested in.

McCaskey felt increasingly uncomfortable as the interview progressed. She felt that Devon was earnestly trying to help her. He seemed to have an excellent technical background and to know what he was doing. It was clear that Devon took pride in doing what he did, and in doing it well. By midmorning, McCaskey began to feel nauseated with herself and the prospect of asking Devon to give her proprietary information on the Silicon 6 plant. As she talked with him, she couldn't help thinking:

> This is a guy who's trying to do good in the world. How can I be doing this? I have an EE degree from CalTech, an MBA from Harvard, and here I am trying to sleaze this guy.

At this point, McCaskey settled on a scheme to end the interview but keep open the option of a second interview with Devon. From the morning's discussion, she was convinced that he had access to the information she needed to complete the Silicon 6 project. Instead of probing for the information, she told Devon that her client had not supplied her with adequately detailed information to focus on a specific technology and plant cost structure. She added that his questions had helped her learn a lot about what she needed to find out from her client before she came back to him. She suggested, however, that if they could put together a representative plant cost structure, it would be useful in going back to her client. Once again, Devon said that he was willing to help her in whatever way he could. He said he had recently helped set up a state-of-the-art facility in Europe that might be similar to the type of plant her client was considering. At this point, McCaskey began to feel that perhaps Devon was being too helpful. She wondered if he might be leading her on to find out who she was working for.

Devon provided her with background on the European plant, including general information about its cost structure and other items on McCaskey's list. McCaskey was so uncomfortable about deceiving him about the purpose of her visit that she barely made it through lunch, even though she had contracted with him for the full day. After lunch, she paid Devon the full day's fee and thanked him. McCaskey said that she would get in touch with him after meeting with her client to see if they could focus on a particular plant design. Devon thanked her, said that he wished he could have been more helpful, and that he looked forward to seeing her again.

A meeting on the Silicon 6 project was scheduled with the client for the following Friday. McCaskey worked over the weekend and through the early part of the next week putting together her slides and presentation. Malone had been out of the office on Monday and Tuesday on another client presentation. On Wednesday, they met and McCaskey provided Malone with an update on her meeting with Devon and with her presentation. She told Malone that she had been unable to get the information. After Malone left, McCaskey once again reflected on the meeting. Devon had seemed so professional. She really wasn't sure how he would have responded to specific questions about the Silicon 6 plant. She felt sure he could have provided her with all the information they needed. On the other hand, although it sounded farfetched, it seemed just possible that Devon was so straight he might have called the police had she asked him for the information. Or, given his prior employment at the target company, Devon might have called someone there about McCaskey's interest in the Silicon 6 plant.

To her surprise, Malone did not press her to try to get more information from Devon. Instead, he asked McCaskey to go through her presentation. When she came to a slide titled "Representative Plant Cost Structure," Malone stopped her, saying that the title should read "Plant Cost Structure." When McCaskey asked him what he meant, Malone told her to cross out the word "Representative." They would conduct the presentation as if this was data they had gathered on the actual Silicon 6 plant. When McCaskey objected, Malone pointed out that the analysis was general enough that no one would know the difference.

Going into the presentation Friday morning, McCaskey had only 30 slides. On other projects she typically had used in excess of 100 slides. To McCaskey's surprise, all of the client's senior plant managers were present for the presentation. She had been under the impression that the meeting was to be a dry run for a more formal presentation later on. The plant managers were courteous, but stopped her 15 minutes into the presentation to say that she was not telling them anything new. If this was all she had, they said, it would be pointless to meet with senior management on the Silicon 6 project, although such a meeting was scheduled for the following month. They then asked her to identify all the sources she had contacted. McCaskey did not mention Devon but the plant managers seemed satisfied with her efforts. Malone then explained that the lack of detailed information was due to the constraint of not being able to contact the target company.

The marketing manager in charge of the Silicon 6 project then asked his secretary to take McCaskey and Malone to his office, while he held a brief meeting with the plant managers. Upon joining McCaskey and Malone, the marketing manager expressed his disappointment with Praxis' handling of the Silicon 6 project. Specifically, he said that his firm had never had any trouble getting such information before. Further, he pointed out how much business they provided for the Industry Analysis division, and that he hoped the relationship could continue. Given their progress on the Silicon 6 project, however, he had doubts. Malone then brought up the possibility of still being able to successfully complete the project. Without mentioning Devon's name, he said that they had just made contact with an ex-employee who could provide them with the necessary information if provided with the proper incentives.

McCaskey was struck by how the marketing manager immediately brightened and told them that he didn't care how they got the information, as long as they got it. He then doubled the original fee that the Industry Analysis division would be paid upon completion of the project, adding that the additional funds should provide their source with an adequate incentive. He also told them that if they could come through on Silicon 6, he had ten more projects just like it for them that would be just as lucrative.

As they climbed into Malone's Ferrari for the ride back to the office, McCaskey felt stunned by the turn of events. First, there had been the unexpected importance of the presentation; then, the marketing manager's proposition; and, now, Malone's enthusiasm for it. Malone could barely contain himself, delighting in how Richardson would react upon hearing how things had worked out. McCaskey just looked at him, shook her head, and said, "You're amazing!" Malone agreed with her, complimented McCaskey in return, and promised her she would be promoted to group manager as soon as she completed Silicon 6.

When they got back, Malone called Hackert into his office with McCaskey and briefed him on the meeting. Hackert's response was that it would be a "piece of cake." All they'd have to do is figure out how to handle Devon. Hackert then suggested that, given the importance of the project, Devon be offered a per diem consulting fee of $4,000 instead of the standard $2,000. Malone responded that he was unsure if that was how they should approach it, but did agree they should make it worthwhile to Devon to provide the necessary information. He then turned to McCaskey and suggested she think about how to proceed with Devon. He also told her not to overlook the option of having someone else, such as Chuck, meet with Devon. She could still manage the overall project. He grinned, and said it would be good training for her upcoming promotion.

# EXHIBITS: Martha McCaskey

### EXHIBIT 1
PROJECT SUMMARY

Develop a competitive profile, in detail, of the Silicon 6 semiconductor manufacturing facility, obtaining:

- Detailed cost information per 1,000 chips
    utilities
    scrap
    depreciation
    other materials
- Salaries for professionals
- Number of people in each category of hourly workers
- How overhead is split out between the different chips

- Equipment
    description, including capacities
    operating temperatures
    actual production rates and expenses
    do they use the same lines for different chips?
- Raw materials
    source
    price
    long-term contracts?
    how account for captive raw materials—transferred at cost or cost plus?
- Marketing and service expenses

### EXHIBIT 2
PRAXIS ASSOCIATES—STAFFING IN THE SAN FRANCISCO OFFICE

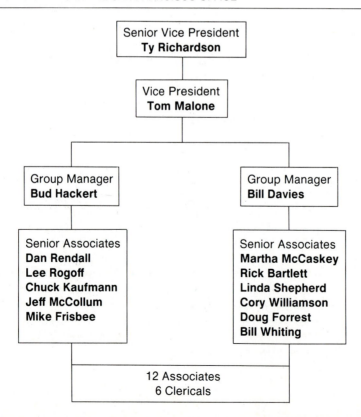

# Ethical Quagmire

These were hardly the best of times for Kevin Stoddard. As a first-year student at Harvard Business School, Kevin—like most of his fellow classmates—had struggled with the adjustment and return to the rigors of an academic environment. Still, despite the ongoing anxiety, he was glad to be charting new waters and sensed that things would soon get better. In any event, he was relieved that his two-year stint in management consulting was behind him.

As an associate consultant at Armstrong Associates, Kevin had spent most of his time developing a performance evaluation system for a medium-sized agency in the federal government. During this extended engagement, Kevin had witnessed and uncovered instances of fraud and conspiracy. The project had been abruptly terminated after the agency accused Armstrong of nonperformance of its contract. Although a subsequent government audit challenged some of the firm's billing practices, the auditor's report lacked evidence to pinpoint guilt. The unhappy episode had been forgotten—or so Kevin had thought.

Now, in late September 1980, Kevin had been called to talk with a federal investigator about his work at Armstrong. Although distressed by what he had observed while at Armstrong, he had, for the most part, remained silent. He had left the firm disillusioned with management consulting in general, disappointed in his work and disturbed by his own actions. As a student, he was no longer under the watchful eyes of Armstrong Associates. There was a lot he could tell that might hurt the firm. It was an opportunity, he thought, to clear his conscience. Yet he had made many friends at Armstrong and, despite the entire ordeal, he retained some genuine affection for the two partners of the firm. They had helped him get started with his career and had warmly welcomed him into their homes and community.

"Why," Kevin asked himself, "did it have to come down to this?"

• • •

The oldest of four children from a middle-class family, Kevin Stoddard had worked hard to pay his way through Harvard College. By his senior year, jobs in the alumni office and student dormitories required 30–40 hours of his time each week. He had especially liked "bumping elbows with the VPs" and at one point thought college administration was his calling. He enjoyed being around people and having supervisory responsibilities for the 30 students in his charge at the dorm.

A realization that he would not make a career in English literature (his major), coupled with the heavy demands on his time, forced him to abandon his senior thesis ("Ralph Waldo Emerson and Transcendentalist Christianity: The Search for a Living Religion"). Consequently, his *summa cum laude* went "out the window." Instead, Kevin graduated with honors in general studies.

Like most college seniors, Kevin had been preoccupied with postgraduate plans. As he later recalled, he "did not know what he was going to do for the rest of his life," so he applied for fellowships, law school, business school, and an assortment of jobs. When Harvard Business School offered him a deferred admission, he decided to pursue a career in business. But he needed to find a job for the interim period of two years.

### "B" LINE TO ARMSTRONG ASSOCIATES

Kevin had planned to sign up for an interview with IBM. It was the "big drop" in the college placement office "B group." As he waited in the long line, a friend suggested he also interview with Armstrong: "It's personnel consulting, people, personnel—that sounds like you." It had sounded interesting. So he added his name to the Armstrong list.

The interview went well. Kevin was invited to visit Armstrong's office, which was located just outside of New York City. Because of a series of mix-ups, that interview never ma-

terialized. Nor did any other job interviews. Graduation day passed without a job offer.

But Kevin was not particularly worried. He had plenty of work at Harvard to occupy him through the summer. He would eventually find a job. In mid-July, Armstrong called back to see if Kevin was available. They had just landed a big two-year contract with the federal government and were adding staff. It was perfect. Kevin explained his plan to attend business school, and Armstrong clearly understood that he would be working for only two years. They seemed impressed that he would someday be an HBS graduate. He was told to rent a car and drive down to their White Plains, New York, office for a Saturday morning visit.

The interview with the firm's partners, Charles (Chuck) Armstrong and Russell Lasker, lasted only an hour but it went smoothly. He was offered a job on the spot. When asked to "give a number," Kevin bashfully suggested a salary of $14,000. Kevin took the job still knowing very little about what the firm did or what he would be doing. One thing was clear: he would be spending a great deal of time in Washington working on the government contract.

### A CURIOUS ORIENTATION

Armstrong Associates, Inc., had been founded in April 1974 for the purpose of providing human resource management counsel to medium and large companies. It was a small firm that employed 20 professionals. Yet its scope of activity was quite broad and included career counseling, labor relations, management development, manpower planning, compensation and benefit programs. Its clients included many "blue chip" American companies. By 1980, Armstrong's billings had topped $1.4 million.

Chuck Armstrong, 46, was not new to the consulting business. After earning his MBA, he had gone to work for his father as a labor relations consultant. He eventually earned a Ph.D. in organizational theory and went on to become a partner of a prestigious New York–based consulting firm. When the lifestyle trade-offs associated with big-time consulting proved too burdensome, he had decided to strike out on his own. Russell Lasker, 41, a long-time friend who had held a number of different personnel jobs, joined as an equal partner. Neither man held the CMC (certified management consultant) designation, nor did either belong to any consulting association.

Kevin started work just after the Labor Day weekend. As an associate consultant, he would be interviewing clients, analyzing data, developing study recommendations, and assisting client executives in the implementation of those recommendations. Kevin arrived in White Plains "wide-eyed" and "full of college innocence." After some brief introductions, Kevin was handed a calculator and a box of computer printouts. He spent the next week "crunching numbers." It hardly seemed like "people work." Nonetheless, it sure was a long way from the days of cleaning bathrooms at Harvard College.

Things improved considerably in the second week as he got to spend some time with members of the firm. Dave Loughlin, 32, and John Blanchard, 33—both two-year veterans at Armstrong—sat him down for an informal orientation. They told him what to wear, what to read, and how to act around Chuck and Russell.

Kevin was startled when Loughlin took him to lunch the following week and announced that he was leaving the firm. Loughlin "tore Chuck and Russ to shreds," saying they "had no idea how to treat people with respect." Loughlin had landed the big contract with DME (a disguised name of a U.S. federal agency) and now was going to be replaced by Dale Crossan. A college classmate of Chuck Armstrong, Crossan worked for the firm on an intermittent basis out of his Denver home. This seemed strange to Kevin, but, then, what did he know about this business of consulting? He figured he would follow Loughlin's original advice—watch, listen and learn.

During the third week of September, Dale Crossan and his assistant, Pam Keller, flew east to meet with Kevin and John Blanchard for the purpose of planning the DME project. After a short briefing from Crossan, Pam Keller pulled Kevin aside to explain the billing procedures. The DME project had been scheduled to begin a month earlier, in August 1978, and was to be completed by February 1980. The $430,000 project would span three of the government's fiscal years and the contract authorized payments for each period in the following manner: FY 78 ($60,000), FY 79 ($300,000), and FY 80 ($70,000). Armstrong was to bill—and presumably work—according to this established schedule or forfeit the period's revenue.

With only a few days remaining in the FY 78 budget, Armstrong still had not started work on the DME project. Facing the loss of $60,000, Pam Keller circulated a memorandum that instructed members of the DME project team on how they should itemize their time sheets. Kevin was told to bill the agency 105 hours for "work performed" during the last three weeks of September. Any work not done by the end of the month would "be made up at a later date." As things turned out, there was never time to catch up for the lost time. DME, unaware of what was happening, paid the $60,000. As far as Kevin could tell, the only thing Armstrong had done was submit the proposal. In his judgment, the agency was paying for the preliminary sales work.

**THE DME CONTRACT**

In August of 1978, Armstrong was awarded a contract for $430,000 by DME to implement a "Performance Evaluation System" (PES) to meet the requirements of the Civil Service Reform Act of 1978. This was a big deal for young Armstrong Associates. The revenue on this project would help the firm turn its first handsome annual profit. It was also the firm's first inroad into the lucrative government-consulting market. A successsful application of PES at DME could help land more valuable government contracts.

Armstrong's PES was essentially an MBO—Management by Objectives—program that was divided into three parts: performance standards, performance evaluation, and performance feedback. When bidding for the contract, Armstrong claimed that its PES had been successfully implemented in several private-sector organizations. Chuck Armstrong had also claimed to have "off-the-shelf" training materials that could be used in PES workshops at DME. In fact, there were few training materials available and Kevin could find client files for only one previous PES job, at a large consumer goods firm.

DME top management, apparently anxious to implement President Carter's civil service reforms, let the contract to Armstrong on a noncompetitive basis. The agency justified the award by pointing to the unique and outstanding qualifications of the firm.

Armstrong had been called in to help DME's personnel department evaluate the work of the agency, which was heavily populated with highly trained engineers and scientists. Specifically, they were to deliver a system that would make it possible to measure the individual performances of the technical field staff. The Armstrong project team—which consisted of Dale Crossan, Pam Keller, John Blanchard, and Kevin Stoddard—soon discovered that measuring technical performance was quite different from using ROI criteria to evaluate the performance of managers in private industry.

## A CORPORAL IN WASHINGTON

The Armstrong contingent arrived in Washington during the last week of September to set up shop. The DME personnel department assumed that the firm had been doing preliminary work on the project in White Plains. Kevin thought it peculiar that DME staff members knew so little about the details of the PES project. Nobody he met at DME seemed overly concerned or mindful of Armstrong's progress or lack thereof. After Crossan and Keller gave DME's top management a general briefing on PES, they flew back to Denver. Blanchard was subsequently called back to White Plains to

help finish up another project. Meanwhile, Kevin had settled into DME's basement office and shared space with the agency's personnel staff. He would do some preliminary on-site research. Once this was completed, he was told, the others would return and the project would get going.

Kevin was charged to study the numerous functions of DME staff—managerial and technical—and to review government personnel and compensation practices. He also had to get a basic understanding of the elements of the Civil Service Reform Act. The PES program would have to incorporate the merit system that had been outlined by the new law. Kevin was disappointed to find Armstrong's PES "was rudimentary at best, incomplete in its design, untested, and hardly ready for sale, let alone implementation." In response to that discovery, he expanded his research to include MBO, performance pay and appraisal systems.

The lack of supervision surprised Kevin. Crossan and Keller came to Washington only on an occasional basis to give DME progress reports. They explained that the PES "fine tuning"—Kevin's work—had taken more time than anticipated. The first PES workshop was postponed. Although top management at the agency was not particularly alarmed by this development, Kevin's office neighbors—the staff in the basement—were puzzled that he had been left alone to do so much of the scoping work. Kevin enjoyed their company and had easily made friends with them, but he did not know nor could he explain the details of the project plan. Pam Keller, who had been elevated to engagement manager for this project (which allowed Armstrong to bill her work at a higher hourly rate), told Kevin she was perfectly satisfied with his performance. He had nothing to worry about.

During the week, Kevin stayed at the Beltway Inn. "It was great," he recalled. "I ate all my meals out and lived like a king." When he learned from DME that his per diem allowance was limited to $50 by the terms of the contract—his hotel bill alone was $45—he immediately sought clarification from Pam Keller. It wasn't a problem, she said; the expenses would be "negotiated" at a later date.

Kevin eventually learned that this was a "time and materials" contract. The agency was billed for time spent on the project and for approved materials (or expenses). DME had agreed to let Armstrong earn roughly 6% on their time. The contract clearly spelled out what items could and could not be charged as materials. Even though photocopying, long-distance telephone calls, and first-class air fare were not to be reimbursed, Armstrong regularly billed and received payment for these items. It was obvious to Kevin that the project was not being carefully monitored. Whenever he would question these billing discrepancies, it was made clear that this was not a matter that should concern him.

## "EGGSHELL" SEASON

By May 1979, Armstrong was ready to run the first of thirty PES workshops. These one-day sessions had been designed to train DME field personnel on the use of the new measurement system. John Blanchard had been picked to run the first workshop. He was perfectly familiar with Armstrong's earlier PES success, but he had spent little time on the DME project because of the competing demands on his time. Kevin, who had written the presentation, was invited along to observe the workshop and assist with administrative duties.

The Chicago workshop turned into a tense affair. The audience was hostile. DME civil servants, satisfied with the annual "step increases" in salary, were angry with President Carter's merit pay idea and were not interested in Armstrong's performance evaluation system. They asked some tough questions and Blanchard was not able to answer them adequately. When Blanchard conceded that he did not know much about their work, the audience had become incensed. Armstrong's team was walking on eggs.

As a result of this debacle, Armstrong was

banned from DME field sites until it could demonstrate competence. Blanchard was fired from the firm. Meanwhile, Crossan and Keller somehow managed to shield themselves from the deadly fallout of the Chicago workshop. Kevin asked to be removed from the project but was told he was "too valuable" to be reassigned. He continued to look for a way out of the PES project and even interviewed for a job back at Harvard. Nobody was interested in hiring him for a one-year stint. Kevin was to stay in the DME basement.

## WATCH WHAT YOU SAY

Word about Armstrong's performance in Chicago spread quickly. The DME project was one of the first attempts to implement the Civil Service reforms. Armstrong's competitors and other government agencies had been watching the PES project with great interest. And by June 1979, the contract had drawn queries from some Congressional offices. Everyone wanted to know how Armstrong could have been awarded the contract on a noncompetitive basis. Questions were raised about the connection between Chuck Armstrong and a former consulting partner who was a high-level DME administrator.

In White Plains, people were frantic about the possibility of an investigation. Employees were instructed not to speak to anyone about the DME job; all calls on that subject would be handled by Chuck alone. Kevin thought that what he knew of DME and its management might be helpful to Chuck, but Chuck seemed far too busy to talk with Kevin. So Kevin waited, sensing that he was getting caught in a gathering storm.

And he worried, too; frustrated that he could never get a straight answer from anyone at the firm, he had already talked. On more than one occasion, he had expressed his disgust with the firm's handling of the project and had apologized to his "basement neighbors" at DME for Armstrong's lapses. Kevin believed the agency's work was important and was bothered that the PES project seemed to be "tracking mud across their floors." He felt terribly awkward. Although he was being paid by Armstrong, he was "working for DME." He felt even more isolated when Dale Crossan and Pam Keller abruptly resigned from the firm. Neither had enjoyed the long commute from Denver to Washington and decided the time had come to concentrate on building a practice in their hometown.

Help arrived with the appointment of a new hire to the project. Anders Kallur was an experienced businessman and had proven himself in the human resources field. He brought instant credibility to the DME project and offered Kevin a strong mentor relationship. Kallur, with Chuck Armstrong's help, convinced the agency to let the firm continue the field workshops.

## WEEKEND RETREAT

Kevin had found a nice place to live in the White Plains area and spent most weekends at home. He joined and taught Sunday school at Chuck's church and had become very friendly with the Armstrong children in his class. Kevin felt almost as if he were a part of their family. He felt comfortable dropping by their house to borrow a lawnmower, or to have a quick chat with a member of the family. In turn, Chuck and his wife were perfectly happy to let Kevin chaperone their children on church-sponsored weekend ski trips.

Aside from Anders Kallur, Chuck was the only person in the firm that Kevin really looked up to. Yet he hardly ever talked business with him. Kevin tended to dismiss the criticisms that he heard directed at Chuck; to him, Chuck seemed like a "decent guy."

## THE ARMSTRONG CURVE

Turnover at Armstrong was rapid. In Kevin's first year at the firm, eleven people had left— all under unpleasant circumstances. One of Kevin's peers in the White Plains office dubbed the phenomenon the "Armstrong Curve." At

first, a new consultant would enjoy the praise and support of the partners. Then, soon, a consultant would be tested in a "trial by fire." Thrown in over their heads, most would usually fail. And finally, continued employment at Armstrong was made an unbearable prospect. As a result, or so the theory went, most left Armstrong with few kind words for the firm's partners.

Kevin believed in the "curve." Chuck Armstrong was a "hard driver" who pushed people a lot. Sometimes, Kevin thought, he had been unfair with people. Maybe that was what it took to be successful in business. Anyway, Kevin managed to keep away from the turmoil and had a pleasant relationship with almost everyone at Armstrong.

Anders Kallur fell off the curve faster than most people. After uncovering weaknesses in the PES concept, he confronted Armstrong with his doubts about the viability of the DME project. Chuck Armstrong exploded when challenged on PES. The work days were repeatedly marked by angry exchanges between Kallur and Armstrong. So, after conducting twenty workshops, Kallur quit and returned to his previous employer. Kevin had lost an important friend—and, for the second time in six months, a boss.

Chuck Armstrong, who had been totally consumed with generating private-sector business, asked Kevin to assume the role of engagement manager in order to fill the void left by Kallur's sudden departure. By this time, the agency, which had been exposed to the Armstrong-Kallur feud, was fed up with the PES project. They had been only marginally satisfied with the PES workshops. Armstrong was behind schedule and had only delivered two of the three system modules. Even though the firm needed to complete just ten more PES workshops (on performance feedback) to finish the project, the agency cancelled the contract in September 1979. Kevin had the dubious distinction of being his own boss on an inoperative project. He subsequently returned to White Plains.

In order to get the last PES module, DME

signed a supplemental contract with Armstrong. Kevin was charged with developing the performance pay workshop materials and sending them to Washington. The DME personnel department would run the workshops without Armstrong trainers. The PES project was finished in January 1980.

DME, however, was not at all satisfied with the total project. It simply could not figure out how to put all three modules together in a workable package. They had been assured by Chuck Armstrong that once the "third leg" was added, the PES program would fall into place. Kevin's friends at DME—the personnel staff responsible for making PES work—kept calling him for help. He cared about these people and wanted to help them. But Chuck Armstrong ordered the project ended. Kevin was to bill them for the supplemental work and explain that no further time could be devoted to DME. The agency would get nothing more than what they had paid for in the contract. Still, the telephone calls from DME kept coming.

Kevin could take no more. On a Friday night, at the end of a particularly grueling week, Kevin's life exploded. He was drunk and had returned to the office late that evening. In five furious minutes he trashed the facility. File cabinets were knocked over, lamps broken, and waste baskets emptied. The place was a real mess. Luckily, a colleague found him and stopped the destruction before he went any further. He sobered up and spent the weekend cleaning up the office. It was a miracle that nobody else in the firm ever learned about the incident. Kevin clearly wanted out. Only five months remained until he would leave for Harvard Business School. He decided to "stick it out" at Armstrong.

### THE FINAL DAYS

Kevin sent DME the final bill for the PES project. He had barely begun work on another project when the agency sent a reply to his billing notice: they wanted to audit Armstrong's books. The audit was allowed under the terms of the government contract. Despite that indisputable fact, Chuck Armstrong at first refused to allow the DME auditor access to the firm's office.

The DME auditor soon discovered a number of billing discrepancies. In one particular instance, Chuck Armstrong had charged $50 for ground transportation to the New York airport; Kevin had charged only $6—the normal bus fare for the ride. It was firm policy to charge $50 for these trips so that money could be set aside to subsidize the firm's private jet. Kevin was told what he should say to the auditor. He had made a mistake, he would tell the auditor. The $50 was the cost for private limousine service. An Armstrong vice president had stood behind him as he answered the auditor's questions to make sure his explanations were clear—and consistent with what others had said. Kevin had been a "nervous wreck" through the entire session. Afterwards, he cornered the Armstrong vice president and vowed that he would "never do that again." It was March 1980 and he had only three months left at the firm.

The DME audit had turned up some questionable billing practices. It had not, however, unearthed anything that could do great harm to the firm. In his final weeks at Armstrong, Kevin was asked to "clean the DME files." As he did so, he came across something he had never seen before—a file folder that contained audio cassettes labeled "July 1978—Telephone Conversations with DME Procurement Office." According to a partial transcript that accompanied the recordings, the DME procurement officer had outlined how Armstrong should fashion its proposal to ensure a noncompetitive award. These notes, scribbled on three pages of a yellow legal pad, were unmistakenly written by Chuck Armstrong. Kevin skimmed the notes, placed all the project papers in chronological order, and slammed the PES file drawer shut.

### A FEW GENERAL QUESTIONS

Kevin left Armstrong Associates as planned in June 1980. Since his car had been demolished in an accident and would not be replaced until

August, he continued to use a company car that Chuck Armstrong had loaned to him. His summer vacation was restful. He had not, however, been able to gather his thoughts about his brief consulting career. Instead, he tried to concentrate on his future plans.

The September telephone call from the Boston DME office had startled him. Kevin had not wanted to relive his Armstrong experience. The DME investigator said he just wanted to ask a few general questions about the PES project. In a somewhat reflexive act, Kevin had agreed to meet with him.

As Kevin sat in his HBS dormitory, looking across the Charles River at Harvard College, he had to consider his next step. What was he going to say about Armstrong? The DME project? He did not want to vilify the firm; but he was angry. As he scolded himself for not having vigorously protested Armstrong's behavior, he wondered how much he had really learned since leaving college.

# Jordan Chemicals, Inc. (A)

It was September 18, 1981. William Royce, president of Jordan Chemicals, Inc., reflected on his situation with both anger and a measure of indignation. "I have enough problems trying to make this company fly economically. How do I make it fly ethically as well?" He had just discovered an employee scheme involving serious misrepresentation of inventories at the company warehouse. The market value of the products involved was approximately $60,000.

## THE COMPANY

Jordan Chemicals was a manufacturer of polyvinyl chloride (PVC) resins. Through a process of carefully monitored temperature changes and chemical additives, such as chlorine and ethylene, vinyl chloride monomer (VCM), a gas, was converted into PVC resin, a fine white powder. PVS was used in the manufacture of pipe, wire, shoes, sheeting, wood-type finishes, etc. It was one of the most widely used plastics in the world, with annual consumption of over 6 billion pounds in the U.S. alone. Other man-

ufacturers were B. F. Goodrich, Diamond Shamrock, Conoco, and Tenneco, all large oil-related companies. Although Jordan Chemicals had "small reactors" (2250 gallons each) and the larger companies had reactors of up to 35,000 gallons each, Jordan was able to compete using a "specialty/regional market segmentation strategy." By specializing in short-run resins (not efficient for large reactors) and local services (within 75 miles), the company was able to penetrate the market without using price incentives. There was one other regional manufacturer in New England the same size as Jordan. Two other small producers (less than 100 million pounds capacity) were located in the Middle Atlantic States.

Jordan Chemicals commenced production of PVC in August 1980, having taken over a dormant Massachusetts plant, constructed in 1974, that operated below capacity until 1978. The manufacturing and sales personnel, including management, numbered 80. It was expected that the new company would have about 18 to 24 months to establish itself before announced additional capacity came on stream, at which time Jordan would become either an attractive addition to a major competitor, a backward-integration opportunity for one of its customers, or a base to acquire other companies in the same field. After some initial start-up difficulties, the plant was operating at full manufacturing and sales capacity by August 1981.

William Royce and two other associates had a management consulting firm that specialized in turnaround situations. This consulting firm entered into an agreement with the financial backer of the reorganization. The agreement was to manage the company for a flat fee plus 20% of the equity in the new venture. Jordan Chemicals, therefore, was the renaming of an existing chemical company in reorganization.

Sales, on an annualized basis, were $17–20 million with production capacity at 72 million pounds (25–30 cents per pound). Exhibit 1 indicates basic price and cost information for the operation.

## PRODUCT MANAGEMENT

The key production imperative of the business was the maintenance of quality throughput, i.e., as little "off-grade" (or "off-spec") PVC as possible. All manufacturers produce some off-grade resins, however, and a rate of 95% "prime" and 5% off-grade was considered acceptable in the industry. Thus Jordan Chemicals expected to have to sell 3 to 4 million pounds of off-grade PVC annually through other than normal customer channels. Prime PVC went directly to manufacturing customers. So as not to diminish the quality image of the product, however, off-grade was commonly sold to resellers (sometimes referred to as "junkies").

Junkies sold off-grade materials for use in applications where appearance was not a factor (e.g., filler for products, black shoe soles) or where strength was not a major factor (e.g., children's toys). They sold to customers who competed with low-cost marginal-quality products such as shopping bags for discount stores, low-priced tape, hose, and plastic pipe.

"Junkies are important because they take the credit and product liability risks of marginal producers," according to Royce. "The material is sold off-grade, as is, no returns or allowances, F.O.B. our plant. They are also important because prime customers don't want the prime suppliers to know that they use off-grade sometimes to improve their profitability and the prime suppliers don't want their prime customers to know that they make less than prime product or more important, how much."

During the process of start-up and in normal operations in 1981, Jordan produced approximately 6 million pounds of off-grade materials that would normally be sold at 50 to 80% of prime prices, depending on the nature of the imperfection.

Royce himself handled the off-grade materials produced by Jordan Chemicals, choosing resellers and setting prices. "This enabled the regular sales force to concentrate on prime customers at prime prices," he explained.

To facilitate the orderly sale of off-grade material, Royce selected an upstate New York company, Tiempo-Endra, Inc., as his exclusive reseller. Tiempo-Endra was a company whose 50% partner was a substantial German trading company. Most other junkies were "desk and telephone" operations.

In Royce's words, "Tiempo-Endra had enough financial muscle to handle the account up to $150,000 and make good through their factors and/or their partner. Other large resellers either would not deal in PVC or would not give the manufacturer a fair price. Traders in this sector are known for shady dealing but we had selected T-E as the best of a bad lot. Working with only one junkie was a basic business decision. Dealing with more than one meant that you would be price-competing with yourself, since the resellers all went to the same customers."

The principals of Tiempo-Endra were Albert Bowman and James Watt. Both had spent many years in the PVC industry. Bowman's career spanned 25 years in sales with two different, but well-known chemical companies. Watt had worked 12 years with one of the same companies.

In September 1981, the recession hit the PVC business. Given the nature of its operation, Jordan was particularly hard hit. Royce's analyses indicated that even at capacity the company would sustain a loss of $3 million in the next several months unless some drastic action was taken. For this reason it was decided to place all but 10 key employees on temporary layoff until industry conditions changed. Shortly after the layoff was implemented, during a check on physical inventories, the problem came to light.

### DISCOVERY OF THE MISREPRESENTATION

It was through George McLain, a local independent trucker who did virtually all of his hauling for Jordan Chemicals, that Royce discovered the misrepresentation.

Dick Jameson, manager of materials, and Gil Kraus, shipping clerk, were responsible for storage and record keeping on all finished products (PVC), whether prime or off-grade. Due to limited storage space at the company's manufacturing facility, significant quantities of both prime and off-grade PVC were stored at an outside warehouse.

"We had asked McLain to take an independent inventory when he was unable to find certain materials that were listed on our inventory as being in the outside warehouse," Royce recalled. "He took an inventory, which Kraus knew about. Kraus asked McLain to give it to him before he showed it to 'management.' McLain gave a copy of his inventory to me and the original to Kraus."

Kraus "doctored" the inventory, eliminating 238,000 pounds of material worth $60,000 on the open market. He then went to McLain's house one weekend to try to convince McLain to submit the "doctored" invoice to Royce. McLain refused to cooperate with Kraus and explained the situation fully to Royce on September 18, the following Monday morning.

## EXHIBITS: Jordan Chemicals, Inc. (A)

**EXHIBIT 1**
PRICE AND COST INFORMATION
(Figures Assume Jordan Chemicals at 100% Capacity)

| | Industry at 80% capacity | | Industry at 65% capacity | |
|---|---|---|---|---|
| | ¢ per lb | % | ¢ per lb | % |
| Selling price | 38.0 | 100 | 28.0 | 100 |
| Off-grade loss | 1.0 | 3 | 1.0 | 3.6 |
| Average selling price | 37.0 | 97 | 27.0 | 96.4 |
| Raw material (VCM) | 20.0 | 52.6 | 20.0 | 71.4 |
| Freight in | 3.0 | 7.8 | 3.0 | 10.7 |
| Gross margin | 14.0 | 36.8 | 4.0 | 14.3 |
| Other costs: | | | | |
| Manufacturing | 6.5 | 17.1 | 6.5 | 23.2 |
| Depreciation | 1.0 | 2.6 | 1.0 | 3.6 |
| Freight out | 1.0 | 2.6 | 1.0 | 3.6 |
| SG & A | 2.5 | 6.5 | 2.5 | 8.9 |
| Interest | 1.0 | 2.6 | 1.0 | 3.6 |
| TOTAL | 12.0 | 31.4 | 12.0 | 42.9 |
| Profit before tax | 2.0 | 5.2 | (8.0) | (28.6) |
| Tax | 1.0 | 2.6 | — | |
| NPAT | 1.0 | 2.6 | (8.0) | (28.6) |

*Source:* Company records.

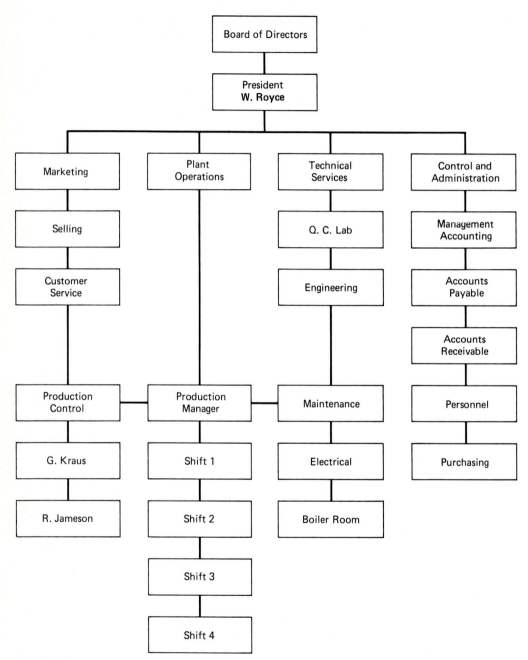

**EXHIBIT 2**
Jordan Chemicals, Inc.: organization chart. (*Source:* Company documents.)

# Jordan Chemicals, Inc. (B)

On September 18, 1981, William Royce, president of Jordan Chemicals, after discovering that two of his employees had been shipping unrecorded inventories worth over $50,000 to one of his company's resale customers, called the Boston office of the Federal Bureau of Investigation. FBI involvement was called for by the size and the interstate nature of the problem. FBI special agent Frank Mertaugh discussed the problem with Royce in Royce's office. "I'll try to help you get all the facts out," Mertaugh said, "but my role in this case, if you press the issue, is criminal investigation and prosecution. I can't help you with a civil recovery of your losses and damages. That will take years."

On September 21, 1981, in the presence of Mertaugh and (eventually) others, Royce called in Gil Kraus and confronted him with the inventory and shipping discrepancies. After four hours of questioning and a final assurance that the company would not demand prosecution, Kraus pulled a slip of paper out of his pocket giving dates, amounts of material, and payoff amounts. "The admission," Royce recalled, "came out in tears when I asked him what he would say to his son ten years from now after his (Kraus's) jail sentence was up."

Kraus explained in his written confession (see Exhibit 1) the main details of the scheme, implicating not only himself but Dick Jameson and Tiempo-Endra's Bowman and Watt. Early the next day, Royce called in Jameson and confronted him with the Kraus confession. In Royce's words, "Jameson stonewalled it for awhile, but eventually signed a confession. Now there was solid evidence aginst Tiempo-Endra."

"I had to decide what to do about Kraus and Jameson and how to deal with Tiempo-Endra," Royce added. "T-E had handled about 6 million pounds of off-grade material during

**EXHIBIT 1**

KRAUS'S CONFESSION

(The following is the text of the Kraus confession as written in the office of William Royce, president of Jordan Chemicals, Inc., on September 21, 1981.)

In February, 1981, Al Bowman of Tiempo-Endra, Inc., asked me if I wanted to make a little extra money by putting a couple of extra skids of resin on the truck and by swapping some prime resin for B-grade resin. I told him I didn't know if I could do it or take the chance. I told him I would have to think about it. Al arranged for my wife and I to go to New York in late February. I paid for the transportation. Al paid for everything else. He talked to me again about shipments to him. In March, we upgraded a few skids for him.

Dick Jameson came to me and complained to me about sending prime resin to Tiempo as off-grade. I told Dick the whole story. In early April, Dick and I took an inventory of the warehouse. We found a lot of resin which had been marked off as having been shipped, but worse still, there were no records of this material at all.

Al called me and I told him of the discrepancies in the inventory. He said when we find out the full story of the inventory, to let him know and he will make arrangements to ship material to him.

On April 17, we (Dick Jameson and I) shipped the first load to Al at Tiempo-Endra. Another load was shipped on April 20, April 24, April 30, June 19 and July 14, 1981.

For these loads, Dick Jameson and I were to receive $1000 each. We have thus far received $4000 each for six loads. Checks were sent to my house, addressed to me. The checks were for $500 each time, one for me and one for Dick Jameson. Checks were made on checking accounts bearing different names each time. Checks were, however, signed by either Al Bowman or James Watt.

Shortly after we shut the plant down, Al called me and asked if I could get more resin sent out. I told him I did not know the inventory in the outside warehouse. He wanted to buy a couple of loads and he was going to send his own truck down to pick them up. I then found we had 238,000 pounds in the warehouse. I was making arrangements to ship this to Tiempo-Endra when the company found out.

All shipments were sent to Tiempo-Endra, using his own trucks. All trucks were loaded at the warehouse. Truck drivers were Fred Sail or Jeff, each at different times.

(Signed)
Gilbert Kraus

the previous year and we had broken off all our other relationships with traders so we wouldn't meet ourselves in the market. Our choice was either to continue to do business with them (they owed us more than $200,000) or to start anew with someone else for the short term until I could get rid of all our remaining inventory in anticipation of the plant starting up again."

Royce picked up the phone and started to dial the number of Albert Bowman.

# Witness for the Corporation

The text that follows consists of verbatim excerpts from the Decision and Order of the State of Maine Public Utilities Commission (PUC), Docket #82-208, September 21, 1983. Names of company employees have been disguised. Only the findings of the commission are presented; the conclusions and action taken are omitted. To facilitate the reading of the narrative, internal page citations of depositions have been removed.

• • •

For several years, Central Maine Power Company, its officers, and employees have conducted activities at least partially in connection with the Company's electric utility business, which they have strongly believed should not be subject to public disclosure. These activities have included public opinion surveys which have been taken by or on behalf of the Company and other clients. Such surveys have in many cases related to political questions, referendum questions, and public image questions which the Company has considered "sensi-

tive." The Company has been reluctant to disclose the results and sometimes the questions under circumstances where there is a risk that the material could be made public. They have further believed any materials provided to the Commission will be in jeopardy of becoming public information, regardless of the issuance of protective orders or other measures designed to prevent public disclosure. This attitude has been held strongly by the Company's President, E. T. Walker, by its Senior Vice Presidents, Robert S. Fenn and Thomas W. Cass, by its Manager of Customer Communications, Robert Warren, and by others.

Mr. Walker has been President of CMP since 1972, and has worked for the Company in various capacities for over 30 years. He has testified and participated in many PUC proceedings. Mr. Walker has known Mr. Fenn for about 25 years and has worked very closely with him for the last decade. Mr. Walker's 1982 salary was $171,866.

Mr. Fenn became Vice President of CMP

in 1974, and was made Senior Vice President in 1977—the last ten years or so of which had been directly under the supervision of Mr. Walker. Mr. Fenn has testified in many PUC proceedings.

Mr. Fenn and Mr. Walker have testified that, until September 23, 1982, no one at CMP had been given reason to doubt Mr. Fenn's integrity. In 1982, Mr. Fenn was paid $81,217.

Mr. Cass joined CMP in 1977, and became a Senior Vice President in 1979. He was the first member of CMP's senior management to have come to the Company from the outside. He has testified in some PUC proceedings. In 1982, Mr. Cass was paid $81,017.

Messrs. Walker, Fenn, and Cass were three of the four highest-ranking employees of CMP in September, 1982.

Mr. Warren has been Manager of Customer Communications for CMP for some two years and has worked for CMP for 17 years. "Manager" positions rank immediately below corporate officers. At the time of Mr. Fenn's testimony, Mr. Warren's salary was $47,600 per year. Before October 1982, he reported to Mr. Fenn and sometimes worked directly with Mr. Walker. He occasionally discussed concerns regarding Mr. Fenn's performance with Mr. Cass. Despite his high position and sensitive responsibilities, he was widely regarded within CMP as "nervous," "excitable," and "an alarmist." His salary was reviewed in May 1983. Because of his involvement in this matter, no increase was awarded.

## EVENTS LEADING UP TO TESTIMONY

In July, 1981, the Company formed Atlantic Research Company ("Atlantic"), a wholly-owned corporate subsidiary, for the purpose of conducting public opinion surveys both for Central Maine Power Company and for outside clients. The primary purpose for the formation of Atlantic was to save money on the cost of surveys which had previously been performed by outside concerns. Additional motivations were the hope of Central Maine Power Com-

pany management that a separate corporate subsidiary could assure greater confidentiality in survey activities for other clients and the hope that a separate polling company could market its services to others for profit.

The officers of Atlantic have included E. T. Walker as President and Robert S. Fenn as Vice President. Thomas Cass has been one of Atlantic's directors. Other officers and directors of Atlantic are also employees of Central Maine Power Company. The bulk of the day-to-day operations have been carried on by Robert L. Warren, Customer Communications Manager of Central Maine Power Company. Mr. Walker and Mr. Fenn have overall supervisory responsibility. Mr. Cass has no responsibility for the operation of Atlantic. Processing of survey results has been performed using a program developed by the Central Maine Power Company and stored in its computer. Atlantic has had no full time employees nor has it had separate office space. Services have been primarily performed by CMP employees, both during and after working hours. Atlantic and the Company have engaged the services of Professor Peter Carlton, Brunswick, Maine, to assist in the development and analysis of polls conducted by Atlantic, to provide other political advice, and to assist the Company in improving its customer communications.

Disclosure of survey material and results within Atlantic and CMP was limited to those persons with "a need to know." For example, Mr. Cass—who was not directly involved in any polling activities—had never seen a copy of any Atlantic polling results until October 7, 1982, in circumstances more fully described below. While no special policy had been formulated regarding retention of survey material, retention was an issue of concern to Atlantic management. Results of surveys were routinely provided to Messrs. Walker, Fenn, Warren, Carlton, Norman Brooks (Vice President of Public Relations), Ad Media (The Company's advertising agency), and Marjorie Jacobs (a CMP computer technician). Mr. Fenn kept an "Atlantic Research file" in which he kept "executive summaries" of all Atlantic surveys. Computer printouts, executive summaries, and a permanent microfiche copy of all surveys were regularly maintained by Mr. Warren or his secretary. Survey results were also retained on magnetic tape in the CMP computer department under a one-year computer records retention policy authorized by Mr. Warren. Prior to September 23, 1982, there was no policy that poll results were to be destroyed or that sensitive questions were to be deleted from completed polls.

In early 1982, a public opinion poll conducted by Cambridge Reports, Inc., on behalf of Central Maine Power Company, was the subject matter of inquiry during the then pending CMP rate case. The Company, through its counsel Gerald A. Manion, was determined to prevent public disclosure of the poll because of its long-standing concern about release of "sensitive" survey information. After some discussion, arrangements were made to have the information made available to the Commission "in camera." To prevent possible public disclosure, the Company decided to eliminate the $15,000 expense for the survey from its test year expenses. Although this incident did not result in public release of survey information, it did cause Mr. Walker concern over the maintenance of confidentiality of the polls in the future. At the time he stated, within the hearing of several others, that the only way to insure that poll results did not become public was to dispose of them as promptly as possible. No other person deposed recalled this statement. No written or generally articulated and circulated policy concerning the retention or destruction of polls or the editing of "sensitive" questions was developed or placed in force at that time or at any other time prior to September 23, 1982.

In early March, 1982, the Company conducted a public opinion survey through Atlantic Research. The purposes of the survey were: (1) to assess the effectiveness of the Company's advertising campaign to upgrade the Company's image, (2) to track public opinion regarding the referendum to close Maine Yankee,[1] and (3) to develop information on customer attitudes toward a conservation loan program. Such a loan program was at that time widely discussed in the Legislature and with the State Energy Office, Maine Housing Authority, Public Advocate's Office, and Maine Public Utilities Commission.

Professor Peter Carlton developed, at the request of Messrs. Fenn and Walker, an initial poll incorporating several general questions from previous polls and several additional questions on the attitude of customers toward weatherization and conservation. The initial questions were reviewed by Mr. Fenn, among others. Mr. Fenn suggested additional questions relating to weatherization and conservation loans. The final poll, including all of the weatherization and conservation loan questions, was reviewed and approved by Mr. Walker. Of the thirty-eight questions in the poll, eight related primarily, if not exclusively, to weatherization and conservation loans.

The poll also contained a question about President Reagan, a question of the attitude of voters concerning the Maine Yankee nuclear referendum, and questions concerning the public's perceptions of E. T. Walker and Central Maine Power Company. The poll was performed in the first few days of March. Five hundred responses were obtained to a telephone survey conducted by part-time labor from the Company's headquarters in Augusta. The survey results from the March poll were promptly run on the computer at the request of Mr. Warren and were distributed in computer printout form to Messrs. Warren, Walker, Brooks, Carlton, and Ms. Jacobs. Several of the distributees and others also received copies of the poll questionnaires with the results penciled in by Mr. Warren. Mr. Fenn received one of these summaries and placed it in his survey file. Mr. Fenn also received two computer printout copies of this survey which he retained in his

---

[1] Maine Yankee was a controversial nuclear power plant in which CMP held a 38% interest.

office. Mr. Warren retained a copy of the computer survey and the executive summary. Mr. Walker received a computer printout of the poll and a copy of the questionnaire including the results. He may not have retained his copies after sometime in April, 1982.

On April 30, 1982, a meeting was held between Mr. Walker, Peter Bradford, then Public Advocate, and Gordon Weil, Director of the Office of Energy Resources, to discuss, among other things, a proposal for a conservation loan program. During the meeting, Mr. Walker went into Mr. Fenn's office and obtained from Mr. Fenn's executive summary of the March survey the results of several questions relating to the conservation loan program.

In May of 1982, Mr. Fenn, in response to an inquiry from Connie Irland, Office of Energy Resources, prepared from his executive summary of the March 1982 poll a letter summarizing the results of six conservation loan and weatherization questions. A copy of the letter summarizing the six questions and responses was sent to Gerald A. Manion, Esquire.

In paragraph 3(c)(5) of its submission of the energy conservation loan program to the Commission in late July and August 1982, the Company made reference to one of the responses to the March survey.

Because the Energy Conservation Loan Program had been developed through negotiations among several interested parties (not including the Commission staff), it was not viewed as a controversial proceeding at CMP.

Staff Data Request 1, Item 2 in the conservation loan program case requested "the results of the CMP telephone survey, referred to in Section C(3)(a)(5) of your program outline, including the questions asked and a summary of the responses thereto." The response to this data request was to be sponsored by Mr. Robert Fenn. The data request was assigned to Mr. Howard Jones for research and initial response preparation. Mr. Jones was referred to Mr. Warren for information on the survey. Mr. Jones' proposed response gave only one question relating to the 10 percent interest rate. The draft was reviewed in a September 10, 1982,

meeting attended by Mr. Fenn and Mr. Manion and others. At Mr. Manion's request, the final response to the data request was expanded to include the response rates at the 0 percent and 5 percent interest levels. The information came to Mr. Jones from Mr. Warren, who had retained a copy of the complete March survey. The response did not include the remaining questions relating to weatherization or energy conservation loans.

At this meeting on September 10, when the data request response was discussed and approved by Mr. Fenn and Mr. Manion, both Mr. Fenn and Mr. Manion were aware that there were more than three questions which dealt with conservation loans and weatherization. The Connie Irland letter, referring to six questions, was present and discussed at that meeting. A second copy of the Irland letter was given to Mr. Manion. At the September 10 meeting, there was no suggestion by any party, including Mr. Fenn, that any survey results had been destroyed.

The usual process followed by CMP in responding to data requests was not followed with regard to the Energy Conservation Loan Program proceeding. Unlike the usual procedure followed at CMP, for example, the draft responses to data requests were not circulated to all those CMP employees participating in the proceeding. Further, even when the responsible CMP personnel did meet to discuss the draft responses, insufficient copies were available. This may have resulted from the fact that the matter was being handled on an expedited basis.

At the prehearing conference on September 7, Commissioner Harrington requested information concerning income levels of respondents to the loan proposal questions on the March survey. Her request was also discussed at the September 10 meeting and assigned to Mr. Jones. He was told to get the information from Mr. Warren. Mr. Warren provided the information to Mr. Jones from the computer-printed cross tabulations. The information for all data requests was supplied by Mr. Warren to Mr. Jones and placed in exhibit or response form to be delivered to the Commission. Copies of the exhibits and responses were given to Mr. Manion.

On the morning of September 23, Robert Warren was aware that Mr. Fenn would be testifying before the Public Utilities Commission and met with him. Mr. Warren learned that the opinion survey information might be the subject of the inquiry. Mr. Warren's lack of confidence in Mr. Fenn's ability to testify on matters relating to opinion surveys caused Mr. Warren considerable concern.

After leaving the meeting with Mr. Fenn, Mr. Warren called Mr. Cass and arranged to meet for coffee in the Company's cafeteria. The two met and Mr. Warren conveyed his concerns regarding Mr. Fenn's upcoming testimony regarding the Atlantic surveys. Mr. Cass took no action in response to Mr. Warren's concerns. Mr. Warren had previously complained to Mr. Cass about Mr. Fenn. Mr. Cass was not inclined to intervene in the relationship between the two, especially because he considered Mr. Warren to be excitable and an alarmist and because his relationship with Mr. Fenn was complicated by the perception that the two of them were rivals to succeed Mr. Walker.

## THE DAY OF TESTIMONY

On or about September 22, preparatory to testifying, Mr. Fenn met with Mr. Manion and went over a draft of his testimony which he had prepared with Mr. Manion's assistance. The parties discussed the presentation of the income breakdown of respondents which had been set forth in a document subsequently identified as CMP Exhibit 4 in Docket 82-145. At no time did Mr. Fenn suggest that any results had been destroyed or were unavailable.

On September 23, Mr. Fenn and Mr. Manion went to the Public Utilities Commission accompanied by Mr. Jones and Mr. Douglas Stevens. The primary Company witness was Mr. Fenn. He testified on direct examination and introduced several exhibits, including CMP Exhibit 4. Upon cross examination, first by Ms. Virginia Davis and then by others including the

Examiner and all three Commissioners, Mr. Fenn was asked a number of questions regarding the content and availability of the March Atlantic survey. Mr. Fenn repeatedly gave answers which he knew were false.

False answers by Mr. Fenn included:

*Q.* I just want to know if that was the only question that you asked, would you borrow up to $1,500 to finance weatherization projects in your home at an interest rate of 10%?

*A.* The only questions that were relevant to this program were those three questions.

*Examiner Donahue:* Mr. Fenn, which data request is that?

*A.* That's 1-MPUC-2.

*Examiner Donahue:* Thank you.

*Q.* That's the only question that was asked?

*A.* Relevant to this program, yes. (Transcript B-77)

*Q.* Can you tell me what those questions were?

*A.* No, I can't.

*Q.* Can you provide us with a copy?

*A.* No, I can't. I don't have them.

*Commissioner Gelder:* I didn't hear that answer.

*A.* I said no, I can't. I don't have them.

*Q.* Who has them?

*A.* They have probably been destroyed.

*Mr. Moskovitz:* The questions or the answers?

*A.* The questions and probably most of the answers. We don't keep them around.

*Commissioner Gelder:* Would you mind checking at the Company to see whether those

*A.* I can double check, but I can pretty much guarantee that they are not available. (Transcript B78-79)

*Q.* What I'm trying to find out is if there was anything else in the survey that limited the question or the response.

*A.* No. I said—maybe you misunderstood

me. I indicated that all there was in the survey that pertained to the conservation loan program were these questions. (Transcript B-81)

*By Commissioner Cheryl Harrington:*

Q. Is that summary report the report that you're uncertain or at least leaning to thinking it doesn't exist any longer? You said you were going to search your files and see if you can find that report.

A. I know it's not in my files.

Q. Well, search the Company's files.

A. Yes. I will ask when I go back this noontime.

Q. If it is not available, would you try to ascertain the date on which it was taken out of your files and destroyed?

A. Yes. That may be very difficult to do. (Transcript B-93)

*By Chairman Peter Bradford:*

Q. Mr. Fenn, would the survey have been destroyed on instruction from someone?

A. Would it have been destroyed on instruction?

Q. Yes.

A. Yes.

Q. From whom?

A. Probably me.

Q. Why would you have given that instruction?

A. Because the survey covers many areas. In order to do a survey you have to ask masking questions. Once we get the answers to the questions we're looking at we get rid of the rest of it.

Q. Why would the report of the answers have been destroyed?

A. Because the report would have included all of the answers to all of the questions.

Q. Maybe I've misunderstood. I thought at some point there was a summary document in existence—summarized answers by number.

A. The summary is complete, or at least the . . .

Q. Why would that have been destroyed?

A. Why would it have been complete?

Q. No. Why would it have been destroyed?

A. Because there are questions and answers on there that were merely masking questions. We just didn't want them around. (Transcript B-94-95)

While Mr. Fenn persisted in his testimony that the March survey had been destroyed, he knew that he had a copy of the complete survey in his desk. Mr. Fenn also knew that Mr. Warren and others had additional copies of the March survey. Mr. Fenn testified falsely in order to protect the confidentiality of the March survey. He feared that, if he acknowledged its existence, he would have to turn it over to the PUC. He thought that it contained much "sensitive" political material. In fact, he had it confused with a more "sensitive" April survey.

Commissioners Harrington and Gelder at different times during the hearings in Docket 82-145 on the morning of September 23 requested Mr. Fenn to search the Company offices for a copy of the March poll during the lunch hour and bring it back in the afternoon to the Commission.

Mr. Manion and other CMP employees present during the hearings were able to discern from the facial expressions and tone of the questions of the other parties that Mr. Fenn's testimony regarding the Atlantic survey was not being believed.

In the latter part of the morning of the 23rd, after there had been extensive examination regarding the content and availability of the March survey, Commissioner Bradford urged the cross-examining parties to expedite the proceedings. These comments were not made on the record. These remarks were, however, heard by Mr. Stevens, but not recalled by Mr. Jones, Mr. Fenn, or Mr. Manion. Mr. Stevens has testified that he recalls telling Mr. Cass, during the noon recess, words to the effect that "Commissioner Bradford had clearly made the point that . . . the Commission wasn't really interested in pursuing something off the subject and would get back on the subject and they would make up their mind based on the facts about the survey that were in the record as it pertained to the loan program." Various Company officials, including Messrs. Warren and Walker, later became aware of the gist of Mr. Steven's view. However, the Chairman's remarks neither cured Mr. Fenn's false testimony nor relieved the Company in any sense of its obligation to provide a copy of the survey if one could be found, an obligation that Mr. Moskovitz emphasized directly to Mr. Stevens later in the day. Furthermore, none of the Company's attorneys ever doubted that the Company was under a legal obligation to produce the survey if it existed.

During the luncheon break on September 23, Robert Fenn left the hearing room. He ordered Mr. Stevens to call Mr. Warren and have him meet him in his office at once. Mr. Fenn rode with Mr. Manion in his car from the Commission hearing room over to the Company offices in Augusta. During the automobile trip, Mr. Manion expressed great concern over Mr. Fenn's lack of credibility in connection with his testimony about Atlantic Research. He urged him to make a careful search to see if some kind of survey information could be produced to be given to the Commission.

Upon arriving at the Central Maine Power Company office, Mr. Fenn and Mr. Manion went into Mr. Fenn's office, where they were almost immediately joined by Mr. Warren. Upon Mr. Warren's arrival, Mr. Fenn asked Mr. Manion to leave the office and said that he wanted to talk to Mr. Warren alone. Mr. Manion was shocked and upset at this request, which had never before occurred in his experience. He left the office and waited outside. By this time Mr. Manion had doubts regarding the truthfulness of Mr. Fenn's statements.

Mr. Fenn closed the door to his office and then told Mr. Warren that he was to destroy the March 1982 survey. Mr. Warren understood that Mr. Fenn intended that the March survey and all other surveys be disposed of so that they would not fall into the hands of the Commission. Mr. Warren stated that persons other than he had copies of the surveys. Mr. Fenn gave him to understand that Mr. Warren was to dispose of those as well. Mr. Fenn told Mr. War-

ren to go home and prepare notes on certain additional weatherization questions from the March survey. Mr. Warren left Mr. Fenn's office. This meeting lasted a few minutes. Mr. Warren proceeded to carry out Mr. Fenn's instructions, except that he decided not to destroy the surveys because of their value in conducting future surveys and because he knew that destruction of the surveys would be dishonest and wrong. Instead, Mr. Warren removed his copies of all survey information and hid the materials in the trunk of his automobile.

After the closed-door meeting with Mr. Warren, Mr. Fenn rejoined Mr. Manion in a small conference room for lunch. He told Mr. Manion that there were no copies of the March poll. Mr. Manion began to impress upon Mr. Fenn the seriousness of the matter, when Mr. Fenn stated that everything was all right and that he would do nothing to break the law. These statements satisfied Mr. Manion. Mr. Manion did not seek from Mr. Fenn an explanation as to what had been discussed with Mr. Warren. Nor did he inquire further as to the alleged destruction of the survey.

At some point, Mr. Stevens joined Mr. Manion and Mr. Fenn, and Mr. Walker also arrived at the conference room. Mr. Walker was informed that the Commission had requested a copy of the March survey, that Fenn had testified that the survey was destroyed, that Fenn's testimony was not being believed by the Commission, that the Commission had requested that Mr. Fenn check over the lunch break to determine whether a copy of the March survey could be provided, and that Mr. Fenn did not have a copy of the survey. In addition, it is likely but not certain that Mr. Walker was told that Mr. Fenn had excluded Mr. Manion from a meeting between himself and Mr. Warren and then had advised Manion that no polls were available. Mr. Manion expressed considerable concern to Mr. Walker about the March survey. According to Mr. Manion (whose account Mr. Walker "emphatically" disagrees with), Mr. Walker stated that he might have a copy of the March survey but was interrupted by Mr. Fenn. Again according to Mr. Manion, Mr. Fenn stated that he knew that Mr. Walker had no such copy, and then Mr. Walker stated that he had no such copy. Mr. Manion and Mr. Fenn left to return to the Commission. As Mr. Manion and Mr. Fenn left the area of Mr. Walker's office to go to the elevator, Mr. Fenn suddenly returned to Mr. Walker's office alone. Either Mr. Fenn or Mr. Warren told Mr. Walker that Mr. Warren would be coming around that afternoon to "pick up the surveys," which, Mr. Walker has testified, he took to mean Maine Yankee surveys because he had just said that he had no copy of the March survey. Mr. Fenn says that he meant the March survey in his conversation with Mr. Walker. Maine Yankee surveys were never mentioned during the meetings between Stevens, Manion, Fenn, and Walker. On September 23 Mr. Walker knew that the Public Utilities Commission had requested a copy of Atlantic's March 1982 survey and that Mr. Fenn had testified that the survey had been destroyed. Mr. Walker knew that the Commission was not provided with a copy of the survey during the afternoon of September 23 or at any other time prior to October 7, 1982.

Still acting on Mr. Fenn's instructions, Mr. Warren went to Mr. Walker's office, informed him that Mr. Fenn had instructed Mr. Warren to get the surveys out of the office, and asked Mr. Walker to give him copies of all survey materials retained by Mr. Walker. He did not single out Maine Yankee surveys. Mr. Walker gave certain materials to Mr. Warren but retained certain current Save Maine Yankee material that he was in the process of reviewing. Despite the pressures of his other duties, Mr. Walker then accompanied Mr. Warren to the offices of Mr. Brooks and Mr. Owens and similarly gathered together copies of survey information. Mr. Walker believed that removing the surveys from the office would prevent the Commission from obtaining copies of the surveys. After gathering the survey information together, Mr. Warren took the materials to his home, where he stayed for the remainder of the afternoon.

Mr. Cass met Messrs. Manion and Fenn in the lobby of the CMP building during the noon hour on September 23 when Mr. Manion and Mr. Fenn had first arrived. Mr. Cass observed that both Manion and Fenn were upset and were in no mood to have any conversation with him. A few minutes later Mr. Cass saw Mr. Manion standing outside of Mr. Fenn's office and noticed that Messrs. Fenn and Warren were meeting in Fenn's office behind closed doors. Mr. Cass saw that Mr. Manion was very disturbed.

Before the noon hour ended Mr. Stevens briefed Mr. Cass on the events of the morning hearing. Mr. Cass was informed that Mr. Fenn was performing poorly. Mr. Stevens also informed Mr. Cass of Chairman Bradford's off-record comments along the lines set forth above.

Mr. Fenn and Mr. Manion returned to the Commission. Prior to the beginning of the afternoon hearings, Mr. Manion advised Mr. Fenn to volunteer efforts to obtain a copy of the March survey from Professor Carlton. Mr. Fenn chose to ignore the advice of his counsel, a decision which Mr. Manion believed to be imprudent but which he did not report to other CMP officers. After his return to the Commission, Mr. Fenn was asked whether he had been able to find a copy of the March survey. Mr. Fenn gave false responses:

*Q.* Were you able to verify over the noon break whether the survey had been shredded or whether it still exists?

*A.* We don't have a copy of the survey. The reason for it is, as I tried to explain before the lunch break, that there is some very sensitive information in those surveys. Once we get the information off it that we want, we want to dispose of it. (Transcript B-109)

*Q.* Now let me come back then to an area that we've discussed probably too long already. The results of this Atlantic Research survey. Are you saying now that you have retained some of the results?

*A.* No. I said earlier this morning that we retained some information on the questions that went with this and that would include the income obviously. (Transcript C-23)

At the midafternoon break on the 23rd, Mr. Moskovitz told Mr. Stevens that he thought that Mr. Fenn was "lying" and that, if his testimony was not corrected, his credibility as a witness before the Commission would be permanently impaired. Mr. Moskovitz indicated that the matter was very serious both for Mr. Fenn and for the Company, and that the only way to correct the damage was to find a copy of the survey and provide it to the Commission. During the evening dinner break, Mr. Stevens reported the gist of this conversation to Mr. Manion.

The Commission session on the 23rd ended after 11:00 P.M. At approximately midnight, Mr. Fenn stopped at the Company offices, picked up his copy of the March poll, and took it home with him. Mr. Fenn then reviewed his copy of the complete March survey and concluded that the survey contained little or no information that could not be disclosed to the Commission. Mr. Fenn did not entertain the thought of providing a copy of the survey to the Commission during the hearings in Docket 82-145 which were continuing the next day.

On Thursday, September 23, between 6:00 and 6:30 in the evening, Mr. Warren called Mr. Thomas Cass at his home and asked him if he could come and talk to him about a serious matter. This call was prompted by a 6:00 P.M. television news story regarding Fenn's testimony. Mr. Cass resisted at first but then agreed to meet with Mr. Warren at Mr. Cass's summer camp where he was then living. Mr. Warren and his wife drove to the Cass summer camp, about a half an hour away. Mr. Warren spent approximately three hours or more with Mr. and Mrs. Cass discussing, among other things, his concern and dissatisfaction with Mr. Fenn's testimony. Mr. Warren "believes" or "suspects" that he told Cass that he had reason to be concerned with the honesty of Fenn's testimony. Mr. Cass says that he did not. Mr. Cass does recall his wife asking Warren what happened and being told, "You don't want to know." At this point Mr. Cass recalls saying, "I don't want to know."

During the evening meeting, Mr. Cass at-tempted to reach Mr. Stevens and others to obtain information that might diminish Mr. Warren's concerns but the attempts were unsuccessful. Based on the continuing misunderstanding of the significance of Chairman Bradford's comments as relayed by Mr. Stevens earlier in the day compounded by Mr. Stevens's failure to tell him of Mr. Moskovitz's midafternoon warning, Mr. Cass told Mr. Warren that he did not believe the Commission was seriously interested in the survey material or was going to pursue it any further. Mr. Cass reassured Mr. Warren that no action was necessary to correct any problems arising from Mr. Fenn's testimony. Mr. Cass's attentiveness to and recollection of the conversation that evening was substantially diminished by his preoccupation at the time with serious personal matters.

**THE DAYS FOLLOWING**

At 6:30 A.M. on September 24, Mr. Fenn called Mr. Warren and asked him for the information which Mr. Warren had been requested on the previous day to abstract from the March poll. Mr. Warren met Mr. Fenn at his office at 7:30 A.M. and delivered to him the handwritten summaries of the questions and answers on weatherization which he had prepared at his home on the preceding afternoon.

On the morning of September 24, an article in the *Kennebec Journal* appeared with the headline "CMP Official Admits to Destroying Loan Survey." The article, which was widely read at CMP, reported Mr. Fenn's testimony the previous day before the Commission. It was read on the morning of the 24th by Mr. Walker, Mr. Cass, Mr. Jenning, Mr. Stevens, Mr. Warren, and Mr. Fenn, as well as other CMP employees and Mr. Manion. At approximately 7:30 A.M., Mr. Walker and Mr. Cass spoke with Mr. Fenn about the *Kennebec Journal* article. Mr. Fenn told them that the headline was inaccurate, but that the newspaper story itself was an accurate report on the morning session. Mr. Fenn assured them vaguely and generally that the matter had been taken care of in the afternoon and that everything was "all right." He did not explain how this had been done. Mr. Walker accepted these assurances. However, he had been given no reason to believe that a copy of the survey had been furnished to the Commission and he did not so conclude. Mr. Walker did not pursue the matter further by, for example, conferring with Mr. Manion. At the same meeting or possibly a different meeting later that morning, Mr. Stevens informed Messrs. Cass, Walker, and Manion that the newspaper story was a fair representation of the hearing.

On the morning of September 24, Mr. Harry Lintner and Ms. Marjorie Jacobs, company employees in the data processing department, approached Mr. Warren. They were concerned about the *Kennebec Journal* article, because it appeared to them that Mr. Fenn's testimony had been inaccurate. They told Mr. Warren that all of the survey results were still on the Company computer. They said that they thought that Mr. Fenn knew or should have known that fact or at least that Mr. Warren kept hard copies and microfiche. Mr. Warren may have assured them that Mr. Fenn had not known that the material was still on the computer and that the Commission was no longer interested in the information anyway. He said that he would pursue the matter further. Mr. Warren reported his conversation with Mr. Lintner and Ms. Jacobs to Mr. Thomas Cass. Mr. Cass referred Mr. Warren to Mr. Walker. Sometime during the day on Friday, September 24, Mr. Warren approached Mr. Walker and advised him of his conversation with Ms. Jacobs and Mr. Lintner, including the fact that they were concerned about the inaccuracy of Mr. Fenn's testimony. Mr. Cass and Mr. Walker did not perceive the need to correct the testimony of the preceding day or to have a computer run of the survey prepared and delivered to the Commission. Mr. Walker expressed surprise that any survey material was still on the computer. He told Mr. Warren to consult with Professor Carlton and see what Professor Carlton's policy was on preservation of survey data in the computer.

Mr. Warren believes that he told Mr. Walker at some point on September 24 about his misgivings regarding Mr. Fenn's conduct. Mr. Walker mentions no such conversation.

On Friday, September 24, or Monday, September 27, Mr. Warren spoke with Professor Carlton and inquired about his policy on survey retention in the computer. Professor Carlton told him that his policy was to purge the survey material from the computer shortly after it had been analyzed in order to save expense. Mr. Warren reported his conversation to Mr. Walker, who told him to remove the survey material from the CMP computer. In Mr. Walker's view, this action did not constitute destruction of documents or records sought by the PUC because Mr. Fenn had told him that same morning that the matter had been taken care of.

All surveys, including the March 1982 survey, were removed from the CMP computer on Monday, September 27 by Marjorie Jacobs on instruction from Mr. Walker through Mr. Warren. Ms. Jacobs had misgivings about removing the surveys but did not feel that she should question the instructions of her superiors. Mr. Lintner also doubted the wisdom of removing the surveys. Later Ms. Jacobs learned that the surveys had also been retained on a backup computer memory device, from which they were not erased.

On the morning of September 24, just before the beginning of a Save Maine Yankee meeting, Mr. Walker approached Michael Worthy, Esq., counsel to the Save Main Yankee Committee, and asked Mr. Worthy if he would, on behalf of Atlantic Research, develop a mechanism to assure the confidentiality of survey results. Mr. Worthy agreed to the representation. Mr. Fenn was present at this meeting.

Over the September 25–26 weekend, Robert S. Fenn took his copy of the executive summary of the March 1982 survey and scissored out certain questions and results and then photocopied the summary onto new sheets to create an edited version of the survey. He placed this new version together with the notes by Mr. Warren in his file. The deleted questions and the remainder of the original survey were destroyed.

On or about Monday, September 27, Mr. Fenn reviewed his Atlantic Research survey files. He re-created the files by destroying or removing copies of polls done for third parties and by deleting the sensitive questions from polls done for CMP. He obtained from Mr. Warren copies of Atlantic Research stationery and prepared two memoranda, one on Atlantic Research stationery, and one on Central Maine Power Company stationery, relating to retention of poll survey material. The memoranda were backdated to May 19, 1982, and purported to have been written on May 19. The memoranda purported to establish Company policy with respect to the retention of surveys done by Atlantic Research for its clients and surveys done for Central Maine Power Company by outside polling firms including Atlantic Research. Mr. Fenn reviewed the backdated memoranda with Mr. Walker. Mr. Walker was aware of the backdating and approved the memoranda. Mr. Fenn also gave copies of the memoranda to Mr. Warren. Prior to September 27, 1982, the policies outlined in the backdated memoranda were not Company policy. During the week of September 27, Mr. Manion called Mr. Fenn to arrange a meeting with Fenn, Manion, and Walker to discuss issues relating to Atlantic and opinion surveys. A mutually agreeable time could not be arranged. On or about September 27, Mr. Walker entered Mr. Fenn's office and observed Mr. Fenn creating an edited version of a public opinion survey. Mr. Walker and Mr. Fenn discussed the new policy of maintaining surveys in edited form.

On Friday, October 1, 1982, the staff of the Public Utilities Commission filed its brief in the conservation loan case and delivered a copy to Mr. Manion, counsel for the Company. The brief commented unfavorably on Mr. Fenn's testimony and credibility with respect to the Atlantic Research surveys.

On Saturday, October 2, Mr. Manion drafted a letter to Messrs. Fenn and Walker requesting a conference to discuss the "problem" of the retention policy concerning the surveys.

This letter was reviewed, redrafted, and hand-delivered to the Company on Monday, October 4. When Mr. Walker read it is not clear.

On October 4, 1982, the Commission held a deliberative session to consider the issues raised by the conservation loan program application. During the course of the session, members of the Commission expressed their concern and dissatisfaction with the testimony of Mr. Fenn and the apparent destruction of the Atlantic Research surveys. The Commission specifically announced during the course of its deliberations that it would further investigate Atlantic Research and its activities during the course of the "reorganization" case then pending before the Commission. The meeting was being monitored by the Company and minutes concerning this meeting were distributed to Messrs. Fenn, Walker, and Cass, among others, on October 4 or 5. It is not clear that they were read by any of them. An oral report on this aspect of the Commission's deliberation was given to Mr. Manion and Mr. Cass.

On October 4 or 5, Mr. Fenn read the last two pages of the Commission staff's brief in 82-145 which pertained to Mr. Fenn's testimony. The assertions angered Mr. Fenn and he decided to resolve the matter by providing his recently edited copy of the March survey to the Commission.

On or about October 4, Mr. Manion met with Mr. Cass and discussed the ratemaking treatment of public opinion surveys generally and the ratemaking implications if all copies of such surveys are destroyed and no longer available for Commission review.

On October 4 or 5, 1982, Thomas Cass advised Robert Fenn that he would need to be briefed and prepared on Atlantic Research, its financial condition, corporate structure, and activities, in preparation for his proposed testimony in the reorganization proceeding later on that week. Mr. Fenn prepared a package of materials for Mr. Cass to have with him during his testimony. The package of materials included a summary of corporate information on Atlantic Research, financial results, and copies of "edited" versions of the executive summaries of several surveys performed by Atlantic Research. One of these edited surveys was a version of the March 1982 survey. Also included was a copy of Mr. Warren's notes concerning the conservation loan questions on the March 1982 survey which Mr. Fenn had requested him to prepare on the afternoon of September 23. The materials were delivered to Mr. Cass on the morning of October 7.

Sometime between October 4 and October 6, Mr. Walker reviewed the portion of the Commission staff's brief relating to Mr. Fenn's credibility. Mr. Walker was concerned and had a brief conversation with Mr. Fenn but failed to obtain a satisfactory explanation. Mr. Walker did not pursue the matter further. He was out of state for part of October 5 and all of October 6.

On October 6, 1982, Mr. Fenn telephoned Michael Worthy in his capacity as attorney for the Committee to Save Maine Yankee. Mr. Fenn advised Mr. Worthy that he had sensitive survey material relating to the Maine nuclear referendum questions that had been generated by Atlantic Research for the Committee. He asked Mr. Worthy what he should do with this material. Mr. Worthy advised him that all such materials should be delivered to him and that Atlantic Research should not retain copies of the survey. Mr. Fenn attempted to have the materials be delivered that day to the headquarters of the Committee to Save Maine Yankee in Augusta. Mr. Worthy then reminded Mr. Fenn that he had been retained by Atlantic Research to advise that company on survey retention and confidentiality matters. Mr. Fenn then asked Mr. Worthy's advice on the disclosure of Atlantic survey materials to the Commission. Mr. Worthy gave Mr. Fenn general impromptu advice on the right of the Commission to order production of survey results and measures to protect confidentiality of surveys done for third parties.

On October 7, 1982, at 7:30 A.M., a meeting was held in Mr. Fenn's office for the purpose of briefing Mr. Cass on Atlantic Research prior to his testimony before the Commission later that day. Present were Mr. Fenn, Mr. Cass, Mr. Jones (outside counsel representing the Company in this case), Mr. Warren, and, for a portion of the meeting, Mr. Walker. At the meeting, all parties, including Mr. Walker, were made aware that among the materials that Mr. Cass had been given by Mr. Fenn was an edited version of the March 1982 Atlantic Research telephone survey. Thus everyone present at this meeting (except perhaps Mr. Jones) had reason to realize that Mr. Fenn's testimony had been inaccurate. Mr. Cass was told by Mr. Fenn that the survey could be made available to the Commission, but none of those present perceived a need to do so immediately (whether or not it happened to come up at the October 7 hearing) in response to the Commission's repeated requests for the survey during the conservation loan proceedings on September 23.

Mr. Fenn's statements during the meeting before Mr. Cass's testimony in the CMP reorganization case caused Mr. Walker to be concerned with the testimony Mr. Fenn had given to the PUC on September 23 regarding the March survey. Mr. Fenn's statements were inconsistent with his previous representations to Mr. Walker. Mr. Walker had a crowded schedule on that morning and did not inquire further. He made a mental note that he should talk with Mr. Fenn to find out what was going on.

Mr. Cass appeared on October 7 and testified at the Commission. During the course of the testimony, he referred to documents lying before him on the witness table. Staff counsel asked to inspect the documents. Because he was concerned about Mr. Cass's handwritten marginal notes and about the relevancy of the March survey to the reorganization case, Mr. Jones unexpectedly objected to the inspection, which was finally granted by the Examiner. These objections came as a surprise to Mr. Cass. During the inspection, staff counsel saw the edited March 1982 Atlantic survey for the first time.

At approximately 12:30 on October 7, Mr. Fenn went to Mr. Manion, who was participating in a meeting on a separate matter at the Company's office, and advised him that a copy of the March survey had just been given to the

Commission by Mr. Cass. At that time, Mr. Manion requested Mr. Fenn to provide him a copy of what Mr. Cass gave to the Commission. Later that day at Mr. Manion's request, Mr. Fenn provided Mr. Manion with a copy of the transcript of the September 23 hearing. Mr. Manion then concluded that Mr. Fenn had lied to him during the noon hour on September 23. In response to Mr. Manion's questions, Mr. Fenn maintained that the Commission had asked for a copy of the entire survey on September 23 and the document provided on October 7 was only a partial survey. Mr. Manion did not know at that time that the edited version had been prepared after September 23. Even without knowing that fact, Mr. Manion found Mr. Fenn's justification "incredible."

Mr. Moskovitz informed CMP General Counsel John Jenning at an afternoon recess at the hearing on October 7 that based upon the documents produced by Mr. Cass, in his opinion Mr. Fenn had given false testimony on September 23. Although Mr. Jenning had read the September 24 *Kennebec Journal* article, he had not inquired into the matter. Consequently, Mr. Moskovitz's statement led to the first realization that Mr. Jenning had that there was any question about the plausibility or truthfulness of Mr. Fenn's testimony. (Mr. Jenning did not receive or review the Commission staff's brief filed October 1 which commented on Mr. Fenn's testimony until sometime after October 7.) Mr. Jenning immediately informed Mr. Cass of Mr. Moskovitz's comment, and Mr. Cass in turn called Mr. Walker and Mr. Fenn. Mr. Jenning then called Mr. Manion at his home to report Mr. Moskovitz's comment and to get Mr. Manion's reaction. Mr. Jenning and Mr. Manion agreed to meet early the next morning in Mr. Jenning's office to discuss the situation further and talk to Mr. Walker about it. When Mr. Jenning arrived at his office the morning of October 8, he obtained a copy of the transcript and reviewed it with respect to the questions asked Mr. Fenn about the March survey, and Mr. Fenn's responses, before Mr. Manion arrived.

On the morning of October 8, 1982, Mr. Manion met with Mr. Jenning and discussed the appearance of the edited version of the March 1982 telephone survey. Mr. Manion and Mr. Jenning agreed that, comparing Mr. Fenn's testimony with the edited survey he had furnished Mr. Cass, Mr. Fenn was potentially liable to criminal charges. Mr. Manion advised Mr. Jenning that the Company should make full disclosure of this document and the circumstances of its nonproduction at the September 23 hearing. He stated to Mr. Jenning that Mr. Fenn should have separate counsel. Mr. Jenning and Mr. Manion then met with Mr. Walker. Mr. Manion advised Mr. Walker of his concern and recommended that Mr. Fenn, who was out of the state on that day, be told to retain separate counsel. He also advised that Mr. Warren have separate counsel. He advised Mr. Walker that he was sending a copy of the survey to the Commission to be included in the record of the conservation loan case. Mr. Jenning and Mr. Walker concurred with this advice. Mr. Manion then delivered a copy of the edited survey with his own covering letter to the Commission.

## AFTERMATH

A full copy of the March survey was turned over to the Commission by the Company on October 12, 1982. The Commission issued its Decision and Order implementing an energy conservation loan program on October 22, 1982. During the interim, the substance of the March survey was not the subject of any inquiry from the Commission to the Company in Docket No. 82-145. . . .

The separate representation of Mr. Walker, Mr. Fenn, and Mr. Warren in all matters relating hereto, including the criminal prosecution of Mr. Fenn, has been paid for by the Company pursuant to the indemnity provisions of Section 7 of its by-laws and specific indemnity agreements entered into with the parties. The payments are subject to reimbursement by the individuals involved only if it is determined that reimbursement is required by the Company's by-laws. Mr. Jenning has recently notified the Commission that the Company does not intend to reimburse Mr. Fenn for any future legal expenses and that the Company has asked Mr. Fenn to repay the expenses that had already been paid by the Company.

On October 16, Mr. Fenn was interviewed by an ad hoc committee of directors regarding Mr. Fenn's actions before, during, and after his September 23 testimony. Mr. Fenn relayed a fabricated story to the ad hoc committee and made false statements to the ad hoc committee to cover up his activities.

On October 21, 1982, at the recommendation of his lawyer, Mr. Fenn again appeared before the ad hoc committee of directors and modified the statement he had given on October 16 "to set the record straight."

Following consultation with the Attorney General, the Commission investigation culminating in this report became active in mid-December 1982. As a result of the Attorney General's investigation, on December 13, 1982, Mr.

Fenn pleaded guilty to false swearing. He was fined $500. In exchange for his guilty plea, Mr. Fenn received a grant of immunity from further prosecution in the form of a December 13 agreement between his counsel and Deputy Attorney General James Brannigan. On December 13, Mr. Fenn resigned his various positions as officer and director of Central Maine Power Company and the various other CMP subsidiaries in which he held an officership or directorship, with the exception of his position as Senior Vice President of Central Maine Power Company. He resigned that office on December 16, 1982. His resignations were requested by Mr. Worthy on behalf of the ad hoc committee. Mr. Fenn has remained an employee of the Company, under suspension. From October 12 through January 16, Mr. Fenn was paid at his former annual rate of approximately $84,000 per annum. On January 16, 1983, Mr. Fenn's salary was reduced to approximately $42,000 per annum.

## APPENDIX: Witness for the Corporation

CAST OF CHARACTERS

| Name | Title/Position |
| --- | --- |
| Peter Bradford | Chairman, PUC |
| Norman Brooks | VP Public Relations, CMP |
| Peter Carlton | Professor, Adviser to Atlantic and CMP |
| Thomas W. Cass | Senior VP CMP and Director Atlantic |
| Robert S. Fenn | Senior VP CMP and VP Atlantic |
| Gelder | Commissioner, PUC |
| Cheryl Harrington | Commissioner, PUC |
| Connie Irland | Office of Energy Resources |
| Marjorie Jacobs | Computer Technician, CMP |
| John Jenning | General Counsel, CMP |
| Howard Jones | Researcher |
| Mr. Jones | Outside Counsel, CMP |
| Gerald A. Manion | Counsel, CMP |
| Mr. Moskovitz | PUC Counsel |
| Douglas Stevens | CMP Staff |
| E. T. Walker | President, CMP and Atlantic |
| Robert L. Warren | Manager, Customer Communications |
| Gordon Weil | Director, Office of Energy Resources |
| Michael Worthy | Counsel, Committee to Save Maine Yankee |

# International Drilling Corporation

Don Taylor[1] sat at his typewriter and sweated. It was hot. Nine months ago, when he had moved his family to Dallas, they had told him the nights would be cool. But this night Taylor was hot. He was chain-smoking again as he bent over to reread what he had written. It was almost dawn and Taylor had been writing all night. The wastebasket was full of discarded papers.

In May of 1971 Don Taylor accepted a job with the International Drilling Corporation (IDC). Taylor was 27 years old, and had graduated from the Harvard Business School in 1968. After receiving his MBA, Taylor spent two years in the Peace Corps. He then worked in New York City for a division of one of the largest industrial concerns in America. Frustrated by what he considered to be "bad management" and "office politics," Don Taylor had

quit his New York job. A close friend and Harvard classmate had suggested he write to Robert Dumont, Chairman of the Board of IDC, a rapidly growing oil and gas company with headquarters in Dallas, Texas. "Dumont's a real entrepreneur," his friend remarked, "and there should be plenty of room for you to test yourself."

Taylor liked the idea of working in a smaller company, and both he and his wife wanted to leave the New York area. After flying to Dallas to interview IDC executives, Taylor was hired as assistant to the president of IDC. Jeff Williams, IDC's President, had been hired in February of 1971. He was 38 years old and had been a successful stockbroker. Robert Dumont, who founded IDC and still owned over 30% of the company, had been impressed with Williams' knowledge of the investment markets and had convinced him to leave the brokerage business and join IDC. Jeff Williams had no experience in managing a natural re-

---

[1]Names of persons, institutions, locations, and dates are disguised.

sources company. When Don Taylor was hired, Williams spoke expansively of "running a tight ship" and "cleaning house," but admitted he hardly knew where to begin. Williams told Taylor in May of 1971 that his primary function would be to help "straighten out the company's internal operations."

## IDC'S BUSINESS

The International Drilling Corporation was engaged in the marketing of limited partnership interests in oil and gas drilling ventures. The company had an established sales force of twenty-five people who functioned as wholesalers to members of the investment community. Broker-dealers then sold the limited partnership interests to investors. These interests were similar to shares in a common stock mutual fund. Unlike mutual funds, however, the IDC drilling funds were set up as a series of partnerships that started each quarter. IDC's first fund, for example, was 1966-4, meaning that it was opened in the final quarter of 1966. Investors put up a minimum of $2,500 each and at the end of the quarter, if at least $200,000 had been raised, the partnership was closed and a new one opened. Investors were not allowed to take out their profits for 10 years (unless they reached age 65). Instead, profits were automatically reinvested in subsequent partnerships. Each year IDC was required to file a detailed prospectus with the Securities and Exchange Commission (SEC) describing its drilling programs.

Persons who purchased shares of IDC's drilling funds were limited partners, as defined under the limited partnership laws of Texas. They had limited liability and could not influence the mangement of the drilling program. Management of all the ventures was vested in IDC, and IDC received a 25% "profits interest" for its management efforts. IDC's prospectus disclosed that IDC would charge each partnership for all of the direct expenses incurred on behalf of the parnership (for example, salaries of the geologists and managers, overhead expenses, etc.). Under the IDC plan, an investor

could "cash out" of a partnership by writing to IDC. IDC published quarterly reports of the "cash surrender value" of each of the partnerships formed under the plan. According to the prospectus, these "cash surrender values" were determined by evaluating all of the drilling activities of each partnership. Independent engineers were required to be used to arrive at the current cash surrender value of each drilling program.

Robert Dumont considered himself the pioneer of this concept. He proudly explained that, through his IDC vehicles, the opportunities of investing in oil and gas, formerly enjoyed only by the very wealthy, were made available to the average individual. Oil and gas drilling were afforded special treatment under the United States tax laws. The expenditures required to locate a potential oil field and drill a well were deductible by the investor for tax purposes, and, if oil or gas was ever produced, a portion of the income generated was also exempt from taxation.

IDC's advertising literature stated that for every $10,000 invested, a $7,500 or $8,000 tax deduction could be expected in the first year. Assuming an investor in the 50% tax bracket, the advertising went on to say that "up to $4,000 of tax savings" were to be had. Thus for a "cost" of only $6,000, an investor could have $10,000 "working for him" in the IDC drilling program.

The IDC drilling programs were extremely popular. When Don Taylor joined the company in May 1971, 18 partnerships had been formed. The initial partnership was formed with $375,000 of investor capital. The first 1971 partnership (closed on March 31, 1971) had $9,500,000 of investor capital.

Aside from its 25 wholesalers, IDC employed a staff of geologists, land men, field managers and support personnel. The company had sales offices in 12 cities in the United States and operations offices in Dallas, Midland, Tulsa, and Calgary.

Robert Dumont was thought to be one of the wealthiest citizens of Dallas. He was on the board of a large local bank and was reputed to have "close" political connections "in Washington."

## THE IDC ORGANIZATION

Don Taylor's first impressions of the IDC organization were very favorable. In spite of Jeff Williams' warnings about "cleaning house," Taylor was impressed with the energy and enthusiasm of the IDC employees. Robert Dumont was held in the highest esteem by everyone Taylor spoke to during his first months on the job. Dumont was seldom seen in the Dallas offices, but it was said that all major decisions affecting IDC were made by him. IDC's common stock had appreciated in price dramatically since the firm went public in 1968, and the rise in value was generally attributed to Dumont's creative ideas and forceful promotional efforts. From its beginnings as an oil exploration enterprise, IDC had diversified and expanded its operations, until by 1971 it was involved in many aspects of international natural resource development. Exhibit 1 presents a corporate description from the 1970 annual report.

There was no formal organization chart and Don Taylor soon learned that Dumont abhorred such formalization. "We are a free-form organization," he was told by Brian Rosenberg, an IDC vice president thought to be particularly close to Dumont. "Everyone has plenty to do and we don't worry about charts. . . . " In spite of the lack of written guidelines, Taylor was able to observe an informal hierarchy at IDC. The sales and marketing staffs had large and richly furnished offices on one floor of the IDC office building in downtown Dallas. The operations staff was officed in

**EXHIBIT 1**
International Drilling Company. (*Source:* 1970 annual report.)

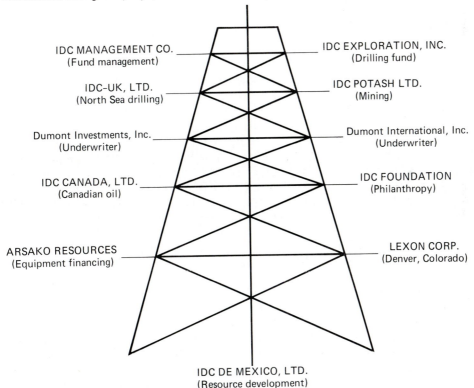

IDC MANAGEMENT CO.
(Fund management)

IDC EXPLORATION, INC.
(Drilling fund)

IDC-UK, LTD.
(North Sea drilling)

IDC POTASH LTD.
(Mining)

Dumont Investments, Inc.
(Underwriter)

Dumont International, Inc.
(Underwriter)

IDC CANADA, LTD.
(Canadian oil)

IDC FOUNDATION
(Philanthropy)

ARSAKO RESOURCES
(Equipment financing)

LEXON CORP.
(Denver, Colorado)

IDC DE MEXICO, LTD.
(Resource development)

comparatively plain surroundings on a separate floor. The office of the president, Jeff Williams, was on the same floor as the sales and marketing personnel. Dumont's offices (on yet another floor) were the most luxurious Taylor had ever seen. There were a group of executives characterized by Jeff Williams as the "brain trust" whose offices were located close to Dumont's. Taylor was told that these executives had been with IDC "from the start" and that they were an instrumental part of the company's rapid expansion and recent success. After several weeks with IDC, Taylor could include in the "brain trust" the following men: Brian Rosenberg, Bill Halpern, and Dave Ford (all vice presidents), Steve Stein and Tom Lowe (both lawyers), and Frank Souring (described as a "special assistant" to Dumont). Except for Lowe and Souring, who were in their early sixties, all of the members of the "brain trust" were in their late thirties. Don Taylor was impressed with their intelligence and their enthusiasm for IDC.

## DON TAYLOR'S FIRST EIGHT MONTHS

Jeff Williams, IDC's President, lived in Los Angeles. When Taylor arrived in Dallas and reported for work, he learned that Mr. Williams was "not going to be in the office this week." Williams commuted to and from Dallas from his Los Angeles home (using an IDC executive jet) and spent much of his time at the IDC sales office in Los Angeles. He had left instructions for Taylor to "get acquainted with things."

Taylor's initial disappointment over the lack of direction given him by Williams soon gave way to enthusiasm. The young MBA found a number of minor projects that needed attention and that allowed him to apply analytic techniques acquired at Business School. Several members of the "brain trust" had staff members and assistants who were Taylor's age and they were more than happy to let Taylor help them with analyses, reports, and cost studies.

Taylor particularly liked Art Weaver, personnel director, and Wendel Toms, one of Brian Rosenberg's assistants. In June of 1971,

Taylor was assigned responsibility for the physical distribution of IDC's sales literature. The mailroom had long been the object of criticism from the IDC sales force. Taylor learned that mailing expenses had exceeded $100,000 in the first five months of 1971, and sales materials were consistently being lost or delayed. He found himself working 12 hours a day to correct the distribution problems.

After six weeks, Taylor had trimmed mailing costs by 75%. He had reorganized mailroom policies so that by utilizing bulk storage and shipping procedures all sales offices were receiving the required sales literature in a timely manner. Even the most particular of the IDC salesmen were complimentary. Although Taylor was proud of the job he had done, he was upset when he overheard Bill Halpern refer to him as "the new mailboy."

In September, Taylor was given a large office adjoining that of Jeff Williams. Although Williams never gave his assistant a list of duties and responsibilities, Taylor soon found himself in the midst of a dozen new projects. He was asked to fly (usually aboard one of the IDC executive jets) to New York, Los Angeles, Denver or San Francisco to "check out" new ventures or potential acquisitions. Jeff Williams began to ask Taylor to represent the president in various staff meetings and Taylor was given a 20% raise in his salary on October 15, 1971.

On October 30, 1971, a meeting was held in Mr. Williams' office that startled and upset Don Taylor. "I want you to listen and take notes," Jeff Williams explained, "but keep your mouth shut." During the meeting Brian Rosenberg, Steve Stein and a lawyer Taylor had never seen before discussed with Williams certain activities which had occurred in 1969 which were in violation of the securities laws. It seems that three broker-dealers were paid commissions for selling partnership interests in excess of what was allowed and disclosed in the prospectus. It was described as a "minor" and "technical" violation and Rosenberg assured Williams that IDC's "tracks were covered."

Williams made a few comments during the meeting. After the others had left he told Taylor he might as well destroy his notes. "The whole mess is so stupid," he remarked, "but there's nothing we can do about it now . . . and there's no sense in making a big deal out of it." Taylor took his notes home and filed them in a desk drawer.

In November, Taylor was put in charge of a companywide budgeting program. He welcomed the opportunity to use his Business School education creatively and to learn more about the various IDC departments. However, before the program was a week old, Taylor was assigned to analyze a major acquisition. Mr. Dumont wanted to purchase a large mutual fund management company. Taylor worked directly with Brian Rosenberg and, for the first time since joining IDC, felt he was part of the "brain trust." After the acquisition study was complete, Taylor asked Williams if he could return to the budgeting program. Williams informed him that Dumont had "killed" the idea.

Taylor was greatly disappointed. On his own he had begun to devise a standard cost control system for Dumont Investments and Dumont International, the two underwriting subsidiaries that sold IDC's partnerships. He felt confident that a simple system of budgets and monthly reports could help reduce corporate overhead and sales expenses. Jeff Williams had often complained that these were "exorbitant."

The aborted budgeting project had also stimulated Taylor to draft several memos for Jeff Williams' signature requesting more detailed operating information from IDC Exploration and IDC Management Co. Regular computerized MIS reports were virtually nonexistent, and those that came to Williams were poorly organized and often inaccurate. Taylor, who prided himself on his skill with numbers, was at a loss to decipher most of the computer reports. His draft memos would have required each of the department heads to write Jeff Williams a summary of each month's activities and expenditures. When the budgeting project was stopped, Williams handed the drafts back to his young assistant: "Good ideas, Don, but we'll have to wait. . . . "

It seemed to Taylor that IDC's rapid growth had led to undue confusion in the accounting departments. Mr. Williams would ask Taylor to "check on that figure" or "find out who authorized that expenditure" and Taylor would be unable to get the required information. A disturbing pattern was emerging. The IDC controller and his assistants seemed helpful and cooperative, but the data, they explained, was "in the computer" or "unavailable." Jeff Williams didn't seem surprised when Taylor reported his failures. "This whole place is a mess," the young president would remark, "and I think Dumont likes it that way."

Taylor also learned from Wendel Toms that Robert Dumont and members of the "brain trust" were heavily invested in oil and gas ventures. Toms said he had seen a summary of these investments and "they were very profitable. . . . Dumont doesn't always invest in the same properties that the IDC partnerships do." Taylor wondered if there was a conflict of interest.

The IDC drilling partnership that "closed" on October 30 was the largest in the company's history, amounting to over $13,000,000. During the spring and summer of 1971, IDC had acquired several more small companies. One was involved in equipment leasing, one was a recreational land development company, and one was an electronics firm. IDC's common stock was selling at an all-time high of $80 per share.

During their first summer in Dallas, the Taylors had become close friends with Mike and Sheila Hull. Mike Hull was editor of a large Dallas newspaper and he and Don Taylor enjoyed playing tennis together. "One of these days, Don, you're going to have to tell me about IDC. Dumont's a mystery here in town. Nobody really knows how he makes all that money." Don Taylor heard himself reply that he, too, was often mystified by IDC's success.

## THE DECEMBER MEETING

In December, Robert Dumont called a special meeting to review the financial position of all of the IDC subsidiaries. The meeting was to be held on a Sunday and Jeff Williams called Don Taylor on Friday night to ask him to attend the meeting in his absence. "Rosenberg, Stein and Halpern are getting all the figures together. All you have to do is show up, listen and report back to me. Dumont won't be there." Taylor was flattered and excited to be included in such a high-level session. On Sunday morning Stein, Rosenberg and Halpern were in jocular moods, but Taylor immediately recognized that their joking was a sign of nervousness. One after another IDC's operations were reviewed. Surprisingly, all seemed to be in great need of working capital. Halpern, a CPA, rapidly recited the facts and figures. Even while reporting increasing profits, almost all operating entities were short of cash. Taylor was shocked. He was acting as the informal secretary of the meeting and, after almost two hours of discussion, sadly announced that almost $20,000,000 would be needed by January 30 if IDC was to continue operating as it had in the past. The current oil and gas partnership was not selling well. Only $900,000 had been raised to date and the recent $13,000,000 partnership was, in actuality, only $4,000,000. Robert Dumont had personally invested almost $8,000,000 to "boost" the figure to record levels.

Taylor also learned that many of the IDC drilling programs had experienced very poor operating performance. Little oil and gas was being pumped and more and more investors were requesting that IDC "buy them out." In the past, IDC had "bought out" old partners with funds raised for new partnerships. This practice was disclosed in the prospectus, but it required that new partnerships be ever larger so that sufficient money would be available to "buy out" old partnership interests as well as to drill new wells. Brian Rosenberg explained the crisis: "We now have almost $1,000,000 of partnership interests to be 'bought out.' If our current partnership is closed with, say $2,000,000, then 50% of the money will have to go towards buying out old interests. The tax deductions have already been taken on these old interests, so the current partnerships will have

a terrible tax shelter potential. Investors will only get a 30% write-off. We'll be dead!"

Don Taylor asked why the old partnerships were valued so high, if so little oil and gas were being discovered and pumped. "Well," smiled Halpern, "the 'cash surrender values' may be a bit overstated. But that's what investors look at when they decide to invest. The higher the 'cash surrender values' on past partnerships, the more credibility the current program will have." Taylor shook his head in disbelief.

Rosenberg, Halpern, Stein and Taylor met for eight hours that Sunday. Once the basic figures were out on the table and Taylor announced the $20,000,000 "cash need," a feeling of camaraderie was felt by the four men. Halpern told Taylor that this was the first time many of these summary figures had ever been discussed at IDC. "Bob Dumont never allowed any one of us to have access to all the facts. That's how IDC has been run. None of the salesmen, for example, really knows how the partnerships are performing. And none of the oil guys knows how the money is raised."

When Taylor returned home at dinnertime, he was exhausted. He had agreed to write a summary report outlining the specific cash needs of each subsidiary. The other three executives had also asked him to write a brief report of their recommendations concerning a basic reorganization of IDC. Halpern, Rosenberg and Stein believed that less emphasis should be placed on "promoting" oil and gas ventures and more placed on operating the ventures themselves. They also recommended that tighter financial controls be established and that Dumont delegate more responsibility to the operating heads of the various subsidiaries and divisions. Although he had not mentioned it at the meeting, Taylor was sure his recent ideas for improved control and reporting would go a long way towards solving these problems.

After thinking about the meeting, Taylor sat down after dinner and organized his thoughts. He was still in a state of shock, but there was more to it than just the financial crisis. Dumont's "brain trust" had carefully reviewed the cash needs and had concluded that by cutting back in certain areas and drawing upon IDC's commercial lines of credit, the necessary funds could be made available. And their willingness to recommend organizational changes was encouraging. He was excited about the possibilities of implementing his reporting system. But, Taylor realized, they had completely ignored the more basic moral implications of the meeting's disclosures. Taylor listed the items which bothered him the most:

• Cash surrender values were "a bit overstated" (remark by Halpern).
• Dumont personally commingled his own funds with those of his IDC companies, often lending them money or borrowing from them (a handwritten footnote to one of Halpern's financial statements where he admitted that even he didn't have up-to-date and complete figures on these "particular transactions").
• Partnership funds were "temporarily" used by other IDC operations from time to time. One of the partnerships formed in 1971 was still "owed" $4,000,000 by the newly acquired IDC real estate company. (When Rosenberg stated this fact in the meeting, Stein had mumbled that "he didn't want to hear about that sort of thing.")
• Partnerships were buying more and more of their oil and gas properties from a little-known IDC subsidiary which was "marking up" the properties as much as 100%. (This remark was made by Rosenberg and both he and Halpern refused to discuss it further when Taylor casually asked them to explain how this operated.)

On Tuesday, when Jeff Williams flew in from Los Angeles, Taylor showed him a draft of the meeting report. "Dumont will never go for the reorganization," he stated. "You guys must have had a ball." Taylor asked if he could have dinner with Williams "to go over some other things that were discussed." Jeff Williams smiled and asked, "Did you get into the ripoffs?

Is that what's worrying you? Yeah, let's have dinner."

Over dinner that night, Taylor described his impressions of "the facts behind the facts" to his boss. Mr. Williams admitted that he was aware of many of the "questionable" dealings and conflicts of interest. "This kind of thing goes on all the time in the oil business. One company sells another a dog; six months later it does the other company a favor and it all evens out. Dumont knows what he's doing and he calls the shots around here." Williams stated that his main concern was to protect the investors who were being "screwed" in the IDC drilling funds. "When I first joined IDC, George Hart (manager of the Tulsa operations office) came to me and described the way Dumont ran the company. I figured I could clean it up a little and we would be OK. But Dumont and his brainboys still make all the decisions. I can't seem to stop them from ripping off the partnerships, but I can limit the ripoff." Williams then explained how he had occasionally vetoed an intercompany deal that was especially "rotten." Dumont, he explained, had backed down when Williams threatened to resign. "Dumont wants to go out for another public offering of IDC stock and he knows that if I quit he'll have trouble getting a decent underwriter."

Taylor was disappointed with Jeff Williams' response to Taylor's disclosures. The president had voiced only mild indignation and portrayed himself as being virtually powerless to correct matters. However, at one point he had been quite firm. "Don, if you and I can tackle the problem of the lack of decent information around here, maybe we can *do* something! Your ideas about new reports and budgets might be the answer." Taylor wondered how other IDC employees felt. For the next ten days he tried to engage other IDC executives in conversations about some of the practices which he had learned about at the December meeting. As Taylor explained to his wife: "I'm beginning to think a lot of people either don't know about what's going on or know and just don't care."

Ten days after the Sunday meeting, Brian

Rosenberg delivered the final draft of the report to Robert Dumont. He called Taylor the following day and said, "He's mad as hell at us for even discussing some of the topics. None of our recommendations will be implemented and I'm supposed to collect and destroy all of our notes on the meeting. Let's just say the meeting never happened. . . . OK?"

Taylor felt completely let down and wondered if he should resign. He thought back to some of the comments Art Weaver had made: "Look, Don, they know what they're doing. I'm sure there's no real problem. . . . you just don't know all the facts. Stop worrying about things that you don't know about."

Dave Ford and Mr. Souring had taken another tack: "There's nothing to bother about that a little belt-tightening and money-raising won't cure. You and Jeff should stop looking for trouble and start selling IDC! Tell Williams to get out there and promote. . . . that's what we need."

Taylor remembered Jeff Williams' response to these comments: "Those two live in a fairy world. Stick around, Taylor, and help me fight that kind of thinking. Maybe we can tackle Dumont and keep him from ruining all of the partnerships."

But Taylor had little confidence in Jeff Williams' ability to reform IDC or Robert Du-

mont. "I don't doubt his sincerity," he sighed to his wife, "but Dumont won't ever let him make any *real* changes. Hell, Dumont is making too much money the way things are!"

Don Taylor was under great pressure. He knew he was backing himself into an uncomfortable corner. From one point of view his job was becoming a real challenge. He was anxious to try out his management ideas. From another point of view, it was turning sour. Too many people were too ignorant of too many transactions. The thought of leaving another job after only nine months added to his feeling of panic. He realized that he had few "hard facts" to confirm his suspicions of corporate wrongdoing, but it seemed that he ought to do something. His wife put it very bluntly: "If there is that kind of hanky-panky going on, you are a part of it. You can't just look the other way. . . . Can you?"

On the night of January 20, 1972, Taylor decided to write a report describing his suspicions of unethical IDC corporate behavior. At least writing it down would enable him to organize his thoughts. He had no idea whom the report would be for: The SEC? The IRS? A local DA? A newspaper? The IDC board of directors? Jeff Williams? Bob Dumont? Himself? Taylor swore silently to himself as he sat at his typewriter.

# Viking Air Compressor, Inc.

As he left the president's office, George Ames[1] wondered what he ought to do. His impulse was to resign, but he knew that could be a costly blot on his employment record. Moreover, there was the possibility that he was seeing things in a distorted way, that he might later regret leaving Viking before he really knew all the facts bearing on his position and its future. He decided to wait for another week before making up his mind, and in the meantime he made an appointment with Professor Farnsworth of the Amos Tuck School of Business Administration at Dartmouth College to get his advice. Mr. Ames had received his MBA degree from the Tuck School the previous June.[2]

The Viking Air Compressor Company was founded in Bradley, Connecticut, in 1908 by Nels Larsen, an inventor and engineer who left the Westinghouse Electric Company to start his own organization. Mr. Larsen had both a successful design for a new type of air compressor and a talent for management. He led Viking to steadily increasing successes in the air compressor industry.

In 1971 Viking held a 25% share of the air compressor business in the United States, with total annual sales of $180 million. Mr. John T. Larsen, grandson of the founder, was chairman of the board and chief executive officer. Three other descendants of the founder were officers of the company, and the rest of the management team had been developed from Viking employees who rose through the ranks. The ownership of Viking was substantially in the Larsen family hands.

In March 1971 Mr. Oscar Stewart, vice president for personnel administration of Viking, visited the Amos Tuck School to talk with MBA candidates interested in a new position to be created in the Viking structure the following

---

[1]Most of the names in this case have been disguised.
[2]Mr. Ames received his A.B. from the University of Michigan in June 1966. He spent three years as an Army officer, concluding as a Captain in Vietnam, before entering Tuck in September 1969. He was married in June 1971.

This case was prepared by John W. Hennessey, Jr., and is intended solely for instructional purposes.

June. Mr. Stewart explained to Dean Robert Y. Kimball, Tuck's Director of Placement, that Viking had never hired MBAs directly from business schools, but wanted to experiment in 1971 with this method of bringing fresh ideas and new techniques into the firm.

The corporate officers had decided, according to Mr. Stewart, to begin to test the effectiveness of the recruitment of MBAs by hiring a business school graduate to become Director of Public Affairs, with the assignment of coordinating the relationships between Viking and outside agencies seeking financial contributions from the company.

As Mr. Stewart described the job to the students he interviewed at Tuck in March 1971, it would contain such tasks as (a) proposing to the Board of Directors the best criteria to use in deciding how to make corporate gifts to charitable organizations of all kinds, (b) supplying the chief officers of the company with information about the participation of Viking employees in public service activities, (c) recommending future strategy for Viking in the employment of women and members of minority groups, and (d) serving as secretary to the newly formed Committee on Corporate Responsibility, which consisted of five members of the Board of Directors.

George Ames accepted the post of Director of Public Affairs at Viking. He had been chosen by Vice President Stewart as the most promising of the five attractive Tuck applicants for the new position. After a short vacation, Mr. Ames reported for work on July 1, 1971, and immediately plunged into the difficult task of gathering information about his new assignment. It soon became clear that his primary task would be to work with the Board Committee on Corporate Responsibility, mainly to propose new policy guidelines to the Board at its September 10th meeting. Mr. Stewart said there were two other areas of high priority: (1) the Corporation's attitude toward public service of employees, and (2) developing criteria for corporate philanthropic giving.

As Vice President Stewart explained to George in early July, the Committee on Corporate Responsibility was created at the January meeting of the Viking Board after unanimous endorsement of the suggestion made by Dr. Thomas A. Barr, pastor of the local Congregational Church and one of the four outside members of the twelve-man Board. Reverend Barr's major support for his recommendation was the observation that the General Motors Corporation had taken a similar step, under some pressure, and that corporate responsibility was an idea whose time had come on the American scene. In response to the question "What will such a committee do?" Reverend Barr replied that there need be no hurry in defining the detailed responsibilities of the Committee, but that furthermore there could not possibly be any harm or drawbacks from setting it up as soon as possible. He added that the public relations value of such a gesture should not be underestimated. In establishing the Committee on Corporate Responsibility, the Board voted to require the first progress report from the Committee in September 1971.

The Committee on Corporate Responsibility met following the February meeting of the Board of Directors and decided to delay any definite action until an Executive Secretary could be hired. Vice President Stewart was asked to keep this post in mind as he interviewed MBA graduates of several of the leading business schools, and so he did.

George Ames met with the Chairman of the Committee on Responsibility at a luncheon on July 21, 1971, arranged by Vice President Stewart. The Committee Chairman was Mr. Paul Merrow, one of the most respected lawyers in Northern Connecticut and the son of one of the first board members of Viking when the company was incorporated in the 1920's. Mr. Merrow expressed his pleasure that George Ames was working on the corporate responsibility question and asked him to prepare a report that might be reviewed by the Committee just prior to the September Board meeting. What he wanted, he explained to Mr. Ames, was an analysis of the three or four possible approaches to corporate responsibility which the Directors ought to consider. He asked for a listing of the pros and cons of these various approaches. He said that Mr. Ames should consider this very much like an assignment in a course at the Tuck School. He would be performing a task which none of the Board members had the time or academic background to do, and thus he would substantially improve the decision making of the Board of Directors.

Mr. Merrow concluded the luncheon by saying that he would like Mr. Ames to proceed on his own during the summer, but that he would be glad to confer with him in early September. Mr. Merrow explained that he was leaving the next day for a legal conference in Europe and would be on an extended vacation until September 6th. He said that he had "the proxies" of the other committee members and that they would prefer not to get involved in working on the committee tasks until after the September Board meeting.

George Ames worked assiduously during August, reading all the articles and books he could find in the area of corporate responsibility, including the background of developments in the General Motors situation. He decided not to talk about this particular assignment with other officers of the company, primarily because of Mr. Merrow's injunction that the Committee itself would prefer not to engage in substantive talk about the issues until the September Board meeting. George feared he would do more harm than good by talking before he knew his subject well.

In early September John Larsen asked George to see him and the following conversation took place:

*John Larsen:* I've asked you to see me this morning and tell me what progress you have been making in developing background materials for the work of the Committee on Corporate Responsibility. Mr. Merrow told me he had asked you to do some digging and that you would have a brief report to make at the September 10th meeting of the Board. I know Mr. Merrow hoped he would be back from Europe in time to talk with you before the Board meeting, but it now appears he will be lucky to make

the meeting at all. He expects to arrive in town about noon on the tenth.

*George Ames:* Mr. Larsen, I appreciate the opportunity I have been given to help Viking by developing recommendations about possible strategies for the company to follow in the area of corporate responsibility. Mr. Merrow told me I ought to develop alternative proposals for recommendations to the Board and I have as recently as yesterday finally been able to narrow the field so that I can make four recommendations with confidence.

I realize the Board may prefer to consider them one at a time, at different meetings, but I would like to tell you about all four so that you will know what my report will contain.

I have decided that the most important issue in the area of corporate responsibility is equal-opportunity hiring. I have been able to develop statistics from the personnel records which show that Viking is rather far behind most major national corporations in the percentage of blacks and women now employed, and, although I am sure conscientious efforts have been made by all officers to remedy this, I cannot stress too strongly how much of a time bomb the present situation is. There will be wide ramifications if we do not improve our record.

The second item of priority which I see is the development of corporate sanctions for public service activities of employees. I believe the company should grant paid leaves of absence for employees who wish to accept public service posts. At present we have done that only for two vice presidents who have been in charge of the Northern Connecticut United Fund. In each case the man was lent to the charitable organization for two full weeks. What I have in mind is a much wider program which would grant employees leaves of absence to work in poverty programs in urban ghettos, or in VISTA projects in Connecticut or neighboring states.

It seems to me a third priority is to develop a committee of consumers who will monitor the safety features and other quality items having to do with our products. If we do not do this we will have Ralph Nader breathing down our necks as has already happened in the automotive industry and some others.

Finally, I strongly recommend that we close our sales contact in Capetown, South Africa, and establish policies which will avoid our being embarrassed as a corporation by discriminatory or dictatorial policies of foreign governments which become critically important political and social issues here in this country.

I feel sure these are great issues of our times and I hope the Board will be willing to debate them at the September 10th meeting. I know I could learn a great deal in my position if such a debate could take place.

*Mr. Larsen:* Young man, I want to congratulate you on how articulately you have told me about some of the things you have learned in the MBA program at the Tuck School. I envy fellows of your generation who go through MBA programs because you get an opportunity to think about policy problems at a much earlier age than my generation ever did. Indeed my only complaint is that the business schools go too far to educate young men to think they know how to run a company long before they have enough real experience to be even a first-line supervisor.

Now, I think you have your assignment all backwards as secretary to the Committee on Corporate Responsibility and I will tell you why I think that. The Committee hasn't even met yet and your remarks make it sound as if you have written the final report. Worse than that it sounds like the final report of the Committee on Corporate Responsibility of the General Motors Company, not Viking. Everybody knows we've done as good a job as we can to hire blacks and women. There just aren't many such people in the work force in our part of Connecticut who could fit our talent standards, and we are going to follow our historical policy of nondiscrimination as we hire the best people to do Viking jobs. We owe it to our stockholders to make a profit, and if we don't do that we don't have the right to do anything else.

Your remarks on public service activities for our employees are equally off target. The first obligation of our employees is to give a fair day's work for a fair day's pay. All public service activities are extracurricular activities, and that's the way they must be. In order for us to sponsor public service on company time we would have to discriminate between good and bad activities and that would get us into partisan politics and preoccupy all of our executive time. How would the company have done if I had been a part-time chief executive officer in the last five years? That is a preposterous idea! At the same time by working harder on my regular job I have been able some evenings and some weekends to work in fund-raising activities for the Boy Scouts, YMCA and heaven knows how many other charitable organizations. I would expect every employee to do the same and not to expect the corporation to subsidize activities in their roles as private citizens. As far as public service is concerned, "Live and let live" should be our corporate motto. If we encourage public service activities and include them as part of our compensation and promotion system we will be bogged down in a fantastic collection of information about private lives which will lead to chaos. Even the most superficial examination of this question should have led you to see the problems with the route your theory took you.

As far as the safety of our products and other demands consumers might make, that's all done through the marketplace, as you will come to understand. If our products were not safe or durable they wouldn't sell. You could have found this out had you talked with our production and marketing people as you certainly should have done by now. It's our responsibility to decide after careful market research what the air-compressor needs of America are and will be in the future. We don't need a special panel of bleeding hearts to lead us along paths where we are already expert.

As for our selling operations in South Africa, I'm afraid you just don't know what you are talking about. As long as there is no plank of American foreign policy or Federal law which tells corporations where they can and where they can't sell their products, American businesses must depend on the free market system. President Nixon is talking about opening the trade doors to mainland China. Do you think for one moment the practices of the Chinese government are any less nefarious in some respects than the practices of the South African government? Of course not. And yet you would probably urge me in your liberal way to establish a selling office in Peking just to go along with the new liberal ideas of our President, and I call that kind of pragmatism ridiculous.

Come to think of it, how could you miss this opportunity to lecture the Board on our responsibilities for pollution control and our ob-

ligations to get out of the military-industrial complex by cancelling all of our air-compressor contracts with the Federal Government!

Young man, you have shown yourself to be a wooly-minded theoretician and I want to tell you that bluntly now so that you will not think me hypocritical at any later point. I will tell the Committee on Corporate Responsibility that you have not had time to prepare your first briefing of the Board of Directors and then I want to have a meeting with you and the Chairman of the Corporate Responsibility Committee on Monday morning September 20th.

That's all I have time for now. I'll see you later.

## PART TWO

# Corporate Values: Looking Inward

Moving from the personal values which are brought to bear in a business context, Parts 2 and 3 introduce a broader platform of moral concerns as we focus on the values and responsibilities of corporations as entities.

The issue of corporate values and social beneficence is not new. Ever since Adam Smith speculated on the possible social benefits which might result from the butcher's, brewer's, and baker's pursuit of self-interest, the moral responsibility that should be attached to economic activity has remained problematic for society. Managers and the general public alike continue to ask such questions as what constitutes the ethical way of doing business, what constraints on self-interest should properly be imposed and by whom, and how far a corporation should extend the range of constituencies to whom it is held responsible.

To complicate matters further, the unit of economic activity has shifted fundamentally since Smith's day—from the individual to the institution—and a host of laws and internal policies concerning the responsibility of and for economic activity has been generated to respond to this organizational reality. From a legal standpoint, the corporation is regarded as an entity whose actions are subject to civil and criminal sanctions. From a managerial standpoint, the corporation's several responsibilities can be generalized and therefore articulated into policy. On this view, the corporation is capable of personification and of having a set of values in much the same way that an individual businessperson has certain standards of conduct for daily work life.

In Parts 2 and 3, we present two series of cases in which corporations as entities have embraced, either implicitly or explicitly, values and responsibilities to guide the decisions of all their members. The moral questions that arose in Part 1 with regard to personal values have not disappeared, but a new level of moral inquiry—the institutional level—is introduced.

The cases in Part 2 involve corporate values of an inward-looking sort, in which individual responsibility and institutional pressures are brought into sharp focus around such questions as the following: From where should the values that influence managerial discretion come? How do institutional values relate to the individual rights and responsibilities of employees? Can meaningful distinctions be drawn between an executive's personal and professional life? Is the corporation, like Emerson's vision of institutions, "the lengthened shadow of one man," or should it accommodate a variety of personal philosophies and styles? It is the nature and legitimacy of moral authority within corporations that is at stake in these cases.

Nowhere is the issue of individual rights versus a manager's responsibility to protect the well-being of the corporation more starkly presented than in "The Individual and the Corporation." This case concerns an article, written by an executive, concerning the assassination of John F. Kennedy, and the possible impact of that article on the executive's company. Although the case was written twenty years ago, the issues that it raises continue to be important.

"American Cyanamid Company" delves simultaneously into two issues of employees' rights—sexual discrimination and safety in the workplace—as a company bars all fertile women from a lead pigment production line. The case offers another opportunity to explore the problems involved when ethical values are in apparent conflict. It also addresses the issue of who should assume responsibility for workers' safety—the federal government, private industry, or the individual workers themselves.

The impact of corporate culture and its values on the individual employee's welfare is explored in "Jim Sawyer," where a problem with alcohol causes further problems in both personal and work life. What policies a corporation ought to adopt and how deeply it should get involved in the personal problems of its employees are among the questions raised.

"Mebel Doran & Company" takes up the question of employees' integrity against the backdrop of institutional policy. It explores the values of the securities industry on three levels: (1) the stated principles of the industry itself, (2) a brokerage firm's procedural interpretation of these principles, and (3) a specific interplay among a broker, an analyst, and a customer. Industry and corporate culture and the location of ultimate responsibility for personal integrity are among the important issues in this case.

A look at the interplay between individual integrity and corporate policy is provided in "H. J. Heinz Company: The Administration of Policy (A)" and "(B)". These two cases take up a problem of questionable or illegal financial reporting practices and explore the manner in which corporate policies can affect executives' behavior. Implicit in the Heinz cases, again, is the impact of the corporation's ethos on individual executives.

In "Duke Power Company and Affirmative Action," a senior executive must make significant layoffs in his work force. The company is not unionized and has recently employed substantial numbers of minority workers. What criteria should govern the layoffs, and to what extent should the executive's personal beliefs influence his management decision?

The *Harvard Business Review* article "Sexual Harassment: Some See It . . . Some Won't" and the "Three Short Cases on Sexual Harassment" offer an opportunity for learning on a particularly sensitive and complex topic in contemporary business. Each of the incidents is based on Harvard Business School students' experience in middle management. The article presents useful empirical information based on a broad survey of managers and a summary of current law on the subject.

The Lex series ("Developing the Guidelines," "Closing Portsmouth Depot," "Work Conditions at Inglesby Shipyard," and "The Reading Pallets Theft") goes back to the very process of developing a set of ethical guidelines for top management. The first case in the series presents the historical and cultural rationale for such an undertaking, the guidelines themselves, and some of the conflicting opinions which Lex's senior managers have about the whole idea. The follow-up cases present three management problems that occurred during the first year after the guidelines were adopted.

"The Beliefs of Borg-Warner" provides an opportunity for a comprehensive inquiry into the decision to articulate a set of values within a large multinational corporation. The case traces the development of the company's statement of beliefs under the leadership of its chief executive officer and invites consideration of the challenges that might be involved in implementing such beliefs at the level of the operating divisions. It serves both as a fitting conclusion to Part 2—on the inward-looking dimensions of corporate values— and as a transition to Part 3, in which the outward-looking dimensions are the primary focus. "Building Trust at Warner Gear," besides offering a window on American labor-management relations amidst comparisons with the Japanese paradigm, takes us into one of the divisions of Borg-Warner in which the corporation's "beliefs" might be tested.

# The Individual and the Corporation

In the 1830s, Alexis de Tocqueville, seeking to describe the social philosophy of the United States, put heavy emphasis on the new nation's reliance upon individualism. He said, "Individualism is a novel expression, to which a novel idea has given birth." By the latter part of the same century, the rapid industrialization of the United States had contributed to the rise of large and increasingly powerful units of economic activity. As new and more complex forms of organization developed in all sectors of life, John D. Rockefeller was led to comment, "Individualism is gone, never to return."

This case concerns one aspect of the relationship between individuals and organizations. Its focus is on the problems that arose when a senior executive of a company wrote an article for a national magazine. The case information came from (1) Donald L. Singleton; (2) annual reports of Summit Petroleum, *Look* magazine, and other published sources; and (3) Lawrence J. Mangum, a senior editor of *Look* magazine. All figures in the case are disguised.

It will be evident from the material below that the case does not present the points of view of all the parties involved in the series of events described.

## THE COMPANY

In the mid-1950s, a European-based oil company established a company called Summit Petroleum, Inc., in the United States. According to the new company's first annual report, Summit represented the European company's first venture in the United States. Control was assured through ownership of more than 50% of the stock of Summit. Corporate headquarters was established in a large eastern city and operating offices were set up in Dallas, Texas. The latter were later to become Summit Petroleum of Texas.

Summit began actual operations after merging with another oil company. Within a short time, the company had a refinery, substantial resources of oil and natural gas, several thousand acres of undeveloped leaseholds, and over 200 gasoline stations located in four Southwestern states.

The company continued to expand, both internally and through acquisitions, in subsequent years. The Summit trademark became increasingly well known in the Southwest and adjacent areas of the United States. By 1959, Summit had nearly 1,800 filling stations, and annual sales were approaching $70,000,000, including several billion cubic feet of natural gas. Most Summit retail gasoline stations were run by independent operators and supplied by independent jobbers, but in some cases, expansion was accelerated by the lease of company-owned stations to independent operators.

By the time the 1960 annual report was issued, Summit operated in nearly 20 states and had over 2,000 filling stations. Sales had increased more than 6% over 1959, as compared to an increase in consumer demand of approximately 1% in Summit's marketing territories. The annual report stated that "The effective advertising and sales promotion programs initiated in 1958 have been responsible in large measure for expanding consumer acceptance of [Summit] products." Although total company sales dipped slightly in 1962, gasoline sales reached an all-time high. In 1963, the acquisition of another oil company almost doubled the company's facilities, gave it an entry into petrochemicals, and added more than 1,000 retail gasoline stations. Many of the latter were immediately converted to Summit colors and station signs. By the end of 1963, annual reports indicated, in brief, that net income had grown to almost $4,500,000 in the comparatively short period of Summit's life, while gross operating income was over $150,000,000.

## THE INDIVIDUAL

The *Dallas Morning News* of April 17, 1964, carried a brief story stating that Summit Petroleum of Texas had confirmed the resignation of Mr. Donald L. Singleton from the Summit organization. The story identified Mr. Singleton as the senior vice president in charge of marketing, refining, pipelines, transportation, and crude oil purchasing for Summit of Texas, and as a vice president and member of the board of directors of Summit Petroleum, Inc. Mr. Singleton had joined the Texas company in Dallas in 1957 as marketing manager. In 1958, he became vice president for marketing of all refined products. By 1962, he had become the senior vice president of the Texas firm. In addition, from 1960 through 1963, the annual reports of Summit Petroleum, Inc., listed Mr. Singleton as Vice President, Marketing, and a member of the board.

Donald Singleton was born in Santa Barbara, California, in 1922 where his father was a sales manager for an oil company in the Los Angeles area. After attending high school at St. Joseph's Academy, Singleton went to St. Mary's College and later transferred to the University of Washington. He graduated in 1943 as a foreign trade major. During his college career, Singleton served as business manager of the university's daily newspaper, belonged to the Naval ROTC, and managed a filling station. On subsequent active duty with the U.S. Navy, he saw action in the Southwest Pacific and the Philippine Islands, was wounded, and received a Bronze Star.

At the end of World War II, Singleton decided to go into business for himself. He returned to the Philippines and set up an import-export business. The business prospered, reaching an annual volume of $12 million within a 6-year period. Singleton and his wife then decided to return to the United States. Their oldest boy was ready for school, and the Singletons preferred an American school. Mr. Singleton also preferred to develop his business career in the United States. Using part of the proceeds from the sale of his import-export business, he established a firm in California that specialized in financing home builders. In addition, after a few months, he decided to enter the oil business. He set up the Singleton Oil Company, became an independent distributor for a major oil company, and phased out his finance business.

Singleton's company doubled his supplier's volume in its territory. In addition, he introduced a line of tires, batteries, and accessories (TBA). Intrigued by the possibilities of innovation in the merchandising and marketing fields, he purchased some old school buses, renovated them, and turned them into "rolling stores" for his TBA lines. In less than three years, Singleton's TBA volume in his rolling stores was $150,000.

Singleton's interest in management and innovation led him to look for an expanding company whose resources and activities would permit a greater degree of experimentation and opportunity for progression. Summit Petroleum appeared to offer such an opportunity, and in 1957 he joined Summit as marketing manager, taking a $10,000 cut in income in order to join the company.

Singleton prospered at Summit. His family and personal background in oil jobbing helped him establish good working relationships with the company's independent jobbers and retailers, and he showed a flair for merchandising, promotion and station design. He was especially interested in design and promotion. The Summit brand attained wide publicity, both in its area and throughout the oil industry, when Singleton developed a new approach in service station design. In a busy industrial section of Dallas, Summit put up a service station that consisted of separate islands offering gasoline, service, and customer facilities. Each island was distinguished by a 30-foot concrete tower of mushroom design. The customer island had a patio and rest areas, and Summit installed air conditioning, floor-to-ceiling drapes, Oriental tile, and Florida red marble. The station received considerable attention in Dallas and was written up in a number of industry publications. Singleton had also been instrumental in the development of mobile, self-powered service stations that offered "Summit à la Carte"; the stations were written up in *Fortune, Business Week,* and other magazines and trade papers.

Summit's Azure Ozone (fictitious name) advertising campaign was originated by Singleton. In the early 1960s, an additive war reflected the keen competition in the oil industry,

as company after company introduced special additives to gasoline to gain competitive advantage. The first additives introduced by the major oil companies attained great prominence, but later ones did not because of conflicting claims and duplication. Singleton and Summit investigated the possibilities of an additive for Summit gasoline. Singleton decided, however, that the use of an additive would be prohibitively expensive, and would be only another "me-too" type of promotion. In his opinion, the industry suffered from too much "me-too-ism" in its advertising and promotion.

As a result, Singleton developed the idea of spoofing gasoline additives as a promotional technique. Together with Summit's advertising agency, he worked out a campaign. The general idea of the promotion was that Summit gasoline had all the additives a car could possibly use. So did all the other Summit products, with the exception of the air that Summit stations put in customers' tires. Summit would, therefore, get to work immediately on the ultimate additive and under the Summit Five-Year Plan, have Azure Ozone available for tires on May 12, 1966; the time was set for 4:30 in the afternoon of that day, because some Summit trucks "don't get around until late in the afternoon." In the meantime, "to help customers through the difficult withdrawal period from regular air, Summit offered azure ballons, azure valve caps, azure asphalt, azure credit cards (for special customers), and Azure Air Room Freshener." The latter was also promoted and sold by a Dallas department store, and achieved national publicity.

The Azure Ozone campaign was concentrated in newspaper advertisements throughout Summit's marketing area, and aided by various kinds of promotion at the service station level. For example, azure-colored asphalt aprons were installed at some stations, and various contests and promotional devices were tied to the concept.

The Azure Ozone approach was praised in trade and advertising journals, and was the least expensive major campaign ever conducted by the company. Consumers found its newness and gentle spoofing interesting. The trade recognized it as an effective promotional device, and it won a number of advertising awards. Singleton himself was in great demand as a speaker before oil industry and advertising media groups.

Thus, by the end of 1963, Summit's promotional campaigns had been extremely successful. Mr. Singleton's contributions to the company's marketing efforts had been substantial, and these and other accomplishments seemed attested to by the steady broadening of his responsibilities and his recognition by various industry journals. For example, in January 1964, *Southwest Advertising and Marketing* said:

> Probably one of the reasons for Summit's phenomenal growth is its aggressive and imaginative young senior vice president [Donald L. Singleton]. Even though he is in direct charge of the company's major operations—refining, marketing, transportation, crude oil acquisition, and other departments—[Singleton] handles the company's advertising personally. . . .

### THE ASSASSINATION OF PRESIDENT KENNEDY

On November 22, 1963, President John Kennedy was assassinated in Dallas. Lawrence J. Mangum (fictitious name), a senior editor of *Look* magazine, was sent from New York to cover the assassination and subsequent developments. Mangum talked to many prominent Dallas citizens, among them government, professional, and business leaders, and was struck by what seemed to him to be an attitude of defensiveness about Dallas. Attacks on the city itself had not yet begun to appear in any volume, but many of those to whom Mangum talked seemed to him to behave and speak as if the city itself were in some way guilty of the presidential assassination and the shooting of Lee Harvey Oswald.

A few days after the assassination, Mr. Mangum met the president of the advertising firm that handled Summit's account. During a discussion of events in Dallas, the agency president suggested that Mangum ought to talk with "Don Singleton, an impressive young guy from the oil industry." He described Singleton as a man who had been a registered Republican in California, an Eisenhower supporter in 1952, a Stevenson man in 1956, and a registered Democrat in Texas "because there was no point in being anything else." The advertising executive said that Singleton had something on his mind, and that it was probably quite different from what Mangum had been encountering.

### SINGLETON'S *LOOK* ARTICLE

Mr. Mangum was favorably impressed by Don Singleton. At a dinner meeting, he found that Singleton had strong feelings about the president's death. Singleton showed Mangum a copy of a letter that he had sent to one of the two leading papers in Dallas, setting forth what he believed should be the city's sense of shame and suggesting that the city erect a suitable memorial to the late president. The letter had not been printed, and Singleton told Mangum that he believed this was because the Dallas papers chose to print only those communications that praised the city itself while condemning acts of violence as isolated events unrelated to its general atmosphere. At the time of his initial meeting with Mangum, Singleton and the advertising agency president were preparing a newspaper advertisement for which Singleton would pay the full cost—the ad would express his feelings about the loss of the president and his dissatisfaction with his own failure to act as a responsible member of the community, and suggest that Dallas itself should erect a memorial appropriate to the memory of Mr. Kennedy.

Mr. Mangum told the casewriter that he had said to Singleton that *Look* sometimes ran articles by nonprofessional writers. He had said that the odds were against publication, but that Singleton could prepare an article if he wished to do so. Singleton's reaction was favorable, and Mangum was impressed by what seemed to be Singleton's desire to help his city reassess its attitudes and actions.

As Mr. Singleton later described his activities to the casewriter, he wrote his article during the next two weeks, spending part of his time in a Dallas hotel. Although carrying on his responsibilities at Summit of Texas, he did not tell anyone at Summit of Texas or Summit Petroleum, Inc., about the article. He considered it a personal venture and the expression of a personal viewpoint that did not concern his company or his fellow employees. He emphasized that neither in the article nor in subsequent statements did he identify the name of his company. In conversations with his wife and Mangum, Singleton had indicated an awareness that the expression of his ideas might have some repercussions. Nevertheless, he went ahead with the preparation of the article. In statements made subsequent to the publication of his article, he said that two factors had prompted him to do so. In regard to President Kennedy, he said:

> It wasn't just that I agreed with most of his policies and his plans for the future; it was his manner and his exuberance and his dignity which made our national government all the more exciting and important.

Singleton's other major reason had to do with Dallas:

> I also believe strongly that open reasoned dialogue on any subject this side of perfection is more likely to produce good results than a monolithic "everything is fine, and even if it isn't don't stir things up" attitude. Before the assassination I was willing to go along with this mystique. . . . I think we should have not only expressed regret at the assassination of President Kennedy, but at the same time should have conceded that the past ugly incidents[1] may have encouraged extremist elements here. It is only human for many outsiders to suspect our motives when they hear nothing but disclaimers that anything at all has even been amiss.

[1]Singleton referred here to incidents involving Adlai Stevenson and Lyndon Johnson.

After Singleton finished his article, Mr. Mangum and his staff documented it.[2] The article was published in the March 24, 1964, issue of *Look.* Excerpts from it are reproduced below; the omissions do not detract materially from the substance of the article, and in no case do they represent excisions of the author's ideas.

### Memo from a Dallas Citizen[3]
### by Donald L. Singleton

We are rich, proud Dallas, "Big D" to Texas, and we have never wanted a lesson in humility from any man. Not even from a murdered President of the United States. We have lived for three months with national tragedy, and I won't be popular for bringing this subject up now. But somebody must. To say nothing, more important, to do nothing, only says to the rest of the world that, as they have read, we shrugged the whole thing off.

• • •

. . . The tragedy would not go away. Day after day, I drove down to the slopes in front of the Texas School Book Depository, and always, no matter when I got there, or whether it rained or snowed, groups of people stood as at a shrine among the madonnas put up by children and the fresh flowers brought by nameless citizens. It still goes on. As I write this, not so much as a street, let alone a stone monument, has been dedicated to Kennedy, but the people have built their own memorial out of their patient presence.

Now, some of our ablest citizens have begun to understand that we can't make sense out of the future until we confront the past. Kennedy's death is a fact. I hope that out of our

[2]In this context, the word "documented" refers to the process of checking on factual statements. For example, Mangum checked on the question of a Kennedy memorial in Dallas, and learned that there was strong sentiment for what he called a "modest marker" at the site of the assassination, with the bulk of the contributions going to the Kennedy Library in Boston, Massachusetts. An ad hoc commission had been established in Dallas to study the question of a fitting memorial.
[3]Reprinted from the March 24, 1964 issue of *Look* magazine. Copyright 1964 by Cowles Magazines and Broadcasting, Inc.

many arguments will come a memorial that is more than a statue. If we are to learn the lessons that President Kennedy came to teach, we must build a living, searching memorial. We could, for instance, buy the Texas School Book Depository, from which the fatal shots were fired, and rebuild it for a better purpose. It would become a civic research center, under Southern Methodist University, dedicated to study of the urban evils that lead to violence and hatred.

• • •

. . . I think Dallas feels shame, not guilt. Many people here are ashamed to have been caught acting like fools—as they have been doing for many months—at the moment when the nation, and their President, needed the best they could give in thought, action and coherent criticism. He came to tell us so. Leaders must be guided by learning and reason, he planned to say, "or else those who confuse rhetoric with reality and the plausible with the possible will gain the popular ascendancy with their seemingly swift and simple solutions to every world problem." He never got to deliver his address, but his death, more than his life, shocked people out of the hysterics they had worked themselves into. Big D's penance for its silly years should lead to a meaningful memorial to its dead teacher. Or his death will be, for Dallas, in vain.

You had to live here in recent years to make sense out of today's confusion. None of us can claim to be blameless. For six years I have been helping build an oil business, a successful one, but at church, civic functions and parties, I have sat on the sidelines like a foreign observer at a tribal rite. I even got so I didn't pay much attention to the "Impeach Earl Warren" stickers on the bumpers in my neighborhood. They were not, it seemed then, much more of an affectation than the genuine alligator cowboy boots and mink chaps worn by people who had every other luxurious distraction our nation can offer.

• • •

. . . A Texan with a cause is formidable, and a Texan doing the work of his Lord is awesome. It was almost as if these people had set up a new religion. They put God aside, for the emergency. . . .

Outsiders make the mistake of thinking that the prominent businesssmen of Dallas led

the Birch chapters, the National Indignation Conference and the other political equivalents of a college panty raid. Not so. The Dallas leaders, the bankers and businessmen who set up the Citizens Council, are an intelligent and dedicated group. They have given the city an efficient government, an honest (if not always efficient) police force, a low tax rate and a booming economy. But they view their leadership in a narrow sense. . . .

• • •

Then it happened. I was sitting over an eight-ounce steak at the Trade Mart, where the President was to speak. When the news came, the first reaction around my table was the one I heard over and over in the next few hours: "I hope the killer didn't come from Dallas." But Dallas was elected by Providence to stand in the hard light of tragedy.

I'll never forget the rest of that terrible day. At the first telephone booth, I called a business friend to cancel an appointment. The telephone operator was sobbing, so I comforted her. She said, "That wonderful man—why did it have to happen in Dallas?" Next, my friend's secretary said, "Oh, Mr. Singleton, I'm broken-hearted. It *must* have been somebody from out of town; nobody in Dallas would do such a thing." My friend said, "Well, they finally got what they wanted." He didn't have to explain to me—or anybody else in town—who he was talking about. I said, "Yes, but suppose it turns out to be a Communist or a Black Muslim?" His answer was loyal Dallasite: "Well, I sure as hell hope that whoever he is, he's from out of town."

• • •

Basically, I suppose, the things that are wrong with Dallas are the things that are wrong with a world whose technology has raced beyond man's ability to shape it to his needs. We know how to get a man into orbit, but we can't find a good way to get to and from work. We can teach machines to think, but not our children. We have shining cities that false-front for stinking, crime-breeding slums; only a very rich society could afford so much poverty. We develop the greatest communications medium mankind has ever dreamed of, and then devote it to trivia and violence. And so on: Make up your own list. It will do, as long as it does not just pass the blame to somebody else—the UN, Washington, the Communist conspiracy, anybody. We can't pass the buck. We have work to do.

In one sense, those who say, "It could have happened anywhere," are quite right. But somehow Big D doesn't derive much comfort from that, nor is it possible. For I'm afraid the record shows all too clearly that in addition to having the world's ills, Dallas has managed to develop a few special complications. For all I know, other cities have our disease, too, but the epidemic broke out *here*. Maybe the President could have caught it anywhere, but he caught it *here*. Here is where the quarantine sign is, and I don't think it will ever really come down until we take it down ourselves.

Will we do it? The answer now is: maybe. Thousands of us are taking inventory of our civic faults. The assassination shocked us into our reappraisal, so our search for solutions should, in justice, be a memorial to the man who died here. A civic research in Kennedy's name could bring the best minds to help us, to keep up the momentum of the work. It won't happen automatically. We still have many who want the whole thing to blow away in the next dust storm.

We need help. If you who don't live here will see the difference between the guilt we don't feel and the shame many of us *do* know, we can succeed. We can bring pride, a better pride, back to Dallas, and make the School Book Depository more than a murderer's sanctuary.

One thing is sure: Thanks to the world's searchlight, we have a magnificently illuminated operating room. Never again will we be able to see our city, its good and bad, as clearly as we do now. We have the opportunity, bought by a great man's life, to treat what ails Dallas and, maybe, the "anywhere" where it didn't happen.

## AFTERMATH

Mr. Singleton told the casewriter that shortly after the March 24 issue of *Look* was published, the president of Summit of Texas and Singleton discussed the latter's article. For a few weeks thereafter, nothing further was said on the subject. Things were less quiet on other fronts, however. Singleton said that he received over 800 letters and 500 phone calls, about 90% of

which praised his position. He did not know how many other letters or calls were received elsewhere in the company, but he believed that the number was large and that the balance of their sentiment was less favorable to him. He knew that a certain number of Summit's credit cards were returned to the company.

On Monday, April 13, another conversation took place between Singleton and Summit's Texas president. The next day, Singleton signed a statement of resignation, which he told the casewriter had been presented to him.

The parent company's board meeting was scheduled for mid-April. As a board member, Singleton had had hotel and plane reservations for some time. Because he was "physically and emotionally tired and thought that a trip might help me unwind," and "just to see what would happen," Singleton went East, but did not visit the board meeting. No one from Summit got in touch with him.

On April 14, the *Dallas Morning News* stated that Summit of Texas had confirmed Singleton's resignation. In a story dated April 17, *Advertising Age* carried the information that Summit's advertising agency had resigned the Summit account, which reportedly amounted to more than $750,000 of commissionable advertising. The story quoted the agency president:

> One of the few privileges you have in the agency field is deciding whose money you want to accept. We just decided that we didn't want Summit's any longer.

The casewriter learned that some time after Singleton's departure from Summit, he and Lawrence Mangum had looked back at the events and forces that might have been involved in his situation. They considered the reactions of suppliers, jobbers, and retailers. The two men knew that some criticisms had come from these sources, but they believed these had been substantially offset by favorable comments from the same sources.

The two men also thought about the reactions of the general public and the press. The range of such reactions is reflected in Exhibits 1–3. Although most of the letters received by Singleton himself had expressed support of his position, as indicated earlier, neither he nor Mangum could be certain about the volume of letters that might have been received elsewhere in the company.

The two had not agreed as to the nature or strength of the reactions of members of the Citizens Council (referred to in the *Look* article), which is described in Exhibit 4. After Singleton's resignation became publicly known, Mangum talked to a number of prominent Dallas citizens, including several important members of the Citizens Council. All expressed regret at what happened to Singleton and emphasized that they had had nothing to do with the Singleton-Summit episode.

Singleton told the casewriter that he had been less certain than Mangum about the reactions of some of the other members of the Citizens Council. He suspected that some of them had expressed dissatisfaction to Summit about his statements. He also knew that one member of the council, in making a speech in April, had said, ". . . If Mr. Singleton would learn to know Dallas better, he would probably like it better.

So much for the gratuitous defectors and journalistic buzzards that are still circling our town. Don't waste your breath lashing back."[4] In any case, Singleton had no reason to suspect any organized activity on the part of the council.

As Singleton himself looked back upon what had happened after the publication of his article, he said,

When I resigned, . . . the impression got around that [Summit] asked for my resignation because it disagreed with what I wrote. This is not what happened and obscures the basic decision that most company men have to make, at one moment or, more likely, on the installment plan.

About a month after the article, and hours after the *Dallas Morning News* took me to its editorial-page woodshed a second time, I was suddenly confronted with a company demand: I must agree never to comment publicly without formally clearing each word in advance and in writing. The issue was not *what* I said, but whether I could say anything at all.[5]

[4]Reported in the *Dallas Morning News,* April 15, 1964.
[5]This quotation from Mr. Singleton has been taken from an article entitled "Memo about a Dallas Citizen," *Look,* August 11, 1964, p. 64, copyright 1964 by Cowles Magazines and Broadcasting, Inc.

## EXHIBITS: The Individual and the Corporation

### EXHIBIT 1
FROM TEXAS PRESS CLIPPING BUREAU—DALLAS

Borger, Texas
*News Herald*
(Cir. D. 9,805 S. 9,962)
March 13, 1964

**LOOK AGAIN**

*Look* magazine, March 24, 1964, on page 88, gives us another one of those among us who have dared to disagree with the progress of socialists, communists, and the world government movement within our government.

The article, entitled "Memo from a Dallas Citi-

zen," was written by [D. L. Singleton], a Dallas citizen.

Mr. [Singleton] is Senior Vice President of the [Summit] Oil Company. His address is [ _____ ], Dallas, Texas.

• • •

**So Sorry!**

When reading this *Look* magazine article by a Dallas citizen, [D. L. Singleton], it is hard to escape the impression that the author would have been a lot happier had the President, John F. Kennedy, been assassinated by someone among us who had dared to exercise the privilege as an American citizen, to disagree with the establishment, the communist-serving bureaucracy in Washington, D.C., instead of being killed, *as he was,* by an admitted communist.

Such hatred as reflected in this article graphically demonstrates why we, who are opposed to socialism, communism, and the loss of our national sovereignty to a world government, should thank God that the murderer of the President was immediately apprehended and as quickly identified as a member of the communist conspiracy.

Had he escaped, it is quite obvious that such unreasonable bitterness as revealed in this article could easily have resulted in either death or imprisonment for American patriots prominent in the conservative movement.

Without the guilty party in custody, it would have been much easier to have saddled the blame upon the conservatives or right-wing element among our citizens.

*But these smear writers and speakers never quit trying!*

## DISAPPOINTED

Since November 22, when President John F. Kennedy was assassinated and Lee Harvey Oswald, who had applied for Russian citizenship, was apprehended as the accused slayer, the news media of this country has been flooded with articles and speeches designed to saddle part of the blame, if not all of the blame, for the assassination on our conservative people, termed rightists.

(Of course, we who oppose the establishment in Washington, D.C., are often described as members of the lunatic fringe.)

These writers and speakers actually seem disappointed that one of us, instead of a communist, *had not* killed our President.

---

**EXHIBIT 2**
LETTER TO SINGLETON

---

March _____, 1964

Dear Mr. [Singleton]:

I have just had an opportunity to read "Memo from a Dallas Citizen" which was written by you and appeared in this month's *Look* magazine. The article was timely. It is excellent. It contains factual matter, most of which are matters of record. However, I am sure you realize that this article is going to call forth . . . your condemnation, with such statements that you are a socialist or communist. Some of them may even go so far as to apply to you the dirtiest word which these extreme rightists know: namely, a Democrat regardless of the hard life one finds in Dallas.

You are well aware of the situation here. Like the members of your church not tolerating sermons that contradict their personal dogma, these [people] will not tolerate any idea that contradicts their personal ideas. For instance, the last sentence in your article implies that there is something "which ails Dallas." These citizens whom I am talking about will not admit that there is anything which ails Dallas. They are still teaching their children that our Federal Government is something to abhor and cuss, instead of pointing out to them the glories of our government.

I am very hopeful that you own your own business, . . . for you may be sure after the article they will do what they can to harm you in any way possible as their dogma and their philosophy cannot stand the light of day and you in this article are throwing a little light upon the ills of Dallas.

Congratulations again for this article, but I am afraid that it will not do Dallas much good because it will just go unheeded like the rest of the suggestions which have been made to cure the ills of Dallas. At least it is refreshing to know that men such as you live in Dallas and are willing to do whatever possible to try and make this city a better place in which to live even at the expense of having adverse criticism cast against you.

With kind regards, I am

Very sincerely,

(Name deleted)

**EXHIBIT 3**
LETTER TO PRESIDENT OF SUMMIT OF TEXAS

(The following is a reproduction of a letter which was sent to the president of Summit of Texas; a carbon of the letter was sent by its author to Mr. Singleton, and this reproduction comes from Mr. Singleton's carbon.)

April ____, 1964

Dear _____:

I was delighted to read in the paper this morning of the resignation from your company of [Don Singleton]. If this is really a cover-up for your discharge of him or if it was due to pressure from you, I want to congratulate you. You will undoubtedly be charged with prejudice and hate by liberal eggheads of [Don Singleton's] persuasion; and, if so, I am sure it was not an easy decision from both your company and personal standpoint.

. . . I remain astounded that an executive of a sizeable public company such as yours would be so stupid as to make such an intemperate charge against his community as did [Singleton] in a national magazine. I am even more astounded by the conclusions drawn by him as expounded in the article, as he is close enough to the community to have felt the true nature of the feeling of this city. It indicates such a prejudice against conservative view as to indicate blindness towards the good things present in Dallas, or such a shallowness of observation as to render him useless for executive position.

Finally, . . . I have heard that [Singleton] did not consult the company management prior to the release of his article. This would be reason enough for the discharge of an executive of a public company, where the article in question could cause serious repercussions to the company. Such an act is simply rank insubordination.

Unfortunately, most news media are written by liberals, who have set the standard that liberals who disagree are merely forward-looking, while conservatives who disagree are vindictive haters. Please know that you have my wholehearted support.

Sincerely,

(Name deleted)

cc: Mr. [D. L. Singleton]
　　[Summit]

**EXHIBIT 4**
THE DALLAS CITIZENS COUNCIL

The Dallas Citizens Council is a highly influential group of over 200 prominent businessmen. Membership is limited to company presidents or board chairmen, and the organization concerns itself with major problems or issues that involve the welfare of Dallas. In recent months, the Citizens Council has been the subject of much attention. For example:

. . . Every person interviewed stated without hesitation that Dallas leadership comes primarily from the business and financial sectors of the community. Throughout the interviews, no contradictory opinion was ever expressed (p. 31).

• • •

In the initial interviews, . . . respondents stressed the role of a Dallas organization called the "Civic Committee" as having "more control over what goes on here" than any other organization (p. 35). . . .

• • •

The Committee as a body, they explained, meets officially only once a year, while the directors meet regularly. Whenever a serious problem arises in the city, the board may be convened quickly to decide what action should be taken.

The power of the organization was described by one of the respondents in this way:

Why, the Board of Education would not think of proposing any bond issue, or doing anything without first clearing it with the Civic Committee. This body has the power to make or break any idea or proposal that certain groups may come up with. It is such a powerful group that nothing can succeed without its support (p. 37). . . .

. . . Recent decision to combine many charity campaigns into a United Fund drive. Other problems included the financial difficulties of the symphony orchestra and of the city-owned zoo, inadequate housing for Negroes, getting a "good slate" of nominees for school board elections, (and getting them elected), juvenile delinquency, school integration, and urban renewal. The range of problems in which the more influential leaders become involved seems unlimited (p. 59). . . .

•  •  •

. . . The Civic Committee . . . functions as a mechanism for coordinating efforts of the various groups and interests within the community concerned with the particular problem at issue. . . . The leaders emphasized, however, that the board of the Civic Committee does not, itself, make decisions. Rather, it is the individual leaders who make the decisions. They use the organization as a tool for mobilizing verbal and financial support for their ideas (p. 61).*

*Fortune* also commented on the Citizens Council in an article that discussed the general question of business's leadership role in Dallas:†

. . . This (Dallas) world would not have survived had it not had many positive qualities—the quality of action, of dynamism, the quality of community service

*These quotations are taken from Carol Estes Thometz, *The Decision Makers, The Power Structure of Dallas,* Southern Methodist University Press, Dallas, 1963. Mrs. Thometz's book began as a master's thesis at Brandeis University and was later expanded and revised into book form. The Citizens Council to which Singleton's article refers is presumably the book's Civic Committee.
†Richard A. Smith, "How Business Failed Dallas," *Fortune,* July 1964, p. 157.

and of high (if localized) morality. And it is this strange mix of the negative and positive that has come to characterize the business leaders of Dallas. Mostly self-made men, they nevertheless place public service above wealth as the supreme symbol of status; the people with the highest standing in Dallas are not necessarily the richest, but those who do the most for the community.

•  •  •

The nine most powerful men in Dallas, the inner circle of its business leadership, have many characteristics in common, including a high degree of individualism. All are directors of the unofficial but omnipotent Citizens Council, four having served as president. . . . Of the eight who are college graduates, only three took degrees outside of Texas. Collectively, the power of these men is enormous; it reaches into every phase of life in Dallas, social, political, cultural, and economic.

•  •  •

Probably not one Dallasite out of five has any real idea of the power and purpose of this twenty-seven-year-old organization. Its membership of 250 maximum is by invitation only and perpetuates the original conception that none but the chief executive officers of the city's biggest corporations—men with the power to say "yes" or "no" to a project and have it binding on the enterprises they head—be invited.

•  •  •

In addition to the work of this organization, the influence of the business leadership is brought to bear on every aspect of community life through interlocking directorates or trusteeships.

# American Cyanamid Company

In June 1981, Nina Klein, corporate medical director of a large, international, U.S.-based chemical company, was rereading a memorandum she had just received from the chief executive officer.

The company was proposing to implement a new set of safety standards, to take account of recent federal and state legislation. The new standards were to focus particularly on reproductive hazards in the workplace. Dr. Klein had been asked for her suggestions in formulating the standards.

While she sat enjoying the late afternoon sunshine, Dr. Klein collected her thoughts on the subject by recalling the kinds of provisions included in the safety standards of chemical companies similar to her own.

In particular, she recalled the fetus protection policy implemented by American Cyanamid three years earlier, which had led to a number of as yet unresolved lawsuits. American Cyanamid was still fighting actions by the Occupational Safety and Health Administra-

tion (OSHA), the American Civil Liberties Union (ACLU), and the individuals who claimed that the fetus protection policy had forced women employees to choose between their jobs and their fertility.

As Dr. Klein mused on the arguments propounded by the various litigants, she wondered what lessons could be learned from the events at Cyanamid's Willow Island plant that would assist her in making proposals for her own company's safety standards.

American Cyanamid Company was incorporated in Maine in 1907 and grew fairly rapidly through related acquisitions in the chemical industry. It had had over $3 billion of revenues derived from operations in 125 countries.

The company was engaged in the manufacture and sale of a highly diversified line of agricultural, medical, specialty chemical, consumer, and formica products. Of approximately 44,000 employees, 48 percent were hourly paid. A large proportion of these hourly paid employees were represented by plant local unions of the International Chemical Workers Union, and the Oil, Chemical, and Atomic Workers Union.

## THE WILLOW ISLAND PLANT

Cyanamid's plant at Willow Island, West Virginia, was one of the more important production facilities in the United States, even though it employed a relatively small number of people. Here, Cyanamid manufactured pigments, dyestuffs, animal feed supplements, melamine, platinum catalysts, plastic antioxidants, and specialty chemicals. The plant represented an important source of employment to an industrially depressed area.

## AMERICAN CYANAMID'S NEW SAFETY STANDARDS

Very few women were employed as production workers by American Cyanamid until 1974, when things began to change. By the end of 1977, 23 women were working on production lines at Willow Island. Legislative activity throughout the 1970s forced companies to become increasingly alert to the hazards of female exposure to fetotoxins, i.e., any substances especially hazardous to fetuses.

Accordingly, in September 1977, American Cyanamid began a corporate-wide campaign to revise safety standards, with particular attention to suspected fetotoxins. From a large list of suspected fetotoxins, five chemicals were identified as being especially hazardous to fetuses. These were lead, hydrazine hydrate, hydrazine sulfate, and two pharmaceuticals, Thiotepa and Methotrexate. For each substance, the company established exposure levels it considered safe for a healthy adult and for a developing fetus. These levels were usually determined by information available in published literature on toxins. Typically, the safe levels for exposure were five to ten times higher for an adult than for a fetus. In the case of lead, the setting of the standards took more than a year.

## THE FETUS PROTECTION POLICY

In January 1978, the American Cyanamid Company announced to employees of its Willow Island pigments manufacturing plant that it intended to implement what it called the "fetus protection policy." This policy, as ultimately implemented, excluded women aged 16 through 50 from production jobs in the lead pigments department unless they could prove that they had been surgically sterilized. The stated purpose of the policy was to protect the fetuses of women exposed to lead, particularly during early pregnancy when the employee might not know of her pregnancy. Similar policies were already practiced in the chemical industry and had been implemented by Allied Chemical, DuPont, Dow Chemical, and General Motors, in areas where workers were exposed to lead.

Twenty-three women at Willow Island were warned at this time that they were working with potentially fetotoxic substances and that new company policies would require their transfer to other work areas if their exposure was found to be hazardous. By October 1978, the policy was put into effect. The only affected area of the Willow Island plant was the lead chromate pigment manufacturing area where eight women worked.

## EVENTS RESULTING FROM THE FETUS PROTECTION POLICY

Between February and July 1978, five women employed in the lead pigments department submitted to surgical sterilization in a hospital not associated with American Cyanamid. The women later claimed that there was considerable confusion over the date when the policy would be implemented, and over its actual effect in practice. They also claimed that they were advised there would not be enough new jobs to go around after their transfer from the lead chromate pigment area, and as a consequence they risked losing their jobs or facing demotion once the guidelines went into effect.

American Cyanamid, on the other hand,

contended that it actively discouraged the five women from undergoing sterilization, and that it offered them perfectly acceptable alternatives in the form of actual or promised jobs with similar status at the same pay level. Nevertheless, the corporate medical director, Dr. Robert Clyne (now retired), agreed that, "If a woman of childbearing age is sterile, she is allowed to work in the pigments area."

As of 1981, the case was still in litigation, and it was not clear where the blame lay. It was, however, certain that the situation was aggravated by the small size of the Willow Island facility. Equivalent jobs were not immediately available for the women, who faced transfer temporarily to lower-status jobs, although with retention of pay for 90 days. It was also certain that the policy caused so much anxiety among those affected that five women chose sterilization over anticipated unemployment or demotion. The youngest woman to undergo the surgery was 25, according to Joan Burton of the ACLU.

Two other fertile women elected to change jobs rather than undergo sterilization. Both were offered janitorial jobs, with the same pay as their previous jobs for 90 days and with special access to other openings in the plant as they became available. Both were offered new jobs at their old pay level during the 90-day period. One took the new job. The other chose to retain the janitorial job, at a lower salary, because the new job involved shift work.

## LAWSUITS AGAINST AMERICAN CYANAMID

Shortly after the initial policy announcement in January 1978, the Oil, Chemical, and Atomic Workers Union (OCAW) and 14 women members of the union filed complaints against the company's policy with OSHA, the West Virginia Human Rights Commission, and with the Equal Employment Opportunity Commission (EEOC) in West Virginia or in Washington, DC. The Union's arbitration grievance and the West Virginia Human Rights Commission investigation were subsequently withdrawn or dismissed.

In January 1979, however, OSHA inspectors visited the Willow Island plant for an investigation of the charges made by OCAW and the 14 women. As a result of the investigation, OSHA brought citations against American Cyanamid. The first citation contended that American Cyanamid was in violation of the lead standard and lead chromate standard mandated by federal law. The exposure level allowed, according to industry standards set by OSHA in April 1979, was 50 micrograms per cubic meter, but 200 micrograms per cubic meter was being permitted as an interim compliance level for pigment plants. The willful and serious violations specified by the OSHA investigation included: failure to identify an area with lead chromate exposure as a regulated area, overexposure to coal dust and noise, allowing workers to use personal protection equipment improperly, and permitting workers to consume food and beverages in a lead exposed area.

Willful violations, according to OSHA definition, existed where evidence showed that the employer committed an intentional and knowing act as contrasted with inadvertent violation, and the employer was conscious of the fact that what it was doing was a violation; or, even though an employer was not consciously violating the OSHA Act, it was aware that the hazardous condition existed and made no reasonable effort to eliminate the condition. Willful violations carried proposed penalties of up to $10,000 each.

Serious violations were defined as those where there was a substantial probability of death or serious physical harm resulting and the employer knew, or could have known with reasonable diligence, of the existence of the hazard. Such violations carried mandatory proposed penalties of up to $1000 each.

OSHA also cited American Cyanamid under the general duty clause of the Occupational Safety and Health Act of 1970. This was the first time that clause had been used to justify an OSHA citation and represented an attempt by OSHA to expand its authority over the setting of safety standards in the workplace.

The purpose of the Act was "to assure so far as possible every working man and woman in the nation safe and healthful working conditions and to preserve our human resources." The general duty clause required each employer to furnish employment and a place of employment free of recognized hazards causing or likely to cause death or serious physical harm. The Act did not, however, define the term "hazard."

By October 1979, OSHA had proposed the maximum fine allowable by law, $10,000, and ordered the company to halt the regulatory violations. American Cyanamid contested the fine and the citations within the 15 days allowable for contesting, and in August 1980, the case was heard by William Brennan, an administrative law judge sitting in Hyattsville, MD.

The citations were dismissed by Brennan on two grounds: first, that OSHA had issued the citations after the six-month statute of limitations had expired. Although the policies mandating exclusion had been announced early in 1978, they were not implemented until October 1978, and OSHA did not issue citations until the middle of 1979. The delays that occurred were partly as a result of confusion about the actual effect of Cyanamid's new policies, and partly because OSHA's legal powers in this area had not been clarified by case law. As a result, the second ground for dismissal of the citations was that OSHA had no jurisdiction over exclusionary policies. OSHA appealed the administrative judge's decision to the OSHA Review Commission, a federal adjudicatory agency designed to hear employer/employee disputes arising from OSHA inspections.

On April 28, 1981, the Review Commission decided that American Cyanamid was not in violation of the general duty clause. The Commission explained that the fetus protection policy was neither a work process nor a work material, and it manifestly could not alter the physical integrity of employees while they were engaged in work or work-related activities. An employee's decision to undergo sterilization in order to gain or retain employment grew out of economic and social factors which operated primarily outside the workplace. The employer neither controlled nor created these factors as it created or controlled work processes and materials. Therefore the policy was not a hazard in the meaning of the general duty clause.

The Review Commission's decision was then appealable by OSHA to the circuit courts. As of 1981 it had not been announced what action OSHA would take.

## AMERICAN CIVIL LIBERTIES SUIT

A second suit against American Cyanamid was brought on January 29, 1980. Thirteen women, represented by the ACLU, filed a class action suit alleging violation of Title VII of the 1964 Civil Rights Act; and in particular that Cyanamid's program wrongfully discriminated against the plaintiffs on the basis of sex, invaded their privacy, perpetrated a fraud, and intentionally inflicted emotional distress upon them. One of the principal allegations of the complaint was that Cyanamid imposed surgical sterilization as a term and condition of continued employment.

The Civil Rights Act upheld the right of employees to hold jobs without suffering discrimination and without threat to reproductive capacity and genetic stability. Among the women represented in this action were four out of the five sterilized women and a number of applicants for employment at the Willow Island plant who were refused work, they claimed, on discriminatory grounds.

Dr. Klein knew that the suit was still in process: if the ACLU should win its case, the women would be entitled to be put in positions they would have been in if no discrimination had occurred, and entitled to receive any money lost through discriminatory practices. American Cyanamid would therefore have to restore to them job opportunities and promotional opportunities. The question of reversing the surgical sterilization also arose. In certain circumstances it was possible to reverse sterilization, although the outcome of such operations in the past had been very uncertain. In addition, the women might be entitled to substantial damages under state tort claims filed at the same time.

The trial was expected to take place at the end of 1981.

## SHAREHOLDERS' CAMPAIGN

American Cyanamid faced attack from a third group. A shareholders' campaign mounted jointly by the International Chemical Workers Union (ICWU) and the Interfaith Center for Corporate Public Responsibility (ICCPR) demanded that American Cyanamid establish a public responsibility committee composed of nonemployee board members; the committee was to be an impartial body set up to study the fetus protection policy and corporate safety standards.

The ICCPR was a shareholder of American Cyanamid, and the ICWU held shares in Cyanamid through members who had received stock options as part of their compensation. The ICCPR held shares in a large number of U.S. corporations. One of its functions was to use its influence as a shareholder to make corporations aware of their social responsibilities. While there were a number of companies that had implemented an exclusionary policy similar to Cyanamid's, the ICCPR selected Cyanamid as a target case. It was felt that in view of the publicity surrounding the sterilizations, Cyanamid would be particularly sensitive, and therefore responsive, to the issue.

Initially, the Board of Directors refused to establish a public responsibility committee, stating that the current mechanism for reviewing safety standards was perfectly adequate. However, on the 31st of January, 1980, a few days after its earlier statement, the Board of Directors, threatened by shareholder resolutions, acceded to the request. The reason for Cyanamid's about-face was unclear, but the ICWU claimed that Cyanamid was particularly concerned about OSHA citations, shortly to come before OSHARC, and about the EEOC's guidelines which were to be published in February of 1980.

The public responsibility committee established by American Cyanamid originally consisted of three members, one of whom later withdrew from the committee. The two remaining members were: Paul MacAvoy, Milton Steinbach Professor of Organization and Management and Economics at Yale University; and George L. Schultz, a private investor. Their report was expected towards the autumn of 1981.

## COMPLAINTS FILED WITH THE EQUAL EMPLOYMENT OPPORTUNITY COMMISSION

Complaints filed with the EEOC by the original 14 women and OCAW were still pending in 1981. The EEOC had taken no action, but had the authority to impose penalties for sex discrimination. The EEOC had, however, a history of involvement in the safety and discrimination issue in general.

## EQUAL EMPLOYMENT OPPORTUNITY COMMISSION GUIDELINES

In April 1978, the EEOC issued a policy statement that fell short of making a decision on exclusionary work practices, but offered some guidelines. It stated that exclusionary employment actions taken hastily or without regard for rigorous adherence to acceptable scientific processes might be viewed as unlawful discrimination. Employers had to make sure that such practices not be instituted without making a serious effort to find alternative methods with a less exclusionary impact.

On February 1, 1980, the EEOC and the Office of Federal Contract Compliance issued proposed guidelines that were somewhat more specific and would have the effect of placing "protective exclusions" within the jurisdiction of the section of the Civil Rights Act of 1964 that prohibited job discrimination. The guidelines, briefly, suggested that an employer's conduct which treated men differently from women raised a presumption of a violation of Title VII. An apparently neutral employment policy, which nevertheless adversely affected either men or women, was an unlawful employment practice. If a workplace hazard was known to affect the fetus through either parent, an exclusionary policy directed only at women would be unlawful. If the hazard was scientifically shown to affect the fetus through women only, the class excluded must be limited to pregnant women and not all women of child-bearing capacity.

A *temporary* exclusion policy, introduced to protect women only, would be allowed provided that the policy was directed only at the individuals who might suffer harm, that it was not introduced until suitable alternatives had been adopted or examined, and that an employer could show that it had thoroughly searched the scientific literature and could find evidence of a similar hazard for the nonexcluded sex. Companies had to begin, within six months of the commencement of the exclusionary policy, research projects to find out whether the chemicals in question also produced adverse reproductive effects on the nonexcluded sex. These research projects had to be conducted under "accepted scientific methods" and produce results within two years. The EEOC solicited industry opinions on the guidelines and received critical responses. Unions, women's and public interest groups supported the guidelines in principle, but found them too vague and subject to misinterpretation. As a result of the lack of support, EEOC withdrew the proposed guidelines on January 13, 1981, stating that:

> Upon reviewing the comments, the agencies have concluded that the most appropriate methods of eliminating employment discrimination in the workplace where there is a potential exposure to reproductive hazards is through investigation and enforcement of the law on a case by case basis, rather than by the issuance of interpretive guidelines.

## SHUTDOWN OF LEAD CHROMATE PIGMENT UNIT AT WILLOW ISLAND

On January 15, 1980, American Cyanamid closed down its lead chromate unit at Willow Island, citing adverse profitability of the operation. Poor profitability was due, the company said, to increased government regulation and the decreasing use of lead chromate pigments in paint. The unit was one of ten production lines at Willow Island. American Cyanamid was thought to have lost some orders after the shutdown because the unit acted as a source for other divisions of the company. Any financial loss, however, was temporary and minimal, especially in view of the probability that the unit would have been phased out in due course as other less hazardous substitutes became readily available in the marketplace. Sixty plant personnel were laid off as a result of the shutdown.

## SUMMARY OF ISSUES

The issues raised were emotional ones, and aroused considerable anger among the people most closely involved with the various suits against American Cyanamid. A casual comment of one ICSU official was typical:

> If a company knew that the result of exposure to fetotoxins would be spontaneous abortion or stillbirth, [it] would be happy to allow women to work in areas where they risked exposure. The company's concern is to avoid expensive lawsuits that might be brought by damaged, but surviving, fetuses.

### Existing Legislation Affecting Fetotoxins

The law in this area was ill-defined as of 1981. State law in West Virginia was also, according to an attorney in the Attorney General's office of West Virginia, somewhat undeveloped. Environmental laws in that state were still relatively new, and many of the issues in the Cyanamid case had not previously arisen.

Federal law was essentially contained in the OSHA Act of 1970 and the Toxic Substances Control Act of 1977. The Acts differentiated between *teratogens* and *mutagens*. Teratogens were agents affecting development of the fetus where only the mother's exposure could endanger the fetus. Mutagens were preconception toxins that altered adults' gametes in such a way to produce mutations in later offspring.

Although the toxic effects of many chemicals were simply not known, in the case of lead there was considerable evidence that harm could accrue to the male reproductive system as well as to the female. A 1974 study had shown that men with levels of blood lead above 60 micrograms (the federal safety standard) suffered reproductive problems, and OSHA explicitly mentions dangers to male workers in the new lead standards of April 1979: "Male workers may be rendered infertile or impotent and both men and women are subject to genetic damage which may affect both the course and outcome of pregnancy." Lead was therefore widely regarded as a *mutagen.*

In theory, then, an employer discovering a mutagen in the workplace had to address the following issues: Does it affect males in a comparable way to females? Can exposure be controlled in some way short of prohibiting access to the workplace of vulnerable groups? Alternative protective measures might include the use of work assignments, engineering controls, and personal protective equipment.

The issue of an employer's liability to a fetus or ultimately born child was also unclear. Legal liability of an employer, however, might arise from a number of sources:

- The employer might be violating a *standard expressly regulated by OSHA.*
- The employer might be violating the *OSHA general duty clause.*
- The employer might be liable to claim by an injured *employee* under state *workmen's compensation statutes* or other occupational illness statutes.
- Under certain circumstances, the employee might not be barred by workmen's compensation from bringing *tort action* against the employer.
- An ultimately born child injured as a result of its parent's exposure to an occupational mutagen might bring a *personal injury lawsuit,* where the employer had substantial liability in tort.

It should be emphasized that an employer would normally face considerably higher costs and damages under a personal injury suit than under a workmen's compensation suit.

### Arguments for American Cyanamid's Fetus Protection Policy

American Cyanamid contended, first of all, that it "absolutely discouraged any surgery to preclude childbearing potential." Jack E. White, plant manager at Willow Island, stated, "Our doctor met with local union committee members who represent the females to explain the company position in this matter." Acceptable alternatives were offered in the form of actual or promised jobs with similar status at the same pay level.

It also contended, in the company of Dow, DuPont, Allied Chemical, and other chemical manufacturers with exclusionary policies, that federal safety standards were often technically or economically unattainable. A case in point was the new lead standard, where the level of pollution of 50 micrograms per cubic meter had not yet been reached even with engineering controls and personal protective apparel. Perry Gehring of Dow Chemical stated that, "If the cost of implementing good industrial hygiene is going to rise exponentially to reach a certain low level for uniquely fetal toxins, then it is justified to take women out of the workplace."

The focus of concern of chemical companies was not so much the health hazards to their employees, who were protected under the worker's compensation act, but to the fetus. Bruce Karrh, medical director of DuPont, stated, "When we remove a woman it is not to protect her reproductive capacity but to protect her fetus."

Further, chemical companies were reluctant to allow women to sign waivers of responsibility for their unborn children. They claimed the unborn children had legal rights that the mothers could not waive and that, if they did not protect the fetus, they would leave themselves open to claims for damages on behalf of children born with birth defects.

Finally, chemical companies were reluctant to allow fertile women in areas exposed to fetotoxins, regardless of whether they intended to become pregnant or not. Major malformations occurred from the 14th to the 40th day of pregnancy, when the major organ systems were being formed. It was usually not possible to detect pregnancy in workers and remove them to a safe workplace before that critical period. While there were methods of ensuring that pregnancies did not take place, or that they were terminated very early in the life of the embryo, these would probably be resisted as unacceptable intrusions into the privacy of employees.

### Arguments against American Cyanamid's Fetus Protection Policy

Critics of the exclusionary policies attacked the chemical companies' position on a number of grounds.

Eula Bingham, formerly of OSHA, felt that such policies allowed companies to avoid real efforts to clean up the workplace in favor of the cheaper and easier alternative of removing those employees most susceptible to the danger.

Further, it had not been proved that a toxic substance that affected the fetus through the mother did not also have a deleterious effect on the male reproductive system. Anthony Robbins, director of the National Institute for Safety and Health (NIOSH), stated that, "There is no reason to believe that the genetic material of a male worker is in any way more resistant to toxic occupational injury than that of the female." There was, in fact, growing evidence to show that a father's exposure to toxic substances might affect the embryo. Dr. Channing Meyer, environmental health specialist at the University of Cincinnati, stated, "Interference with the normal development of human sperm

may result in reduced numbers of sperm, improperly shaped sperm, abnormal sperm movement and genetic abnormalities in the sperm cell."

Male workers' exposure to toxins could affect the fetus directly through interference in sperm development, and indirectly through carrying toxins from the workplace to the home. In August 1980, the United States Court of Appeals for the District of Columbia Circuit upheld the portion of the OSHA standard that provided the same safeguards for both men and women working with lead, which was commonly regarded as being hazardous to the male reproductive system. Petitions regarding the standard were brought by a variety of parties, including the United Steelworkers of America, the United Automobile Workers, General Motors Corporation, National Construction Association, and others who said the standard was too strict; other unions, however, wanted the standard stricter. The decision was being appealed to the Supreme Court.

Women's rights groups were concerned that the policies would contribute to the myth of "permanent pregnancy": that is, that all fertile women at any one time are assumed to be pregnant. The right and ability of women to make a choice about pregnancy should not be curtailed. Eighty percent of blue-collar workers then used some form of contraception. Exclusionary policies seemed to deny the fact that women were now free to make their own choices about childbearing.

Finally, the ICWU and other groups were concerned about the dangers inherent in discriminating on genetic grounds. Should the exclusionary policies be allowed to stand, it might open a path to companies screening out other minority groups on the basis of "genetic susceptibility." The *New York Times* published a series of articles in February 1980, on this subject. Excerpts from the articles follow:

Petrochemical companies have quietly tested thousands of American workers to determine if any of the genes they were born with are what industry doctors call "defective," making the employees especially vulnerable to certain chemicals in the workplace. The process is called genetic screening. . . .

Employers say the purpose of the tests is to provide a protective barrier keeping "hypersusceptible" workers away from industrial poisons. . . .

Some scientists, union leaders, and industrial hygienists reject assertions that the tests protect the workers. . . .

They say the genetic approach is indeed a barrier, but one that threatens workers with sexual, racial, or ethnic discrimination. They oppose an employment philosophy that would label a particular group of people as unfit for certain jobs because of their genetic make-up. This approach shifts the focus of the problem to the genes of the workers, rather than to the presence of industrial poisons in the workplace.

# Jim Sawyer

It had been a long, hot summer day and Robert Taylor, vice president of finance, United Industries' Plastics Division (UIPD), was troubled and confused. An incident earlier that day had led him to file the following disciplinary report with Richard Hammond, UIPD's vice president of personnel.

---

**To:** Personnel file of Jim L. Sawyer

**Date:** July 9, 1980

After lunch (about 1:00 P.M.) I looked for Jim to discuss a problem. He was not back from lunch so I tried several times later and he still had not returned. At 3:20 P.M., on a hunch, I walked down to Gino's Bar and found Jim and Art Wentworth having an extended lunch, including beer, and enjoying some kind of dice game. I told them I wanted to speak with them in my office. I told Jim his behavior (extended lunch hour) was not in keeping with his position as a manager and that it was totally unacceptable. He apologized and admitted that he had been doing this at times over the past year. He said it would not recur.

    E. M. Sanchez will speak with Art about this problem on July 10.

R. J. Taylor

---

## COMPANY BACKGROUND

United Industries was a multinational corporation with headquarters in Cleveland, Ohio. Sales for 1980 were $2.36 billion with net earnings after taxes of $112.8 million. Sales resulted from four major operating groups: Air Conditioning ($520m), Automotive Equipment ($788m), Industrial Products ($458m), and Plastics ($594m). Because of its diversified activities, United Industries was a highly decentralized operation with many policy decisions delegated to each of the operating companies, particularly those associated with product development and personnel.

United Industries Plastics Division exemplified the independent spirit found within the corporation. Headquartered along the Ohio River in Huntington, Kentucky, UIPD was proud of its accomplishments. Its sales and earnings growth were at the top of its industry; furthermore, the company had recently introduced a new line of highly profitable plastic resins. Though the division was successfully driven by its marketing department, UIPD executives were especially proud of its employee orientation. As UIPD President Gordon Marshall put it, "The business *is* the people. . . . My job is to get them excited about our goals."

Many people liked the fact that United Industries was a paternalistic employer. With over half of the 3,500 UIPD employees located in Huntington, United Industries was the town's major employer. Even though many of its competitors were closely located along the river, the town was a friendly place. The people enjoyed the business rivalry, and the competition actually fostered a strong spirit of community cooperation. It was a working town of 50,000 people who appreciated its rural identity and relative isolation.

Many people spent their entire lives in the Huntington area. After completing school, graduates could usually choose from a number of opportunities among local plastics manufacturers. Like its competition, United had a high

percentage of home-grown personnel. UIPD was certainly not tied to the idea of only hiring local talent, however, and it often recruited outside the area for technical and managerial positions. Furthermore, United's corporate staff had always encouraged some interdivisional transfers to develop the management ranks in each of the company's divisions.

Gordon Marshall, 53, a Canadian by birth and educated as a chemical engineer, had spent 28 years with the firm before being named worldwide UIPD president in early 1980. He served the community as a director for the Huntington Chamber of Commerce and the Huntington National Bank. He also acted as an adviser to a number of local small business enterprises. (See Figure A for the individuals described and their working relationships.)

Richard Hammond, 54, served as Mar-

**FIGURE A**
Partial organization chart, Plastics Division. (*Source:* Company documents.)

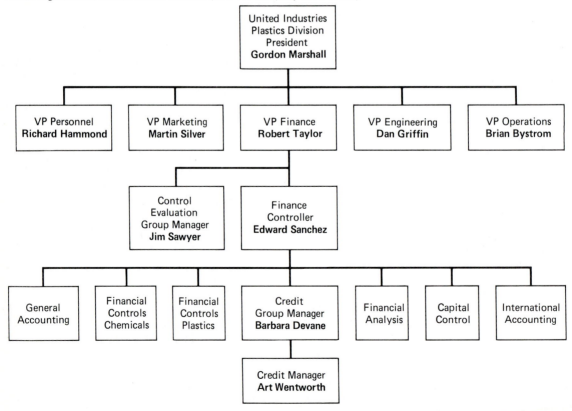

shall's second-in-command. He had been with the company for 18 years, serving in a variety of functional areas before being named vice president in 1972. Hammond was personally involved with almost every hiring decision as well as every employee termination. No UIPD employee could be fired until Hammond and Marshall were certain that the decision was a fair and just one. Hammond would often act as an advocate for the employee during such performance reviews. Because of this unusual high-level review, hiring choices were made with utmost care and consideration. Hammond believed that a decision to terminate an employee was the most drastic job decision any United manager would ever make. Hammond insisted that dismissals should never come as a surprise to any employee. He demanded that UIPD managers explicitly note and discuss performance weaknesses with employees during appraisal sessions. Then each worker would be given an honest chance to overcome weak points and to succeed at United.

Robert Taylor, 48, had spent 18 years with UIPD, serving in various accounting and financial positions. Edward Sanchez, 30, a Harvard Business School graduate, had joined UIPD in 1973 and served as controller, reporting to Robert Taylor. Jim Sawyer, 40, who also joined UIPD in 1973, was control evaluation manager and likewise reported directly to Taylor.

### JIM SAWYER

Jim Sawyer was considered an intelligent and highly ambitious individual who had potential growth at United Industries. He joined UIPD in March 1973 after nine years of related industrial experience and assumed the job of business analyst within the finance department. Within three years, Sawyer was promoted to credit manager responsible for managing new and existing credit accounts. Although he was seen as a capable credit manager, his aggressive manner alienated some clients accustomed to a more easygoing relationship with people at UIPD. When antagonisms developed between Sawyer and his supervisor at that time, Barbara Devane, Taylor decided to transfer him to an-

other group within the department. Sawyer had expressed some interest in securing a marketing assignment, but management believed that his career would develop with additional experience in the finance area.

In March 1979 Sawyer was appointed control evaluation manager reporting directly to Taylor. He was responsible for managing a small task force assigned to audit and review UIPD's operations and policies. According to Taylor, the group required minimal supervision from him, thus permitting Sawyer a great deal of individual discretion and freedom.

### SIGNPOSTS

The July incident at Gino's had irritated Taylor. He had not enjoyed an especially warm relationship with Sawyer, but nevertheless he recognized that Sawyer had significant potential for development. Jim was a quick thinker who was good with numbers and had a lot to offer the finance department. Inexplicably, however, his performance had begun to falter; he was not meeting deadlines and his work was barely meeting management's expectations.

Taylor had heard that Sawyer was having domestic difficulties and wondered whether this personal distraction explained his failure to meet certain business obligations. He also wondered if Sawyer was feeling trapped in his job; Taylor thought that Sawyer might still be angry about the lateral transfer from the previous year. He knew from experience that Sawyer was an intense person who could easily become frustrated. Sawyer had once written United's CEO imploring him to exert more pressure on corporate executives to implement the quality-of-work-life (QWL) program. This kind of end run around divisional management had been viewed as an impulsive act that had embarrassed both Sawyer and the company. As the summer progressed, Taylor became more alarmed as Sawyer missed work deadlines and occasionally arrived late for work on Monday mornings. Taylor wondered what Sawyer's problem was.

In addition to filing his July memorandum, Taylor had sought Hammond's professional guidance in trying to reverse Sawyer's performance setbacks. Hammond lived near Sawyer's home and had known his family since their arrival in Huntington. He had a polite relationship with Sawyer but they rarely met socially outside of the office. Hammond was fond of Sawyer's children, having come to know them in their teenage years as neighborhood newspaper carriers. He had occasionally talked with Sawyer's wife, Marion, when out for a walk around the neighborhood.

Hammond suspected that the trouble ran deeper than family problems. He recalled seeing Sawyer at a community meeting, where his breath smelled of whiskey. Hammond sometimes had lunch at Gino's and he remembered seeing the same group at the bar with a long line of beer cans before them. He also noticed Sawyer's lateness on Monday mornings and was concerned about performance slips. In addition, Hammond thought he detected a change in Sawyer's physical appearance; his palms and cheekbones appeared red and blotched. Something, Hammond realized, had gone wrong. Taylor and Hammond kept their apprehensions about Sawyer to themselves. They had talked with each other frequently in an effort to find the causes of Sawyer's difficulties, but neither was totally certain about what should or could be done to rectify the situation.

In mid-August 1980 Taylor departed for an overseas business trip and left Edward Sanchez in charge of the finance department. Meanwhile, Hammond continued to investigate the problem of alcoholism and sought professional advice from several public and private alcoholic treatment centers. Hammond had recently been forced to terminate a high-level clerical employee who had faltered on the job because of a drinking problem. The employee had denied having a problem with alcohol abuse and refused to accept any help or treatment. Finally, after repeated performance lapses, he was fired. Hammond distinctly remembered the words of one professional counselor: "People who are having problems with alcohol abuse don't wear a badge that tells everyone they are alcoholic. Correctly identifying the disease of alcoholism is the first step toward successful treatment." (Exhibits 1, 2, and 3 contain literature about alcoholism that Hammond had obtained from local alcoholic treatment centers.)

Friday afternoon before the Labor Day weekend Sawyer could not be found, and his desk had been left strewn with work papers. Sanchez had called an impromptu meeting to review a report for the corporate staff and he needed Sawyer's input. A secretary recalled seeing Sawyer earlier in the day but had no idea where he had gone. After searching UIPD's headquarters, Sanchez went to see Hammond. Hammond told Sanchez to stop searching while he took responsibility for locating Sawyer.

Hammond found Sawyer with another UIPD employee at Gino's Bar. Hammond walked into Gino's, made eye contact with Sawyer, then turned around and walked out the door. Sawyer's lunch partner, sensing trouble, ran back to his office to remind his supervisor, Sanchez, that he was on a legitimately scheduled vacation day. Sawyer, however, never returned to his desk that day.

Taylor returned from his overseas trip during the long Labor Day weekend. Hammond believed that the time had come to confront Sawyer with his suspicions. To prepare for their encounter once business resumed following the holiday, Hammond telephoned Taylor at home to tell him about the second incident at Gino's. Taylor was furious: "Why should I be concerned about Jim's problem when he doesn't appear concerned about it! I just don't need this problem. I know he's having personal difficulties, but how many chances can I give him?" Hammond shared this sense of exasperation but believed that the company should try to help Sawyer and his family.

It was Labor Day, September 1, 1980. Taylor and Hammond had to decide what to do about Jim Sawyer when he reported to work the next day. If they could not reach an agreement, they would have to take the matter directly to Marshall.

# EXHIBITS: Jim Sawyer

**EXHIBIT 1**
FACTS ON ALCOHOLISM*

Alcohol is America's favorite recreational drug. It is also the nation's number one drug of abuse. Alcohol is a mood changer, as are tranquilizers, heroin, cocaine, barbiturates, and amphetamines. The chronic alcoholic is physically and psychologically addicted.

In 1956, alcoholism was recognized by the American Medical Association as a disease with identifiable and progressive symptoms. This position is endorsed by the American Hospital Association, the American Bar Association, the American Psychiatric Association, and the World Health Organization.

Fifty-two percent of all male admissions to state mental hospitals suffer from alcohol-related problems.

There are an estimated 12–15 million alcoholic persons in America today. Of the 100 million persons in this country who drink, one in ten is prone to alcoholism.

Alcoholism is one of the top three killer diseases, along with cancer and heart disease. Persons afflicted with alcoholism are sick, as are people who suffer from heart disease or cancer. If not treated, alcoholism ends in permanent mental damage, physical incapacity, or early death.

The average alcoholic is in his or her mid-forties with a responsible job and a family. Fewer than 5 percent of all alcoholics are found on Skid Row.

*Source: Statistics were taken from material published by the National Institute on Alcohol Abuse and Alcoholism (NIAAA) 1977–1978.

Ninety-five percent are employed or employable, like many people you see every day.

Fifty percent of all fatal accidents occurring on the roads involve alcohol, and half of these involve an alcoholic.

Alcoholism involves both sexes and crosses all ethnic, religious, economic and sociocultural groups. While there are as many women alcoholics as there are men, only 25 percent of the women receive treatment.

Thirty-one percent of those who take their own lives are alcoholics. The suicide rate among alcoholics is 58 times that of the general population.

Alcoholism costs the nation $54.1 billion annually. Industry alone picks up a $25.2 billion tab for lost work time, health and welfare service benefits, property damage, medical expenses, and overhead costs of insurance and wage losses.

Eighty percent of all violence in the American home is alcohol related.

Children of alcoholic parents are 50 percent more likely to marry an alcoholic person.

Alcoholism is a treatable disease.

Education, early detection, and community treatment facilities are the greatest forces operating today for the control and reduction of alcoholism. Prevention and intervention through programs of information and education have been primary objectives of the National Council on Alcoholism since its founding in 1944.

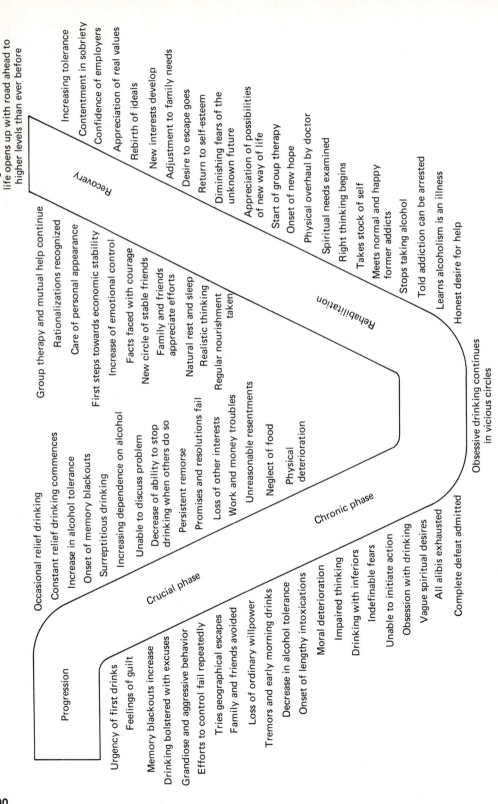

The progression and recovery of the alcoholic in the disease of alcoholism. To be read from left to right. (*Source:* Comprehensive Care Corporation. Copyright © 1982. Reprinted by permission.)

**EXHIBIT 2**

Progression

Occasional relief drinking
Constant relief drinking commences
Increase in alcohol tolerance
Onset of memory blackouts
Surreptitious drinking
Increasing dependence on alcohol
Unable to discuss problem
Decrease of ability to stop drinking when others do so
Persistent remorse
Promises and resolutions fail
Loss of other interests
Work and money troubles
Unreasonable resentments
Neglect of food
Physical deterioration

Crucial phase

Urgency of first drinks
Feelings of guilt
Memory blackouts increase
Drinking bolstered with excuses
Grandiose and aggressive behavior
Efforts to control fail repeatedly
Tries geographical escapes
Family and friends avoided
Loss of ordinary willpower
Decrease in alcohol tolerance
Onset of lengthy intoxications
Moral deterioration
Impaired thinking
Drinking with inferiors
Indefinable fears
Unable to initiate action
Obsession with drinking
Vague spiritual desires
All alibis exhausted
Complete defeat admitted

Chronic phase

Tremors and early morning drinks

Obsessive drinking continues in vicious circles

Rehabilitation

Group therapy and mutual help continue
Rationalizations recognized
Care of personal appearance
First steps towards economic stability
Increase of emotional control
Facts faced with courage
New circle of stable friends
Family and friends appreciate efforts
Natural rest and sleep
Realistic thinking
Regular nourishment taken

Honest desire for help
Learns alcoholism is an illness
Told addiction can be arrested
Stops taking alcohol
Meets normal and happy former addicts
Takes stock of self
Right thinking begins
Spiritual needs examined
Physical overhaul by doctor
Onset of new hope
Start of group therapy
Appreciation of possibilities of new way of life
Diminishing fears of the unknown future
Return to self-esteem
Desire to escape goes
Adjustment to family needs
New interests develop
Rebirth of ideals
Appreciation of real values
Confidence of employers
Contentment in sobriety
Increasing tolerance

Recovery

Enlightened and interesting way of life opens up with road ahead to higher levels than ever before

100

# Alcoholism is hurting your business.

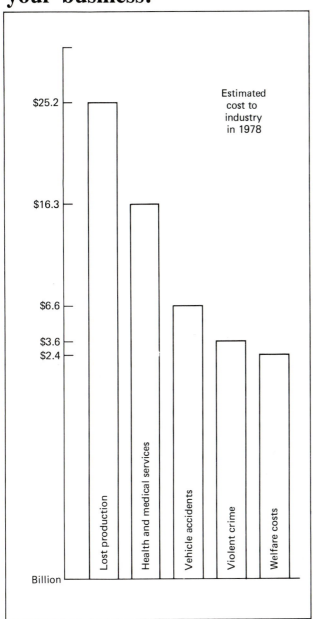

Estimated
cost to
industry
in 1978

$25.2

$16.3

$6.6

$3.6
$2.4

Lost production

Health and medical services

Vehicle accidents

Violent crime

Welfare costs

Billion

## It cost business $54.2 billion a year.

All the alcoholics in the world aren't on Skid Row. One out of every 10 employed persons is an alcoholic.

It means:
Inefficiency
Increased absenteeism
Overtime pay
Faulty decision making
More on-the-job accidents
Low employee morale

The effects of alcoholism can cost your company an additional 25 percent of each alcoholic employee's salary. Despite the extra costs, however, alcoholic employees are often the most valued in the organization. They usually average 15–30 years with the company, and the cost to replace their skills, expertise, and experience is incalculable.

Like cancer and diabetes, alcoholism is a disease. It is not a moral issue. Alcoholism can be treated and controlled.

Treating and retaining the alcoholic employee is good business. Every dollar your company invests in employee assistance programs for the problem drinker yields at least a $17 return. Alcoholic treatment expenses are covered by most health insurance policies. For the price of the premium you are probably already paying, you can correct the damage done to the bottom line of your profit and loss statement by alcoholism.

**EXHIBIT 3**
"Alcoholism is hurting your business." (*Source:* Comprehensive Care Corporation. Copyright © 1982. Reprinted by permission.)

# Mebel Doran & Company

It was Monday, February 23, 1987, and Harvey Hegarty, President and Chief Executive Officer of Mebel Doran & Company, a major investment banking firm based in New York, had been following the unfolding developments in the insider trading cases with a mixture of shock, fascination, and secret relief that, to the best of his knowledge, his firm was untouched by the spreading accusations of abuse. The revelations and charges had made him freshly aware of just how important an unimpeachable reputation was to a securities firm seeking to maintain its current client and customer base as well as to pursue new business. He resolved that his firm would redouble its efforts to provide internal control procedures that would continue to protect Mebel Doran against abuses in the future.

At that point, Stephen Claire, one of Mr. Hegarty's partners, came into his office and informed Mr. Hegarty that he had just received a phone call from the Chairman of the Knox Corporation, one of Mebel Doran's oldest clients, voicing anger and alarm at the recent run-up in the share price of another company which Knox had secretly targeted for acquisition. Professionals in Mebel Doran's mergers and acquisitions group had been working with Knox on these takeover plans for some months and were well aware that management of the potential target, Power-Tie Corporation of Wilmington, Delaware, had publicly stated its hostility to any merger proposals that would threaten that company's independence.

The CEO of Knox had not-too-obliquely accused Mebel Doran of being the source of a leak of its plans. Mr. Claire had assured the client that this was highly unlikely, since the firm had devised elaborate procedures to assure the confidentiality of information entrusted to it by its clients and others. Nonetheless, he had promised to investigate immediately and report back to the client as soon as possible.

## MEBEL DORAN & COMPANY

Mebel Doran had been founded in Philadelphia in 1873 as merchants, importers, and shippers. Over the years the company had gradually moved more and more heavily into financing operations, first as discounters of notes of local tradesmen in the Philadelphia area and later as financial backers of fledgling manufacturing enterprises in the Delaware Valley. In 1913, shortly before the outbreak of World War I, the firm had sold its ocean shipping business, and in 1922 it had disposed of several textile mills that it had run since the late 1800s. This left it free to concentrate on the business of merchant banking, in which role it had raised funds for a broad variety of manufacturing and retailing businesses. It also had established several closed-end mutual funds during the 1920s that had been sold to retail investors through its small but effective cadre of salesmen operating out of the main Philadelphia office as well as offices in Pittsburgh and in Allentown, Pennsylvania. A New York office was also established after World War I to handle the clearing for an increasing volume of securities trades on the New York Stock Exchange and other exchanges. By the end of the 1920s, the New York branch had grown in size and scope of activities such that it began to rival in importance the main office in Philadelphia.

The stock market crash in 1929 and the malaise which subsequently beset the securities industry hit Mebel Doran with particular force. As prices fell, the firm sustained substantial losses on its securities positions, and the mutual funds which had been sponsored and managed by the firm saw values of their portfolios shrink by 85% between 1929 and 1932. Unwanted publicity had also dogged the firm as government hearings singled out Mebel Doran for particular censor for its alleged use of these captive mutual funds to purchase excess securities in slow-moving underwritings managed by the firm.

Sizable losses were sustained from 1930 to 1933 and a number of the firm's partners sought to withdraw their remaining capital, thus threatening the very existence of the firm. It was only when a Boston-based manufacturer, John Hegarty, agreed to invest a substantial sum of additional capital in return for a controlling interest that the firm's survival was assured.

Mebel Doran prospered in the post-World War II U.S. economy along with a number of other securities firms that had also suffered severe reverses during the Depression years of the 1930s. It participated as a "major bracket" underwriter in debt and equity underwritings and it enjoyed a substantial stable of client relationships that either had carried over from the pre-Depression period or had been cultivated since the end of the war. One of the firm's special strengths had been a nationwide network of branches catering to high-net-worth individuals. Although the center of the firm's operations had shifted to New York City, Philadelphia and the Delaware Valley area continued to be a region of special strength for the firm, among investors as well as corporate and financial service clients.

Although initially slow to recognize the trend toward the institutionalization of savings, Mebel Doran had ultimately moved aggressively to establish itself as an important competitor in the institutional stock and bond marketplace. Its research analysts were usually prominently represented among *Institutional Investor*'s "All American" list, and its institutional trading services were highly rated by portfolio managers, as reflected in several annual trade surveys, including the Greenwich Research polls.

As the nature and mix of the securities business shifted during the 1970s and early 1980s, Mebel Doran sought to maintain its competitive edge in the marketplace. Although not one of the "bulge group" of six leading investment banking firms, Mebel nonetheless occupied a respected niche in the group ranking just below those firms. It had been among the first to see the growing importance of mergers and acquisitions as a source of revenue to securities firms (see Exhibit 1) and had what it believed was one of the most sophisticated and experienced groups of professionals available anywhere on Wall Street. It had also perceived that in the post-shelf registration era it would be important to be capable of bidding strictly on a price basis for underwriting business that offered little if any direct profit but which was an entrée to other higher-margin business. Partially in response to that, Mebel Doran had made the momentous decision to "go public" in 1984 as a means of raising a large amount of capital that would be permanently available to the firm in the future (see Exhibit 2).

Mebel Doran was proud of its long operating history and of the stature that had come to be attached to its name. Its reputation for excellence and integrity had been an effective calling card when approaching potential clients and investors, and had also enabled the firm to compete head to head with other leading securities firms for new employees at the top U.S. graduate business schools.

## THE CLIENT COMPANY

The Knox Corporation, a diversified manufacturing firm based in Philadelphia, had been a long-time client of Mebel Doran. The firm had brought Knox "public" in 1951 and had undertaken a number of financings for the company in succeeding years. Mebel Doran had also counseled the company in connection with its acquisition activities, which had been instrumental in the company's growth from sales of $75 million in 1960 to more than $1.7 billion in 1986 (see Exhibit 3). In late 1985, Knox had itself become the target of an outsider raid and, after several abortive attempts to find a friendly third-party merger partner, had implemented a public restructuring of its capitalization with the assistance of experts in Mebel Doran's mergers and acquisitions group. Some 43% of the company's common stock had been repurchased at a substantial premium above the prevailing market. The stock repurchase had been financed by drawing down Knox's cash reserves, selling off much of its real estate holdings and other redundant assets, and floating additional senior and junior debt securities

such that the company's debt-to-capitalization ratio moved from 27% to almost 74% (see Exhibit 4). Coverage ratios (ratio of earnings before income taxes to interest expense) had plummeted, not unexpectedly, from 8.4 times in 1984 to barely 2.0 times in 1986 (see Exhibit 3). The bond rating on the company's debt had also dropped from Baa to B, thus placing it in the "clearly speculative" category of investment risk.

In September 1986, a representative of Mebel Doran's M&A group had approached Knox with the idea of acquiring the Dover, Delaware-based Power-Tie Corporation, a publicly traded manufacturer with a product line which overlapped and extended that of one of the Knox divisions. Potential operating economies from the hoped-for combination were projected to boost Knox's operating income by approximately 15% even after the incremental financing costs had been deducted.

Power-Tie, which had been trading on the New York Stock Exchange in the $30 to $33 range for several months, had approximately 10 million shares outstanding which were fairly widely held. Historically, institutional interest in the company had been only modest. Knox had acquired 4.9% of the shares in carefully orchestrated open market purchases over the past month and a half, and the confidential plan was to structure a tender offer that would seek a total of 51% of the outstanding equity in a cash transaction. This would then be followed by a merger in which the remaining shares of Power-Tie would be exchanged for a package of Knox securities, including high-yield debt instruments.

Mebel Doran's staff had been collaborating with Knox in arranging bridge financing for the proposed tender offer, even though they had not revealed the name of the potential target to the commercial bankers with whom they were talking. The net need for long-term funds would be somewhat reduced by the fact that Mebel Doran had identified substantial redundant assets at Power-Tie in addition to the fairly sizable cash balances carried on the company's balance sheet.

Mebel Doran's arrangement with Knox called for a front-end fee of $2 million for its work in developing the strategy for acquiring Power-Tie. The agreement also called for payment of a contingent fee of 1% of the principal value of the merger transaction in the event that the acquisition was consummated, with the $2 million fee being credited against the total. The bulk of the preliminary preparation work was now completed and Mebel Doran was at the point in late February 1987 of sending an invoice to Knox for payment of the $2 million fee.

## FURTHER INQUIRIES

Mr. Hegarty was quite disturbed by the information that his partner had just related. A check of the trading volume and price action of Power-Tie's common stock confirmed that there had indeed been a sharp increase in share price accompanied by heavy volume. He decided to go down and talk with the M&A professionals who had been working most closely on this deal.

In talking with an M&A vice president and two young associates who had been directly assigned to the project, he learned that in the course of their efforts to engineer a viable tender offer proposal, they had consulted with one of the traders in Mebel Doran's risk arbitrage[1] group about the specifics of the Knox situation. Although Mebel Doran had always maintained a "Chinese Wall" between its M&A group and its risk arbitrage desk, there were situations in which the expertise and market savvy of these specialized traders constituted an important resource for the M&A specialists working to structure financial strategies on behalf of various of the firm's corporate clients. This type of contact between the two Mebel Doran entities had not been considered a real breach of the "Wall" because the securities of the companies

in question were automatically placed on Mebel Doran's "restricted" list and therefore barred from trading by the firm's arbitrage desk. Further, the arbitrage personnel who were consulted in this capacity understood explicitly that the intrafirm inquiry was being made in the strictest confidence and that it constituted "insider information" in a legal sense of the term.

Mr. Hegarty next went down seven floors from the M&A headquarters to the offices of the risk arbitrage group to speak with the partner in charge of the unit, as well as with the trader with whom the M&A specialists had consulted. Mebel Doran's risk arbitrage activity was a profit center of long standing within the firm. It dated back to the days just before and after World War II when a large quantity of new securities were issued in various railroad reorganizations; this offered an attractive opportunity for "arbitraging" the newly issued securities against the old ones being surrendered. Over more than four decades, this arbitrage activity, almost completely financed with the firm's own capital, had been among the most profitable parts of the securities business. During the past several years, the amount of capital committed to arbitrage by Mebel Doran had grown enormously, so that in 1986 it was the largest capital commitment next to the firm's fixed income inventory. Moreover, the profitability of the arbitrage desk had grown so large that by 1986 it contributed more than a quarter of Mebel Doran's after-tax profits (versus the M&A group's contribution of 40% of the firm's profits).

When questioned, the arbitrageurs expressed puzzlement at the recent price and volume patterns in the Power-Tie stock and wondered if someone else was interested in taking over the company and had therefore caused the recent price run-up. Under further questioning, however, Mr. Hegarty learned that one of the group's traders had gotten an inquiry about Power-Tie the week before from an arbitrageur at another securities firm. The caller had made the standard query as to whether Mebel Doran knew of any new developments regarding

---

[1]"Risk arbitrage" is roughly defined as the business of investing in takeover stocks, when a takeover is being negotiated, on the basis of the probable risk of the takeover's success.

Power-Tie. The trader had given noncommittal answers but, when the caller had asked whether Power-Tie was on Mebel Doran's "restricted" list, the trader had replied that he was "not in a position to talk about that."

Mr. Hegarty was angry and somewhat shaken at the way this inquiry had been handled and the implicit signal which it sent. He directed the partner in charge to initiate quiet inquiries to try to determine whether this particular arbitrageur had in fact been active in the Power-Tie stock trading. Three hours later, his partner reported back that, based on the bits and pieces that they had been able to put together, the arbitrageur in question had indeed been an active buyer of the Power-Tie shares over the past week. At this point, he was believed to be holding somewhat short of 5% of the company's outstanding equity in his inventory.

After directing his secretary to hold all his calls, he closed his office door and settled down to weigh just what he should do next.

As he reflected, he became more and more aware of the porosity of the financial community within which he and his firm operated day in and day out. He recognized that people talked to each other all the time and were very careful listeners, weighing *what* they were hearing and *who* they were hearing it from. He could recall more than one conversation he had had with one of his firm's arbitrageurs that was interrupted by a telephone call to the latter from a trader at another house. There would be what appeared to be a casual chit-chat about this and that stock and Mr. Hegarty would become aware that his colleague was asking some rather elliptical questions about one of the stocks in particular. When the telephone conversation had ended, the Mebel Doran arbitrageur might well pick up the phone to the firm's own trading desk, order a transaction in that particular stock, and direct that the execution be given to the trader who had just called him.

In light of this familiar pattern, Mr. Hegarty wondered why he should allow himself the luxury of believing that the "dropping" of the confidential information had been inadvertent? Wasn't it at least as likely that it had been a calculated signal to the other market trader and therefore a clear violation of the insider information rules?

If that was the case, he asked himself whether he would find he was in the position of covering up an illegal act? What would be the consequences of such a move, if disclosed, for both the firm of Mebel Doran and for himself as chief executive officer? How could he stay "clean" on this thing?

# EXHIBITS: Mebel Doran & Company

**EXHIBIT 1**
CONSOLIDATED STATEMENTS OF INCOME
(in thousands)

| | Years ended March 31 | | | | |
|---|---|---|---|---|---|
| | **1982** | **1983** | **1984** | **1985** | **1986** |
| **Revenues** | | | | | |
| Commission | $114,673 | $112,066 | $ 166,468 | $ 194,054 | $ 182,193 |
| Principal transactions | 105,844 | 118,166 | 173,156 | 55,039 | 163,192 |
| Investment banking | 39,636 | 31,676 | 65,106 | 89,237 | 98,950 |
| Interest and dividends | 91,451 | 144,591 | 598,550 | 858,167 | 1,178,061 |
| Other income | 1,981 | 874 | 1,771 | 2,397 | 1,437 |
| Total revenues | 353,584 | 406,773 | 1,005,051 | 1,198,894 | 1,623,833 |
| **Expenses** | | | | | |
| Partner and employee compensation | 114,299 | 121,839 | 181,427 | 205,205 | 239,612 |
| Interest | 78,001 | 124,936 | 533,586 | 711,511 | 1,066,594 |
| Floor brokerage, exchange, and clearance fees | 14,422 | 15,939 | 25,366 | 28,838 | 29,558 |
| Communications | 11,371 | 14,296 | 17,356 | 22,206 | 25,582 |
| Professional fees | 2,990 | 3,000 | 6,054 | 8,718 | 12,010 |
| Depreciation and amortization | 1,695 | 2,694 | 4,554 | 6,142 | 8,529 |
| Taxes on income | 117 | 1,343 | 2,606 | 1,962 | 1,710 |
| Other taxes | 3,784 | 4,963 | 6,079 | 7,966 | 10,129 |
| Occupancy | 5,357 | 7,173 | 9,254 | 11,641 | 19,390 |
| Advertising and market development | 5,588 | 7,150 | 9,292 | 11,707 | 14,324 |
| Data processing and equipment | 7,771 | 11,328 | 13,104 | 14,757 | 16,096 |
| Other expenses | 11,315 | 12,688 | 16,395 | 20,805 | 28,417 |
| Total expenses | 256,700 | 327,735 | 825,073 | 1,051,459 | 1,471,981 |
| Net income | 96,884 | 79,421 | 179,978 | 147,435 | 151,852 |

**EXHIBIT 2**
CONSOLIDATED BALANCE SHEETS
(in thousands)

| Assets | 1985 | 1986 |
|---|---|---|
| Cash and cash equivalent | $ 11,546 | $ 692,000 |
| Cash and securities deposited with clearing organizations or segregated in compliance with federal regulations (market value of securities $12,800 in 1984 and $46,378 in 1985) | 63,911 | 116,299 |
| Securities purchased under agreements to resell | 5,750,843 | 8,153,585 |
| Receivable from brokers, dealers, and clearing organizations | 856,622 | 1,651,709 |
| Receivable from customers | 1,388,622 | 1,663,508 |
| Marketable securities and commodities owned—at market value: | | |
| United States government | 6,600,241 | 8,649,598 |
| State and municipal | 62,606 | 106,705 |
| Other | 1,353,699 | 1,005,040 |
| Furniture, equipment, and leasehold improvements— at cost, less accumulated depreciation and amortization of $18,365 in 1984 and $26,895 in 1985 | 20,843 | 38,796 |
| Other assets | 49,000 | 71,821 |
| Total assets | $16,158,085 | $21,526,281 |

| Liabilities and equity capital | | |
|---|---|---|
| Money borrowed | 454,522 | 564,711 |
| Drafts payable | 66,521 | 95,292 |
| Installment sale notes payable | 107,297 | 61,447 |
| Securities sold under agreements to repurchase | 6,440,523 | 12,295,771 |
| Payable to brokers, dealers, and clearing organizations | 667,808 | 836,343 |
| Payable to customers | 1,016,806 | 2,109,001 |
| Marketable securities and commodities sold, but not yet purchased—at market value: | | |
| United States government | 5,749,339 | 4,333,544 |
| State and municipal | 7,165 | 10,299 |
| Other | 984,236 | 440,677 |
| Accrued employee compensation and benefits | 58,450 | 71,358 |
| Other liabilities, accrued expenses, taxes and reserves | 213,632 | 242,245 |
| Senior subordinates notes | 117,000 | 147,600 |
| Other subordinates notes | 2,993 | 2,993 |
| Equity capital | 271,800 | 315,000 |
| Total liabilities and capital | $16,158,085 | $21,526,281 |

**EXHIBIT 3**
CONSOLIDATED STATEMENT OF EARNINGS
The Knox Corporation and Subsidiares for the twelve months ending December 31, 1986 (in thousands)

| | |
|---|---:|
| Net sales revenue | $1,784,637 |
| Expenses | |
| Cost of sales | 1,356,230 |
| Depreciation expense | 35,737 |
| Selling and administrative expense | 212,004 |
| Interest expense | 64,287 |
| Total expenses | $1,668,258 |
| Earnings from continuing operations before income taxes | $ 116,379 |
| Provision for income taxes | 61,910 |
| Earnings from continuing operations | 54,469 |
| Loss from discontinued operations | (80,272) |
| Net earnings (loss) | $ (25,803) |

**EXHIBIT 4**
CONSOLIDATED BALANCE SHEET
The Knox Corporation
December 31, 1986
(in millions)

| **Current assets** | | | **Current liabilities** | | |
|---|---:|---|---|---:|---|
| Cash and marketable securities | $ 8 | | Notes payable to banks | $ 16 | |
| Accounts and notes receivable | 241 | | Accounts payable | 117 | |
| Inventories | 346 | | Accrued expenses | 182 | |
| Other current | 129 | | Current portion of liabilities of discontinued operations | 38 | |
| Total current assets | $ 724 | | Total current liabilities | $ 353 | |
| **Long-term assets** | | | **Long-term liabilities** | | |
| Property, plant & equipment (net) | $ 336 | | Liabilities of discontinued operations | $ 23 | |
| | | | Long-term debt | 570 | |
| **Other assets** | $ 30 | | **Shareholders' equity** | $ 152 | |
| **Total assets** | $1,098 | | **Total liabilities, shareholders' equity** | $1,098 | |

# H. J. Heinz Company: The Administration of Policy (A)

In April 1979 James Cunningham, H. J. Heinz Company's president and chief operating officer, learned that since 1972 certain Heinz divisions had allegedly engaged in improper income transferal practices. Payments had been made to certain vendors in a particular fiscal year, then repaid or exchanged for services in the succeeding fiscal year.[1]

These allegations came out during the investigation of an unrelated antitrust matter. Apparent improprieties were discovered in the records of the Heinz USA division's relationship with one of its advertising agencies. Joseph Stangerson—senior vice president, secretary, and general counsel for Heinz—asked the advertising agency about the alleged practices. Not only had the agency personnel confirmed the allegation about Heinz USA, it indicated that similar practices had been used by Star-Kist Foods, another Heinz division. The divisions allegedly solicited improper invoices from the advertising agency in fiscal year (FY) 1974 so that they could transfer income to FY 1975. While the invoices were paid in FY 1974, the services described on the invoices were not rendered until sometime during FY 1975. Rather than capitalizing the amount as a prepaid expense, the amount was charged as an expense in FY 1974. The result was an understatement of FY 1974 income and an equivalent overstatement of FY 1975 income.

Stangerson reported the problem to John Bailey, vice chairman and chief executive officer; to Robert Kelly, senior vice president–finance and treasurer; and to Cunningham. Bailey, CEO since 1966, had presided over 13 uninterrupted years of earnings growth. He was scheduled to retire as vice chairman and CEO on July 1 and would remain as a member of the board of directors. James Cunningham, who had been president and chief operating officer since 1972, was to become chief executive officer on July 1, 1979.

[1] H. J. Heinz Company, form 8-K, April 27, 1979, p. 2.

Subsequent reports indicate that neither the scope of the practice nor the amounts involved were known. There was no apparent reason to believe that the amounts involved would have had a material effect on Heinz's reported earnings during the time period, including earnings for FY 1979 ending May 2. (Heinz reported financial results on the basis of a 52–53 week fiscal year ending on the Wednesday closest to April 30.) Stangerson was not prepared to say whether the alleged practices were legal or illegal. "This thing could be something terrible or it could be merely a department head using conservative accounting practices; we don't know,"[2] one Heinz senior official stated to the press.

## BACKGROUND

Henry J. Heinz, on founding the company in 1869 in Pittsburgh, Pennsylvania, said: "This is my goal—to bring home-cooking standards into canned foods, making them so altogether wholesome and delicious and at the same time so reasonable that people everywhere will enjoy them in abundance."[3] The company's involvement in food products never changed, and in 1979 Heinz operated some 30 companies with products reaching 150 countries. Heinz reported sales of over $2.2 billion and net income of $99.1 million in FY 1978.

After a sluggish period in the early 1960s, a reorganization was undertaken to position Heinz for growth. Under the guidance of John Bailey and James Cunningham, Heinz prospered through a major recession, government price controls, and major currency fluctuations. The 1978 annual report reflected management's pride in Heinz's remarkably consistent growth:

> Fiscal 1978 went into the books as the fifteenth consecutive year of record results for Heinz.

Earnings rose to another new high. Sales reached more than $2 billion only six years after we had passed the $1 billion mark for the first time in our century-long history. We are determined to maintain the financial integrity of our enterprise and support its future growth toward ever-higher levels. [Exhibit 1 presents a financial summary of fiscal years 1972–1978.]

Although Heinz was a multinational firm, domestic operations accounted for 62% of sales and 67% of earnings in FY 1978. Five major divisions operated in the United States in 1979.

Throughout the 1970s Heinz's major objective was consistent growth in earnings. While Heinz management did not consider acquisitions to be crucial to continuing growth, it looked favorably on purchase opportunities in areas where Heinz had demonstrated capabilities. Bailey and Cunningham stressed profit increases through the elimination of marginally profitable products. Increased advertising of successful traditional products and new product development efforts also contributed to Heinz's growth. Heinz's commitment to decentralized authority as an organizational principle aided the management of internal growth as well as acquisitions.

## ORGANIZATION

In 1979 Heinz was organized on two primary levels. The corporate world headquarters, located in Pittsburgh, consisted of the principal corporate officers and historically small staffs (management described the world headquarters as lean). World headquarters had the responsibility for "the decentralized coordination and control needed to set overall standards and ensure performance in accordance with them."[4] Some Heinz operating divisions reported directly to the president; others reported through senior vice presidents who were designated area directors (see Exhibit 2). World headquarters officers worked with division senior managers in

[2]"Heinz to Probe Prepayments to Suppliers by Using Outside Lawyers, Accountants," *Wall Street Journal,* April 30, 1979, p. 5.
[3]H. J. Heinz Company, annual report, 1976.

[4]H. J. Heinz Company, form 8-K, May 7, 1980, p. 7.

areas such as planning, product and market development, and capital programs.

Heinz's divisions were largely autonomous operating companies. Division managers were directly responsible for the division's products and services, and they operated their own research and development, manufacturing, and marketing facilities. Division staff reported directly to division managers and had neither formal reporting nor dotted-line relationships with corporate staff.

World headquarters officers monitored division performance through conventional business budgets and financial reports. If reported performance was in line with corporate financial goals, little inquiry into the details of division operation was made. On the other hand, variations from planned performance drew a great deal of attention from world headquarters; then, divisions were pressured to improve results. A review was held near the end of the third fiscal quarter to discuss expected year-end results. If shortfalls were apparent, other divisions were often encouraged to improve their performance. The aim was to meet projected consolidated earnings and goals. Predictability was a watchword and surprises were to be avoided.[5] A consistent growth in earnings attended this management philosophy.

## MANAGEMENT INCENTIVE PLAN

Designed by a prominent management consulting firm, the management incentive plan (MIP) was regarded as a prime management tool used to achieve corporate goals.[6] MIP comprised roughly 225 employees, including corporate officers, senior world headquarters personnel, and senior personnel of most divisions. Incentive compensation was awarded on the basis of an earned number of MIP points and in some cases reached 40% of total compensation.

MIP points could be earned through the achievement of personal goals. These goals were established at the beginning of each fiscal year in consultation with the participant's immediate supervisor. Points were awarded by the supervisor at the end of the year, based on goal achievement. In practice, personal goal point awards fell out on a curve, with few individuals receiving very high or very low awards.

MIP points were also awarded based on net profit after tax (NPAT) goals. (On occasion, other goals such as increased inventory turnover or improved cash flow were included in MIP goals.) Corporate NPAT goals were set at the beginning of the fiscal year by the management development and compensation committee (MDC) of the board of directors. The chief executive officer, the chief operating officer, the senior vice president–finance, and the senior vice president–corporate development then set MIP goals for each division, with the aggregate of division goals usually exceeding the corporate goal. Two goals were set—a fair goal, which was consistently higher than the preceding year's NPAT, and a higher outstanding goal. The full number of MIP points was earned by achieving the outstanding goal.

Senior corporate managers were responsible for executing the system. While divisional input was not uncommon, division NPAT goals were set unilaterally and did not necessarily reflect a division's budgeted profits. Once set, goals were seldom changed during the year. The officers who set the goals awarded MIP points at the end of the fiscal year. No points were awarded to personnel in a division that failed to achieve its fair goal, and points were weighted to favor results at or near the outstanding goal. One or more bonus points might be awarded if the outstanding goal was exceeded. Corporate officers also had the authority to make adjustments or award arbitrary points in special circumstances. The basis for these adjustments was not discussed with division personnel.

MIP points for consolidated corporate performance were awarded by the MDC committee of the board. Corporate points were credited by all MIP participants except those in a division that did not achieve its fair goal. The MDC

[5]Ibid, p. 8.
[6]Ibid, pp. 10–12.

committee could also award company bonus points.

Heinz also had a long-term incentive plan based on a revolving three-year cycle. Participation was limited to senior corporate management and division presidents or managing directors for a total of 19 persons.

## CORPORATE ETHICAL POLICY

Heinz had an explicit corporate ethical policy that was adopted in May 1976.[7] Among other things, it stated that no division should:

1   Have any form of unrecorded assets or false entries on its books or records
2   Make or approve any payment with the intention or understanding that any part of such payment was to be used for any purpose other than that described by the documents supporting the payment
3   Make political contributions
4   Make payments or gifts to public officials or customers
5   Accept gifts or payments of more than a nominal amount

Each year the president or managing director and the chief financial officer of each division

---

[7]Ibid, p. 12.

were required to sign a representation letter which, among other things, confirmed compliance with the corporate Code of Ethics.

## APRIL 1979

Heinz itself had originated the antitrust proceedings that led to the discovery of the alleged practices. In 1976 Heinz filed a private antitrust suit against the Campbell Soup Company, accusing Campbell of monopolistic practices in the canned soup market. Campbell promptly countersued, charging that Heinz monopolized the ketchup market.[8] Campbell attorneys, preparing for court action, subpoenaed Heinz documents reflecting its financial relationships with one of its advertising agencies. In April 1979, while taking a deposition from Arthur West, president of the Heinz USA division, Campbell attorneys asked about flows of funds, "certain items which can be called off-book accounts." West refused to answer, claiming Fifth Amendment protection from self-incrimination.[9] Stangerson then spoke with the advertising agency and received confirmation of the invoicing practices.

---

[8]"Heinz slow growth behind juggling tactic?" *Advertising Age,* March 24, 1980, p. 88.
[9]"Results in Probe of Heinz Income Juggling Expected to Be Announced by Early April," *Wall Street Journal,* March 18, 1980, p. 7.

# EXHIBITS: H. J. Heinz Company (A)

**EXHIBIT 1**
FINANCIAL SUMMARY, FISCAL YEARS 1972–1978
($ thousands except per share data)

| | 1978 | 1977 | 1976 | 1975 | 1974 | 1973 | 1972 |
|---|---|---|---|---|---|---|---|
| **Summary of operations** | | | | | | | |
| Sales | $2,150,027 | $1,868,820 | $1,749,691 | $1,564,930 | $1,349,091 | $1,116,551 | $1,020,958 |
| Cost of products sold | 1,439,249 | 1,262,260 | 1,228,229 | 1,097,093 | 939,565 | 772,525 | 700,530 |
| Interest expense | 18,859 | 16,332 | 22,909 | 31,027 | 21,077 | 13,813 | 11,463 |
| Provision for income taxes | 69,561 | 71,119 | 53,675 | 49,958 | 36,730 | 30,913 | 30,702 |
| Income from continuing operations | 99,171 | 83,816 | 73,960 | 66,567 | 55,520 | 50,082 | 44,679 |
| Loss for discontinued and expropriated operations | — | — | — | — | — | 3,530 | 2,392 |
| Income before extraordinary items | 99,171 | 83,816 | 73,960 | 66,567 | 55,520 | 46,552 | 42,287 |
| Extraordinary items | — | — | — | — | 8,800 | (25,000) | — |
| Net income | 99,171 | 83,816 | 73,960 | 66,567 | 64,320 | 21,552 | 42,287 |
| **Per common share amounts** | | | | | | | |
| Income from continuing operations | 4.25 | 3.55 | 3.21 | 2.93 | 2.45 | 2.21 | 1.98 |
| Loss from discontinued and expropriated operations | — | — | — | — | — | .16 | .11 |
| Income before extraordinary items | 4.25 | 3.55 | 3.21 | 2.93 | 2.45 | 2.05 | 1.87 |
| Extraordinary items | — | — | — | — | .39 | (1.10) | — |
| Net income | 4.25 | 3.55 | 3.21 | 2.93 | 2.84 | .95 | 1.87 |
| **Other data** | | | | | | | |
| Dividends paid | | | | | | | |
| Common, per share | 1.42 | 1.06⅔ | .86⅔ | .77⅓ | .72⅔ | .70 | .67⅓ |
| Common, total | 32,143 | 24,260 | 19,671 | 17,502 | 16,427 | 15,814 | 15,718 |
| Preferred, total | 3,147 | 3,166 | 1,024 | 139 | 146 | 165 | 184 |
| Capital expenditures | 95,408 | 53,679 | 34,682 | 57,219 | 44,096 | 48,322 | 28,067 |
| Depreciation | 31,564 | 29,697 | 27,900 | 25,090 | 22,535 | 20,950 | 20,143 |
| Shareholders' equity | 702,736 | 655,480 | 598,613 | 502,796 | 447,434 | 399,607 | 394,519 |
| Total debt | 228,002 | 220,779 | 219,387 | 295,051 | 266,617 | 249,161 | 196,309 |
| Average number of common shares outstanding | 22,609,613 | 22,743,233 | 22,696,484 | 22,633,115 | 22,604,720 | 22,591,287 | 22,538,309 |
| Book value per common share | 28.96 | 26.27 | 23,79 | 22.04 | 19.61 | 17.50 | 17.26 |
| Price range of common stock | | | | | | | |
| High | 40 | 34⅛ | 38 | 34⅜ | 34⅞ | 30⅞ | 31½ |
| Low | 28¾ | 26½ | 28⅞ | 18 | 24⅞ | 25⅜ | 25⅞ |
| Sales (%) | | | | | | | |
| Domestic | 62 | 62 | 59 | 58 | 59 | 58 | 57 |
| Foreign | 38 | 38 | 41 | 42 | 41 | 42 | 43 |
| Income (%) | | | | | | | |
| Domestic | 67 | 78 | 66 | 71 | 57 | 53 | 54 |
| Foreign | 33 | 22 | 34 | 29 | 43 | 47 | 46 |

*Source:* Company records.

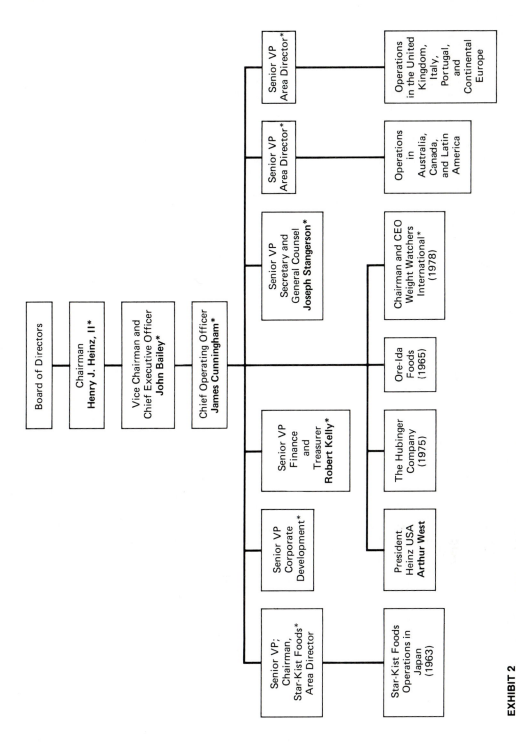

**EXHIBIT 2**
Organization chart, April 1979. Asterisk indicates member of the board of directors.
Date in parentheses indicates year acquired.

**Board of Directors**

**Chairman**
**Henry J. Heinz, II***

**Vice Chairman and Chief Executive Officer**
**John Bailey***

**Chief Operating Officer**
**James Cunningham***

Senior VP;
Chairman,
Star-Kist Foods*
Area Director

Senior VP
Corporate
Development*

Senior VP
Finance
and
Treasurer
**Robert Kelly***

Senior VP
Secretary and
General Counsel
**Joseph Stangerson***

Senior VP
Area Director*

Senior VP
Area Director*

Star-Kist Foods
Operations in
Japan (1963)

President
Heinz USA
**Arthur West**

The Hubinger
Company
(1975)

Ore-Ida
Foods
(1965)

Chairman and CEO
Weight Watchers
International*
(1978)

Operations
in
Australia,
Canada, and Latin
America

Operations
in the United
Kingdom,
Italy,
Portugal,
and
Continental
Europe

115

# H. J. Heinz Company: The Administration of Policy (B)

In April 1979 Heinz's senior management learned of improper practices concerning the transfer of an undetermined amount of reported income from one fiscal year to the next. At two of the Heinz operating divisions payments had been made to vendors in one fiscal year, then repaid or exchanged for services in the succeeding fiscal year. The scope of the practice and the amounts involved were not then known.

Aware that the practice might have affected the company's reported income over the past seven fiscal years, management consulted an outside legal firm for an opinion on the seriousness of the problem. Based on that opinion, John Bailey, Heinz's chief executive officer, notified the Audit Committee of the board of directors. Composed entirely of outside directors, this committee was responsible for working with internal auditors and financial officers and with the firm's outside auditors, thus preserving the integrity of financial information published by Heinz.

The Audit Committee held a special meeting on April 26, 1979. After hearing from outside counsel and from Joseph Stangerson (Heinz's general counsel) about the practices, the committee adopted a resolution retaining an outside law firm and independent public accountants to assist in a full investigation of the matter.[1]

An attorney from Cravath, Swaine & Moore, the outside law firm, accompanied Stangerson to Washington to advise the Securities and Exchange Commission of the information available and of the investigation then under way. (An excerpt from form 8-K filed with the SEC is attached as Exhibit 1.) The two

[1] "Report of the Audit Committee to the Board of Directors: Income Transferal and Other Practices," H. J. Heinz Company, form 8-K, May 7, 1980.

also informed the IRS of possible tax consequences of the practice.

On April 27, 1979, Heinz publicly announced its investigation. "At this stage," the formal statement said, "it isn't possible to determine the scope of the practice or the total amounts involved." It also stated that there "isn't any reason to believe there will be any material effect on the company's reported earnings for any fiscal year including the current fiscal year." While the investigation would cover the period from 1972 to 1979, Heinz would not identify the divisions or vendors involved. Stangerson stated: "We aren't prepared to say whether [the practices] were legal or illegal." He added that the company had informed the SEC and the IRS.[2]

## THE INVESTIGATION

The Audit Committee supervised the conduct of the investigation. Teams composed of lawyers and accountants from the two outside firms interviewed present and former company and vendor personnel about possible improprieties. The investigators focused on the following areas:

1 Practices that affected the accuracy of company accounts or the security of company assets
2 Practices in violation of the company's Code of Ethics
3 Illegal political contributions
4 Illegal, improper, or otherwise questionable payments
5 Factors contributing to the existence, continuance, or nondisclosure of any of the above

The investigating teams interviewed over 325 Heinz employees, many of them more than once. The teams also interviewed personnel employed by many of Heinz's vendors, including advertising agencies. Accounting records, correspondence, and other files were examined. The board of directors at its regular May meeting asked for the cooperation of all officers and employees.[3]

On May 10, 1979, Heinz announced that a settlement had been reached in its private antitrust suit against the Campbell Soup Company. The settlement resulted in the dismissal of Heinz's action against Campbell, which had been brought in 1976, and of Campbell's counterclaim against Heinz. The court ordered the record of the suit sealed and kept secret.[4]

On June 29, 1979, Heinz disclosed a preliminary figure of $5.5 million of after-tax income associated with the income transferal practices. Stressing that this was a "very soft number," the company indicated that it was delaying release of audited results for FY 1979 (ended May 2, 1979) and that its annual meeting, scheduled for September 12, would be postponed until the investigation (which could continue well into the fall) was completed. The preliminary unaudited figures released by Heinz showed net income of $113.4 million ($4.95 per share) on sales of $2.4 billion, after the $5.5 million deduction. Press reports indicated the investigation was being broadened to include Heinz's foreign units.[5]

On September 13, 1979, it was reported that the preliminary figure had grown to $8.5 million. Heinz's statement, filed with its first quarter FY 1980 earnings report, also stated FY 1979 income as $110.4 million or $4.80 per share. Most of the $3 million growth was attributed to the discovery of improper treatment of sales in addition to the improper treatment of prepaid expenses discovered earlier.[6]

Heinz's 1979 annual report contained au-

[2]"Results in Probe of Heinz Income Juggling Expected to Be Announced by Early April," *Wall Street Journal,* March 18, 1980, p. 7.

[3]Audit Committee Report, form 8-K, May 7, 1980, p. 4.
[4]H. J. Heinz Company, form 8-K, May 10, 1979, p. 2; *Wall Street Journal,* March 18, 1980, p. 7.
[5]"Initial Study of Some Heinz Units Finds $5.5 Million in Profit Juggling Practices," *Wall Street Journal,* July 2, 1979, p. 8.
[6]"Heinz Discloses Profit Switching at Units Was Much Broader Than First Realized," *Wall Street Journal,* September 13, 1979, p. 15.

dited financial statements for FY 1979 and restated financial statements for FY 1978. The report contained an unqualified opinion from Peat, Marwick, Mitchell & Company, Heinz's auditors, dated November 14, 1979. In Note 2 to the 1979 financial statements, the report also contained a restatement and reconciliation of sales, net income, and earnings per share for the previous eight fiscal years. (The 1979 results are shown in Exhibit 2. The restatement of FY 1971–FY 1978 are shown in Exhibit 3.) This information was filed with the Securities and Exchange Commission on November 20, 1979.[7]

In February 1980 Heinz reorganized its top management structure (see Exhibit 4). Arthur West, formerly president of Heinz USA, was promoted to world headquarters as area director. He assumed responsibility for the Hubinger Company and Weight Watchers International, both of which had previously reported directly to James Cunningham, Heinz's president and new CEO. West was also to be responsible for Heinz's Canadian subsidiary. Heinz USA would now report through Kevin Voight, senior vice president, rather than directly to Cunningham. Unlike other area directors, West would be neither a senior vice president nor a member of the board of directors.[8]

In April 1980 Doyle Dane Bernbach, the only publicly held firm among the advertising and consulting firms included in the Audit Committee's investigation, admitted in an SEC filing that it had participated in the income-juggling practices by prebilling and issuing bills that did not accurately describe the services provided.[9]

On May 7, 1980, the Audit Committee presented its report to the Heinz board of directors. The 80-page report was filed on form 8-K with the SEC on May 9, 1980. (The remainder of this case is derived substantially from the Audit Committee's report.)

[7]Audit Committee report, form 8-K, May 7, 1980, p. 2.
[8]"H. J. Heinz Realigns Its Senior Management in Consolidation Move," *Wall Street Journal,* February 19, 1980.
[9]"DDB admits Heinz role," *Advertising Age,* April 28, 1980, pp. 1, 88.

## THE FINDINGS

The Audit Committee reported widespread use of improper billing, accounting, and reporting procedures at Heinz's divisions, including Heinz USA, Ore-Ida, and Star-Kist, and a number of Heinz's foreign operations. The two major areas of impropriety were:

1  *Improper recognition of expenses.* These were most often advertising and market research expenses, improperly recorded in the current fiscal period when in fact the services were performed or goods delivered in a later fiscal period. This treatment resulted in an overstatement of expenses (and understatement of income) in one period and a comparable understatement of expenses (and overstatement of income) in a later fiscal period.
2  *Improper recognition of sales.* Sales were recorded in a fiscal period other than that in which those sales should have been recorded under generally accepted accounting principles.

Table A indicates the amounts involved. The accumulated effects of such practices on shareholders' equity and working capital did not exceed 2%.

The Audit Committee indicated that these income transferal practices were designed to adjust the income reported by divisions to corporate headquarters and were motivated primarily by a desire to meet the constantly increasing profit objectives set by world headquarters. While division management supported the publicly announced goal of steadily increasing profits, the committee reported that the management incentive program (MIP) under which the goals were administered created significant pressures. Aside from obvious personal financial considerations, many division-level personnel reportedly viewed the achievement of MIP goals as the key to advancement at Heinz. One manager told the committee that failure to achieve these goals constituted a "mortal sin."

**TABLE A**
INCREASE (DECREASE) OF CONSOLIDATED INCOME BEFORE TAX, NET OF RECOVERIES
($ Thousands)

| | Improper recognition | | | Net income before tax | | |
| --- | --- | --- | --- | --- | --- | --- |
| FY | Expenses | Sales | Other practices | Increase (decrease) | Total after restatement | % effects of restatement |
| 1972 | $ (513) | — | — | $ (513) | $ 75,894 | (.7) |
| 1973 | (1,814) | $(1,968) | — | (3,782) | 84,777 | (4.5) |
| 1974 | (4,250) | (309) | $(1,364) | (5,923) | 98,173 | (6.0) |
| 1975 | 2,476 | 1,527 | (615) | 3,388 | 113,137 | 3.0 |
| 1976 | (111) | (1,815) | 877 | (1,049) | 128,682 | (.8) |
| 1977 | (4,139) | (1,294) | 268 | (5,165) | 160,101 | 3.2) |
| 1978 | 734 | (2,872) | 671 | (1,467) | 170,198 | (.9) |
| 1979 | 8,888 | 7,085 | 396 | 16,369 | 183,178 | 8.9 |
| 1980 | 76 | (354) | (233) | (511) | — | — |

The Heinz principle of decentralized authority extended to financial reporting and internal control procedures. Division financial officers were not responsible to corporate headquarters but to their division president or managing director. The MIP goal pressures provided the incentive, and autonomous control the opportunity, for adopting the improper practices being reported.

One reason for using such reporting techniques was explained to the committee:

> If this fiscal year's goal is, say, $20 million net profit after tax (NPAT), it can be anticipated that next year's goal will be, say, 15% higher, or $23 million NPAT. This year seems to be a good one and it is anticipated that earnings will be $24 million NPAT. But, if that figure is reported to world headquarters, it is likely that next year's goal will be about 15% higher than the $24 million NPAT, or approximately $27 million NPAT. Of course, there is no assurance that there will not be some unforeseen disaster next year. Thus, if it is possible to mislead world headquarters as to the true state of the earnings of the [division] and report only the $20 million NPAT, which is the current fiscal year's goal, and have the additional $4 million NPAT carried forward into next year, the [division] will have a good start toward achieving its expected $23 million NPAT goal next year and will not have to reach $27 million NPAT.

Explanations for accepting these practices at lower levels included job security and the desire to impress superiors.

The committee's report stated: "There is no evidence that any employee of the company sought or obtained any direct personal gain in connection with any of the transactions or practices described in this report. Nor did the investigation find any evidence that any officer or personnel at world headquarters participated in any of the income transferal practices described in this report." The report went on to describe activities at each division in greater detail.

## DIVISION INCOME TRANSFER PRACTICES

### Heinz USA

Income transfer at Heinz USA started late in FY 1974 when world headquarters realized that Heinz USA might report profits in excess of those allowed by the wage and price controls in effect at the time. World headquarters sought to have Heinz USA report lower profits, although no evidence indicates that any world headquarters personnel intended GAAP to be violated. After some commodity transactions lowered expected profits, there was a reluctance in Heinz USA to reduce its expected profits further. Nevertheless, to accomplish the further reduction, $2 million in invoices for services that would not be performed were obtained from an advertising agency and recorded as an expense in FY 1974.

Heinz USA reported FY 1974 NPAT of $4,614,000. NPAT goals for the year were $4.9 million (fair) and $5.5 million (outstanding). In calculating NPAT for MIP purposes, world headquarters allowed an adjustment of $2 million ($1 million after tax) for advertising. This adjustment resulted in Heinz USA achieving its outstanding goal for FY 1974. The division also received a bonus point. The use of improper invoices to manage reported income continued after FY 1974 at Heinz USA, although there was no evidence that world headquarters personnel knew about these transactions.

Beginning in FY 1977, additional income transfer methods were developed. Distribution centers were instructed to stop shipments for the last few days of the fiscal year to allow the recording of sales in the subsequent year. These instructions presented practical difficulties and some of the shipments were not held up. Without the authorization of division senior management, paperwork was apparently altered or misdated to record the sales as desired.

Vendors' credits were often deferred and processed in the subsequent fiscal year to assist the income management program. Detailed schedules were privately maintained that served as the basis for discussions on income management. One employee had the job of maintaining private records to ensure the recovery (in subsequent fiscal years) of amounts paid to vendors on improper invoices.

The use of improper invoices spread to the departmental level as well. Individual department managers used either prepaid billing or delayed billing, as required, to ensure complete use of their departmental budget without overspending. This practice provided protection against future budget cuts during those periods when the full budget would not otherwise have been spent. Division management actively discouraged these transactions.

Vendor cooperation was not difficult to obtain. One Heinz manager described it as "the price of doing business with us." During the period in question, 10 vendors participated in improper invoicing at Heinz USA, and 8 participated at the department level. Most vendors' fiscal years did not coincide with Heinz's.

In FY 1975 a sugar inventory write-down was used to transfer income. Sugar inventory, valued at an average cost of 37 cents per pound, was written down to 25 cents per pound. This adjustment, which amounted to an increase in FY 1975 expense of $1,390,360, was justified on the basis of an expected decline in price early in the next fiscal year. This would result in lower selling prices in FY 1976 for some division products. The lower NPAT figure that resulted was used for establishing FY 1976 goals, but when FY 1975 performance was evaluated, world headquarters adjusted Heinz USA's income up by the amount of the sugar write-down. The anticipated price decline did not occur.

At other times, inflated accruals, inventory adjustments, commodity transactions, and at least one customer rebate were used to report income other than that required by GAAP.

### Ore-Ida

Improper invoices to transfer income were also used at Ore-Ida during that period, and the issue of obtaining these invoices was discussed at meetings of Ore-Ida's management board. Even though the invoices contained descriptions of services that were generic or had no correlation to the actual services to be rendered, members of the management board believed the practice was appropriate because comparable services would have been purchased at some point. During two fiscal years Ore-Ida received interest payments from an advertising agency in connection with the payment of these invoices.

Ore-Ida's management believed that members of world headquarters' management were aware of the income transfer practices, but raised no objections to them. Documents submitted to world headquarters by Ore-Ida contained references to special media billing, pre-bills, year-end media billing, special billing adjustments, and advertising and promotion prebilling. Some documents indicated that these items actually applied to the fiscal year following that of expense recognition. The amount of these expenses was indicated each year to world headquarters' management (in one year, the amount was understated). In FY 1974 corporate management increased Ore-Ida's income before tax by the amount of the prebilled advertising expense for MIP award purposes. Ore-Ida's management did not know if world headquarters' management appreciated the fact that this practice did not conform to GAAP.

### Star-Kist

Both improper expense recognition and improper sales recognition were used to adjust reported income at Star-Kist. Improper invoices were solicited from vendors to accumulate an advertising savings account. Sales during the last month of a fiscal year were recorded during the first month of the next fiscal year by preventing selected documents from entering the sales accounting system. These practices were apparently present only in Star-Kist's marketing department.

Similar practices were also discovered at some of Heinz's foreign subsidiaries.

### OTHER IMPROPER PRACTICES

Although it focused primarily on income transferal practices, the investigation uncovered a number of other practices. Again, the committee stated that no member of world headquarters' management appeared to have any knowledge of these practices, and no employee sought or obtained any personal financial gain. All of these transactions took place outside the United States. None of the countries in which the transactions took place was identified by the committee.

In one country six questionable payments totaling $80,000 were made during FY 1978 and FY 1979. Two were made to lower-level

government employees in connection with alleged violations of import regulations. One was made to a lower-level government employee in connection with the settlement of a labor dispute. Municipal employees received one payment in connection with real estate assessments. Labor union officials received the remaining two payments. In January 1979 three of these payments were reported by division management to world headquarters. A brief investigation ensued and the board of directors reprimanded certain officers of the division.

Star-Kist was involved in several transactions listed in the following section of the report.

1   In one country the payment of interest to nonresidents was prohibited. Star-Kist collected interest on its loans to fishing fleets through the falsification of invoices indicating the purchase by Star-Kist of supplies for the fleets.

2   In another country Star-Kist acted as a conduit through which funds flowed to facilitate a fish purchase involving two other companies. Letters of credit requiring the approval of the exchange authorities were used.

3   In a third country Star-Kist received checks from a fish supplier and endorsed those checks to a wholly owned U.S. subsidiary of the supplier. These transactions were not recorded in Star-Kist's accounts.

The Heinz operating company in yet another country made payments for goods to individual or designated bank accounts rather than to the supplier involved. These payments were not made through the normal cash disbursement procedure; rather, the division was acting at the supplier's request.

### CONTRIBUTING FACTORS

The Audit Committee reported that only a small part of the failure to detect these practices could be attributed to weakness in Heinz's internal controls. In most cases, those controls were circumvented by or with the concurrence of division management. With the autonomy enjoyed by division management, it would have been difficult for world headquarters personnel to detect these practices.

The committee attributed part of the problem to a lack of control consciousness throughout the corporation. *Control consciousness* referred to the atmosphere in which accounting controls existed and it reflected senior management attitudes about the importance of such controls. Clearly, control consciousness was not then present in most Heinz divisions. The committee blamed world headquarters' senior management for creating an environment that was seen as endorsing poor control consciousness:

> If world headquarters' senior management had established a satisfactory control consciousness, internal accounting controls that were cost/benefit justified should have been able to survive reasonable pressures to meet or exceed the defined economic goals. In establishing this atmosphere, world headquarters' senior management apparently did not consider the effect on individuals in the [divisions] of the pressures to which they were subjected.

Other factors cited by the committee included:

- Corporate internal auditing personnel report to their respective division managers and not to the director–corporate audit
- The lack of an effective Code of Ethics compliance procedure
- The lack of standardized accounting and reporting procedures for all Heinz divisions
- The lack of an effective budget review and monitoring process
- The lack of enough competent financial personnel at world headquarters and at the divisions
- The lack of a world headquarters electronic data processing manager responsible for the control procedures of the divisions' EDP departments

## CONCLUSIONS OF THE AUDIT COMMITTEE

1 The amounts involved in the income transferal practices were not material to the consolidated net income or shareholder's equity of the company in the aggregate during the investigatory period (FY 1972–FY 1978).

2 The income transferal practices were achieved primarily through circumvention of existing internal controls by division personnel who should have exercised responsibility in the enforcement of such controls. Such practices were also assisted by certain inadequacies in the internal control systems of the divisions.

3 Although world headquarters' personnel did not authorize or participate in the income transferal practices, their continuance was facilitated by the company's philosophy of decentralized management and the role played by world headquarters' financial personnel in reviewing the financial reports from divisions.

4 No individual employee obtained any direct financial benefit from the practices uncovered in the investigation.

5 Perceived or de facto pressures for achievement of MIP goals contributed to the divisions' desirability of providing a cushion against future business uncertainties.

6 The income transferal practices did not serve any valid corporate need.

7 The income transferal practices and other questionable practices described in this report [of the Audit Committee] indicate the lack of sufficient control consciousness within the corporate structure; that is, an understanding throughout the company and the divisions that responsible and ethical practices are required in connection with all transactions.

8 The entrepreneurial spirit of the divisions fostered by the philosophy of decentralized autonomy should be continued for the good of the company and its shareholders.

9 World headquarters did not have the number of competent financial personnel needed to fulfill its role.

10   The continuance of the income transferal practices was aided by the independence of division financial personnel from world headquarters.

11   The continuance of the income transferal practices was aided by the reporting relationships of the internal audit staffs within the company.

12   The administration of the MIP and the goal-setting process thereunder did not result in adequate dialogue between senior world headquarters management and managements of the divisions.

13   The board of directors and management of the company have the duty to take all steps practicable to ensure safeguarding the assets of the company and that all transactions are properly recorded on the books, records and accounts of the company.

## EXHIBITS: H. J. Heinz Company (B)

**EXHIBIT 1**
FORM 8-K EXCERPT, APRIL 27, 1979

### Item 5: Other Materially Important Events

On April 27, 1979, the registrant announced that it had become aware that since 1972 in certain of its divisions or subsidiaries payments have been made to certain of its vendors in a particular fiscal year, which were repaid or exchanged for services by such vendors in the succeeding fiscal year.

The registrant stated that at this stage it was not possible to determine the scope of the practice or the total amounts involved, but that there was no reason to believe there would be any material effect on the registrant's reported earnings for any fiscal year including the fiscal year ending May 2, 1979.

The Audit Committee of the registrant's board of directors has retained the law firm of Cravath, Swaine & Moore, independent outside counsel, to conduct a full inquiry of the practice. Cravath, Swaine & Moore will retain independent public accounts to assist in the investigation.

The registrant has heretofore advised the Securities and Exchange Commission and the Internal Revenue Service of the foregoing. At this time the registrant is unable to estimate the extent of any adjustments which may be necessary for tax purposes.

**Note**: Exhibits 2, 3, and 4 appear on pages 124–127.

**EXHIBIT 2**
FINANCIAL SUMMARY, 1979
($ Thousands Except Per Share Data)

|  | 1979 | 1978* | Change |
|---|---|---|---|
| Sales | $2,470,883 | $2,159,436 | 14.4% |
| Operating income | 214,735 | 187,062 | 14.8 |
| Net income | 110,430 | 99,946 | 10.5 |
| Per common share amounts |  |  |  |
| Net income | $4.80 | $4.28 | 12.1% |
| Net income (fully diluted) | 4.64 | 4.17 | 11.3 |
| Dividends | 1.85 | 1.42 | 30.3 |
| Book value | 32.29 | 29.33 | 10.1 |
| Capital expenditures | $ 118,156 | 95,408 | 23.8% |
| Depreciation expense | 38,317 | 31,564 | 21.4 |
| Net property | 481,688 | 412,334 | 16.8 |
| Cash and short-term investments | $ 122,281 | $ 84,044 | 45.5% |
| Working capital | 401,169 | 453,517 | (11.5) |
| Total debt | 342,918 | 228,002 | 50.4 |
| Shareholders' equity | 778,397 | 711,126 | 9.5 |
| Average number of common shares outstanding | 22,330 | 22,610 |  |
| Current ratio | 1.70 | 2.14 |  |
| Debt/invested capital | 30.9% | 24.7% |  |
| Pretax return on average invested capital | 20.7% | 20.7% |  |
| Return on average shareholders' equity | 14.8% | 14.5% |  |

*As restated.
*Source:* 1979 annual report.

**EXHIBIT 3**
RESTATED FINANCIAL DATA, 1971–1978
(Change in Sales, Net Income, and Earnings Per Share)

| In thousands except for per share amounts | 1971 | 1972 | 1973 | 1974 | 1975 | 1976 | 1977 | 1978 |
|---|---|---|---|---|---|---|---|---|
| Sales as previously reported | $876,451 | $1,020,958 | $1,116,551 | $1,349,091 | $1,564,930 | $1,749,691 | $1,868,820 | $2,150,027 |
| Net increase (decrease) resulting from restatement to correct improper treatment of sales | — | — | 14,821 | (1,777) | (4,747) | 4,725 | 8,480 | 9,409 |
| Sales as restated | $876,451 | $1,020,958 | $1,131,372 | $1,347,314 | $1,560,183 | $1,754,416 | $1,877,300 | $2,159,436 |
| Net income as previously reported | $37,668* | $42,287* | $21,552* | $64,320* | $66,567 | $73,960 | $83,816 | $99,171 |
| Net increase (decrease) in income before income taxes resulting from restatement: | | | | | | | | |
| Correct improper treatment of sales, net of related costs | — | — | 1,968 | 309 | (1,527) | 1,815 | 1,294 | 2,872 |
| Correct improper recognition of income/expense | 1,290 | 512 | 1,813 | 5,615 | (1,861) | (684) | 3,822 | (1,417) |
| | 1,290 | 512 | 3,781 | 5,924 | (3,388) | 1,131 | 5,116 | 1,455 |
| Income tax effect | (671) | (263) | (1,566) | (2,698) | 1,254 | (604) | (2,203) | (680) |
| Net adjustments | 619 | 249 | 2,215 | 3,226 | (2,134) | 527 | 2,913 | 775 |
| Net income as restated | $38,287 | $42,536 | $23,767 | $67,546 | $64,433 | $74,487 | $86,729 | $99,946 |
| Income per common share amounts: | | | | | | | | |
| Income from continuing operations as previously reported | $1.71 | $1.98 | $2.21 | $2.45 | $2.93 | $3.21 | $3.55 | $4.25 |
| Net increase (decrease) from restatement | .02 | .01 | .09 | .14 | (.09) | .03 | .12 | .03 |
| Income from continuing operations as restated | 1.73 | 1.99 | 2.30 | 2.59 | 2.84 | 3.24 | 3.67 | 4.28 |
| Loss from discontinued and expropriated operations | .02 | .11 | .16 | — | — | — | — | — |
| Income before extraordinary items | 1.71 | 1.88 | 2.14 | 2.59 | 2.84 | 3.24 | 3.67 | 4.28 |
| Extraordinary items | — | — | (1.10) | .39 | — | — | — | — |
| Net income | $1.71 | $1.88 | $1.04 | $2.98 | $2.84 | $3.24 | $3.67 | $4.28 |

Footnotes on page 126.

(Continued.)

**EXHIBIT 2**
CONTINUED

| In thousands | Income from continuing operations | Loss from discontinued and expropriated operations | Extraordinary items | Net income as previously reported |
|---|---|---|---|---|
| 1971 | $38,171 | $ (503) | $    — | $37,668 |
| 1972 | 44,679 | (2,392) | — | 42,287 |
| 1973 | 50,082 | (3,530) | (25,000) | 21,552 |
| 1974 | 55,520 | — | 8,800 | 64,320 |

(The Following Table Presents the As-Reported and As-Restated Interim Results, Which Are Unaudited, for 1978 and 1979)

| In thousands except per share amounts | Sales | | Gross profit | | Net income | | Earnings per share | |
|---|---|---|---|---|---|---|---|---|
| | As reported | As restated | As reported | As restated | As reported | As restated | As reported | As restated |
| **1978** | | | | | | | | |
| First quarter | $ 491,469 | $ 472,955 | $156,538 | $152,639 | $19,645 | $ 17,621 | $ .83 | $ .74 |
| Second quarter | 520,051 | 525,440 | 169,476 | 170,348 | 23,613 | 22,676 | 1.00 | .96 |
| Third quarter | 523,640 | 517,738 | 170,621 | 169,001 | 19,901 | 20,208 | .85 | .86 |
| Fourth quarter | 614,867 | 643,303 | 214,143 | 221,992 | 36,012 | 39,441 | 1.57 | 1.72 |
| Total | $2,150,027 | $2,159,436 | $710,778 | $713,980 | $99,171 | $ 99,946 | $4.25 | $4.28 |
| **1979** | | | | | | | | |
| First quarter | $ 555,558 | $ 536,301 | $178,250 | $171,330 | $21,161 | $ 16,783 | $ .91 | $ .72 |
| Second quarter | 620,230 | 619,627 | 203,708 | 203,964 | 28,204 | 26,026 | 1.23 | 1.13 |
| Third quarter | 575,410 | 566,747 | 202,171 | 199,497 | 23,301 | 21,192 | 1.01 | .91 |
| Fourth quarter | — | 748,208† | — | 267,584† | — | 46,429† | — | 2.04† |
| Total | $    — | $2,470,883† | $    — | $842,375† | $    — | $110,430† | $    — | $4.80† |

*Net income as previously reported above includes losses from discontinued and expropriated operations and extraordinary items as shown.
†Not previously reported.
*Source:* 1979 annual report.

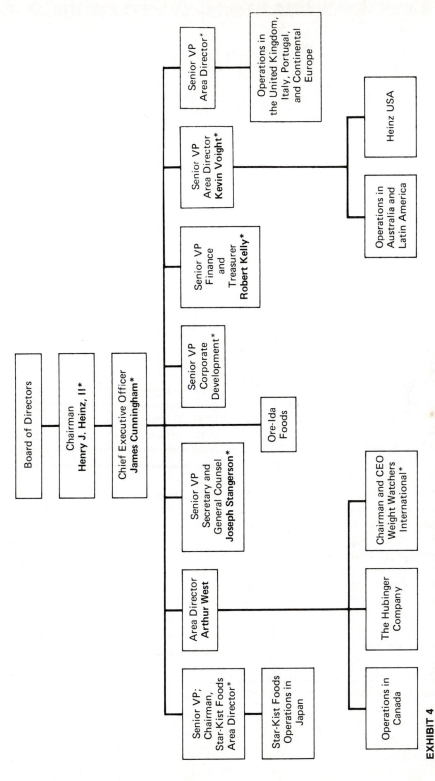

**EXHIBIT 4**
Organization chart, February 1980. Asterisk indicates member of the board of directors.

# Duke Power Company and Affirmative Action

In the mid-1970s, for the first time in its history, the financial condition of Duke Power Company required layoffs. The board of directors had decided to make major cutbacks in construction that would require dismissing about 1,500 of its 4,646 construction workers.

Bill Lee, senior vice president–engineering and construction, was not sure how he should handle the layoffs. In the past, individuals had been discharged only on the basis of performance. He was bothered, however, by the amount of subjectivity involved in using performance as the criterion. If he used "last hired, first fired" as a standard, the company would undo much of the progress it had made in increasing the number of its minority employees. Going by inverse seniority, he estimated that everyone with less than three years' experience would be discharged, including most of the black construction workers. The alternative of protecting minority workers from being laid off would require firing white construction workers with up to seven years' seniority. This might provoke considerable resentment and lead to demands for a union. Bill Lee also did not want to compromise the company's high standards for quality of construction. Maintaining that standard required a skilled and experienced work force.

A prompt decision was necessary. Lee arranged a meeting with his superior, B. B. Parker, for 8:00 A.M. the next day, August 22, 1974, to tell him what he wanted to do. He talked with Bob Dick, vice president–construction, to find out how many employees in each trade were needed for the projects scheduled for completion. Bill Grigg, senior vice president–legal and finance, told him that the law allowed him to do what he chose in this situation (see Figure A for organization chart). That night Lee prayed long and hard; by morning, he knew what he would do.

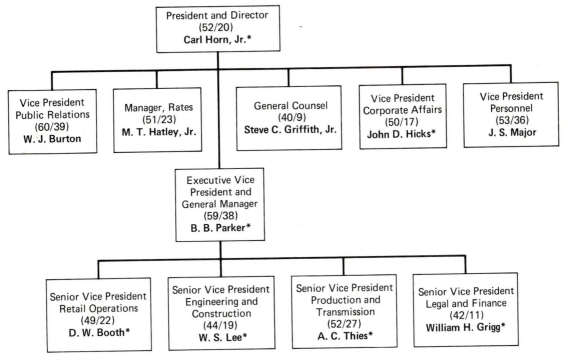

**FIGURE A**
Organization chart, August 1974. Figures in parentheses denote age and length of service.
Asterisk indicates director and member of executive committee.

## COMPANY BACKGROUND

Duke Power Company was an electric utility engaged in the generation, transmission, and distribution of electric power to the general public and industry in North and South Carolina. The company was originally incorporated in New Jersey in 1917 as the Wateree Electric Company. The name was changed to Duke Power Company in 1924, and in June 1964 incorporation was shifted to North Carolina.

In 1974 Duke Power was the sixth largest investor-owned utility in the United States. It served approximately 1,100,000 customers, and its service area encompassed some 20,000 square miles throughout the industrial Piedmont of the two states. Generating capability at the start of 1974 was 8.5 million kilowatts (kw). This consisted of 5.9 million kw from fossil-fueled steam stations, 0.8 million kw from nu-clear-fueled steam stations, 1.1 million kw from hydroelectric stations, 0.4 million kw from combustion turbines, and purchased power of 0.3 million kw. Duke Power's home office was in Charlotte, North Carolina, with retail customers served locally through 98 district and branch offices. In 1974 there were 13,063 employees. (Figure B shows the company's service area, its facilities, and work in progress.)

Duke Power owned three subsidiaries. The Crescent Land and Timber Corporation was formed in 1963 to manage the company's non-utility lands. The Eastover Mining Company and Eastover Land Company were organized in 1970 to purchase and develop coal properties in Virginia and eastern Kentucky. The Mill Power Supply was chartered in 1910 and was an authorized distributor for many of the largest electrical equipment manufacturers in the country. In addition to selling items to Duke

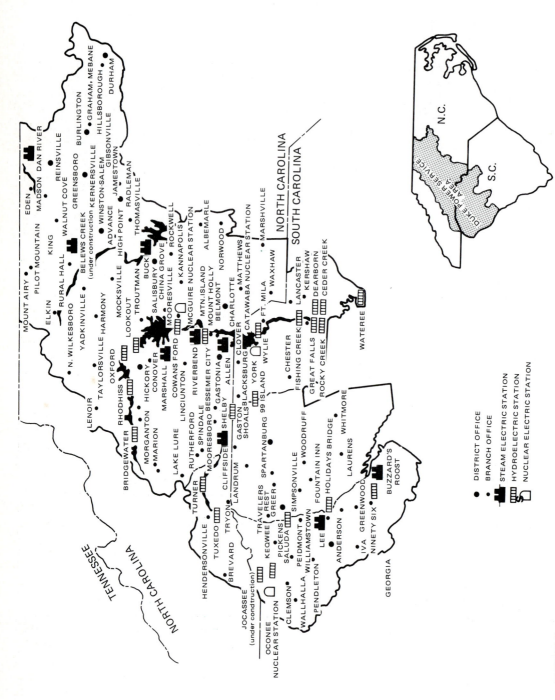

**FIGURE B**
Duke Power service area.

Power and others as a wholesale distributor, Mill Power Supply purchased virtually all supplies, equipment, and fuel required by the parent company.

The company was the only major U.S. utility to design and construct its own power plants. In 1974 it undertook new construction at the rate of over $3 million every working day. If ranked by output, its construction department would have been in the top dozen construction companies in the country. It had an excellent reputation for efficient construction and operation of generating facilities. The Marshall Steam Station had been acclaimed as the most efficient coal-burning plant in the nation for the past seven years; for the past two years, the steam-electric generating system had been rated #1 by the Federal Power Commission (FPC).

Rates were set by the FPC for wholesale customers and by the North Carolina Utilities Commission (NCUC) and the Public Service Commission of South Carolina (PSCSC) for retail customers. Economies of scale and new technology made the utility industry a declining costs industry up to 1969. Combined with Duke Power's efficiency, this had resulted in six major rate reductions for Duke Power's customers in the 1960s. In 1969 its retail prices were 18% below the national average.

Organizational culture at Duke Power was similar to a family-run business, especially prior to the company's rapid expansion in 1969. Things were done informally with few written policies or procedures. Even multimillion-dollar contracts had often been finalized by a handshake. Heads of departments had considerable autonomy. Those who had problems in their departments were expected to make recommendations and, if approved, to take responsibility for implementing them. There was also a norm for rapid decision making and implementation.

## MINORITY EMPLOYEES

In November 1966 the 13 black workers at Duke Power's Dan River plant filed suit against the company. They claimed that the educational and testing requirements used by Duke Power were discriminatory and invalid, and that prior to the Civil Rights Act of 1964, blacks had been relegated to the lowest-paying department. The plaintiffs also argued that centuries of cultural and educational discrimination had placed them at a disadvantage when competing with whites for positions allocated by education or performance on standardized tests.

*Griggs v. Duke Power,* as the case was known, was heard by the Federal District Court and the Fourth Circuit Court of Appeals with mixed results before the Supreme Court agreed to review the case. The Federal District Court ruled that Duke Power had followed a policy of overt racial discrimination prior to the Civil Rights Act, but it acknowledged that such conduct had since ceased. In 1970, the Supreme Court ruled 8 to 0 that although it was not Duke Power's intent to discriminate against blacks, the educational and testing requirements used by the company were not related to job performance and thus were illegal. It was also stated that these requirements would operate to "freeze the status quo of prior discriminatory employment practices." Closely followed by the press, the decision was a landmark in labor relations and heralded as a victory for blacks.

In 1973 the company hired Dewitt Reid as director of equal employment opportunity (EEO). Reid, age 46, was a native of Charlotte, had been a teacher for 20 years and had worked in personnel at another company for 7 years. He reported through the manager of employee relations to Joseph Major, vice president–personnel.

Reid's formal job responsibilities were to help Duke Power reach its affirmative action goals and monitor its compliance with EEO guidelines. He also made himself available as a consultant to managers on minority issues. Because of his position and his personality, black employees often voiced their concerns to him. Reid himself was particularly interested not only in the company's long-range goal of having the same proportion of blacks working at Duke Power as there was in Duke's service area, but also in having blacks receive their fair share of management positions. (In 1970 about 23% of the population of Charlotte was black.) In January 1974 there were 19 black managers among the company's 1,229 managers and officers.

In 1974 top management believed that there had been more affirmative action progress in the past three years than in all the company's history. Special attention had been paid to increasing the number of minorities and making Duke Power a more attractive place for minorities to work. The company was especially concerned with increasing the number of minorities in the construction department where the percentage of blacks was among the lowest. In 1970 the department had started an employee-orientation program for minorities to make working at Duke Power easier. It also had a learner's progressive skills (LPS) program in which workers were taught trades other than those they already knew. The company, and especially Reid, had encouraged blacks to use this program as a means of gaining the opportunity to move out of utility, or common laborer, positions. Most blacks in construction were unskilled and worked as cement finishers. Although desirous of adding blacks to the payroll as engineers or highly skilled workers, management found it difficult to locate qualified people. The department's search to hire its own director of minority affairs in the early 1970s was unsuccessful because it could not find a suitable person.

Duke Power did not keep statistics on minority employment before 1966, and because of inconsistent counting methods the company had no reliable figures before 1970. In that year a computerized and standardized system was established.

Table A presents the number of Duke construction workers and the minority percentages from 1970 to 1974. During that time the percentage of minorities companywide changed from 7.6% to 10.3%.

**TABLE A**
MINORITIES IN CONSTRUCTION AT DUKE POWER

| | Construction total | Minorities | |
|---|---|---|---|
| | | Number | % |
| 1970 | 2,853 | 204 | 7.2 |
| 1971 | 3,407 | 256 | 7.5 |
| 1972 | 4,290 | 327 | 7.6 |
| 1973 | 4,894 | 379 | 7.7 |
| 1974 | 4,646 | 360 | 7.7 |

*Source:* Data compiled by Duke Power Company from EEO-1 reports.

## LABOR RELATIONS IN THE CONSTRUCTION DEPARTMENT

Duke Power's labor practices not only enabled the company to have the lowest construction costs per unit of output of any utility in the nation, but also provided an unusual degree of job security for its skilled construction workers. When one project was completed the company would transfer its skilled workers to another project and pay their relocation expenses. The LPS program also enabled the company to shift employees from one trade to another, as needed. This would not have been possible if the work force had been unionized.

Although there had been several attempts at labor organization, in 1974 there were no unions in the construction department. In 1968 the Buildings and Trades Council union was defeated 7 to 1 in a vote at the Oconee Nuclear Station. In 1972 the ironworkers union was defeated in its vote at the McGuire nuclear plant. In 1972 the International Brotherhood of Electrical Workers was also defeated in a construction department election. In addition, there had been several occasions in the early 1970s when unions had withdrawn petitions on the day before an election because they believed they would be defeated.

From 1970 to 1973 coal miners at the Brookside mine in Harlan County, Kentucky, were represented by the Southern Labor Union (SLU). Brookside was operated by Duke Power's subsidiary, the Eastover Mining Company. In July 1973 miners at Brookside voted to have the United Mine Workers (UMW) represent them. The company would not agree to some of the terms of the UMW contract and the miners went on strike. The UMW took out full-page ads in newspapers in Duke Power's service area urging Duke's customers to oppose the company's rate increase requests. It also launched an ad campaign in the *Wall Street Journal* to discourage potential investors in Duke Power securities. Eventually the company agreed to the union's major demands.

In the spring of 1974 Bob Dick was concerned that the personnel function had been particularly slow to develop in the construction department. There were no written statements of policy for promotions, discipline, transfers, or termination, for example. Such decisions were based almost exclusively on the recommendations of supervisors as to employees' work quality. Dick felt that in too many cases this resulted in discharge or discipline because the supervisor "didn't like the way the man parted his hair." He wanted to change this way of operating, although he knew that both supervisors and foremen liked the tradition of hiring and firing based on performance.

## THE ECSTASY

Business was booming for Duke Power in 1969. Earnings per share were a record $2.05 and return on common equity was 13%. Common stock had reached a record market high of $43.50 with a book value of $16.62. The company's bond rating was AAA.

In the 1960s, peak load growth for most utilities had averaged about 7% a year. (*Peak load* refers to the greatest demand on the company's generating system during a particular time period.) Projections for the next several years indicated an annual growth rate of over 9% for the company's service area. The 1969 annual report pointed out that "every company record involving the sale of electricity for residential purposes was smashed." Duke Power had aggressively promoted "total electric living" and was proud of the fact that it led the country in the number of total electric units added each year and that average use per customer was 40% higher than the national average. Industrial, commercial, and agricultural uses were projected to show similar increases.

Duke Power's peak loads had increased from 2.48 million kw in 1959 to 5.61 million kw in 1969. Throughout the early 1960s peak loads had consistently exceeded forecasts. Reserve generating capacity declined from 22% in 1959 to 3% in 1969, although the company had firm purchases of an additional 8% to meet unexpected demand that year. It was generally held in the industry that a minimum of 20% reserve capacity was safe.

Based on its projections and experience, the company embarked in 1969 on the most ambitious expansion and modernization program in its history. Utilities across the nation were doing the same.

Expansion plans included nuclear, coal, and hydroelectric facilities. The planned construction and the work in progress would double Duke Power's generating capacity by 1977. In 1969 investment in new power generation, transmission, distribution, and other plant facilities was a record $283 million, more than $43 million above the previous high in 1968. Projected capital expenditures from 1969 through 1971 totaled $1.04 billion. During these boom years, Bob Dick had said that the company was "beating the bushes" to find and hire enough qualified construction workers.

## THE AGONY

After 1969 a gradual downward spiral began. The single most damaging event was the unexpected increase in the cost of coal. In 1969 coal was priced at $7.80 per ton. The next year the price jumped to $11.00 per ton and cost the company an unexpected $49 million. In 1974, a year after the Arab oil embargo, coal soared to $27.64 per ton. From 1969 to 1974 investment and operating costs also increased due to inflation, delays in construction, and the installation of air pollution equipment.

Top management responded in a variety of ways to increase revenues and lower operating expenses. The company began applying for unprecedented rate increases as early as 1969, but it had a difficult time obtaining adequate increases due to regulatory lag. The utility commissions set rates by examining the company's performance over a test period in its recent past. Based on what was considered a reasonable rate of return on equity, they would then establish rates. Throughout the 1960s the commissions had allowed Duke Power a return on equity of 12%–13%. Since requests usually took six months to a year to be acted on, the increases no longer covered actual operating costs by the time they were approved.

From April 1970 to August 1974 the company filed over 16 applications for increases. About 75% of the requested amounts were granted. Although none of the company's revenues came from rate increases in 1969, in 1973 24% of total revenues were from rate increases. Despite these increases, the company was not able to maintain its customary return on equity. As requests were approved, prices to residential customers increased 50% from 1970 to 1974. Protests from these customers made it even more difficult to obtain further increases.

Duke Power was also hampered by not having a fuel-adjustment clause that would allow it to pass on to its customers the increased costs of fuel. Although it applied for such a clause in April 1969, it was not until April 1973 that the FPC approved a coal-adjustment clause for wholesale customers. And only in January 1974 was the company given the initial approval by the state utility commissions for residential customers.

Although the company's financial condition had declined, projections for high energy demands caused Duke Power to announce plans in 1973 to build an additional eight nuclear plants and another hydroelectric facility.

Construction work in progress in that year totaled $866 million.

Earnings per share dropped from $2.05 in 1969 to $1.57 in 1973 and by 1974 were still only $1.74. By 1974 return on equity was down to 8.8%. The company's fixed charges coverage dropped from 6:1 in 1965 to 2:1 in 1969. Its bond rating dropped from AAA to A.

The deterioration in Duke Power's fixed charges coverage had forced the company on four occasions since 1971 to meet its expenses by obtaining short-term loans at rates substantially above what would have been required if conventional sources of capital had been available. On three of these occasions short-term borrowing exceeded available lines of credit. By 1974 cost increases outstripped revenue increases. (Figure C shows changes in revenues, earnings, and costs from 1969.)

In 1969 the company had 23.2 million shares of common stock outstanding and by the beginning of 1974 had sold an additional 15.3 million shares. As the market value of its stock dropped below book value, each offering of common stock diluted its value. In April 1974 additional shares of common stock were sold at 75% of book value.

In mid-July 1974 the company was faced with $200 million cash shortage. Although Bill Grigg worked feverishly for several weeks, he was only able to raise $2 million. In a desperation move, the company sold $100,000,000 of unsecured five-year notes at 13%, the highest rate of interest ever paid by an electric utility.

## EMERGENCY MEASURES

On August 20, 1974, the board of directors authorized significant cutbacks in construction. "Duke has thoroughly investigated all available means of financing and is convinced it is impossible to raise the huge sums needed to maintain the former construction schedule," announced Carl Horn, Jr., CEO, in a statement to the press. The cutbacks would reduce capital expenditures $150 million through 1975 and would total $1.5 billion through 1979. Under

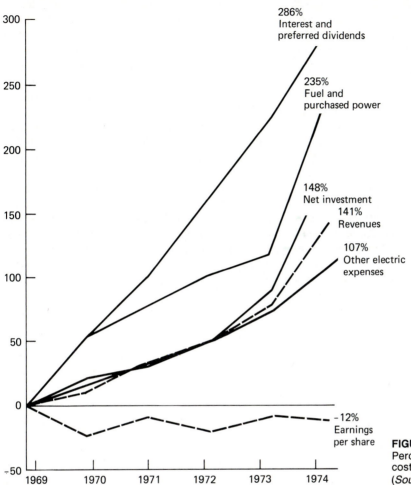

**286%**
Interest and
preferred dividends

**235%**
Fuel and
purchased power

**148%**
Net investment
**141%**
Revenues

**107%**
Other electric
expenses

−12%
Earnings
per share

**FIGURE C**
Percent change in revenues, major
costs, and earnings, 1969–1974.
(*Source:* Duke Power Company.)

the new construction schedule, completion of
nuclear stations then in progress would be delayed up to two years. Despite a decrease of 2.5
million kw in the company's peak load projec-
tion, there would be a reserve capacity in 1980
of only 12%. Citing the national energy supply
situation and the need to ensure that the cutbacks would not curtail the company's ability
to provide electricity, Horn also announced
that a load management program would be developed to reduce total system load and peak
loads.

**BILL LEE**

"He's been a dynamic leader in anything he's
undertaken. He just doesn't know the word
'failure.' It isn't in his vocabulary," was the way
one of Bill Lee's peers described him.

Lee was the grandson of the company's
first chief engineer. He joined Duke Power in
1955 as a junior designer. Named vice president–engineering in 1965, he was promoted to
senior vice president–engineering and construction in 1971. The Marshall Steam Station

and the Keowee-Toxaway project, both of which won national awards for engineering excellence, had been largely designed by him. In 1972 he won the American Society of Mechanical Engineers' George Westinghouse gold medal award for engineering.

Bill Lee was also highly regarded as a manager. His associates felt that he brought out the best in the people who worked for him and that he had a genuine personal concern for Duke Power's employees. He took pleasure in the fact that before the company expanded rapidly in the late 1960s, he knew many of the construction workers by their first names. Reflecting on his job, he had said: "We won't be remembered for our power plants, but for what kind of people we leave to design and manage them."

Lee was known as a thorough but fast decision maker. In October 1969 he left a meeting in which he learned that completion of the Oconee plant would be delayed and went immediately to a pay telephone. He asked his boss for approval to begin construction at once on another power plant. From that phone booth, in the next 45 minutes, he ordered $40 million worth of equipment.

Bill Lee also had a reputation for being fair and trying to use the Golden Rule as a guide for running the construction department. Besides being an Elder in the Presbyterian church, he was active in numerous community service organizations. Lee was particularly pleased about the relationships he had cultivated with the black community. He had promoted Duke Power as a work place for minorities by speaking at local black colleges and at meetings of black business leaders.

# Sexual Harassment: Some See It . . . Some Won't

"This entire subject is a perfect example of a minor special interest group's ability to blow up any 'issue' to a level of importance which in no way relates to the reality of the world in which we live and work."—*A 38-year-old plant manager (male) for a large manufacturer of industrial goods.*

"A vice president of the company where I worked made overt advances following a company banquet. This included stroking my buttocks and continually rubbing himself against me. At one point he got me alone—away from the group—and put his hand down my dress. I finally managed to get rid of him. For several weeks afterward he kept calling me at work. When I talked to my supervisor about it, his only reaction was amusement. A few months later, my supervisor started making advances. When I found another job, I left. It's much better where I am now."—*A 27-year-old computer specialist (female) in a large public utility.*

"In my own circumstances, sexual harassment included jokes about my anatomy, off-color remarks, sly innuendo in front of customers—in short, turning everything and anything into a sexual reference was an almost daily occurrence. I have just left this company [a big chemical manufacturer] partially for this reason."—*A 34-year-old first-level manager in environmental engineering (female) for a large producer of industrial goods.*

"I'm baffled by this issue. I used to believe it was a subject that was being exaggerated by paranoid women and sensational journalists. Now I think the problem is real but somewhat overdrawn. My *impression* is that my own company is relatively free of sexual harassment. But I don't know the

This article, which originally appeared in the March–April 1981 issue of *Harvard Business Review*, is based on a joint survey conducted by the *Review* and *Redbook Magazine*.

*Harvard Business Review* reprint 81203.

facts."—*A 53-year-old senior vice president (male) of a medium-sized financial institution.*

Is sexual harassment a manufactured issue? Is it widespread? Should it concern top management? To try to answer these and other questions, the editors of HBR and *Redbook* maga-zine surveyed 7,408 HBR subscribers (1,846, or nearly 25%, of whom responded) in the United States. (See the ruled insert for a complete description of how the survey was conducted.)

Our major findings are:

• Sexual harassment is seen as an issue of power. In four out of six situations that we

---

## SURVEY APPROACH

This survey, conducted jointly by *Redbook* magazine and HBR, aimed to measure opinions on and awareness of the issue of sexual harassment in the workplace. We mailed a questionnaire to 7,408 HBR subscribers in the United States and tabulated 1,846 replies, a 24.9% response. (A further 234 completed questionnaires were returned after the cut-off date and could not be included.)

To serve as a benchmark for respondents and give them a certain amount of information as a starting point, we listed the EEOC guidelines on sexual harassment in the introduction to the questionnaire.

We divided the survey into three sections. In the first, to elicit definitions and attitudes we offered readers 11 statements and asked whether they agreed with them or not. We also listed 14 comments that have been made about the behavior of men toward women at work and asked whether the behavior described constituted sexual harassment and whether people had heard of or observed this behavior in their organizations.

In the second section, we described four vignettes and asked what action to take. The third set of questions concerned EEOC guidelines and company policies, and the fourth section was statistical.

In the first section we split the sample in half to get at differing attitudes that might not otherwise be revealed. Of the 14 comments on behavior, 8 differed between the white and colored forms. The four vignettes in the second section were also worded differently between the two forms.

In examining the data, we discovered a certain amount of conditioning. In the 8 split-sample statements on behavior, the aggressor in the colored form was always a supervisor, while in the white form he was a co-worker. In the other 6 questions in the group that were the same in both forms, those who returned the colored questionnaires were more likely to term an action harassment than those who returned the white ones.

We excluded all non-U.S. subscribers (22% of HBR's total number of subscribers) from the sample because we wanted to probe the issue from a strictly American viewpoint. We also skewed the sample another way: To ensure a representative response from women, we mailed a questionnaire to virtually every female subscriber, for a male/female ratio of 68% to 32%. This bias resulted in a response of 52% male and 44% female (and 4% who gave no indication of gender)—compared with HBR's U.S. subscriber proportion of 93% male and 7% female.

The administrative levels of the survey group broke down as follows: top management, 24%; middle management, 33%; lower management, 34%; and other, 7%. Nearly three-quarters of the group were in the 25 to 45 age bracket. The breakdown was: under 25, 3%; 25 to 35, 42%; 36 to 45, 32%; 46 to 55, 15%; 56 to 65, 6%; and over 65, less than 1%; 1% did not answer.

The salaries of about one-quarter of the group fell into the $20,000 to $29,999 range, another one-quarter in the $30,000 to $39,999 range, while 11% earned less than $20,000, and 6% more than $100,000. Some 49% held graduate degrees and 35%, college degrees.

The sizes of the organizations for which the individuals worked were spread widely, the most significant categories being 1,000 to 9,999 employees (23%), more than 20,000 (16%), and under 50 (13%).

On average, the survey group was at a lower management level than our U.S. subscribers overall. Respondents were generally younger and earned less but were about as well educated. We ascribe the differences between respondents and HBR's subscriber group to the fact that our sample was skewed to include more women, who have not reached the higher echelons of U.S. corporations in great numbers.

described to readers, they rate a supervisor's behavior as considerably more serious and threatening than the same action by a co-worker.

- Men and women generally agree in theory on what sexual harassment is but disagree on how often it occurs. Nearly two-thirds of the men, compared with less than one-third of the women, agree (or partly agree) with the statement, "The amount of sexual harassment at work is greatly exaggerated."

- Top management appears isolated from occurrences of harassment, and middle-level managers are somewhat less aware of misconduct than lower-level managers.

- Most respondents favor company policies against harassment, but few organizations have any policies to address it. For example, 29% of respondents work in companies where top executives have issued statements to employees disapproving of sexual misconduct, but 73% favor such statements.

- In general, most see the Equal Employment Opportunity Commission (EEOC) guidelines issued in 1980 as reasonable and necessary and agree that they will not be difficult to follow. But the returns show that the mildest and most pervasive forms, such as innuendo and dirty jokes—to many women the most obnoxious forms—are harder to prove and often impractical to take action on, even though the guidelines cover them.

- Most respondents think sexual harassment can be a very serious matter. Ten percent report they have heard of or observed a situation as extreme as the following in their organizations: "Mr. X has asked me to have sex with him. I refused, but now I learn that he's given me a poor evaluation."

Regardless of the perceived seriousness of the problem, however, the findings cannot reveal how pervasive sexual harassment is. Obviously, those who were most interested or involved completed the questionnaire; we do not know about the experiences of others who did not answer or who were not included in the survey.

- Finally, many people—nearly one out of three—took the time to write about their concerns and uncertainties regarding this issue. In their comments, many women despair of gaining top management's understanding of how harassment damages them.

Until recently, consciousness of sexual harassment has been low. But people have become aware of it as more women have arrived at levels of authority in the workplace, feminist groups have focused attention on rape and other violence against women, and students have felt freer to report perceived abuse by professors. (Although the survey was designed to investigate mainly women's experiences, we recognize—and the answers to the questionnaire make clear—that harassment of men by women and homosexual harassment do occur, also with distressing consequences to the victims.)

In the last five years, other studies have also shown that sexual misconduct is a big problem. For example, in a recently published survey of federal employees, 42% of 694,000 women and 15% of 1,168,000 men said they had experienced some form of harassment.[1]

In November 1980, the EEOC adopted its final guidelines for employers to deal with the problem. The new guidelines define sexual harassment as "unwelcome sexual advances, requests for sexual favors, and other verbal or physical conduct of a sexual nature" that take place under any of the following circumstances:

**1**  When submission to the sexual advance is a condition of keeping or getting a job,

[1]Merit Systems Protection Board Report on Sexual Harassment in the Federal Workplace, given before the Subcommittee on Investigations, Committee on the Post Office and Civil Service, U.S. House of Representatives, September 1980. See also Frank J. Till, "Sexual Harassment: A Report on the Sexual Harassment of Students," National Advisory Council on Women's Educational Programs, U.S. Department of Education, August 1980; Catherine A. MacKinnon, *Sexual Harassment of Working Women* (New Haven: Yale University Press, 1979); and Claire Safran, "What Men Do to Women on the Job," *Redbook,* November 1976, p. 149.

whether expressed in explicit or implicit terms.

2  When a supervisor or boss makes a personnel decision based on an employee's submission to or rejection of sexual advances.

3  When sexual conduct unreasonably interferes with a person's work performance or creates an intimidating, hostile, offensive work environment.

According to the EEOC, employers have "an affirmative duty" to prevent and eliminate sexual abuse. Additionally, the guidelines make the employer responsible for misbehavior by supervisory personnel, their assistants, co-workers, or outside personnel. (See the Appendix for the legal issues.)

Top managers, middle and lower-level managers, women, and men do not always agree on what constitutes harassment or even whether it is prevalent. But because so many perceive it as a problem, and because the EEOC has issued guidelines and raised the prospect of stepped-up litigation by employees, top management of for-profit and nonprofit organizations clearly should pay attention to the issue.

In this article we explore what some of our readers think sexual harassment is and how much they think it occurs in their organizations. In doing so, we report what they think about the EEOC guidelines, company policies, and, more personally, how they feel when harassed.

## WHAT IS IT AND HOW MUCH?

"I attended a meeting of department heads (only two women were classified as department heads). There, 40- to 45-year-old men—department heads and elected officials—were tossing a prophylactic back and forth, with the usual comments accompanying the tosses. I don't know if this show was for the benefit of the two women present or if they just found out what the item was used for. We tried to ignore their behavior. Another department head sug-

gested they pay attention and grow up." *(female)*

"Constant 'small' examples show lack of awareness, such as from a boss: 'You deserve a pat on the fanny for a good job.'" *(female)*

"I have heard much 'joking' about sex in regard to women's bodies in the office. I have seen this going on for years. Since it is supposedly said in jest, it is apparently supposed to be ignored. But most of the female employees get very uncomfortable when these remarks are made. The men enjoy every minute of it and it seems to amuse them even more if the women get embarrassed. This has happened in one-on-one situations and in group situations." *(female)*

"There is a great deal of fondness in my company, particularly my division, but I'm confident it does not include the necessary element of harassment, i.e., indebtedness. Maybe I'm naive. Better yet, maybe my businesslike deportment prevents any encouragement of innuendos or allows me to be 'one of the boys.' There is an unusually high comfort level among the men and women in our company. I attribute most of that to the age of the group (30 to 35) and the fact that they've been brought up in a more aware time." *(female)*

"I have supervised many women and have found them very sensitive especially to biases of their male bosses. Many times their sensitivity is more acute than my own—that is, I saw nothing obvious but they were quite sure of the bias. As a result, I am unsure whether accusations of sexual bias are not just disguises of—or poorly stated initial reactions to—some other underlying management problem (or perception)." *(male)*

Not surprisingly, respondents to our survey agree about which extreme situations constitute sexual harassment but differ over the more ambiguous cases. For instance, 87% think that the following statement definitely indicates abuse: "I have been having an affair with the head of my division. Now I've told him I want to break it off, but he says I will lose out on the promotion I've been expecting." (Exhibit I shows the 4 instances of 14 we described that most people think constitute misconduct.)

Opinions on these extreme cases differ little between men and women and between top and lower-level management. For example, 89% of the men and 92% of the women think the first statement in Exhibit I is harassment ("I can't seem to go in and out of my boss's office without being patted or pinched"). Nearly 87% of top management and 91% of lower-level management also think it is.

In other, less extreme situations, however, people are less certain about the interpretation but still consider the behavior quite offensive (see Exhibit II). An average of 40% say the situation where a man starts each day with a sexual remark and insists it's an innocent social comment is harassment; an average of 48% say it is possibly; 8% say it is not; and 4% don't know. According to many readers, a situation where a man often puts his hand on a woman's arm when making a point is even more innocent (see Exhibit II).

The perceived seriousness of the harassment seems to depend on who is making the advance, the degree of interpreted intent, and the victim's perception of the consequences. The amount the victim appears to suffer, however, does not necessarily vary with the perceived seriousness. In many comments, for instance, the writers seemed more vexed by persistent low-level misbehavior, which, although covered by EEOC guidelines, is impractical to do something about and is often harder to prove than more extreme forms.

A 26-year-old female market research analyst for an industrial goods manufacturer wrote: "It is not easy for a smart woman to avoid sexual harassment. Case in point—a male in our DP department continually makes comments and gestures to me. I reacted at first by being 'cool and silent.' When this did not

have any effect, I requested that he stop, as I found it offensive. I must deal with this person professionally, and I feel that our relationship has been hindered. We both found each other's actions and reactions offensive."

Harassment is not, of course, limited to the office. Wrote a 30-year-old male foundry materials manager for an industrial goods producer: "When secretaries walk through the shop, there are whistles and catcalls. However, management has not seen this as a problem. It does not interfere with promotion or pay, but I find it an offensive situation."

To test whether a supervisor's behavior is seen as more threatening and serious than a co-worker's, the survey included a split sample in which we asked readers' opinions of statements made by female employees about male co-workers and supervisors (see Exhibit II). For example, the colored survey form, sent to half the subscribers polled, stated, "Whenever I go into the office, my supervisor eyes me up and down, making me feel uncomfortable." On the white form, which was sent to the other half, "my supervisor" became "a man I work with" (Exhibit II).

In four of these six less extreme cases, a higher percentage view the supervisor's behavior as worse than the co-worker's. Quite clearly, the perceived seriousness of the action correlates with the power of the person making the advances. (The two situations where the co-worker is seen as more blameworthy—continually glancing at the woman, part C, and putting a hand on her arm when making a point, part F—are rather ambiguous, and the behavior is certainly less threatening in relation to work but more repugnant because it constitutes unwanted intimacy.)

Many people commented on how power influences perceptions of harassment. As one reader put it, "The indebtedness increases the harassment's potency." Some of our male readers were very aware of the implications of power differences: "There is a male code of silence regarding harassment of females that has to be broken, particularly in the area of male 'power' figures and females without power," said the 38-year-old male vice president of marketing in a large insurance company. "Either too many men never recover from being high school jocks or they understand that corporate power can be a new way to be attractive. Having suffered through both lessons, I feel free to comment."

The power phenomenon is not necessarily restricted to men, either. "The more power people have, the more able they are to let go of their inhibitions and act on their desires," testified a 36-year-old government administrator. "As a woman manager, I must admit to temptation! It is when the overtures are unwanted, persistent, and *power* based that they are unhealthy organizationally."

In five of the six split-sample cases, more women than men consider the behavior offensive, whether the statement is about a supervisor or a co-worker. For instance, in the situation where the man eyes the woman up and down (Exhibit II, part A), 24% of all women, compared with 8% of all men, think it is harassment. (Since it was not possible to include all the survey data in the exhibits, here and in a few other instances, the data have been extrapolated.)

In the remaining split-sample case—where the man kisses the woman every time they meet (part D)—somewhat more men than women, proportionately, rate the action objectionable whether by a supervisor or a fellow worker. Perhaps women are often more conscious of social formalities and tend to accept this kind of behavior from supervisors, whereas men are more likely to consider it merely an encounter between the sexes.

In response to two other statements that were more conventionally social—where the man often offers to drive the woman home and where the married man and the woman have dinner together and go to a nightclub while on a business trip—slightly more men than women also think these are possibly harassment.

Additionally, as all the split-sample responses in this section testify, top managers say that the behavior by supervisors is more blameworthy than the same behavior by co-workers.

Answers to the split sample clearly demonstrate that the power relationship implicitly carries a coercive threat. But what about co-workers? Why do only a third of top managers who completed the white form think that being greeted each day with a sexual remark from a co-worker is harassment?

Throughout the survey we found answers that could be explained only by a "that's the way men are" assessment on the part of both men and women—resignation or acceptance bred of recurring experience. Perhaps the more one sees behavior like that we described, the less one is stirred to call it misconduct.

### How Much?

Except for the incident where the man kisses the woman on the cheek every time they meet (Exhibit II, part D), all the situations in Exhibit II have been heard of or seen by many people. For example, an average of one-third say that they have heard of or observed persistent requests for a date by men in their organizations.

The four activities our sample considers the most objectionable (Exhibit I) they have seen or heard of the least. Understandably, these are the least likely to occur, be detected, or be admitted to.

In general, of those who have knowledge of certain sexual behavior in their organizations, a higher proportion assert that such behavior is not harassment. For example, 10% of the people who have seen or heard of someone starting each day with a sexual remark say it is not harassment, compared with 5% of those who haven't heard of or seen such behavior.

The spread appears greater when we look at the co-worker/supervisor split sample. In cases where the supervisor makes the advance, people are much more likely to call it harassment when they have no knowledge of its occurrence in their own organizations. (Does familiarity breed contempt?) In all these cases, however, interpretation of intent may cloud the statistics.

The most striking finding on the question of how much abuse actually takes place is the difference in perception between men and women and between high-level and lower-level management. (Because most high-level managers in our survey were men and more lower-level managers were women, the two sets of responses often parallel each other.) The answers to the statement, "The amount of sexual harassment at work is greatly exaggerated," are:

|                        | Agree or partly agree | Disagree or partly disagree |
|------------------------|-----------------------|-----------------------------|
| Top management         | 63%                   | 22%                         |
| Middle management      | 52                    | 30                          |
| Lower-level management | 44                    | 40                          |
| Women                  | 32%                   | 52%                         |
| Men                    | 66                    | 17                          |

In most instances substantial differences appear in men's and women's perceptions of how frequently sexual harassment occurs. For example, one-third of the men, but a full half of the women, have witnessed or heard of a case where the man starts each day with a sexual remark that he insists is an innocent social comment (Exhibit II, part B).

How can we explain the differences in viewpoint? Sexual harassment may not take place when male managers are around to observe it; and even if it does, they may not "see" it as women do. Consider this account from a 30-year-old female project leader in the finance department of a large company: "Not a day passes without my boss either sharing a particularly lewd joke with me or asking me what I did with my boyfriend the night before—complete with leers and smirks. My requests for him to cease have fallen on deaf ears; he seems to enjoy my discomfort and chides me for being a 'poor sport.' Prior to my divorce he was totally inoffensive."

That such an attitude on the part of male managers is discouraging for women is evident from many comments we received. Typical was this remark from a 32-year-old financial officer in a small company: "I was the victim of harassment and it was a miserable experience. When I voiced complaints to my so-called feminist male boss and male colleagues, I was made

to feel crazy, dirty—as if I were the troublemaker." Another woman wrote, "Sexual harassment eats away at the core of a woman's being, destroys self-confidence, and can contribute to a lowered feeling of self-worth."

Even though men generally agree in the abstract with women about what harassment is, the gap in perception of what actually happens is real and significant. From the comments in the returns, a visitor from another planet might conclude that men and women work in separate organizations.

One factor that may help explain the difference in perception is social conditioning. For example, 44% of the women view the statement about the man who starts each day with a sexual remark (Exhibit II, part B) as only "possibly" misconduct. "Many incidents go unnoticed by both parties because of conditioning," wrote a 30-year-old female radio station manager. "Men are 'expected' to do such things, women are 'expected' to have to cope with that type of behavior." Perhaps some women, accustomed to accept such incidents as a price of survival in the business world, have lost sensitivity. They, as well as men, suffer from sexual astigmatism.

One reader, a 30-year-old female vice president of marketing in a large financial institution, wrote, "Senior people are the wrong people to ask about such behavior because they may not know much. The 'little people' are afraid to complain." The survey corroborates her observation, perhaps because the "little people" are afraid of exposure, embarrassment, and retribution.

In extreme cases, higher-level executives report that they are generally unaware of what's going on. Perhaps one of the worst examples of abuse in our survey is epitomized by Exhibit I, part C—where the man gives the woman a poor evaluation because she refuses to have sex with him. Ten percent of all respondents have heard of or observed this situation. The response by management level breaks down this way: top management, 5%; middle management, 9%; lower-level management, 13%; persons other than managers (a small number), 19%.

As in other situations, more women than

men testify to knowledge of the situation described in Exhibit I, part C—16% against 5%. Whether conditioning, denial, or lack of awareness explains these disparities, the gap in perception between different levels of management and between men and women poses a serious problem for policymakers.

## WHAT WOULD YOU DO?

"Men in my company are not penalized for sexual encounters with co-workers, whereas women are. You feel [helpless] trying to confront silent accusations and using the company complaint channels where the men you talk to share a common, somewhat negative philosophy about women." *(female)*

"I have worked successfully in good positions all my life. Since I was both attractive and smart, [the problem] was always the boss. I either had to learn to say no graciously, or lose every good job I got. I find that a woman must defend herself every day, and I don't believe you can find rules for the top men. The world is made of men and women who either get along or don't. If they do get along, the men invariably try to have a physical attachment. I think it's inborn in a man." *(female)*

"I was in an elevator along with the president and some other men. One man made a dirty comment, and the president came back with a remark telling this employee to keep his locker room comments to the locker room and not make them around any women in the firm." *(female)*

The problem of disparities in perception appears throughout the survey. To probe differing attitudes, we sent two different versions of four vignettes in our split-sample questionnaire. In one we asked readers to say what they would do as managers in these situations; in the other, what typical managers would do (see Exhibit III). One can draw many conclusions from the

answers, but three disparities in perception stand out: (1) the differential treatment men and women employees receive after an unwanted advance; (2) how women should handle themselves; and (3) how responsible managers ought to act in the workplace.

### Perceived Differential Treatment

The responses to the vignettes show that men and women hold very different opinions on how top managers will act in an ambiguous situation. Their opinions also differ depending on whether the victim is a female or male executive, a female executive or secretary, and on who is making the advance.

For example, in the first vignette a company president walks into his sales manager's office and finds him standing near his secretary, who looks upset and flustered (Exhibit III, part A). On the colored questionnaire we asked what the typical president would do, and on the white form we asked what "you" would do. Nearly two-thirds of the women who filled out the colored form believed that the typical president would do nothing—being unaware of what happened or unwilling to confront the sales manager on a personal matter—while fewer than half the men voted this way.

In thinking that the typical president would do nothing, most of the women chose avoidance of confrontation as the motivation, while most men selected ignorance as the reason for inactivity. Women, it seems, tend to think that male executives take an uninvolved stance even when they know what is happening (and even when it is addressed in the guidelines). "Unless women make an issue of harassment, management will be more than willing to bury their collective heads and say they have no problem," wrote a 31-year-old female manager of training and development in a petrochemical services company.

This assumption by women of how male executives will behave reveals itself in another vignette. We described a scene in an elevator where a male executive makes a remark about a female occupant's body to another male executive (Exhibit III, part B). In the white form one man was senior; in the colored form the two executives were peers.

Of the women who answered the colored questionnaire, 41% asserted that the second executive, the peer, would share the first's amusement, while only 14% of the men chose this option. On the white form, 23% of the women decided that the senior executive would join in the joke, while only 7% of the men said that he would find the remark amusing. Instead, 37% of the men who filled out the white form asking them what the senior executive would do said he would express verbal disapproval when alone with the other executive [option f]. In contrast, the prime choice of men who returned the colored form asking what the peer executive would do was option c, where he would remain silent.

Given the same facts, men and women expect vastly different reactions from senior executives and even from two peer males together. On both forms, "share the joke" received more votes from women than any other choice. Here is a representative view from a 32-year-old female manager of customer services in a large insurance company: "Our CEO thinks sexual innuendo, risqué jokes, and flirtations are a natural part of male-female relationships inside and outside the office."

We wonder whether the disparity in perception stems from women's cynicism or from their realism. Are things really as bad as women think? Are the men who answered our questions realistic or are they unaware?

In another vignette, we asked readers who got the white forms to say what they would do if confronted by a female secretary complaining about unwanted advances from a boss (Exhibit III, part C). In the colored form, a woman executive complained.

The responses to this vignette clearly show that women take harassment more seriously than men. In the case of the secretary, almost two-thirds of the female respondents voted to inform the boss that if his behavior continues, it will harm his career—while only 48% of the men selected that action. (In response to a question about the impact of harassment on the workplace, 75% of the women had "quitting or firing" as one choice, while 62% of the men selected that severe outcome.)

The responses to this vignette also reveal perceived differential treatment of executive women and secretaries. Women disapprove of the activity slightly more when the victim is a secretary (40%) than when she is an executive (36%). One-quarter of all our respondents would express their disapproval to the secretary's boss, while one-fifth would do so on behalf of the executive. If secretaries are unprotected, executive women are even more so, although more respondents say they would give advice on how to deal with the behavior to executives than to secretaries (11% to 6%).

Whatever the sources of this difference, it crops up again. In another vignette, the white form featured a male executive and the colored form a female, receiving unwanted advances from a client of the opposite sex. When asked to rate what the typical division head would do, the male and female respondents differ sharply in their answers (see Exhibit III, part D).

In both variants, most male readers assume that the typical manager would advise the executive—whether male or female—to handle the client with tact, regardless of the consequences. Most women, on the other hand (perhaps reasoning that the typical division head would regard the client as more important than the employee), believe that the boss would encourage the male executive to parry the advances and, most important, would offer to transfer the female from the account before doing anything else.

If we look at the order of options that our female respondents think a typical division manager would choose in the case of a woman executive, we see a discouraging picture of how much support women think management will give them in the face of sexual harassment. Rather than buttress them with a team (their next-to-last choice), back them regardless of the consequences, or encourage them to parry the advance, women assume that the division managers would want to transfer them. Whether women fear this most as the outcome or base their opinions on personal experience, their perceptions of how management would act should ring alarms for top officers.

## What Can a Woman Handle?

Do men and women hold different views on how women should or can deal with sexual advances? Women disagree among themselves here. Some think that women, to survive in the business world, have to handle whatever comes their way. A 43-year-old female office manager in a small transportation company wrote: "Women should stop feeling sorry or deprived, trying to play both sides to get the career they want, and act more like businesspeople—as men do. Furthermore, the so-called liberated women are probably the ones who are causing this commotion after all. It would be better for everyone if women would start acting more like people."

Other women think that harassment within organizations is too much for any person to handle alone. The following comment by a 34-year-old administrative assistant in an average-sized consumer services company is representative of many made by women: "In every incident in my organization, every woman has been fired, encouraged to resign or transfer, or demoted. Never has a man been in any way disciplined or punished for sexual harassment. Even when a complaint is won, the work situation continues to be uncomfortable. It is far easier to change jobs."

We asked our readers whether "a smart woman employee ought to have no trouble handling an unwanted sexual approach." Fifty-nine percent of the women disagree or partly disagree and the same proportion of men agree or partly agree. Men seem to think that women can overcome sexual overtures through tact, as in the vignettes of the female executive with the client (Exhibit III, part D) and the female executive and the secretary who complain about their bosses' advances (part C). In other words, it's her problem. That fewer women chose sanctions against the two female executives' bosses

than against the secretary's boss indicates that some women think female executives *should* be able to or can handle more.

Most women are less sure that they can deal with an unwanted sexual approach and, in fact, they wonder whether *anything* they do would make them safe from such behavior in the workplace. A full 78% of them disagree with the statement, "If a woman dresses and behaves properly, she will not be the target of unwanted sexual approaches at work."

The same proportion of women, however, agree or partly agree with the statement, "Women can and often do use their sexual attractiveness to their own advantage" (compared with 86% of the men). As one woman who is a 55-year-old supervisor in a large financial institution noted: "Although I do not side with sexual harassment from *any* source at the office, many young women invite this sort of response by their behavior and the type of clothing they wear. Whether it is intentional makes little difference. When dealing with the human factor, you (male or female) should know what can happen and avoid it on the job."

Although we cannot assume that the opposite of the statement—"If a woman dresses and behaves properly, she will not be the target of unwanted sexual approaches at work"—is true, the strong female disagreement with it indicates that women feel vulnerable on the issue. If they cannot avoid unwanted advances themselves, what is the manager's duty here? What do our respondents and the top managers among them think about managerial responsibility?

## How Much Can a Manager Know?

In dealing with the ambiguity in part A of Exhibit III—where the company president finds the sales manager standing very close to his secretary, who looks upset and flustered—63% of high-level managers who answered the white form said they would "suggest to the sales manager that even the appearance of sexual behavior was unwise." On the colored form, 42% indicated that the typical president would choose that option. However, 30% of this latter group feel that the typical president would do nothing because they think the executive would be ignorant of the facts or their importance—or of the EEOC guidelines.

Although top managers are convinced that they themselves *would* do something, apparently many people see real problems for most presidents in reacting to the ambiguity. Also, most think top managers are in no position to know about misconduct if it occurs; half of them disagree with the statement, "A good manager will know if it's happening in his or her department." Not surprisingly, lower-level managers and women are in even greater disagreement (56% for both groups).

The 27% of top managers filling out the white form who pleaded ignorance about part A of Exhibit III by marking option a—doing nothing, not knowing what had happened—were playing it very safe considering that they also had option c—suggesting to the sales manager that even the appearance of sexual behavior was unwise. This situation may or may not be harassment, but it should be confronted regardless.

Do women and lower-ranking managers—who may have heard of and observed much more sexual harassment than men and upper-level managers—really know how difficult it is for top managers to be aware of the problem? Does high-level management deceive itself about the difficulty of detecting abusive behavior? Are top managers aware mainly of the grosser forms and less knowledgeable about the daily "accepted" forms that annoy our female readers?

In part D of Exhibit III, in which the executive faces unwanted advances from the client, top managers' first choice (43%) was a tactful response, when a woman is the object of the advances. Lower-level managers also selected tact first (34%) but spread themselves much more evenly among the other options.

Given that two-thirds of high-level executives agree or partly agree that the reported amount of sexual harassment at work is greatly exaggerated, it might follow that for the *per-ceived* seriousness of the problem, "tact" would be a sufficient response. But since so many of our women respondents think tact is insufficient, what can a manager do? Will the new EEOC guidelines solve the problem? Should company policies and procedures address directly the subtler, varied, and more covert forms of misconduct that (although covered by the guidelines) are difficult to take action on or prove? If so, which policies would work?

## EEOC GUIDELINES AND COMPANY POLICIES

"The guidelines will be hard to implement because of 41,000 years of habit." *(male)*

"We have several store managers involved with women and harassment issues. We have a company policy which allows managers who find the need to transfer to another unit. Counseling is available. We don't want to lose people, but if a harassment charge is proven correct, we terminate that management person. Within the last year we have had to terminate three managers for harassment. Interestingly, the problem continues to plague us. Heart-to-heart, man-to-man talks, policy statements, and a proven corporate response have been no visible deterrent." *(male)*

"I do not know of a significant incident of sexual harassment at the company recently. The issue came up at seminars on male-female relationships run by the company in January and February 1980—much to the surprise of most males attending (including me). The general issue was problems of atmosphere—sexual remarks, innuendo, etc. As a result, management took a clear position on proper behavior at a series of meetings of all management personnel. I believe the situation has improved, but it is not the type of problem that is ever going to be solved by one action or policy." *(male)*

"This is a middle-western conservative work force, stable, with little turnover, and closely managed [20,000-plus employees]. Any individual having a problem could quickly and easily get support through peer relationships or by contacting another manager. Any manager demonstrating such immaturity and insecurity would immediately find his career declining and would be told the reason. This would be done without publicity." *(male)*

"Women would have to be brought under a new and stricter dress code." *(male)*

As one might expect, the degree to which people see the EEOC rules as reasonable and necessary correlates closely with the degree to which they think sexual misbehavior is a problem at work. Exhibit IV shows opinions on the guidelines.

In their comments many respondents maintain that, while the guidelines are reasonable in theory, it is unreasonable to expect much success in implementing them. These people consider them vague and unworkable because so much male-female interaction is ambiguous, private, and varied.

A 31-year-old man who manages special projects in a small trade association observed: "Too much of whatever harassment and/or sexual activity that occurs between employees is subject to interpretation. While employees who are clearly harassing others can be disciplined, I suspect that clear-cut cases will be hard to identify or prove."

Consistent with their perception of the seriousness of the problem, most male managers (68%) think the guidelines will be "not difficult" to implement. Others expressed concern that the guidelines will "become a crutch for disgruntled employees." Asserted a 35-year-old advertising promotion manager for a very large manufacturer of consumer goods, "It could be used as a smokescreen to defend against legitimate performance reviews."

A number of the men agree with a 44-year-old CEO who declared that his bank could "take care of misconduct without government snoopervision." Even more men (and a few women) expressed sentiments like the following from the 40-year-old personnel director of a large health care enterprise: "The guidelines are procedurally OK, but people are reluctant to change deep-seated, culturally reinforced attitudes."

Replies to a question on company policies again show how lack of experience with them, as much as experience, affects opinions on the issue. For instance, although 68% of the men and 58% of the women think the EEOC guidelines will not be difficult to implement, few work for companies that have any rules governing harassment. As Exhibit V shows, a significant gap also exists between what most people favor as policy and what their organizations actually have. (Implementing such rules can sometimes mitigate corporate liability but is not an absolute defense as far as individual liability is concerned.)

The policies listed in Exhibit V received substantial support, except for the management statement disapproving of office flirtations. The lukewarm reception for this is consistent with the concern, expressed by younger people particularly, over legislation against love affairs and condemnation of camaraderie. Elsewhere, some 20% of the sample expressed neutrality, rather than agreement or disagreement, on the statement, "A little flirtation makes the workday more interesting." The 51-year-old male vice president of a large company wrote, "I do not favor any legislative attempts to interfere with natural female-male forms of communication. Vive la différence!"

Judging from many comments, smaller organizations rely more on peer pressure and informal controls to deal with misbehavior. Since such organizations in general do not suffer from the impersonal atmosphere of those with thousands of workers, they perhaps feel less need for written and formally enunciated rules. (Whether they ought to is another issue.) Wrote the male president of a professional service firm with fewer than 50 employees, "We wouldn't tolerate sexual harassment any more than we would lying or theft. However, we don't have formal procedures for dealing with any of these forms of misconduct."

That many companies fail to communicate to employees the directives they do have is clear from the responses. And we found a significant difference in men's and women's opinions as to whether their companies even have certain policies. The difference is described in the following table (the letters refer to the list in Exhibit V).

| Policy | Percent of respondents who say their company has this policy | |
| --- | --- | --- |
| | Men | Women |
| A | 33% | 25% |
| C | 20 | 14 |
| D | 15 | 11 |
| F | 19 | 14 |

Why this difference? Do respondents really understand whether the policy exists, or have some answered according to their perception of whether the policy is working? Women, who are predominantly in the lower echelons of organizations, may not know what company policy is—especially the sanctions developed for sexual harassers (policy A) and management directives asking department heads to take responsibility for preventing harassment (policy F). And managers may just assume that the policies exist or are working.

Which policies and approaches work? Which really promote an understanding of harassment, its damaging effects on employees, and its divisiveness? And which support women and men in their stands against such abuse? Here are respondents' suggestions:

- Make known, in a firm but subdued manner, the chief executive's attitude about sexual misconduct.
- Install an all-purpose procedure, bypassing any union channels, that allows people to

voice their concerns—including complaints of harassment—confidentially.
- Hold in-house consciousness-raising seminars to inform managers of the consequences of misbehavior.
- Assign responsibility for cases of harassment to a high-level person—a vice president or assistant to the chief executive. This person should be seen to have the ear and respect of senior management and have credibility in other issues as well.
- Foster strong peer relationships among women employees.
- Encourage women to confront harassers by letter, after a confidential consultation with an appropriate officer of the company.

The last suggestion is clearly crucial because no enunciated or implied policies, however firmly and evenly applied, can be effective unless victims attack the problem themselves. Also, the situations are so varied that they need individual responses. Sometimes harassment calls for forthright action, such as that recommended by the 56-year-old female treasurer of a small manufacturer of industrial goods: "I have been in the work force for 40 years and find that the female visual and verbal attitude of 'hands off' works. When I was an airline stewardess in 1946, I perfected a devastating hands-off look that still works today. 'Develop the look' is my advice to my daughters and employees."

At other times, a casual confrontation is more appropriate and effective. A 33-year-old woman, the general manager of a management consulting firm, wrote, "My boss has a habit of making sexual innuendos and jokes to female managers. We have not filed a complaint but have instead raised his consciousness. We immediately offer to take him up on his suggestion. I've said, 'OK, let's get on with it if you're that hot to trot.' He is generally a good guy and this embarrasses him and improves his behavior."

Numbers of men indicate that they don't know "where the line is"—don't know when a joke that is funny to them is offensive to women. They believe it is up to women to tell men when a remark is not funny. In our opinion, by failing to take action right away, the woman risks letting the harasser think that it is welcome. Before women feel safe enough to speak up, however, managers must promote a supportive atmosphere through enforced company policies that make clear what behavior is not permitted.

## A COMPLEX PROBLEM

"A lot of women hesitate to report sexual harassment because women: (1) don't think they'll be believed; (2) will be punished by smaller raises or cruddy jobs; (3) will be ostracized by male and female employees; (4) will be accused of inviting the advance; (5) have guilt feelings that perhaps it was invited subconsciously; (6) fear publicity; (7) are unsure exactly what is harassment and what is just interaction of people." *(female)*

The problem is not just an artificiality created by the numbers and the varying responses to our probing; it is real. We give the last word to the 37-year-old director of communications for a large financial institution. She wrote:

Sexual harassment is corporate rape and, as with rape on the streets, many people see the victim as responsible. Most of the time the victim who complains falls under suspicion and is thought of as "dingy."

Our company has a formal complaint system that allows employees to take problems to the chairman of the board without retribution. This procedure should be adequate to deal with complaints of sexual harassment, but it is not. It puts the burden of action on the victim, forc-

ing her to complain and continue complaining until something is done.

Always the "real world" issue surfaces. Women can't expect protection from confrontations that are offensive to them in one way or another. Can we hope to achieve in the workplace what we have never been able to achieve anywhere else in society? Women have to take responsibility for managing the conflicts in their lives. Most of us do.

Something that occurred in my office illustrates the problem for women and managers. A male employee who worked for me recently resigned his position. After he left, four women came forward and complained about his sexual overtures, which included statements about his ability to help them in their jobs. One of the women reported directly to him. All four had handled the situation deftly themselves.

The story points up a serious issue. If no one complains, how can management know? Here I sit, a female executive appalled by the idea of sexual harassment, while a male manager who reported to me was practicing it. (All of this is complicated, of course, by the fact that what one woman thinks is sexual harassment, another may never notice.)

Some evidence exists that the situation is changing but, regardless, I think it is extremely difficult for a man to understand the demeaning nature of sexual harassment to a woman and to investigate it objectively. Men don't understand what it is, and I find this to be true without exception. It is hard to recognize something as negative when it has been part of your own way of thinking, and harassment has survived in corporate locker room attitudes for a long time.

A man's view will always be colored by the way he behaves toward women and what he finds acceptable. . . . I do not mean to malign the motives of men, but simply to say they cannot understand what they have never experienced or been educated about. The more we women educate them, the better they'll be able to deal with this subject.

# EXHIBITS: Sexual Harassment

**EXHIBIT I**
VIEWS ON EXTREME BEHAVIOR
By percent of total respondents: 1,846*

|  |  | Not harassment | Possibly harassment | Sexual harassment | Don't know | Heard of or observed in company | Not heard of or observed in company |
|---|---|---|---|---|---|---|---|
| A. | "I can't seem to go in and out of my boss's office without being patted or pinched." | 1% | 8% | 90% | 1% | 14% | 83% |
| B. | "Mr. X has told me that it would be good for my career if we went out together. I guess that means it would be bad for my career if I said no." | 2 | 17 | 79 | 2 | 12 | 85 |
| C. | "Mr. X has asked me to have sex with him. I refused, but now I learn that he's given me a poor evaluation." | 1 | 20 | 78 | 1 | 10 | 87 |
| D. | "I have been having an affair with the head of my division. Now I've told him I want to break it off, but he says I will lose out on the promotion I've been expecting." | 4 | 7 | 87 | 2 | 7 | 90 |

*In some cases, throughout the exhibits, not all people answered all questions.

**EXHIBIT II**
VIEWS ON LESS EXTREME BEHAVIOR ACCORDING TO SUPERVISOR/COWORKER SPLIT
SAMPLE
(White form statements in boldface, colored form statements in lightface)

| | | Not harassment | Possibly harassment | Sexual harassment | Don't know | Heard of or observed in company | Not heard of or observed in company |
|---|---|---|---|---|---|---|---|
| A. | "Whenever I go into the office, my supervisor **(a man I work with)** eyes me up and down, making me feel uncomfortable." | 20% | 60% | 16% | 4% | 61% | 37% |
| | | **26** | **54** | **15** | **4** | **71** | **27** |
| B. | "My supervisor **(A man I work with)** starts each day with a sexual remark. He insists it's an innocent social comment." | 5 | 46 | 44 | 4 | 35 | 63 |
| | | **10** | **49** | **37** | **4** | **45** | **53** |
| C. | "Often in meetings my supervisor **(a man I work with)** continually glances at me." | 62 | 26 | 1 | 10 | 50 | 47 |
| | | **65** | **26** | **2** | **6** | **61** | **36** |
| D. | "Every time we meet, my supervisor **(a man I work with)** kisses me on the cheek." | 4 | 43 | 46 | 7 | 11 | 86 |
| | | **17** | **47** | **20** | **10** | **18** | **79** |
| E. | "My supervisor **(A man I work with)** asked me out on a date. Although I refused, he continues to ask me." | 10 | 39 | 48 | 4 | 26 | 71 |
| | | **33** | **41** | **20** | **5** | **42** | **56** |
| F. | "My supervisor **(A man I work with)** puts his hand on my arm when making a point." | 43 | 44 | 3 | 10 | 59 | 36 |
| | | **46** | **42** | **4** | **9** | **63** | **33** |

**EXHIBIT III**
SPLIT-SAMPLE RESPONSES TO FOUR VIGNETTES*
(White form statements in boldface, colored form statements in lightface)

| | Male | Female | Top management | Middle management | Lower management | Other |
|---|---|---|---|---|---|---|
| Number responding, colored form* | 489 | 412 | 245 | 332 | 289 | 62 |
| white form | 470 | 391 | 192 | 277 | 347 | 61 |

A. The president of a company walks into the office of his sales manager to congratulate him on setting a new record in sales. When he enters the office, he finds the sales manager standing very close to his secretary, who looks upset and flustered. When the president and sales manager are alone, what do you think the president would do—if he were typical of company presidents you have known or heard about? **(If you were the president, what would you do when you were alone with the sales manager?)**

| | | Male | Female | Top management | Middle management | Lower management | Other |
|---|---|---|---|---|---|---|---|
| a. | He **(I)** would do nothing, not knowing what had happened. | 33% | 30% | 30% | 33% | 32% | 35% |
| | | **30** | **25** | **27** | **30** | **29** | **15** |
| b. | He **(I)** would do nothing, not wanting to confront the sales manager on a personal matter such as this. | 13 | 36 | 20 | 24 | 26 | 29 |
| | | **1** | **1** | **1** | **1** | **1** | **2** |
| c. | He **(I)** would suggest to the sales manager that even the appearance of sexual behavior was unwise. | 47 | 3 | 42 | 39 | 37 | 27 |
| | | **61** | **66** | **63** | **61** | **63** | **77** |
| d. | He **(I)** would express strong disapproval to the sales manager. | 4 | 2 | 4 | 3 | 2 | 3 |
| | | **4** | **4** | **4** | **5** | **3** | **3** |
| e. | He **(I)** would tell the sales manager that if such behavior continued, it would have an adverse effect on his career. | 2 | 3 | 3 | 1 | 2 | 3 |
| | | **2** | **3** | **4** | **1** | **3** | **2** |

B. Two middle-level male executives **(A senior executive and a junior executive)** enter an elevator. One of them **(The junior executive)** turns to the other occupant, a female employee, and makes a suggestive remark about her body. Then he winks in amusement at his companion **(the senior executive).** If the companion **(senior executive)** were typical of those in your company, what would his response be?

| | | Male | Female | Top management | Middle management | Lower management | Other |
|---|---|---|---|---|---|---|---|
| a. | He would share the first executive's amusement. | 14% | 41% | 17% | 25% | 33% | 36% |
| | | **7** | **23** | **6** | **12** | **20** | **18** |
| b. | He would feel neutral, believing that if the woman objects, it's up to her to say so. | 19 | 21 | 21 | 25 | 18 | 36 |
| | | **9** | **17** | **13** | **13** | **13** | **13** |

Footnote on page 155.

(*Continued*)

**EXHIBIT III**
CONTINUED

| | | Male | Female | Top management | Middle management | Lower management | Other |
|---|---|---|---|---|---|---|---|
| c. | He would remain silent because it's an embarrassing issue to raise. | 23 | 21 | 24 | 22 | 19 | 24 |
| | | **7** | **14** | **8** | **10** | **12** | **10** |
| d. | He would indicate his disapproval by his coolness or aloofness. | 22 | 8 | 17 | 15 | 16 | 11 |
| | | **30** | **20** | **26** | **26** | **24** | **30** |
| e. | He would express disapproval within the woman's hearing. | 4 | 5 | 6 | 4 | 2 | 7 |
| | | **8** | **6** | **9** | **7** | **7** | **8** |
| f. | He would express disapproval when he and the other executive were alone. | 17 | 5 | 16 | 10 | 12 | 8 |
| | | **37** | **18** | **37** | **30** | **24** | **21** |

C. A female executive earning $40,000 a year is one of the most promising executives of either sex in her insurance company. She complains to the executive vice president in charge of her division **(A secretary complains to the vice president in charge of her division)** that her boss has been making unwelcome and persistent sexual advances to her. The vice president has reason to believe her even though, in a private talk, her boss insists that the woman has mistaken his "innocent" remarks and gestures. If you were the executive vice president, what would you do?

| | | Male | Female | Top management | Middle management | Lower management | Other |
|---|---|---|---|---|---|---|---|
| a. | I would wonder about the woman's ability to handle interpersonal relationships. | 4% | 2% | 4% | 3% | 3% | 3% |
| | | **1** | **1** | **1** | **1** | **1** | **2** |
| b. | I would advise the woman on how she might better deal with such behavior. | 20 | 20 | 15 | 23 | 20 | 18 |
| | | **12** | **11** | **14** | **13** | **9** | **10** |
| c. | I would offer the woman a transfer to another division. | 2 | 4 | 2 | 3 | 4 | 3 |
| | | **9** | **5** | **6** | **8** | **9** | **3** |
| d. | I would express my strong disapproval to the boss. | 25 | 16 | 23 | 21 | 18 | 13 |
| | | **29** | **21** | **27** | **27** | **25** | **26** |
| e. | I would inform the boss that if such behavior continued, it could have an adverse effect on his career. | 45 | 56 | 52 | 47 | 52 | 58 |
| | | **48** | **60** | **53** | **49** | **55** | **59** |

(Continued)

**EXHIBIT III**
CONTINUED

| | | Male | Female | Top management | Middle management | Lower management | Other |
|---|---|---|---|---|---|---|---|
| f. | I would discreetly arrange a transfer for the boss. | 3 | 3 | 3 | 3 | 4 | 3 |
| | | 1 | 2 | 1 | 1 | 1 | 0 |

D.  A female **(male)** executive with a large manufacturing company has been the object of persistent sexual advances from the male **(female)** vice president of a major customer. She **(He)** has tried to discourage these advances tactfully, but in the course of negotiating a new contract, the customer has suggested that she **(he)** might lose the contract if she **(he)** were not "friendlier." The woman **(man)** discussed the problem with the head of her **(his)** division. What do you think the typical division head would do?†

| | | Male | Female | Top management | Middle management | Lower management | Other |
|---|---|---|---|---|---|---|---|
| a. | Offer to transfer the woman **(man)** from the account. | 23% | 35% | 27% | 24% | 30% | 42% |
| | | 15 | 18 | 16 | 16 | 18 | 21 |
| b. | Encourage the woman **(man)** to parry the advances without offending the client. | 21 | 32 | 23 | 26 | 25 | 36 |
| | | 28 | 36 | 26 | 35 | 33 | 34 |
| c. | Encourage the woman **(man)** to be tactful but firm, regardless of the consequences | 45 | 28 | 43 | 38 | 34 | 31 |
| | | 33 | 26 | 35 | 29 | 28 | 25 |
| d. | Send a team to future negotiations with the client. | 33 | 30 | 36 | 29 | 32 | 34 |
| | | 24 | 33 | 27 | 29 | 27 | 31 |
| e. | Indicate disapproval to the client. | 7 | 3 | 4 | 6 | 6 | 6 |
| | | 1 | 2 | 1 | 2 | 1 | 0 |
| f. | Other | 6 | 4 | 7 | 6 | 6 | 2 |
| | | 9 | 9 | 7 | 7 | 8 | 7 |
| g. | Don't know. | 2 | 4 | 3 | 3 | 4 | 2 |
| | | 6 | 9 | 5 | 6 | 10 | 8 |

*Throughout the four sections of this exhibit, in order to determine readers' intuitive responses to the vignettes, we did not include as an option the correct legal approach—starting a full investigation in each situation depicted.
†Respondents were not limited to a single choice.

**EXHIBIT IV**

OPINIONS ON WHETHER THE EEOC GUIDELINES ARE REASONABLE AND NECESSARY
AND WHETHER THEY WILL BE DIFFICULT TO ADJUST TO

|  | Highly reasonable, very necessary | Reasonable, necessary | Reasonable, unnecessary | Unreasonable, very unnecessary | Not difficult |
|---|---|---|---|---|---|
| Total | 15% | 57% | 16% | 7% | 63% |
| Male | 5 | 51 | 27 | 11 | 68 |
| Female | 27 | 64 | 4 | 2 | 58 |
| Top management | 9 | 44 | 27 | 14 | 69 |
| Middle management | 13 | 59 | 17 | 6 | 64 |
| Lower management | 19 | 62 | 11 | 4 | 61 |

**EXHIBIT V**

OPINIONS ON COMPANY POLICIES

|  |  | Do you favor this policy? | Does your company have this policy? |
|---|---|---|---|
| A. | A management statement to all employees disapproving of sexual harassment. | 73% | 29% |
| B. | A management statement disapproving of office flirtations, even when mutual. | 28 | 9 |
| C. | Developing appropriate sanctions for sexual harassers. | 68 | 17 |
| D. | Orientation programs to make all new employees aware of company policy on sexual behavior at work. | 59 | 13 |
| E. | Developing materials—employee manuals, films, and so forth—to make all employees aware of this issue. | 44 | 8 |
| F. | A management directive that asks each department head to take responsibility for preventing sexual harassment in his or her department. | 68 | 16 |

# APPENDIX: The Legal Context

*by Grace L. Mastalli*

The law provides a variety of means by which victims of sexual harassment in the workplace can seek redress through legal action against their employers, directly against the harassers, or (as is often the case) against both.

## TITLE VII

The primary basis for action against employers is Title VII of the 1964 Civil Rights Act (as amended), which prohibits discrimination on the basis of sex in employment and provides the legal authority for the final interpretive guidelines on sexual harassment issued by the EEOC.* The final guidelines provide that:

"Unwelcome sexual advances, requests for sexual favors, and other verbal or physical conduct of a sexual nature constitute sexual harassment when (1) submission to such conduct is made either explicitly or implicitly a term or condition of an individual's employment, (2) submission to or rejection of such conduct by an individual is used as the basis for employment decisions affecting such individual, or (3) such conduct has the purpose or effect of unreasonably interfering with an individual's work performance or creating an intimidating, hostile, or offensive working environment."

The guidelines impose absolute liability on employers for the acts of supervisors regardless of whether the conduct was known to, or authorized or forbidden by, the particular employer.

The standard of employer liability for the acts of co-workers is somewhat less stringent. An employer is responsible for such acts if the employer knew, or should have known, of the conduct in question—unless the employer can demonstrate that it took immediate and appropriate action to correct the problem on learning of it.

Grace L. Mastalli, a lawyer, is senior associate of the Law and Public Management Program, National Institute of Education. She is also a member of the employment discrimination committee of the Women's Legal Defense Fund.

*"Guidelines on Discrimination on the Basis of Sex" (Washington, D.C.: Equal Employment Opportunity Commission, November 10, 1980).

Similarly, under the guidelines an employer may be liable for acts in the workplace committed by nonemployees if the employer knew, or should have known, of the conduct and failed to take appropriate corrective action. Moreover, a controversial section of the guidelines states that an employer may be held liable for sex discrimination against qualified third parties who have been denied opportunities or benefits granted to another who provided sexual favors to a mutual supervisor.

In addition to establishing standards for imposing liability, the guidelines make employers responsible for developing programs to prevent sexual misconduct in the workplace. The elements of an adequate prevention program are not specified, but they would probably include the adoption and dissemination of a strong policy statement prohibiting sexual harassment, presentation of the subject in employee training materials and orientation sessions, and development and publication of procedures for handling complaints in the organization—including a range of sanctions and remedies and information about employee rights.

Under the guidelines, an employer must also thoroughly investigate all complaints alleging sexual harassment and all instances potentially constituting harassment that come to the employer's attention through means other than formal complaints. Following an investigation, an employer is required to take immediate and appropriate corrective action to remedy any illegality detected and prevent its recurrence. Failure to do so constitutes a violation of Title VII as interpreted by the EEOC.

Although the guidelines in and of themselves lack the force of law, the courts accorded them some weight while they were still in interim form, and courts are likely to rely on them substantially in the future. In fact, to a large extent the guidelines only restate and amplify the evolving line of Title VII cases establishing employer liability for the sexual harassment of employees by other employees. For example, in a leading Title VII case on the issue of employer liability, *Miller* v. *Bank of America,* the U.S. Court of Appeals for the Ninth Circuit held an employer to be liable for the sexually harassing acts of its supervisors, even if the company has a policy prohibiting such conduct and even if the victim did not formally notify the employer of the problem.†

†600 F.2d 211 (1979).

This is also the standard articulated by the guidelines. However, in the provisions concerning any conduct that is offensive, conduct by co-workers and nonemployees, and third-party rights in the guidelines, the EEOC went beyond what the courts had established as harassment constituting sex discrimination under Title VII. Pending further litigation, it is difficult to assess whether the courts will adopt or qualify the EEOC's broad assignment of liability for and liberal definition of sexual harassment. However, in what may be a bellwether case, the guidelines recently received significant support from the U.S. Court of Appeals in Washington, D.C. In January 1981, the court ruled in effect that sexual harassment in and of itself is a violation of Title VII. The court said that the law does not require the victim to prove she resisted harassment and was penalized for the resistance. According to the decision in *Bundy* v. *Jackson,* employers are liable for sexual harassment in the workplace because it creates an offensive "discriminatory environment" by "poisoning the atmosphere of employment."

(Incidentally, employer reliance on the guidelines provides a defense to charges of discrimination where the acts of alleged discrimination were taken in reliance on the EEOC's interpretation.)

## CIVIL SUITS

Victims of sexual harassment are not limited to a Title VII cause of action; they may combine the sex discrimination claim with other civil charges against an employer in order to obtain a more extensive remedy and/or damages. Common law doctrines on assault, battery, and intentional infliction of distress—as well as actions for breach of contract— may be used to establish employer liability for sexual harassment in some circumstances where the elements of a *prima facie* Title VII case may be lacking.

The wide range of compensatory relief, including damages, available through common law actions, combined with what may be more easily met standards of proof, has encouraged victims of employment-related harassment to seek recovery directly from their harassers and, under the tort law doctrine of *respondeat superior,* to hold employers liable for the misconduct of their workers. (*Respon-*

*deat superior* is the theory that an employer is liable for all the acts of an employee committed "within the scope of employment.")

Case law suggests that the courts may broadly construe what constitutes "the scope of employment" in order to establish employer liability for acts of sexual harassment. In such cases, however, some damages could be mitigated by the existence of a strong employer-sponsored harassment prevention program.

Sexual harassment that results in the wrongful dismissal of the victim and economic loss may also provide the basis for a suit against the employer for interference with an employment contract or breach of contract. In such cases an employer may be liable for back pay and conceivably even for damages awarded for mental suffering that the harassment causes. (As a rule, courts do not award damages for mental suffering in breach of contract actions unless the breach is of such a kind that serious emotional disturbance is to be expected or likely.)

Similarly, although litigation of this issue is not complete, employers may be subject to liability for breach of contract involving sexual harassment in instances where the victim is unable to demonstrate the degree of harm required under tort law.

## CRIMINAL ACTIONS

An extreme instance of sexual harassment in the workplace may also constitute a criminal offense— ranging from criminal assault and battery to self-exposure to rape or other sexual assault—and may subject the perpetrator to prosecution. The nature of such actions varies with state jurisdiction but normally would not involve employer liability. Under certain circumstances and in some jurisdictions, however, employers may be subject to civil liability related to such criminal actions for failing to provide a safe and secure work environment.

## SUMMARY

The combination of Title VII, as broadly construed by the EEOC, and the availability of a wide range of other civil actions provides a multitude of ways to establish employer liability for sexual harassment in the workplace. The courts can fashion remedies involving substantial victim compensation for harassment without making a finding of discrimination. Moreover, the flexibility afforded by this combination means that one or more claims against the employer could emerge from the factual circumstances surrounding almost any charge of work-related sexual harassment.

The employer's sole protection against liability is prevention of harassment. In those cases where prevention proves impossible, the employer's actions will, at least under common law, help limit damages.

# Three Short Cases on Sexual Harassment

## WITHOUT RECOURSE*

Jane, a new graduate from Cornell and a deferred admit to HBS, had accepted a job with Elexon, Inc., a high-tech company located in San Francisco. She had been impressed with the Elexon representative, Mr. Lindsay, who had interviewed on campus, and was thrilled to discover, upon accepting the offer, that he would be her supervisor.

Upon reporting for work on September 1, 1980, Jane found to her disappointment that Mr. Lindsay had been promoted, and her supervisor was to be a middle-aged engineer, Mr. Wang. The post was Mr. Wang's first management position.

For her first assignment, Jane was assigned to work with a Harvard MBA, Mike Furnell, on a short, six-week project. Mike intimated to Jane that in the absence of a training program, she could use him as an information source on everything that was happening in the company.

After the first month at work, during which Jane felt she was learning a lot and enjoying it, Mike invited Jane and other office mates on a day-long bicycle ride. (Jane had decided not to mix her social and professional lives, but not having any friends in San Francisco, she agreed to go along.) It was an enjoyable day. However, Jane refused when one week later, Mike proposed that they go on a hiking trip together.

During the following week, Mike pestered Jane, who continued to refuse his advances. In mid-October Jane arrived back to her desk to find a one-page note from Mike criticizing her for sloppy work on the project which they had just completed. Jane believed she had performed well, and took Mike's criticisms as "sour grapes." She approached Mike, who replied that "she had the means to change his opinion."

In the ensuing month, Mike began to circulate derogatory rumors about Jane in the office. He followed this with two more letters again accusing her of poor performance. At this point, the office atmosphere, as perceived by

Jane, had become very strained because of the number of rumors circulating.

One Saturday evening, Mike visited Jane's apartment building, demanding that she let him into her apartment. She was frightened, but refused. Instead, she called her parents in New York, who advised her to tell all to her supervisor, who was also Mike's boss.

Jane presented Mr. Wang with the letters on the following Monday and told him the full details of the situation. To her shock, he was unmoved, and said it was none of his business, that it was her own personal matter and she should look after it.

Jane then met with a higher-level manager who was also unhelpful, but said he would see what he could do. At this stage, Jane wondered whether, indeed, it was she who was naive and overreacting. She found she could no longer concentrate and began to dread coming to work in the morning. She avoided Mike as much as possible.

## THE RISK OF KNOWLEDGE*

On Friday morning, Claudia Schneider arrived at her office at the usual time of 7:30 and was surprised to see Janet Cronin seated in the reception area of the Human Resources Department. Janet was visibly distressed and looked as if she had been crying for some time. Claudia ushered her into her office, where Janet told her, even before she removed her coat, that she was resigning, effective immediately.

Janet had been hired 4½ months earlier as senior secretary to Jonah Albert, 54, division head at Academic, Inc. Janet was a graduate of Katherine Gibbs Secretarial School and had joined Academic, Inc. immediately after her graduation from the program.

As part of Janet's orientation to Academic, Inc., Claudia had been responsible for providing explanations of corporate policies and em-

*Copyright © 1984 by the President and Fellows of Harvard College.
Harvard Business School case 9·384·274.

ployment benefits. Her presentation included a discussion of laws governing equal opportunity, affirmative action, and sexual harassment. All new employees received an employee handbook which confirmed the company's commitment to compliance with the above regulations.

The reason Janet gave for her resignation was sexual harassment by her immediate supervisor. The single incident involved had occurred the previous evening. Janet had worked several nights during the week in order to complete an extensive report for her boss. As a nonexempt employee, she would receive additional compensation, at time and one-half, for all hours over 40 worked during the week. By Thursday evening at 8:15, she had completed the typing of the report and was preparing to leave when her supervisor stepped out of his office and thanked her for her effort over the past few days. He suggested that he buy her dinner in appreciation of her dedication. In the past, whenever they had to work late, Mr. Albert would treat any of his staff still in the office to a sandwich, or occasionally they would send out for Chinese food. Tonight, though, since their work was done and they were heading home, he suggested eating out to "celebrate" the completion of the report. Because of its proximity to their office, Mr. Albert chose one of his favorite restaurants, Locke-Ober's.

Janet went on to describe a sumptuous dinner, complete with a before-dinner drink, wine during the meal, and brandy in the lounge afterward. It was clear from her tone and the details she recalled that Janet had never previously enjoyed such an impressive or costly meal. It was approaching 10:30 when they finished, and Mr. Albert, wary of public transportation at such a late hour, offered to drive Janet to her home. When she declined, he pressed a $10 bill into her hand and stood with her in the restaurant lobby until the taxi he had called arrived. As she stepped into the cab, he thanked her again for her effort on the report and for the pleasure of her company during dinner.

Reminding Janet that all conversations she had with employees were held in the strictest confidence, Claudia asked, "But what *else* did he say? What did he actually *do?*" Janet looked embarrassed and answered, "He spent over $100 on me last night. He took me to a restaurant I thought I'd never see the inside of and kept telling me what a terrific secretary I was. He didn't have to do or say anything more. It was clear what he wanted."

Claudia wondered what she should say next to Janet and what she would tell Mr. Albert when he called later that morning to say that Janet had neither come to work nor called with an explanation.

## THIS SIDE UP*

As Randy walked back to his office, he replayed the events of the last half-hour in his mind. He was not certain that what he had witnessed in the conference room fell under the company's EEOC guidelines—he was even less sure what he should do about it, if anything.

The event that concerned him occurred during a company-sponsored "going away" party for Karen Douglas, an engineering supervisor who had been transferred to another district office. Karen had been in the district for several years, first as an engineer and now as a supervisor. In an industry dominated by men, Karen had been very successful in performing all her duties, and had established good relationships with everyone she worked with. She often joined co-workers and subordinates in after-hours parties and seemed to enjoy the joking and camaraderie of being "one of the boys."

The party tradition was long-standing in the district. Everyone in the office who knew the guest of honor was welcome to attend the conference room party which featured cake and soft drinks (provided by the company) on company time. Over the years, the parties began to include a "celebrity roast," in which the co-workers of the honoree would present both gag gifts and nice gifts, accompanied by numerous

"embarrassing moment" stories. For the most part, the history of the roasts was trouble-free. But Randy did recall that the tradition had been discontinued for a short time a few years earlier due to a particularly crude roast that involved a male engineer and a "gift" of a half-dressed female doll.

Today's roast had started well enough. Because Karen was so well known in the district, over 50 people (male and female) from all departments and all levels of management turned out. Several of the engineers (all male) who worked in Karen's group had spoken, telling stories and presenting some nice gifts—a camera lens, a collage of pictures, etc. Finally, the last of the speakers, also a subordinate of Karen's, began. Ron had been with the company about three years, and had come to the district during the last year. Karen was the first woman supervisor Ron had worked for. Ron's presentation today was long, but its message was clear. He spent 15 minutes describing (in fun, Randy thought at first) the difficulties of having a woman for a boss, particularly of trying to explain to outsiders that the woman he was with in the field *was* his boss. He concluded the talk by presenting Karen with a T-shirt on the back of which was printed "That ain't no lady, that's my boss."

"Had he stopped there," Randy thought, "I probably wouldn't have considered the event an EEOC problem."

But Ron didn't stop here. As he explained to the gathering, "I wouldn't want people in the new district making the same mistake with Karen." And then he showed the front of the shirt to the audience—"This Side Up." The faces of the people in the crowd mirrored Randy's own dismay, and only a few embarrassed chuckles broke the silence that followed. Karen, who usually took kidding in stride, flushed a deep red and folded the T-shirt so only the back could be seen.

Now, Randy had to decide what to do. As the engineering manager for the district, he was responsible for appraising and counseling the engineers and supervisors who worked under him. As part of the management team, he had

*Copyright © 1984 by the President and Fellows of Harvard College.
Harvard Business School case 9·384·275.

an even greater responsibility to see that the policies of the company were followed. The company did have a stated EEOC policy, which included a rating of "EEO Sensitivity" on the formal appraisal form. As far as he knew, though, no one had ever invoked the rating and even if they did, he was not sure what it would mean. Besides, formal appraisals were six months off, and the problem could blow over in a day. On the other hand, Randy had to consider what to do if Karen decided to press the issue on a legal basis.

# Lex Service Group, Ltd.: Developing the Guidelines (A)

In 1978 the British firm of Lex Service Group Ltd. decided to shifts its organization away from its current highly centralized form towards a more decentralized management structure. In the past the company had been heavily dependent on the values and decision making of its chairman and chief executive officer, Trevor Chinn—and on those of his father before him, who had been the previous CEO. Although Trevor Chinn was convinced that devolution[1] was a necessary organizational structure for Lex Service Group Ltd., and although he had the utmost confidence in his senior managers, in reviewing the firm's devolution efforts a year later, he and Lex's senior management agreed that they needed some formal means for insuring that the corporation maintain a cohesive character and strategy as its decision making became less dependent on Chinn's own personal judgment. Consequently, Chinn and his policy group drafted a set of twenty statements, here entitled the "Guidelines," which summarized the values and financial objectives of the company as they perceived them. The statement was then circulated to the senior managers in the firm to obtain their comments, and a final draft of the Guidelines was examined at length at a senior managers meeting in September of 1979. A short while later the revised Guidelines were adopted and the appropriate authority and role of each senior managerial level was determined within the context of that statement (for full text see Exhibit 1). The following cases represent some of the major problems which occurred in the first year of applying the Guidelines. Although some of the situations are a composite of several managers' experiences, all opinions expressed herein are direct quotations or close paraphrases of statements made by Lex senior management.

---

[1] Originally a government term for the federal status of Scotland and Wales, "devolution" was adopted by British business to signify a partially decentralized organization.

**EXHIBIT 1**
GUIDELINES FOR CORPORATE CONDUCT

1  The company will operate a diversified range of service and distribution businesses on an international basis, aiming to develop over the next decade so that 50% of profits before interest and tax are earned outside the U.K., with no single business activity in any country contributing more than 25% of profits before interest and tax.

2  The company will be honest and responsible in its dealings with all its stakeholders, considering shareholders and employees to be of equal importance.

3  The company will operate as a management company, and as part of the process of continual improvement in management capability will seek to recruit only those managers whose intelligence, as well as qualifications or experience place them in the top quartile of their roles by national standards.

4  The company will not permit discrimination between employees or in recruitment on the grounds of sex, nationality, creed or color.

5  The company will work within the laws of any country in which it operates.

6  The company will not operate in a country where the standards of business conduct do not allow the company to meet its own values, policies and constraints.

7  The company will offer each employee the fullest possible opportunity to develop his or her potential within the organization.

8  The company will provide all its customers with a quality of product/service which is substantially above the average for the market segment in which it is operating at a price which yields a sufficient value for money to encourage long-term customer loyalty.

9  The company aims to increase pretax earnings per share, when measured over five years,
   • At least as fast as the upper quartile of U.K. companies of comparable size.
   • Noticeably faster than the weighted average rate of inflation for the countries in which the company operates.

10  The company aims to achieve a pretax return on shareholders' funds of at least 25% per annum.

11  The company will develop an adequate supply of qualified, competent personnel to allow for a choice of internal candidates for all managerial positions.

12  The company will not close a business activity unless all the following conditions are met:
   • The scale of its performance shortfall is such that it threatens the long-term achievement of the relevant business group's objectives.
   • It is demonstrated that all possibilities for alternative developments for the business have been exhausted.
   • There is no possibility of sale of the business rather than closure within a timescale which would protect the business group's objectives.

13  The company will:
   • Provide working and off-work* conditions which are amongst the best for relevant occupations, particularly in respect of safety, and in no circumstances will such conditions fall below statutory or nationally agreed minimum standards.
   • Offer all employees a remuneration and benefits package which reflects upper quartile practice (with special reference to the practice of high performance companies in that segment) for the appropriate industry or activity (overall industrial practice in the case of managers).
   • Be honest and open towards employees on issues that affect them, provided that the disclosure of the information involved would not be prejudicial to the interests of the business or of other employees.
   • Provide all employees with adequate training to enable them to perform their duties efficiently and the appropriate

*On the Lex site but away from the actual place where work is conducted.

(Continued.)

**EXHIBIT 1**
CONTINUED

training to enable them to develop their potential.

- Not dismiss any employee for inadequate performance unless a full disciplinary procedure at least meeting the company's standards has been followed to its conclusion. Such conclusion does not preclude a fair and mutually acceptable financial settlement.
- Not make any employee redundant prior to the offer of any vacant position of a suitable nature in the company. If such an offer is declined, or if no such position exists, compensation must be at least equal to the company's minimum standards.
- Not dismiss any employee who has been overpromoted prior to the offer of any vacant position at their former level for which they are suitably qualified. If such an offer is declined, or if no such position exists, compensation must be at least equal to the company's minimum standards.
- Give any employee who transfers with a business which is purchased from Lex, and who is not offered the alternative of continued employment with Lex in a suitable position, reasonable compensation for any reduction in benefits suffered as a result of the transfer, together with a guarantee of at least Lex redundancy terms should that employee be made redundant by the purchasing company within the first year following the transfer.
- Give every employee the right to appeal to higher management through an established grievance procedure if they feel that their treatment by their immediate manager is unfair.

14 The company is committed to a policy of promotion from within, and will prefer an internal candidate for a vacant position whenever this is consistent with the maintenance of adequate managerial stability and the need to meet the objective of employing top quartile managers.

15 The company will be relatively high geared, in order to fund a high rate of growth and maximize returns on shareholders' funds.

16 In order to ensure that there is a very low probability of any financial pressures threatening the corporate values, the company will maintain an acceptable balance between the equity base and borrowings in the light of the risks inherent in the trading activities and in the external environment.

- Net borrowings will not normally exceed 75% of shareholders' funds less goodwill and will never exceed 90%. Net borrowings will only be allowed to exceed 75% if there are clearly implementable plans to return to this ratio within the next twelve months.
- Interest charges, recalculating interest at 12%, will be covered not less than $3\frac{1}{2}$ times by profit before interest and tax.
- Current assets will not be used to secure debt.

17 The amount of goodwill in the balance sheet will not exceed 25% of shareholders' funds, including goodwill.

18 Debt maturities will be spread as evenly as possible over future years and will extend as far as possible. Not more than 10% of total debt will be repayable in any of the next five years.

19 Each Business Group must be organized so as to be able to seek technological solutions towards enhancing its competitive position and meeting its own and corporate objectives and goals.

20 The performance of each business, in relation to its specified strategic plans and goals, must be measured constantly against the performance of its competitors.

## HISTORY OF THE COMPANY

Lex Service Group Ltd. was a publicly owned, diversified company with reported net revenues of approximately £500 million and retained profit of £15 million in 1979 (at the time, approximately $30 million). Although its headquarters were located in central London, the company's six decentralized business groups (in U.S. terms, divisions) were comprised of approximately 30 subsidiary companies located throughout the U.K. Lex had recently made substantial acquisitions in the United States and was planning over the next five years to expand its overseas operations until they yielded 50% of the company's profits before interest and tax.

Originally a string of parking garages and petrol stations, Lex was publicly incorporated in 1928 in London, and the company name (then Lex Garages Limited) was derived from the location of the first garage on the corner of Lexington and Brewer Streets. In 1945 Mssrs. Rosser and Norman Chinn became directors of Lex, and in 1954 Chinn Family Holdings Ltd. acquired the company's total issued share capital, which was again issued publicly in 1960. In 1980 the Chinn family owned less than 10% of the firm's shares.

Under Chinn leadership, Lex began a long series of acquisitions which continued steadily to the present time. In the 1950s and early '60s Lex's new subsidiaries bore some relationship to the historical origins of the firm: vehicle sales and servicing operations were expanded, and an exclusive franchise to import and distribute Volvo automobiles was obtained. In 1968 Trevor Chinn assumed the role of chief executive at the age of 33 upon the retirement of his father, Rosser. By 1970 Lex had become the largest British Leyland car distribution group, the second largest distributor for Rolls Royce, and the largest distributor of heavy trucks in the U.K. Over the next three years Lex also moved into nonautomotive service businesses which included the acquisition of transportation and leasing firms, several hotels, and an employment agency. Following this period of rapid diversification, the company was forced to stop expansion and capital investment and to start on a process of extensive rationalization in order to survive Britain's 1973–74 economic crisis. Wishing to avoid a repeat of that experience, Lex resolved to diminish its U.K. dependency. It expanded its involvement in the deluxe hotel market by acquiring four hotels in the U.S., including the Whitehall in Chicago and the Royal Orleans, and in 1979 acquired two vehicle parts distribution concerns in California. The acquisition of a leading U.S. industrial distributor of electronic components in 1981 furthered the company's commitment to non-U.K. expansion.

From the outset of his leadership, Trevor Chinn had played a very strong role in the company's strategic and organizational decision making, particularly during the '73–'74 crisis. Chinn, however, believed that as the company became larger and more diversified, and its financial position more stable, it would be best for him to diminish his own involvement in the operational decisions of the firm. While Lex had nominally adopted a divisional, decentralized structure as early as 1970, it was not until 1978 that the company fully addressed the issue of decentralization and formally devolved into six business groups, each of which was headed by a group manager and had its own functional staff. A corporate staff was centered in London and the chairman's policy group comprised the two chief operating officers, who supervised the U.S. and U.K. groups, respectively, and the directors of finance, personnel and corporate strategy. Like Trevor Chinn, the firm's senior management was unusually young by British standards: one of the chief operating officers and several group managers were under age 40, and none was over age 50. All of them had been with the firm during its unstable strategic and organizational shifts during the '70s, and had personally witnessed the company's chaotic series of rapid hirings, firings, and promotions during that period.

When the Guidelines were proposed in 1979, none of the group managers found the statements to be extraordinarily different from his or her own way of doing business. Trevor Chinn's profound religious beliefs were well known in the corporation and had always been expressed in practical terms: in his private life he was an active Zionist and also served on several secular British public service committees, while as chairman of Lex Service Group Ltd. he had always emphasized a concern for customer service and employee welfare. The Guidelines seemed to be a consistent—if somewhat ideal- ized—articulation of those same beliefs, and group managers did not find it difficult to agree to comply with the twenty statements for a year's trial period. At the end of that time, it was found that, as could be expected, the Guidelines had been less easy to interpret and follow when applied to practical problems. But after a serious review of those problems at the 1980 senior managers' meeting, it was agreed to retain the Guidelines at Lex Service Group Ltd.

# Lex Service Group, Ltd.: Closing Portsmouth Depot (B)

Keith Hampson,[1] group manager (in U.S. terms a divisional president) for Lex Service Group Ltd., had just completed what he himself defined as one of the worst times in his career. Two months ago it had been finally decided that the Portsmouth Depot had to be closed or sold, and, although Lex had found a buyer who was willing to employ 50 Lex workers, and another 15 could be relocated within his own group, Keith and his personnel staff had spent the next two months working out arrangements for the other 50 employees who were slated to lose their jobs. Although the company had a firm policy that, wherever possible, alternative jobs would be offered the workers when a location was closed or sold, in this instance there were no other Lex facilities in the Portsmouth area, and few workers had been happy about the idea of relocation. Keith had just finished the last employee negotiation and it had been

one of the most painful discussions of all: John Sargent, the Portsmouth facilities manager, age 57, with 30 years of service at Lex, had had to be made redundant. There simply were no comparable positions for which he would be suited in the Lex company.

It was precisely in considering seven department managers at Portsmouth who, like John, all had over 25 years with Lex and were about ten years away from retirement, that the Board of Directors had almost rejected Hampson's proposal to sell the Portsmouth Depot. Hampson had had to argue long and hard for the Portsmouth sale—preparation for that particular proposal had taken four months—and in the end he was not really certain that he had made the right decision.

## LAYARD MOTOR TRANSPORT LTD. AND THE PORTSMOUTH DEPOT

Keith Hampson had been with Lex Service Group for 11 years, and at age 49 was one of its

---

[1] With the exception of the chairman, the names of all Lex employees and subsidiaries are disguised.

oldest senior managers. His business group, Layard Motor Transport Ltd., consisted of five subsidiary companies which specialized in heavy hauling. The Portsmouth Depot was one of four depots comprised by Victoria Transport Ltd., a Layard subsidiary, servicing the transport of steel in the southern half of the U.K. That particular subsidiary, which was acquired with heavy investment in 1970, was now sorely handicapped by British Steel's alarming production problems, and it had been losing its market share at the rate of about 20% in the first half of 1980. Keith Hampson felt that there were too many Victoria depots in the southern region, and that the overall number should be reduced from four to three. Portsmouth was the obvious choice: its shortfall had been worse than those of the other three depots, partially because local zoning laws restricted the hours during which the lorries could operate, and the business was smaller there than in the other three locations. With the loss of 40% of its business in 1979, Portsmouth's return on investment had dropped from 26% the previous year to 8%. Moreover, its operating costs were higher than average because previous rationalizations of Layard depots in the region had left Portsmouth with a staff level that was higher than was strictly necessary. The two depots which were closest to Portsmouth would be able to absorb the Portsmouth business easily, but Hampson could not justify financially the continued employment of the seven special category department managers with long-term service: to retain them, Layard Motors would have to place them in "nonjobs" at the other depots, which would cost the company £50,000 per annum. Hampson suspected that several might even welcome redundancy over relocation if the settlement were high enough.

The Board, however, was very reluctant to approve a closure. As Chairman Trevor Chinn put it, "We just don't have the option of putting 100 people out of work—we've got nothing to offer them instead." Some members even felt that business might pick up in a year, and that it would be better to wait for the industry to turn the corner than lose 100 experienced em-

ployees and a facility which might be needed later.

Throughout the Portsmouth discussions two statements in particular from the Guidelines had been appealed to as a basis for the Board's decision:

1  The company will not close a business activity unless all the following conditions are met:

   • The scale of its performance shortfall is such that it threatens the long-term achievement of the relevant Business Group's objectives.
   • It is demonstrated that all possibilities for alternative developments for the business have been exhausted.
   • There is no possibility of sale of the business rather than closure within a time scale which would protect the Business Group's objectives.

2  The company will be honest and responsible in its dealings with all its stakeholders, considering shareholders and employees to be of equal importance.

Before deciding to recommend a shutdown of the facilities, Hampson had tried to find a solution that would meet the financial needs of the company and still keep the Portsmouth people under Lex employment. He scouted the area and conducted an extensive study of the possibilities of undertaking a similar business at Portsmouth, but was unable to discover a viable alternative. Even if he *had* found another transport business, inherent problems at that particular location and a general shortfall of productivity in comparison with the other three depots suggested that the steel industry was not the only reason for the depot's bad return, and that a new business would not necessarily provide any better margin. But despite these problems and threatening forecasts, Keith Hampson was personally unsure whether he could honestly say that the Portsmouth Depot's performance "threatened the long-term achievement" of his Business Group's objectives, as the Guidelines prescribed. In fact, he personally believed that no single business in his group would ever be substantial enough to threaten the whole.

Joe Stearns, director of Corporate Strategy, felt otherwise:

> You may argue that no one subsidiary could threaten the company, but we could find a combination of many small events which would certainly threaten the corporate strategy if not the ultimate existence of the company. We've already decided that we need to make some dramatic changes in the businesses we've got now if we're going to generate a higher gross and higher profitability. Our whole U.S. expansion seeks to break our dependency on the U.K. economy and particularly on industries like British Steel, and now you want to keep a losing business open. It can't be done. We've got to move large numbers around, and that's going to mean either lots of redundancy, lots of closure, or being able to sell big chunks of the company and simultaneously take the even bigger risk of moving into new ventures. If you don't feel free to move in a lot of small instances in order to be able to make the larger, grander moves, then in a sense the small instances do threaten the whole.

Morey Lear, Corporate Personnel director, strongly disagreed:

> Look, these closure constraints aren't absolute. You can't pretend Keith's divestment analysis is based on a precise science—the long-term advantages of closure or continuing Portsmouth are quite unclear. But you can be sure that even the very best rationalization would still leave at least 100 people out of a job, and although we have another policy which forbids making any employee redundant prior to the offer of a vacant position of a suitable nature at Lex Service Group, you and I both know that Portsmouth people aren't going to relocate to a Newcastle just to work with us. That means, given the 12% unemployment rate in the Portsmouth area, that we will be putting those people on the dole. Besides, for every one driver Keith might look

to relocate, another group manager will have six more he'd like to send to Keith.

Joe Stearns intervened:

> Aren't you really talking about two different issues? There's a long-term consideration which absolutely must be given the first priority, and then we can adjust the short-term decision making accordingly. Now the number one issue is whether Portsmouth fits into the long-term objectives of the company: cash generation, less dependence on the automotive and steel industries and on the U.K. economy as a whole, with substantial expansion abroad. At this point employee welfare is not really the main consideration. Once we have the financial considerations fully in line, and perhaps decide to close Portsmouth, *then* we can return to that portion of the Guidelines dealing with employee redundancy and closure constraints, and we can very well follow the spirit of the statement. But to try to justify the main decision by fooling around with the wording in the Guidelines is just silly. If Hampson's financial analysis is not a precise science, the same holds even more strongly for the relationship between employee welfare and shareholder interest. It's helpful to ensure that we don't transgress the spirit of the Guidelines, but I'm afraid Layard Motors' particular role at the moment is to generate cash. And if Portsmouth's productivity is as hopeless as it appears in Keith's analysis, then the real responsibility is to manage divestiture as humanely as possible. That's a very important role, but I'm not sure the Guidelines emphasize this part of our management philosophy strongly enough.

Although he remained quiet and heard out everyone's view, Trevor Chinn had become increasingly agitated during the discussions. The memory of the 1973–74 divestments and redundancies was still very sharp, and he blamed much of that scramble for survival on his own failure to anticipate long-term consequences during the acquisitions of the '60s. That and the sudden downturn of the British economy, the announcement of a massive increase in oil prices by OPEC, and the upsurge of Japanese competition in the steel industry had forced

Lex Service Group and many other U.K. firms to make some very drastic short-term decisions. That period in the company's history had been marked by an extremely aggressive management style, and Trevor now wanted a more secure top management team which was able to consider both the long and the short term and be willing to assess these factors on their own but with less coldbloodedness than in the past.

The problem was that the company had thrived on bright young managers who were very good—perhaps even inspired—at handling the short-term implications of the corporation's strategy, and Trevor himself freely admitted to putting too much pressure on the short term in the past when things got difficult. In a sense the Guidelines had evolved out of a desire to correct this tendency, to provide greater security for employees, and better value for money for the customers through long-term stability of the businesses. Trevor was now prepared to allow for a certain amount of time and training in order to implement a truly decentralized management team which could be relied upon to consider customarily the long-term implications of its decision making, but in this case the financial and employee considerations seemed to him squarely equal, and he feared that his group managers were tending to recommend divestment of facilities in the course of which Lex would lose some very good people. He fully understood and admired the long-term strategic planning which Hampson had prepared, but he was also afraid that the short-term adaptation—a Portsmouth divestment which would cost at least 50–100 people (some with very long service) their jobs—was not consistent with the company standards as agreed upon in the Guidelines. Why wouldn't it be possible to meet the company's long-term objectives by closing more recently acquired businesses where Lex did not have such long service from its employees? Or wait out the short term and reduce headcount through natural wastage?

The Board of Directors had been unable to reach a decision, and subsequently Keith Hampson was able to find two companies in unrelated kinds of businesses which were willing to buy the Portsmouth Depot. One potential buyer had offered a substantially higher price than the other, but the lower bidder had also indicated that it was willing to keep some of the current Lex employees. The different nature of that business, however, precluded its taking on any of Layard Motors' department managers at the Portsmouth facility. Keith estimated that the sale to the lower bidder would cost Lex approximately £100,000 altogether in redundancy pay, plus employee retraining and cleaning up the Portsmouth property.

Hampson's own inclinations were to sell Portsmouth to the lower bidder on the condition that 50 of the Lex employees be offered positions with the new company, and that any redundancies among them in the first year would be accompanied by settlements equal to or better than Lex standards. While this decision was not ideal—even after relocations within Lex, approximately 50 employees at Victoria Transport would still lose their jobs—Hampson felt that if the business weren't sold now, it would be closed later, all 115 employees would be out of work, and the costs to Lex Service Group Ltd. would be even higher. As one group manager put it, "Some employees have to suffer for the greater good. We can't have 1% of the company threatening the welfare of the other 99%."

The Chairman of the Board eventually agreed to a sale to the lower bidder, but continued to chafe at the decision. He was heard to remark as he left the meeting, "I still have my conscience: I don't like this idea that whenever the company makes a big mistake, other people—not management—end up paying. That's one of the biggest problems in business today. Well, we're going to do everything we can to be fair with those Portsmouth people, even if it costs us more than we would otherwise have to pay."

• • •

After the Board's decision to sell Portsmouth, Keith Hampson had called together all his personnel directors at Layard Motors Transport to discuss the Portsmouth sale, and to determine which fifty employees would be rehired by the purchasing company, which employees might be relocated to other Lex businesses, and which would be made redundant.

Hampson felt that the Lex Guidelines clearly indicated that every employee should have the opportunity to relocate if at all possible, and that the first task of the personnel people was to hunt out all available positions within the company. After they had a better idea of how many redundancies they were actually facing, they would decide the basis on which employees would be kept or be made redundant, and the terms of the redundancy. Some of the directors had real difficulties with the relocation policy. One argued that there were so few job openings that the issue was irrelevant anyway, while another, Adam Mills, expressed his long-standing opinion that Lex Service Group Ltd. was generally too inclined to hire and promote from within even when an employee was ill-qualified for the job.

A major problem lay with four general managers with 30 years' service who were too young to retire early but not really suited for a promotion to a higher position. (It had been decided that the three others, who were in their early 60s, would retire early with larger-than-usual pensions.) Adam Mills argued that it would be cruel to promote them beyond their competency and cited cases where line managers had been moved up and out of Layard into other parts of Lex simply because they had been "good lads," and he felt that those moves had ultimately led to their quitting Lex altogether with a great deal of mental anguish and company cost besides. Placing them in nonjobs was not the answer either. Mills had seen too many examples where jobs had been created which in the end gave little to anyone or to the company—moreover, he worried that that kind of organizational window dressing set a very bad precedent.

We have one structure; we change it; then we say to the world, "We created this job because the change is right." Then when it doesn't work out we change it back again. Wouldn't it be better to sit down and say, "Look, we have a problem. What can we do about it together?" That way people can retain their pride and can probably end up doing something else outside the organization or within it that they can do com-

fortably; therefore they're happier because they're under less stress, and everybody's faced it honorably.

Hampson disagreed. He felt that the long-service people had a particular attachment to Lex that transcended their position or salary, and that they had stayed with the company in part because they liked its character and wanted to work for such a firm. Lex in turn owed them its fullest possible consideration, and Hampson argued for a first-in, last-out redundancy policy.

Walter Royce, the youngest personnel director at Layard Motor Transport, argued strongly for a meritocracy. The older managers should be judged on the same basis as everyone else. Maybe the fact that they weren't really promotable indicated that they had been falling off in their performance. To keep them and others like them would only mean a gradually worsening rate of productivity throughout the rest of Layard. It would mean four fairly important positions in the revised depots might be filled by people who were not very competent, but on whom the success or failure of three depots and the jobs of over a thousand people would be dependent. Besides, on the first-in, last-out principle, the work force kept getting older and older with each rationalization, and that only aggravated the problem. That was in part why Portsmouth was where it was currently: previous rationalizations at Victoria Transport had always favored those with long service. Walter also questioned the loyalty of these people, which Hampson had felt was implied in their continued stay at Lex: "These managers won't be heartbroken; they've stayed because we pay them such high salaries they can't afford to leave. We've bound them to Lex with golden handcuffs. I feel more sorry for the younger managers whose salaries have been so high that they're now totally priced out of the market. Where will they go?"

When Hampson had later shared this discussion over a pint with another group manager, John Price, Price had absolutely exploded.

This whole relocation thing is a sham! It's a positive insult. Here are people who are relatively poor, who live in subsidized housing, and we'll say to them, "We've got a job for you in Newcastle. We can't give you a rented house in Newcastle, but we'll give you the company transfer payment, which is not particularly favorable if you're living in rented and going to rented accommodations. And your motorbike won't do up there, you'll have to get a car for that weather, but I'm sure you'll agree that we're trying to be fair." That just salves our conscience. Then we can say no one *had* to go. They won't relocate, they'd rather have redundancy. That way their subsidized rent is reduced and they get a lump of money besides. In my group we've offered 200 employees continuing employment at other depots and to date no one has accepted the offer. Put yourself in their position: you've got a corporate strategy that projects 50% of the company profit overseas. Would *you* relocate to the U.S.?

How much time have you spent discussing relocation anyway? How much has *that* cost the company? And I suppose you're going to offer them all huge redundancy benefits. I agree with the idea of fairness, but we're positively over-generous. We corrupt them. We offer them the alternative of a huge lump of money, bigger than they've probably ever had before, or the opportunity to move to a strange place at great cost. Which would you take? They'd be better off with a job, but they'll never take it. The only way to make money in this company is to do your job badly—at least you get a good settlement when you're made redundant.

I find this whole employee concern overplayed. There's no such security for management. Aren't we employees, too? When we were hired we knew Lex was a high-performance, high-pay company, and that means when the performance is down you're out. That's all right. I can live with that, and so can most people here. What we shouldn't be doing is creating a climate where being kicked out pays well. That just encourages abuse. I had a guy who took his redundancy on the Morrisgate closure, . . . dragged his feet, expressed his sorrow, got a lot of dough from us to ease our conscience, and then he signed up with our competitor.

In spite of Price's protest, Hampson and the corporate personnel director had worked out a plan which gave about 12% of the employees a chance for relocation. An added 40% would be hired by the new buyer. When these were added to the early retirements, disciplinary dismissals, and a bit of natural wastage, about forty-five people would have to be told that they were being made redundant. Hampson expected many of the employees to refuse relocation, and was prepared to offer each of them around £2,000 settlement on the average, and assist them in finding alternative jobs. Disclosing the sale of the Portsmouth Depot had not been easy.

It had been decided that because of the Guidelines on honesty to employees, the department managers would have to be told of the sale immediately. It was felt, however, that it would be detrimental to the interest of the company to tell the trade union at that time, since the regional official was on holiday and the company was hesitant to begin negotiations with an unknown union official. The morale of the department managers immediately dropped, and they had a difficult time planning the changes of personnel and transferring Portsmouth operations to the other two depots. The entire changeover had taken six weeks, and one manager had even approached Hampson with a demand for a payoff to keep quiet about the sale "so as to facilitate the shutdown."

Hampson eventually called all the Portsmouth employees together and announced the sale. Local press, radio and television reported the announcement, and one station tied it into a feature on the effect of Japanese steel production on Britain's steel industry. Over the following week the trade union pressed the company very hard to allow unlimited voluntary redundancy before applying LIFO (last-in, first-out). Hampson had resisted voluntary redundancy out of a fear that it might unbalance the mix of skills which the other depots required for available business. Even his desire to serve the needs of the special category long-service employees was thrown aside: the union was much more concerned about securing better compensation for shorter-service employees than it was about making special provisions for older employees with long service.

Negotiations had not been helped by a long-standing rivalry between the Victoria Transport depots at Portsmouth and Plymouth (where some of the workers were to be offered a chance to transfer), or by the timing of the union consultation. Layard was under a legislative requirement to consult with the trade union on any redundancy proposal "at the earliest opportunity . . . and in any event begin consultation . . . "; union officials expressed privately that they felt that they were being presented with a fait accompli which was not in line with the spirit of that legislation. Hampson had felt that any earlier consultation would have opened the way to negotiation, which would not only be unfair to the nonunion people, but would also introduce the possibility that Layard would be forced to make a settlement which was not in line with Lex's stated redundancy policies. Either he would be forced to propose too low a settlement and run the risk of having it accepted (in which case he would violate the minimal requirements of the Guidelines), or he would be forced to succumb to union clout and settle too high. By the end of the third meeting with the union and Portsmouth's general manager, Hampson began to wonder if Lex's redundancy policies were placing its own perceptions of what was right above the wishes of the people being made redundant and whether the company had a right to decide this issue for the workers.

A week after the announcement of the Portsmouth sale, negotiations with the union were finally settled and Hampson and the personnel director began conducting individual discussions with employees to review their situations and opportunities, juggle with staff at the other depots, and determine redundancy settlements. These discussions could not have been completed in any event in under two weeks, and production problems at another Layard business made it necessary for Hampson to take three weeks. Fifty employees were scheduled to be made redundant at an average cost of £2,000 each, and the highest settlement was £12,000 ($30,000).

The last days at Portsmouth had been absolute torture, and Hampson could not stop thinking of his conversation with John Sargent, the facilities manager who was 57 years old. John had worked 30 years at Lex, 10 of them with Keith Hampson, and had always been a quiet, dependable, and honest worker. Hampson had thought he might be able to place Sargent at the Plymouth Depot and so had delayed making a final settlement until the last minute. When the position had not become available and Hampson had told John he would have to leave Lex, John had expressed little surprise or emotion. After the redundancy terms were worked out, he simply said:

> I know you've always tried to have a concern for the employees, and I know you care about their security. And I understand from what you say that these Guidelines are an attempt to formalize that concern, but in reality, where does that get me? Sacked. Where's *my* protection? What does your statement say about *that?*

# Lex Service Group, Ltd.: Work Conditions at Inglesby Shipyard (C)

Sweating, slums, the sense of semislavery in labour, must go. We must cultivate a sense of manhood by treating men as men.—David Lloyd George

Sarah Markham[1] had every reason to be very proud of her Business Group (in U.S. terms, a division). Her Webster Hire had managed to meet the margins which she had projected a year earlier despite a recession in the British economy and a very sudden rise in the nation's unemployment rate to the extent that in August 1980, Britain's total of jobless workers had passed the 1930s' figure for the first time since the Great Depression.

Webster Hire, one of six business groups at Lex Service Group Ltd., was primarily a fork truck hire business with a £20 million turnover and an operating profit of £2.5 million in 1979. This return was particularly impressive when

one considered that many of the Webster Hire subsidiaries serviced the hardest-hit industries in the country: steel, textiles, shipbuilding, and the automotive industry. Sarah, who had been group manager for Webster for the last three years, felt that part of this performance could be attributed directly to the character of her particular business group. She had fewer unions to deal with than some of the other groups in which she had previously worked during her twelve years at Lex Service Group Ltd., and as group manager she had sought to cultivate a spirit of employee-management cooperation in all the Webster subsidiaries. Her own door was always open, and she tried to work out as many of the normal management problems as possible at the committee meetings which she held once a month with the regional managers. They, in turn, met every month with the depot managers, and the discussions at these meetings were communicated to the employees whenever practicable. Three times a year Webster conducted a formal briefing all the way

[1]With the exception of the chairman, the names of all Lex employees and subsidiaries are disguised.

down the line regarding closure reports, productivity, and the general goals of the Webster businesses.

At Sarah's regional sessions the managers would raise and air their own difficulties of the past month and have a chance to comment on and compare conditions among the depots. Sarah felt that her own role was primarily as mediator between the broader objectives and values at Lex and the specific concerns of the Webster managers, but she also tried to develop as independent a management force as possible. During three years of such meetings a bond of trust had developed between her and her managers which ensured a general belief on both sides that everyone would work toward the general welfare of the employees and the company, and that everyone would consistently attempt to resolve problems in an open and fair way.

This ethos had developed in part out of the general values of the corporation, and partly out of Sarah's own past experience as corporate personnel director. Her knowledge of the company's business was broad, and her commitment to treating employees as individuals was the chief operating value behind what she privately called her "reasonable style." She in turn required great commitment from each employee, and had helped ensure this not only through her own management style but by instituting an extensive series of training seminars at every depot and a separate training school for the service engineers at the Webster headquarters. In 1979 the average achievement of preventive maintenance targets was 94%, and customer breakdown calls averaged 1.8 hours against the guaranteed four hours' response. Sarah made it known that she was willing to provide everything in her power to help facilitate employee performance, and last year's record-breaking productivity figures at Webster had reinforced the mutual trust and respect which the managers and employees shared.

It was precisely this same climate of trust which had enabled Webster Hire to implement rigorous cost cutting and increased productivity demands with only minimal complaints from the general managers and employees. Many traditional employee benefits such as the annual depot outing also had had to be omitted that year, but as a result of these efforts very few people had had to be made redundant at a time when unemployment levels were soaring, and the breakdown rate in 1979 had been reduced by 30% over a 50% reduction the year before.

In view of the overall cooperation which Webster people had exhibited in the last year, Sarah found the corporation's recent adoption of a general set of guidelines, which emphasized an equal consideration of employee and shareholder interests (see Exhibit 1, page 130, for a complete copy), to be quite consistent with her own management approach. Trevor Chinn, Chairman and CEO of Lex Service Group Ltd., had introduced the Guidelines at the last annual senior managers meeting, and for the most part Sarah thought that they were a reasonably accurate statement both of what she felt to be Trevor Chinn's personal beliefs and of what she herself could comfortably live with as a group manager with high performance expectations.

She was less sure, however, that a business could ever come up with a consensus of values which would be capable of adoption at all levels of the organization. One might agree to a principle in theory and still find it necessary to suspend it momentarily in an actual business situation, and the problem was that no two people would agree on which situation would justify putting the Guidelines aside for the moment. Sarah could envision her regional managers' meetings dissolving into a chaos of misunderstanding if too many people tried to stick too literally to the Guidelines' policies and constraints.

The Guidelines, she reflected, would only work if you regarded the groups as consisting of one or two top people. Sarah, for example, had jokingly entitled Terry Rockford, group personnel director, the "guardian of the group's values," and she could depend on him to interpret a situation in a way that was very consistent with the corporation's general beliefs: he would always endeavour to hit upon a "fair" solution that considered employee and shareholder interests and ultimately to give the customer value for money at the same time. Rockford also tended to favor the former in any really thorny discussion, and Sarah was constantly forced to emphasize the costs of his recommendations and their effect on the price of the service to the customer. Sarah felt comfortable in discussing these issues with her personnel director, but was not so sure that she would want to have to make explicit or defend how she viewed the balance between these interests to every one of her regional or depot managers—never mind the line employees!

Still, all in all, she thought the Guidelines were a good idea—at least as a standard to strive for—and she recalled with admiration the chairman's introduction of them. As in many meetings, Trevor Chinn had displayed a genuine concern for his employees and intellectually accepted—no, pushed—the idea of a decentralized senior management, but emotionally he was still very much a patriarch: when it came to questions of corporate values, he tended to rely heavily on his own personal beliefs. Sarah found that to be fine, and the personal tenor of the Guidelines was all to the good in that everyone had always looked to Trevor for the company's values anyway.

Trevor Chinn himself had wrestled with his role as leader in a decentralized firm during that last senior managers meeting. In introducing the Guidelines he had said,

> I think that these are issues that are the responsibility of the chief executive. I don't believe in paternalism, but I do believe in the chief executive knowing those matters in which he must get involved, and in being prepared to make explicit statements about them. That is something that he cannot delegate. It is affected by his own attitudes and morality. He's got to think it through, and then work with his senior management in the company to come to some explicit statements that everyone can live with. But he can't leave it to somebody else because if he doesn't care about it, nobody else will. At the same time, I think it is very important not to believe that you are the only guardian of the truth. You have to keep questioning, and I expect everyone here to do the same.

Sarah wondered if she would ever as a group manager have the perspective that Trevor Chinn had, a perspective that colored his application of the Guidelines so strongly. She remembered how, when she had been at corporate headquarters as personnel director, Trevor would say, "Sarah, you've got to make sure that every employee counts. You save one life, you save the whole world—it's a Jewish concept." How would Trevor apply the Guidelines, she speculated, to Inglesby Shipyard? The position in the Guidelines seemed fairly straightforward:

> The company will provide working and off-work conditions which are amongst the best for relevant occupations, particularly in respect of safety, and in no circumstances will such conditions fall below statutory or nationally agreed minimum standards.

But when one looked at a case such as Inglesby, the proper course of action was less clear. That situation had been a bother to Sarah for three years now, and was still totally insoluble as far as she could see.

### THE INGLESBY SITE

Webster Hire had leased a small working area on the Inglesby Shipyard site in Southampton, where it contracted to supply and service 16 fork trucks for the shipyard's use. The Inglesby depot ran three shifts a day and had spare trucks ready at all times to service the shipyard's needs as fully as possible. Although Inglesby was the service base of a larger operating unit nearby which had 120 trucks, it provided close to 50% of the unit's profits before tax (= £20,000 per year). The Inglesby depot was in reality a minimal structure erected over a pounded dirt floor. It had no heating facilities, it was too small to maneuver in, and there was no place to rest. On Sarah Markham's last visit, the dirt had been ferocious and the roof leaked. Every year Sarah tried to negotiate with Inglesby Shipyard to improve the site, and every year Inglesby had refused to put any money into it at all. At one point she had considered investing Webster Hire money in the location, but a rough estimate of the costs of putting up a new depot came to £100,000. Although the Inglesby contract was extremely lucrative, that company was absolutely firm about signing with Webster Transport for no more than one year at a time, and shipbuilding was currently one of the national industries with the highest unemployment rates.

Sarah felt that without a long-term contract she couldn't authorize the investment to improve the site, and yet she had always hesitated to close the whole operation down, both because of the subsequent loss of revenue and because of the three Inglesby service engineers. One of them, Joey Barton, had the longest employment of any Webster worker in the southern region. In fact, Joey had personally secured the Inglesby business for Webster Transport ten years ago, and he loved working the shipyard. Joey felt that at the smaller operation he was really running the show—which he was—while he would have been lost at the larger depot. None of the Inglesby service people had really complained about the working conditions, and Sarah had approved whatever portable facilities she could to improve the site: she had had installed a local electric heater and had instituted extra breaks in winter; an electric kettle had been set up in one corner of the depot, and they had installed a chemical toilet at the back.

But the facilities were still far below Lex standards, and ironically, Sarah Markham had always prided herself on maintaining in general the safest work places in the industry. In fact, she had almost decided to pull out of the Inglesby contract last year when there seemed no possibility of improving the depot without taking an inordinate financial risk, but there had been no comparable positions for Joey and the other two workers in the Southampton region. To ask him to take a subordinate position at one of the larger sites would be the equivalent of firing him. For Joey to accept those conditions of employment would mean the loss of his dignity and self-respect. Sarah simply would not be so absurd as to drop the job just because it did not meet company working standards.

Terry Rockford, Webster's group personnel director, knew how much the Inglesby situation bothered Sarah, but he himself had no problem with keeping the site open. He did not disguise the fact that he thought Sarah was making too big a fuss over the depot, and never failed to rib her about it when the subject came up. The last time they discussed the negotiations to renew the Inglesby contract, Terry had remarked blackly, "Yeah, you'd better close it. Joey's a heavy smoker, and most likely he'll get emphysema and sue Lex Service Group for keeping him in substandard work conditions."

Shortly after the senior managers' meeting, Terry, who had seen the Guidelines, dropped by Sarah's office and remarked, "Trevor Chinn's new personnel director wants to visit Webster's southern region next week, and I'm trying to work out a schedule. Will you be taking him for a tour of Inglesby?"

# Lex Service Group, Ltd.: The Reading Pallets Theft (D)

It was ten o'clock in the evening when Frank Heathrow's[1] wife came into his study.

"It's for you, Frank. It's the Reading police." Bewildered, Frank took the phone.

"Hello. Is this Mr. Frank Heathrow, group manager for Devon Parcel Service? Mr. Heathrow, we're sorry to bother you at this time of night, but we've just arrested a Mr. Barney Snide, who has been receiving stolen pallets and reselling them for £3–4 apiece down here in Reading. Among his suppliers were three of your employees from Devon's Reading depot. They've been selling Barney about twelve of your customers' pallets a week for £1 a piece for the last six months, and we'd like your permission to arrest them tomorrow morning at the depot."

"Are you sure these men were stealing the pallets from us?"

---

[1] With the exception of the chairman, the names of all Lex employees and subsidiaries are disguised.

"Oh, yes, sir, there's absolutely no mistake. After it came to our attention that Barney was selling pallets with other company names stamped on them, we began watching his place. Six Devon Parcel Service trucks were spotted at the back of his warehouse and the drivers were seen unloading pallets from the truck. We have the names of three of them and would like to make the arrests tomorrow."

"Well, okay, go ahead, but please try to be as discreet as possible while you're at the depot. By the way, who are they?"

"Billy Simpson, Gerald Rose, and Johnny Miller, sir. Thank you very much, sir, and good night."

## THE COMPANY

Devon Parcel Service was a Lex subsidiary which distributed packages in the south and west regions of England. Employing 140 workers, including 40 drivers, the main depot for sorting parcels was located in Oxford, and in 1979 reported a £650,000 profit with an 18% return on investment. Drivers in the south and west regions would pick up parcels, take them to Oxford or sometimes a local depot for sorting, and then deliver the packages to receivers in the same region. Because of its size, the Reading area had its own depot out of which 12 Devon drivers and the same number of trucks picked up, sorted, and delivered local packages. Each driver delivered approximately 120 parcels a day, and collected a hundred or more which were unloaded at the Reading depot. Drivers ran about 100 miles per day and made £125 per week on the average. The dockers at the Reading depot were paid £95 per week.

## THE PALLET THEFT

When a large parcel or group of parcels was collected, the customer supplied a pallet (a flat wooden slat platform normally costing £4–5) on which the packages were stacked and loaded onto the truck. At the parcel service depot the packages were unloaded, sorted, and reloaded onto other trucks, and anywhere from 25–50 pallets went in and out of the depot each day. Some of the pallets were reused in deliveries, and the remainder were either returned to the customer at his own arrangement or stacked at the parcel depot. Pallets usually had the owner's name stamped on them, but in practice were employed interchangeably, and one could find an assortment of pallets stored up behind most warehouses. Apparently some of the Devon drivers, as they were loading their trucks at the Reading depot, were having the dockers pile a few extra pallets in the back of the truck for "delivery" to Barney Snide.

The morning after his telephone call from the police, Heathrow called Paul Harris, his personnel manager in Reading, to inform him of the police's intended visit that day. He briefly outlined the incident to Harris, and they agreed that the three employees should be fired. Harris, who had a reputation for being "soft" with the employees, and had run into disagreements with Heathrow on firings in the past, was

particularly eager to lend his support to Heathrow's suggestion since the case was such a clearcut incident of employee dishonesty. It was unfortunate, however, since Simpson, Rose, and Miller also happened to be by far the most productive workers at the depot.

Later that same day Heathrow casually mentioned his late-night call from the Reading police to Dave Tucker, the group personnel director.

"What did you do?" asked Dave.

"Oh, I told Harris to fire them, of course, and he agreed. We're all sorry to see them go—they're the best workers on the lot—but we can't have that sort of thing going on, can we?"

To Heathrow's surprise, Tucker got all upset.

"Wait a minute," said Tucker. "Don't you think we'd better get the whole story here? When I used to be a depot manager, those pallets were just throwaways. They stacked up behind the warehouse and they were a pain in the neck. Half the customers forget all about them or can't be bothered to take them back, and then we're stuck with them. Why, I once donated a huge pile of them to the Boy Scout's annual bonfire. You know, the one where they sell tickets to benefit handicapped children, and local businesses donate burnables and contribute toward the tickets? These Boy Scouts came 'round, and we had a huge pile of pallets that were just getting in the way, and I gave them the lot. Was I stealing from the customers? I guess I was. Arrest *me*. Besides, I'll bet you any thing the depot supervisor knew all about this. Those guys probably said, 'Look, all these pallets are in the way. Would you like us to take them off your hands?' *He* knew they weren't offering out of the goodness of their hearts. Shouldn't he be fired too?"

Heathrow was stunned. "I thought you were the hard one, Tucker. You're always going on about higher work standards at the depot."

"Look, all I know is, this kind of thing goes on all the time, and probably everyone there knew about it and ignored it. Why should those three lose their jobs?"

At that point the Devon financial planner

walked by and jumped into the argument. He pointed out that casual theft in the parcel industry was almost a recognized way of life, and said that he had heard that in the States a maritime union had secured adjustments in its contracts to make up for lost income when the shippers shifted over to sealed containers. The financial planner looked Heathrow in the eye and said, "If everyone knows it's going on, how can it be stealing?"

Heathrow promised to reconsider his decision. That afternoon he called the trade union and informed them of the problem. He asked them if they planned to discipline the three employees, and the union replied that it had no intention of getting involved in the incident.

# The Beliefs of Borg-Warner

It was May 19, 1982, the last day of Borg-Warner's 1982 chairman's meeting, and CEO James Beré closed the final session of the meeting by speaking about the development of "The Beliefs of Borg-Warner":

> For some time, Borg-Warner has been a company in search of an identity. I am not sure that during most of the half-century of our history we ever really ourselves questioned what we stood for, what needs we fulfill, or where we were going. But before we can know surely where we are going, we must first know *what* we are. So we are beginning a long reexamination. Why now? Because right now we are at a turning point in a long and massive transition in this company; . . . because in a sea of violent change, guidelines are vital to avoid being swamped; . . . because values and profits are inseparable.[1]

[1]*Note:* References throughout the case to company history and documents come from H. Lee Geist's *Borg-Warner: The First Fifty Years* (Chicago, Borg-Warner Corporation, 1978).

He also talked about what the "Beliefs" meant and how they would affect the company:

> With this formal document, we are saying, both as a corporation and as individuals, that we believe that inherent values are as applicable in our work as in our personal lives. In fact, these values may be even more important on the job, since our business actions affect far more people than do our personal affairs.
>
> So if it sounds familiar, please do not dismiss it. These are not one-day-a-week precepts—they are basic guidelines to the day-to-day running of a business.
>
> We know we are not going to change our activities and our personality overnight. It has taken us a full decade to shift from a stodgy manufacturing company dominated by the auto industry to the degree of balance that we have now. Events move faster today—but it would still be a mistake to expect us to become something radically different very quickly.
>
> But we know we *will* change. We have a very strong base of people, and operations, and financial structure to build upon. With an equally strong framework of shared values to

THE BELIEFS OF BORG-WARNER: TO REACH BEYOND THE MINIMAL

Any business is a member of a social system, entitled to the rights and bound by the responsibilities of that membership. Its freedom to pursue economic goals is constrained by law and channeled by the forces of a free market. But these demands are minimal, requiring only that a business provide wanted goods and services, compete fairly, and cause no obvious harm. For some companies, that is enough. It is not enough for Borg-Warner. We impose upon ourselves an obligation to reach beyond the minimal. We do so convinced that by making a larger contribution to the society that sustains us, we best assure not only its future vitality, but our own.

This is what we believe.

**We believe in the dignity of the individual.**

However large and complex a business may be, its work is still done by people dealing with people. Each person involved is a unique human being, with pride, needs, values, and innate personal worth. For Borg-Warner to succeed, we must operate in a climate of openness and trust, in which each of us freely grants others the same respect, cooperation, and decency we seek for ourselves.

**We believe in our responsibility to the common good.**

Because Borg-Warner is both an economic and social force, our responsibilities to the public are large. The spur of competition and the sanctions of the law give strong guidance to our behavior, but alone do not inspire our best. For that we must heed the voice of our natural concern for others. Our challenge is to supply goods and services that are of superior value to those who use them; to create jobs that provide meaning for those who do them; to honor and enhance human life; and to offer our talents and our wealth to help improve the world we share.

**We believe in the endless quest for excellence.**

Though we may be better today than we were yesterday, we are not as good as we must become. Borg-Warner chooses to be a leader—in serving our customers, advancing our technologies, and rewarding all who invest in us their time, money, and trust. None of us can settle for doing less than our best, and we can never stop trying to surpass what already has been achieved.

**We believe in continuous renewal.**

A corporation endures and prospers only by moving forward. The past has given us the present to build on. But to follow our visions to the future, we must see the difference between traditions that give us continuity and strength, and conventions that no longer serve us—and have the courage to act on that knowledge. Most can adapt after change has occurred; we must be among the few who anticipate change, shape it to our purpose, and act as its agents.

**We believe in the commonwealth of Borg-Warner and its people.**

Borg-Warner is both a federation of businesses and a community of people. Our goal is to preserve the freedom each of us needs to find personal satisfaction while building the strength that comes from unity. True unity is more than a melding of self-interests; it results when values and ideals also are shared. Some of ours are spelled out in these statements of belief. Others include faith in our political, economic, and spiritual heritage; pride in our work and our company; the knowledge that loyalty must flow in many directions, and a conviction that power is strongest when shared. We look to the unifying force of these beliefs as a source of energy to brighten the future of our company and all who depend upon it.

*Source:* Company document. Copyright © 1982 Borg-Warner Corporation. Reprinted by permission.

---

guide and strengthen us, I believe we can become *anything* we want to.

Beré ended his speech by asking the company's managers to commit themselves to the "Beliefs" and to make them meaningful through their own words and actions: "One of the noble houses of England has as its motto a Latin phrase that translates essentially as, 'What I promise, I will do.' This statement today is our promise to the future. Please join me in that promise."

## THE CHAIRMAN'S MEETING

Once every two years the 100 senior managers of Borg-Warner, along with spouses, would gather at the chairman's meeting to discuss important long-range issues. Whereas the annual president's meeting afforded a regular opportunity to discuss operating business issues, the chairman's meeting was viewed as a special session that allowed a retreat from the daily pressures of management so that participants could reflect on the company's health and direction. With a theme of shared values, the 1982 chairman's meeting had concluded with the release of "The Beliefs of Borg-Warner."

The development of this statement of beliefs had begun long before the 1982 chairman's meeting was even scheduled. While the "Beliefs" had only come to fruition after 10 months of intensive work, they were also the product of the company's long history, its culture, and the ideals of its chief executive officer.

### Company History

Borg-Warner Corporation was born at a time when America's love affair with the automobile was in full bloom. A whole new social, economic, and transportation pattern had developed around the motorized wheels. Yet, despite the big annual increases in car production during the 1920s, the industry was going through a stage of consolidation.

### Early Acquisitions

On June 5, 1928, Borg-Warner was created when four established auto parts manufacturers agreed to consolidate their assets in a holding company. "What we want," said George Borg, first president of Borg-Warner, "is a corporation which cannot be made or broken by the fortunes of any single division, or the market for any one product." Each of the participants maintained its identity and operating methods while the corporation supplied the "fiscal glue."

In just over a year Borg-Warner added five more operations, thus establishing itself as a major force in the automotive industry. A published company history explained developments:

> These nine tribal fiefdoms were to remain the heart of Borg-Warner for almost 25 years. . . . The nine companies had the same customers and parallel technology in common—but little else. Each considered itself as still independent. . . . Borg-Warner was not considered as a parent—it was known as the "central office." The charter of the corporation stated that "individual divisions retain all powers not expressly limited to the central corporation."
>
> The philosophies that were to guide, or to dominate, the operations of Borg-Warner through much of its history, and to be the roots of both its strengths and its weaknesses were really established from the day the merger began.

Charles S. Davis, Borg-Warner's chairman, served as a referee who helped maintain the growth of the independent divisions. In an effort to lessen Borg-Warner's dependence on the automotive industry, Davis helped acquire an electric refrigeration business, a small chemical operation, and an aviation supply firm.

In 1950 Roy C. Ingersoll, an entrepreneurial division executive, became CEO. Whereas Davis had been content in his role as central banker, Ingersoll wanted to *run* the corporation. He was frustrated, however, as were his successors, by the organization of the company: 44 people reported directly to him—35 division heads and an assortment of staff people—representing a wide spectrum of activities and policies and a wider range of operations. There was little time for communication, and, given the tradition of decentralization and divisional autonomy, there seemed little that Ingersoll could do about the organization. A company document stated that "the central office had only two real controls over a division: it could refuse to allocate further capital funds, or it could fire the division president." Ingersoll eventually presided over the first restructuring in the company's history, thus improving communication within the organization.

## Period of Redevelopment

Once a consensus developed that Borg-Warner needed to reduce its dependence on Detroit (a full two-thirds of the company's business was going to the automotive industry), Roy Ingersoll set the transition in motion. Existing operations—the electric refrigeration and chemical businesses—were rebuilt and expanded. New operations—oilfield supply-service and air conditioning businesses—were acquired.

In 1961 Robert Ingersoll became CEO only after his father reluctantly agreed to step aside at age 73. While Roy Ingersoll had instinctively been a dynasty builder, his son offered a different style of leadership. "Bob Ingersoll was a new type at Borg-Warner. Neither a driver like his father, nor a negotiator like Davis, he was probably a better manager than either one."

Robert Ingersoll succeeded in grouping the divisions more along business lines, and set up group administrations through vice presidents who would have responsibility for compatible industries—such as automotive, chemical, construction, industrial, and so forth. By 1964 his new group organization was in place and attitudes slowly started to change. Communication between divisions and the corporate office improved and it became possible to find out what the divisions were doing ahead of time, rather than after the fact. The corporate office knew how earnings projections were arrived at and which "losers" among division products had been maintained and protected. The central office was referred to as a central bank and sometimes as a management consultant.

Robert Ingersoll introduced a new policy by ending the tradition that the company acquired operations but never got rid of them. Long-term commitment to an operation was a great ideal—but he insisted on justification for that commitment. Although a large number of persons objected to any divestiture, Robert Ingersoll sold the electric refrigeration business—it was the first real divestiture the company had ever had in its 40-year history. Other, smaller divestitures followed and included companies that had been acquired under his father's direction. He oversaw other fundamental changes in

the character of the company. International operations accelerated and the chemical operation spawned a highly successful plastics business that held great promise.

## THE BERÉ YEARS

In 1972 Robert Ingersoll left the company when President Richard M. Nixon appointed him U.S. ambassador to Japan. James F. Beré was chosen to be the next CEO, representing yet another style of leadership. As a company observer noted: "Beré was the company's first professional manager, one with strong humanistic overtones, as keenly aware of a big company's obligations to society in general as to its stockholders. He was also the first chief executive with no personal connection to the 'early days'— and probably the first one to make decisions on a basis of company needs rather than company traditions." Beré joined Borg-Warner in 1961 as a seasoned business executive, and in an unusual move he was immediately named president of an automotive parts division. Subsequently, he occupied the group vice president's chair, acting as an ombudsman between the divisions and corporate staff. He established his reputation as an operating manager even though it was not his strong point. This reputation did, however, help him win the confidence of Robert Ingersoll and eventually gain the position as Borg-Warner's president. He had only been with Borg-Warner for seven years, but his lack of experience with the company was viewed as one of his assets in getting the job. Beré preferred to involve himself in long-term policy and strategic matters, while Chairman Ingersoll consistently involved himself in the day-to-day division affairs. Even though Ingersoll remained the boss until he left, the two men had apparently worked out an unconscious role reversal, one which made their working relationship strong. When Ingersoll stepped down, Beré was ready to assume the formal title of CEO.

After the shock of the 1974–1975 economic downturn, Beré realized that he had to improve communications between corporate staff and division management. In late 1975

Borg-Warner introduced a strategic planning system that involved many more people than previously, including division-level people all the way down to individual product areas. The operating manager now had to ask hard questions: What business am I really in? What future does the business have? Should we be in it at all? The discipline of such self-examination forced groups and divisions to make their own hard decisions about how to allocate their resources to the areas providing or promoting the best return. For the first time, the operating people aimed for clearer goals other than just next week, next month, or at most, next year.

By 1976 Borg Warner's nonproductive activities had been shed and modern management systems installed. The transportation equipment business remained the largest segment of the company, accounting for one-third of total earnings. The air conditioning, chemical and plastics, and finance operations had helped to diversify the corporation's earnings base. Beré continued to believe the company needed some new directions.

Recognizing that consumption of services was beginning to exceed consumption of manufactured products in the economy at large, Borg-Warner's management began to think about adding a service business. In 1977 the company acquired Baker Industries and gained a substantial foothold in the protective services industry. During late 1978 Borg-Warner and Firestone Tire and Rubber Company, with annual sales twice those of Borg-Warner, mutually agreed to consider a merger of their companies. After serious negotiations, each company decided to retain its independence, and the merger talks ended. In mid-1982 Borg-Warner acquired Burns International Security Services and thereby became the largest protective services operation in the world.

In 1982 Borg-Warner Corporation was a diverse, multinational corporation that was listed among the 500 largest industrial corporations in the United States. According to *Fortune,* it ranked 154 with sales of $2,761.2 million, 117 with net earnings of $172.1 million, and 71 with 55,700 employees. (Exhibits 1 and 2 present a corporate profile and selected financial data.) Table A illustrates the change in the character of the company over the 1970–1980 decade.

## EARLY ATTEMPTS AT DEVELOPING A CORPORATE CREED

Borg-Warner's first attempt to formally articulate a statement of beliefs occurred in 1970.

**TABLE A**
CHANGING CORPORATE BUSINESS MIX

|  | Early 1970s | Early 1980s |
| --- | --- | --- |
| **Net earnings** | $50 million | $170 million |
| **Manufacturing:** Air conditioning group, chemicals and plastics group, energy and industrial equipment group, and transportation equipment group | 88% | 40% |
| **Services:** Financial services group and protective services group | 10% | 27% |
| **Affiliates:** Major equity investments including a 19% interest in Hughes Tool Company, a 22% interest in Echlin, and a 24% interest in Amedco | 2% | 33% |

*Source:* Borg-Warner's Investor Facts, 1982.

During Robert Ingersoll's administration, the public relations department drafted a "Borg-Warner Creed" that mentioned the company's obligations to shareholders, employees, customers, suppliers—and society (see Exhibit 3). While many U.S. companies publicly adopted similar codes of ethics around this time, Borg-Warner was unable to achieve a consensus on any such statement. Initial efforts fizzled in the company's policy committee.

Ingersoll had frequently urged company management to reexamine attitudes and beliefs about work and the role of the corporation in modern society. As a company document explained:

> He was the bridge between the old attitude that an employee was literally nothing but a cents-per-hour cost, and the current belief that the employee, at all levels, has an individual personality and individual rights.
>
> When he interviewed someone for an upper level job—he often started the interview with a thoroughly unexpected question: "What is your philosophy of life?" He was looking for honesty and a sense of dedication to company and customer, rather than followers of the old tradition of "make a buck any way you can."

While Ingersoll's beliefs were well known, his successor had to formalize a corporate statement of ethics. During a visit to a Texas Instruments' facility in early 1974, Beré had been handed a copy of its code of ethics and was impressed. He decided the time had come for Borg-Warner to articulate a statement of values and beliefs.

### "Borg-Warner's Ethics"

After several drafts, "Borg-Warner's Ethics" was published as a booklet for senior management review. As its foreword suggested, this was food for larger thought. It asked such questions as: "What ultimate standards do we cling to at Borg-Warner?" "In conflicts of purpose, how do we expect you to choose [what is best]?" The booklet was meant to offer guid-

ance to managers wrestling with ethical dilemmas. The seven parts dealt with the law, company policy, affirmations of ethics, employee relations, consumer affairs, community relations, and corporate "sociology."

Although a senior management committee recommended that "Borg-Warner's Ethics" should eventually be published in a book, it suggested that management first establish a foothold for such a standard of ethical conduct. The committee thought the company had not yet attained the standards set forth in the drafted statements. Like the earlier effort, therefore, this attempt also sputtered.

### Beré's Concerns about Corporate Ethics

Following widespread reports of illegal and improper conduct during the first half of the 1970s by employees of public companies, Beré rekindled the discussion about corporate ethics in mid-1976. In a letter to all company employees, Beré stated that "Borg-Warner does not want you to act in any way contrary to your ethical principles." He urged employees to seek guidance from their supervisors or co-workers if in doubt about the morality of a certain action (see Exhibit 4).

The 1976 annual report included a discussion about the social responsibility of business, along with the usual reporting of sales and earnings results. Beré began to speak more frequently about "building the character of our company," and he argued that Borg-Warner had to manage its business so as to create public confidence by considering the "economic *and* social needs of its constituents."

At the 1977 annual shareholder's meeting, Beré delivered a special "Report on the Noneconomic Side of the Business," addressing the public's dissatisfaction with big business:

> Americans are dissatisfied with business, not because of complaints about its economic performance, but because they see corporations and their managers as too self-serving, too remote, too purely economic in our approach to human needs.

The public today judges corporations more by our social performance—that is, by the effect of our routine conduct of business on the quality of life of people we touch: our employees, the people in our plant communities, our customers and the ultimate users of our products or services.

In the future, managers of Borg-Warner's businesses would be required to assess and respond to the needs of their customers, general public, and civic officials as part of the strategic planning process. At a senior management conference in late 1977 Beré declared that managers would be judged on their ability to meet social performance goals. As he put it, "Our objective will be to generate public approval based upon a sense of commitment to the company, employees, and society."

According to one corporate officer, "Beré had the right idea [about a code of ethics] but the timing was wrong. There were powerful people around Borg-Warner who still gave only lip service to the concept. The 'snicker index' was simply too high." Since Beré's own thoughts had solidified, he believed that some progress could finally be made to articulate a corporate statement of ethics. One senior manager noted that Beré was still quite vague about what such a statement would actually say. "But," he said, "Beré was determined to develop one—soon." Beré was often heard to say that "when we have a code of beliefs it should include . . . "

### Developing a Statement of Beliefs

In summer 1981 Beré made another attempt to develop a corporate statement of beliefs. During an officer's meeting then, he reviewed his own initial attempts to develop a corporate statement:

I did not have the nerve to issue a statement of beliefs in the mid-1970s. I had gone to some of our senior managers with the concept and they told me it was a stupid idea because, as they said, "We have actions in our company that cannot measure up to a standard of ethics." I finally became mature enough to realize, that regardless of any past mistakes, a norm was essential to this company. Others, like our public relations people, believed it was a good idea, but were dubious that we could live up to it. Some also felt it would detract from the business of running the company.

When asked why such a project should be attempted under such difficult economic conditions, he talked about the things that had prompted him to proceed:

Why do it in 1981? There is a mosaic of factors that has triggered my actions.

First, I attended a seminar sponsored by the American Enterprise Institute and was moved by the words of one of the speakers, Michael Novak. Novak was convinced that we had a leadership dilemma in our society. Political leaders, he felt, would not speak from an ethical point of view—because it was not in their self-interest. The church, he argued, was divided and had lost its way—it was not providing people with needed guidance. Schools had lost their capability of providing an ethical norm for society. The family structure was in a state of decay. Novak made a strong plea: "If we are going to have true beliefs in the business sector, you, as business leaders, better stand up and realize that it is time to decide what your culture is—and give it some beliefs." I was convinced he was right! There had been a deterioration of ethics in our society. The norm was gone, and people were looking for leadership—but they wanted *quality* leadership.

Secondly, I have been CEO long enough so there is no way people are going to detach my actions from what I plan to publish.

Thirdly, I have confidence in our corporate communications department. They are the professional communicators and I know they will have to play a major role in shaping this document. When they appeared receptive to the idea, I felt confident we could proceed.

Lastly, when I visited our management training sessions, I heard a lot of our managers, particularly the younger ones, say they wanted to identify with a company that stands for something, that has a vision about what it is doing. For many of them, something was missing.

Beré was convinced that business could provide quality leadership by developing norms and went on to talk about the duties and rights of the modern corporation:

> I think I have an obligation as a corporate leader to establish standards. I do *not* think I have a right to be so exclusive that I become a bigot. But I do think I have a right to not deal with the extreme 10 percent in society. My job is to cater to the middle 80 percent in society— any person with qualifications, regardless of background, is permitted to come. But we are not going to take the whole range of society. What I am saying is . . . we have a right to have beliefs in a company, to tell you what they are, before you join us.
>
> A corporate statement of beliefs can give people a norm. . . . It is similar to athletics. The best athletic events all have rules. You do not play basketball without a set of rules. I happen to think that people in business, which is also highly competitive, really admire a person who has made it big . . . as long as they have played by the rules. They absolutely despise a person who has cheated.
>
> While we have an obligation as leaders to establish that norm, we must remain humble enough to realize that the norm may be wrong. It is not something that is fixed in concrete.

By mid-1981 a great deal of spadework had already been done to develop a corporate statement of beliefs. Yet, as one company officer put it, "We were shooting arrows and drawing the target around the points where they landed." Few understood what a corporate statement of beliefs was going to say and do.

## DEVELOPING SHARED VALUES

In September 1981, Beré put the task of developing a set of corporate beliefs before the company's senior managers. Speaking at the annual president's meeting, he talked about the company's strategy and performance:

In the business world, there is a tendency to think of strategy as some cosmic approach that somehow takes place on the top floor of a corporate headquarters. We've had a certain amount of confusion about it in this company, too. For instance, we've said we wanted to reduce our dependence on the highly cyclical automotive market. We've said that with the country swinging steadily toward a service economy, we had to direct more interest to the service sector ourselves. Well, we've done both of these things.

He believed the company's view of strategic planning had to be enlarged:

> Now I think it may be time to redefine our understanding of what strategy should mean to Borg-Warner. Part of that goes back to the original meaning of the word *company.* [It is] a group of persons with common interests banded together to achieve a common goal. Common interests. Common goals . . . I am not sure we ever really had enough of them.
>
> To my mind, shared values—a companywide set of principles against which all business decisions can be measured and tested—must be the base upon which concrete long-term objectives are built.

The Japanese, he argued, offered a model worthy of emulation but not outright imitation:

> In large Japanese companies, for instance, there is an understanding, often unspoken, but spread through the ranks, of where the company wants to go, what it wants to be, and what it will do, and how to gain those results. That really is possible here, too.
>
> I do not believe that the Japanese style of management by consensus really holds promise for close imitation in the United States. There is a homogeneity of approach and tradition in Japan that carries over from the culture to the work place. I hope Americans never lose the sense of drive, of individual achievement, that made this country great in the first place.
>
> But I do believe that in the American system, there is a great deal of room and flexibility for individual achievement within the larger

framework of group achievement—room for both independence and interdependence.

As he finished his speech, Beré started the clock ticking toward the next gathering of Borg-Warner's senior management: "We are going to raise our strategic sights now. . . . We are going to try to codify and publish the values that will guide us. . . . All of you must be involved. . . . The theme of our chairman's meeting next May is going to be where we stand, what we believe, what our shared values really are. We would like to have our compendium (of beliefs) ready by then if we can."

## MANAGEMENT'S RESPONSE TO DRAFTING A STATEMENT OF BELIEFS

Only seven months remained to discuss, develop, and publish the actual words for a company statement of beliefs. Beré asked each manager to think about the actual contents of such a corporate statement and to write to him with suggestions. (Exhibit 5 presents excerpts from some of the 40 responses out of about 90 managers who attended the meeting.) It was critical for Beré and the company to achieve wide participation. Otherwise, he felt the beliefs would mean very little to the company's employees. To do this, Beré looked to Robert Morris, vice president of communications, for assistance.

Morris was familiar with the work of other companies that had undertaken similar efforts—notably, his previous employer, IBM. He began by spending a great deal of time talking with Beré to flesh out what he was asking for. Although the quantity of responses from management had been fairly good, the content of the letters indicated that there was considerable confusion about Beré's request for help in drafting a statement of beliefs.

Morris advocated more discussion with the company's management. He solicited more letters from division management; he also considered setting up field interviews and round-table "rap sessions" to widen the discussion. When he realized that his department lacked the resources to undertake such an effort, he went outside the corporation for help.

In early January 1982 Management Analysis Center (MAC) was retained to interview a select group of 35 managers and to analyze their responses on the proposed statement of beliefs. According to Morris, MAC did a good job of categorizing the issues and, most importantly, helped build the perception that this statement was being developed in a democratic fashion.

### Beré's List

Meanwhile, Beré was developing his own list of items that he thought should be in the statement of beliefs. He kept an index card in his pocket during the day and would often jot down words or phrases that he felt belonged with the company's philosophy. His words were then combined with the suggestions generated by management. For Morris, Beré's list proved critical in drafting a specific statement from what was originally an abstract concept:

> Sense of belonging
> Work ethic
> Competitive zeal
> Company loyalty
> Rational decision making
> Employee ideas
> Risk taking
> Agents of change
> Citizenship
> Share power
> Gratitude
> Belief in the economic system
> The whole person
> Diversity

Morris and his staff worked feverishly to prepare a draft of the beliefs since only a few months remained to the chairman's meeting. When Beré resisted words in one draft that were attributable to Socrates, Morris and his staff had to begin anew. Beré insisted that the statement be grounded in Judeo-Christian values.

To arouse enthusiasm for the development of the beliefs, Morris had an expert on corporate culture address an officers' luncheon on the subject of institutional values. It turned out to be a disaster. The top circle of management left the session more confused than ever about how values and beliefs would affect their strategic thinking.

Morris enlisted help from a philosopher at a well-known university whose teaching and research centered on ethics and business. The philosopher helped Beré and his staff find a historical springboard for each of the principles included in the draft statement. Beré later said: "He was a real catalyst—he boosted my confidence that we could finally articulate a meaningful statement of philosophy for Borg-Warner."

### The Chairman's Meeting

By early March the agenda for the May 1982 chairman's meeting had been established (see Exhibit 6). Guests would hear prominent speakers from industry and academia address issues on shared values and corporate policy. Yet the beliefs, to be released at that meeting's conclusion, were still not fully formulated.

When the actual principles in the statement started to come together, Beré realized that a preamble—a philosophical foundation—was needed to properly introduce the company's beliefs. Two approaches were considered: one could talk about how an enterprise making money could do good things for the community; or, conversely, one could talk about how an enterprise could do good things for the community and then expect to find profits flow as a natural consequence of its behavior. When Borg-Warner settled on the second choice, the statement of beliefs was ready to be presented at the chairman's meeting.

Important questions were raised during the three-day session. Division management was concerned that a corporatewide statement of philosophy might reduce division autonomy. Beré was convinced that the sharing of

common values would allow operating personnel to make difficult decisions *without* looking to headquarters for help. Centralization, he insisted, came when people relied too heavily upon the "mystical powers" of their leader. In this instance, he thought, the "Beliefs" would give power to a broader base of management—sharing beliefs meant sharing power.

When asked what steps would follow the chairman's meeting, Beré talked in general terms:

> The starting point for communicating these beliefs begins here—how I practice what is written down in this statement "to reach beyond the minimal."
>
> These beliefs are signposts, guides, goals—a vehicle for discussion. We must tell our people that these are *not* schoolroom rules—after all, they are *not* a bunch of kids. We need to start a training program to explain why we have beliefs. We need to continue to discuss the operating implications of these beliefs—how it will affect management behavior. We will have to become a lot more selective in the type of people we bring in [to Borg-Warner]. We must come up forward to tell people—this is the culture of our company, this is what we believe in!
>
> Lastly, we have to make this a living document of our company activity—no different than our accounting system. To me, the "Beliefs" are another professional tool of management to be utilized to reach our common goals.

He also reminded everyone of the relationship between philosophy and profit making:

> I contend that unless you do what we are doing in terms of beliefs, you will *not* have a profitable company. Therefore, to those who attack me and say "this is none of your business—your job is to make money for the stockholders"—I say I am optimizing the stockholder's holdings. If I do what I am now doing, I will attract talent and release creativity to the point of making this a better company. This is what I believe.

The chairman's meeting was termed a great success. The invited speakers had triggered thoughtful management discussions on the subject of corporate philosophy and ethics. As the company's senior managers filed out of the conference room following the closing remarks, each received a portfolio of the "Beliefs," personally signed by Beré. It was a gratifying moment for Beré and his staff. Yet, he knew that the real job of sharing and communicating the "Beliefs" had just begun.

### Incorporating the "Beliefs"

A plan would have to be developed over the next several months that would move "The Beliefs of Borg-Warner" beyond the status of high-sounding rhetoric. Steps would need to be taken to clarify, communicate, and put into practice such phrases as "to reach beyond the minimal." It was important, as one officer put it, "that these words not disappear like spit on sand."

Almost everyone in the company recognized that Beré was deeply committed to the "Beliefs," but many wondered how such principles could meaningfully be shared in a large and decentralized organization whose divisions treasured their operating independence.

The axiom that policy formulation is empty without careful attention to implementation was something that Beré understood very well; however, the "Beliefs" of Borg-Warner were not just ordinary policies.

## EXHIBITS: The Beliefs of Borg-Warner

### EXHIBIT 1
CORPORATE PROFILE

In 1982 Borg-Warner was a $2.7 billion diversified manufacturing and services company involved in eight markets basic to the world's economy: transportation, construction, consumer products, machinery, agribusiness, energy, financial, and protective services. Borg-Warner had operations in 20 countries on 6 continents. Its more than 100 operating units were organized into six product and service groups, described below.

### AIR CONDITIONING

This group manufactured a broad range of air conditioning, refrigeration, and heating equipment under the York®, Fraser-Johnston®, Luxaire® and Moncrief® brand names. These included engineered systems for large buildings; industrial refrigeration equipment for the petrochemicals, food and other process industries; commercial air conditioning equipment for small buildings, schools, factories and apartment buildings; and residential air conditioning systems, heat pumps and furnaces. In 1981 sales for the group were $571 million and operating profit was $30 million.

### CHEMICALS AND PLASTICS

Borg-Warner Chemicals was the largest producer of ABS—a family of engineering thermoplastics used in a growing variety of applications around the world. Borg-Warner Chemicals also was in the specialty chemicals business with a growing line of intermediates, additives and alkylphenols. The group produced styrene monomer for Cycolac® ABS and for sale on the open market. Group sales in 1981 were $664 million; operating profit was $61 million.

### ENERGY AND INDUSTRIAL EQUIPMENT

Major products in this group included centrifugal pumps for power plants, petroleum production, processing and pipelines, agriculture and general industrial applications; precision seals for pumps and compressors; valves; chains; bearings; and other power transmission products for general industrial applications. The group also made a.v. educational systems. In 1981 sales were $480 million and operating profit was $36 million.

## FINANCIAL SERVICES

Borg-Warner Acceptance Corporation (BWAC), the twelfth largest independent U.S. finance company in 1981, was the group's major unit. With more than 330 branches throughout the world, BWAC was the largest consumer durables floor-planning organization in the country, excluding captive automobile finance companies. BWAC also provided commercial, industrial and leveraged lease financing; insurance premium financing and other insurance-related services to businesses; it also provided marine, agribusiness, and automotive financing. The unconsolidated units which made up the financial services group contributed $32 million of net earnings in 1981.

## PROTECTIVE SERVICES

Acquired in 1977, Baker Industries offered the broadest range of protective services in the security field. It provided Wells Fargo® alarm, guard and armored services; Pony Express® courier service;

and Pyrotronics fire and smoke detection and extinguishment systems. In mid-1982, Borg-Warner also acquired Burns International Security Services. The combined Burns and Baker operations made Borg-Warner the largest protective services entity in the world, with the world's largest security guard service operation. On an annual basis, the group's revenue approached $700 million. In 1981, before the Burns acquisition, revenues were $364 million (not included in the consolidated financial data) and operating profit was $33 million.

## TRANSPORTATION EQUIPMENT

This group supplied component products to the manufacturers of automobiles, trucks, and off-highway vehicles and to replacement part distributors. Included were transmissions and transmission parts, clutches, axles, four-wheel-drive units, electronic sensors, control devices, and engine-timing components. Sales for the group in 1981 were $1.02 billion and operating profit was $78 million.

**Note**: Exhibits 2 to 6 appear on pages 195–201.

**EXHIBIT 2**

SELECTED FINANCIAL DATA, 1971–1981

(Millions of Dollars Except Per Share Data)

| Earnings | Year ended December 31 | 1981 | 1980 | 1979 | 1978‡ | 1977 | 1976 | 1975 | 1974 | 1973 | 1972 | 1971 |
|---|---|---|---|---|---|---|---|---|---|---|---|---|
| | Sales and other income: | | | | | | | | | | | |
| | Net sales | $2,761.2 | $2,673.3 | $2,717.4 | $2,326.0 | $2,031.9 | $1,862.4 | $1,639.0 | $1,767.8 | $1,546.8 | $1,283.2 | $1,148.2 |
| | Other income | 35.1 | 15.7 | 9.7 | 12.6 | 12.5 | 18.3 | 8.8 | 4.8 | 4.2 | 3.3 | 4.2 |
| | | 2,796.3 | 2,689.0 | 2,727.1 | 2,338.6 | 2,044.4 | 1,880.7 | 1,647.8 | 1,772.6 | 1,551.0 | 1,286.5 | 1,152.4 |
| | Costs and expenses: | | | | | | | | | | | |
| | Cost of sales | 2,179.6 | 2,134.3 | 2,133.8 | 1,780.7 | 1,554.8 | 1,440.2 | 1,308.2 | 1,419.9 | 1,179.8 | 973.0 | 885.4 |
| | Depreciation | 73.8 | 64.4 | 59.6 | 55.2 | 50.9 | 43.4 | 42.8 | 43.1 | 40.5 | 37.3 | 34.7 |
| | Selling, general and administrative expenses | 375.0 | 334.9 | 310.2 | 290.8 | 252.6 | 231.3 | 206.4 | 206.3 | 182.3 | 153.5 | 131.8 |
| | Interest expense | 23.0 | 31.4 | 20.9 | 16.7 | 16.7 | 16.6 | 24.3 | 31.1 | 16.7 | 13.1 | 13.6 |
| | Finance charges from related companies | 19.1 | 17.6 | 12.2 | 10.0 | 9.1 | 9.4 | 12.1 | 7.0 | 5.0 | 4.0 | 3.8 |
| | Minority interests | 5.1 | 4.3 | 2.6 | 3.0 | 2.6 | 2.7 | 2.1 | 2.0 | 2.0 | 1.2 | .9 |
| | Provision for income taxes | 56.5 | 47.1 | 68.2 | 81.3 | 71.4 | 66.8 | 21.0 | 21.9 | 61.6 | 52.8 | 40.2 |
| | | 2,732.1 | 2,634.0 | 2,607.5 | 2,237.7 | 1,958.1 | 1,810.4 | 1,616.9 | 1,731.3 | 1,487.9 | 1,234.9 | 1,110.4 |
| | Earnings from consolidated operations | 64.2 | 55.0 | 119.6 | 100.9 | 86.3 | 70.3 | 30.9 | 41.3 | 63.1 | 51.6 | 42.0 |
| | Equity in earnings of affiliates | 62.9 | 35.3 | 8.7 | 6.9 | 4.9 | .8 | 5.5 | 1.5 | 1.4 | 1.4 | .4 |
| | Earnings from manufacturing operations | 127.1 | 90.3 | 128.3 | 107.8 | 91.2 | 71.1 | 36.4 | 42.8 | 64.5 | 53.0 | 42.4 |
| | Earnings from financial services companies | 32.0 | 27.2 | 21.1 | 16.1 | 12.8 | 10.6 | 8.1 | 8.0 | 6.8 | 6.2 | 5.0 |
| | Earnings from protective services companies | 13.0 | 8.6 | 6.2 | 1.9 | | | | | | | |
| | Net earnings | $ 172.1 | $ 126.1 | $ 155.6 | $ 125.8 | $ 104.0 | $ 81.7 | $ 44.5 | $ 50.8 | $ 71.3 | $ 59.5** | $ 47.4 |
| **Per common share** | Net earnings† | $ 4.00 | $ 2.93 | $ 3.63 | $ 2.94 | $ 2.47 | $ 2.11 | $ 1.15 | $ 1.33* | $ 1.85 | $ 1.52** | $ 1.23 |

Footnotes on page 196.

*(Continued)*

**EXHIBIT 2**
CONTINUED

| | | 1981 | 1980 | 1979 | 1978 | 1977 | 1976 | 1975 | 1974 | 1973 | 1972 | 1971 |
|---|---|---|---|---|---|---|---|---|---|---|---|---|
| **Operating data** | Year ended December 31 | 1981 | 1980 | 1979 | 1978 | 1977 | 1976 | 1975 | 1974 | 1973 | 1972 | 1971 |
| | Return on sales | 6.2% | 4.7 | 5.7% | 5.4% | 5.1% | 4.4% | 2.7% | 2.9%* | 4.6% | 4.6%** | 4.1% |
| | Return on sales from consolidated operations | 2.3 | 2.1 | 4.4 | 4.3 | 4.2 | 3.8 | 1.9 | 2.3* | 4.1 | 4.0** | 3.7 |
| | Dividends | $ 53.9 | $ 49.6 | $ 43.8 | $ 39.3 | $ 34.5 | $ 27.5 | $ 26.4 | $ 26.1 | $ 26.4 | $ 24.6 | $ 24.5 |
| | Per common share paid† | 1.28 | 1.17 | 1.04 | .93 | .83 | .71 | .68 | .68 | .68 | .63 | .63 |
| | Capital expenditures | 175.8 | 134.2 | 130.7 | 115.3 | 77.0 | 36.0 | 55.9 | 83.0 | 69.6 | 62.8 | 55.2 |
| | Research and development expense | 66.5 | 63.9 | 55.8 | 49.1 | 45.3 | 44.2 | 42.2 | 42.2 | 41.2 | 42.7 | 39.2 |
| **Financial data** | December 31 | 1981 | 1980 | 1979 | 1978 | 1977 | 1976 | 1975 | 1974 | 1973 | 1972 | 1971 |
| | Current assets | $ 826.8 | $ 757.9 | $ 851.9 | $ 795.8 | $ 648.7 | $ 688.5 | $ 589.5 | $ 687.5 | $ 641.9 | $ 528.3 | $ 502.1 |
| | Current liabilities | 560.4 | 446.2 | 460.1 | 401.3 | 315.5 | 318.6 | 243.5 | 264.2 | 291.4 | 188.0 | 168.7 |
| | Net working capital | *266.4 | 311.7 | 391.8 | 394.5 | 333.2 | 369.9 | 346.0 | 423.3 | 350.5 | 340.3 | 333.4 |
| | Current ratio | 1.48 to 1 | 1.70 to 1 | 1.85 to 1 | 1.98 to 1 | 2.06 to 1 | 2.16 to 1 | 2.42 to 1 | 2.60 to 1 | 2.20 to 1 | 2.81 to 1 | 2.98 to 1 |
| | Investments and advances | 664.1 | 519.1 | 393.9 | 351.5 | 343.8 | 209.5 | 188.6 | 166.3 | 113.1 | 97.7 | 75.8 |
| | Property, plant and equipment, net | 673.2 | 606.7 | 556.0 | 493.7 | 443.5 | 423.6 | 397.6 | 412.8 | 400.8 | 377.8 | 364.8 |
| | Total assets | 2,191.2 | 1,908.3 | 1,823.4 | 1,658.7 | 1,450.2 | 1,340.3 | 1,192.5 | 1,284.6 | 1,171.5 | 1,021.4 | 963.0 |
| | Notes payable and long-term debt | 258.1 | 226.4 | 219.1 | 194.6 | 171.3 | 206.1 | 180.9 | 301.5 | 214.6 | 174.3 | 183.2 |
| | Debt to equity ratio | 20.9% | 19.8 | 20.5% | 20.3% | 19.6% | 27.8% | 26.3% | 45.0% | 33.4% | 28.6% | 31.9% |
| | Shareholders' equity | 1,235.9 | 1,145.7 | 1,068.9 | 958.1 | 872.2 | 742.3 | 689.1 | 670.0 | 642.4 | 610.4 | 574.9 |
| | Return on average equity | 14.5% | 11.4 | 15.4% | 13.7% | 12.9% | 11.4% | 6.6% | 7.7%* | 11.4% | 10.0% | 8.4% |
| | Book value per common share† | 29.52 | 27.06 | 25.30 | 22.63 | 20.54 | 19.18 | 17.76 | 17.31 | 16.74 | 15.47 | 14.70 |
| **Other data (Thousands)** | Average number of common shares outstanding† | 43,030 | 43,088 | 42,890 | 42,832 | 42,186 | 38,828 | 38,532 | 38,214 | 38,544 | 39,280 | 38,658 |
| | Number of stockholders at year end | 47.0 | 50.0 | 53.6 | 55.9 | 57.0 | 58.6 | 63.3 | 63.7 | 61.6 | 60.8 | 64.3 |
| | Average number of employees | 55.7 | 55.2 | 55.4 | 47.0 | 38.9 | 38.9 | 39.6 | 46.5 | 46.3 | 42.9 | 41.4 |

*Includes net expense of $20.5 million, or $.54 per share of common stock, resulting from accounting changes, principally to reflect the cost of substantially all domestic inventories at LIFO (last-in, first-out).
**After extraordinary items, net of tax, of $260 thousand or one cent per share of common stock.
†Adjusted for two-for-one stock split effective November 25, 1981.
‡Restated for accrual of compensated absences.
Source: Borg-Warner Corporation, 1981 annual report.

**EXHIBIT 3**
PROPOSED BORG-WARNER CREED, 1970*

Borg-Warner Corporation is owned by the shareholders who supply its capital funds, but is responsible also to employees, customers, suppliers, and to society. Operating within a free enterprise economy, the corporation acknowledges its obligations to the following groups:

### OBLIGATIONS TO SHAREHOLDERS

To earn a return on their investment that compares favorably with other leading companies in our industries, enhancing over the long term the value of that investment. To pay out a fair proportion of income in dividends, consistent with the corporation's continuing need for capital for growth.

### OBLIGATIONS TO EMPLOYEES

To pay an adequate wage to each employee commensurate with his individual contribution to the corporation's work, and at least at the average level of the community where he is employed. To provide the best and safest possible working conditions. To give each Borg-Warner employee equal opportunity for personal achievement and recognition for such achievement. To provide a work environment in

*Source: Draft company proposal, September 16, 1970.

which initiative and creativity are recognized and rewarded.

### OBLIGATIONS TO CUSTOMERS

To develop, through skill, innovation and enterprise, products and services of the highest quality for the purpose intended, and sell them at a price competitive with other producers. To be guided in developing products by the needs of present and prospective customers. To strive always to be a reliable supplier, justifying a reputation for dependability and good service.

### OBLIGATIONS TO SUPPLIERS

To be a reliable customer, working with suppliers as business partners to ensure mutually satisfactory standards of quality and schedules for delivery. To follow business practices that are fair and responsible.

### OBLIGATIONS TO SOCIETY

Shareholders, employees, customers and suppliers all are people who live within a society. To provide for the interests of all these groups, Borg-Warner is obligated to preserve that which it considers good for society, and to take the necessary steps, including the commitment of corporate resources, to improve it when practical.

**EXHIBIT 4**
BERÉ'S LETTER TO EMPLOYEES

June 23, 1976

Borg-Warner Corporation
200 South Michigan Avenue
Chicago, Illinois 60604
Telephone: (312) 663-2060

**To:** Borg-Warner Employees

In view of widespread reports of illegal or improper conduct by employees of public companies, you may have asked yourself: What standard of conduct does Borg-Warner expect of me as its representative?

In the past we have stated that our policy is to comply with the letter and spirit of all laws, wherever we operate. In addition, we will soon issue an expanded statement that reaffirms this policy and deals with political contributions and improper payments.

Such policies are concerned with laws and regulations, and therefore are relatively specific. However, the question itself is broader, relating to the ethical aspects of actions we take on Borg-Warner's behalf that might violate no law, but could violate our personal codes and consciences.

Borg-Warner's philosophy of management puts a premium on individual judgment. We believe most decisions should be made by managers close to the action—not by corporate decree. However, you should know what we expect of you in dealing with the moral and ethical content of decisions.

Briefly stated, it is this: *In carrying out your duties, Borg-Warner does not want you to act in any way contrary to your ethical principles.*

I realize that business is conducted by people whose personal standards vary widely. However, at Borg-Warner, we traditionally seek to hire only people of high moral standards and, believing we have done so, we trust you to maintain those standards in your service with us.

Should there be any doubt about the morality of any action you are considering on Borg-Warner's behalf, ask yourself these questions:

Would I be willing to tell my family about the actions I am contemplating?

Would I be willing to go before a community meeting, a congressional hearing, or any public forum, to describe the action?

In any case, if you would not be willing to do so, Borg-Warner would not want you to go ahead with the action on the assumption it would help the company.

I might make a final suggestion, based on the variations in interpreting ethical conduct, even among well-meaning people.

If you apply the above test and still have doubt about what to do, discuss it with others in the company for whom you have respect—whether peers, subordinates or superiors. I am sure this will help to guide you.

In summary: Your actions in representing Borg-Warner should be always lawful and proper, always capable of withstanding public disclosure, and always guided by your personal code of conduct.

I am confident each of you will abide by that standard.

Very truly yours,

James F. Beré
Chairman and Chief Executive Officer

**EXHIBIT 5**
EXCERPTS FROM MANAGEMENT LETTERS

There are several areas that I feel should be addressed in this policy statement:

1 The philosophy should be customer oriented so that the policy will clearly support our new "marketing" orientation and can serve as a sales tool.
2 The philosophy should as clearly as possible describe the kinds of businesses and products we wish to have in our corporate lineup.
3 Clearly define the financial objectives of the corporation.
4 Describe the interaction between the employee and the corporation. What is expected of the employee and what the employee can expect should be described at least in general terms.

I have purposely excluded a discussion of business ethics since our current policy seems completely clear on the subject.—*A manager, Transportation Equipment Group*

In response to this request, I submit the following:

> To create an environment which will assure the *long-term viability* of Borg-Warner or its successors by supplying *quality goods* and *services* in world markets that generate adequate capital to finance *growth* in *new, existing and emerging markets.*—*A manager, Transportation Equipment Group*

Bill Kieschnick, Atlantic Richfield's new president, made the following value statements during a recent speech:

> "Atlantic Richfield Company believes that to serve its owners, employees and society well, it must have a consistent and coherent set of values on which it premises all of its policies and actions."—*A manager, Energy Equipment Group*

As management's relationship with employees is such an important ingredient in any formula for suc-

cess, I propose to limit any further comments to one particular aspect that worries me—the apparent conflict between the company's support for QWL [quality of worklife] programmes and its policy of divestment where a business unit is not considered to fit into its long-term business strategy.

The fact is that, especially in Europe, there are large numbers of employees very worried and insecure about their future because they surmise that their units are up for sale or may be closed. The attitude of these employees is not unnaturally tempered by the circumstances, but would, I'm sure, be greatly improved if they could be assured that divestment is always the action of last resort.

Although probably a question of policy rather than philosophy, I do feel that a code of divestment practice is needed that employees will accept as fair and reasonable. As mentioned earlier, I also feel that an essential element of such a code would be that divestiture or closure will be an act of last resort, authorised only when every possible effort has been made to effect a "cure" by some other means.—*A manager, Overseas Corporate Office*

In response to your request at the president's meeting that we set down some suggestions for "Principles of Borg-Warner," I have distilled my thoughts to the following:

*Philosophy*
Borg-Warner wants to be the *best company* in any area in which it operates. It wants to be *flexible* in attainment of its strategies. *Decisions* are to be made at the *lowest level* (i.e., nearest to the facts) with an *acceptance* of the fact that taking risks sometimes entails making errors.

The company's people will have a *trust* in each other and *share* in its successes and failures. *The company, through its people, will be dedicated to balanced service to its several constituencies*, i.e., stockholders, customers, suppliers, community and employees. Its people will *contribute* as they are able and be *credited* according to their contributions.

*Goals*
The company shall have goals of *profitable growth* in the value of its stockholders' investment, *personal*

*development* of its people and a strong orientation to *improving service to its customers.—A manager, Transportation Equipment Group*

Obviously, as an outside director, the potential for a meaningful contribution is limited, so I hope you will not be disappointed by my thin offering.

You have sponsored a high regard for the individual and good participation by all parties—as evidenced by the procedures in this program. There seems ample evidence of decentralization and participation, and perhaps more importantly, of a human face to the entire organization.

There is one area where I believe focus and consistency could be greater. As a descendant of a parts manufacturing operation, it is not surprising that Borg-Warner does not appear to demonstrate a high degree of marketing sensitivity. What seems to happen is that you at the center supply the strategic insights on market potential, which leads to acquisitions and divestitures. But in a way, these rather severe approaches are a substitution for marketing sensitivity and responsiveness in the traditional units. Perhaps organizational evolution and modernization would be a smoother process if it were more organic.

Accordingly, I suggest that somewhere in the beliefs and practices you have a fundamental statement of purpose that you succeed by finding customer needs and by responding to them with unique quality, service, and price.—*An outside director*

**EXHIBIT 6**

AGENDA FOR 1982 CHAIRMAN'S MEETING

**Monday, May 17**

7:45 A.M.  Continental breakfast

8:30 A.M.  General meeting session
Peter Valli, moderator

"Shared Values"
Jim Beré

"The Power of Belief"
Professor John R. Hale
University College, London

"The Spirit of Democratic Capitalism"
Michael Novak
American Enterprise Institute

"Personal Values"
Dr. Robert Kelly
professor and consultant to business

Lunch and afternoon free

6:00 P.M.  Reception

7:00 P.M.  Mexican fiesta

**Tuesday, May 18**

7:45 A.M.  Continental breakfast

8:30 A.M.  General meeting sesion
Bill Blalock, moderator

"Choices"
Jerry Dempsey

"What Americans Believe"
Florence Skelly, president
Yankelovich, Skelly & White, Inc.

"Running Scared"
Thomas J. Watson, Jr.,
chairman emeritus,
IBM Corporation

"Gossamer Aircraft and Creativity"
Dr. Paul MacCready,
founder and president,
AeroVironment, Inc.

Lunch and afternoon free

5:45 P.M.  Trip to Rawhide

**Wednesday, May 19**

7:45 A.M.  Continental breakfast

8:30 A.M.  General meeting session
Len Harvey, moderator

"What Businesses Can Do"
Amitai Etzioni, professor of sociology
George Washington University,
founder and director of
Center for Policy Research

"Beliefs at Work"
Robert Patchin
Director of productivity programs
Northrop Corporation

"The Entrepreneurial Spirit"
Bob LaRoche

"Marketing and Moral Vision"
Professor Peter E. Gibson
Harvard University

Closing remarks
Jim Beré

Lunch and afternoon free

6:00 P.M.  Reception

7:00 P.M.  Dinner dance

# Building Trust at Warner Gear

Jim Doyle sat back in his chair and smiled. He had just received word that management had won a dispute over the employee health insurance plan. It had taken over a year to get a decision on the arbitration, but Doyle, vice president of human resources management, thought it had been worth the wait. Prior to 1983, the health plan had paid for all employee hospitalization costs. Now Warner Gear would save over a million dollars a year by using a new insurance plan that required employees to pay for more of their health care. Furthermore, the union (UAW Local 287) and management now had a "winner take all" agreement: Whoever lost the arbitration paid all of the legal fees.

Doyle savored the victory, but had other reasons to feel pleased. Arbitrations like this one were becoming scarce. Union grievances were down from 300–400 per year in the 1970s to 12–14 in the past two years. With sales up, manufacturing costs down, and morale high in April 1985, things looked better than ever at Warner Gear.

## COMPANY BACKGROUND—A STORMY PAST

Warner Gear was founded in 1901 in Muncie, Indiana. In 1928 the gear manufacturer united with the Borg and Beck Company, a producer of clutch plates and universal joints, to form the Borg-Warner Corporation. Borg-Warner later diversified into air conditioning, chemicals and plastics, industrial products, and protective services. Nevertheless, the automotive group had always accounted for the largest portion of corporate sales and earnings (see Exhibit 1). Employing 2,600 people, Warner Gear operated on three shifts, 24 hours per day. It produced mechanical and hydraulic transmissions for cars, trucks, and marine engines; also gears for industrial applications, locking hubs, and transfer cases for four-wheel drive vehicles.

George Inman, manager of labor relations, had worked at Warner Gear since 1955. He remembered how, "during the big years of the auto industry [1950s and 1960s], we were making so much money that we couldn't really argue with the union. We just settled with them and went on to avoid strikes. At the time, we usually waited to see how the big three auto companies negotiated their union contracts with the UAW and then followed suit." Ted James, the general manager, said, "People in the automobile business—both labor and management—were fat, dumb, and happy all the way up to 1970. There were bad feelings between labor and management back then too, but as long as wages and profits kept going up, both sides were content to leave well enough alone."

In 1970 troubles began to surface. Warner Gear lost its biggest client, American Motors.[1] Foreign competition and the oil crisis put unprecedented strains on the automotive industry. Labor relations were marked by constant posturing and shows of strength between labor and management. Even the company newsletter had ceased to function. In 1972 Doyle's job was to stop illegal strike activity. Ex-union president Max Daniels described the situation as "a game to see who could tell the biggest lie. No one kept promises and both sides would do anything to win a point." Union activist Tom Armstrong recalled that wildcat strikes were so frequent that "one time a guy walked out midday to go fishing and the rest of the shop followed him. After that, men leaving work early had to wave their passes over their heads so that the rest of the shop wouldn't follow."

There was a temporary reprieve in 1973. Business picked up when Warner Gear contracted to produce automatic transmissions for Ford. One thousand new people were hired. But when the recession of 1974 hit, they were laid off. Tensions continued to mount. Warner Gear was in trouble, but few people knew exactly how much trouble. Financial information was only shared with a handful of top managers. Since management had lied to the union in the past, the union was not ready to believe them when they suddenly "cried poverty." Said

Armstrong, "When you don't know how much a person has in his pockets, you tend to ask for everything."

In 1975, management, hoping to involve workers in the reduction of scrap costs, introduced a productivity bonus plan.[2] The plan was not effective because, according to Doyle, the employee groups were too large and workers could not identify with what they had done. There were also communications problems. "Basically, communications between management and labor consisted of squabbling over grievances on a continuous basis," said George Inman. There were mass disciplinary meetings which one union member referred to as "kangaroo courts." Said Inman, "The union would defend their people whether they were right or wrong and management would hand out suspensions—everything went on paper because the only form of communication was confrontation."

The company's labor disputes were complicated by other problems. Engineering research and development had been regarded as an operating expense rather than a long-term investment. As a result, the engineering department shrank and failed to develop new products. Warner Gear was losing customers to the better products and lower prices of foreign competition. One union member observed that "Borg-Warner had been raping this company—they just took the money and ran—machines were old and the place was falling apart."

## A FIRST STEP

"By the end of 1976," said Inman, "an overall evaluation [of this company] would have said that there was no way we could stay in business. Borg-Warner Corporation told us we would not get any more capital investment unless we negotiated a viable union contract." Thus, in 1977 it was crucial for Warner Gear to negoti-

[1]Warner Gear's competition comes from its clients, since most car manufacturers also produce transmissions. One of their major American competitors was New Process Gear, the transmission division of Chrysler Corporation.

[2]When a gear or other metal part was defective, it was discarded and turned into scrap. The price of metal scrap was lower than the price of the metal, so scrap costs were of great concern to this industry.

ate a labor contract which it could afford. But the union was hostile and ready to "slug it out." Consequently, management decided to open its books. They made a videotape presentation in which the financial condition of the company was explained in detail, demonstrating that Warner Gear would fail if the union did not cooperate.

The strategy worked and the resulting contract rewrote the collective bargaining agreement and changed the incentive system. The new incentive system provided a flat 1% in pay for 1% in production. The contract also changed seniority retention from five years to three years, which meant that Warner Gear was not required to rehire those workers that it laid off in 1974. Left with little choice, the union grudgingly ratified the contract but told its members to save their money because in three years there would be a strike.

With a viable contract, the Borg-Warner Corporation provided capital to Warner Gear, which then invested heavily in the engineering department. Their strategy was to develop the best products on the market. In 1978 a new "world class" five-speed gear system called the T-5 was developed. It was suitable for jeeps, trucks, and high-performance cars (e.g., Trans Am, Firebird, Z28, Camaro, Thunderbird, and the Nissan 300ZX). Another product developed was transfer cases for four-wheel drive pick-up trucks. Although Warner Gear had had no previous business in this area, it eventually succeeded in becoming Ford Motor Company's sole supplier of transfer cases. Warner Gear's third success was a dramatic award-winning innovation: a "shift on the fly" option, which allowed the driver of a four-wheel drive vehicle to shift from two-wheel to four-wheel drive with the push of a button.

## THE "HUMAN" PROBLEM

While the engineering department in 1978 and 1979 was making steady progress, tensions from the last union contract continued to grow between labor and management. Jim Doyle said that "the human side of the problem was

the real killer. If we didn't get that licked, it would be all over." Max Daniels, the union president at the time, also knew that things had to change. He said, "We [the union] didn't believe anything that management said, so we would have slowdowns and walkouts—there was no way for us to deal with our mistrust except by shows of strength."

In addition to mistrust, widespread drug and alcohol abuse caused further disciplinary problems. One union member boasted that in the early 1970s "you could get the best dope in Indiana at Warner Gear—we were the UAW, we had more money, so we could buy the best." Over the years, employees and the union covered up for people with substance abuse problems while management tried to punish them through suspensions. Hank Smith, a 54-year-old toolmaker, believed that people with such problems should be given help. He began, on his own time during lunch and after work, to help individuals find assistance for their drug and alcohol problems. With the cooperation of the assistant manager of labor relations, Ed Stone, an Employee Assistance Program (EAP) was formulated in 1978. The EAP provided a free and confidential referral service to all employees for substance abuse, psychological problems, and family problems. Management hoped that, by showing genuine concern for the welfare of its employees, it could gain their trust. The rank and file did not initially accept the program, worrying that it was "a management trick" to gain personal information on employees that could be used to fire them. "Union leaders," said Smith, "did not want to look silly for having trusted a management that they had never trusted before."

Doyle had learned that managing trust and mistrust was a complicated but not impossible task. In 1976, because of family concerns, he had taken a course in Parent Effectiveness Training (PET).[3] Doyle found what he learned in this course was so helpful that he and Phil Day, training and management development

[3]Thomas Gordon, *Parent Effectiveness Training* (New York: Bantam Books, 1970).

manager, took a similar course in Leadership Effectiveness Training (LET) in 1979.[4] The training program focused on active listening (i.e., listening so as to understand the speaker's feelings and needs), effective confrontation and problem identification, and most importantly win/win conflict resolution in which outcomes acceptable to both parties were sought. Essentially, the training provided useful ways to establish and maintain constructive relationships among parties with different interests.

LET had a profound effect on Doyle's management style and philosophy. He became convinced that Warner Gear needed to change its combative atmosphere into a cooperative one. To this end he began to investigate "Employee Involvement Circles" (EICs). These were groups in which employees discussed solutions to on-the-job problems. In other companies, those who worked daily on the line had played a creative role in formulating improvements. Doyle decided that EICs could pool production know-how and, while saving the company money, might also help to improve labor relations. At first trial EICs were set up in the shop and office area. Employees were organized into groups of four to ten. They were to raise work-related problems and, when a solution was suggested, check its feasibility with an engineer or other specialist. Doyle hoped to implement the plan throughout Warner Gear in the beginning of 1980. That year, however, turned out to be a time of struggles and surprises.

### 1980—A ROLLER COASTER YEAR

When Doyle had unveiled his plan for EICs, the rank and file were as skeptical as they had been with the EAP. "Another management program," they said, "a new form of manipulation." The circles were operative for two weeks, whereupon the union decided to boycott them. The union hoped to use this boycott as a bargaining chip in pending grievance discussions.

[4]Thomas Gordon, *Leader Effectiveness Training* (New York: Bantam Books, 1977).

Doyle refused to yield to what he referred to as "blackmail" on quality of work life programs such as the EAP and the EIC.

In the spring of 1980 there was a three-week strike. Sales were down but relations between the union leaders and management had been improving. Management again offered to open its books to union leaders, who could then see for themselves the financial condition of the company. The union leaders, however, refused. Doyle said that it was because "if they saw the figures, they would have had to be responsible." Union president Max Daniels said it was because they weren't sure that they were being shown the correct figures. When union leaders finally reached a settlement with management, the rank and file rejected it. This was a sobering event for the labor leaders and management—both were out of touch with the rank and file. A second proposal, not significantly different from the first, was accepted by union members two weeks later. Four hundred people were laid off after the contract was ratified. The union leaders knew that the company was in financial trouble. Union president Max Daniels said, "We all realized that we were in the same boat and that we had to sit down and decide that we wouldn't lie to each other no matter what."

Both offered gestures of trust. The union pledged to give full support to the Employee Assistance Program and union members ended their boycott of the EICs. Management, in return, promised to give workers regular updates on the company's financial situation. Doyle said that "it was obvious that we had to become more open if we expected more cooperation." These agreements were "sealed with a handshake" and not written into the contract.

### SHARING FINANCIAL INFORMATION

Jeff Bell became the vice president of finance in 1980. He had worked for the automotive division of Borg-Warner in Japan and Great Britain. He had never wanted to work at Warner Gear because of its reputation for labor problems and its "unruly size." However, the innovations that were under way when he arrived pleasantly surprised him. He was particularly pleased with the EICs because he had observed how well they worked in Japan.

In Bell's opinion, the 1980 strike had occurred because the union and its members did not sufficiently understand the financial information they were given. He decided to rectify this problem by conveying timely financial information to both management and employees. In business, he said, "there are no quantum leaps—you need to see things improving daily." Using charts and diagrams, he conducted weekly meetings in which he gave key financial data on productivity and compared that data with the figures forecasted for that week. These meetings were attended by managers, the union president, and the chairman of the union negotiating committee. Some of the shared information was sensitive, such as the margin Warner Gear had on certain products. Doyle realized the trade-off: "If the competition got hold of this information they could undercharge us, but if you don't share information with the employees, then they will not work with you—the union has no more reason to leak this information than a manager," said Doyle.

Employees were further kept up to date by a monthly profit-sharing newsletter and a semi-annual presentation to all employees. In the presentation, Bell disclosed financial information on sales and operating income which included a breakdown of how much business Warner Gear did with each customer. He also discussed various problems and business opportunities and reserved the end of each session for questions.

Bell discovered many misconceptions and recognized the need to make complex issues clear. He explained the stresses of international business on the automotive industry and why companies had to tighten their belts in order to be competitive. He also tried to clear up misconceptions that employees had about corporate finances. For example, some thought that Warner Gear could make up for losses on its tax return. "The challenge," said Bell, "was to get some of these economic issues to make

sense." He liked being accountable to management and employees on a regular basis. "A financial officer must be willing to be challenged," he affirmed.

## LIFE IN THE BOZO TANK

The first real test of whether the labor climate was starting to change came with the company picnic in August 1980. Labor and management pooled money and manpower to organize a picnic for hourly and salaried employees of Warner Gear. It was to be held in a park owned by the union. Doyle remembers that some workers insisted there was "no way that salaried people would set foot in a union park." Union dissidents threatened to boycott the picnic and put up signs that said: "Enjoy the picnic with your COLA," which referred to the freeze on cost of living adjustments in the new union contract. Both Doyle and union president Daniels heard rumors that no one would show up for the picnic. But Doyle said, "Let's do it anyway." This was their first joint social event—its success was considered important.

When the day arrived, between six and eight thousand people showed up. This included the families of employees and retirees of Warner Gear. Doyle and Daniels volunteered to sit in the Bozo tank. (The Bozo tank is part of a game in which people would throw balls at a target, causing the person in the tank to fall into the water.) When Doyle noticed that union members were lining up behind the children who were playing the game, he thought that the good-natured fun might be over. But the union sharpshooters attacked both men and gave each an equally good dunking. Doyle believed that the picnic was an important turning point in labor relations. "If two hundred salaried and hourly employees were able to work together on this, there was no reason why we couldn't work together every Monday morning," he said.

## QUALITY OF WORK LIFE PROGRAMS

The initial six-month union boycott of EICs had ended in the fall of 1980. "It was a blessing in disguise," said Doyle. Many managers, particularly line managers, had resisted the idea because they did not want to lose control. Doyle worked one on one with his managers to sell the concept, and he believed that his job was made somewhat easier by an influx of younger managers in 1980. "We realized that involvement circles had to belong to everyone," said Doyle. "Otherwise all of this sharing of information and responsibility would have been just a false promise." Hence, all circles were open to both hourly and salaried employees and there were circles for each shift in every department.

Max Daniels indicated he would support the circles as long as the union had equal participation in running them. He appointed the leader of the circle boycott to be the first facilitator (group leader) of an EIC. Phil Day carefully selected other group facilitators on the basis of leadership qualities and "personal charisma." All group facilitators then took LET. As a result they became a tightly knit group.

By February of 1981 a series of quality of work life programs was formally launched by the joint efforts of the union and management. Because these programs were agreed upon in the absence of a written agreement, the ongoing need for consensus extended the time it took for implementation. The programs included LET for managers and union leaders, Effectiveness Training for Women,[5] joint communications including the *Warner Gear News,* fitness programs, the yearly employee picnic, the Employee Assistance Program (EAP), Employee Involvement Circles, and team building.[6] Daniels observed that "the new feeling of trust helped make the programs successful. Once employees saw that the programs gave them a chance to upgrade their working conditions, they became pretty enthusiastic."

When fully operational in 1981, the quality circles met once a week for an hour, usually at the end of a shift. There were only a few minor problems. Some line supervisors were resistant to the circles, because they claimed that they lost an hour of productivity from their workers. Also, since the end of the shift was the busiest time for a supervisor, it was inconvenient for supervisors to take part in circles.

The circles tried to solve problems efficiently. They were given immediate access to management, even though some circle solutions could be implemented without management clearance. There were results. One night-shift circle, called the "Night Owls," wanted to help reduce scrap wastes by keeping gears from being run through a machine twice. Their solution was to have the plant carpenter build a barrier to prevent the gears from being cut a second time. The barrier cost $120 to build and saved the company an estimated $5,000 per year. Another group, called the "Cast Iron Elite," enlisted management and engineering support and saved the company about $98,000 a year by retooling a machine so that it could perform two processes on a part rather than moving the part to separate machines for each process. All of these innovations were praised and publicized in the company newsletter.

Employees also began to use the Employee Assistance Program. Joan Carey, a trained social worker, was hired as EAP administrator for salaried employees. Hank Smith, who had informally been playing such a role in the plant, was named EAP administrator for hourly employees. Although Smith had no formal training in the area (he hadn't even finished high school), he was warmly referred to as a "teddy bear" who really cared about people. Smith and Carey had met while doing volunteer work drug rehabilitation center and worked gether. Eventually, formal arrange to personal choices—manager ployees consulted the adr best.

The EAP pr family memb through loc and drug a problems,

---

[5] A form of LET for women as outlined in Linda Adams, *Effectiveness Training for Women* (New York: G. P. Putnam's Sons, 1979).
[6] Team building was used to develop self-managing work groups.

personal concerns such as legal or financial problems. Said Carey, "The program worked well because people saw results—when you cure the company drunk, people notice." The community was so impressed by the EAP that when judges heard drunk-driving cases involving Warner Gear employees, they referred them to the company EAP.

## THE 1983 CONTRACT

Throughout 1982 labor-management relations continued to get better. The quality of work life programs had improved communications and the employee meetings led by Jeff Bell gave workers a better understanding of the company's finances. The path was cleared for contract negotiations. But sales were down again and this time around Doyle wanted to make some changes in the union contract.

In the fall of 1982, Warner Gear needed to know what their labor costs would be for the following year because of some potential new business with Ford. Consequently Doyle decided to press for a contract by December 1982. Max Daniels told Doyle that the union would not be ready until January of 1983, which was when they had expected to negotiate the contract. Doyle responded that, if they waited until January, Warner Gear would go out of business. The Borg-Warner Corporation later told Doyle that he had "no right" to tell the union that Warner Gear would go out of business, but as Doyle pointed out, "the contract was already signed."

Three days after Doyle's forceful request the union came to the negotiating table. The provisions of the 1983 contract rolled back many of the benefits gained in previous UAW ~tracts. After some deliberation the union ac-~ed but objected to the insurance plan. ~e was taken to the courts for arbitration ~it 2).

~workers made some advances as ~d the opportunity to share in the ~. This paid off the following ~ct, employee cooperation, ~nd the efforts of the en-

gineering department all made 1983 a profitable year for Warner Gear.

About 1,200 new (and younger) employees were hired in 1983–1984 under the terms of the new contract. In the past, the company had simply selected people and put them on the line with little training. Now each new employee was given a 40-hour orientation course in which management and the union familiarized them with the physical plant and the quality of work life programs, and gave instructions on whom to go to for various types of problems. One union member remembered how, when he was hired ten years earlier, "they just lined everyone up and selected the big guys to work on the parts of the line that required heavy lifting. None of us knew what we were doing. We broke machines and produced a lot of scrap."

## THE "SALUTE TO THE WINNERS"

On March 4, 1984, Warner Gear employees received $1.01 in profit for each hour that they worked. Most employees received a profit-sharing check for about $2,000 for the 1983 fiscal year. The company distributed the checks and celebrated their success at a special program at the Ball State University Auditorium.

The program opened with a recording of Carly Simon singing "Nobody Does It Better" to a darkened auditorium illuminated by a 60-foot-long slide of Warner Gear employees at work. "It was the kind of experience that gave you goose bumps," said Doyle. When the lights came up there were speeches. General manager Ted James thanked everyone for their sacrifices over the past few years. Doyle emphasized the new spirit of cooperation that had resulted from the quality of work life programs and the improvement in productivity and in the bottom line. Union president Daniels said that "trust was something that had slipped away from us." He expressed the hope that "labor and management would continue to be honest with each other and nurture mutual trust and respect in the future."

Union members, however, retained one fear—namely, that management would not continue to give them financial information when the company was making money. While the ceremony of 1984 allayed some doubts, union members still wondered about the future.

## CONTINUED IMPROVEMENT

1984 was an even better year for Warner Gear.[7] In another ceremony, employees received their share of a profit that had grown by $1.4 million from the previous year. This time each employee received $1.19 for every hour worked. Investments in machinery, engineering, and people were reflected in the following areas:

- The average value-added per employee, a measurement which included all facets of the operation and was determined by subtracting the cost of purchases from sales and then dividing by the number of employees, increased from $34,000 to $47,000 between 1978 and 1984.
- In 1982 total sales were $167 million, amounting to an average of $93,192 per employee. By 1984, sales had risen to $331.5 million and sales per employee to $127,700.
- Inventory turns, or the relationship between inventory and sales, showed a remarkable improvement over three years:

| 1982 | 1983 | 1984 |
|------|------|------|
| 4.2  | 7.8  | 8.6  |

This meant that there was a 50% reduction of inventory or double sales volume with the same inventory level.

- The scrap cost for all products made at Warner Gear had gone from 2.1% of sales in 1982 to 1.8% in 1984, a 14% reduction. In one area, the scrap level of the 4- and 5-speed gear systems (which were 35% of the business) was $7.47 per unit in 1982, $5.28 per unit in 1983, and $4.01 in 1984. This

[7]Sales to Ford accounted for 42% of their business in 1984.

represented a 46% reduction in waste from 1982 to 1984.
- The cost of reworking defective parts had declined from 8.31% of cost of sales in 1983 to 6.17% in 1984, a 26% reduction.
- The cost of materials to sales for 1984 decreased .3% from 1983. When combined with the producer price index inflation figure, this showed an actual cost improvement of 1.6%.
- Company savings from EICs were more than $2,000,000 in 1984 (a 14:1 return on the company's investment in the circles), and the total savings from cost-cutting programs amounted to $14,548,930.

In addition to increased productivity and substantial savings, there were no strikes in 1984 and grievances showed a steady decline.

By April 1985 there were 80 EICs with approximately 800 participants. Enthusiasm for the circles was high. "When the quality circles first started," one union member said, "I thought that they were all bull. Not now. We have communication here like we never had before." Another said, "I'm a union man. They wanted us to get involved. Now it's a way of life. It's not just saving money; it's building people." Said a circle member, "Before you felt like you had no one to talk to—now you can talk to management—it gives us a chance to have a positive influence." "Circles are," said one woman, "the best source of information." And one circle member boasted, "We have one of the main leaders of union walkouts in our group."

## VISIONS OF THE FUTURE

Between 1979 and 1984, the management of Warner Gear had conducted internal and external studies of the organization. The external studies included assistance from organizational design and development consultants as well as staff assistance from Borg-Warner.

Jim Doyle was excited about the results of these studies and had big plans for the future. For example, he felt that by reducing layers and focusing the business units, it would be possible to achieve a "supervisorless" facility. It was Doyle's opinion that such a step, although considered by many to be radical, was a logical extension of the already successful quality of work life programs in place at Warner Gear.

Three million dollars was set aside to train selected team members. In the factory, focused production units would use robotics and numerically controlled (computerized) machines. In order to learn how to repair new equipment, 76 skilled tradesmen and operators would be sent to the machine vendors' factories. Said Doyle, "I want this place to get to the point where the machine operator becomes like the owner-operator."

The first teams would be specially selected by management and the new leaders would take an LET course. In the future, teams would select their own managers and the factory would be run entirely by workers. Management development manager Phil Day, however, was skeptical—"no way that will ever happen." Doyle pointed out in reply that "a few years ago no one would have thought that union members would sit in quality circles and worry about saving the company money."

"The days of the big labor strikes are over," said union member Tom Armstrong. "The key to the future of the UAW is problem solving." The success of the quality of work life programs was due, according to Armstrong, to the union—"they are not programs, but a way of life." Labor relations were good, said Armstrong, "but a union will always be needed to guard the terms of the labor contract. They [management] have a different life style. Many of them don't get down to the factory floor enough, so they don't live in the same everyday reality." One example that Armstrong gave of this "different reality" was the time in November of 1984 when a manager removed a coffee pot from one of the work stations because a worker was filling the pot on company time. The other workers resented this—the task did not take up much time and proceeds from the coffee pot funded retirement and Christmas

parties. The new union president was so outraged that he began to fill the pot and was supended for six hours by management. The Muncie newspaper ran a story on the incident with the headline "Coffee Pot Boils Over at Warner Gear." Eventually, the coffee pot was put back in operation. Armstrong pointed out that "management doesn't realize that for many people the factory is the center of their social life."

One problem on the horizon for the union was the issue of what constituted a full workday. Management had traditionally defined a full workday in terms of the maximum utilization of workers and not according to what was produced. They claimed 7.1 hours and wanted workers to remain at their machines until the end of a shift. The union said that a full workday was the time it took to produce 121.25% over the base incentive rate. In reality, said Armstrong, most employees worked their hardest in the first four hours—with some working through breaks and lunch to finish early. Max Daniels also emphasized productivity. "We get paid for what we do. The guys in the factory will police themselves—if someone on the line goofs off, we make sure that he doesn't get his incentive pay. Everyone in a UAW shop quits early on Fridays. It's a tradition—they 'kill snakes' to get out early. If you were to make them stay on the machines until the end of the shift, you'd get 70% less production."

After the 1983 contract was signed, Daniels lost the union election to a younger man who ran on a platform that opposed all of the quality of work life programs. Union campaigns could be vicious affairs; candidates had been known to get into fist fights, and to write letters slandering the candidate and sometimes his or her family. "Nice guys don't make it in the UAW," said Armstrong. "When I ran for shop steward, the other candidate sent around a letter saying that I played golf all the time and wouldn't have time for my union duties." In Daniels' case the other candidate spent money on T-shirts and buttons, and won a landslide victory. Ironically, when Daniels' opponent became president, he began to support all of the programs that he had campaigned against. "The outs always want in," observed Daniels.

Daniels was proud of his six years as union president. He believed that management should show an interest in their employees and that honesty and trust were necessary for the survival of a business. Daniels said, "I may not like what you say, but if I can believe it, we can work problems out." While he thought that employees should have a say in work-related decisions, Daniels did not think that workers should manage the plant. "The current problem is that supervisors are hired off the street and not from inside the plant. The supervisors today are too lax. They act like they don't want to stir up the waters. What we should do is hire fewer supervisors and pay them more money—supervisors should be paid more than workers. It is management's job to manage and the union's job to make sure that the work agreement is met."

• • •

Max Daniels put a piece of chewing tobacco under his lip and stared out at the snowy April sky. At 61 his legs were beginning to get sore at the end of a day. But with the 1986 union elections less than a year away, Daniels was not ready to stop working. "I have one more thing that I want to do before I retire," he said, "I want to be union president again so I can get back the insurance plan that we lost in the 1983 arbitration."

# EXHIBITS: Building Trust at Warner Gear

**EXHIBIT 1**
SALES FOR BORG-WARNER CORPORATION AND ITS
AUTOMOTIVE GROUP
(in millions of $)

| Year | Borg-Warner Corporation | Automotive group |
|------|------------------------|------------------|
| 1970 | 952.0 | 402.5 |
| 1971 | 995.3 | 387.3 |
| 1972 | 1,138.4 | 452.4 |
| 1973 | 1,386.5 | 560.8 |
| 1974 | 1,648.6 | 651.1 |
| 1975 | 1,608.7 | 620.6 |
| 1976 | 1,814.4 | 652.4 |
| 1977 | 2,013.8 | 718.5 |
| 1978 | 2,307.6 | 844.5 |
| 1979 | 2,254.0 | 909.8 |
| 1980 | 2,293.8 | 832.8 |
| 1981 | 2,515.8 | 960.8 |
| 1982 | 2,444.6 | 905.5 |
| 1983 | 2,763.2 | 1,037.0 |
| 1984 | 3,009.6 | 1,168.0 |

*Source:* Borg-Warner 1975, 1979, and 1984 annual reports. According to company records, Warner Gear's average contribution to Automotive Group sales during this period was just under 20%, with a high of 28% and a low of 12%.

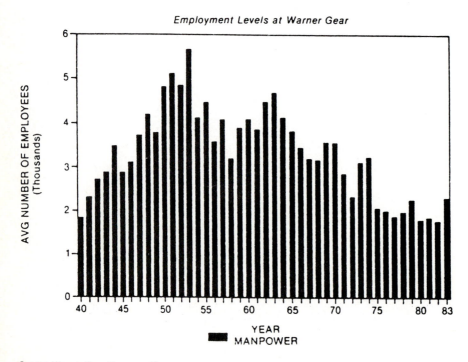

*Employment Levels at Warner Gear*

YEAR
MANPOWER

*Source:* Warner Gear Company History.

**EXHIBIT 2**
THE 1983 CONTRACT

**WAGE/FRINGE PROVISIONS**

- A 42- (rather than 36-) month contract term
- A 24-month wage freeze for salaried employees
- Cost-of-living adjustments eliminated for 24 months
- Wage scales reduced by 20% for new employees
- 2 holidays and 2 personal days per year eliminated
- Year-end bonus for new employees delayed for 2 years
- Company/union panel established for productivity and quality recommendations
- Profit-sharing plan initiated

**INSURANCE PROVISIONS**

- Levels of hospital insurance coverage capped at "usual and customary" as of April 1, 1983 (this went into arbitration)
- Substance abuse program modified to restrict frequency of enrollment
- Disability benefits reduced to same level as unemployment compensation
- Disability claims cannot exceed 52 weeks out of 24 months
- New employee group insurance plan [instituted] for those hired after January 1, 1983
- Pension plan continued at present level

## PART THREE

# Corporate Values: Looking Outward

In Parts 1 and 2 of this book, the cases concerned problems that focused either on individuals or on situations largely internal to corporations. Nevertheless, it will already have become apparent from the discussion of several cases—such as "The Individual and the Corporation" and the series on Lex Service Group, Ltd.—that there may be another important set of constituencies to whom the corporation has obligations—that is, those to be found "outside" the boundaries of the firm. Whether those persons or groups represent themselves or are represented by a government body, it is clear that today's corporation cannot and does not operate in a social vacuum. And because the corporation can affect the lives and livelihoods of people outside, it is a kind of "moral agent" in society.

Part 3 presents a wide range of cases in which corporate behavior and policy affect the welfare of the larger society or some segment of it—from the safety of a specific product to the implied value system that choices of advertising messages and programs help to convey. We acknowledge that there are a multitude of topics that could be covered from this perspective, and so we have tried to select cases of significance to many kinds of companies and industries and to many sectors of society.

We begin with "Tennessee Coal and Iron" and look back in time at the racial tensions in Birmingham, Alabama, during the 1960s, as one of the major companies in that city considers actions it might or should take to mitigate the social effects of a highly segregated society. As the company's president considers the role of his corporation regarding segregation, he is faced with a variety of conflicting pressures and views from the local community, the national press, and the federal government.

In "The Poletown Dilemma," General Motors and the city of Detroit are the institutional players. The residents of Poletown are among those affected by their decisions. How much loyalty can and should a large corporation have to its city of origin, the community it has served since its founding? Are the shareholders well served by such loyalty? Are other stakeholders? On the other hand, how much loyalty does the city owe to the corporation? To the residents who will be displaced if the corporation builds its new plant in Detroit?

In "Massachusetts High Technology Council," a major industry association considers how it should best promote its belief that a reform of the state's personal income tax structure is essential to ensuring the continuing development of high-tech industry and employment. The council must decide with whom it is willing to ally itself and what strategy it should adopt to pursue its goal of influencing public policy on an important economic and social issue.

In "Dayton Hudson Corporation: Conscience and Control," we witness a hostile takeover attempt with significant implications. A company that has an outstanding record of corporate community involvement is suddenly plunged into a major economical and political crisis as its various shareholders become active. This case invites careful reflection on the meaning of ownership and governance in the modern corporation.

The question as to who legitimately holds moral authority both within a company and in society as a whole is expanded, this time as it relates to marketing policy, in "Consolidated Foods Corporation (A)" and "(B)" and "Note on the TV Advertising and Programming Controversy, 1981."\* When Consolidated acquires Hanes Hosiery, it suddenly finds itself in the middle of a heated controversy over some of the Hanes advertising messages and programming decisions. Company executives must decide how to respond to criticisms and how to balance the social and economic impacts of their ads and programs.

Like Consolidated Foods, Alco Beverage Company must determine to what degree it is its "brother's keeper," but the challenge in the latter case is directly related to its principal product: beverage alcohol. Is it simply prudence, or is it ethics, or is it beyond the call of duty to encourage moderation in the use of one's own product? Can the issues in this case be generalized to other products and other industries?

In the series of Managing Product Safety cases, we explore various considerations that affect the development and marketing of products. Four cases on very different products that carry potentially serious threats of injury to consumers are presented in retrospect, from both a company and a public interest point of view, to reflect the panoply of problems that managers face in deciding what to market and what liabilities may or do exist. An introductory "Note on Product Safety" accompanies this series and furnishes information on the economic, legal, and ethical aspects of product safety problems.

Next we present several cases that develop the product safety theme within a much wider framework—business ethics and the environment. "Col-

---

\*We direct the reader's attention to the "Illustrative Case Analysis for Consolidated Foods Corporation (A)" in the Appendix. Case "(B)" offers an opportunity for further discussion, particularly in conjunction with the Note on TV Advertising and Programming, which provides an overview of the concerns that various sectors of society have expressed about the quality and influence of American network television.

laborative Research, Inc." along with the "Note on the Biotechnology Industry" invite reflection on just how much general managers can be expected to
anticipate potential product-related hazards and abuses.

"Environmental Pressures: The Pollution Problem" is a description of the
"classic pollution case"—Reserve Mining Company's alleged deposit of iron
ore tailings in the waters of Lake Superior. In tracing Reserve's strategy for
dealing with environmental issues since the founding of the operation in the
late 1940s, the reader has an opportunity to consider what he or she believes
is the proper company posture regarding pollution under a variety of changing
legislative requirements. The company must also deal with a complex array of
government policies and political processes in order to resolve the issue.

"DuPont Freon Products Division" and "Ashland Oil, Inc." involve more
recent environmental challenges. In the DuPont case, a corporation must confront the economic implications of discontinuing and the ethical implications
of continuing ozone-depleting fluorocarbon production. In the Ashland case,
economics and ethics again meet. This time the issue is how candid the CEO
should be about a massive diesel fuel discharge into the Ohio River from one
of his company's storage terminals.

To conclude Part 3, and as a natural transition to Part 4, we consider
"Braniff International: The Ethics of Bankruptcy." Both inward-looking and
outward-looking corporate values are at stake in this case as Howard Putnam
struggles to manage responsibly a company in economic decline.

# Tennessee Coal and Iron

In the early 1960s, the Tennessee Coal and Iron Division (TCI) of United States Steel Corporation (USS) was one of that corporation's largest divisions. Originally an independent company, TCI became a subsidiary of USS in 1907. It continued to grow, and added quarries, mines, reservoirs, electric power systems, and coke, wire, and many other kinds of plants and steel facilities over the years. By the beginning of World War II, TCI was by far the largest producer of primary steel and many other products in the 11-state region that it served. It moved from subsidiary to divisional status in 1953.

TCI's peak employment was in 1942, when a total of 33,000 was attained. A number of factors, e.g., decline in steel demand and a switch to imported ores, reduced the number of TCI employees to about 24,000 in 1955–57 and to 16,000 in 1964. Nearly 12,000 of these were production and maintenance employees, and about one-third of the 12,000 were black. All, or nearly all, of the production and mainte- nance employees were covered by a contract between USS and the United Steelworkers of America (USW). Despite the decline in its employment rolls, TCI continued to be by far the largest employer in Birmingham and the Jefferson County area of Alabama. Mr. Arthur Wiebel, President of TCI, estimated that the next largest employer was about one-third the size of TCI. Birmingham had a civilian male labor force of 78,000 and Jefferson County, of which Birmingham was the center, a civilian male labor force of about 155,000. The ratio of whites to blacks was about 2 to 1 in Jefferson County, and about 2 to 1⅛ in Birmingham itself.

In 1963, the attention of the nation was focused on racial disturbances in various parts of the South. Some of the most violent occurred in Birmingham. Bombings of black churches, incidents of personal violence, and threats of all types occurred as the drive toward racial integration kindled or kept alive old racial hatreds.

The movement toward integration was also taking place inside TCI's many plants in and around Birmingham. USS had had, orally since 1902 and in writing since 1918, a policy that employment at USS would be made available without regard to race, color, creed, or national origin. This policy, however, was affected by labor agreements, and a portion of the USS Policy Manual had, for several years, read as follows:

> Application of this policy as it relates to union-represented employees will be in accordance with applicable provisions of labor agreements.

Thus, for many years prior to the 1960s, the combined effects of seniority, contracts at individual plant and local union levels, strike threats, and local racial customs had resulted in a high degree of racial segregation within TCI's plants. It was against this backdrop that senior officials of USS, TCI, and the USW had to work to bring about a lessening of racial discrimination within TCI.

Three major events occurred to help these officials in their efforts. A Human Relations Committee was formed in 1960 by 11 major steel producers and the USW as a mechanism for exploring and solving common problems. In March 1961, President John F. Kennedy issued Executive Order 10925. The Order was intended to prevent discrimination within companies bidding or holding government contracts; it also established the Committee on Equal Employment Opportunity, and Vice President Lyndon B. Johnson was appointed chairman of the committee. Finally, there was a continuing decline in demand for TCI's products, which made it more difficult for senior employees to hold their jobs in spite of the more than 1000 separate and rigid lines of promotion among the production and maintenance workers.

These several factors, plus months of hard and laborious work by company and union officials, bore fruit. Lines of promotion were broadened, and all claims of racial discrimina-

tion brought before the CEEO were closed out by June 1963. As a result of this, and a new 1962 contract between the USW and the 11 major steel producers that provided for sweeping changes, Hobart Taylor, Jr., executive vice chairman of the CEEO, wrote a letter to USS which included the following paragraph.

> May I thank you, too, for the example which U.S. Steel has given the rest of the managers in this country by its courageous move in Birmingham at a time of great social tension in the area. This was an important milestone toward true equal employment opportunity. You have earned the gratitude of those of us who are also working toward this important national goal.

In spite of the major accomplishments toward integration within TCI's plants and mines, however, TCI's role in the community had been an issue for some time, and was to become a major one in the summer of 1963. The remainder of this case concerns that issue.

By summer's end, 1963, officials of the United States Steel Corporation (USS) and its Tennessee Coal and Iron Division (TCI) believed that the problems of job integration among TCI's 12,000 white and black production and maintenance workers had been solved in satisfactory fashion. In addition, the physical violence that had permeated the Birmingham area in the spring and early summer of that year had greatly abated.

The tension that had preceded and accompanied the violence, however, continued to exist in the community at large. In discussing the situation, James Reston made the following comment in *The New York Times* (Sept. 22, 1963):

> The point, then, is not that Birmingham is lacking in young leaders, and not that it is lacking in biracial committees, but that the real power structure of the city—the older men who run the industries, banks and insurance companies that in turn influence the stores and big law firms—are not leading the peace effort.

There are about a dozen men in this group, some of whom have worked quietly for a compromise, some of whom have tried and then withdrawn. But at no time have they all worked together.

• • •

(The Reston story listed 13 prominent Birmingham businessmen and lawyers, among them "Arthur W. Weible [sic], president of the Tennessee Coal and Iron Division of United States Steel.")

• • •

There is general agreement here that these men, working together with the leaders of the local clergy of both races, could do more to produce a compromise in a month than Federal troops, Federal officials and all the national Negro organizations put together could in years.

The question is who, if anybody, can get them together. They damn "The Kennedys" and concede that Senator Goldwater would carry Alabama against the President tomorrow, but even this prospect only creates a new dilemma.

On October 22, a *New York Times* reporter met with Mr. Wiebel, Mr. C. Thomas Spivey (TCI director of personnel services), and Mr. Clinton Milstead (TCI director of public relations) in Mr. Wiebel's conference room. The meeting lasted from 9:00 A.M. until 2:30 P.M., and was largely concerned with the work of TCI and union officials in bringing about job integration within TCI.

During his visit, the reporter also asked Mr. Wiebel whether TCI would use its economic power to speed integration in the community itself. According to Mr. Wiebel, the reporter suggested that TCI might put pressure on its suppliers, its bank connections, and some of its customers to aid the cause of Birmingham's blacks.

Both the question and the suggestion came as a surprise to Mr. Wiebel and his associates. In the preceding months, TCI officials had held extended conversations with union officers, representatives of the President's Committee on Equal Employment Opportunity, General Royall and Colonel Blaik, and black leaders.

No question about the use of economic pressure by TCI had arisen in any discussion with these groups and no suggestions concerning its use had been made officially, although unofficially USS had been criticized in the press.

Mr. Wiebel told the reporter that there were two major reasons why TCI would not resort to economic coercion, as the area's largest employer, to try to solve Birmingham's racial problems. He pointed out that neither TCI nor USS had sufficient economic power in the area to solve the problem, and that neither had the right to tell people what they ought or ought not to do. He also stated that, if TCI were to do what the reporter suggested, charges would be made that TCI and USS were trying to run Birmingham.

Three days later, under an October 25 dateline, *The New York Times* carried a 2-column story about TCI and racial integration in Birmingham. Much of the story concerned activities within TCI. Only the lead paragraphs, which discussed the issue of the division's economic influence in the community, are reproduced here:

**The New York Times**
**October 25, 1963**

The United States Steel Corporation, the largest employer in Birmingham, appears to be making significant strides in opening up Negro job opportunities in its Alabama plants.

But the nation's biggest steel maker appears to be making little effort to wield its economic influence to help solve the community's racial problems.

These conclusions emerge from talks with officials of U.S. Steel's Tennessee Coal and Iron Division here, as well as with others in both the North and South familiar with the situation.

Critics have contended that Roger M. Blough, U.S. Steel chairman, could contribute greatly toward stemming the racial strife here by simply instructing local officials to exert their power toward that end. . . . But company officials here insist they do not have that much power, and in any event they show no signs of using what power they do have on the community's racial front.

• • •

On October 29, at a press conference called to announce the results of USS operations during the preceding quarter, Mr. Roger M. Blough, Chairman of the USS Board of Directors, was asked to comment on USS policies in its TCI operation and, more particularly, on the use of its "economic influence" in the Birmingham area as a means of influencing local opinion. The portion of his response dealing with the latter issue follows:

Now, the criticism that U.S. Steel hasn't used what some people refer to as ... economic influence, which I presume to mean some kind of economic force to bring about some kind of a change, is, I think, an improper matter upon which to criticize either Mr. Wiebel or U.S. Steel. I think I would have to take considerable time to fully explain this point, but very briefly, I'd like to say this—that I do not either believe that it would be a wise thing for U.S. Steel to be other than a good citizen in a community, or to attempt to have its ideas of what is right for the community enforced upon that community by some sort of economic means. This is repugnant to me personally, and I am sure it is repugnant to my fellow officers in U.S. Steel. I doubt very much that this in principle is a good thing for any corporation to follow. When we as individuals are citizens in a community, we can exercise what small influence we may have as citizens, but for a corporation to attempt to exert any kind of economic compulsion to achieve a particular end in the social area seems to me to be quite beyond what a corporation should do, and I will say also, quite beyond what a corporation can do.

... We have fulfilled our responsibility in the Birmingham area—whatever responsibility we have as a corporation or as individuals working with a corporation, because, after all, a corporation is nothing but individuals.

The October 30 issue of *The New York Times* carried a front-page story devoted primarily to Mr. Blough's comments about the Birmingham-TCI situation, and on October 31 the following editorial appeared in the paper:

### Corporate Race Relations

When it comes to speaking out on business matters Roger Blough, chairman of the United States Steel Corporation, does not mince words. Mr. Blough is a firm believer in freedom of action for corporate management, a position he made clear in his battle with the Administration last year. But he also has put some severe limits on the exercise of corporate responsibility, for he rejects the suggestion that U.S. Steel, the biggest employer in Birmingham, Ala., should use its economic influence to erase racial tensions. Mr. Blough feels that U.S. Steel has fulfilled its responsibilities by following a nondiscriminatory hiring policy in Birmingham, and looks upon any other measures as both "repugnant" and "quite beyond what a corporation should do" to improve conditions.

This hands-off strategy surely underestimates the potential influence of a corporation as big as U.S. Steel, particularly at the local level. It could, without affecting its profit margins adversely or getting itself directly involved in politics, actively work with those groups in Birmingham trying to better race relations. Steel is not sold on the retail level, so U.S. Steel has not been faced with the economic pressure used against the branches of national chain stores.

Many corporations have belatedly recognized that it is in their own self-interest to promote an improvement in Negro opportunities. As one of the nation's biggest corporations, U.S. Steel and its shareholders have as great a stake in eliminating the economic imbalances associated with racial discrimination as any company. Corporate responsibility is not easy to define or to measure, but in refusing to take a stand in Birmingham, Mr. Blough appears to have a rather narrow, limited concept of his influence.

Also on October 31, the *Congressional Record* contained remarks made by Representative Ryan of the State of New York:

Mr. Speaker, yesterday's *New York Times* carried two stories—one of high corporate indifference, the other of high corporate profits. The statement of Roger Blough, Chairman of the Board of United States Steel Corp., that the corporation should not use its influence to improve racial conditions in strife-torn Birmingham is the epitome of corporate irresponsibility and callousness.

United States Steel willingly accepts all the benefits of our laws and constitution which guarantee the rights of corporations and of private property, but refuses to accept its obligation to support the same laws and constitution which also declare all men equal.

Apparently United States Steel sees [that] its only responsibility is to make profits. Public welfare is not its concern. This callous attitude is a giant step backward by a giant corporation.

It is ironic that, in the same conference, Roger Blough reported a sharp increase in third-quarter sales and earnings. Who is responsible for these profits? Roger Blough in his plush New York office did not bring this about by himself. Behind the profits are some 15,000 steelworkers in Birmingham, many of whom are black, who mine the ore, melt the steel, cut it, shape it, and by their hard labor create the product with which the profits are made. These steelworkers and their families live in a town of terror—a town with segregated schools and bigoted police where our citizens are denied their constitutional rights. United States Steel says to these workers, "Give us your labor but do not expect us to be concerned with your lives or the lives of your children."

United States Steel also says to American Society, "We will benefit from the advantages of American Society and its economic system and its laws but do not expect us to share any responsibility for improving human relations in that society."

Even a schoolboy knows that citizenship has obligations as well as privileges. If all citizens, whether private or corporate, insisted on privileges while refusing obligations, our free democratic society would disintegrate.

Mr. Speaker, power without responsibility is tyranny. United States Steel's policy of inaction is in reality a policy of action. Birmingham and other southern cities are permitted to abuse American citizens and deny to them the right to live decently because the so-called respectable

and responsible people and organizations remain silent. In the case of United States Steel this unconscionable silence in Birmingham is shocking. As a giant of industry, it has a moral obligation to speak out. In Birmingham, where it is the largest employer, this corporation could use its tremendous influence to bring about substantial and constructive change.

I urge all members and all citizens to raise their voice in protest against this callous irresponsibility and indifference. It is time for United States Steel to put people ahead of profits.

President Kennedy, at a press conference on Thursday, November 1, was asked to comment on Mr. Blough's stand. The question and the President's answer follow:

*Question:* The United States Steel Corporation has rejected the idea that it should use economic pressure in an effort to improve race relations in Birmingham, Alabama. Do you have any comment on that position, and do you have any counsel for management and labor in general as to their social responsibility in the areas of tension of this kind?

*The President:* Actually Mr. Blough has been somewhat helpful in one or two cases that I can think of in Birmingham. I don't think he should narrowly interpret his responsibility for the future. That is a very influential company in Birmingham, and he wants to see that city prosper, as do we all. Obviously the Federal government cannot solve this matter. So that business has a responsibility—labor and, of course, every citizen. So I would think that particularly a company which is as influential as United States Steel in Birmingham I would hope would use its influence on the side of comity between the races.

Otherwise, the future of Birmingham, of course, is not as happy as we hope it would be. In other words, it can't be decided—this matter—in Washington. It has to be decided by citizens everywhere. Mr. Blough is an influential citizen. I am sure he will do the best he can.

On November 4, the *Congressional Record*

carried the following remarks by Representative George Huddleston, Jr., of Alabama:

*Mr. Huddleston:* Mr. Speaker, in recent days, what I consider unjustifiable criticism has been lodged at Mr. Roger M. Blough, chairman of the board of the United States Steel Corp., as a result of comments he made in a press conference held in New York on Tuesday, October 29, in which he discussed the role of business in race relations, with particular reference to the Birmingham situation. Some misunderstanding has arisen as a result of this criticism and I feel that, in all fairness to the United States Steel Corp., Mr. Blough, and the people of Birmingham, the record should be clarified. For this purpose, I insert herewith in the *Congressional Record* a verbatim transcript of Mr. Blough's press conference of October 29.

I want to especially call the attention of the Members of Congress to Mr. Blough's comments regarding whether business should attempt to apply economic sanctions to a community in order to further so-called social or moral reforms. Mr. Blough states that such effort by business is repugnant to him and his company, and I think I speak for the overwhelming majority of the citizens of Birmingham in applauding his firm and forthright stand. For any enterprise, Government or private, to attempt to exert economic pressures on the people of any community to bring about social changes is truly repugnant to the American way of life.

We in Birmingham are proud of the contributions that United States Steel's TCI division has over the years made to the economy of our city and look forward to continued cooperation for our mutual benefit in the future.

*The New York Times* of Nov. 7 contained a letter from Mr. Blough:

*To the editor of the New York Times:*

From your Oct. 31 editorial "Corporate Race Relations" it would appear that you are under considerable misapprehension as to what I said in my press conference of the previous day concerning the policy and actions of United States Steel in Birmingham. For example, you said:

"Mr. Blough feels that U.S. Steel has fulfilled its responsibilities by following a nondiscriminatory hiring policy in Birmingham, and looks upon any other measures as both 'repugnant' and 'quite beyond what a corporation should' do to improve conditions."

Quite to the contrary, I recounted in some detail the efforts of U.S. Steel management to use its influence in Birmingham to promote better communications and better understanding between the races—not just during the recent crises but over a period of many years.

Unfortunately, the able representatives of *The Times* who attended that press conference made only casual reference to this part of my remarks in their stories. For your information therefore, and for the information of your readers, I should like to summarize the specific statements I made on this point:

The present president of our Tennessee Coal and Iron Division, Arthur Wiebel, has been working since 1946 toward developing understanding and strengthening communications between the races in Birmingham.

In 1949 he became a trustee of the Jefferson County Coordinating Council of Social Forces devoted to civic and social improvement.

... In 1951 an interracial committee of this council, with Mr. Wiebel as a member, was formed to improve the lot of the Negroes in many fields: health, sanitation, safety, business, housing and cultural and recreational opportunities. That same year the committee made a formal request that the Birmingham city government employ Negro policemen. That request was denied.

Mr. Wiebel worked, for example, for a Negro upper-middle-class housing project considered as attractive as any in that economic range anywhere in the nation. He helped get Negro insurance companies and investors in Birmingham to make home mortgage money available to Negroes.

From 1953 to 1961 he was a trustee of Tuskegee Institute, an outstanding Negro institution of higher learning.

As a member of the Senior Citizens Committee, last May when serious racial problems occurred in Birmingham he devoted as much time and effort as anyone there in trying to resolve this matter. More recently he has worked in cooperation with General Royall and Colonel Blaik, and was one of 44 business leaders endorsing a recent public appeal for the employment of qualified Negroes on the Birmingham police force.

. . . Mr. Wiebel has also been active in the United Fund, which supports Negro welfare activities, and in the Red Cross. He is a charter member of the Committee of a Hundred, devoted to bringing new industry to Birmingham, and in more ways than I can recount he has tried to carry out what is our overall U.S. Steel policy of being a good citizen in the community in which we live.

I also said that as individuals we can exercise what influence we may have as citizens, but for a corporation to attempt to exert any kind of economic compulsion to achieve a particular end in the social area seems to me to be quite beyond what a corporation should do, and quite beyond what a corporation can do.

To recapitulate, then, let me make our position perfectly clear:

I believe that U.S. Steel in its own plants should provide equal opportunities for all employees, and that it does so in Birmingham, as *The Times* recently reported.

I believe that U.S. Steel management people, as citizens, should use their influence persuasively to help resolve the problems of their communities wherever they may be—and that they are doing so in Birmingham.

I believe that while government—through the proper exercise of its legislative and administrative powers—may seek to compel social reforms, any attempt by a private organization like U.S. Steel to impose its views, its beliefs and its will upon the community by resorting to economic compulsion or coercion would be repugnant to our American constitutional concepts, and that appropriate steps to correct this abuse of corporate power would be universally demanded by public opinion, by Government and by *The New York Times*.

So, even if U.S. Steel possessed such economic power—which it certainly does not—I would be unalterably opposed to its use in this fashion.

We shall, however, continue to use our best efforts in Birmingham to be as helpful as possible.

Roger Blough

Chairman, Board of Directors
United States Steel Corporation
New York, Nov. 2, 1963

The matter of the possible use of economic pressure by business firms to speed the process of racial integration drew considerable attention in newspapers throughout the country. News stories, editorials, and letters from readers took various positions on Mr. Blough's stand and on President Kennedy's remarks. Several such comments follow:

Somehow Mr. Blough seems to say that the injunction "we are our brother's keepers" does not apply to corporations, or at least not to U.S. Steel. I am sure that even a most casual examination of this proposition will destroy it. Many large enterprises, including U.S. Steel, have made substantial contributions to the welfare of the community or the nation, beyond the necessities of profit and loss.

What I am afraid Mr. Blough means is that in the current effort to eliminate all the remaining vestiges of a servile history he would prefer to be neutral, at least in deed if not in thought. If we cannot be sure as to what is morally correct in this struggle, when ever will we be able to know right from wrong?

If U.S. Steel strong and great as it is, will not exert its strength for justice, what can be expected from lesser mortals? What strength U.S. Steel has in Birmingham is best known to it, but that it should be used, I have no doubt.

Carl Rachlin

General Counsel, CORE
New York, Nov. 8, 1963

• • •

**Big Steel and Civil Rights**
**(American Metal Market, November 11, 1963)**

What is the extent of the moral responsibilities of the modern, impersonal, publicly owned corporation? The question has been raised in acute fashion in Birmingham, Ala., where the city's largest single employer is the Tennessee Coal and Iron division of U.S. Steel Corp.

U.S. Steel, and Tennessee president Arthur Wiebel in particular, have been under pressure from civil rights activists to do more to promote the individual rights of Negroes in that embattled city. In response to criticism, the corporation recently disclosed that it has been moving quietly to erase some traditional barriers that have held hundreds of Negroes to low-paying jobs. U.S. Steel has merged into one line previously separate lines of promotion for Negroes and whites in its steel plants. For instance, Negroes in the open hearth shop can now rise along with whites to a job class which pays $3.83 an hour and offers a 40% incentive. Previously they had been limited to a maximum job class offering $2.78 and a 15% incentive. Moreover, in the corporation's Fairfield plant, whites are working under Negroes for the first time. The situation reportedly has caused some discontent among white workers. But U.S. Steel has been strict in the application of its policy. Workers who object are sent home. According to a corporation official, the objectors usually return quickly to the plant. Jobs, after all, are not so easy to get in the steel industry these days.

Beyond taking these forthright steps in its own operations in Birmingham, however, U.S. Steel is inclined to go no further. According to Roger M. Blough, U.S. Steel chairman, the idea that a company should "attempt to have its ideas of what is right for the community enforced upon that community by some sort of economic means" is "clearly repugnant to me personally" and "repugnant to my fellow officers" at U.S. Steel. "We have fulfilled our responsibility in the Birmingham area," Mr. Blough said at the corporation's recent third-quarter press conference. For a corporation to attempt to exert any kind of economic compulsion to achieve a particular end in the social area "seems to be quite beyond what a corporation should do, and . . . quite beyond what a corporation can do." But corporate officials who are citizens in a community "can exercise what small influence we may have as citizens," Mr. Blough said. Apparently, U.S. Steel's chairman was referring among other things to Mr. Wiebel's recent support of a move to put Negro policemen on the Birmingham police force.

A careful study of America's industrial past would probably make it difficult for Mr. Blough to support in factual detail the argument that corporations are prevented from achieving particular ends in "the social area." State and local taxes, for instance, clearly play an important social role in the community, and large corporations can wield enormous influence over tax policy. But Birmingham is a unique situation, as puzzling to politicians as it is to businessmen. Even the Federal government has been reluctant to apply economic sanctions by withholding Federal funds from states which defy negro rights. Can U.S. Steel be expected to do more?

Indeed Big Steel has left little doubt of its sincerity in advancing civil rights in its own operations. If other businesses . . . and more particularly unions . . . were to follow the corporation's example of on-the-job reforms in the South, the civil rights problems of cities like Birmingham would be a lot closer to solution.

In the realm of morality, one positive example may be worth a dozen damaging sanctions in promoting a worthy end.

• • •

**The Wall Street Journal**
**Monday, November 4, 1963**

**The Company in the Community**

There are still a lot of people around who remember the old "company towns"—those communities so dominated by one business enterprise that the politics, the business and very often even the social customs of the people were ordained in the company boardroom.

Some of these company towns were run badly. But many were actually run very well, the company managements having a sincere interest in the well-being of the community. In many places the company out of necessity provided housing, streets, schools, hospitals, recreation centers, churches and a host of other things which the people would otherwise not have had. Often the resulting municipal government was a model of good management.

Yet even in the best run such communities the people always chafed. However high-minded the motives, high-handed power was rightly resented and people found intolerable the economic power that could tell the banker to whom he should lend, the shopkeeper whom he should hire, the town councillors what laws they should pass. Thus today companies make their very considerable contributions to the community in other ways—in good jobs, in gifts to local services and in lending their influence to civic progress—and, like other outmoded institutions, the "company town" has passed without mourning.

Or anyway, so it was until lately. Now in the new context of the civil rights struggle, there are voices demanding that our large corporations use exactly this sort of power to force their desired moral standards on the communities in which they live.

Specifically this has been urged by otherwise thoughtful people in the case of Birmingham. Just the other day Roger Blough of U.S. Steel had to devote the major part of a business press conference to "explaining" why the company did not use its economic power to compel that unhappy city to mend its ways.

The question here was not about U.S. Steel's own practices. Nationwide it follows a practice of nondiscrimination in employment; upwards of 10% of its employes are Negroes, including a number in clerical jobs, supervisory assignments, skilled trades and professional positions. In Birmingham itself, according to Mr. Blough, the U.S. Steel subsidiary has about 30% Negroes among its employes.

Nor is there any argument here about the duty of a company or its officers to provide moral leadership for what they believe to be right, whether in Birmingham or anywhere else.

In this instance the present president of the U.S. Steel division in Birmingham, Arthur Wiebel, has since 1946 been active in groups working for better race relations; since 1951 he has served on the integration committee formed by local citizens, white and Negro; he is a trustee of Tuskegee Institute, a Negro college; and in the latest difficulties he played an active and prominent role in the quiet citizens' group which has worked hard to improve the situation for Negroes in Birmingham.

Mr. Blough made it quite clear that he approved and encouraged this kind of leadership. But to the voices of impatience this is not enough. It is said by some that companies like U.S. Steel should not merely persuade but coerce the community into adopting the policies they believe to be right.

It is probably true, as these voices say, that a company as large as U.S. Steel could wield powerful weapons against the people of Birmingham. It could, as some clamor that it should, boycott local suppliers who did not act as U.S. Steel thinks they should; it could threaten to take away all or a part of its business if the city authorities didn't do as it wishes; it could even halt its contributions to local civic organizations, from hospitals to recreation facilities, if they did not conduct their affairs in an approved fashion.

Perhaps, although we gravely doubt it, such coercion might win some immediate point for the Negroes of Birmingham. But it would certainly do an injury to all the people of Birmingham and most of all a grievous injury to good government and society everywhere.

Mr. Blough himself put it well: "I do not believe it would be a wise thing for U.S. Steel to be other than a good citizen in a community, to attempt to have its ideas of what is right for the community enforced upon the community."

As a good citizen, business can use its influence for good, but the old-fashioned "company town" is better buried. And no one—least of all those who seek wider democracy—should wish for its resurrection.

# The Poletown Dilemma

In May of 1980 executives of General Motors Corporation were facing a business environment more difficult than any since the Depression.[1] Sitting in their offices on the fourteenth floor of the company's world headquarters in Detroit, they looked out over the city which had been home to General Motors and the American automobile industry since its founding. Both the industry and Detroit were in economic trouble. Battered by recession, changing consumer tastes, and strong competition from foreign automobile manufacturers, sales and profits of the Big Three American auto makers had dropped sharply. This decline resulted in cutbacks in production and widespread layoffs of workers in the industry. Over a quarter of the Big Three's hourly work force—some 211,000 people—were laid off, as well as one-third of the work force in auto-related supplier industries.

To meet the challenge of the new environment, General Motors realized that it would have to make major changes in its operations. It had announced a $40 billion five-year capital investment program, to begin in 1980, which was designed to recondition or replace outmoded production plants. Two of the facilities targeted for replacement, the Cadillac Assembly and the Fisher Body Fleetwood plants, were located in Detroit. The decision now facing the executives was where to build the new plant which would replace these old ones.

## THE STRUCTURE OF THE AUTOMOTIVE INDUSTRY

### History

Almost from its beginnings in the early twentieth century, the automotive industry had been highly concentrated. Ford Motor Company, the

---

[1]Much of the material for this case is drawn from Bryan D. Jones, Lynn W. Bachelor, and Carter Wilson, *The Sustaining Hand* (Lawrence: University Press of Kansas, 1986); and from Joseph Auerbach, "The Poletown Dilemma," *Harvard Business Review,* May–June 1985.

early industry leader, captured a 50.3% share of the market in 1923 while General Motors held a 20% share. General Motors pulled ahead in the late 1920s and remained the dominant manufacturer from then until the present. Together with Chrysler Corporation, the smallest of the Big Three, General Motors and Ford accounted for 80% of the market by the 1930s. By the 1950s, only American Motors remained as a minor producer to challenge the Big Three's control of the domestic automobile market.

The strategy which gave Ford its early success was an emphasis on standardization, quality, and low prices. However, the market for automobiles shifted in the 1920s toward replacement buyers. While Ford continued to compete on the basis of price, General Motors introduced a strategy of market differentiation, producing a "full line" of automobiles ranging from economy to luxury models. General Motors also recognized the importance of frequent model changeovers to further stimulate replacement purchases. In the new automobile market this strategy proved to be the most successful, and Ford's market share dropped to 25% by 1926.

The annual model changeover strategy raised high barriers to entry into the automobile manufacturing industry. It meant that high sales volume was required to pay for the cost of design and retooling of new models over a much shorter production period than previously. While this development did not produce the high concentration which already existed in the industry, it eliminated the possibility of small-scale new entrants, and presaged the decline of minor independent producers in all but specialty markets.

As an oligopolistic industry, automobile manufacturing was a cautious one. Technological innovation was not emphasized, nor was it encouraged by the dominant American consumer demand for comfort as opposed to economy and quality in the product. Alfred P. Sloan, Jr., former president (1923–1937) and chairperson (1937–1956) of General Motors and the person primarily responsible for the development of the corporation, asserted that it was "not necessary to lead in design or run the risk of untried experiment."[2] Fundamental changes in technology, even if they might result in more efficient or safer automobiles, presented risks which a conservative and well-positioned company was not willing to take. Until 1970 the attention of management was focused on the complex task of coordinating the production of the full line of automobiles.

### General Motors

In 1980 General Motors was the largest industrial corporation in the United States. Its 1979 annual statement showed worldwide sales of $66.3 billion, of which $62 billion were in its core business of automotive products. (See Exhibit 1.) The company employed over 850,000 people worldwide. Operations were carried out in six "nameplate" divisions, each of which produced its own line of vehicles. Five of these divisions (Chevrolet, Pontiac, Cadillac, Buick, and Oldsmobile) were descendants of independent companies before the formation of General Motors. A sixth division, GMC, made trucks.

General Motors also had a number of divisions which were not dedicated to particular product lines. The Assembly Division, created in the 1960s, controlled automobile assembly in all but the five "home" plants of the car divisions which were operating when General Motors was formed. Other divisions produced automotive parts for the nameplate and the Assembly divisions. Finally, Argonaut Realty was a separate division of the company responsible for acquiring property.

### THE CHANGING ENVIRONMENT

#### Two Major Forces

In the 1970s two external forces came to prominence in the decision making of automotive industry managers. The first was government regulation which came in the wake of consumer

---

[2]Cited in Jones, et al., p. 58.

activist Ralph Nader's investigations in the 1960s on automobile safety. The initial reaction of General Motors to Nader's investigations was extremely negative. The company hired detectives to probe Nader's past; their harassment of the consumer activist resulted in a successful lawsuit by Nader against General Motors, and a public apology by the General Motors' chairperson. However, the affair damaged the company's credibility, and encouraged the imposition of regulation on the industry.

Minimum safety standards for automobiles were enacted beginning in 1966, including fuel system safety regulations in the early 1970s. In 1968, regulations were also established for automobile exhaust emissions, and in the late 1970s, for fuel economy standards. Although these standards did produce safer, cleaner, and more efficient automobiles, the cost of complying with them added almost $2,000 to the price of an automobile. The most recent set of regulations, scheduled to go into effect in 1983, applied to pollution emitted by production plants. Most of the industry's existing facilities would not meet these standards. General Motors estimated that to bring its assembly plants into compliance with them would cost $3.5 billion.

The second external force was foreign competition. The share of foreign automobile manufacturers in the domestic market had climbed from almost zero in the 1950s to well over 20% in 1979, and was approaching 30% in 1980. When gasoline prices jumped sharply following the Arab oil embargo in 1973, and again after the cut-off of oil from Iran during its revolution in 1979, foreign manufacturers had been quicker than the Big Three to respond to the new consumer demand for smaller, more fuel-efficient automobiles. They had developed a reputation for superior quality, and had exploited cost advantages, which included lower wage rates and more efficient methods of production. One of these methods was the "just-in-time" inventory management process, which yielded savings in working capital requirements by reducing the level of materials in inventory.

### Effects on General Motors

The result of these forces was a large drop in the number of cars sold by domestic auto makers, from a record high of about 9.5 million sales in the early 1970s to a projected low of under 6.5 million in 1980, the lowest level since the early 1960s. This drop in sales was accompanied by a dismal profit performance for the automobile manufacturing industry, projected for 1980 to be a return on equity of about *negative* 10%. While the industry historically was much more volatile than manufacturing generally, the magnitude of these losses was unprecedented. For General Motors, profits in 1979 were at their lowest level since the recession in 1975, and projections for 1980 indicated a loss for the year of $750 million. It would be only the second loss in the corporation's history and its first since 1921.

The executives of General Motors knew that they had to take drastic action to turn the situation around. The company decided to abandon its long-successful strategy of producing a full line of automobiles, and concentrate instead upon production of the "world car" which would satisfy the new consumer demands. The company planned to design all its new models as front-wheel drive cars, and to down-size all cars, including luxury models. Such large-scale innovation would require far more investment than a typical model changeover. The $40 billion five-year capital spending program represented a significant increase over historical spending levels of $1 billion to $3 billion per year. Replacement and reconditioning of old plants would account for two-thirds of the investment, while the remainder would pay for the new tools and equipment necessary to produce smaller, fuel-efficient, front-wheel drive automobiles.

### FACTORS IN SITE SELECTION

There were a variety of technical, economic, and social factors which entered into the selection of a site for the new General Motors assembly plant. Wherever it was built, however, the plant construction and equipment costs would be about $500 million and there would be little difference in operating costs.

The parcel of land for the new plant had to be rectangular and approximately 500 acres in size. The plant itself would take up 3 million square feet to accommodate a state-of-the-art one-story assembly line which would wind through the building. Additional space on the site was required for a marshaling yard for the trains which would carry parts and raw materials directly into the plant. Under the new "just-in-time" inventory process which General Motors planned to use, deliveries would be coordinated with suppliers so that the parts arrived at the time they were needed for the production line. The size of the train yard was dictated by the turning radius of the train cars. Finally, space would be required for employee parking lots, a power plant, treatment and storage areas for storm water, storage of completed cars, and landscaping for the facility.

The new plant had to have access to both a long-haul railroad and freeways, to provide links with suppliers and routes to ship finished cars.

Proximity to suppliers was also important if the adoption of "just-in-time" inventory methods was to be successful. A General Motors executive at another assembly plant location commented that 99% of parts needed for assembly were available within a 300-mile radius (i.e., about a day's transit distance), 93% within 200 miles, and 83% within 100 miles. Yet in implementing "just-in-time" inventory methods, he intended to encourage suppliers to locate even closer to his plant. (See Exhibit 2 for data on General Motors plant locations.)

General Motors recognized the advantages of remaining in the immediate area around Detroit. It could employ the existing labor force from the Cadillac and Fisher Body plants, thereby avoiding the $40 million to $50 million cost to train an inexperienced work force for assembly plant jobs. The new plant would employ 6,150 workers in two shifts. Furthermore, under the collective bargaining agreement negotiated with the United Auto Workers, the company was required to provide supplemental unemployment and relocation benefits for workers idled by plant closings if the replacement plant were built more than 50 miles from the site of the closed facility. Under this contract, the expected cost of relocating workers for the new assembly plant was estimated to be $50 million to $55 million.

However, the benefits of retaining the Detroit work force were unclear. General Motors planned to equip the new assembly plant with the latest technology, including robots. The existing work force would require substantial training to unlearn old methods and to learn new ones. Some industry observers felt that training an inexperienced labor force in the new technologies would be no more difficult or expensive than retraining the existing workers, with the incremental cost estimated at $25 million to $30 million.

General Motors wanted to have the new plant ready for production of the 1983 model year cars which would begin in September of 1982. Therefore, the land for the plant would have to be available for the commencement of construction in the middle of 1981.

## DETROIT: THE FATE OF OLD CITIES IN NEW TIMES

### The Big Picture

Between 1950 and 1980, Detroit lost 35% of its population; between 1970 and 1980 alone, the loss was 21%. This change was not and isolated phenomenon, but a characteristic trend among the aging industrial cities of America. In the same 30-year period, the St. Louis population dropped by 47%; Buffalo, by 38%; and both Pittsburgh and Cleveland, by 37%.[3] In increasing numbers, Americans were forsaking large cities and the older suburbs which surrounded them, because prosperity permitted them to live where they wanted to. In a national poll in February 1985, George Gallup asked the ques-

[3]George Sternlieb, *Patterns of Development* (New Brunswick, NJ: Center for Urban Policy Research, 1986), p. 110.

tion, "If you could live anywhere you wished, which one of these places would you prefer?" The responses were:[4]

| | |
|---|---|
| Large city (1 million or more population) | 7% |
| Medium city (100,000 to 1 million) | 15 |
| Small city (50,000 to 100,000) | 16 |
| Large town (10,000 to 50,000) | 13 |
| Small town (2,500 to 10,000) | 23 |
| Rural area, on a farm | 17 |
| Rural area, not on a farm | 8 |
| Don't know | 1 |

More and more, the people living in central cities were the old and the poor, the disadvantaged and the minorities who were unable to move out. Lack of employment for them in the cities kept them in poverty.

The unemployment problem was not the result of a lack of jobs in the United States as a whole: during the decade from 1970 to 1980, total nonagricultural employment grew by nearly 20 million to 90 million. However, manufacturing employment remained almost constant in the range of 18 million to 20 million, unchanged since 1965.[5] The growth was due largely to service employment, both skilled and unskilled. Inner-city residents without skills were unable to find jobs, because the increases in unskilled employment took place in the outlying areas of increasing population.

With the departure of the middle class, the cities were becoming polarized between rich and poor. Downtown development which produced new skyscrapers, convention centers, and pedestrian malls provided jobs mainly for professionals commuting in from distant suburbs, and accommodations and attractions for tourists. Philadelphia illustrated the structural unemployment problem of the old cities:

> When the city of Philadelphia, which is a major manufacturing city, loses a hundred manufacturing jobs, seventy of those are held by municipal residents. When the city gains one hundred office jobs, only thirty are held by central city residents—thus the mismatch function.[6]

The "gentrification" of decayed city neighborhoods, resulting from prosperous young professionals moving in and rehabilitating old housing, a phenomenon praised and denounced in the media, had only a minor effect on the demographics of the cities. The number of "gentry" was far too small either to reverse the decline or to displace the bulk of the residents of poor areas.

The movement of people and industry out of inner cities and into the suburbs and beyond was spurred by government incentives. The federal government's guarantees and subsidies of home mortgages encouraged the purchase of homes in the suburbs. Express highways in metropolitan areas made it easier for people working in the city to live outside of it. Furthermore, the roads fragmented the city, cutting through and destroying neighborhoods. As the most productive people left the cities, the industries followed them. However, industrial relocation was also encouraged by tax policies such as accelerated depreciation schedules which made construction of new facilities economically more attractive than rehabilitation of old ones. State governments and local governments outside central cities also encouraged the migration, the former by locating facilities in and building roads through less-developed areas, and the latter by competing with each other in offering generous tax incentives and subsidies for new business development.

Businesses also preferred exurban locations for new facilities because they allowed room for landscaping and other amenities which attracted employees. In addition, they deserted central industrial areas in favor of less-developed states with lower levels of unionization, often not for lower wage rates, but for

[4]John Herbers, *The New Heartland* (New York: Times Books, 1986), p. 188.
[5]Sternlieb, p. 102.
[6]Sternlieb, p. 91.

greater flexibility in work rules and job classifications.[7]

Central cities faced a grim future. Declining population meant declining tax base, at a time when infrastructure repairs and services for the poor required increasing amounts of revenue. At the same time, the movement of population to the less developed areas shifted political power. The people living in exurban areas, isolated from the poor and the disadvantaged, believed in independence and self-help and distrusted government intervention.

### Demographics

Detroit's history paralleled the experience of many old industrial cities. During the late 19th and early 20th century, Detroit was composed of separate and autonomous ethnic communities. By 1920, however, the separate hierarchies and opportunities for advancement of these communities had largely given way to a single structure for economic opportunity. In the early 1940s, Detroit's 100,000 black residents were 7.6% of the population; by 1960, blacks made up 29% of the city. Following the race riots in the summer of 1967, white migration to the suburbs increased, and the black population grew to 44% of the 1,514,000 city residents in 1970, and to 63% of 1,192,000 by 1980.

### Local Economy

Economically, Detroit was suffering badly. The survey of employers taken in 1972 had indicated that firms representing 28% of Detroit area employment thought it was probable that they would leave the area within the next five years. Shift reductions and plant closings by auto makers had eliminated thousands of jobs. The closing of General Motors' Cadillac and Fisher Body Fleetwood assembly plants would add another 5,000 workers to the ranks of the unemployed, on top of the 5,000 who had already been laid off from the two plants because of production cuts.

[7]Herbers, p. 147.

### City Finances

Financially, Detroit's city government was in a deteriorating position. (See Exhibit 3.) Its bonded debt had increased in recent years to nearly a billion dollars. In four out of the last five years the city's general fund expenses exceeded revenues. The tax burden was high: property taxes were over 7.5% of state-equalized value (i.e., approximately half of market value), and the city also levied a 2% income tax on residents and ½% on nonresident workers. (By contrast, property taxes in Orion Township, Michigan, where General Motors was building another new assembly plant, were only a little over 5% of state-equalized value, and there was no township income tax.)

### Politics

In 1980 Coleman A. Young was the mayor of Detroit. His political roots went back to the United Auto Workers union, where he was regarded as an articulate and politically able radical. The racial discrimination which he felt at that time made him a passionate fighter for justice and equal rights for black people. From 1964 to 1973 he was a senator in the Michigan Senate, and in 1973 was elected by a narrow margin as mayor of Detroit. His first term was controversial as he implemented an affirmative action program in the city's bureaucracy and struggled with the municipal unions, especially the police union, which had opposed his election. However, in 1977 Young was reelected by a large margin, and by 1980 his approval rating in Detroit stood at 93% among the black population and 47% among the white, or 72% overall.

Young was the strongest mayor in the history of Detroit. His strength came not only from his firm support in the black community, but also from constitutional change. At the time of Young's election in 1973 a change in the city's charter expanded the powers of the mayor in financial affairs and in appointments, at the expense of the city council. Young used his strength to promote three basic goals: increasing opportunities for blacks in Detroit's bureaucracies, forming coalitions with the private sector elites of Detroit to promote economic development, and working with state and federal officials to increase intergovernmental funds for the city.

In 1980 Young had the resources of a professional city bureaucracy skilled in obtaining funds from state and federal government programs to support city services and local economic development. As an early supporter of President Jimmy Carter he had powerful allies in the administration in Washington, D.C. His director of economic development, Emmett Moten, had been an aide to Moon Landrieu, the former mayor of New Orleans who was now secretary of the Department of Housing and Urban Development. Thus, Young had the political power, the skills, and the connections to make a large-scale industrial redevelopment project in Detroit successful.

Young had made his position on Detroit plant closings and relocations clear to General Motors' chairperson Thomas A. Murphy. In September of 1979, well before the company announced plans to close its Detroit Cadillac and Fleetwood plants, the mayor had attended a meeting in Murphy's office in which Murphy announced that General Motors was relocating an assembly line from one of its Detroit plants. The announcement was in part a formality to fulfill a promise that Detroit would have a chance to bid on the next company facility. Young reacted angrily, saying:

> You knew we couldn't do that. When you ask us to do something, and you give us 24 hours, you know up front that we can't produce. When will the day be when you come to us and say, "Here are our plans; let's sit down and plan together"?[8]

[8]Cited in Jones, et al., p. 73.

Murphy, on the defensive, promised to consider Detroit seriously for the next plant.

## THE SEARCH FOR SITES

General Motors began its site selection process in the summer of 1979. The search was carried out by a task force administered by Argonaut Realty and included representatives from real estate, plant engineering, industry-government relations, labor relations, personnel, public affairs, the corporate staff, and the Assembly Division. The focus of the search was on the area within 50 miles of Detroit, although the company knew of an out-of-state location in another part of the Midwest which met its criteria. Sites within Detroit, however, were initially rejected because of lack of rail access, or because the number of homes and businesses that had to be removed would delay the project beyond the company's construction deadlines. After nine months of searching the task force was also unable to find any sites outside of Detroit but within 50 miles of the city which met General Motors' conditions.

In April of 1980, making good on his promise to Young in September of 1979, Murphy formally invited Detroit to join with the company in an effort to locate a site within the city. Nine locations were reviewed, and each one had problems. (See Exhibit 4.) Only the Central Industrial Park site (A) met all of General Motors' requirements for site characteristics; yet it was heavily settled and would require a major residential and commercial relocation effort before a plant could be built there.

### Eminent Domain

Under their power of eminent domain, governments have the right to demand that private owners sell their property to them, in return for just compensation, if the property is needed for a public purpose. A typical use of this power by governments is to acquire land for constructing new roads which would benefit the entire community; it has also been used for urban renewal projects. However, property owners could delay the acquisition through court challenges over the adequacy of compensation. Thus, even if Detroit were to exercise eminent domain to acquire the land in the Central Industrial Park site for General Motors' new assembly plant, a small number of property owners could file lawsuits against the city and effectively kill the project by delaying it beyond the company's deadlines.

Such delays had hindered urban renewal projects in the past, and in response to the problem the Michigan State Legislature had adopted Public Act 87 of 1980 in April of 1980, a statute which came to be known as the "quick take law." Under P.A. 87, cities were permitted to take title to property by eminent domain before agreeing with owners on a purchase price. Thus, court challenges over compensation for the taking of the property could not delay the start of a project. It was Emmett Moten who realized that the passage of the quick take law made the Central Industrial Park site feasible within General Motors' timetable for the construction of a new assembly plant.

### Profile of Central Industrial Park Site

Of all potential sites in Detroit which were studied, the Central Industrial Park site involved the largest amount of relocation. Part of the site lay within Hamtramck, an independent city completely surrounded by Detroit. Most of the Hamtramck section of the site was occupied by the old Dodge main assembly plant, which Chrysler had closed in January of 1980, eliminating 3,000 jobs. Acquisition of this property was not expected to be difficult, as Chrysler was experiencing severe financial problems and would be eager to sell. In addition, the people and government of Hamtramck strongly supported the construction of a new plant as a source of jobs for the community.

However, the Detroit portion of the site included about one-third of the Detroit district of Poletown. Nearly 3,500 people lived in this area in about 1,176 homes; the population was half black and half white, with the whites mostly of Polish descent. The Poles were all

older, many of them retired or nearly so; most had been in the community for 20 to 50 years and had strong ties to it; some of them had never been outside of Poletown in their lives. A deterioration of ethnic identity in the Polish community was also a likely result of relocating the community. The commitment of these people to their neighborhood was evident in statements such as:

> The church we belong to, the bingo, my friends, everything we know is in that neighborhood. . . . I own that home free and clear, and they come along and tell you you've got to get out. I'm here to fight![9]

Sixteen churches served as focal points for the community, including eleven Protestant congregations with predominantly black membership and three Roman Catholic churches to which the Poles belonged. Two of these three churches, Immaculate Conception and St. John's, were within the project area.

Economically, the area was poor, but not destitute: 25% of Poletown families earned more than $15,000 per year. Housing was mostly detached single and two-family homes. Although in economic decline, Poletown was still a community. Abandoned property, which constituted about one-third of each block, was situated next to well-maintained homes. The area contained 150 businesses, including 28 manufacturing firms. In addition, the Poletown Area Revitalization Task Force (PARTF), a group founded in 1977 and run by local community activists, was attempting to encourage redevelopment in Poletown and had received funding grants from a number of sources, including the city of Detroit.

Opposition to the Poletown site was coordinated by the Poletown Neighborhood Council (PNC). This group was formed after the PARTF had disbanded upon announcement of plans to build a General Motors plant in Poletown, and was led by former members of the PARTF. Thomas Olechowski, a resident of

---

[9]Cited in Jones, et al., p. 145.

Poletown and an administrative aide to a Detroit state senator, served as president; Richard Hodas, a local businessperson and community activist, was vice president. The PNC's headquarters were in the Immaculate Conception church, and many parishioners, as well as former members of the PARTF, joined the group.

In early communications with the Detroit city government and with General Motors, the PNC emphasized its willingness to negotiate and to assist in implementing the project. In return for its cooperation, however, it required that the other parties (1) recognize the PNC's role in the planning of the project, (2) treat Poletown as a single entity, including both the project and nonproject areas, (3) develop specific revitalization programs for the nonproject part of Poletown, and (4) fully disclose all facts, plans, and meetings pertaining to the project, to demonstrate the necessity to relocate several thousands of citizens from their homes.

The PNC's great weaknesses were, first, that it was supported by no more than half of the people living in the project area, primarily the Poles who had lived there for many years. Many of the other residents were relatively recent arrivals and had no particular stake in Poletown. In fact, they would welcome a chance to relocate from an area they saw as deteriorating, in return for a generous settlement payment. Second, the PNC was not supported by the larger Polish community, particularly in the predominantly Polish Hamtramck, because of their own interest in the jobs created by a new assembly plant.

### Acquisition Costs

The expense of acquiring and preparing the Central Industrial Park site for construction of the new plant was estimated at over $200 million. This figure included payment of $62 million to area residents for their property, $28 million for relocating residents to new homes, $35 million for demolition, and $88 million for site preparation (improvements to roads and railways, relocation of public facilities, and professional services).[10]

In sharp contrast, alternative sites in neighboring midwest states would cost $5 to 7 million for the unimproved land, plus $60 million to $80 million for site preparation. Several states were eager to attract light industry and were prepared to help General Motors secure a site. The resulting ease and speed appealed to at least several of the members of the company's site selection task force.

### LABOR RELATIONS[11]

In the United States, General Motors' hourly labor force belonged to the United Auto Workers union. General Motors had fought the union's right to represent workers in its early years, and had only reluctantly agreed to negotiate with it following a sit-down strike in the middle 1930s. However, it had gradually accepted additions to the issues discussed during contract negotiations, including wages based on the corporation's "ability to pay" (1946), cost of living escalation clauses in wage contracts (1948), employee benefits (1950), and unemployment benefits (1955).

In the early 1970s, faced with growing worker dissatisfaction resulting in higher rates of absenteeism, grievances, and in some extreme cases wildcat strikes and sabotage on the assembly line, General Motors in cooperation with the UAW instituted a "Quality of Work Life" (QWL) program. The goal of the program was to increase job satisfaction by involving workers in decisions affecting their working conditions. The company hoped that the program would lead to increased productivity and quality, both necessary to compete against the

---

[10]Detroit Community and Economic Development Department, *Final Environmental Impact Statement, Central Industrial Park,* December 1980, p. V-87.

[11]Much of the material in this section is taken from the Harvard Business School cases, "Contract and Consensus at General Motors, 1900–1984" (376·170, rev. 11/87); and "General Motors and the United Auto Workers" (481·142).

high-quality and low-cost Japanese imports. "Conservatives" in both General Motors and the union distrusted the new program because it undermined management authority and softened the adversarial relationship between the company and the union. However, the leadership of both General Motors and the UAW recognized the need for cooperation to reduce costs, improve quality, and stop the soaring levels of imported cars.

In an agreement signed in 1979, General Motors in effect committed itself to automatic union recognition at all newly opened plants. The UAW no longer needed to fear the replacement of union by nonunion jobs in a relocation. However, any loss of jobs for workers in Detroit was of concern to the UAW, for the union membership wanted protection for their existing jobs. Therefore, the national union strongly supported the construction of a plant at the Central Industrial Park site, even though it meant the demolition of the neighborhood. Only the leader of a radical faction of a UAW local union whose headquarters were in the project area expressed support for the PNC.

### GENERAL MOTORS CORPORATE CULTURE

Historically, the corporate culture of General Motors had enshrined the values of free enterprise and emphasized returns to shareholders as a primary measure of success. In his autobiography Alfred Sloan clearly expressed these values:[12]

> ... General Motors could hardly be imagined to exist anywhere but in this country, with its very active and enterprising people; its resources, in-

cluding its science and technology and its business and industrial know-how; its vast spaces, roads, and rich markets; its characteristics of change, mobility, and mass production; its great industrial expansion in this century, and its system of freedom in general and free competitive enterprise in particular.... If in turn we have contributed to the style of the United States as expressed in the automobile, this has been by interaction.

• • •

If I have expressed or implied in this book a so-called ideology, it is, I suppose, that I believe in competition as an article of faith, a means of progress, and a way of life.... We set out to produce not for the chosen few but for the whole consumer public on the assumption of a continuously rising standard of living....

• • •

... It is as I see it the strategic aim of a business to earn a return on capital, and if in any particular case the return in the long run is not satisfactory, the deficiency should be corrected or the activity abandoned for a more favorable one.

• • •

The measure of the worth of a business enterprise as a *business* ... is not merely growth in sales or assets but return on the shareholders' investment, since it is their capital that is being risked and it is in their interests first of all that the corporation is supposed to be run in the private-enterprise scheme of things....

### CURRENT SITUATION

The task force felt pressure to reach a decision soon. Mayor Young, suddenly aware of the possible loss of jobs, was pressing Murphy for a commitment to stay in Detroit; the neighborhood was escalating its resistance; and the Assembly Division constantly reminded the task force that a site, fully prepared for construction, was needed by mid-1981. Time was running out.

---

[12]Alfred P. Sloan, Jr., *My Years with General Motors* (New York: Doubleday & Company, Inc., 1964), pp. xxi, xxiv, 49, 213, and 199.

# EXHIBITS: THE POLETOWN DILEMMA

**EXHIBIT 1**

GENERAL MOTORS CORPORATION: FINANCIAL HISTORY
(All references to shares are to common stock only.)

| | 1970 | 1971 | 1972 | 1973 | 1974 | 1975 | 1976 | 1977 | 1978 | 1979 |
|---|---|---|---|---|---|---|---|---|---|---|
| Sales (millions) | $18,752 | $28,264 | $30,435 | $35,798 | $31,550 | $35,725 | $47,181 | $54,961 | $63,221 | $66,311 |
| Net income (millions) | 609 | 1,936 | 2,163 | 2,398 | 950 | 1,253 | 2,903 | 3,338 | 3,508 | 2,893 |
| Assets (millions) | 14,174 | 18,242 | 18,273 | 20,297 | 19,874 | 21,557 | 24,442 | 26,658 | 30,598 | 32,216 |
| Stockholders' equity (millions) | 9,854 | 10,805 | 11,683 | 12,567 | 12,531 | 13,082 | 14,385 | 15,767 | 17,570 | 19,179 |
| Return on assets (%) | 4% | 11% | 12% | 12% | 5% | 6% | 12% | 13% | 11% | 9% |
| Return on stockholders' equity (%) | 6 | 18 | 19 | 19 | 8 | 10 | 20 | 21 | 20 | 15 |
| Earnings per share | $2.09 | $6.72 | $7.51 | $8.34 | $3.27 | $4.32 | $10.08 | $11.62 | $12.24 | $10.04 |
| Dividends per share | 3.40 | 3.40 | 4.45 | 5.25 | 3.40 | 2.40 | 5.55 | 6.80 | 6.00 | 5.30 |
| Share price: high | 81⅜ | 91⅛ | 84¾ | 84⅝ | 55½ | 59⅛ | 78⅞ | 78½ | 66⅞ | 65⅞ |
| low | 59½ | 73⅜ | 71¼ | 44⅞ | 28⅞ | 31¼ | 57¾ | 61⅛ | 53¾ | 49⅜ |
| Price/earnings: high | 39 | 14 | 11 | 10 | 17 | 14 | 8 | 7 | 5 | 7 |
| low | 28 | 11 | 9 | 5 | 9 | 7 | 6 | 5 | 4 | 5 |
| Times charges earned: | | | | | | | | | | |
| Before income taxes | 16 | 64 | 57 | 44 | 11 | 9 | 20 | 23 | 20 | 15 |
| After income taxes | 13 | 36 | 30 | 24 | 7 | 5 | 11 | 13 | 11 | 9 |
| Senior debt rating | Aaa | Aaa | Aaa | Aaa | Aaa | Aaa | Aaa | Aaa | Aaa | Aaa |

*Source: Moody's Industrial Manual.*

**EXHIBIT 2**
GENERAL MOTORS CORPORATION: U.S. CAR AND TRUCK/BODY AND ASSEMBLY
GROUPS PLANT LOCATIONS IN 1979

| | Fisher Body Division | Chevrolet Motor | GM Assembly | Guide | Buick Motor | Cadillac Motor Car | GMC Truck and Coach | Oldsmobile | Pontiac Motor | Total |
|---|---|---|---|---|---|---|---|---|---|---|
| Detroit | 4 | 3 | | | | 1 | | | | 8 |
| Other Michigan | 10 | 12 | 1 | | 1 | | 1 | 1 | 1 | 27 |
| Other East North Central | 9 | 6 | 3 | 1 | | | | | | 19 |
| East North Central | 23 | 21 | 4 | 1 | 1 | 1 | 1 | 1 | 1 | 54 |
| Middle Atlantic | 3 | 4 | 2 | | | | | | | 9 |
| South Atlantic | | | 4 | | | | | | | 4 |
| West South Central | | | 2 | 1 | | | | | | 3 |
| West North Central | | | 3 | | | | | | | 3 |
| Pacific | | | 3 | | | | | | | 3 |
| New England | | | 1 | | | | | | | 1 |
| Total | 26 | 25 | 19 | 2 | 1 | 1 | 1 | 1 | 1 | 77 |

*Source: Moody's Industrial Manual.*

**EXHIBIT 3**
DETROIT: FINANCIAL STATISTICS

|  | 1970 | 1971 | 1972 | 1973 | 1974 | 1975 | 1976 | 1977 | 1978 | 1979 |
|---|---|---|---|---|---|---|---|---|---|---|
| Property tax rates per $1,000 of assessed value | $54.113 | $57.060 | $57.712 | $53.000 | $65.370 | $64.518 | $65.202 | $71.833 | $74.813 | $75.079 |
| General fund (millions): |  |  |  |  |  |  |  |  |  |  |
| Revenues | 368.4 | 391.0 | 456.2 | 555.9 | 542.0 | 527.4 | 524.3 | 608.5 | 657.9 | 685.1 |
| Expenses | 384.9 | 405.1 | 447.6 | 496.1 | 533.7 | 563.0 | 547.0 | 557.0 | 682.2 | 700.6 |
| Excess (deficit) | (16.5) | (14.1) | 8.6 | 59.8 | 8.3 | (35.6) | (22.7) | 51.5 | (24.4) | (15.5) |
| Bond rating (general obligations) | Baa | Baa | Baa | Baa | Baa | Baa | Baa | Baa | Baa | Baa |

Source: Moody's Municipal and Government Manual.
Notes: Assessed value is based on state-equalized value, which is equal to one-half of fair value. Property tax rates include taxes payable to local government units in addition to Detroit (e.g., school districts, county government).
Income taxes of 2% and ½% are levied on the income of residents and nonresident workers, respectively.
Numbers may not total due to rounding.

**EXHIBIT 4**
SITE COMPARISON

A CENTRAL INDUSTRIAL PARK
B HUBER SOUTH
C AIRPORT SOUTH
D CITY AIRPORT
E LYNCH ROAD COMPLEX
F RIVERSIDE INDUSTRIAL PARK
G FOREST PARK REHABILITATION
H RIVER ROUGE PARK
I SOUTHWEST DETROIT INDUSTRIAL

Source: City of Detroit Community and Economic Development Department, *Final Environmental Impact Statement, Central Industrial Park Project.*

**EXHIBIT 4**
SITE COMPARISON (*Continued*)

| Basic site selection considerations | (A) Dodge Main | (B) Huber South | (C) Airport South | (D) Airport | (E) Lynch Road | (F) Riverside Industrial | (G) Forest Park | (H) Rouge Park | (I) Southwest |
|---|---|---|---|---|---|---|---|---|---|
| Size (450–500) acres) | X* | X | X | X | X | 0† | 0 | X | 0 |
| Configuration (¾ × 1 mile) | X | X | X | X | X | 0 | 0 | X | 0 |
| Railroad access‡ | X | 0 | 0 | 0 | X | 0 | 0 | X | X |
| Freeway access | X | X | X | 0 | 0 | 0 | X | 0 | X |
| Readily available | X | 0 | 0 | X | 0 | X | 0 | 0 | 0 |
| Other related deficiencies | Relocation of numerous residential commercial and industrial structures. | Relocation of many commercial and residential structures and recreational services. | Relocation of numerous residential and commercial structures. Conflict with airport. | Elimination of active viable airport. | Relocation of active industrial facilities. | Riverfront land not appropriate. Recreation land displaced. | Urban renewal land for residential. | Removal of major parkland. Flood plain area. | Historical Fort Wayne impacted. School and railroad relocated. |

*Source:* City of Detroit Community and Economic Development Department, *Final Environmental Impact Statement, Central Industrial Park Project.*

*X—meets basic site selection criterion.
†0—does not meet basic site selection criterion.
‡Railroad must provide access to other GM Michigan plants that would be providing components and parts for the proposed assembly facility with a minimum time delay.

*Source:* City of Detroit Community and Economic Development Department, *Final Environmental Impact Statement, Central Industrial Park Project.*

# Massachusetts High Technology Council

<table>
<tr><td>To:</td><td>BOARD OF DIRECTORS</td></tr>
<tr><td>From:</td><td>HOWARD P. FOLEY</td></tr>
<tr><td>Date:</td><td>JULY 3, 1980</td></tr>
</table>

YESTERDAY AT APPROXIMATELY 5:30 P.M. ON A VOTE OF 97 TO 91 WILLIAM M. BULGER, PRESIDING OFFICER OF THE LEGISLATURE'S CONSTITUTIONAL CONVENTION, ADJOURNED THE CONVENTION WITHOUT ACTING ON OUR PENDING CONSTITUTIONAL AMENDMENT TO LIMIT STATE AND LOCAL TAXES.

WE EXPECTED A TOUGH FIGHT—AND WERE PREPARED FOR IT—BUT WE NEVER EXPECTED TO BE DENIED A VOTE! WE FEEL THAT THE CONSTITUTION HAS BEEN VIOLATED, THAT THE PROCESS WHICH WE HAVE BEEN INVOLVED IN FOR THE BETTER PART OF THE PAST TWO YEARS HAS BEEN PROSTITUTED, AND THAT 60,000 CITIZENS OF THE COMMONWEALTH WHO SIGNED OUR PETITION, AS WELL AS EVERYONE ELSE WHO BELIEVES IN THE CONSTITUTION OF THE COMMONWEALTH, HAVE BEEN CHEATED.

WE INTEND TO EXPLORE ALL AVAILABLE LEGAL AND OTHER MEANS TO ENSURE THAT THIS INITIATIVE AMENDMENT IS AT LEAST VOTED ON BY THE MASSACHUSETTS LEGISLATURE BEFORE THIS BIENNIUM ENDS.

Massachusetts High Technology Council, Inc.
60 State Street, Boston, Massachusetts 02109
Telephone (617) 227-4855

Howard Foley was still shocked after having spent the July 4th weekend at home reflecting upon the events of the previous week. The Massachusetts legislature, ignoring a constitutional requirement, had adjourned its final session as a Constitutional Convention *before* considering an initiative amendment petition designed to limit state and local taxes. While some legislators may have simply been anxious to start campaigning for the fast-approaching September primaries, it was clear to most informed political observers that the legislative leadership intended to block any measures aimed at limiting state or local taxation. State lawmakers were apparently reluctant to debate the two potentially difficult political issues that remained on their agenda—the death penalty and tax limitation.

As president of the Massachusetts High Technology Council (MHTC), Howard Foley had fought hard to dispel the notion held by many council members—chief executive officers (CEOs) of local technology companies—that business cannot win issues in the arena of state politics. Slowly, through such efforts as the tax limitation amendment, he had convinced the council that they could be heard and that they could do something. With the adjournment of the Constitutional Convention, it now looked as if the MHTC initiative had come to an unexpected halt.

Despite this sudden setback, Foley did not sit still for long. After witnessing the adjournment from the fourth floor gallery, he stormed down to the third floor and barged into Governor King's office to demonstrate his disgust with the situation and to demand a recall of state lawmakers. In the days that immediately followed, Foley pursued the recall issue during a series of telephone conversations and meetings with the governor. The council attempted to mobilize interest groups outside the high tech industry to demand a recall of state lawmakers. The business community had not reached any broad consensus, however, regarding either the tax limitation amendment or the recall of legislators. Despite a modest amount of public pressure to "call them back," Governor King had still not committed himself to reconvene the Constitutional Convention.

As Howard Foley sat in his downtown Boston office on July 8, 1980, he was well aware of the urgency of the situation. The next four months would be important for proponents of tax reform. The September party primaries and the November general election would mark a decisive juncture in this grassroots movement. Foley had to devise a plan of action for the council, and MHTC members had to determine the strategic interest of their respective corporations. As he sat back in his chair and read through his memo to MHTC's Board of Directors, he began to measure the distance the council had traveled since its beginning almost three years earlier.

• • •

## THE COUNCIL'S BEGINNINGS

On October 13, 1977, after several months of informal meetings, 38 chief executive officers of Massachusetts high technology companies founded the Massachusetts High Technology Council. While their businesses were healthy and operations in Massachusetts were expanding, the executives could see limits to that growth: limits imposed by state and local government's fiscal policies which kept personal tax burdens climbing; limits imposed by the insufficient supply of engineers, computer scientists, and managers within the state; and limits imposed by the difficulty the executives experienced when they tried to entice new employees to Massachusetts. During their informal discussions, these high tech executives were mindful of the problems that had plagued the textile, leather, and footwear industries, each of which had eventually abandoned New England.

Ray Stata of Analog Devices, Inc., opened the first meeting of the Council as its president in October 1977. He spoke of its mission:

> We are all here because we share a common belief that there are some serious problems in Massachusetts which interfere with the successful growth of our companies and that by working together we have a much better chance of setting things straight than we do by working separately.
>
> There is a broad and growing recognition that the economic health of this region will depend on the expansion of the high technology industry segment which we represent. Employment opportunity is coming to the top of the list of our elected officials not so much due to their visionary wisdom but due to pressure from voters who are concerned about jobs.
>
> The time is ripe for this organization to be effective in influencing state and local government policy. Nearly everyone I have talked to about this organization in the last six months—including bankers, politicians and educators—is enthusiastic to learn that this vitally important segment of our economy will take constructive steps in clarifying what has to be done to improve the prospects for employment growth.
>
> Our recommendation is that we concentrate our attention strictly on issues in our immediate Massachusetts communities that are vital to growing, high technology companies. These are mostly concerned with state and local government policies, but we must also be concerned with the educational institutions which develop the human resources that are vital to our success.

Council members believed from the outset that success could be achieved only by forming a unique critical mass held together by personal commitments from the heads of Massachusetts companies. (Exhibit 1 lists original council members.) Unlike many trade associations and lobby groups, the MHTC would be run by member CEOs and served by a small staff organization. Through the council, the CEOs would define the problems they saw facing the Commonwealth, perform the research, and make their voices heard in political and educational circles. The original council members employed 42,000 people within Massachusetts in 1977.

Council members initially represented about 20% (and eventually would grow to represent 50%) of the total high technology employment in the state. By 1977, the high technology industry accounted for 31% of the Massachusetts manufacturing work force. High technology, while usually associated with the computer business, actually covered a wider range of industries, including electronic components, medical equipment, scientific instruments, communications gear, and genetic engineering. Most of the companies had relatively large research and development budgets and had a high percentage of engineers and scientists in their work force.

At its founding, the MHTC's goals included:

- Slowing the growth of state and local spending to a point where the Commonwealth's overall tax burden was no higher than the average of 17[1] states competing with Massachusetts for critical manpower.
- Working cooperatively with government and public and private educational institutions to better match the knowledge and skills of the state's work force with the needs of its member companies.

Political activity was to become more visible, but it was viewed as a subset of an overall human resource program.

Although outwardly the council appeared to be harmonious, there were differences of opinion and differences in personality that sometimes made a consensus difficult to achieve. Natural differences in perspective between small and large firms were exacerbated by the fact that new ventures were often the result of spin-offs from previous employers. Occasionally, divisions would also arise between members who were quite active in the affairs of the council and those who played a more passive role.

The Massachusetts High Technology Council stood in marked contrast to other business associations within the state. Dominated by young companies, the high tech business and its leaders were perceived as rebellious upstarts by many in the more established business community. The Massachusetts Taxpayers Foundation, representing the largest banks, insurance and utility companies, and Associated Industries of Massachusetts (AIM), representing most traditional capital-intensive manufacturing firms, urged high tech leaders to be cautious when dealing with state lawmakers. These business groups were generally perceived to be much more conservative in their lobbying efforts, since their businesses were subject to constant oversight and regulation by state agencies and did not have the option to relocate to other states.

## PROPOSAL FOR RESPONSIBLE FISCAL POLICY

Past economic debates in Massachusetts mostly involved the simplistic complaint that taxes were too high or the notion that only property tax relief was needed. The state had been dubbed "Taxachusetts" by many of its residents because of the above-average tax burden. While most complaints focused on the heavy rate of taxation, many were also directed

---

[1]The 17 competing states, defined as neighboring states and industrial states with a developing base of high technology industry, included: Arizona, California, Connecticut, Illinois, Maine, Maryland, Michigan, New Hampshire, New Jersey, New York, North Carolina, Ohio, Pennsylvania, Rhode Island, Texas, Vermont and Washington.

at the quality of services delivered within the state. According to one member of the legislature, these views were partly inspired by "an unhappy history of unscrupulous management within state government." Many legislators felt a direct comparison to other states did not tell the complete story. They argued that high energy costs and the concentration of an extraordinary number of tax-exempt institutions in the state had to be figured into any such equation. With greater service and welfare costs than other states, the state budget had been balanced precariously during recent years.

According to the Massachusetts League of Women Voters (a voter information group), the distribution of the tax burden had indeed gone awry.

> Our income tax, while somewhat inequitably assessed, is a relatively progressive tax, the impact of which is about average for industrial states. We depend less than most states on sales and excise taxes and on fees. Our property tax, however, is completely out of proportion— about 70% above the norm.

The Massachusetts High Technology Council cited evidence that the tax burden in Massachusetts had grown much more rapidly during the 1970s than it had in the 17 states with which Massachusetts competed. By 1978, the per capita (state and local) tax burden was 17.6% of personal income, in contrast to the 15.7% tax burden of the 17-state average. MHTC believed that the tax differential constituted an impediment to anyone considering coming to work in the state, and that it was a significant factor behind the decisions of many home-grown, high technology workers and graduates to relocate to other states. In addition to the loss of highly educated and trained workers, MHTC cited the expansion of firms outside of Massachusetts as a particularly damaging consequence of an unfavorable business climate.

As an initial effort at tax reform, the council decided that repeal of the 7.5% surtax on personal income should be its first priority.

This surtax was created in 1975 under Democratic Governor Michael Dukakis as a temporary measure to prevent an extremely dangerous statewide fiscal crisis from getting even worse. Arguing that the fiscal crisis was now over (a budget surplus was projected for FY 1978), MHTC sought repeal of the surtax so that it would not become a permanent addition to the tax base. In the face of an energetic campaign to achieve repeal, Governor Dukakis vowed to veto any such measure.

The council drafted its Proposal for Responsible Fiscal Policy in July 1978, which was a broad statement regarding state revenue generation and spending. The council urged Massachusetts to address its fiscal and social problems by stimulating growth in the private sector—especially in the high technology industry—with tax policies that would make the state competitive. Specifically, this proposal called for elimination of the surtax on personal income, reduction of tax rates on unearned income, and reduction of property taxes.

As illustrated in Figure A (page 186), MHTC projected that the average tax burden in the 17-state comparison group would decline slightly from 15.7% to 15.3% over the next four years. The council proposed that Massachusetts gradually reduce its tax burden so as to achieve parity with the other states by 1982.

MHTC members knew they faced a difficult battle to win tax limitation because Governor Dukakis was likely to resist many of their tax-cutting initiatives. Since 1978 was a gubernatorial election year, many high technology firms turned their attention to seeking a political alternative to the incumbent governor.

## NOVEMBER 1978 ELECTION: AN UPSET AND A NEW GOVERNOR

Frustrated by the unsympathetic response to their pleas, many members of the Council began actively to support and campaign for Edward J. King, a relatively unknown Democrat who was challenging Michael Dukakis in the September 1978 party primaries. Governor Dukakis, perceived as a champion of "honest

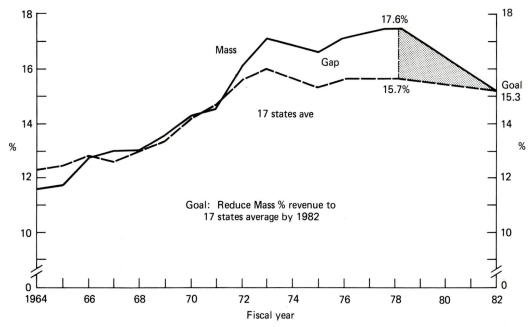

**FIGURE A**
State and local general revenue from own sources as percent of personal income.
(*Source:* MHTC Proposal for Responsible Fiscal Policy.)

and efficient state government," was considered an easy favorite to retain his own party's support in the primary election. Although he campaigned for the popular cause of property tax reduction, King's victory was seen as a major political upset.

With the support of a Democratic electorate, King proceeded to win the November election by narrowly defeating his Republican opponent. Considered "pro-business" in outlook, King had received substantial financial support from the business community, including strong backing from the high technology industry. The new governor's initial political appointments reflected his sympathies toward business and, according to some observers, revealed his support for the high technology industry.

As MHTC began its second year of activity, the prospects for tax relief and a more favorable business climate looked encouraging.

At this time, Howard Foley joined the council to serve as its full-time president, responsible to MHTC's Board of Directors and membership for implementation of its plans and programs. (Exhibit 2 provides a profile of Howard Foley.)

**THE SOCIAL CONTRACT**

In the first exercise of its new State House muscle, the high tech council offered the recently inaugurated governor a *social contract* which highlighted the industry's ability to create thousands of jobs if the state would cut taxes. This symbolic contract was signed by Governor King on February 9, 1979. King's Secretary of Economic Affairs, George S. Kariotis, expressed his agreement with the concept, saying, " . . . The *social contract* has started to wake people up to the problem of attracting skilled personnel to work in the high technology industry in Massachusetts."

The terms of the agreement were summarized as follows:

Council member firms believe they can create as many as 60,000 new jobs in Massachusetts over the next four years (1979–1982) if the Commonwealth takes substantive steps to restore competitive conditions and to establish a healthy climate for the growth of the high technology industry here. The proposed *social contract* is not a binding agreement; it is an implicit understanding between government and business that there are important benefits to be derived by working together toward the common goal of job creation.

The beneficiaries of positive action by both government and industry will be all the citizens of Massachusetts. The benefits to be derived by 1982 are:

- 60,000 new high technology jobs, plus an additional 90,000 new jobs in manufacturing and support services.
- A $2 billion annual increase in personal income by 1982 and $300 million annual increase in state and local revenues to fund state and local tax reductions and to support worthy social goals.

No one could prove the *social contract* would work, but the council was relying upon past experience which suggested that lower personal tax burdens would indeed be an important first step.

## HUMAN RESOURCES— BRIDGING THE "PEOPLE GAP"

Although tax reduction and reform in state fiscal policies would make it easier to attract engineering and management talent, the council had been working since its beginning on other fronts to solve its human resources problem. With the assistance of Coopers & Lybrand, the Council conducted a comprehensive study of MHTC-member human resources needs in technical areas. The survey results revealed a significant shortfall of experienced engineers, technicians and managers which was, in

MHTC's opinion, limiting the growth of employment in the high technology industry. A summary of the survey is presented in Table A (page 188).

In a collective effort to narrow its own human resource gap, the council undertook the following measures:

- A film designed to tell high school students and counselors about careers in high technology was produced and shown in Massachusetts schools.
- A MHTC subcommittee on university relations was formed to increase the number of recruits from out-of-state colleges and universities.
- A MHTC subcommittee focused on skills training and developed a pilot program to train surplus teachers as programmers.
- A MHTC initiative was launched to encourage closer ties between industry and educators. MHTC sought incentives for industry to give equipment and funds to technical schools.

The council hoped that increased collaboration with educational institutions and the Massachusetts educational authorities would help to improve the human resource outlook for the state's high tech employers.

## PETITION FOR A CONSTITUTIONAL AMENDMENT

Although they were heartened by the governor's favorable reception to the *social contract*, MHTC members recognized that it would be difficult to produce a lasting tax limitation law. A new tax law would have to come from a legislature that had historically been unable to deal effectively with tax reform. Nevertheless, pleas for tax relief were now beginning to reach sympathetic ears within the Statehouse. MHTC members were encouraged by this new political climate and hoped it might inspire passage of tax legislation that would place Massachusetts

**TABLE A**

MHTC SURVEY ON HUMAN RESOURCE NEEDS
(Prepared by Coopers & Lybrand)

### Projected annual compounded growth in Massachusetts, high demand job categories

| | Employment, 6/30/79 | Projected needs, 7/1/79– 12/31/82 | Total projected employment, 12/31/82 | Projected annual compounded growth rate |
|---|---|---|---|---|
| **Technical professionals** | | | | |
| Electronic/electrical engineers | 3,979 | 4,180 | 8,159 | 23% |
| Mechanical engineers | 942 | 832 | 1,774 | 20% |
| Computer sciences | 2,425 | 3,329 | 5,754 | 28% |
| Chemistry/chemical | 512 | 904 | 1,416 | 34% |
| Other* | 3,703 | 2,400 | 6,103 | 15% |
| Totals | 11,561 | 11,645 | 23,206 | 22% |
| **Technical paraprofessionals** | | | | |
| Technicians | 4,576 | 5,871 | 10,447 | 26% |
| Computer programmers | 368 | 510 | 878 | 28% |
| Drafters | 488 | 507 | 995 | 22% |
| Other* | 3,167 | 3,650 | 6,817 | 24% |
| Totals | 8,599 | 10,538 | 19,137 | 25% |
| Assemblers/production operators | 11,456 | 11,245 | 22,701 | 21% |
| Total high demand job categories | 31,616† | 33,428 | 65,044 | 23% |
| Other Massachusetts employment | 47,835 | 19,110 | 66,945 | 10% |
| Total Massachusetts employment | 79,451 | 52,538‡ | 131,989 | 16% |

*Certain participants reported total analysis data with no indication of specific function or position. Such total amounts have been included in "Other."
†Human resource gap (unfilled jobs) was 8% in high demand job categories, during previous year.
‡Projected needs (7/1/79 to 12/31/82) of 52,538 employees in this report equates to a 4-year (1/1/79 to 12/31/82) forecast of 60,043 employees which was mentioned in the *social contract*.

in a more competitive position with other states. The Council realized, however, that another sudden change in the political winds could dissipate any gains in the tax reform effort. MHTC members were still uncertain state legislators would enact a new tax law; they were even less confident that such a law would survive likely challenges from politically active lobbies operating at the Statehouse.

The Council believed that a tax limitation constitutional amendment, as opposed to a law, would be more likely to bring lasting tax relief to Massachusetts residents. The task of amending the state's constitution was a long and complicated process. If a citizen group wanted to initiate a change in the state constitution, it would need to petition the legislature asking for consideration of a proposed amendment. In 1979, petitioners were required to collect signatures from approximately 60,000 registered voters. If enough valid signatures were collected, the legislature would vote on the citizen initiative for a constitutional amendment when it convened during a joint session as a Constitutional Convention during 1980. The legislature would need to approve the proposed amendment during two separate conventions over a four-year period. If the proposed amendment received approval during both convention sessions, the proposal would then be presented to voters on a statewide ballot. Once ratified by voters, the amendment would then be incorporated into the state's constitution.

"We have debated the taxation issue long enough. Now it is time to get to work—to put up or shut up!" Rallied by those words, the council decided the time had come to engage in referendum politics. With that decision, the council committed itself to a petition drive to collect enough signatures to win lasting tax reform.

In the summer of 1979, the Massachusetts High Technology Council (MHTC), working in conjunction with Associated Industries of Massachusetts (AIM), wrote two similarly worded tax petitions—one for a *law* and the other for a constitutional *amendment*. The AIM-MHTC proposals would not only cap property taxes but would limit the total state and local tax revenue to a percent of personal income that was competitive with other states. Meanwhile, Citizens for Limited Taxation (CLT)—a grassroots organization of taxpayers—was planning to collect signatures for its *law* and *amendment* petitions that were designed to limit property taxes. In September of 1979, Foley proposed and each group agreed to work with the other to collect the necessary signatures in order to get the best "bang for the buck." The AIM-MHTC petition called for a constitutional amendment for an overall tax limit and the CLT law called for a local property tax limit.

AIM-MHTC and CLT were not alone in their petition campaigns. In fact, the autumn air was filled with referendum petitions. Business groups, labor unions, public employees, teacher associations, consumer advocates, and taxpayer organizations each had plans to mount petition drives. The Massachusetts Teachers Association (MTA)—a large and prominent teacher union group—had mounted the most significant counterproposal to the AIM-MHTC and CLT petitions.

By January 1980, AIM-MHTC and CLT had collected 59,227 signatures (359 above the minimum legal requirement) for their *amendment* petition and 60,529 signatures (1,661 above the minimum legal requirement) for

their *law* petition. Before these two petitions could be formally presented to the legislature for consideration, however, both AIM-MHTC and CLT had to fight legal challenges by the Massachusetts Teachers Association (MTA), which questioned the validity of a small portion of the signatures on each petition. Of all the groups that started petition drives, the MTA was the only other organization to successfully gather enough signatures for its proposal. After AIM-MHTC and CLT won the legal challenge, they then turned attention to winning passage of a new tax law. As MHTC prepared to do battle with the teachers' association, it was clear that many, including the legislature, would be watching MHTC, the "new kid" on the political block.

## PETITION FOR A NEW TAX LAW

As the legislature began to consider the merits of CLT's petition for a law to limit property taxes, the issue of tax limitation started to gain public attention. The CLT petition—dubbed Proposition 2½ because it would cap local property taxes at 2.5% of fair market value within each city and town—fanned a fire of tax reform debate. Editorials that criticized the measure worried aloud about the potentially devastating impact it could have on cities and towns with low property values. The League of Women Voters, while noting the need for tax justice in Massachusetts, called Proposition 2½ "a wolf in sheep's clothing" and argued that such a statewide mandate would interfere with the home rule of local municipalities. CLT and MHTC denied these claims and cited the need to "send a message to the legislature," a legislature that had failed to enact any of the 125 tax-limiting proposals brought before it during the last 50 years.

In May 1980, state lawmakers rejected the CLT proposal—Proposition 2½—by an overwhelming 173 to 5 margin. Although discouraged by this outcome, CLT vowed to continue its fight and began another petition drive seeking an additional 10,000 signatures. This supplementary petition would bring Proposition

2½ directly to voters on the November 1980 ballot.

In June 1980, Citizens for Limited Taxation was having organizational problems. With its funds depleted, the full-time salaried CLT director resigned his post and a CLT staff member, Barbara Anderson, assumed day-to-day direction of the organization. Meanwhile, the MTA had developed a well-funded campaign to defeat Proposition 2½ should it appear on the ballot. At the same time, the MTA had also decided *not* to commit any of its financial resources to win voter approval of its own more moderate tax reform proposal.

## THE CONSTITUTIONAL CONVENTION

When Howard Foley took his seat in the Statehouse gallery, he was not certain how the Constitutional Convention (a special session of the state legislature) would receive the AIM-MHTC proposal for a tax-limiting constitutional amendment. While he was fully aware of the negative reception to Proposition 2½, he believed the AIM-MHTC proposal was more moderate and broader in scope. So, when legislators voted to adjourn their convention without even discussing the amendment initiative, Foley and MHTC members were outraged by what they felt was an abuse of political power.

• • •

As Howard Foley sat behind his desk on that July 8, 1980 morning, he had to decide on a course of action. He could continue to press Governor King to exercise his constitutional duty to reconvene the Constitutional Convention and thereby force legislators to deal with the AIM-MHTC proposal. Since Proposition 2½ was facing organizational, financial and political obstacles, the MHTC membership might also consider lending their resources—time and money—to help Citizens for Limited Taxation. Council Chairman Alex d'Arbeloff had called a meeting for the following month inviting the executive committee of MHTC's board of directors to review their progress and consider alternatives for gaining a tax limitation measure. (Exhibit 3 provides a list of council members in July 1980.)

As one CEO looked to the upcoming August meeting, he commented on the recent course of events:

When I found out about the adjournment, I was livid. After all, we do have constitutional rights like anyone else. This sort of thing makes me wonder about the kind of state we live in. . . . Is there or is there not a process?

I realize that the power brokerage system has been around for a long time and I know we probably threaten that system. Information *is* power. . . . If we try to make people aware of economic realities facing high technology, we believe they will listen. . . . One thing we won't be involved with is peddling influence with money. . . . It happens, but we will not play that game. As far as I'm concerned, our democratic process is at stake. . . .

The basic issue is creation of an equitable tax policy that is in line with other competing states—this is not just a high tech need, it's a need for all of Massachusetts. The Council is "solution oriented." . . . We don't believe in studying things to death. We are really frustrated by the lack of decisions. . . .

Another CEO remarked:

We are really involved in a struggle for power and should not be dismayed by disagreements, power politics or immorality on the part of others. If we want to change things, we had better be ready to stand up and fight. . . . If we want tax reform, maybe we had better play power politics. . . . We don't want to railroad this issue. . . . All that we ask is that voters be given a chance to express their will. . . .

I believe in enlightened self-interest. . . . An individual ought to be able to keep the fruits of his labor. . . . On the other hand, compassion is necessary in any civilized society. Someone must be ready to help the sick and lame . . . but, in this case, the definition of who is sick and lame has lost its bounds.

Since I moved to Massachusetts six years ago . . . my taxes have doubled and my services were cut in half! People talk about the cultural attractions within the state. . . . I think we are being taken by this mystique. Tax reform is not a trivial issue. . . . If something doesn't happen soon the state will bankrupt its economy. . . .

People are nervous about discussing tax limitation in public. . . . They fear criticism from neighbors . . . and think people will consider them greedy. . . . That kind of anxiety also exists within the Council. We need to articulate a philosophy . . . an intellectual springboard to explain our gut feelings. . . .

Still confident, but nevertheless uncertain about the outcome of this tax reform effort, Howard Foley added a handwritten footnote below his memorandum to the Board of Directors—"July 8th: TO ALL MEMBERS—WE ARE GOING FORWARD!"

# EXHIBITS: Massachusetts High Technology Council

**EXHIBIT 1**
MEMBERSHIP LIST (OCTOBER 1977)

**Officers:**

| | | |
|---|---|---|
| Ray Stata | D. V. d'Arbeloff | Donald J. Evans, Esq. |
| President | Treasurer | Secretary and Clerk |

**Board of Directors:**

| | | |
|---|---|---|
| Frank Wezniak | Martin Allen | Jay Barger |
| President | President | President |
| Adar Associates, Inc. | Computervision Corporation | Dynatech Corporation |
| Ray Stata | Marvin Stolberg | William Thurston |
| President | President | President |
| Analog Devices, Inc. | New England Nuclear Corp. | GenRad, Inc. |
| Bernard Gordon | Edson deCastro | D. V. d'Arbeloff |
| President | President | President |
| Analogic Corporation | Data General Corporation | Millipore Corporation |
| Carl Dantas | Andrew Knowles | George Berman |
| President | Vice President | President |
| Compugraphic Corporation | Digital Equipment Corporation | Unitrode Corporation |

**Members:**

| | | |
|---|---|---|
| Accutest Corporation | Data General Corporation | LFE Corporation |
| Adams-Russell Company, Inc. | Digital Equipment Corporation | Microwave Associates |
| Adar Associates, Inc. | Dynatech Corporation | Megapulse |
| Alpha Industries, Inc. | GenRad, Inc. | Millipore Corporation |
| Analog Devices, Inc. | Germanium Power Devices | New England Nuclear Corporation |
| Analogic Corporation | Gould, Inc. | Prime Computer |
| Augat, Inc. | Hewlett-Packard Co. | Semicon, Inc. |
| BBF, Inc. | Incoterm Corporation | Teradyne Corporation |
| Bolt, Beranek & Newman | Inforex, Inc. | Unitrode Corporation |
| Codex Corporation | Instrumentation Laboratory, Inc. | Valtec Corporation |
| Compugraphic Corporation | Ionics, Inc. | Wang Laboratories |
| Computer Devices, Inc. | Itek Corporation | Waters Associates, Inc. |
| Computervision Corporation | | |

**EXHIBIT 2**
PROFILE: HOWARD P. FOLEY

As president of the Massachusetts High Technology Council, Inc., Howard P. Foley is responsible to its board of directors and rapidly growing membership for successful implementation of the Council's plans and programs.

Prior to joining the Council in November 1978, Mr. Foley held the position of executive vice president of Jobs for Massachusetts, Inc. from its inception in April 1972. Jobs is a private nonprofit economic development corporation made up of leaders from business, labor and both the legislative and executive branches of state government.

Before his work with Jobs for Massachusetts, Mr. Foley was a marketing manager in IBM's Data Processing Division Office, Boston, Massachusetts. In that position, one he held from September 1969 to April 1972, he directed the marketing and systems engineering personnel responsible for IBM's data processing business in the banking and securities industries.

From December 1961 to September 1969, he was a data processing salesman in Boston, and a staff instructor and sales school coordinator at IBM's Poughkeepsie, New York, Education Center teaching computer applications and salesmanship to hundreds of IBM personnel. Prior to his promotion back to Boston, he was special assistant to the division's vice president of marketing in White Plains, New York.

Upon graduating in 1960 from the University of Notre Dame with a B.B.A. in marketing, Mr. Foley served as a 1st Lieutenant and Platoon Leader in the Infantry of the U.S. Army.

In 1973, Mr. Foley was the Industrial Division chairman of the Massachusetts Bay United Fund Drive. He was also president (1973) and director of the Boston Business Resource Center (1973–1977), a nonprofit corporation established to assist minority business enterprises. He currently serves as a member of the Board of Overseers' Visiting Committee for Continuing Education in the Faculty of Arts and Sciences at Harvard College and as a member of the Board of Advisors to the New England Congressional Institute.

Mr. Foley was born in New York City in 1938 and now lives in Wayland, Massachusetts, with his wife, Marylee, and their three children, Cass, Matthew and Megan.

**EXHIBIT 3**
MEMBERSHIP LIST (JULY 1980)

**Officers:**

Alexander V. d'Arbeloff
Chairman

D. V. d'Arbeloff
Vice Chairman and Treasurer

Howard P. Foley
President

Donald J. Evans, Esq.
Secretary and Clerk

**Board of Directors
(Executive Committee):**

Ray Stata
Chairman
Analog Devices, Inc.

Roger Wellington
Chairman
Augat, Inc.

Carl E. Dantas
President
Compugraphic Corp.

Edson de Castro
President
Data General Corp.

Andrew C. Knowles
Vice President
Digital Equipment Corp.

William R. Thurston
President
GenRad, Inc.

Arthur L. Goldstein
President
Ionics, Inc.

D. V. d'Arbeloff
Chairman
Millipore Corp.

Kenneth G. Fisher
President
Prime Computer, Inc.

Alexander V. d'Arbeloff
President
Teradyne, Inc.

**Members:**

Accutest Corp.
Adage, Inc.
* Adams-Russell Co., Inc.
* Adar/Scientific Atlanta, Inc.
Aerovox Incorporated
* Alpha Industries, Inc.
Altron, Inc.
American Pacemaker Corp.
Amicon Corp.
* Analog Devices, Inc.
Applicon, Inc.
Aritech Corp.
* Arthur D. Little, Inc.
ATEX, Inc.
* Augat, Inc.
Baird Corp.
* BASF Systems, Inc.
* BBF, Inc.
Bolt, Beranek & Newman
BTU Engineering Corp.
Burroughs Corp.
Chomerics, Inc.
Codex Corp.
* Compugraphic Corp.
Computek, Inc.
* Computer Devices, Inc.
* Computervision Corp.
Concord Computing Corp.
Control Logic, Inc.
Controlonics Corp.
Corning Glass Works
Coulter Systems Corp.
Cullinane Corp.
dataCon, Inc.
* Data General Corp.
* Data Terminal Systems
Data Translation, Inc.
Daymarc Corp.

Dennison Kybe Corp.
* Digital Equipment Corp.
Dynamics Research Corp.
* Dynatech Corp.
E G & G, Inc.
Eikonix Corp.
Environmental Sciences
   Associates, Inc.
Epsco, Inc.
* Foxboro Co.
Frequency Sources, Inc.
* GCA Corp.
General Scanning, Inc.
* GenRad, Inc.
* Germanium Power Devices
GTE Laboratories Inc.
Haemonetics Corp.
Harbridge House, Inc.
* Hewlett-Packard Co.
Honeywell Information Systems
Hybrid Technology Corp.
Hybrid Systems Corp.
Hy-Sil/MADICO
Inforex, Inc.
Instron Corp.
Insul-Tab, Inc.
Intermetrics, Inc.
Intronics, Inc.
* Ionics, Inc.
Itek Corp.
JBF Scientific Corp.
Kalba Bowen Associates,
   Inc.
Kaye Instruments, Inc.
Keane, Inc.
Kurzweil Computer
   Products, Inc.
LFE Corp.
LTX Corp.
M/A COM, Inc.

Management Decision
   Systems, Inc.
Medical Information
   Technology, Inc.
MEDI-TECH, Inc.
Megapulse, Inc.
* Metal Bellows Corp.
Microfab, Inc.
Micro Networks Corp.
* Millipore Corp.
Minnesota Mining
   & Manufacturing Co.
Gould, Inc.
National Medical Care, Inc.
* New England Nuclear Co.
Nixdorf Computer Corp.
Nuclear Metals, Inc.
Nypro, Inc.
Omni Spectra, Inc.
Orion Research Inc.
Ortho Instruments
* Prime Computer, Inc.
* Printed Circuit Corp.
Semicon, Inc.
Shipley Co., Inc.
Sigma Instruments, Inc.
* Sippican Corp.
SofTech, Inc.
Sperry Research Center
Sprague Electric Co.
Technical Communications
   Corp.
Technical Operations, Inc.
* Teradyne, Inc.
The Analytic Sciences Corp.
Thermo Electron Corp.
* Unitrode Corp.
Valtec Corp.
Walker Magnetics Group, Inc.
Wang Laboratories

*Member, Board of Directors.

## Associate Members:

Alex. Brown & Sons
American Research
 & Development
Arthur Andersen & Co.
Arthur Young & Co.
Barclays Bank International, Ltd.
Bear, Stearns & Co.
Berg & Co., Inc.
Blyth Eastman Paine Webber,
 Inc.

Burgess & Leith, Inc.
Cambridge Trust Co.
Coopers & Lybrand
Deloitte Haskins & Sells
Ernst & Whinney
First Boston Corp.
Goldman, Sachs & Co.
Hay Associates
Linden Sales, Inc.

Merrill Lynch, White Weld
Moseley, Hallgarten
 & Estabrook, Inc.
Peat, Marwick, Mitchell & Co.
Price Waterhouse & Company
Shawmut Community Bank, N.A.
Shawmut County Bank, N.A.
The Carlson Corp.
The Strayton Corp.

# Dayton Hudson Corporation: Conscience and Control (A)

*To those who assert that business should operate only in its own best interests, I contend that corporate social responsibility is in our best interest. It is in the interest of our survival.*

— Bruce B. Dayton
Chairman, Executive Committee
Dayton Hudson Corporation
May 20, 1976

Just before lunch, the legal team reentered the meeting to share what they had been discussing. They said they had a possible "showstopper," an alternative that might permit the company to remain independent in its current form. Kenneth A. Macke, 48, CEO of the Minneapolis-based Dayton Hudson Corporation (DHC), listened intently.

Only a short time before, Macke had made it clear that he was dissatisfied with the strategies that had been discussed during the morning meeting. He had scheduled the meeting for Thursday, June 11, 1987, and opened it as a general might convene a council of war. With him were some of the senior managers of the company and a number of outside advisers, assembled to formulate a strategy for defending the company against an emerging hostile takeover threat. These advisers included representatives of Goldman Sachs (DHC's investment bankers), Kekst and Co., and the New York law firm of Wachtell, Lipton, Rosen, and Katz. One discussion focused on the financial options, while in another room DHC's legal staff and their advisers discussed legal defenses. The debate in each group ranged widely, and at one point or another, in the words of one participant, "every imaginable option" was considered.

To the financial team it was clear that every alternative entailed fighting the battle for the company's future in New York. They considered attempts to block the raider's access to needed financial resources as well as various plans to restructure the company and make it unattractive to the raider. Every participant was aware of the need for quick and decisive action.

Eight days earlier, on Wednesday, June 3, 1987, DHC's stock had increased in value by nearly $3 per share in unusually heavy trading, to close at about $50.62 (see Exhibits 1, 2). To the casual observer, this increase was puzzling, for the company had, only a few months earlier, reported its first earnings decline in sixteen years (see Exhibit 3). Since then, the stock had traded between about $42 and $45, and volume had been relatively low. Furthermore, nothing obvious had happened to account for the sudden increase in price and volume.

To the professional observer, however, the change was not so surprising. Once a favorite of Wall Street because of its consistently strong earnings, the company had fallen out of favor.

In the opinion of many observers, its earnings decline was caused by the poor performance of one of its four operating companies. Furthermore, management had not kept investors and analysts well-informed about efforts to correct the problems. As a result, DHC's stock traded at a price that some analysts felt undervalued the company.

Macke was confident that DHC would rebound and post strong earnings growth within a year or two. In late May and early June, however, he watched his company's stock with growing concern. SEC regulations specified that anyone acquiring 5% or more of a company's stock must file a disclosure. No such disclosure had been filed. However, alerted by the unusual market activity, and by rumors circulating on Wall Street, Macke and his management team feared that the company might become the target of a hostile takeover attempt. By June 3 this appeared highly likely, and shortly afterword, in response to the probable threat, Macke called together a task force of senior managers that had been formed some years earlier to deal with such a situation. Included in this group were Boake Sells (president and COO), Willard Schull (CFO), James Hale (senior vice president and general counsel), Peter Hutchinson (vice president for external affairs and chairman of the Dayton Hudson Foundation), and Ann Barkelew (vice president for corporate public relations).

With the help of their Wall Street advisers the team was able to identify the likely raider as the Dart Group Corporation, a Maryland-based discounter with a recent history of unsuccessful takeover attempts. Though the Dart Group had not made a concrete proposal, nor even publicly acknowledged its interest in the company, Macke and his team were aware that they needed to act quickly if they were to protect the company from being put in play.* On Wednesday, June 10, DHC's stock was the second most heavily traded on the New York Stock Exchange. Since June 3 it had risen in value by over $4.50.

## THE DAYTON HUDSON CORPORATION

The Dayton Hudson Corporation described itself as "a growth company focusing exclusively on retailing." Headquartered in Minneapolis, the company operated 475 stores in 34 states at the end of 1986, employing some 120,000 people nationwide (full-time and part-time). In that year it had pretax earnings of $494.2 million on sales of $9,259.1 million.

In 1902 George Draper Dayton, a Minneapolis banker and real estate developer, entered into a partnership to operate a dry goods store in a building he owned in the downtown area of the city. The Dayton Company went on to become the most prominent retailer in Minnesota, and the Dayton family among the most important of the state's citizens. Unlike most of the state's other major employers, DHC is incorporated under Minnesota law. In 1987, DHC employed some 34,000 Minnesotans, about 20,000 of whom worked for the company part-time. That year DHC's payroll for Minnesota employees was nearly $278 million.

Through a combination of mergers, acquisitions, and retailing innovations, the company grew dramatically in the 1950s and 1960s. At one time it had interests in real estate (development and management of shopping centers) and specialty retail outlets (jewelry, books, and consumer electronics) as well as large department stores. The company was taken public in 1967, and in 1969 it merged with the J. L. Hudson Company of Detroit to form the Dayton Hudson Corporation (see Exhibit 4).

In 1962, DHC opened its first three Target stores, offering name brand merchandise at discount prices. By 1975 the Target division was DHC's largest revenue producer. In 1978 DHC acquired Mervyn's, a West Coast retailer, to become the seventh largest non-food retailer in the United States. In 1984, the University of Southern California's School of Business Ad-

---

*When a company's stockholder base becomes destabilized, i.e., when a large proportion of the stock is in the hands of short-term holders (arbitrageurs, for example), the company's stock is said to be "in play." Up to this point, strictly speaking, DHC's efforts were focused on preventing the stock from being put in play.

*customer
shareholders
community*

ministration named DHC the best managed company in America and awarded it the Vanguard Corporation Award for its uncompromising ethical standards and unusual dynamism.

By 1987 DHC had disposed of its real estate and most of its small format, specialty retail businesses to focus exclusively on what management concluded to be the company's greatest strength: operating large retail stores.

Macke joined DHC as a merchandise trainee with Dayton's in 1961, immediately after his graduation from Drake University (Iowa). Rising through the ranks, he became president and CEO of the Target division in 1976, and chairman the following year. Under his leadership, Target grew in four years from 49 stores to 137 stores, and more than doubled its operating profit to become the top profitmaker for DHC. In 1981 Macke was named president of DHC. He became CEO in 1983, and chairman of the board in 1984.

Stephen Watson, chairman and CEO of the Dayton Hudson Department Store Company (a division of DHC), described Macke as a "needler," someone who "constantly needles you about areas of the business that need improvement." On the other hand, in situations where important decisions needed to be made, he was a good listener. His practice was to give a full hearing to his subordinates and advisers, and then to choose what he saw to be the best course of action. To some, Macke's management style bordered on the abrasive, but others admired his decisiveness and his commitment to DHC.

### Operating Structures and Policies

DHC was composed of four operating companies and a corporate headquarters. This structure reflected DHC's fundamental management philosophy which favored decentralization. The operating companies were:

Target: an upscale discount store chain. In 1986 Target produced 47% of DHC's revenues and 47.4% of pretax profits, with earnings of $311 million on sales of $4,355 million.

Mervyn's: a highly promotional, popularly priced, value-oriented department store company. In 1986 Mervyn's produced 31% of DHC's revenues and 24.4% of pretax profits, with earnings of $160 million on sales of $2,862 million.

Dayton Hudson Department Store Company (DHDSC): the largest traditional department store operation in the United States. In 1986 DHDSC produced 17% of DHC's revenues and 25.2% of pretax profits, with earnings of $166 million on sales of $1,566 million.

Lechmere's: a hard goods retail store company. In 1986 Lechmere's produced 5% of DHC's revenues and 3% of pretax profits, with earnings of $19.5 million on sales of $476 million.

The operating companies made autonomous decisions about merchandising and buying, and had responsibility for profits and return on investment. They were made accountable to corporate headquarters through an annual planning cycle, considered to be crucial to DHC's management process. This annual planning cycle included a strategy and human resources review, an agreement on capital allocation, the setting of financial goals, and a performance appraisal. However, despite the apparent autonomy granted to the operating companies, Macke continued to pay close attention to details and "needle" his executives in an effort to improve performance.

*Fin. objs.*

### Financial Policies

DHC's stated financial goal was to provide its shareholders with a superior return on their investment while maintaining a conservative financial position. More particularly, the company preferred to own assets where possible, to meet external needs with long-term debt, and to maintain a maximum debt ratio of 45% (including capital and operating leases). The majority of the company's growth was financed through internally generated funds.

In its 1986 Annual Report, DHC stated that its performance objectives were to "earn an after-tax return on beginning shareholders' equity (ROE) of 18%," to "sustain an annual growth in earnings per share (EPS) of 15%," and to "maintain a strong rating of [its] senior debt." The report also noted that "the incentive compensation of corporate management and the management of each operating company is based on return on investment, as well as growth in earnings."

These goals, however, were not extrapolated from past performance. The ROE had averaged 15.3% in the period 1975–86, and the earnings per share growth had only been above 15% five times in those twelve years (see Exhibits 5, 6).

Though DHC remained a profitable company, 1986 was a disappointing year. Revenues increased by 12% and passed the $9 billion mark, but net earnings per share dropped by 9% (see Exhibit 7). The principal reason appears to have been difficulty with the Mervyn's division, where operating profits fell by more than 34%. DHC's Annual Report for 1986 acknowledged a problem with Mervyn's and attributed the dramatic decline in profits to an organizational restructuring and to a need to reduce margins in order to remain competitive.

More specifically, Mervyn's had expanded significantly in Texas, adding buying and sales offices there in 1984 which duplicated some services performed at its California headquarters. The oil price collapse made these functions redundant and the company was forced to close that office and reorganize at considerable expense. These difficulties distracted management attention and marketing mistakes were made. Coupled with increased competition, these factors, and the efforts made to correct for them, were responsible for poor performance in 1986.

This was the second year of poor performance for Mervyn's (in 1985 operating profits had increased by only 9.7%), a sharp contrast to the previous two years, when profits had increased by 21% each year. Since the decline began when Macke became chairman, some observers raised questions about his ability to manage the corporation.

## Customer Service

DHC was strongly customer-oriented. The stated merchandising objective of each of the operating companies was to fulfill the value expectations of customers more effectively than the competition. They consciously aimed to do this by providing superior value in five categories: assortment, quality, fashion, convenience and pricing. One concrete sign of this orientation was the longstanding corporate policy of accepting the return of merchandise for a full refund, no questions asked. Stories abounded, especially in Minnesota, about the lengths to which the company was willing to go to honor this policy. One customer told a story about an experience she had had in the china department.

> Not long ago a woman went to Dayton Hudson's flagship department store in Minneapolis to purchase a wedding gift in the china department. Before she could make her purchase she was annoyed to have to wait for a young woman who apparently wished to return some china. Her annoyance turned to astonishment when she heard the young woman's story. It seems that for some years the young woman's mother had been purchasing place settings and other pieces of a particular pattern and saving them for her daughter's wedding. Quite a number of pieces had been accumulated, and now the daughter was indeed to be married. However, she did not like the pattern and decided to return the entire collection to Dayton's for a refund. It turned out that the pattern had been discontinued by the manufacturer. Nevertheless, despite some understandable initial reluctance on the part of the clerk, the policy prevailed and the young woman received her refund.

What was remarkable was that people in the Twin Cities did *not* seem to find such stories unusual.

## Corporate Community Involvement

In 1946 the Dayton Company became the first major American corporation to initiate a policy by which it donated 5% of its federal taxable income to nonprofit organizations. (It was a charter member of Minnesota's "5% Club," an or-

*Store Closings*

ganization founded in 1976 whose membership consisted of corporations that donated 5% of their annual taxable income.) This policy had continued without interruption, and in 1987 DHC's contributions totaled nearly $20 million (principally to arts and social action organizations.) These contributions were distributed throughout the states in which DHC did business. The four states which generated the largest revenues for the company were California, Minnesota, Texas, and Michigan, but contributions were not proportioned to revenues (see Exhibit 8).

Eighty percent of DHC's contributions were made in two areas: the arts and social action,* each receiving roughly equal amounts (see Exhibit 9). The remaining community giving funds were contributed to other programs and projects that addressed responsiveness to special community needs and opportunities; and innovative partnerships with other community leaders. The company was Minnesota's largest private donor and a mainstay of many of the arts organizations in the Twin Cities. In the past, it had helped fund such activities as job creation programs, neighborhood renovations, and child care and chemical abuse programs.

Observers considered DHC's community involvement program to be distinctive in several ways. Among these was the company's commitment to maintain a professional staff, "held to standards as rigorous as any profit center within the corporation, with specific goals, objectives, and performance review." Another was the decision to commit 6% of their giving budget to emerging issues in social action and the arts. As Peter Hutchinson, chairman of the Dayton Hudson Foundation, commented, "Armed with an integrated view of needs and opportunities, we must . . . adapt our programs to changing circumstances. . . . Regardless of the means, our goals must be to bring programs and constitu-

ents together in a common vision and commitment for the future."

DHC's concern for social responsibility extended into other aspects of its business as well. In 1978, for example, Kenneth Dayton (then chairman and CEO of the company) was one of the principal organizers of the Minnesota Project on Corporate Responsibility. This organization sponsored seminars and other programs aimed at encouraging and strengthening a sense of social responsiveness in Minnesota corporations. James Shannon, then executive director of the General Mills Foundation, commented in a guest editorial in the *Minneapolis Star Tribune,* "In a community nationally known for its corporate support of the arts, social services, and education, the Dayton Hudson Corp. is the flagship for dozens of other publicly and privately held corporations committed to the proposition that a successful company has an obligation to be a good corporate citizen."

DHC's relations with the public were not always smooth, however. There were times when its concern for communities was questioned. In 1983, for example, Hudson's flagship store in downtown Detroit was closed. From DHC's perspective the store had become old and inefficient, and the business climate in downtown Detroit unsupportive. Mayor Coleman Young's view was different. As he told the *Detroit Free Press,* "I don't think Hudson's demonstrated any sense of responsibility or citizenship after growing in this city and off this city for almost 100 years."

The following year, 1984, Dayton's and Hudson's operations were consolidated into the Dayton Hudson Department Store Company, with a single headquarters in Minneapolis. Once again, Detroit objected, since the move resulted in the loss of about 1,000 jobs for the city, many of them well-paid management positions. Ann Barkelew, DHC's vice president for public relations, commented in the *Minneapolis Star Tribune,* "Our decision to bring the headquarters [to Minneapolis] was a business decision. The whole purpose in combining the companies was to do things better."

---

*A very wide variety of social action projects were funded, including literacy programs, job skills training programs, development programs for minority businesses, and neighborhood renewal programs.

*diff. than DHC.*

## THE DART GROUP CORPORATION

The Dart Group Corporation's 1987 Annual Report (year ending January 31, 1987) was spartan and no-nonsense. Its only two photographs, which appeared on the first page, were of Herbert Haft, founder and chairman, and Robert Haft, president and Herbert's older son. There were no photographs of the discount retail outlets they operated or of satisfied customers, nor did other members of management or the board of directors appear. Instead, attention was focused exclusively on information about Dart's operations and finances. And not without reason, for Dart's net income more than tripled in fiscal 1987 (see Exhibit 10).

According to the Annual Report, Dart operated retail discount auto parts stores through the Trak Auto Corporation, operated retail discount bookstores through the Crown Books Corporation, and operated a financial business which dealt in bankers' acceptances. The present company was a successor to Dart Drug, a Washington, D.C., retail drugstore chain founded by Herbert Haft. Haft built a chain of stores from one store he opened in 1954 by selling most of his merchandise at discount prices. At the time the minimum price for many brand-name products was set by the manufacturer, and Haft was often in violation of fair trade laws in selling at a discount. While the practice provoked a number of supplier suits, it also attracted thousands of customers. As the suburbs of Washington grew, Dart Drug grew with them. In the 1970s, Dart pioneered the concept of a "super" drugstore that sold not only the traditional drugs and cosmetics, but beer, lawn furniture, lumber, auto parts, and almost anything else the Hafts could find.

While Robert Haft was a student at the Harvard Business School in the mid-1970s, he wrote a paper exploring the idea of selling books through discount retail outlets. By some accounts, he was motivated to set the idea in motion after listening to a Dayton Hudson executive who spoke at Harvard. Dayton Hudson operated B. Dalton Booksellers at the time and

the executive claimed that a discount book chain could not be successful. Robert earned an MBA in 1977 and later established Crown Books, which sold both hardcover and paperback books at a discount. By 1986 Crown Books operated about 200 stores nationally, with 1986 earnings of $5.5 million on revenues of $154 million.

In 1984, Dart's drugstore division was sold to its employees. In the three years prior to the sale the Hafts boosted profitability by sharply cutting costs. They accomplished this in part by dramatic reductions in inventory (e.g., stocking far fewer sizes and varieties of merchandise), and customer services (e.g., declining to give cash refunds). According to a *Fortune* magazine article, they were well known among their suppliers as tough customers. They acquired a reputation of paying late and demanding discounts. Suppliers were frequently reluctant to insist on their terms and risk losing a large customer, so they often made concessions. By 1987, the independent Dart Drug Stores were struggling to survive, burdened with large interest payments and a poor reputation. In an effort to win back customers, the new owners ran ads in the *Washington Post* announcing that the stores were no longer owned or operated by the Hafts.

### Attempts to Acquire Other Businesses

DHC was not the first corporation in which the Hafts took an interest. Between 1983 and 1986 they attempted to acquire Supermarkets General Corp., Jack Eckerd Drug Stores, Revco Inc., Federated Department Stores, May Department Stores and the giant supermarket chain, Safeway Stores. In each case they failed, but their failures were spectacularly profitable. They realized a $9 million profit on the sale of their Jack Eckerd stock, $40 million in their unsuccessful attempt to purchase Supermarkets General, and $97 million when they failed to take over Safeway. Not surprisingly, the value of Dart Group stock rose from $10.75 in 1982 to over $150 per share in 1987.

Target companies have seriously questioned, and seriously resisted, the Haft's attempts to acquire them. Like many other corporate raiders, the Hafts relied on "junk bonds" as part of the financial component of their proposals, and issuers like Drexel Burnham Lambert indicated that they were "highly confident" that financing could be arranged. Yet unlike many other raiders, the Hafts always targeted businesses close to their own experience. They remained in the retail industry and attempted to acquire chains, especially where their low-margin expertise might be valuable. Since they were always unsuccessful in their acquisition attempts, accusations by critics that they intended to sell off the major assets of the target companies were, while speculative, not entirely unreasonable. For their part, the Hafts insisted that they planned to operate, rather than break up, the companies they targeted.

However, even when a takeover attempt failed, the target company could face a difficult time. In 1986, the Dart Group was unsuccessful in an attempt to acquire Safeway Stores. The management of Safeway eluded the Hafts by taking the company private with a leveraged buyout. This involved taking on $4.2 billion in debt in order to purchase outstanding stock. As a result, Safeway, once the largest supermarket chain in the United States, was compelled to sell off profitable British and Australian holdings. In addition, it sold or closed 251 stores in the United States. Many of these stores were in small towns that had complained bitterly about the move. While Safeway's streamlining substantially improved profitability, it was still left with an enormous debt burden to service.

### The Events Leading Up to Early June 1987

In 1986, DHC offered its B. Dalton division for sale. At that time B. Dalton, founded by one of the Dayton brothers in the 1960s, was one of the two largest and most successful retail bookselling chains in the United States. However, DHC had decided to pursue a strategy focused on the operation of large stores that offered a broad spectrum of merchandise. The typical B. Dalton store was fairly small and specialized in books and computer software. Among those seriously interested in acquiring B. Dalton was the Dart Group. Ultimately they were unsuccessful, and the division was sold to Barnes and Noble. According to one rumor, the negotiations broke down when personal hostilities flared up between senior executives of DHC and the Hafts.

Nevertheless, in their negotiations the Hafts had the opportunity to become familiar with DHC. While they recognized value in the company, they were critical of DHC's management. In a later interview with the *Minneapolis Star Tribune,* Robert Haft criticized DHC's retail strategies. "This thing is slowly going downhill," he said. According to *Business Week,* they felt that their own successful experience in managing discount retail outlets made them well suited to manage DHC properly.

In the spring of 1987, when DHC announced its first decline in earnings in sixteen years, the Hafts saw an opportunity. Though the significant drop in DHC's stock price discouraged some investors, the Hafts felt there was good reason to think that the company still had the potential for solid earnings. The Target division had acquired a number of important leases in California and was poised for expansion. With proper management, Mervyn's could certainly be turned around. Moreover, the board of directors and senior management collectively owned a very small portion of DHC's stock, far less than would be required to exercise a controlling influence.

By that same spring the legal climate was becoming less conducive to hostile takeovers. Provisions of an Indiana law that gave the state considerable power to restrict such takeovers had been upheld by the U.S. Supreme Court in April. Some Minnesota corporations (though not DHC) had lobbied hard for similar legislation in 1984, but it had failed to pass, partly because many legislators felt that it would not be upheld by the courts. The Supreme Court's decision, however, came too late to influence the 1987 session of the Minnesota legislature, which adjourned on May 18.

## ANOTHER ALTERNATIVE?

During the week of June 8, the Task Force met frequently and Macke remained in constant communication with the board of directors. As alternatives were generated, however, each one seemed unacceptable to management and the board.

At the meeting on June 11, Macke himself made clear his opposition to a "bust up" take-over, one that would require breaking up the corporation and selling off parts to repay the debts incurred by the takeover. He and his management team were convinced that it was best for all the corporation's constituencies—stockholders, customers, employees, and communities—that the company remain intact. As the

*"Greenmail" is a payment made to a raider, and not to other stockholders, by a target company in exchange for the raider's stock, where the price paid is higher than the market value of the stock.

possibilities were discussed, some were set aside rather easily. They found greenmail,* in the words of one participant, to be a "repugnant" alternative. They were also repelled by various schemes to take on debt or sell off assets, which, as another participant put it, would involve doing to themselves exactly what they feared the Hafts would do. Nor were they convinced that the financial defenses would be successful. They realized that if they chose to fight a financial battle, the action would take place in New York, where they had less influence. On the other hand, they had considerable influence in Minnesota, but it was not clear how to bring that influence to bear.

As Macke listened to the legal team, he anticipated the direction of their proposal. Would this alternative take advantage of DHC's strengths and preserve the integrity of the company? Or would it be flawed like all the others?

# EXHIBITS: Dayton Hudson Corporation: Conscience and Control (A)

**EXHIBIT 1**
CLOSING PRICE OF COMMON STOCK, MAY–JUNE 1987

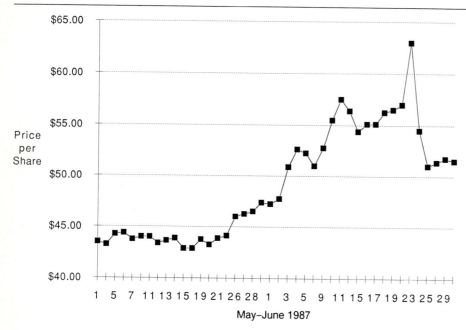

Source: Standard & Poor's *Daily Stock Price Record*, New York
Stock Exchange, 1987.

**EXHIBIT 2**
VOLUME OF COMMON STOCK TRADED, MAY–JUNE 1987

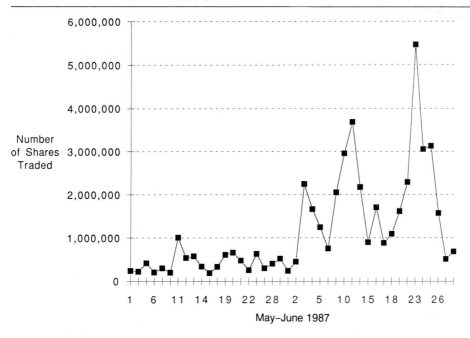

*Source:* Standard & Poor's *Daily Stock Price Record,* New York
Stock Exchange, 1987.

**EXHIBIT 3**
EARNINGS PER SHARE, 1970–1986

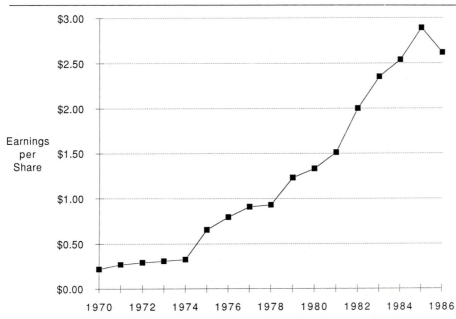

*Source:* Dayton Hudson Corporation Annual Reports, 1979, 1986.

**EXHIBIT 4**
HIGHLIGHTS FROM COMPANY HISTORY

1881  The J. L. Hudson Company founded in Detroit.

1902  The Dayton Company, later to become Dayton Corporation, founded in Minneapolis.

1956  The Dayton Company opens Southdale, the world's first fully enclosed two-level shopping center in suburban Minneapolis.

1962  The Dayton Company enters low-margin merchandising with the opening of three Target stores.

1966  The Dayton Company enters specialty book retailing through the creation of B. Dalton Booksellers.

1967  Dayton Corporation has first public offering of common stock.

1968  Department store expansion to the West through merger with Lipmans in Oregon and Diamond's in Arizona. Acquisition of Pickwick Book Shops in Los Angeles, later to be combined with B. Dalton.

1969  Merger of the Dayton Corporation and the J. L. Hudson Company to form Dayton Hudson Corporation, then the nation's 14th largest general merchandise retailer. Listing of Dayton Hudson common stock on the New York Stock Exchange.

1971  Revenues top the $1-billion mark.

1973  Corporation becomes nation's 11th largest general merchandise retailer.

1975  Target becomes corporation's top revenue producer.

1977  Corporation passes the $2-billion mark in annual revenues.

1978  Merger with Mervyn's. Corporation becomes the country's seventh largest general merchandise retailer. Dayton Hudson discontinues real estate line of business. The sale of nine regional shopping centers brings more than $300 million.

1979  Corporation passes $3-billion mark in annual revenues.

1980  Corporation purchases Ayr-Way, Indianapolis-based chain of 40 low-margin stores. Ayr-Way stores are converted to Target stores. Dayton Hudson passes $4-billion mark in annual revenues.

1981  Target passes $2-billion mark in annual revenues. Mervyn's reaches $1 billion.

1982  Sale of Dayton Hudson Jewelers. Corporation reaches $5 billion in annual revenues.

1983  Dayton Hudson moves up to fifth largest general merchandise retailer, opens 1,000th store and passes $6-billion mark in revenues.

1984  Hudson's and Dayton's combined to form Dayton Hudson Department Store Company, the largest individual department store company in the nation. Annual revenues reach $8 billion.

1986  B. Dalton Booksellers sold. Target negotiates major West Coast real estate transaction.

1987  Dayton Hudson receives and rejects unsolicited merger proposal from Dart Group Corporation.

*Source:* Dayton Hudson Information Booklet, Dayton Hudson Public Relations.

**EXHIBIT 5**
RETURN ON BEGINNING EQUITY (ROE), 1971–86

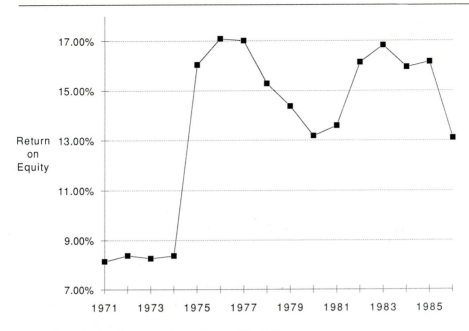

*Source:* Dayton Hudson Corporation Annual Reports, 1979, 1986.

**EXHIBIT 6**
EARNINGS PER SHARE GROWTH RATES, 1971–86

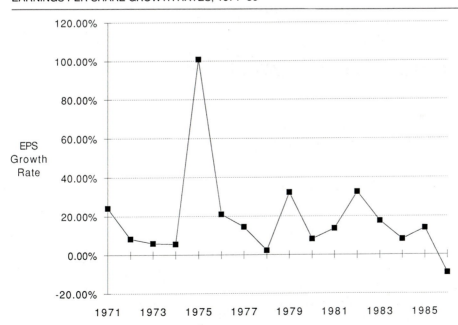

*Source:* Calculated from Dayton Hudson Corporation Annual Reports, 1979, 1986.

**EXHIBIT 7**
CONSOLIDATED RESULTS OF OPERATIONS
Dayton Hudson Corporation and Subsidiaries

| (Millions of dollars, except per-share data) | 1986 | 1985 | 1984 |
|---|---|---|---|
| Revenues | $9,259.1 | $8,255.3 | $7,519.2 |
| Costs and expenses | | | |
| Cost of retail sales, buying and occupancy | 6,705.2 | 5,908.3 | 5,392.1 |
| Selling, publicity and administrative | 1,538.1 | 1,365.9 | 1,234.4 |
| Depreciation | 182.7 | 158.2 | 144.9 |
| Rental expense | 73.1 | 69.0 | 69.5 |
| Interest expense, net | 117.5 | 99.8 | 97.7 |
| Taxes other than income taxes | 148.3 | 136.3 | 127.1 |
| | 8,764.9 | 7,737.5 | 7,065.7 |
| Earnings from continuing operations before income taxes and extraordinary charge | 494.2 | 517.8 | 453.5 |
| Provision for income taxes | 239.2 | 237.3 | 207.9 |
| Net earnings from continuing operations before extraordinary charge | 255.0 | 280.5 | 245.6 |
| Net earnings from discontinued operations | | | |
| Earnings from operations | 2.1 | 3.1 | 13.7 |
| Gain on sale of B. Dalton | 85.2 | — | — |
| Net earnings before extraordinary charge | 342.3 | 283.6 | 259.3 |
| Extraordinary charge from purchase and redemption of debt. Net of tax benefit | (32.3) | — | — |
| Consolidated net earnings | $ 310.0 | $ 283.6 | $ 259.3 |
| Net earnings per share | | | |
| Continuing operations | $ 2.62 | $ 2.89 | $ 2.54 |
| Discontinued operations | | | |
| Earnings from operations | .02 | .03 | .14 |
| Gain on sale of B. Dalton | .88 | — | — |
| Earnings before extraordinary charge | 3.52 | 2.92 | 2.68 |
| Extraordinary charge | (.33) | — | — |
| Consolidated | $ 3.19 | $ 2.92 | $ 2.68 |

*Source:* Dayton Hudson Corporation Annual Report, 1986.

**EXHIBIT 8**
CORPORATE OVERVIEW

⟶

*Source:* DHC Community Involvement Annual Report, 1987.

# DAYTON HUDSON CORPORATION

## WHO WE ARE

| Operating Companies | 1987 Revenues | Stores | States |
|---|---|---|---|
| ⊙ TARGET | $5.3 Billion | 317 | 24 |
| MERVYN'S | $3.2 Billion | 199 | 13 |
| Ⓓ Ⓗ | $1.6 Billion | 37 | 7 |
| LECHMERE | $636 Million | 24 | 8 |

Dayton Hudson Corporation is a growth company focused exclusively on retailing.

The Corporation's principal strategy is to provide exceptional value to the American consumer through multiple retail formats.

Our customers know us as: Target, an upscale discount store chain; Mervyn's, a highly promotional, popular-priced, value-oriented department store company; Dayton Hudson Department Store Company, emphasizing fashion leadership, quality merchandise, broad selections and customer service; and Lechmere, a hardlines retail company.

## WHERE WE DO BUSINESS

| | | | |
|---|---|---|---|
| Arizona | Iowa | Nebraska | Oregon |
| Arkansas | Kansas | Nevada | Rhode Island |
| California | Kentucky | New Hampshire | South Dakota |
| Colorado | Louisiana | New Mexico | Tennessee |
| Connecticut | Massachusetts | New York | Texas |
| Florida | Michigan | North Carolina | Utah |
| Georgia | Minnesota | North Dakota | Washington |
| Illinois | Missouri | Ohio | Wisconsin |
| Indiana | Montana | Oklahoma | Wyoming |

## ECONOMIC IMPACT IN TEN LARGEST STATES

| States | Companies | Revenues | Payroll | Giving Funds |
|---|---|---|---|---|
| Arizona | T/M | $ 397,470,000 | $ 33,651,000 | $ 180,000 |
| California | T/M | 3,163,750,000 | 406,313,000 | 2,728,000 |
| Colorado | T/M | 411,610,000 | 38,033,000 | 496,000 |
| Indiana | T/D | 466,140,000 | 45,679,000 | 518,000 |
| Iowa | T | 271,350,000 | 20,365,000 | 275,000 |
| Massachusetts | L | 358,700,000 | 44,103,000 | 224,000 |
| Michigan | D/M/T | 879,950,000 | 118,087,000 | 1,881,000 |
| Minnesota | T/D/F | 1,357,940,000 | 277,884,000 | 9,253,000 |
| Texas | T/M | 1,189,210,000 | 113,708,000 | 1,165,000 |
| Wisconsin | T/D | 218,330,000 | 17,632,000 | 242,000 |
| All other states | T/M/D/L | 1,962,900,000 | 183,511,000 | 2,419,000 |
| Total | | $10,677,350,000 | $1,298,966,000 | $19,381,000 |

**T** Target/**M** Mervyn's/**D** Dayton Hudson Department Store Company/**L** Lechmere/**F** Dayton Hudson Foundation

**EXHIBIT 9**
CORPORATE GIVING

# 1987 COMMUNITY INVOLVEMENT REPORT

## FINANCIAL HIGHLIGHTS

We concentrate our community involvement on programs that offer the potential for achieving results and demonstrating leadership.

We do 80 percent of our giving in two focus areas where we believe we can have significant impact: Social Action and the Arts. The other 20 percent of our giving responds to special community needs and opportunities.

| | |
|---|---|
| **Social Action** | **$ 8,658,275** |
| **Arts** | **$ 7,738,094** |
| **Miscellaneous** | **$ 2,984,141** |
| **Total 1987 Giving** | **$19,380,510** |

**Social Action**

Forty percent of community giving funds are contributed to programs and projects that result in: **a** the economic and social progress of individuals; and/or **b** the development of community and neighborhood strategies that respond effectively to critical community social and economic concerns.

**Arts**

Forty percent of community giving funds are contributed to programs and projects that result in: **a** artistic excellence and stronger artistic leadership in communities; and/or **b** increased access to and use of the arts as a means of community expression.

**Miscellaneous**

Twenty percent of community giving funds are contributed to programs and projects outside Social Action and the Arts that result in: **a** our responsiveness to special community needs and opportunities; and/or **b** innovative partnerships with other community leaders.

*Source:* DHC Community Involvement Annual Report.

**EXHIBIT 10**
DART GROUP CORPORATION AND SUBSIDIARIES
Consolidated Statements of Income

| | Years ended January 31 | | |
| --- | --- | --- | --- |
| | 1987 | 1986 | 1985 |
| Sales | $338,008,000 | $97,833,000 | $73,834,000 |
| Income from bankers' acceptances (Dart Group Financial Corporation) | 10,563,000 | 7,315,000 | — |
| Other interest and other income | 18,830,000 | 14,201,000 | 16,391,000 |
| | 367,401,000 | 119,349,000 | 90,225,000 |
| Expenses: | | | |
| Cost of sales, store occupancy and warehousing | 271,119,000 | 75,540,000 | 54,388,000 |
| Selling and administrative | 62,165,000 | 22,271,000 | 17,300,000 |
| Depreciation and amortization | 4,978,000 | 1,189,000 | 666,000 |
| Interest | 36,357,000 | 12,738,000 | 522,000 |
| | 374,619,000 | 111,738,000 | 72,876,000 |
| Income (loss) before unusual items, income taxes, equity in loss of affiliates, preacquisition minority interest in losses of purchased subsidiary, minority interest, discontinued operations and extraordinary item | (7,218,000) | 7,611,000 | 17,349,000 |
| Unusual items | 78,294,000 | 13,275,000 | — |
| Income before income taxes, equity in loss of affiliates, preacquisition minority interest in losses of purchased subsidiary, minority interest, discontinued operations and extraordinary item | 71,076,000 | 20,886,000 | 17,349,000 |
| Income taxes | 28,423,000 | 9,648,000 | 7,917,000 |
| Income before equity in loss of affiliates, preacquisition minority interest in losses of purchased subsidiary, minority interest, discontinued operations and extraordinary item | 42,653,000 | 11,238,000 | 9,432,000 |
| Equity in loss of affiliates | — | (1,098,000) | (2,027,000) |
| Preacquisition minority interest in losses of purchased subsidiary | 519,000 | — | — |
| Minority interest in income of consolidated subsidiaries and partnerships | (7,187,000) | (270,000) | (1,093,000) |
| Income from continuing operations before extraordinary item | 35,985,000 | 9,870,000 | 6,312,000 |
| Discontinued operations | | | |
| Income from operations of discontinued division (net of taxes of $1,010,000 for the year ended January 31, 1985) | — | — | 1,010,000 |
| Gain on sale of discontinued division (net of taxes of $39,000,000) | — | — | 75,000,000 |
| Extraordinary item | | | |
| Loss on reacquisition of debentures, net of income tax benefit of $5,212,000 | (5,258,000) | — | — |
| Net income | $ 30,727,000 | $ 9,870,000 | $ 82,322,000 |
| Earnings per common share and common share equivalent: | | | |
| Income from continuing operations before extraordinary item | $19.24 | $5.28 | $ 3.46 |
| Discontinued operations | — | — | .55 |
| Gain on sale of discontinued division | — | — | 41.14 |
| Extraordinary item: | | | |
| Loss on reacquisition of debentures | (2.81) | — | — |
| Net income | $16.43 | $5.28 | $45.15 |
| Weighted average common share and common share equivalent outstanding | 1,870,000 | 1,868,000 | 1,823,000 |

Source: Dart Group Corporation Annual Report, 1987.

# Dayton Hudson Corporation: Conscience and Control (B)

On Thursday, June 11, while Macke and his management team were meeting with their advisers, Wendy McDowall was beginning a well-earned fishing vacation. Director of Government Affairs for DHC, she had finished several grueling months as the company's chief lobbyist at the Minnesota legislature. The 1987 session, which adjourned May 18, had been more difficult than most and everyone involved was relieved to see it end. By this morning Wendy had been at a cabin on the North Shore of Lake Superior for only a day or two. As she sipped a cup of coffee she turned on the radio and was stunned by the news she heard. DHC's stock had been the second most actively traded issue the day before. Although she did not know quite what she could do to help, she quickly decided that she could not continue fishing while her company was in danger. Within the hour she was in her car speeding back to Minneapolis.

That afternoon, after listening to discussion about alternative defenses, Macke had made it clear to his team that the responsibility for the decision would be his. Later that evening, after consulting with the board of directors, he decided to approach the governor regarding a special session of the legislature to strengthen Minnesota's corporate takeover statute. It seemed to be the alternative that took best advantage of the company's strengths, all things considered, and the one most likely to succeed. But many obstacles still lay in the path.

### Friday, June 12

D. J. Leary remembered the afternoon very well. Friday afternoons during summer in the Twin Cities were usually not busy times, certainly not good times to do business. People leave the cities by the tens of thousands, clogging the northbound highways, heading for a weekend "at the lake."

Leary himself was leaving the office a bit early, around 4:00 P.M. He had pulled off his tie and settled into the seat of his car, waiting for the air conditioner to take effect, when his car phone beeped. Wendy McDowall was calling from DHC's corporate headquarters to ask Leary to come by as soon as possible. She needed to talk with him about something too sensitive to discuss over the phone.

Something serious was obviously happening. Leary, a former aide to Minnesota's premier politician, Hubert Humphrey, and a prominent legislative lobbyist and public relations consultant, hurried to McDowall's office. When he arrived she told him that the company was "in play," and that she had been asked to help plan a strategy for approaching the legislature in a special session, one called by the governor just for this purpose. She asked Leary if he would join the team being formed to work on the project, specifically to help develop a media strategy.

Leary was stunned. One of the most difficult sessions in recent memory had just concluded. How could anyone ask the governor to call a special session now? Special sessions were notoriously unpopular in Minnesota, not least among the legislators themselves. But Leary agreed to consider the problem, and over the weekend he began to put together the pieces of a plan. On Monday he reported back with some thoughts about how it could be done.

### Wednesday, June 17

The pieces of DHC's action plan were falling into place, and a large implementation team had been gathered under the direction of the Task Force members. As a beginning step, Robert Hentges, an attorney with a local firm advising DHC about the legislative option, called Gerry Nelson, communications director for Minnesota's Democratic governor, Rudy Perpich. Hentges' message was cryptic. First, he inquired about Perpich's schedule for the next day. Then, Nelson recalled, "He said there might be some people who have to see [the governor] on an urgent matter." Nelson said that something could be arranged and as he put his phone down, he puzzled about what might be brewing.

### Thursday, June 18

At 9:30 in the morning Hentges called Terry Montgomery, Governor Perpich's chief of staff. Telling Montgomery that Macke had an urgent matter to discuss with the governor that day, he said, "He'll meet any place, any time!" Montgomery rearranged Perpich's schedule and set a meeting for 3:00 P.M. in Macke's office.

When Montgomery and Perpich met with Macke that afternoon, they were told that DHC had become the target of the Dart Group, and that millions of shares of stock were changing hands. Macke outlined the options identified by the Task Force and explained why he had decided on seeking a change in Minnesota's takeover statute. He asked Perpich to call a special session of the legislature as soon as possible to enact the changes. That same afternoon, Boake Sells, DHC's president and COO, called Minnesota Attorney General Skip Humphrey to tell him about their plan. Humphrey called in his office's expert in takeover law to prepare him to examine DHC's proposal. In a third meeting, Ann Barkelew and Leary met with Gerry Nelson to discuss the media aspects of the plan.

Perpich was taken completely by surprise and agreed merely to explore the possibility with legislative leaders. That evening, during a birthday party held for him at a downtown Minneapolis hotel, Perpich slipped away to consult with a handful of legislators. They were willing to consider a special session under the circumstances, but insisted that hearings be held to explore the matter first. For his part, Perpich refused to call a special session unless legislative leaders supported the idea and could agree on a limited agenda and specific provisions for a new takeover bill.

But Perpich's efforts to keep DHC's request private were in vain. By that evening the information had leaked out and Perpich was besieged by reporters at the birthday party. As a result, he scheduled a press conference to be carried live at 10:30 P.M., immediately following the local television news broadcasts.

Both the media and DHC people were caught off guard by the governor's abrupt decision to call a news conference. Macke was expected to be present, but he was at home on a sticky summer evening, getting ready to go to bed. Peter Hutchinson, DHC's vice president for external affairs, called Macke with the news. He dressed as quickly as he could and dashed back

*Had comm. support*
*asked favors of media.*

downtown from his suburban home to join Perpich. He arrived just in time.

Moments after Macke arrived, Perpich told reporters and a live television audience that DHC had asked for a special session. He went on to say that he had agreed to consider it.

### Friday, June 19

Commerce Commissioner Mike Hatch canceled his morning schedule to prepare for an 11:00 A.M. meeting with Perpich. Some years earlier, Hatch had written a law review article on Minnesota's takeover statute and was quite familiar with the issues. His principal concerns were to protect shareholders and to see restrictions imposed on golden parachutes and greenmail. When he met with Perpich and his staff to explain his position, DHC's attorneys, who had been working for nearly ten days on a detailed plan to amend the statute, had not yet delivered their proposal.

In downtown Minneapolis the phones were ringing frantically at DHC's corporate headquarters. Some of the most urgent calls were directed to the Dayton Hudson Foundation, and to its chairman, Peter Hutchinson. As vice president for external affairs, Hutchinson had been heavily involved in the activities of the previous weeks. Many of the callers represented arts and social action organizations that received major funding from DHC. They wanted to know what was going to happen if the Dart Group succeeded. Hutchinson and his staff quickly realized that too many calls were coming in to be handled effectively, so they scheduled an informational meeting for 1:30 P.M. that afternoon at the Children's Theater in Minneapolis. DHC routinely used that auditorium for its shareholder meetings and for other company events.

Shortly after noon, DHC's formal proposal was delivered to Perpich at the Capitol. Soon afterward, the acting Speaker of the House, Robert Vanasek, shared the proposal with Rep. Wayne Simoneau, the author of the 1984 takeover bill that DHC declined to support. Vanasek asked Simoneau if he would sponsor the bill in the House. Simoneau was delighted to see that some

of the provisions paralleled those in his earlier bill and agreed to be the sponsor.

At about the time that Simoneau became sponsor of DHC's proposal, Macke and Leary were meeting with the editorial board of the *Minneapolis Star Tribune*. Leary recognized the crucial value of favorable editorials in the upcoming Sunday editions, with their statewide circulation and influence. They explained the situation and asked for help in getting their message across to readers. Later, they also met with the editorial board of the *St. Paul Pioneer Press Dispatch*.

Shortly after 1:00 P.M., Peter Hutchinson arrived at the Children's Theater auditorium. He was uncharacteristically nervous and what he saw on the way in did not put him at ease. He and his staff had contacted scores of people about the meeting, but barely a hundred seats were filled and the auditorium looked empty. Hutchinson went backstage to prepare. When he walked out a few minutes later he was shocked and amazed to see that the auditorium was full.

People called by DHC had spontaneously called others and word of the meeting had spread throughout the community. Even people from organizations who had never received funding from DHC had come. Television crews, who had not been called by DHC, began to set up their lights and microphones. Neither Hutchinson nor his staff were prepared for a response like this.

Not knowing quite what to say, he began the meeting by explaining why DHC had called it. "Since so many of you have called in with questions, we felt it was the best way to communicate with you," he said, "and to tell you what is going on." He then outlined the events of the previous weeks. He told them what a hostile takeover was, what the company's position was, and what steps they were taking. No one could know, he said, what would happen if the Hafts were successful. After about ten minutes he stopped and asked if there were any questions.

Someone raised the question that was on everyone's mind, "What can we do to help?" Hutchinson replied that they had not called the meeting to recommend tactics but merely to provide information. Silence fell over the auditorium. Suddenly, a woman sitting on the left side stood up. "I'll tell you what you can do," she shouted. "Call the governor! His number is 296-0093." "I have a pocketful of quarters, and a list of legislators" shouted another person, "Let's call right now!" For the next twenty minutes audience members made suggestions to one another. Then the meeting broke up as people spilled out of the auditorium determined to do something.

While Hutchinson was meeting with the people from the community at the Children's Theater, DHC's attorneys were conferring with the state's attorneys. Later that afternoon, Perpich's office requested an evaluation of DHC's proposal from the Attorney General's office. Meanwhile, Wendy McDowall was beginning to implement the plan that she and Leary had devised earlier in the week. Having divided the legislature into three groups of descending importance, she began her lobbying efforts.

DHC found that the governor's announcement the previous evening had set off a string of reactions that management had not anticipated and could barely control. Store managers began to call headquarters asking for directions. They wanted to know what they should tell employees to do. Senior management was preoccupied with other pressing tasks, so at first they told employees to do nothing. But when managers insisted that their employees were determined to do something, Macke sent a letter to all of them explaining the situation and suggesting that they communicate with their legislators (see Exhibit 1). That evening employees began doing just that.

### Saturday, June 20

The strategy that DHC laid out with respect to the legislators was simple in theory, but was complicated to execute in such a short time. Their aim was to help legislators understand clearly what was at stake and to help them become comfortable with the idea of a special session *and* with amending the statute. To accomplish this they did five things.

First, they hired some of the most experienced professional lobbyists in the state to ensure that every legislator would be contacted personally. Second, they commissioned an opinion poll to discover the reaction of citizens to DHC's plight and the proposed special session. Third, they prepared an information packet for each legislator. By coincidence, the June 22, 1987, issue of *Fortune* magazine carried an article on the Hafts' entitled "The Most Feared Family in Retailing." The article, which was included in an information packet, described the Hafts' businesses and detailed their efforts to acquire a national retailer, with a special sidebar about the damage done to Safeway.

Fourth, they made strenuous efforts to contact newspapers in rural Minnesota and urge them to publish editorials supporting the special session. Fifth, they planned to send DHC executives to every community in the state where DHC had a store and where there was an important media instrument.

Some tactics, however, were rejected. DHC's advertising department had been asked earlier in the week to develop some ideas for advertisements that could be placed in newspapers to inform the public and gather support. On the afternoon of the 20th, management discussed what to do with the proposed ads. A couple of years earlier, Dayton's department stores had offered a small, white stuffed bear as a Christmas premium to customers. The response to "Santabear" had been overwhelming and the company had become closely associated with the toy, especially in Minnesota (see Exhibit 2). Some of the ads attempted to capture attention by suggesting that Santabear was at risk. After considerable debate a decision was made not to use the ads. Management was concerned that they might be perceived as too manipulative.

### Sunday, June 21

Lobbying efforts were put on hold for Father's Day. In the afternoon, Commerce Commissioner Hatch drove to Montevideo, a rural town not far from the Twin Cities, to attend a parade. He asked people there what they thought about calling a special session to address DHC's prob-

*Macke testifies*

lem. For the most part they were not enthusiastic about the plan.

In the evening, two lawyers from the Attorney General's office completed a memo evaluating DHC's proposed bill. They concluded that it probably did not violate the state constitution.

### Monday, June 22

Early in the morning, Steve Watson, president of the Dayton Hudson Department Store Company, and Leary boarded the company plane to fly around the state implementing their plan to make media appearances and meet with legislators. By evening they had visited four different cities.

In the afternoon, Hatch reviewed options with Perpich. They could (a) call the special session and try to pass the proposal, (b) modify the proposal and recommend only those provisions that had been tested in the courts, (c) promote strong provisions restraining greenmail and golden parachutes, or (d) do nothing at all. In the evening, Hatch attended a fund raiser in St. Cloud, in the heart of Minnesota's farming community. Once again he asked people about the plan to call a special session. Once again he received a negative response. People in attendance wanted to know when a special session would be called to help farmers in danger of losing their land.

### Tuesday, June 23

In the morning, the results of the opinion poll commissioned over the weekend were released. A large majority of citizens, 85%, favored the special session and the proposed toughening of the takeover statute. At the Capitol, a joint meeting of the House Judiciary and Commerce committees convened. Macke was the first to testify, but, as the *Minneapolis Star-Tribune* reported, his performance was anything but smooth. Out of his element and disconcerted by recent developments, he seemed nervous and abrupt. He told the committees that he not only believed in a free market, but also in a fair market. "During the last three weeks," he said, "30 percent of our stock was traded. This means that 30 percent of our stock is owned by people who have held it for less than three weeks." Later, an attorney representing DHC reported, "In 10 minutes or less, more than 3 percent of the stock changed hands this morning."

But the most startling moment came when Macke announced that another attempt to acquire the company had begun that morning. A $6.8 billion offer had been made by a Cincinnati stock analyst thought to be representing a wealthy Ohio family. In a matter of hours, the paper value of the company increased by nearly a billion dollars. By the afternoon, however, the offer was shown to be bogus and the stock analyst was found to have had a history of mental illness. The incident graphically underscored the volatility of the circumstances in which the company found itself, and drove home the urgency of the situation to the legislators.

Also that morning a variety of demands began to surface for additional agenda items, threatening to force the special session out of control. By afternoon, it became clear that compromises were necessary and that DHC needed to make some concessions in its proposed amendments.

No decision was reached by the committees that night, except to postpone a recommendation for the governor until the following day. Macke and his team closed the day not knowing what recommendation to expect.

DAYTON HUDSON CORPORATION

777 Nicollet Mall
Minneapolis, Minnesota 55402-2055
612/370-6948

June 19, 1987

Dear Dayton Hudson Corporation Employee:

I'm sure that you are aware that for the past several weeks there has been very heavy trading in Dayton Hudson common stock.

We want you to know that we believe it is in the long-term interests of our shareholders, employees, customers and communities for Dayton Hudson to remain independent in its present form. To support this belief, we have taken two recent actions. First, we met with Minnesota Governor Rudy Perpich yesterday to express our concern over the growing problem of hostile takeovers. And second, we are communicating today with an aggressive buyer of our stock that we are not interested in being acquired.

We applaud Governor Perpich in considering a special session of the legislature to enact tougher corporate anti-takeover laws. The proposed legislation will strengthen our existing laws to protect Minnesota companies from the disruptive and irreparable damage to a corporation's shareholders, employees, customers and communities that frequently results from stock market raids and other abusive tactics.

The new legislation will provide Minnesota companies with protection from threatened takeovers and restructurings similar to the protection offered to corporations in certain other states. It is also consistent with a recent decision of the U.S. Supreme Court and the present mood of many other state legislatures.

We need everyone's help in this matter. If you have friends, family or other relatives who live in Minnesota, ask them to contact their Governor and legislators to support this special legislation.

Working together we can keep Dayton Hudson a healthy and independent company.


Sincerely yours,



Kenneth A. Macke
Chairman and Chief Executive Officer

*Source:* Dayton Hudson Department Store Company—Public Relations.

**EXHIBIT 2**
SANTABEAR

*Source:* Dayton Hudson Corporation, Public Relations Department.

# Dayton Hudson Corporation: Conscience and Control (C)

*Acceptance of proposal*

*creating the bill*

The joint House committees agreed on Wednesday, June 24, to recommend a special session to the governor, and endorsed a bill quite similar to what DHC proposed. But the hearings on the Senate side ran into trouble. Commerce Commissioner Hatch was determined to see that provisions were contained in the bill that made golden parachutes illegal and strongly discouraged greenmail. He threatened to recommend against a special session if he failed to receive support on these issues. "If you don't include them," he told the Senate hearing, "it's just big business crawling into bed with big government." DHC, however, opposed the greenmail provision. After considerable discussion, all sides agreed to language severely restricting both golden parachutes and greenmail. Senate leaders then decided to join the House in recommending a special session.

Legislative leaders met with Perpich in the afternoon and agreed on a very limited agenda for the special session. However, disagreement between the House and Senate versions of the bill surfaced. Perpich refused to call the special session until everyone agreed on one bill, and insisted that agreement be reached in time for an announcement on the 10:00 P.M. news.

Negotiations involving legislators from both houses and DHC lawyers began at 7:30 in the evening, and two hours later the House members left the meeting in frustration when they could not reach agreement over the question of a "sunset" provision.* Communication resumed, however, and minutes before the 10:00 P.M. deadline, agreement was reached by phone. Perpich announced the special session on television and ordered the legislature to convene at 2:00 P.M. the following day.

*The bill*

## The Provisions of the Bill

In 1986, the Indiana legislature passed the Control Share Acquisitions Act (CSAA). As suggested in the "A" case, this statute placed restrictions on attempts to acquire a controlling

---

*A sunset provision causes a statute to expire after a specified date unless the legislature enacts an extension.

interest in a company without approval of the board of directors, but only applied to those Indiana corporations that elected to be covered. Shortly after it went into effect, a company that was the apparent target of a hostile takeover chose to be protected by the act. The bidder immediately sued and a lower court found in its favor, as did the court of appeals. However, in April 1987, the U.S. Supreme Court reversed the decision and upheld the statute. Indiana's CSAA subsequently became the model for DHC's proposal, as well as for similar legislation in other states.

The bill proposed in the Minnesota legislature aimed to protect companies by addressing the problem of tender offers. It required approval of the majority of disinterested shareholders before a bidder could gain voting rights for a controlling share of the stock. It also required the approval of a majority of the disinterested members of the board of directors (i.e., those who were neither managers nor representatives of bidders) before the bidder could enter any business combination with the target. Furthermore, and perhaps most importantly, it prohibited the sale of a target company's assets to pay debts incurred in financing a hostile takeover for a period of five years.

One of the most controversial provisions of the Minnesota bill, however, was the stipulation that the board of directors of a target company could legitimately take into consideration the interests of a wide range of groups in exercising their "business judgment." In discharging their duties, directors were authorized to consider "the interests of the corporation's employees, customers, suppliers, and creditors, the economy of the state and nation, community and societal considerations, and the long-term as well as short-term interests of the corporation and its shareholders including the possibility that these interests may be best served by the continued independence of the corporation."

Finally, the bill introduced measures which virtually prohibited golden parachutes and the payment of greenmail, but the greenmail provision was not scheduled to become effective until some months afterward.

### Thursday, June 25

The debate on the floor of the House was broadcast in the afternoon over Minnesota Public Radio. Several representatives rose to oppose the bill. They argued that it would not only violate the rights of shareholders but that it was also an unjustified government interference with the freedom of the market. Members clearly felt pressured by the emergency atmosphere of a special session.

At DHC headquarters, management and staff members were glued to their radios. The longer the debate went on, the more worried they became. During one of the speeches, Wendy McDowall, DHC's director of Government Affairs, called the office to get a message and spoke to Inez, one of the secretaries:

"Wendy, have you been listening to the debate? Do you think many of the House members feel that way?"

"No, Inez, I haven't been listening just now. In fact, I haven't gone to the House chamber this afternoon."

"You didn't go over there! But Wendy, it sounds like we're going to lose. Everybody here is getting pretty discouraged."

"Inez, turn off your radio! It's going to be all right."

And indeed it was. Despite the rhetoric of the opposing speeches, the bill passed by an overwhelming margin: 120–5 in the House and 57–0 in the Senate. Perpich made the 10:00 P.M. news as he signed the bill into law. (See Exhibits 1, 2 for a sampling of editorial responses to the legislation.)

### Friday, June 26

Macke sent a letter to DHC's employees in Minnesota thanking them for their support. He also urged them to write their legislators once more to express their appreciation, and he invited them to corporate headquarters that day to sign a banner to be given to the governor (see Exhibit 3).

DHC's corporate headquarters occupied several floors of the IDS Center, the tallest building in downtown Minneapolis. On the first floor of that building was a large enclosed courtyard and it was there that DHC held an enormous ice cream social for anyone who cared to come. A life-sized Santabear worked the crowd and hundreds of DHC employees stopped by to sign the giant banner that read simply, "Thanks, Minnesota." (See Exhibit 4 for an ad with the same theme that appeared in newspapers throughout Minnesota.)

## EXHIBITS: Dayton Hudson Corporation: Conscience and Control (C)

**EXHIBIT 1**
DAYTON HUDSON
Irwin L. Jacobs,* letter to *City Business,* July 15, 1987

Dayton Hudson certainly enhanced its "can-do" reputation in the business world when it "took over" the state of Minnesota one afternoon last week and had a well-tailored and highly polished and manicured management-entrenching law passed by *its* governor and *its* Legislature. The law will hereafter be known as the "Dayton Hudson Protective Act of 1987."

It is not difficult to believe the Legislature would pass a bill that will further regulate a market. The history of our Legislature is much the same as that of other state legislatures: "If it moves, let's tax it and regulate it" and "Let's try and get a competitive advantage in Minnesota over South Dakota, or Wisconsin, or Tennessee, etc."

Also, the attitude of the governor—a long-time minion of Control Data Corp. and William Norris—was certainly never in question.

However, the Dayton's executive group that lobbied and fought for the new antitakeover bill is indeed a mystery. Doesn't the group have golden parachutes, poison pills, and every other known protective device in place? The executive group crying over the prospect of the Dart Group Corp. coming in with an unsolicited tender offer for Dayton Hudson is much like Chicken Little crying over the falling sky. Where is the so-called imminent offer? Don't fear, "Imminent Suitor"—there is still time, thanks to the Dayton Hudson Protective Act of 1987, which allows greenmail payments until March of 1988.

It is little wonder that the Legislature welcomed Dayton's with open arms. The IOU's now will most certainly abound; the Dayton's executives can count on receiving campaign solicitations from state legislators for the next decade. Isn't it also true that Dayton's lobbying position on many crucial business issues in the future will be greatly compromised because of its rash rush to seek legislative protection from the Dart bullies?

My position on the tendency of large corporations to get bloated, inefficient, and unimaginative like government bureaucracies is certainly no secret. Dayton's now certainly can fall within the definition of a "corporacracy," as a minion of the state of Minnesota. The management has deserted its principal constituency—Dayton's shareholders—in favor of its suppliers, charities, state legislators, employees, and customers. Maybe Dayton's management can convince the state during a regular session of the Legislature to tender for its stock; then it would be completely free from any attempt at a takeover from other states.

Dayton's, the governor, and the state Legislature deserve each other. Dayton's shareholders deserve better, and they should now sell their stock and find a corporation to invest in that has not abandoned its shareholders. Or there is another solution: *a proxy fight to throw the rascals out.*

*Irwin L. Jacobs was a Minneapolis-based entrepreneur engaged in corporate acquisition.

**EXHIBIT 2**
EXCERPTS FROM "DAYTON HUDSON REAPS BENEFIT OF ITS GOOD IMAGE"
James Shannon,* *Minneapolis Star Tribune,* July 5, 1987.

. . . The onus and the bonus of [its] impressive corporate image came into sharp focus in Minnesota two weeks ago when Dayton Hudson announced that it might be the target of a takeover by the Dart Group of Maryland, which had then acquired a significant stake in Dayton Hudson stock. What the Dayton Hudson managers, the governor of Minnesota and the Legislature have done since June 18 to impede a hostile takeover of Dayton Hudson is an illustration of how community good will toward a publicly held corporation can be translated into political muscle.

On June 19 at the Children's Theater in Minneapolis, Peter Hutchinson, chairman of the Dayton Hudson Foundation, addressed an emergency meeting of more than 500 community leaders to explain the elements and the dangers of a possible takeover. At that meeting Gleason Glover, president of the Urban League of Minneapolis, urged people to write the governor and their legislators to endorse the calling of a special session of the Legislature and the passage of legislation designed to impede or prevent the hostile takeover of Minnesota-based corporations. Several legislators have said since then that no single issue has ever generated as much mail or as many phone calls to their offices as the threat of a hostile takeover of Dayton Hudson.

On June 22 the House Judiciary Committee met to hear testimony on whether to have a special session; the Senate Judiciary Committee met on June 23 for the same purpose. On June 24 Gov. Rudy Perpich called for a special session; on the 25th both houses convened. In three hours they enacted a new anti-takeover statute modeled on an Indiana law that in

*James Shannon was Executive Director of the General Mills Foundation.

April was found constitutional by the U.S. Supreme Court.

The takeover threat seems to have eased. The Dart Group still has not commented publicly on its plans. But given the new Minnesota statute, which would deny a raider the chance to break up a company like Dayton Hudson and sell off pieces of it to pay for his takeover debt, the Dart Group or any other future raider eyeing a Minnesota target company will need lots of money in hand to pay for its purchase before it puts the desired company "in play."

The new Minnesota statute is not a panacea. But it has bought precious time for all companies incorporated in Minnesota. Granted, this new law was occasioned by the threat to Dayton Hudson, but its benefits flow to every publicly held Minnesota corporation.

A key element is that the directors of a target company may now take into consideration the benefit or the harm to the community from a takeover. Heretofore directors of such companies have felt legally compelled to consider only the financial benefit or loss that their shareholders would sustain in a takeover. It is doubtful, at least to this writer, whether any company in the nation was in a better position than Dayton Hudson, because of its good public image, to orchestrate such a campaign for urgently needed legislative protection for community values in this age of whirlwind and disastrous takeovers.

There is an abundance of legal precedent, in our statutes and in court decisions, defending the rights of shareholders in takeover battles. The new Minnesota statute breaks new ground in saying that there are also community values that directors, judges and raiders should evaluate in deciding when a takeover serves the common weal. Caveat raider.

**EXHIBIT 3**
MACKE'S MEMO TO EMPLOYEES

 DAYTON HUDSON CORPORATION

777 Nicollet Mall
Minneapolis, Minnesota 55402-2055
612/370-6948

June 26, 1987

Dear Dayton Hudson Corporation Employee,

With your help, Minnesota has achieved something we believe is unprecedented: we have taken important steps to deter corporate raiders from hostile takeovers of Minnesota businesses.

On Wednesday, Governor Rudy Perpich called a special legislative session. Yesterday, the Minnesota legislature took action to toughen the state's anti-takeover laws.

While there are no absolute guarantees that Dayton Hudson cannot be taken over (nor do we believe, philosophically, there should be), we believe that the new law will prevent many abusive tactics used by raiders, including "bust-up" hostile takeovers.

For that, we have many of you to thank. You were great! With thousands of letters and phone calls, you let the Governor and the legislature know, in no uncertain terms, what was at stake.

Because this state has taken historic action, I'd like to ask you to help us say "Thanks, Minnesota" by writing your state representative and state senator one more time. Tell them how much you appreciate what they have done, and what this legislation means for Minnesota's entire quality-of-life, because it helps preserve this as a "headquarters state."

Also, if your work schedule permits, come sign the giant "Thanks, Minnesota" banner in the IDS Crystal Court between 11:30 a.m. and 1 p.m. today. Once signed it will be displayed on Nicollet Mall.

I'd like to make one additional request: Say "Thanks, Minnesota" in the way you do better than anybody I know — by serving our customers the very best way you know how.

Let's redouble our efforts to make Dayton Hudson the best retailer in the country — one that provides exceptional value to its customers, employees, communities, and its long-term shareholders.

That is the best way — indeed, the only way — to ensure that Dayton Hudson continues to be a growing, dynamic, and independent company.

Again, thank you for your extraordinary teamwork. I am honored and proud to be able to say, "I'm part of the Dayton Hudson family of companies."

Sincerely,

Kenneth A. Macke
Chairman and Chief Executive Officer

*Source:* Dayton Hudson Corporation, Public Relations Department.

**EXHIBIT 4**
THANKS, MINNESOTA

# There's no place like home.

*Thanks, Minnesota*

🔲 DAYTON HUDSON CORPORATION

TARGET    MERVYN'S    DAYTON HUDSON DEPARTMENT STORES    LECHMERE    BRANDEN'S    PRIMENET

*Source:* Dayton Hudson Department Store Company—Public Relations.

# Consolidated Foods Corporation (A)

Much like individual citizens, Consolidated Foods has an obligation to act in a socially responsible manner. In addition, we are keenly aware of the votes cast each day by consumers through their purchase decisions in our extremely competitive marketplace. Thus, your comments are taken seriously into account.— *Corporate response to consumer ad complaint.*

It was mid-June 1981 and top management at Consolidated Food Corporation (CFC) in Chicago was concerned about consumer complaints and threatened boycotts. Some of these concerns related to the TV and print ad content of its recently acquired Hanes division and others related to sponsoring TV programs thought to portray excessive sex or violence. The tactics of the organized groups had become progressively more sophisticated, evolving from simple letter-writing campaigns to elaborate TV monitoring and publicity efforts. In addition the targets of the groups had shifted from the networks to advertisers and their parent companies.

John H. Bryan, Jr., chief executive officer of CFC, had been receiving numerous individual consumer complaint letters as well as communications from organized groups. Like many of the people in the civic and religious groups forming the coalition, Bryan was raised in the conservative Christian South. He shared many of the protesters' values. Yet his corporate role demanded that he look at the issues more broadly. He did not watch much television, though on occasion he had been dismayed by what was passing for entertainment on the networks. Sex and violence were being depicted with increasing boldness to attract viewers and ultimately to sell consumer products.

On his desk were several documents, including a copy of the fall 1980 results of a TV monitoring campaign organized by the National Federation for Decency. Though Consolidated Foods was not mentioned among the sponsors of offending programs, it received top billing among "Users of Sex in Commercials," and Bryan's name and home address were listed with those of other chief executive officers (see Exhibit 1). There was also a memorandum from the recently formed Coalition for Better Television listing Consolidated Foods interim scores in the latest monitoring effort (see Exhibit 2). The memorandum clearly implied that a boycott was likely for those whose scores did not measure up. Finally, there was a copy of a policy statement on advertising that had just been passed by the Public Responsibility Committee of Consolidated's board of directors (see Exhibit 3).

Bryan reflected on these materials before him, wondering what course of action to take: What could or should the corporation do that it had not already done? Obviously, it was not in the interest of Consolidated Foods or any of its operating units to advertise in ways that would lose rather than gain sales. General guidelines pertaining to truthfulness and good taste in ads and media had been in place for years in several of the operating units. Moreover, elaborate consumer testing of ads, though not directly aimed at measuring variables like offensiveness, was almost certain to pick up information that would signal any of these problems. As a general rule, Bryan believed that direct corporate involvement in division-level policy on such matters was inappropriate and that the Hanes division was doing a responsible job. He also believed that the threat of a well-orchestrated boycott of Hanes products, and possibly other Consolidated Foods products, was a serious matter.

## CORPORATION BACKGROUND

Consolidated Foods Corporation had grown during its 42-year history from a small Baltimore distributor of sugar, coffee, and tea to a $5.6 billion diversified company active in three major business segments: consumer packaged goods, food services, and consumer direct sales. Its founder, Nathan Cummings, guided the company through complex acquisitions and divestitures for nearly 30 years, retiring to the role of honorary chairman of the board in 1968. (See Exhibit 4 for a brief chronology of the company.)

Years of uninterrupted gains came to a halt during the 1973–1974 fiscal year; then, in FY 1975, earnings fell dramatically. The stock, which had traded as high as $51 a few years previously, bottomed out at $10½. The chairman resigned in February 1975 and Bryan, age 38, president of the company, became chief executive officer. Bryan had come to CFC's headquarters on April 1, 1974, from the position of president of the Mississippi-based Bryan Foods division. John J. Cardwell, who joined the company in mid-1976 as president, spoke of Bryan in an interview: "[He] took a number of write-downs, established an internal audit group at the headquarters, sold off a few furniture companies and otherwise set the stage for the subsequent turnaround." FY 1976 already began to show the results of the new strategy. In FY 1977 67% of the operating units were generating a return on net operating assets below 24%. By FY 1982, fewer than 16% of the operating units would be earning below the 24% return rate. At about the midpoint of the turnaround period, 1976–1981, Consolidated Foods added a major element to its consumer product mix by acquiring the Hanes Corporation of Winston-Salem, North Carolina.

## HANES GROUP

Hanes Corporation was formed in 1965 by the merger to two successful companies, Hanes Hosiery Mills and P. H. Hanes Knitting Company, both headquartered in Winston-Salem. A market-oriented consumer products company, its line included women's seamless hosiery, support hosiery, and panty hose; brassieres, girdles, swimwear, and cosmetics; men's and boys' underwear, casual wear, knit sport shirts, sweaters, and socks. Among the better-known brand names for Hanes products were Hanes and L'eggs hosiery, Bali bras, L'erin cosmetics, and Hanes underwear.

Hanes Corporation had 5 operating units, 23 manufacturing plants, and more than 13,000 employees in North Carolina, South Carolina, Virginia, Pennsylvania, New Mexico, Puerto Rico, Mexico, and the Dominican Republic.

The corporation also operated an extensive system of customer service centers and warehouses in strategic locations throughout the United States, as well as New York sales offices. International trade specialists conducted export sales, overseas market development, and foreign licensing for Hanes products.

Hanes hosiery was a pioneer in the production and marketing of seamless nylon hosiery for women and was generally credited with being the principal force in the industry's change from full-fashioned (seamed) to seamless hosiery. Similarly, Hanes hosiery was credited with being the first major hosiery manufacturer and marketer to recognize the potential of a first-quality, nationally advertised brand of hosiery products in food and drug stores. This brand, L'eggs, was introduced into four test markets in March 1970, and in less than two years, it became the leading U.S. manufacturer's brand. By 1979 L'eggs enjoyed a 30% share of the $1.5 billion hosiery market.

Consolidated Foods' annual report for 1979 described the Hanes acquisition: "[It provides] a strong consumer packaged goods company that fits well with the corporation's other packaged goods businesses. Its orientation is toward high margin products with strong brand identification, supported by heavy advertising and aggressive promotion. In addition, Hanes capitalizes on the trend of women purchasing more nongrocery items at the grocery store."

At the completion of the acquisition in January 1979, Hanes Corporation was combined with Aris (gloves), Canadelle (brassieres), and Sirena (swimwear) to form the Hanes Group. Robert E. Elberson, former president and chief executive officer of Hanes Corporation, was made an executive vice president and a director of Consolidated Foods, with responsibility for the Hanes Group and three other operating units. (Financial information on CFC and an organization chart appear as Exhibits 5 and 6.)

By 1981 Consolidated Foods had met most of its turnaround goals and was planning modest shifts in corporate organization that would signal less emphasis on acquisition and more corporate participation in guiding internal growth. In an interview Cardwell described this new orientation:

> All our businesses are more execution-sensitive than strategy-sensitive. (Maybe all businesses are.) But that means, if we are fully to discharge our corporate responsibilities, that the corporate center must have a considerable involvement in execution, and not limit itself to providing only broad direction and ex-post review. In effect, we have completed the first phase of corporate redirection, and are now in our "second act." That act focuses almost exclusively on growth from within; hence the necessity of now paying greatly increased attention to execution; hence the requirement for a more directive style of management and a more prominent corporate presence.

## ADVERTISING AT HANES

For many years advertising had played a central role in the marketing of Hanes products. And with the acquisition of Hanes, advertising began to be a much more important factor in the business of Consolidated Foods. Hanes expenditures on advertising and promotion represented about one-third of total corporate spending in this category.

The development and placement of TV commercials and print ads at Hanes followed a pattern widely used among consumer packaged goods companies. Strategic marketing decisions at company headquarters in Winston-Salem led to product-related positioning statements that were shared with advertising agency teams in New York.

Dancer, Fitzgerald, Sample (DFS), for example, was one of a small number of major agencies used by the Hanes Group. It had responsibility for several Hanes products, including L'eggs hosiery. Using the positioning statements from Hanes, DFS would develop more focused advertising copy and creative ideas for both TV commercials and print ads; then Hanes management would select from DFS's proposals. At this stage a typical TV commercial was presented as a storyboard—a series of

10–20 drawings depicting image and voice messages to guide further production.

Selected storyboards were then rendered as animatics—cartoon-like videotapes suitable for market testing. This stage was important because it kept investment manageable ($5,000–10,000) by comparison with finished commercials ($100,000–150,000).

Animatics were then market tested in various ways. "Ad labs" were convened in which groups (women in the case of Hanes hosiery) would be asked to give their reactions to the animated commercials. If testing results at this stage were positive, then a commercial would be produced in final (nonanimated) form. Further local broadcast testing of the final commercial assessed impact and recall before advertising placement, the last phase of the process, was completed.

Hanes management turned to DFS for guidance on ad placement. Demographic statistics and target, frequency, and reach information would be used to determine appropriate local and network time slots. Prime-time network programming would also be prescreened (when possible) by DFS staff to ensure compliance with Hanes advertising guidelines. Finally, the commercial would run in its carefully selected program environment.

## CORPORATE AND GROUP ADVERTISING POLICIES

Since October 1977 Consolidated Foods had a Public Responsibility Committee (PRC) of the board of directors. Beyond responsibility for corporate contributions, the "Statement of Purpose" of the committee provided that "oversight and guidance" be exercised "in the areas of employee safety and equal employment opportunity programs and performance." The committee also undertook any activities "deemed necessary and advisable to monitor or improve the corporation acting in the public interest."[1]

[1]Minutes of Public Responsibility Committee meeting, April 1978.

At its August 1980 meeting, the PRC reviewed existing advertising guidelines at three operating companies with a view toward preparing a general corporate advertising policy. It was thought that such a statement could be used in answering inquiries or complaints on advertising. A statement was approved by the PRC at its January 1981 meeting and was to be conveyed to key operating unit managers by Bryan.

Since the mid-1970s Hanes Corporation had maintained its own written guidelines on advertising placement, pertaining to both TV programming and print media. The implementation of these guidelines was left primarily to the advertising agencies employed by the corporation, but the agencies were advised that from time to time they would be requested to demonstrate "that their judgment coincides with that of Hanes Corporation senior management." (The guidelines in effect in June 1981 are reproduced as Exhibit 7.)

## PRESSURES DURING 1980

During 1980 Hanes management as well as Bryan at corporate headquarters received increasing numbers of consumer complaints. Some of the letters dealt with ad content, expressing offense at commercial themes like "Gentlemen Prefer Hanes" and "Show Us Your Underalls." Others dealt with Hanes sponsorship of various TV programs thought to be too violent or too sexually permissive (e.g., "Dallas," "Charlie's Angels," "Three's Company," and certain TV movies). Similarities in style, content, and timing among some of the complaints made it clear that they were occasioned by organized groups' newsletters like those of the Joelton Church of Christ and the National Federation for Decency. Each letter received a formal response from top managers at Hanes as well as a response from communications staff at corporate headquarters.

In November 1980 Hanes management received a warning letter from the Reverend John Hurt, leader of the Joelton, Tennessee, Clean Up TV campaign. In essence, the letter threatened a boycott similar to one called by Rev.

Hurt against General Foods and American Home Products. It referred to eight TV programs, several of which Hanes had sponsored in the past, implying that future sponsorship would result in a boycott of Hanes and other CFC products. The letter read in part:

> During the coming months, the shows . . . will continue to be monitored, and on a selected date, the first (suitable) sponsor whose ad is first to appear on each of these shows will immediately be selected and a nationwide boycott of all of their products begun without further warning. (In order to clarify this point, if a beer commercial, for example, is put on first, we shall simply bypass it and instead select the first suitable company whose ad appears on each program. Parent companies will also be held accountable for ads placed by their divisions.)
>
> Since our records indicate that your company has advertised on one or more of these shows within the past several months, this is your formal notice of our intended action. In view of the fact that the names of all of the companies who continue to help support these programs will probably also be made public even when a boycott is not involved, it would be to your advantage to give serious consideration to selecting other programs which will not be in the public spotlight. Monitors from almost every state, however, will also regularly report on companies who help to sponsor any of the new shows which contain similar offensive material and appropriate action will be taken. This will include morally offensive movies and TV specials.
>
> We are very hopeful that your company will see fit to make clear your genuine concern for moral decency and for the feelings of a very large segment of the public. The purpose of the campaign is not to remove programs from the air but to insist that they improve the moral content of their presentations.

Paul Fulton, general manager of the Hanes Group, did not respond to the letter, but subsequently no ads for Hanes products appeared on any of the eight programs. In an interview Fulton spoke of how he expressed his concern to corporate headquarters as well as to his immediate division subordinates: "I reviewed the situation in detail with Dancer-Fitzgerald-Sample with regard to its present impact and possible future implications. We are very concerned about what could develop out of this campaign, particularly if the Moral Majority becomes involved." Fulton went on to observe that avoidance of the eight programs in question would not "significantly limit our ability to effectively reach our consumers" so that reducing company exposure seemed to be the best course. "This position will obviously have to be reevaluated," he added, "if objectionable programs expand significantly."

Bryan had heard from the Reverend Donald Wildmon once before in September 1980 when he had written to Bryan about a specific program, "The Women's Room," that Consolidated Foods had helped sponsor. Bryan had not seen the program, but he could remember having inquired about its content and found that he shared Rev. Wildmon's dismay. Bryan could also remember thinking long and hard about whether and how to reply to his letter. (The letter and reply appear as Exhibits 8 and 9.)

## PRESSURES MOUNT, 1981

The wide distribution given to the fall 1980 ratings resulted in a new wave of complaint letters to both CFC and Hanes during March and April 1981. The number more than doubled from the previous year, and many of the letters were being sent directly to Bryan's home address.

Bryan was perplexed. He felt strongly that advertisers, for self-interest if for no other motive, had to exercise great care in choosing both ads and programs for sponsorship. Good taste and social awareness were essential to the marketing effectiveness of any consumer goods company. On the other hand, the products (women's hosiery) and target markets of the Hanes division seemed to demand a somewhat "sexy" image and a programming policy that reached the right customers. Nielsen ratings were important indicators of what the relevant public apparently enjoyed watching. The consumer was, in some sense, getting no more and no less than he or she wanted in this domain. Was it a corporation's place to do anything but follow the market? He knew that these organized efforts for better television would not just disappear. The social and political environment was ripe for a reaffirmation of traditional values. Yet as sympathetic as he was to some of the complaints about the quality of TV programming and even TV advertising, he did not think that the values of Consolidated Foods or its operating units differed from any but the most narrowly conservative values.

The idea of Consolidated Foods or Hanes being singled out for criticism by CBTV or any other group was not appealing. Neither was the idea of caving in to this kind of pressure. Bryan reread the documents on his desk as he thought about how to respond to the threat of a boycott.

## EXHIBITS: Consolidated Foods Corporation (A)

**EXHIBIT 1**
REPORT OF THE FALL 1980 TV MONITORING PROGRAM:
NATIONAL FEDERATION FOR DECENCY

**Sex incidents per hour**

|  | 1980 | 1979 |
|---|---|---|
| ABC | 9.38 | 5.64 |
| CBS | 7.44 | 5.51 |
| NBC | 4.11 | 4.96 |
| Total avg. per programming hour | 6.97 | |

83.74% of all sex depicted outside marriage. Using intercourse and comments only viewers are exposed to 13,213 incidents over a period of one year of prime-time viewing. Using intercourse and comments and skin scenes viewers are exposed to 23,921 incidents. 73.87% of all programs contained sexual content. 59.87% of all programs contained profanity. 48.75% of all programs contained sex and profanity. 85% of all programs contained either sex and/or profanity.

**Top users of sex in commercials**

| 1 Consolidated Foods | 53 |
|---|---|
| 2 Ford Motor Company | 19 |
| 3 Avon Products | 15 |
| 4 Gulf & Western Industries | 10 |
| 4 Revlon | 10 |

**Ten top sex-oriented programs**

| 1 It's A Living | 43.00 | ABC |
|---|---|---|
| 2 Three's Company | 40.90 | ABC |
| 3 Ladies Man | 33.60 | CBS |
| 4 Soap | 32.50 | ABC |
| 5 Laverne & Shirley | 32.22 | ABC |
| 6 Happy Days | 22.25 | ABC |
| 6 Taxi | 22.25 | ABC |
| 7 One Day At A Time | 19.25 | CBS |
| 8 Love Boat | 16.66 | ABC |
| 9 Too Close For Comfort | 15.20 | ABC |

**Ten least sex-oriented programs**

| 1 Wonderful World of Disney | 0.0833 | NBC |
|---|---|---|
| 1 NBC Sports | 0.0833 | NBC |
| 2 Little House On The Prairie | 0.1904 | NBC |
| 3 The Waltons | 0.3333 | CBS |
| 4 ABC Sports | 0.4677 | ABC |
| 5 Those Amazing Animals | 0.5833 | ABC |
| 6 Quincy | 1.000 | NBC |
| 7 That's Incredible | 1.083 | ABC |
| 8 NBC Magazine | 1.250 | NBC |
| 9 The Incredible Hulk | 1.375 | CBS |
| 10 Games People Play | 1.428 | NBC |

**Top sponsors of sex**

| 1 Revlon | 18.50 |
|---|---|
| 2 Noxell | 17.92 |
| 3 Beecham | 16.28 |
| 4 Gulf & Western | 15.30 |
| 5 American Motors | 15.26 |
| 6 Carnation | 14.95 |
| 7 Heublein | 14.62 |
| 8 Clorox | 14.60 |
| 9 Pfizer | 13.58 |
| 10 Warner-Lambert | 13.14 |

**Least sponsors of sex**

| 1 Timex | 1.74 |
|---|---|
| 2 Hallmark | 2.13 |
| 3 Philip Morris | 2.53 |
| 4 Nissan Motors | 3.62 |
| 5 IT&T | 4.25 |
| 6 Zenith | 4.97 |
| 7 RCA | 5.09 |
| 8 Hershey | 5.28 |
| 9 Eastman Kodak | 5.44 |
| 10 General Mills | 5.50 |

*( Continued )*

**EXHIBIT 1**
CONTINUED

**CONSTRUCTIVE
PROGRAMS AND SPONSORS**

**Top ten constructive programs**
(Based on minimum 120 minutes air time)

| | | |
|---|---|---|
| 1 NBC Sports | 9.000 | NBC |
| 2 Little House on the Prairie | 8.730 | NBC |
| 3 Wonderful World of Disney | 8.680 | NBC |
| 4 Those Amazing Animals | 8.550 | ABC |
| 5 Quincy | 8.220 | NBC |
| 6 60 Minutes | 8.183 | CBS |
| 7 The Waltons | 7.933 | CBS |
| 8 NBC Magazine | 7.513 | NBC |
| 9 Trapper John M.D. | 7.440 | CBS |
| 10 CBS Specials | 7.394 | CBS |

**Ten least constructive programs**
(Based on minimum 120 minutes air time)

| | | |
|---|---|---|
| 1 Ladies Man | 2.480 | CBS |
| 2 Soap | 2.640 | ABC |
| 3 It's A Living | 2.850 | ABC |
| 4 Taxi | 3.050 | ABC |
| 5 Three's Company | 3.164 | ABC |
| 6 Flo | 3.980 | CBS |
| 7 Laverne & Shirley | 4.033 | ABC |
| 8 WKRP in Cincinnati | 4.264 | CBS |
| 9 Vegas | 4.289 | ABC |
| 10 The Dukes of Hazzard | 4.300 | CBS |

**Ten most constructive
programming sponsors**

| | |
|---|---|
| 1 Timex | 7.624 |
| 2 Hallmark | 6.595 |
| 3 Kelloggs | 6.506 |
| 4 Eastman Kodak | 6.494 |
| 5 Hershey | 6.493 |
| 6 General Electric | 6.479 |
| 7 PepsiCo | 6.475 |
| 8 Philip Morris | 6.434 |
| 9 Polaroid | 6.420 |
| 10 American Telephone & Telegraph | 6.320 |

**Ten least constructive
programming sponsors**

| | |
|---|---|
| 1 Revlon | 4.718 |
| 2 Dow Chemical | 4.958 |
| 3 Noxell Corporation | 5.083 |
| 4 Gulf & Western | 5.131 |
| 5 Beecham | 5.182 |
| 6 American Motors | 5.277 |
| 7 Nestle Company | 5.363 |
| 8 Richardson-Merrell | 5.363 |
| 9 Warner-Lambert | 5.443 |
| 10 Sterling Drug | 5.469 |

*Note:* Prime-Time Viewing Sept. 14–Dec. 6, 1980

PARTIAL LIST OF ADDRESSES

**American Home Products**
Chrm. W. F. LaPorte
435 East 52nd St.
New York, NY 10022
212-986-1000
Anacin. Easy-Off. Woolite

**Bristol-Myers Co.**
Chrm. Richard L. Gelb
1060 Fifth Avenue
New York, NY 10028
212-644-2100
Tickle. Clairol. Bufferin.
Excedrin. Vanish

**Carnation Co.**
Chrm. H. E. Olson
448 N. Las Palmas Ave.
Los Angeles, CA 90004
213-931-1911
Friskies. Come and Get It
dogfood. Carnation foods

**Consolidated Foods Corp.**
Chrm. John H. Bryan, Jr.
140 Melrose
Kenilworth, IL 60043
312-726-6414
Hanes hosiery. L'eggs.
Underalls. Shasta beverages.
Tyco toys

**General Mills, Inc.**
Chrm. Robert E. Kinney
1520 Xanthus Lane
Wayzata, MN 55391
612-540-2311
Cheerios. Betty Crocker.
Wheaties. Cocoa Puffs

**Hallmark Cards, Inc.**
Chrm. Joyce C. Hall
2501 McGee
Kansas City, MO 64108
816-274-5111
Cards. giftwrap. books

( *Continued* )

**EXHIBIT 1**
CONTINUED

---

**Kellogg Co.**
Chrm. Joe E. Lonning
222 Lincoln Hill Dr.
Battle Creek, MI 49015
616-966-2000
Cereals. Mrs. Smith's Pies

**Milton Bradley**
Chrm. James J. Shea, Jr.
1500 Main St.
Springfield, MA 01115
413-525-6411
Toys. Playskool

**Polaroid Corp.**
Chrm. Edwin H. Land
Brattle Street
Cambridge, MA 02139
617-864-6000
Cameras & Film

**Revlon, Inc.**
Chrm. Michael C. Bergerac
767 5th Avenue
New York, NY 10022
212-522-5000
Charlie. Jontue. Flex balsam.
cosmetics. Tums

**Volkswagen of America, Inc.**
Chrm. Toni Schmuecker
27621 Parkview Blvd.
Warren, MI 48092
313-574-3300
Automobiles

**Wm. Wrigley Jr. Co.**
Pres. William Wrigley
60 North Lake Shore Drive
Lake Geneva, WI 53147
312-644-2121
Doublemint. Juicy Fruit.
Spearmint. Big Red gum

---

**EXHIBIT 2**
MEMORANDUM: COALITION FOR BETTER TELEVISION

April 10, 1981

**To:** Network advertisers
**Re:** Monitoring results

Below are scores for your company for the first four weeks of monitoring which includes March 1–28. We felt you might be interested in them. To get an idea of where your company stands figure that a combined total of your ad ratio for sex, violence and profanity of 14 or more would put you in the top sponsors of sex, violence and profanity. If your constructive rating is less than 4.400 then you would fall in the bottom of constructive sponsors. The higher your combined ad ratio score the poorer your practice and the lower the constructive rating the poorer your practice.

If you desire more complete information on how to interpret the scores feel free to contact us. Remember that the scores are based on the first four weeks of monitoring. Several companies are making a serious effort to bring their scores down which means that companies on the borderline who don't make an effort will move up.

Company    CONSOLIDATED FOODS

Sex score
   Volume    **162**
   Ad ratio   **4.15**

Profanity score
   Volume    **211**
   Ad ratio   **5.41**

Violence score
   Volume    **176**
   Ad ratio   **4.51**

Constructive rating **4.549**

Sincerely,

Donald E. Wildmon

**EXHIBIT 3**
CORPORATE POLICY AND PROCEDURES MEMORANDUM*

April 20, 1981

**Department Division:** Corporate Affairs
**Subject:** Advertising policy

Consolidated Foods Corporation has [subscribed], and will continue to subscribe, to a philosophy of responsible corporate citizenship. This responsibility requires that advertisements representing the products and services of Consolidated Foods Corporation be truthful and free of statements, illustrations or implications offensive to reasonable standards of good taste.

*Source:* Company files.

Consolidated Foods Corporation is opposed to the placement of its advertisements in publications or broadcast programs which make gratuitous, exploitive or excessive use of violence or sexual themes, as well as those that demean human dignity or abuse particular segments of society. However, the corporation is unable to exercise control over the presentation of its products which may infrequently appear as a result of editorial use.

The monitoring of advertising policies and placement of advertisements, including the use of randomly placed spot broadcast advertisements, remains the responsibility of the senior executive at each operating company, regardless of whether internal or agency advertising resources are utilized.

**EXHIBIT 4**
CONSOLIDATED FOODS CHRONOLOGY*

**1939** Nathan Cummings purchased C. D. Kenny Co., a small wholesale distributor of sugar and packager of coffee and tea, located in Baltimore.
**1942** Acquisition of Sprague Warner Co., located in Chicago, and distributor of the famous Richelieu brand of fine foods.
**1945** Acquisition of Reid, Murdoch and Co., nationally recognized for its Monarch quality brand. Company entered food processing business. Name changed to Consolidated Grocers Corporation.
**1946** Landmark year for company; stock offered to the public for the first time and company sales grew to $123 million.
**1951** Acquisition of Union Sugar.
**1954** Name changed to Consolidated Foods Corporation. Acquisition of Piggly Wiggly and Eagle Food Centers.

*Source:* In-house newsletter.

**1956** Acquisition of Kitchens of Sara Lee.
**1959** Acquisition of Lawson's, Shasta, Booth Fisheries, Popsicle, Kahn's, PYA, and Hollywood Brands.
**1962** First overseas acquisition of Jonker Fris.
**1966** Federal Trade Commission ordered division of food manufacturing and retail activities. Company sold Eagle. Acquisition of nonfood companies, such as Electrolux, Fuller Brush and Oxford Chemicals, began.
**1967** Sales reached $1 billion.
**1968** Founder Nathan Cummings retired and became honorary chairman of the board and chairman of the executive committee. Acquisition of Bryan Foods.
**1976** John Bryan moved up from president to chairman of the corporation; John Cardwell named president.
**1978** Investment of 65% controlling interest in Douwe Egberts. Acquisition of Chef Pierre.
**1979** Acquisition of Hanes Corporation. Fiscal year sales reached $4.7 billion.

**EXHIBIT 5**
CONSOLIDATED FOODS CORPORATION AND SUBSIDIARIES
OPERATING RESULTS BY INDUSTRY SEGMENT,* 1976–1981
(In Millions)

| | 1981 | | 1980 | | 1979 | | 1978 | | 1977 | | 1976¶ | |
|---|---|---|---|---|---|---|---|---|---|---|---|---|
| | Sales | Pre-tax income | Sales | Pre-tax income | Sales | Pre-tax income | Sales | Pre-tax income | Sales | Pre-tax income | Sales | Pre-tax income |
| Consumer packaged goods | | | | | | | | | | | | |
| Beverages | $1,348 | $ 88 | $1,402 | $ 97 | $1,112 | $ 84 | $ 597 | $ 58‡ | $ 181 | $ 10 | $ 173 | $ 9 |
| Hanes group | 792 | 46 | 715 | 44 | 397 | 6† | 76 | 9 | 61 | 7 | 51 | 6 |
| Specialty meats | 874 | 45 | 743 | 43 | 699 | 32 | 534 | 26 | 459 | 23 | 441 | 20 |
| Frozen foods | 643 | 28 | 598 | 32 | 551 | 35 | 496 | 34 | 428 | 30 | 396 | 26 |
| Other consumer products | 417 | 46 | 437 | 32 | 542 | 30 | 603 | 40 | 684 | 45 | 677 | 43 |
| Total consumer packaged goods | 4,074 | 253 | 3,895 | 248 | 3,301 | 187 | 2,306 | 167 | 1,813 | 115 | 1,738 | 104 |
| Food services | 1,075 | 31 | 978 | 39 | 902 | 35 | 739 | 26 | 643 | 25 | 601 | 25 |
| Consumer direct sales | 543 | 57 | 536 | 47 | 575 | 65 | 545 | 69 | 522 | 68 | 497 | 57 |
| Total | 5,692 | 341 | 5,409 | 334 | 4,778 | 287 | 3,590 | 262 | 2,978 | 208 | 2,836 | 186 |
| Intersegment sales* | (78) | — | (66) | — | (58) | — | (54) | — | (45) | — | (48) | — |
| Interest, net | — | (28) | — | (41) | — | (34) | — | (14) | — | (10) | — | (11) |
| Unallocated corporate expense | — | (30) | — | (28) | — | (18) | — | (15) | — | (18) | — | (17) |
| Net sales and pre-tax income | $5,614 | $283 | $5,343 | $265 | $4,720 | $235 | $3,536 | $233 | $2,933 | $180 | $2,788 | $158 |

*Sales by segment include sales to outside customers and sales between segments. Intersegment sales are at transfer prices which are equivalent to market value.
†Reduced by $30 as a result of valuing Hanes' inventory at fair market value at the date of acquisition.
‡Increased by $24 as a result of valuing Douwe Egberts' inventory acquired net of deferred taxes at the date of acquisition.
¶Fifty-three-week accounting year.

(Continued)

294

**EXHIBIT 5**
CONTINUED

(Included in the Above Table Are Sales and Pre-Tax Income of Businesses Sold as Follows, in Millions)

| | 1981 | | 1980 | | 1979 | | 1978 | | 1977 | | 1976 | |
|---|---|---|---|---|---|---|---|---|---|---|---|---|
| | Sales | Pre-tax income | Sales | Pre-tax income | Sales | Pre-tax income | Sales | Pre-tax income | Sales | Pre-tax income | Sales | Pre-tax income |
| Other consumer products | $ 63 | $ 7 | $ 132 | $ (1) | $ 262 | $ 7 | $ 350 | $ 21 | $ 443 | $ 22 | $ 435 | $ 17 |
| Food services | — | — | — | — | — | — | — | — | 53 | 3 | 51 | 2 |
| Consumer direct sales | — | — | 33 | 2 | 79 | 6 | 73 | 5 | 68 | 4 | 64 | 4 |

**Description of industry segments**

The corporation is a diversified company primarily engaged in the manufacture and distribution of a broad range of branded products and services. These products and services have been classified into the following three industry segments:

**Consumer packaged goods.** This segment manufactures and distributes hot and cold beverages; hosiery, undergarments, gloves, swimwear, and cosmetics; processed and fresh meats; frozen baked goods, fish, seafood, potatoes and confection products; and personal care products, sugar and a variety of canned and processed fruits and vegetables.

**Food services.** This segment distributes food and related grocery products to volume feeding operations and operates restaurants and convenience retail food stores.

**Consumer direct sales.** This group produces and sells home cleaning appliances, household and personal care products, specialty chemicals and commercial vehicle cleaning equipment, and provides building maintenance and security services.

*Note:* The Notes to Financial Statements should be read in conjunction with the Operating Results by Industry Segment.
*Source:* 1981 annual report.

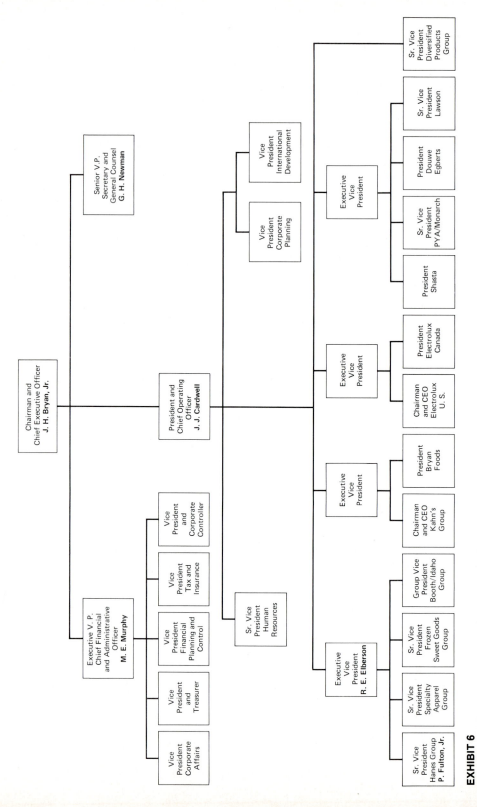

**EXHIBIT 6**

Organization chart, June 1981. (*Source:* Company documents.)

**EXHIBIT 7**
HANES CORPORATION ADVERTISING GUIDELINES, MARCH 31, 1978

## SCOPE

The primary purpose of this document is to establish advertising placement guidelines which respond to public concern over the display of violence and sensitive moral issues on television and lack of good taste in magazines.

## TELEVISION

1 *Violence*
Hanes Corporation will avoid commercial participation in all TV programs judged to be excessively or gratuitously violent under any of the following criteria:
   - *Violence for the sake of violence.* Portrayals of violent actions not necessary to either story or character development.
   - *Glorification of violent acts.* Programming which makes the committing of violent actions appear to be appealing or which appears to condone the use of more than necessary violence on the part of the police, soldiers, etc., in the line of their duty.
   - *Overly graphic violence.* Portrayals which dwell on violent actions for excessively long periods or are unnecessarily descriptive in describing their effects either visually or verbally.

2 *Controversial moral issues*
Hanes Corporation will avoid commercial participation in TV programming that may be offensive to a significant proportion of the population. Specifically, Hanes Corporation will avoid programs which:
   - Graphically depict sexual behavior—this is defined as full or partial nudity, explicit visual and verbal sexual descriptions/language and excessively passionate lovemaking.
   - Deal with polarizing moral issues such as abortion and homosexuality as major or minor themes.
   - Involve aberrant sexual behavior such as incest and sodomy even in a minor way.
   - Deal with any of the following subjects as primary themes or major subplots—nymphomania, statutory rape or prostitution.

   - May be offensive to large numbers of pe in specific religious or ethnic groups.

## MAGAZINES

Magazine readership is generally restricted to adults or to a select audience by virtue of magazine availability. Therefore, advertising placement standards for magazines can provide wider ranges of tolerance. General standards of good taste provide a suitable editorial environment for Hanes products. Hanes Corporation will avoid advertising in all magazines which go beyond these standards. Specifically proscribed are: (a) frontal male nudity; (b) simulated sexual activities; (c) excessive use of verbal obscenities; and (d) an overwhelming sexual environment created editorially and/or by a preponderance of sexually oriented advertising.

In judging new magazines, no commitment will be made until there is time to evaluate the first one or two issues to determine whether the new magazine will violate the above standards.

## IMPLEMENTATION

1 Advertising media buyers will be supplied with the above guidelines and will advise the TV networks and magazine publishers of this policy. Primary responsibility for judging which programs or magazines comply with the above guidelines will rest with the advertising agency.

2 In the case of TV advertising, the TV networks will be periodically supplied with lists of specific programming deemed unacceptable.

3 Prescreening should be utilized for all prime time TV programming. (Prime time is defined as the period between 8:00 P.M. and 11:00 P.M.) Evaluation of non-prime time programs must be based on the title, reputation or random checking due to their magnitude.

4 Each advertising agency employed by Hanes will be requested, from time to time, to demonstrate through specific examples that its judgment coincides with that of Hanes Corporation senior management.

er 18, 1980

Mr. John H. Bryan, Jr.
140 Melrose
Kenilworth, IL 60043

Dear Mr. Bryan:

Last Sunday evening, September 14, ABC aired a program entitled "The Women's Room" which Consolidated Foods helped sponsor. All the advance reviews of the program indicated it to be a vicious attack on marriage and the family. I must confess that it was exactly that. ABC said that the purpose of the film was to "make people angry." I must confess, also, that it did that.

We plan to run a list of the sponsors and their products in our next NFD Newsletter. If you care to explain your reason behind helping sponsor "The Women's Room" we would be happy to share it with our readers and supporters. Since much of our paper is reprinted in several hundred local and regional newsletters, I feel you might desire to share the reason why you chose to help sponsor such an obviously biased and prejudicial movie.

I look forward to hearing from you. I am sure your media people can bring you up to date on this program.

Sincerely,

Donald E. Wildmon

**EXHIBIT 9**
EXECUTIVE OFFICES' CORPORATE RESPONSE

October 8, 1980

Mr. Donald E. Wildmon
Executive Director
National Federation for Decency
P.O. Box 1398
Tupelo, Mississippi 38801

Dear Mr. Wildmon:

Mr. John Bryan has asked me to respond to your recent letter regarding a L'erin cosmetics commercial that aired during ABC's "The Women's Room." While neither Mr. Bryan nor myself saw the program, the information we have received indicates that your concern about it being an attack on marriage and the family structure is well founded.

I would like first to explain the manner in which our companies operate. They have a great deal of autonomy, and, because of the variety of products marketed, have the responsibility for developing and implementing their own advertising programs.

L'erin cosmetics, part of our Hanes Group, has in effect specific advertising guidelines relating to TV program content and the purchase of commercial time. L'erin's advertising agency has the responsibility to prescreen TV programs and movies shown during prime time. The agency is instructed not to place commercials on programs that relate predominately and specifically to sex and violence. The guidelines, as they now stand, do not specifically address programs which may be antifamily or marriage, or, for that matter antibusiness, antilabor, etc. On the surface, the agency did not believe "The Women's Room" violated the guidelines; thus a commercial for L'erin did air in certain local markets.

Your letter has prompted us to reexamine whether more expansive guidelines concerning matters of this type should be developed. In any case, I am forwarding copies of your letter and this response to Mr. John F. Ward, president of L'erin cosmetics, who, I'm sure, will be interested in your comments.

Your point of view concerning this specific program is well taken and we thank you for taking the time to bring this matter to our attention.

Very truly,

Richard D. Kemplin
Vice President—Corporate Affairs

cc: John F. Ward

# Consolidated Foods Corporation (B)

Top management at Consolidated Foods Corporation in Chicago had been concerned about consumer complaints and threatened boycotts throughout early 1981, some relating to the TV and print ad content of its newly acquired Hanes division and others relating to sponsorship of TV programs thought to portray excessive sex or violence.[1] Contrary to expectations, a boycott was not called in June 1981. Press reports suggested that the Reverend Donald Wildmon and the Reverend Jerry Falwell, president of Moral Majority, differed over the need for a boycott. The Coalition for Better Television (CBTV) announced a delay until new monitoring data could be gathered in the fall.

[1]*Note*: Events leading up to mid-June 1981 and company background are detailed in "Consolidated Foods Corporation (A)" HBS Case Services No. 382-158. An overview of external developments is presented in "Note on the TV Advertising and Programming Controversy," HBS Case Services No. 382-160.

Nevertheless, the momentum of the better television campaign continued. And Hanes, along with Consolidated Foods, would receive publicity twice more before the end of the summer.

On July 23, 1981, the *Wall Street Journal* carried an article entitled "Poll Suggests TV Advertisers Can't Ignore Matters of Taste." It reported on the results of a study by Warwick, Welsh & Miller, a New York ad agency, aimed at assessing the public's true feeling about the tastefulness of TV programming and advertising. Ads for Hanes' Underalls panty hose were mentioned among those that respondents cited as offensive:

> Underalls advertising, for example, features shots of women's backsides while an announcer says, "OK, America, show us your Underalls." William Karnbach, marketing vice-president at Hanes, maker of the pantyhose, maintains that any company that makes a commercial that is noticeable is "going to get people who aren't going to like it."

Mr. Karnbach is less impressed by War-wick, Welsh & Miller's survey than he is by Underalls' popularity: 27 million pairs, worth more than $100 million at retail, are sold annually.

In August, another coalition entered the picture. The National Coalition on Television Violence (NCTV) verged on being hostile to the New Right's preoccupation with TV sex and profanity. It focused more on common liberal concerns such as the social and psychological effects of violent scenes and themes in TV programming.

Despite differences in moral focus, however, the two coalitions employed similar tactics; they conducted elaborate monitoring surveys aimed at boycotting and otherwise calling attention to sponsors of offending shows.

The July-August 1981 issue of *NCTV News* (Volume 2, Number 4) listed the L'eggs division of Hanes among the 10 heaviest sponsors of prime-time violence. The newsletter called for a boycott of L'eggs hosiery and it published the Winston-Salem office address of Joseph Neely, president of L'eggs products. Predictably, a significant new round of letters was received at Hanes's management offices. Reaction at Hanes was swift, and efforts were made to identify and evaluate sponsorship of the offending programs.

## REVISED GUIDELINES AT HANES

In the wake of the NCTV ratings and mindful of a new fall offensive by CBTV, top management at Hanes Group undertook a careful revision and expansion of its advertising guidelines. A draft of the revised guidelines was circulated in late September. It offered not only advertising media, but advertising content, trademark usage, substantiation of claims, legal review procedures, and recommendations on the handling of consumer complaints. Imple-mentation would include closer cooperation between Hanes and its ad agencies on all fronts.

## FALL 1981

In October 1981 Rev. Wildmon reported that the canceled boycott had indeed not been forgotten: "We are in another monitoring process. . . . We had committed ourselves to look at the programs this fall." Pending the results of this monitoring process, the boycott was now to be regarded as "delayed until at least January."[2]

By November 1981 business and media observers were able to reflect on the year's events in light of their impact on programming and its sponsorship. There seemed to be general agreement that the networks had been affected by the events of the summer.

In its "Roundup" article on the impact of the boycott threat, *Advertising Age* concluded: "Few advertisers . . . liked admitting it on the record, but it was clear that the vast majority felt the hullabaloo raised over the past year by groups such as the Moral Majority and Coalition for Better Television has had a significant effect."[3]

One ad agency executive put it this way: "I hate to give these groups something to crow about, but there's no doubt that the state of TV last year handed them an issue and they got results. . . . Their influence is strong and they've gotten the attention of our top management; we have to factor it into every decision we present."[4]

On December 8, 1981, the *Boston Globe* reported that the coalition's Rev. Donald Wildmon was threatening a boycott for February 1982 to continue pressuring the networks and advertisers.

[2]*New York Times,* October 5, 1981, Sect. 4, p. 12.
[3]*Advertising Age,* November 16, 1981, p. 3.
[4]Ibid.

# Note on the TV Advertising and Programming Controversy, 1981

We take the view that television is now teaching—even advancing—a particular moral viewpoint. . . . Just look at any of the shows Norman Lear produces. Extramarital sex is OK; the practice of homosexuality is OK; booze, you name it . . . and now and then they throw in a couple hours of "Little House on the Prairie" to satisfy the moralist part of the audience. We're not saying that viewpoint should never be treated. Conservatives like sex as much as anybody else—maybe even more. What we are talking about is balance. The Norman Lear people have their influence, and we want to have ours, too.

With these comments Cal Thomas, vice president–communications of the Moral Majority, fired one of the opening salvos of a battle that would occupy the attention of TV networks, advertising agencies, corporate advertisers, and the American public in 1980 and 1981.[1]

Organized efforts to change the quality of TV programming were not new to the American scene. Groups as diverse as the Knights of Columbus (a Roman Catholic fraternal society), the National Council of Churches (representing mainstream Protestantism), the Anti-Defamation League (representing the Jewish faith), the National Federation for Decency (a conservative Christian group), and the National PTA Action Center (an association devoted to close communication between parents and teachers on the educational environment of the young) had all attempted to influence what enters American homes in the form of TV entertainment.

The efforts of 1980 and 1981, however, bore the imprint of increased organization and a concerted drive to influence TV programming through direct appeals and threats to those advertisers whose sponsorship made such programming possible. These appeals and threats were couched in terms of boycotts whereby religious groups claimed the ability to deliver large numbers of consumers who would refuse

[1]Mark Miller, "New Move to Bridle TV," *Marketing and Media Decisions,* January 1981, Vol. 16, No. 1, p. 58. Reprinted by permission.

to patronize the products or services of sponsors of offending programs.

The threat of a TV boycott itself was also not new to the American public. In 1978, for example, the National Federation for Decency attempted to exert boycott pressure on Sears, Roebuck and Company for sponsoring programs allegedly containing excessive sex, violence, and profanity. Other early targets of boycott efforts had been General Foods and American Home Products (in this case, by Clean Up TV, a group sponsored by the National Churches of Christ).

In response to these earlier efforts, General Foods' representatives had pointed out they annually dropped 100 programs that did not meet corporate standards regarding sex and violence, and that only 3% of General Foods' advertising budget went into shows which Clean Up TV found objectionable. The company maintained, however, that "we're in the market to buy time, and not everything we buy will please every viewer. . . . We don't believe any one group should be able to dictate to all others what their choices should be."[2] This response was not adequate for the church groups and a boycott ensued.

The church groups, however, were emboldened by the response of another major corporation to these early boycott threats. Warner-Lambert reported dropping several shows as a result of Clean Up TV's campaign. A Warner-Lambert spokesperson observed:

> We had a policy since 1971 that . . . we should be associated with wholesome entertainment—programs that don't exploit sex or violence, or demean human dignity. And to carry out that policy, we have a practice of prescreening everything that we're on. For instance, we were advertising on "Saturday Night Live," which of course is impossible to prescreen because it is broadcast live. We stopped advertising on that show—not because of a moral judgment, but

because we couldn't prescreen. In fact, we're now off a number of shows that we had been on. You might say that our sensitivity to the matter has been heightened.[3]

On November 9, 1980, the *New York Times* reported that Warner-Lambert had dropped sponsorship of "The Newlywed Game," "The Dating Game," "Three's Company," and "Saturday Night Live." All of these programs had been on Clean Up TV's target list.

## 1981 BOYCOTT, SPRING PHASE

With some initial success behind them, and encouraged by what many perceived as a shift of mood within the American public away from liberal social standards toward more traditional ones, church groups prepared a major assault on advertisers and programming for 1981. Leading the assault was the Coalition for Better Televison (CBTV), a group headed by the Reverend Donald Wildmon of Tupelo, Mississippi, and supported by the following groups: the Moral Majority of the Reverend Jerry Falwell, the Church of Christ, the American Life Lobby, Concerned Women for America, and the Eagle Forum (Phyllis Schlafly's group). CBTV reported that it had scores of volunteers across the country who were monitoring all TV programming for offensive content. The output of this monitoring effort would be a list of those advertisers who consistently sponsored programs that CBTV rated as offensive. These advertisers in turn would be threatened with nationwide boycotts if they continued to sponsor questionable programming. (Excerpts from Rev. Wildmon's press statement announcing the formation of CBTV appear as Exhibit 1.)

The potential impact of this effort on the advertising budgets for the 1981–1982 season was swiftly recognized. According to one network official: "Though I still believe there are sponsors in control of their advertising destiny,

[2]General Foods spokesperson, quoted in *Marketing and Media Decisions*, art. cit., January 1981, Vol. 16, No. 1, p. 107.

[3]Ibid.

the fuss kicked up by CBTV will be a factor in the pricing of our shows, especially those meriting a clean bill of health and appealing to the family audience."[4]

An agency buyer observed: "The bottom line is that the networks have to make the bucks. With the pressures building on the advertisers, they are going to look for programs with strong moral values and tone down anything considered too offensive."[5]

According to a network buyer: "Let's face it, go into any meeting today, and the Moral Majority is all anyone is talking about. . . . The producers don't really give a damn about Wildmon or the Moral Majority, but once it begins to affect their pocketbooks—well, if it's clean that sells, then that's what they will deliver."[6]

On March 23, 1981, the Moral Majority took out a full-page ad in newspapers across the country explaining its position. The campaign was reported to cost over $100,000, and it had as its central point a defense of the group's role in society: "Moral Majority, Inc., is made up of millions of Americans, including 72,000 ministers, priests, and rabbis, who are deeply concerned about the moral decline of our nation and who are sick and tired of the way many amoral and secular humanists and other liberals are destroying the traditional family and moral values on which our nation was built."[7]

As the potential impact of the organized religious groups became clear, network executives became increasingly nervous. In April 1981 the presidents of the three major networks presented their case at the annual meeting of the American Association of Advertising Agencies.

According to NBC's Fred Silverman, threats of boycotts were "the coalition's sneak attack on the foundation of democracy." Gene Jankowski of CBS warned of "the disenfranchisement of the real majority by a determined

minority." ABC's Fred Pierce pleaded with the advertisers and their agencies to stand "side by side" with the networks in resistance to the "coercive tactics" of the "self-appointed censors" within the coalition.[8]

The agency people did not appear to respond favorably to these pleas. Their responses included those voiced by executives who felt that the networks were less than consistent in their desire for cooperation with the agencies ("What partnership? Where were these fellows when we were trying to talk to them about . . . rate increases?"). Other responses asserted reluctant sympathy with complaints about programming quality: "I don't want censors like the Moral Majority, Jerry Falwell or any of them. But I don't want 'Three's Company' either—and that is what I get. The networks program offensive shows, pure trash, and they expect us to defend them."[9]

The network executives, on the other hand, suggested that the mass of viewers be allowed to decide what should be on the air, rather than any special interest groups. As Jankowski observed: "If they (the viewers) are disenchanted with what is offered . . . that fact registers quite clearly. They can be and ought to be trusted to go on doing their own voting with their own dials."[10]

Others disputed this perspective and argued that, in many cases, a program's rating reflected not so much a program's worth as the lack of any superior competition. On this hypothesis, a TV program might have received high ratings because it was the most interesting or appealing of a bad lot in a given time spot—a tribute to the fact that people who are going to watch television will give high ratings to a particular program for want of any meaningful alternative. These same observers also argued that ratings fail to measure a grassroots dissatisfaction with what television is offered. They suggested that the right people were not being

[4]*Advertising Age,* March 30, 1981, p. 1.
[5]Ibid., p. 80.
[6]Ibid.
[7]*New York Times,* March 23, 1981, p. B 11.

[8]*Advertising Age,* April 13, 1981, p. 1.
[9]Ibid.
[10]*Advertising Age,* April 13, 1981, p. 103.

polled for their opinions regarding what is on the air. Moral Majority's Thompson observed:

> I do a lot of public speaking around the country and in place after place that I go, I take my own polls. I ask for a show of hands of anybody who has *ever* been surveyed by Nielsen or Arbitron, or anybody who has ever been contacted by a pollster with questions about TV programs. I've spoken to tens of thousands of people, and I've never met anyone yet who has ever raised a hand in the affirmative. I don't know who they're polling, but they're polling the wrong people.[11]

## A DIVERSE SET OF STAKEHOLDERS

It is difficult to estimate the potential impact of a boycott such as the coalition was planning without examining the roles of various stakeholders. Since the response of the advertisers themselves will be considered below, the reader's attention is here called to other parties: agencies, networks, educational leaders, religious leaders, and finally the American public.

### Agencies and Networks

The network leaders failed to find a sympathetic audience among the agency executives. The agency people seemed to be caught between their obligations to procure popular and lucrative time slots for their clients on the one hand, and their reported distaste for potentially objectionable programming on the other. Leo-Arthur Kelmenson, president and CEO of Kenyon and Eckhardt, an advertising agency, deplored the state of television when he wrote: "I don't think I'll get much argument from reasonable people that such [objectionable] program content is damaging to society in general and to impressionable young people in particular."[12]

At the same time, Kelmenson articulated the dilemma faced by the agency executives:

> Only if the decision to forgo rating points for moral principles is mandated in the corporate boardroom—only when the networks rise to the programming challenges they will then face—will agency media buyers feel free to make program credibility one of the evaluative criteria. . . . Given sufficient support at these three levels, perhaps we can hope that . . . [the sex and violence] type of program will stop proliferating. Until then, let society beware.[13]

The networks' financial stakes were substantial. Each Nielsen point advantage was worth $40 million in annual advertising revenue to the individual network. It was feared that programs branded as objectionable by the Moral Majority could have their ad rates fall by as much as 30%.

Throughout the debate, network leaders maintained that they were the targets of unfair, even unconstitutional, tactics. In response to these perceived threats, prominent media, religious, and political leaders joined together to form a group called People for the American Way to battle what it described as a "climate of fear and repression."[14] The groups produced public service announcements with the aid of Norman Lear and featured, among others, Carol Burnett, Goldie Hawn, and Muhammad Ali. Supporters of the group included the Reverend M. William Howard, president of the National Council of Churches, and Barbara Jordan, former Democratic representative of Texas.

One of the central themes of the network response had been summed up by NBC's Fred Silverman in his description of the boycott tactics as an attack on the foundations of democracy. The Rev. Wildmon was quick to respond: "A boycott is as legal and as American as apple pie. Didn't Martin Luther King lead boycotts?

---

[11]*Marketing and Media Decisions,* January 1981, p. 58.
[12]"Vast Wasteland Revisited," *Harvard Business Review,* November-December 1980, p. 29.

[13]Ibid.
[14]*New York Times,* June 25, 1981, p. C 14.

... I'm not seeking to have a law passed. These are public airwaves and I'm just saying that if an advertiser wants my business, he has to treat me with respect. If there's no public support for our position, the boycott will fail and we'll disappear."[15]

### Educational and Religious Leaders

Even moderate voices tended to disagree with the network executives in their protests. Everett Parker, head of the communications office of the United Church of Christ, was a well-known advocate of improved TV programming. Parker, who opposed boycotts as a means to achieve this end, observed: "I think all these speeches they're [network broadcasters] making about censorship are hypocritical. ... For years they've been putting out all these sleazy programs and thumbing their noses at people who object to them. They've never listened to sensible people, because they knew sensible people wouldn't attack them this way. The coalition has gone for the jugular."[16]

The Reverend Timothy S. Healy, S. J., president of Georgetown University, was another opponent of boycotts and a critic of the Moral Majority. Nonetheless, he recognized the strength of these efforts: "What it [CBTV] is trying to do is as old as American politics and every bit as legal. As long as there is a significant public support behind the pressure it brings, the coalition will be effective." While Healy believed that the boycott threats would ultimately fade because of their excessively negative tone, he observed that CBTV had struck the networks in a weak spot and that it was now in the process of exploiting this weakness: "These are real problems. And because of the problems, elements like the coalition ... can pressure ... and hard."[17]

The strongest critique of the Moral Majority and its tactics from the academic community was the assessment of A. Bartlett Giamatti, president of Yale University. In a speech prepared for delivery to Yale's 1981 incoming class, Giamatti painted this picture of Rev. Falwell's group: "Angry at change, rigid in the application of chauvinistic slogans, absolutistic in morality, they threaten through political pressure or public communication whoever dares to disagree with their authoritarian positions. ... Using television, direct mail, and economic boycott, they would sweep before them anyone who holds a different opinion."[18]

The Moral Majority was quick to respond, accusing Giamatti of an "unprovoked diatribe." A Moral Majority spokesperson contended that the organization "just wants [its] side to be heard and that it became involved in TV programming to seek a better balance than the violence and permissiveness that is broadcast now."[19]

### The American People: Would They Boycott?

Another central theme of the network responses was the contention that only a small minority of viewers would actually respond to boycotts:

> A poll commissioned by ABC ... showed that a maximum of 1.3 percent of the American public would consider supporting a boycott; of that group, only one-half of one percent were Moral Majority members. CBS News found that 30 percent of the groups listed by Wildmon as coalition members said they did not belong to it. An NBC survey concluded that only two programs—"Three's Company" and "Soap"— would be turned off the screen by as many as 3 percent of the public because of sex, profanity or violence they exhibit; twelve would be turned off by 1 percent or less. In other words, boycott or not, a lot of people would keep tuning in to watch "Dallas" and "The Dukes of Hazzard."[20]

[15]*New York Times,* June 22, 1981, p. A 12.
[16]Ibid.
[17]*Advertising Age,* August 3, 1981, pp. 33–34.

[18]*New York Times,* September 1, 1981, p. 1.
[19]*New York Times,* September 2, 1981, p. A 16.
[20]*New York Times,* July 5, 1981, Sect. 4, p. 16.

As Kelmenson observed: "The American public ... does not seem at all repelled by this type of program. A 1977 study by the J. Walter Thompson Company revealed that a mere 1.5 percent of viewers said they had actually boycotted advertisers of violent programs."[21]

During the early months of 1981, NBC had commissioned the Roper Organization to conduct a nationwide survey "to determine the reaction of the adult American public to specific entertainment programs." Though not aimed directly at assessing the likely impact of a boycott, the study clearly had this as an indirect purpose. The results of the study, which network executives interpreted favorably, were eventually shared with both advertisers and ad agencies. Roper summarized the findings:

> Relatively few Americans are critical of any of these shows on sex or violence grounds. Also, there is disagreement on sex and violence: some like the content that others object to. . . . People of strong fundamentalist persuasion are significantly more concerned about sex and profanity than are nonfundamentalists. Yet even this small group watches these shows and is more likely to express favorable than unfavorable opinions of them. . . . NBC concludes from this study that Americans generally like the programs they watch on television and relatively few object to specific network programs on sex and violence grounds. Further, a majority of the very people who are the constituency of the fundamentalist leadership seem to hold attitudes towards programs which are quite similar to those of the general public.

Other studies carried less sanguine messages for advertisers. In Portland, Oregon, a poll taken in the spring of 1981 by the *Oregon Journal* found that 72% of those sampled believed that "the public should boycott the products of those companies sponsoring programs with sex, violence, and profanity."

The *Wall Street Journal* reported on another study done in early summer 1981 by Warwick, Welsh and Miller, a New York ad agency. Though focused primarily on the content of TV commercials, the survey of 3,440 people concluded that while 40% found TV commercials to be in poor taste, 20% found *programs* to be in poor taste. The report of the survey added that although 55% said they shun products with objectionable advertising, four-fifths of those people said they never complained directly to an advertiser or TV station."[22]

In a somewhat philosophical reflection, Daniel Yankelovich, president of the social research firm Yankelovich, Skelly and White, observed that it was concern for children that gave force and legitimacy to the television protests. Yankelovich concluded in an article in *Psychology Today* that "we have been neglecting the question, broadly put, of what is best for our children because we have been too busy with the question of what is best for us as adults, assuming—all too comfortably—that the same answer would do for both questions" (see Exhibit 2).

## PROCTER & GAMBLE'S RESPONSE

Owen B. Butler, chairman of the nation's largest TV advertiser, Procter & Gamble Co., appeared before the Academy of Television Arts and Sciences in Los Angeles on June 15, 1981. Butler announced that P&G, which spent over $480,000,000 on TV advertising in 1980,[23] had "withdrawn sponsorship from over 50 programs, including movies, for reasons of taste" during the year. Butler's presentation went into some depth regarding the reasons for this decision:

> Generations of Americans are being taught far more powerfully about virtues and vices, about morality, about society and individual responsibility by the things which you [academy members] create and produce. There is a large,

[21] Ibid., p. 29.

[22] *Wall Street Journal,* July 23, 1981.

[23] *Wall Street Journal,* June 16, 1981, p. 39.

serious and increasingly vocal segment of our population who believe that much of what you are teaching is destructive, that it tears at the character which has enabled this country to become ... the finest society yet built by mankind.[24]

He expressed concern over the tactics chosen by the CBTV, but concluded that "the coalition may well believe that this was the only way they could ever get very many people to listen." Butler pointed out occasions in the past when P&G had refused to bow to threats of boycott because the company believed in the correctness of sponsoring specific programs. While he also expressed concern over the coalition's data-gathering procedures, he was able to draw the following conclusions:

Despite this concern about the technique, we think the coalition is expressing some very important and broadly held views about gratuitous sex, violence and profanity. I can assure you that we are listening very carefully to what they say.... For example, while we can't agree with their method of establishing ratings, the fact is that their list of the top ten sex-oriented programs includes seven programs which we had previously decided either to avoid entirely, or schedule only rarely, because of the difficulty of finding episodes which are consistent with our guidelines governing excessive and gratuitous sex. We review every program on which we schedule advertising, and even beyond the coalition's list, we find it necessary to withdraw sponsorships periodically because of offensive program content.

For sound commercial reasons, we are not going to let our advertising messages appear in an environment which we think many of our potential customers will find distasteful. Beyond that, we are going to be guided by our conscience on the kind of material we sponsor. A corporation is not without personality and character and conscience. A corporation like ours has a character which is the sum of all the tens

of thousands of people who have made up that corporation for more than 140 years, and our definition of the kind of media which we would support with our advertising has always involved some moral considerations.... It is completely within our character not only to screen out problem programs, but also to actively seek programs of exceptional artistic quality, which are truly inspirational and which challenge the very best in human nature.[25]

The Rev. Jerry Falwell quickly commended P&G's actions, noting that the company would avoid a boycott "if what this speech means is that P&G is in fact pulling away from the most offensive programs."[26]

Advertising executives appeared to be taken by surprise when they learned of the reaction to Butler's remarks. David B. McCall, chairman of McCaffrey and McCall, described the attention that the P&G chairman's speech was receiving as "much ado about nothing." The ad executives claimed that all major advertisers screen programming either directly or through hired agents. Withdrawal of support from programming that was not up to the company's standards was described as routine. "None of us can understand the motivation of the announcement, since it is common practice in the business," said J. Walter Thompson's Chairman, Burt Manning. Others were more skeptical. James J. Jordan, chairman of Jordan, Case and McGrath suggested that "Procter & Gamble was trying to focus the attention of the Reverend Jerry Falwell ... on prime time in order to distract him from daytime programming, where several P&G soap operas are a daily feature." Jordan was also perturbed that Reverend Falwell had "taken it [Butler's speech] out of context [and] and was using it for a license to put the Procter & Gamble seal of approval on his entire campaign."[27]

Despite the hesitations of the advertising agency executives, the Procter & Gamble deci-

---

[24]"Television Can Show and Tell, but Can It Listen?" Speech before the Academy of Television Arts and Sciences, June 15, 1981.

[25]Ibid., *Speech.*
[26]*Wall Street Journal,* June 16, 1981, p. 39.
[27]*New York Times,* June 24, 1981, p. D 18.

sion seemed to have a ripple effect throughout the business world. Shortly after Butler's speech, Thomas of the Moral Majority observed: "It's like the prime rate. . . . When No. 1 announces, a lot of others follow. The response we've gotten from advertisers since the Procter & Gamble speech has been very gratifying."[28]

The issue had clearly been joined and would not die.

[28] *New York Times,* June 27, 1981, p. 48.

## EXHIBITS: Note on the TV Advertising and Programming Controversy, 1981

### EXHIBIT 1
EXCERPTS FROM PRESS STATEMENT BY THE REVEREND DONALD E. WILDMON, CHAIRMAN, COALITION FOR BETTER TELEVISION, FEBRUARY 2, 1981

---

Tom Shales, noted TV critic for the *Washington Post,* wrote in his column a few weeks ago this item. "An experienced Hollywood screen writer who works occasionally in TV will never forget what a network executive told him when handing back one of the writer's scripts. The executive said, 'Dirty it up a little, will you?'"

Gary Deeb, TV critic for the *Chicago Sun-Times,* wrote a few months back about an interview with Tony Randall. "A CBS executive told my head writer," Mr. Randall is quoted, "to put more t—and a—into the show. . . . These guys would put pornography on television tomorrow if they could get away with it."

Lee Rich, producer of "Dallas," "Knots Landing," "Midland Heights" and several other programs, recently told *TV Guide* his show about teenage sex would be "hot stuff" and laughed, "I'm going to be the porno king of television."

For years concerned citizens have urged, pleaded and even begged the networks to halt the trend toward increasing amounts of sex, violence, and profanity. In reply, they have received answers ranging from a polite "We appreciate your opinion," to a sarcastic "If you don't like what is on, turn it off." The concern of millions of Americans has fallen on deaf ears.

Instead of reason, restraint, and responsibility, the networks have rather displayed an arrogance and indifference rarely matched in the history of corporate America.

We feel that television prides itself on being able to sell products while disclaiming any ability to sell ideas or values.

In the past the networks have attacked those of us who have activated our concern by doing what they are experts at—stereotyping. They have said that we are a small group of religious fanatics whose concerns and cares are to be dismissed and ignored.

If that be true, then we have some good company. People like Erma Bombeck, who wrote in one of her columns: "You told me violence was necessary because it was 'real.' Throwing up is 'real,' but I don't want to see it in color."

And people like Red Skelton. "Then," Mr. Skelton said, "they sell violence. Now they say this doesn't affect your mind in any way whatsoever, but if you can subliminally sell a product in 30 seconds, what does one hour of filth or violence do to your brain?"

To properly do their stereotyping the networks must also include Kathleen Nolan, who, as president of the Screen Actors Guild, said: "The heads of the networks are parasites and tasteless mercenaries. They've trashed up the airwaves almost beyond repair. It's a subhuman situation."

The networks must include in the "religious fanatic" stereotyping Dr. Rose K. Goldsen, professor of sociology at Cornell University. Dr. Goldsen had this to say: "TV is more than just a little fun and entertainment. It's a whole environment and what it does bears an unpleasant resemblance to behavior modification—on a mass scale."

Lucille Ball said: "Television's treatment of sex has gone too far. . . . Romance has been taken out of sex." Miss Ball's observations were confirmed by Harvard University's Project on Human Sexual

Development whose study on television reported that 70% of allusions to intercourse on television occur between unmarried couples or involve a prostitute. "Much of TV's erotic activity involves violence against women," the report stated.

In addition to the networks, the sponsors of TV programs must also share responsibility for the increasing amounts of violence, vulgarity, sex, and profanity. For they have been quick to support these programs with their dollars.

Because of this situation, we are today announcing the formation of a Coalition for Better Television. As of this morning the coalition includes more than 150 national and regional organizations. We expect that number to continue to grow.

Beginning March 1 the coalition will monitor TV programs for their violent, sexual, and profane content. The monitoring will continue through the months of March, April, and May. At the end of the three-month period the coalition will select one or more advertisers who rank among the top sponsors in the categories mentioned and ask for a one-year voluntary boycott of all their products. In addition, we will select one or more advertisers who support basically quality programs and ask that their products be chosen over their competitors.

It is regrettable and unfortunate that such action is necessary. Most of us who are involved would prefer to be doing something other than dealing with this issue. However, let no one question our resolve.

The networks will respond with the only reply they know—by crying censorship. Censorship, however, is an official act by some official body at some level of government. The clearest expression of the First Amendment is the right of a person to spend his money where he so desires. With our plan of action the networks have the right to spend their money where they desire, the advertisers have the right to spend their money where they desire, and consumers have the right to spend their money where they desire.

Several groups, including those in civil rights and the National Organization of Women, have used economic leverage and, I might add, without the criticism of the networks.

**EXHIBIT 2**
THE PUBLIC MIND—DANIEL YANKELOVICH*

---

## STEPCHILDREN OF THE MORAL MAJORITY

Ever since the emergence of the Moral Majority, the takers of the public pulse—politicians, pollsters, network executives, educators, newspeople—have nervously been trying to gauge its political strength and its staying power. Usually these efforts have amounted to one or another kind of survey. Side by side the results present a confusing picture. Last year, 14 months after the Reverend Jerry Falwell founded the organization, the *New York Times* reported its membership at 400,000. Soon after, the Moral Majority claimed that it registered 3 million new voters in the 1980 Presidential election. This year, an ABC-TV survey concluded that 2.9 percent of those interviewed—or a projected 4.6 million Americans—supported the Moral Majority's "attempts to influence [TV] programs to conform to their standards and values" and tentatively projected a membership of 10.6 million. A New York Times/CBS Poll suggested the Moral Majority could be equated with evangelical Christians and thereby implied that the number of people who share the organization's outlook might extend to the stratospheric height of 67 million.

The ludicrously wide range of these estimates, from 400,000 all the way to 67 million, suggests a failure of clear thinking about what is being measured, and why. I suspect that what people want to learn about the Moral Majority is neither how many dues-paying members it has, nor how many voters it recruited in the last election, nor how large is the religious group from whose members some—but not all—moral majoritarians are drawn. What we really want to know is whether the Moral Majority is a passing fad or will take hold in the mainstream of American life.

The key to exploring the potential impact of the Moral Majority is not numbers but issues. What is

*Reprinted by permission from *Psychology Today* (November 1981), © 1981 by Ziff-Davis Publishing Company.

the basis of the organization's appeal? More specifically, is there a critical social issue that gives it a potential constituency beyond its official membership, whatever that number may be? Once this question is asked, several insights come quickly to light.

We see immediately that the Moral Majority draws its vitality from a concern shared by millions of Americans for whom the Moral Majority is otherwise anathema. The organization's connection with this concern gives the Moral Majority its plausibility and claim to attention as a potentially significant social movement. It leads people who would ordinarily reject its proposals out of hand to say, at least tacitly, "Well, maybe they have a point. . . ."

What is this concern? It is that Americans are growing ever more uneasy about the influence of the prevailing moral climate on their children. Let me put the issue first in terms of several imaginary examples. Say I am a parent who believes everyone over the age of consent is entitled to engage in the sexual behavior he or she finds most satisfying (short of compelling others to do something against their will). Say I am a parent who believes in freedom of speech. I am sufficiently committed to these beliefs, in fact, to vote against people who, in one way or another, seem to oppose them—which is one reason I oppose the Moral Majority. But still I am not happy about the fact that my 13-year-old son can buy *Hustler* on the newstand. I am not happy, but I am not sure what to do about it.

Say I want to decriminalize marijuana. But I am very concerned already about the easy availability of many kinds of drugs in the high school my 15-year-old daughter attends. Or say that, as a matter of principle, I do not forbid my children to attend any movie or watch any television program or read any book. But the gross violence in many movies they go to see, the deliberately sensational treatment of social problems like urban crime and pregnant teenagers on the television dramas they frequently watch distress me. Must I deny my own principles to do what I, however confusedly, feel is right for my children?

Now I am convinced that many Americans, especially parents, are increasingly uncomfortable with the sweeping permissiveness that their own pursuit of permissiveness has created for young people.

One piece of supporting evidence is provided by the ABC-TV survey I referred to earlier. Not only did it find that 4.6 million Americans supported the Moral Majority's "attempts to influence [TV] programs to conform to their standards and values," it also found that about 33 million (20.5 percent of those interviewed) would support a group using tactics such as organized boycotts to shape TV programming to their moral preferences.

Another item is the finding in a recent nationwide study of the American family conducted by Yankelovich, Skelly, and White that even the most untraditional parents—those who stress self-fulfillment and deemphasize money, work, marriage, and obligations to others—nevertheless raise their children according to traditional moral precepts. These parents (slightly over 40 percent of the sample) are just about as likely as traditionalist parents to teach children that duty comes before pleasure, that sex outside of marriage is wrong, that "my country right or wrong" is the proper attitude.

Are such parents hypocritical? Perhaps. Even if they are, the question is why. I see them as hedging their bets. Uncertain and confused about the full import of their own values, they fall back upon simpler, less individualistic, less *ad hoc* principles—values that exist, as it were, "out there": patriotism, duty, sexual fidelity.

Such parents have not yet made a whole piece of their lives or their principles. Up to now, they have neglected to think through whether the behavior that they consider morally right for themselves as adults—setting personal choices above socially approved ways of life—creates a sound moral world for their children. In their preoccupation with self, they have not devoted the time and energy to wrestle with the question, What kind of social world, what range of individual choices, provides children with healthy security and healthy freedom?

To a member of the Moral Majority, the issue of the moral care and feeding of the young is quite clear. The country is too permissive. This freedom to sin is seen in television programs that sport as their main attraction the exploits of provocatively clothed young women; in legislation that gives women the right to abort fetuses and thus (from this point of view) go through life without accepting responsibility for their sexual conduct; in the willingness of many people to allow homosexuals to teach in schools. To a large portion of the American population, these examples are instances in which people are expressing choices about how to live their lives. But to the Moral Majority, they represent instances in which society unblinkingly allows people to make the wrong choices, even encourages such choices; the very existence of these choices in the public realm creates immorality.

This firm and unquestioned view is integral to the program of the Moral Majority. Briefly, it opposes abortion, busing, the Equal Rights Amendment, homosexuality, pornography, premarital sex, easy divorce; and it supports prayer in schools, community censorship of textbooks, capital punishment, military superiority over the Soviet Union, a strong and traditional family. All of these varied positions express the core of the Moral Majority's conservatism—an explicit rejection of what it calls "secular humanism," the tradition of modernism that promotes the individual, pluralism, tolerance, and skepticism toward the authority of government and other institutions.

Like all conservative movements, the Moral Majority seeks to strengthen authority, especially the authority of parents over their children. Thus it supports Senator Paul Laxalt's Family Protection Act, which would exclude all forms of corporal punishment from child-abuse laws, give parents the right to censor textbooks and local school boards the right to prevent boys and girls from participating in sports together. Falwell was quoted in a *New York Times* article on children's rights as follows: "I believe that children should be subservient to their parents. Children have the right to expect their parents to love them and to give them the correct discipline to develop their character. They have the right to be punished properly when they do wrong but never to be abused."

Given all this, how could the majority of parents, people who want their lives to be based on choice and want the same for their children, conceivably find any common ground with the Moral Majority? The answer lies in the intrinsically uneasy tension between the activists in any social movement and its broader constituency. It is in the nature of a social movement that many people can align themselves with it without supporting the full range of its program.

One example is the student movement during the war in Vietnam. Its activists largely held a New Left orientation. But at no time were more than 10 percent of all college students sympathetic to its overall viewpoint, despite the fact that the vast majority of students were against the war. As soon as the war ended, differences surfaced and the movement disappeared.

The women's movement offers a different example. Among the militant activists have been women who despise the traditional role of women as "mere" wives and mothers. But most women are not opposed in principle to that choice. Their objective is simply to expand their range of choices. The interests of the activists and the general constituency are hardly congruent, they overlap only at the edges; but it is on the basis of this overlap that the women's movement has become one of the most influential of our time.

As with both these movements, so with the Moral Majority. In my view, its program overlaps only to a small degree with the broad social concerns of many of its sympathizers. The resonant issue that forges the link between them is the social climate within which children perforce must grow up. I believe this issue, in a qualified form, also gives credibility to the Moral Majority among many people who shun the idea of identifying with the style of a Jerry Falwell and certainly oppose any efforts to restrict their own freedom.

Whether the Moral Majority goes the way of the New Left after the war in Vietnam or the way of the women's movement depends on two contingencies.

The first is the fate of the economy. If we have a severe and prolonged economic setback, which I do not think will happen, then the Moral Majority will grow stronger. We should remember that there is a deep-rooted American tradition of blaming economic setbacks on failures of moral rectitude. Historian Robert Wiebe recounts the many periods of soul-searching that coincided with recessions in 19th-century America. "Throughout the 19th century a great many looked upon economic downturns as moral judgment, precise punishment for the nation's sins." Not far below the surface of Americans' consciousness there lingers the conviction that today's inflation and other economic ills can be traced to the nation's moral looseness. If, throughout the 1980s, the economy shows moderate health, the Moral Majority will lose one of its least visible but most powerful supports.

The second contingency is what happens to the concern about the moral welfare of young people. If there is polarization at the extremes—total permissiveness versus total restrictiveness—then I believe the restrictive extreme will prevail. When people sense that a situation is out of control, the temptation to fall back on restrictive measures grows overwhelming. If the only voices expressing concern about and offering programs of action to improve the moral climate for children come from the cultural right, those voices will set the agenda. But if a moderate middle ground can be found, the Moral Majority will go the way of the New Left and shrink back to become one of the many minor ideological movements on the fringes of American life.

For such a middle ground we need new thinking about the influences that affect the moral development of children. We need to confront the possibility that adults who now live a life of choice while keeping their own moral center intact are capable of doing so because their upbringing instilled in them a clear sense of right and wrong. We need to recognize that we have been neglecting the question, broadly put, of what is best for our chidren because we have been too busy with the question of what is best for us as adults, assuming—all too comfortably—that the same answer would do for both questions. It will not. A continuing failure to face this reality will serve to strengthen the Moral Majority.

# Alco Beverage Company and Moderation Advertising

*Moderation is essential to the enjoyment of everything.*

—Ralph Waldo Emerson

At 6:00 on a Monday morning in August 1986, Edward Phillips struggled to finish the last mile of his daily six-mile run around Minneapolis' Lake Calhoun and Lake of the Isles. Despite the exercise, Phillips was tense. As president of Alco Beverage Company, Phillips knew that he and his top executives faced some difficult decisions today.

There was no doubt about it: Americans were consuming less beverage alcohol. Increased alcohol taxes, social pressure and nationwide concern about driving under the influence were part of the national trend toward moderation in drinking—a trend likely to continue in the short term. The company had a profitable record with Alco Standard, but the reality of reduced consumption demanded a fresh strategy to accomplish several objectives: maintain record sales and increased earnings, gain market share in key product categories, maintain Phillips' high return on capital, *and* continue to promote responsible alcohol consumption with the company's moderation campaign.

Still sweating from the run, Edward Phillips knew in his heart that while the company must keep its advertising fresh, eye-catching and unique, responsible consumption was fundamental to the image he wanted for the company. Should the company continue the campaign per se, try variations on the central theme, or had the moderation concept run its course?

## THE EARLY DAYS

Back in 1912, Jay Phillips and his father, the late Ed Phillips, opened a wholesale distributorship for out-of-town newspapers and began what was to become a very successful enterprise—Ed. Phillips & Sons Company. Within two years, the Phillips company expanded to include cigars, tobacco, candies, and specialties. By 1918, Ed. Phillips & Sons Company had become a full-line distributing house for leading brands. The delivery system consisted of one truck.

Making customer goodwill the primary

goal, in 1920 the Phillips family decided to align with suppliers who had strong brand-building programs, and developed merchandising techniques that would augment their suppliers' efforts and provide goods profitably to retailers and value to consumers. The early days of the Phillips company witnessed important changes in the way products were merchandised—from bulk to brand and from cracker barrel to labeled package. This dawn of the era of intense brand merchandising introduced such giants as Coca Cola, Camel, Chesterfield, Wrigley, and Hershey. The young Phillips company hitched its wagon to these stars-to-be. Committed to the policy of never compromising quality for price, and building brands and brand loyalty, Phillips made steady progress with known brands, good service, and increased profits for its customers.

Between 1920 and 1930, the company expanded its markets in Wisconsin and Minnesota and opened several distributing houses. Headquartered in Minneapolis, Minnesota, the company devoted significant time to the training of a new sales force and the cultivation of an expanding retail clientele. By 1930, the company had achieved its goal: it had a well-trained organization, good relationships with suppliers, and the confidence of its retailers as their favored distributor of nationally known brands of quality. The company had quickly become a sought-after distributorship. Customer goodwill remained the primary goal of all of its business relationships.

## THE REPEAL OF PROHIBITION

During the 1930s, Ed. Phillips & Sons Company continued its expansion, consolidated its position, and strengthened its belief that strong national brands could withstand the economic upheaval of the Depression. Suppliers who carried nationally known brands looked for progressive and well-organized distributorships, and retailers found that nationally recognized brands could survive economic hard times.

With the repeal of the 18th Amendment and the end of Prohibition, the company found a further possibility for expanding its distributorships. The renewed alcoholic beverage business made it an attractive distribution channel. As Jay Phillips recounted:

> A majority of our customers were venturing into the liquor business as retailers and were urging us, as their prime supplier, to broaden the scope of our activities to include alcoholic beverages and increase the extent of the services which we were rendering to them.
>
> I knew nothing about liquor. I knew nothing about the quality of liquor and, as everyone now knows, there were no established brands to speak of. Many were entering the wholesale liquor distributing business, but it was purely a question of hit or miss. On the other hand, here was a consumer item that offered tremendous marketing opportunity.

Alcoholic beverages were rushed to market to satisfy the new national demand. Given the company's history of doing business with only those firms who carried nationally advertised and accepted brands, it set out to associate with those it saw as well-established firms in the distilling industry. The company continued to distribute candies, tobacco, and specialty items in Wisconsin, while the expanding distributorships focused on beverage alcohol. In 1933, one of the company's first beverage alcohol suppliers was Hiram Walker. Several years later National Distillers came on board and "Phillips-land" has consistently been that company's best market. Bacardi Importers, Brown Forman, Canadaigua, Heublein, Paddington Corporation (J & B Scotch), Seagrams—Phillips became a "who's who" of beverage alcohol staples.

In 1937, Ed. Phillips & Sons began its own bottling operation, producing distilled spirits under its own proprietary labels and bottling wine for such companies as Italian Swiss Colony. This production division acted as a "blocking back" in support of its nationally distributed brands and helped minimize the infusion of "private labels" in the Phillips market.

During World War II, many suppliers were unable to support the product needs of their distributors—especially cordials. The company reacted by expanding its own product line—"THE PHILLIPS FAMILY OF FINE SPIRITS."

## GROWTH AND SUCCESS

The geographic dimensions of the company continued to expand with the acquisition of companies in its state of origin—Wisconsin—as well as North Dakota, Nebraska, Colorado, and New Mexico. Each distributing company became a local enterprise directed by local residents. With a pledge of responsibility to its customers and to the communities it served, the company made long-term commitments to assure a continued supply for its markets. Nationally advertised brands of merchandise were always available to the retailer—as well as service, advantageous buying conditions, merchandising assistance and support in both trade and public relations. Phillips sought to assure not only consumer satisfaction, but maximum turnover with maximum profits for retailers.

The company eventually became the largest independent wine and spirits distribution organization in the country. On the occasion of its 50th anniversary, Jay Phillips underscored the key to the company's long-standing success:

> The key to our future as a business institution is to keep our company focused on people—on our customers, our employees, and our suppliers. In other words, our starting point is with people whose needs and desires we think we can satisfy in a way that is helpful and profitable to them as well as to Ed. Phillips & Sons. This is what built our business and is what will continue to make it grow.

In 1964, Jay Phillips' son, Morton, became president of the company and Jay Phillips became chairman of the board. The Phillips Foundation owned more than 50% of the company and the 1968 Tax Reform Act mandated divestiture. While investigating a public offer-

ing, the family was introduced to Alco Standard, an emerging conglomerate known as "The Corporate Partnership." Alco's commitment of operating autonomy and a perpetuation of Ed. Phillips & Sons' corporate culture was pivotal to the decision to sell—which was accomplished in September 1971 (see Exhibits 1 and 2).

Edward Phillips, Morton's son, joined the company in 1973 and became president in 1975 at the age of 30. He describes this succession as the "acid test" of Alco's commitment to family management. Fifteen years after joining Alco, Edward Phillips recounted laughingly, his associates were still waiting for changes to occur! "The beauty of Alco," said Phillips, "is its ability to protect the sanctity of the original corporate culture while overlaying a strong pride in Alco and its culture."

## A NEW LAW FOR MINNESOTA—1973

Although balanced through multiple markets and Phillips' own products, the Minnesota operation continued to be the largest in terms of sales and profits. It was a full-service wine and spirits wholesaler, selling to retail stores, hotels, and restaurants. As a full-service organization, the company hired and trained its own sales force and added value by helping its customers with merchandising, product information, display advice and services, credit, and inventory management.

In 1973, the Minnesota legislature introduced the Liquor Reform Act, which dramatically altered the distribution of alcoholic beverages. Minnesota would be the first and only state in the U.S. to disenfranchise beverage alcohol distributors. The new law required suppliers to provide all wholesalers and distributors of spirits with the same products, on an equal basis. This forced intrabrand competition and intrabrand distribution. The Reform Act was based on the 21st Amendment, which gave states extraordinary power to regulate the distribution and sale of alcoholic beverages.

The new law had tremendous significance

for the company. It meant loss of exclusivity in Minnesota, its largest market. Howard Karon, executive vice president of Alco Beverage, described the company's response:

> We were shocked, how could this happen? Never in the history of the industry had companies that spent years and years building brands with a huge investment of time and effort been disenfranchised and suddenly told by law that you no longer have the brands that you've built; that anyone could have them, anyone could start up in the business; anyone could get a license. We were good, solid citizens of this community. We saw ourselves as responsible, caring business people who contributed to and supported everything good in the community.

Edward Phillips saw this as more than a legislative defeat:

> Clearly, we were victims of the "image" of our industry which had never fully shed its Prohibition trappings in the public eye. Exclusive franchises were very much the norm in consumer products; yet the media painted these exclusive franchises as "brand monopolies" and for sake of brevity, simply "monopolies."

The industry fought the law in court, but to no avail. In 1975, the Liquor Reform Act was finally judged to be legal as the U.S. Supreme Court denied *certiorari* (i.e., refused to review the case as decided by the Court of Appeals). The result for the company was loss of market position and the potential end of brand promotion. While the industry had always been highly competitive, the Liquor Reform Act forced distributors in Minnesota to compete for the *same* bottle of liquor. Said Karon:

> The loss of exclusivity resulted in price wars and totally eliminated our profit for about two years. We lost a tremendous amount of money and retailers couldn't wait to meet each other with their new lower prices.

Four major distributors closed because they could not compete in this new environment. Alco Beverage weathered the storm, due

in part to its affiliates outside Minnesota, its exclusive hold on the Phillips label, and the fact that the new legislation did not apply to wine distribution.

The Liquor Reform Act added one more constraint to an already highly regulated industry: consumption laws, selling laws, advertising laws, and distribution channel laws; laws pertaining to driving while intoxicated and a minimum distance of retailers from schools and churches; no advertising of distilled spirits on radio or television; limitations against producers owning wholesalers and wholesalers owning retailers. The result was a mixture of state and federal regulations and laws, some dating back to 1934.

## MODERATION ADVERTISING

Toward the end of 1975, the company gathered off-site for purposes of strategic planning. Once again, "industry image" was identified as both a weakness and a threat.

"We resolved," recalled Phillips, "that although the image of our industry and company was unfounded and unfair, we could either continue to feel sorry for ourselves or actually seek to change this common misperception."

He argued that the Liquor Reform Act was a reflection of the public's image of the beverage alcohol industry, a negative image that had origins in the early days of Prohibition. Howard Karon described that image, often portrayed by the press, as "those less than first-class citizens who made their living on liquor—an industry with a lack of concern for who used its products and in what quantities." With the entire industry mired in advertising sameness, best described as "bottle and glass" and "lifestyle" themes, the company chose to differentiate itself through public relations.

Edward Phillips formulated the strategy: "As the largest regional producer of distilled spirits in the U.S., our products should only be used in moderation and with responsibility." He added, "We are seeking the moderate use of our products by our consumers, with the full understanding that this may mean a reduction in sales. Someone in the liquor industry should take a responsible stand on the issue of moderation." He convinced his own management that regardless of whether the negative image was deserved, the responsibility to foster change rested with their company:

> The Phillips family represents four generations of dependable and responsible business conduct. This is the reason we underwrite this moderation campaign with pride and confidence that it will be read and respected. Healthy enjoyment of our products is our objective.

The company's first moderation message (Exhibit 3) was largely autobiographical and reflected the real concerns shared by Edward Phillips and his executive team.

The advertising campaign—drink in moderation—was based on the assumption that alcohol abuse was a "people" problem, not a "product" problem. The company recognized the importance of credibility in this new venture and actively solicited the advice of experts in the field of alcoholism such as Harvard's Norman Zinberg. "Ain't Charlie a Scream?" (Exhibit 4) reflected Dr. Zinberg's conclusions that during periods of peak alcohol-related problems in history, a double standard of behavior was socially condoned.

"The Birds and the Bees . . . and Booze" (Exhibit 5) was based upon Dr. Zinberg's conviction that education about the proper role of alcohol in a person's life was a parental responsibility which must be addressed. Treating drinking as a forbidden subject, he believed, only heightened emotionalism and misunderstanding.

"Our objective," said Phillips, "is responsibility; we feel much can be gained by conditioning the linkage of *enjoyment* of beverage alcohol to *moderation*." The company carefully defined "the right not to drink" as a proper alternative to moderate consumption. Karon added: "We want to build a business with those people who can properly use our product and add somehow to their life or to their social well-being."

The company sought to introduce this new image to the public, the media, opinion leaders and elected officials. Edward Phillips traveled and talked—representing his industry on radio and television shows, establishing dialogue with the press, and venturing into schools and talking with students about responsible decisions."

The risks associated with the new strategy were substantial. Would friends within the retail tier be concerned? Would alcoholics and their loved ones feel that the company was making light of a serious matter? Would skeptics say that the company was only attempting to sell more products to *anyone?* Although Edward Phillips did not have answers to these questions, he was sure that there were enough threats to the industry that a more radical marketing campaign was needed.[1]

Joseph Strauss, president of Ed. Phillips & Sons, Minnesota, worked long hours during 1977, using the moderation message as a vehicle to introduce himself and the company to legislators:

> What I did for almost an entire six months was first to send out the moderation kit, through the mail, to friends of mine who were in the legislature, and just asked them for their input. What do you think about this kind of thing? Do you see it as having a significant impact on some of the issues that you are working on? How could state government use it? How could we interact with state government? Then I took the kit and literally drove the state of Minnesota from Sunday night until Saturday morning and

---

[1]Concerns included: the doubling of federal excise tax, Minnesota state tax increases, chemical dependency and drunk-driving program funding, proscription against the use of broadcast media (radio and television) to advertise malt beverages and wine, nondeductibility and advertising expenses, an increase in the legal drinking age, reduced selling hours, limitations on the number of outlets, and intoxication laws using a .5 blood alcohol level. Gallup polls in 1977 tracked the public opinion behind these threats: 81% of those surveyed reported alcohol abuse as a major national problem, 47% believed drinking could lead to the use of other drugs, 66% indicated drinking had been a cause of trouble in their family, and 19% (almost one in five) favored a return to prohibition.

called on legislators, knocking on their doors. While they were out in the farm throwing hay, I put on my old grubbies and went out there and threw hay with them and had fun and sat in their parlors and chatted and we got to know each other. I talked about the moderation campaign and what we were trying to accomplish with it by way of taking a responsible position in our industry and attempting to deal with some of these broader issues that may have been sitting there festering for some time and being ignored. The results of that were first of all that I built up personal friendships with a number of legislators. I think we also were with people who were not typically supportive of our industry. You always have the wet and dry phenomenon in the political arena.

Strauss quickly came to believe that the company was headed in the right direction:

It became very clear that some people should not consume beverage alcohol at all, and that we had an obligation to communicate that to the public. The second part of that being, that if you do consume it, there is a concomitant responsibility in the consumption of our product.

Strauss' meetings with legislators yielded more than Edward Phillips had anticipated. Ideas evolved concerning possible joint efforts by state government and the industry for dealing with social issues such as drunk driving law enforcement, age of consumption, education in grade schools and high schools, and public service messages. If the company and government worked together, from Edward Phillips' point of view, its own credibility and that of the industry would be enhanced. It was this relationship with government that helped protect the exclusivity of Phillips' own label. It also helped safeguard its wine business. Starting in 1977, alliances were established with a myriad of agencies nationally who were concerned about alcohol issues.

In a few years the company began to gain the exposure and credibility it was seeking. In Strauss' words, "We were kind of alone in the industry with a new message that people have a choice not to drink, and if that is the choice, don't pressure people in social settings to consume it."

In 1978, Alco Beverage Company was the first producer of beverage alcohol in the world to offer a friendly reminder on the front label of all of its own products: "Enjoy in Moderation." (Company officials pointed out that "the label was *not* a warning label. A warning label is essentially negative and psychological research concluded that as warning labels become more severe they become less effective.")

During the ensuing years, Phillips produced multiple print messages (see Exhibits 6 to 9), and several radio and television ads. The television messages were an industry first, as Edward Phillips explained:

In the past, various trade associations have utilized public service television time to encourage moderation, and other liquor firms have utilized magazines and newspapers with the same objective, but to my knowledge this is the first time a *producer* of distilled spirits has used television to promote moderation in the use of its own product.

In one 30-second commercial a bartender cautioned against the overuse of the product, then clearly stated: "If you have any doubt about your ability to handle alcohol, don't even start!" Produced in cooperation with various local government agencies and drug abuse organizations, the spots were furnished to local television stations at no charge, and the stations were encouraged to run them as public service announcements throughout their programming schedules.

By 1982, approximately 80% of the company's advertising budget was devoted to the moderation campaign. "A primary objective of our program," Edward Phillips said, "has been the effective positioning of our company as an ally—not an adversary—with government, private organizations, and the public."

In business, it is common to measure success by return on investment, Phillips explained:

> I am convinced the return from our investment—although difficult to immediately quantify—would satisfy the most stringent of hurdle rates. When we, as an industry, succeed in de-emotionalizing beverage alcohol, we can anticipate an environment where sales and profits will grow in a healthy manner and where we shall be perceived as aligned with—not opposed to—the common good, because moderation is the mark of maturity.

## THE EFFECTS OF MODERATION

By 1983, the national trend toward moderation was clear. Popular media were full of moderation and abstinence messages—in format similar to the themes pioneered by the company in 1976. There had been a nearly two-gallon per capita decline in beverage alcohol consumption since 1980. Beer consumption had also declined, although much less dramatically. Table wine had increased in sales, but the increase had slowed over the previous decade. To meet this increased interest in moderation in alcohol consumption, many in the industry developed beverages with reduced proof content or no alcohol at all.

Despite the trends toward lower consumption, the company continued to gain market share in 1984, particularly in wines, cordials and the proprietary Phillips product line. During 1984, the company's annual production increased from 1 million to 1.3 million cases. The company expanded its products to include alcohol-free prepared cocktail mixes, sparkling waters and de-alcoholized wine.

Increasing social pressure to reduce alcohol consumption and the rise in federal alcohol taxes (as of October 1985) were expected to keep consumption of beverage alcohol from growing in the short term. Alco Beverage Company showed satisfactory results in 1984 with $7.9 million in operating income and record sales of $225 million—a revenue increase of 26% from 1983. And they had an excellent 1985 with $9.4 million in operating income and $238 million in sales (see Exhibit 10).

It was difficult to determine what the effects of Phillips' moderation campaign had been in terms of changing the image of the beverage alcohol industry. Market research could not easily isolate the consumer impact of the company's unique approach to marketing. What Edward Phillips did know through thousands of consumer letters was that many people were buying Phillips-labeled products because of the moderation theme. Research at Michigan State University supported this perception—consumers will gravitate toward the products of companies they respect. What started out as a public relations endeavor had accomplished an advertising (sell-through) result as well.

The company continued to promote responsible drinking through its moderation ad campaign, but in 1986 considerably less than 80% of its advertising budget was allocated for this purpose. While Edward Phillips remained devoted to taking a leadership role in "social responsibility, citizenship, and self-regulation," his initial push for this campaign had been tempered by a new environment: an industry facing slower growth, intensified competition, higher prices because of higher excise taxes, and a general weakening of sales and profits from beverage alcohol.

## THE FUTURE

In preparing for Monday's long-range strategic planning session, Edward Phillips reviewed the situation. While Alco Beverage Company continued to be a profitable organization, clearly it faced the question of marketing to a new and fast-changing environment.

The future of the distilled spirits industry was in question, in view of the continued trend toward lower consumption. The moderation strategy had succeeded in differentiating the image of the company and in successfully introducing its products to new markets.

Should the moderation message fade into the background? Should the company shift the focus in some way, perhaps distributing the message at point-of-purchase or using outdoor, billboard advertising? What about establishing a direct link with the consumer through an 800 number? Edward Phillips was not at all prepared to neglect his original objective: to change the image of the industry *and* maintain the company's competitive edge. But this would not be easy, and in this new environment it would be difficult to maintain a business where the major product, beverage alcohol, continued to show declining consumption. Phillips explained:

> We are now widely recognized as the responsible marketers in our industry. All of the women and men with whom I work share a strong sense of pride in this corporate endeavor. We have been embraced as allies by many well-intentioned, effective organizations who traditionally have perceived us as adversaries. No aspect of our business excites me more.

Phillips also wondered if associated product lines would strain his marketing organization. Would he have to restructure the organization? Operate separate distribution centers? Train separate sales forces? Would costs increase? Would diversification dilute the company's image as the outstanding distributor of beverage alcohol?

# Exhibits: Alco Beverage Company and Moderation Advertising

**EXHIBIT 1**
ALCO STANDARD CORPORATION

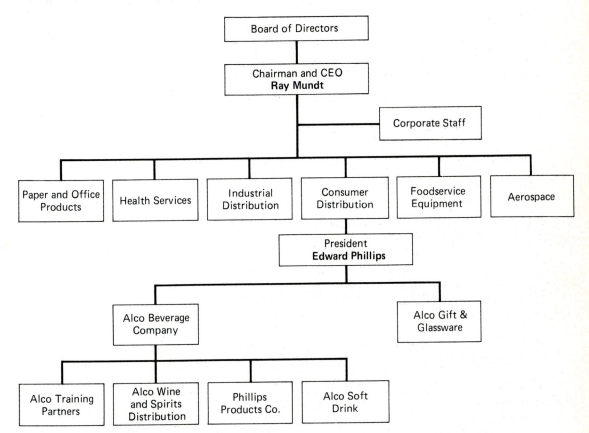

**EXHIBIT 2**
ALCO BEVERAGE COMPANY

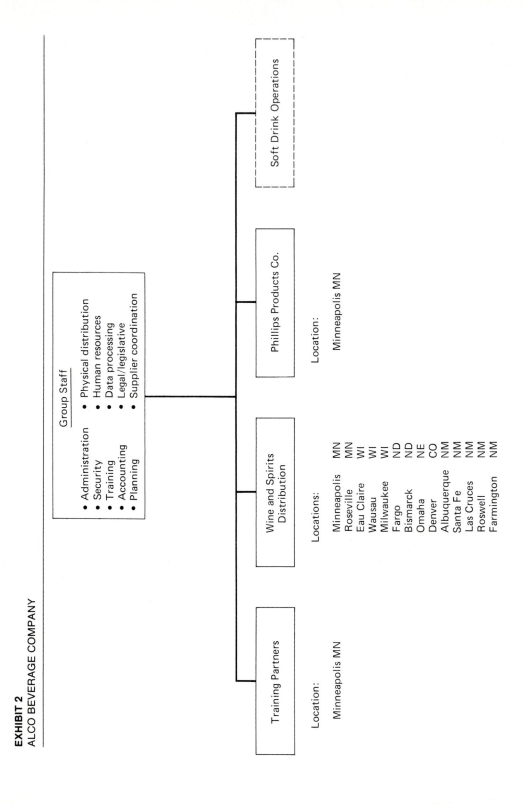

Group Staff

- Administration
- Security
- Training
- Accounting
- Planning

- Physical distribution
- Human resources
- Data processing
- Legal/legislative
- Supplier coordination

**Training Partners**

Location:

Minneapolis MN

**Wine and Spirits Distribution**

Locations:

| | |
|---|---|
| Minneapolis | MN |
| Roseville | MN |
| Eau Claire | WI |
| Wausau | WI |
| Milwaukee | WI |
| Fargo | ND |
| Bismarck | ND |
| Omaha | NE |
| Denver | CO |
| Albuquerque | NM |
| Santa Fe | NM |
| Las Cruces | NM |
| Roswell | NM |
| Farmington | NM |

**Phillips Products Co.**

Location:

Minneapolis MN

**Soft Drink Operations**

**EXHIBIT 3**
1978 PRINT AD

# DRUNKEN DRIVER KILLS TWO

## Thoughts after reading the morning paper:

It's enough to make a man want to sell his business. But then the man I sold it to wouldn't be buying it to discontinue it.

Another thought: What if everybody in the liquor business just quit selling liquor? Would that do it? Would that prevent those tragic accidents we read about almost daily?

I'm afraid not. As a matter of fact, that's been tried. It was called "Prohibition." As those of you who are old enough to remember know, it created more ills than it cured.

So what's the solution? How about educating the public on the importance of moderation in drinking?

After all, a sociable drink is a fine old American custom ... enjoyed by sensible people. It's those poor individuals who don't know when to stop who cause all the problems.

So why not educate the young people? Publicize the importance of moderate, responsible consumption.

Yes, that's the answer. That's what we'll do.

It's working already. You're reading this ad.

Get the message?

Pass it along.

If you can think of anyone who could use a little guidance on moderation, send for our booklet, "Know Your Limits." It includes the latest information on this subject, and it's free for the writing. Ed. Phillips & Sons Co., 2345 Kennedy St. N.E., Minneapolis, Minn. 55413.

**EXHIBIT 4**
1978 PRINT AD

# Ain't Charlie a scream?

The fat man with a lampshade on his head entertaining his friends and their wives may be a "scream" at a party. But the scream could turn into one of terror should good, ol' Charlie decide to drive home in that condition .

There is nothing funny about drinking too much or any kind of excess for that matter—be it with food or exercise, smoking, or exceeding the speed limit.

A poll asking people how they felt about alcohol yielded opinions ranging from *alcohol is poison,* to *the more you drink the better the party.*

Somewhere in between lies a sensible answer: moderation. **Moderation is the mark of maturity.**

Those who abuse alcohol are abusing their rights as members of a free society. And the cost of their misbehavior falls on you and me.

Fun is fun, and an occasional drink is accepted as part of the traditional American scene.

But that doesn't mean that excessive drinking gives you the right to interfere with my enjoyment of life—or to injure me for life—or to take my life.

There is a role for each of us in this battle against alcohol abuse.

That's why education on moderation is so important.

We can begin by adopting a responsible attitude toward the use of beverage alcohol and promoting that attitude among others.

We can respect the rights of abstainers and demand that respect of others if we do not drink.

We can learn and teach that there is a point in time when pleasure turns into punishment.

That's why we're offering a pamphlet, "Know Your Limits." It may be of help to you—or someone you know. Send for it today.

For free pamphlet, write Ed. Phillips & Sons Co. 2345 Kennedy St. N.E., Minneapolis, Minn. 55413

**EXHIBIT 5**
1979 PRINT AD

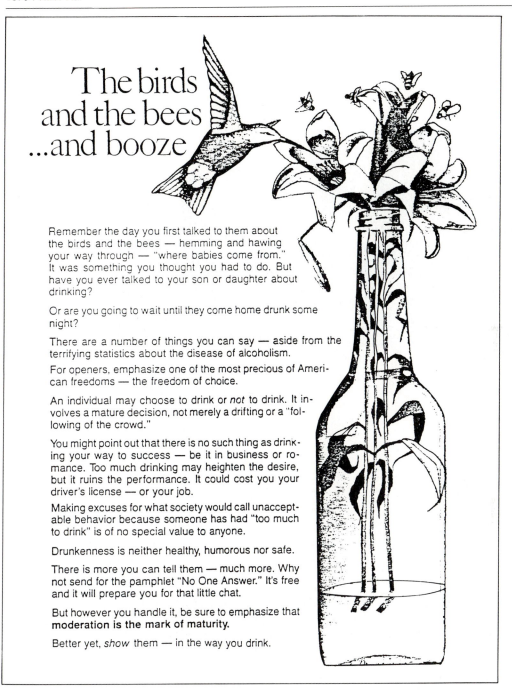

# The birds and the bees ...and booze

Remember the day you first talked to them about the birds and the bees — hemming and hawing your way through — "where babies come from." It was something you thought you had to do. But have you ever talked to your son or daughter about drinking?

Or are you going to wait until they come home drunk some night?

There are a number of things you can say — aside from the terrifying statistics about the disease of alcoholism.

For openers, emphasize one of the most precious of American freedoms — the freedom of choice.

An individual may choose to drink or *not* to drink. It involves a mature decision, not merely a drifting or a "following of the crowd."

You might point out that there is no such thing as drinking your way to success — be it in business or romance. Too much drinking may heighten the desire, but it ruins the performance. It could cost you your driver's license — or your job.

Making excuses for what society would call unacceptable behavior because someone has had "too much to drink" is of no special value to anyone.

Drunkenness is neither healthy, humorous nor safe.

There is more you can tell them — much more. Why not send for the pamphlet "No One Answer." It's free and it will prepare you for that little chat.

But however you handle it, be sure to emphasize that **moderation is the mark of maturity.**

Better yet, *show* them — in the way you drink.

**EXHIBIT 6**
1979 PRINT AD

The congenial host begins to pour the liquor: "Say when." One of the sure signs of maturity is the ability to make the right response. Some people don't know *when,* and abuse the use of alcohol. For others with special sensitivities to alcohol, the answer to *when* is *never.*

Knowing when to exercise restraint applies not only to alcohol but to how much food you consume, how much tobacco you use, how fast you drive your car, or even how hard you drive *yourself.*

When someone tries to talk you into having *just one more* and you know you have had enough, say so. The decision is yours, as are a lot of other say-when choices you make daily. If you decide to drink at all, **remember moderation is the mark of maturity.**

The pamphlet, "Know Your Limits," contains helpful information on the subject of responsible drinking. It's free, send for it today. Write Ed Phillips & Sons Co., 2345 Kennedy St., Minneapolis, Minn. 55413.

# Ed. Phillips & Sons Co.

Fine Wines and Spirits
for Four Generations

© 1979 Ed Phillips & Sons Co.

**EXHIBIT 7**
1981 PRINT AD

# A Friendly Reminder:
# Enjoy in Moderation

It may strike you as curious that one of America's largest producers and distributors of wine and spirits, Ed. Phillips & Sons Company, would be sponsoring messages to the public urging moderation in drinking.

The reason is logical: In addition to being a part of the liquor industry, we are also a part of a society that suffers gravely if the products we produce and sell are used irresponsibly.

Recent statistics* indicate that there are approximately 11 million problem drinkers in the U.S. That is roughly 5 percent of the population. In other words, there are more than 210 million Americans who are *not* alcoholics, some of whom may enjoy an occasional drink — and are *not* part of the problem.

Not everyone can drink. Not everyone should drink. The cost of excess is a burden to us all.

Some years ago we launched an educational program based on the theme, "Moderation is the mark of maturity."

And now we have added the message on the label.

The next time you're in a liquor store, look at the label on a Phillips bottle, and you'll see the friendly reminder: "Enjoy in Moderation."

*Source *Statistics on Consumption of Alcohol and on Alcoholism,* Rutger Center of Alcohol Studies — 1976

**EXHIBIT 8**
1984 PRINT AD

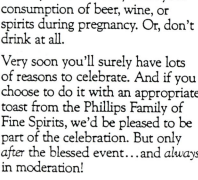
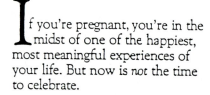

# TWO WELL-KNOWN BOTTLES

## TO BE USED ONLY AFTER THE BLESSED EVENT.

If you're pregnant, you're in the midst of one of the happiest, most meaningful experiences of your life. But now is *not* the time to celebrate.

There is a medical condition with the complex name of "fetal alcohol syndrome", which could possibly affect unborn children. While there is still a lot to learn about this condition, your physician may advise you to carefully limit your consumption of beer, wine, or spirits during pregnancy. Or, don't drink at all.

Very soon you'll surely have lots of reasons to celebrate. And if you choose to do it with an appropriate toast from the Phillips Family of Fine Spirits, we'd be pleased to be part of the celebration. But only *after* the blessed event...and *always* in moderation!

**EXHIBIT 9**
1983 PRINT AD

# A Message of Moderation from Phillips, Producer of Spirits.

## "You've gotta respect this stuff."

For years now Ed. Phillips & Sons, the nation's largest regional producer of spirits, has been telling the people of Minnesota that "moderation is the mark of maturity." We've done it in newspaper ads…public service radio spots… and through the first moderation television announcements ever produced and distributed by a liquor company.

The problem is that "moderation" can be a vague term. And with the introduction of Minnesota's new driving laws, the need to be *specific* about "moderation" becomes more important than ever. We hope this ad will help clarify the situation.

To begin with, exceeding your personal drinking limits is a function of several factors. Foremost among these are the alcohol content of the beverage being consumed, and the size of the individual. Here's a little blood alcohol percentage chart, which you may wish to clip and keep, to help explain:

| Drinks | Body Weight in Pounds | | | | | | | | |
|---|---|---|---|---|---|---|---|---|---|
| | 100 | 120 | 140 | 160 | 180 | 200 | 220 | 240 | Influenced |
| 1 | .04 | .03 | .03 | .02 | .02 | .02 | .02 | .02 | Rarely |
| 2 | .08 | .06 | .05 | .05 | .04 | .04 | .03 | .03 | |
| 3 | .11 | .09 | .08 | .07 | .06 | .06 | .05 | .05 | |
| 4 | .15 | .12 | .11 | .09 | .08 | .08 | .07 | .06 | |
| 5 | .19 | .16 | .13 | .12 | .11 | .09 | .09 | .08 | Possibly |
| 6 | .23 | .19 | .16 | .14 | .13 | .11 | .10 | .09 | |
| 7 | .26 | .22 | .19 | .16 | .15 | .13 | .12 | .11 | |
| 8 | .30 | .25 | .21 | .19 | .17 | .15 | .14 | .13 | Definitely |
| 9 | .34 | .28 | .24 | .21 | .19 | .17 | .15 | .14 | |
| 10 | .38 | .31 | .27 | .23 | .21 | .19 | .17 | .16 | |

Subtract .01% for each 40 minutes of drinking

How can you tell how much alcohol is in the beverages you consume? Here's a simple way to remember what one drink represents in the above chart:

| 1.5 oz. 80 proof spirits | = | 5 ozs. table wine | = | 12 oz. strong beer. |

Now that we've described some facts on consuming alcohol, let us give you a few tips on how *not* to consume it. When you don't feel like a drink, say so. When you're the host or hostess, don't press. If you're entertaining, we're naturally pleased when you have the Phillips Family of Fine Spirits on hand to offer your guests. But be sure to offer non-alcohol beverages, too.

And whether you're enjoying an evening with your friends at your local tavern, or you are a guest in a private home …always remember that *moderation is the mark of maturity.*

*For free reprints of this "Know Your Limits" chart, in wallet size, write to Ed Phillips & Sons, P.O. Box 1185, Minneapolis, Minn 55440*

**EXHIBIT 10**
ALCO BEVERAGE COMPANY
(in millions)

|      | Revenues | Adjusted operating income | Investment |
|------|----------|---------------------------|------------|
| 1985 | $238     | $9.4                      | 34.9%      |
| 1984 | 225      | 7.9                       | 27.2       |
| 1983 | 179      | 7.4                       | 31.2       |
| 1982 | 176      | 6.8                       | 38.6       |
| 1981 | 154      | 5.9                       | 42.7       |

*Source:* Company files.

# Background on the U.S. Beverage Alcohol Industry

The 1980s have been years of challenge for the U.S. beverage alcohol industry. Overall consumption of alcoholic beverages in the United States has declined due to various factors, especially those concerning "lifestyle" changes and intensified public concern about substance abuse. Domestic producers of alcohol products also face increasing imports, principally beer and wine, that flourished with the strong dollar and have continued to be popular even with a weaker dollar.

Lifestyle changes have been most influential in reducing alcohol consumption. Among those in the 20–40 age group, the most important consumers, health-consciousness has become a preoccupation, and this group has indicated preferences for drinks lower in calories and in alcoholic content. This change correlates with a public desire for a trim, physically fit appearance, derived from a more stringently regulated diet and consistent exercising. Substance abuse has become a focus of national attention due to a greater awareness of the effects of drug and alcohol consumption at the workplace, on the highways, and in schools.

Nevertheless, alcohol is one of man's earliest recorded discoveries, with the Babylonians referring to beer as a "gift from God" around 5,000 B.C. Wine made its first recorded appearance about 2,000 years later, and soon thereafter appeared the written recognition that differing amounts of wine or beer were required to produce intoxication. By the eighth century A.D., Arabian alchemists had created even stronger "spirits" than wine or beer. The "spirits" were produced from wine during the fermentation process, along with impurities. When the impurities were burned away, the isolated liquid was concentrated. This liquid was called, in Arabic, *al kuhul,* from which the English "alcohol" is derived. These three primary categories of alcoholic beverages—distilled "spirits," beer, and wine—are used throughout this note.

## PRODUCTS

### Distilled Spirits

The production of every distilled spirit is similar. Distillation begins with a fermented liquid in which natural sugar has been converted into alcohol through the action of selected yeasts. Some raw materials like grapes or molasses (used as the base for rum) already contain sugar before fermentation. Because it boils at a lower temperature than water, alcohol is released when the fermented liquid is boiled in a vat. The "spirit" condenses as it emerges.

A basic distinction in distilled spirits is between "neutral" and "noble" (although "white" and "brown" are also used). Neutral spirits are continuously distilled and rectified (adjusting the proof* by adding water or other liquids). They can be sold in a flavorless state or have tastes added; for example, gin distillers can inject a dose of spirits flavored with juniper berries and other herbs into the basic mixture. Neutral spirits can be produced continuously, sold as soon as they are distilled, and are readily mixable with soda or fruit juices. Gin, vodka, rum, and tequila are examples of neutral spirits.

Noble spirits, on the other hand, are not produced continuously but in batches in "pot stills." The capacity of these stills cannot be increased without damaging the quality of the product by removing too many of the distinctive properties of the grain or fruit from which it is made. Noble spirits—for example, cognac and brandy—are then carefully aged in expensive oak casks, sometimes for several years—a costly process.

The distinction between neutral and noble spirits is not absolute, however. Bourbon whiskey, for example, is continuously distilled, but because it must be made—by law—from carefully specified types of grain and then aged in oak casks, it is considered a noble drink. Rum, though sometimes aged in wood, is considered a neutral spirit.

*"Proof" (or proof spirit) is a mixture of alcohol and water, with a standard amount of alcohol; in the United States this amount is 100 proof = 50% of ethyl alcohol by volume at 60°F.

### Beer

Beer production begins with a malting process: grain is soaked, usually for about 24 hours, then heated until it begins to sprout; the grain starch turns to sugar. Water is added and the result mashed. Yeast is added and fermentation begins. The liquid is clarified and then aged, for varying periods. "Blonde" beer is malted less and has less alcohol, and the grain is used for the mash as soon as it begins to sprout. "Dark" beers are malted longer until the grain is toasted; therefore, the beer is darker and the product is usually "heavier." The alcohol content of beer ranges from 3.2% to 8%.

### Wine

Wine products are also divided into different categories. "Table" wines, the dominant category, are made from fermented fruit juice, contain no flavor additives, and have less than 16% alcohol. Several other factors distinguish these products: color, grape variety, and vintage. White, red, and rosé wines result from pressing different types of grapes; contact between the pressed juice and the grape skins and stems also changes the color of the final product.

"Dessert" wines contain added grape spirits (or grape alcohol), which raises the total alcohol content to more than 14%. These wines include port, sherry, and vermouth, and are sweeter than most table wines. "Sparkling" wines are natural wines with carbonation (a minimum of seven pounds per square inch) and an alcohol content of no more than 14%. Other special natural wines include still and carbonated wines with either less or more than 14% alcohol containing two or more fruit sources for flavoring.

## CONSUMERS AND CONSUMPTION

After the repeal of Prohibition (1933), alcohol drinking increased gradually through the remainder of that decade, the World War II period, and then sharply rose during the 1960s, when per capita consumption of all forms of alcohol increased by almost 25% (according to the reports of licensed manufacturers). In the 1970s, per capita consumption of distilled spirits began to level off, with mid-decade figures about 2.7 gallons per year for those over age 14 (1). At that time there were far more younger drinkers, in part due to many states' lowering the drinking age, but also because there was more illegal drinking among teenagers. Market studies showed that young people provided most of the new business (2).

Consumption of distilled spirits per adult peaked at three gallons in 1978 and has been on a steady decline since then (3). Wine consumption, however, sharply rose during the 1970s: wine shipments increased 37%, greater than any other beverage alcohol category. Beer, traditionally the largest single source of alcohol intake in this country, showed increased consumption during the 1960s and 1970s as well, but it rose more slowly in comparison to wine and distilled spirits. Although beer is considered a moderate* drink, more than half of total beer sales were to a small minority of heavy drinkers.

Looking at the consumption patterns for all alcoholic beverages, then, Americans were drinking less heavily in the 1970s as compared to the 1960s, but the 1970s showed an increase in the number of light drinkers.

By the 1980s, however, the U.S. beverage alcohol industry faced a shrinking market. *Impact,* a trade association publication, estimates that the total distilled spirits market, at 434 million gallons of production by 1984, will drop to 401 million gallons by 1990 and to 370 million gallons by 2000 (see Exhibit 1 for distribution and market share information). According to DISCUS, a Washington-based trade association representing major distillers, domestic beer consumption dropped slightly in 1984 after two flat years. Domestic brewers suffered their first slump since 1957.

Wine's growth rate, which had accelerated since the 1970s, also slowed. Only consumption of wine and imported beer is up. Further,

Americans are spending less of their income on beverage alcohol: they currently spend about 1%, as compared with 2.5% during the 1970s and 3.25% during the 1960s (4). Exhibit 2 shows consumption preferences for 1985.

One consuming group is increasing, however, and is expected to continue to grow: women. *Impact* projects that women's purchases of alcoholic beverages will total close to $30 billion in 1994, compared to $20 billion in 1985. Studies have found that women currently purchase more distilled spirits in supermarkets, buying 57% of the gin sold, 75% of the brandy, and about 50% of the vodka (although it is not clear if they are simply buying the product and/or actually consuming it). It is estimated that 55% of all wine drinkers are women, drinking 48% of all consumed.

## ADVERTISING

According to *Beverage World's* 1986/87 Databank, the top company worldwide ranked by overall beverage sales is the Coca-Cola Company. Anheuser-Busch (Budweiser and Michelob beer products) and Philip Morris (Miller beer products) occupy the second and third positions, then followed by PepsiCo, and Seagram Company. Altogether, of the top 20 companies in *Beverage World's* list, 14 have subsidiaries in the beverage alcohol area (see Exhibit 3 for more company information).

Advertising of beverage alcohol products has increased in sophistication and quantity. Experienced marketers like Philip Morris have created "lifestyle" ads that appeal to specific audiences. Promotion and packaging currently include college campus beer representatives, dollars-off coupons, rock concert sponsorship, sports "personalities" in advertising, partial sponsorship of the Olympics; products are packaged in plastic bottles and wine comes in six-packs.

For the period 1970–1981, advertising expenditures by companies with alcohol products rose 203%; in 1981, alcohol ad budgets went beyond $1 billion for the first time. TV advertising by the wine industry jumped 30% in the first nine months of 1982, compared to 1981, while

---

*"Light" drinkers consume one or two drinks a few times per month, while "moderate" drinkers may have up to four drinks per week.

beer advertising increased 17% in the same period (5). (Exhibit 4 gives additional information on advertising expenditures.)

Various studies have explored whether increases in the amount and quality of marketing expenditures contribute to increased consumption. One study, commissioned by the Bureau of Alcohol, Tobacco, and Firearms, the Federal Trade Commission, and the Department of Transportation, concluded that advertising increases consumption by at least 10%, prompts excessive drinking, and influences the behavior of consumers—in particular, adolescents (6). Other research supports the view that there is little association between ads, alcohol consumption, and problematic outcomes (7).

Some alcohol industry representatives claim that for the most part, any relationship between increased advertising and increased consumption is coincidental. Advertising and promotion are intended, rather, to shift drinkers from one brand to another; the point is brand competition within an established market, with the purpose of advertising to appeal to existing drinkers, not to vulnerable groups like heavy drinkers or young people.

The industry has sought to maintain an image of responsibility and respectability. Trade associations representing the majority of domestic spirits, wine, and beer producers have established advertising codes, which are voluntary guidelines for ethical practices in advertising. The most widely known code restriction is the prohibition against advertising distilled spirits on television and radio. Some codes discourage appeals to children, the use of sexuality, and the exploitation of women, blacks, or ethnic groups.

DISCUS (the Distilled Spirits Council of the United States) adopted a *Code of Good Practice* in 1975, which includes the following statement: "All ads of distilled spirits shall be modest, dignified, and in good taste." The U.S. Brewers Association's *Guideline for Beer Ads* discourages appeals to overindulgence, links to dangerous or criminal activities, loss of control, using young models, and the depiction of "unkempt taverns." The Wine Institute's *Code of Advertising Standards* (1978) discourages the kind of "lifestyle ads" that are the mainstay of beer and spirits advertising: "Any attempt to suggest that wine directly contributes to success or achievement is unacceptable. . . . Wine shall not be presented as being essential to personal performance, social attainment, achievement, success, or wealth."

Federal laws and regulations pertaining to the advertising of alcohol are overseen by the Federal Trade Commission (FTC) and the Bureau of Alcohol, Tobacco, and Firearms (BATF), a division of the Treasury Department. The FTC forbids "unfair or deceptive" marketing practices but does nothing specifically related to beverage alcohol ads. The BATF regulations are more narrowly focused, prohibiting "false," "misleading," "obscene," or "indecent" statements. These federal regulations are not regularly monitored in any systematic way.

## REGULATION

As early as the seventeenth century, New England settlers were brewing beer and other fermented drinks made from pumpkins, parsnips, grapes, and currants. The distillation of molasses into rum was the most profitable manufactured article of the times, with a flourishing rum trade between New England and the Caribbean Islands.

By the eighteenth century, distilling was a frequent farming activity, as rye and corn whiskey became popular beverages. Inns and taverns became social and community centers; businessmen and shopkeepers kept barrels of rum on tap for their favorite customers; laborers were given a daily morning break for "bitters"; farmers also provided rum for their hired hands.

Drunkenness soon became a significant industrial problem, however. The country was changing from a nation of small farms and shops to one of large factories, and too much drinking caused absenteeism and poor performance on the job. It also caused social problems: many drunkards wound up in jail or in public almshouses that were soon filled beyond capacity (8). Some people considered intoxication a potential threat to law and order and contemplated prohibition as a legal solution.

In 1826, the American Temperance Union was formed, which opposed whiskey, rum, and brandy, but not beer, wine, and cider. In 1833, the U.S. Supreme Court ruled that state governments could regulate their own liquor trade; therefore, states could adopt prohibition laws if so desired. The Women's Christian Temperance Union, the first important nationwide prohibition organization, was founded in 1874, to be followed by the Anti-Saloon League of America in 1893. By 1917, as the United States entered World War I, some Americans accepted "temporary" prohibition as a measure to help the war effort (9), but many prohibitionists pushed to banish liquor nationally by constitutional amendment. And in January 1919, the National Prohibition Act (the Volstead Act) was passed by Congress, effective the following year.

This "noble experiment," as the Eighteenth Amendment was called, prohibited the manufacturing, sale, giving away, or transporting of any alcoholic beverage. In the United States at that time were 122 million people and an estimated 2 billion gallons of alcohol products consumed each year.

Prohibition created a host of unanticipated results: bootlegging, bribery of public officials, a doubling of the federal prison population in its first three years, lost liquor taxes, and the growth of organized crime. All these combined to argue for repeal, which was accomplished by Congress in 1933. It was now up to states to set their own rules concerning beverage alcohol.

In 39 states, local government makes decisions on alcohol sales issues by ballot; in the remainder, state governments have direct control. Once alcohol outlets are licensed, states may impose certain restrictions. As part of state government, Alcohol Beverage Control (ABC) agencies regulate how, when, and where alcohol can be made available, with the purpose of protecting the community's health and welfare. Six areas of state regulation are:

1 Screening license applicants to ensure they have no previous criminal record and are of "good repute" and moral character.
2 Determining who may purchase or be served alcoholic beverages. All states have a minimum drinking age, which ranges from 18 to 21; some minimum age laws restrict minors from entering licensed premises. Many states have raised the legal age to 21 in part due to recent federal laws restricting highway fund allocation.
3 Restricting the interlocking of industry interests with on-premise or retail regulations (i.e., retailers, wholesalers, and producers cannot invest or have any control over companies in another tier of the industry).
4 Imposing state excise taxes, resale price maintenance ("fair trade") statutes, or other provisions to restrict product discounting. In state-run liquor stores, retail prices are fixed for all products; in privately owned wholesale or retail outlets, state revenues come from excise taxes, sales and enforcement taxes, and fees for operating licenses.
5 Restricting the hours and days of sales.
6 Prescribing the design and location of outlets. Different states either require or prohibit the visibility of the premises from outside as a criterion for issuing a license. These policies are based on the following: (a) outside visibility may moderate drinking inside; or (b) the visibility of patrons drinking by those outside could have a corrupting influence, particularly on children. Several states require that establishments remain inaccessible to other rooms or buildings. The location of outlets can also be restricted; for example, they cannot be in proximity to schools, churches, parks, and other institutions.

### Server Liability

Many states have also instituted "server liability" laws making bar and restaurant ("on-premise") operators liable for the conduct of patrons or guests who become intoxicated in the server's establishment; such statutes currently exist in 37 states. The on-premise operators face soaring insurance rates because of increasing numbers of lawsuits filed by victims of intoxicated patrons who cause automobile accidents; their property and casualty insurance has grown tenfold or more, tripling since 1982. The suits are based on the claim that "contributory negligence" exists when a server continues to provide alcoholic beverages to someone who is already—when served—intoxicated, or who is a minor. To insurance companies this "dram shop" coverage is high-risk and therefore merits high premiums, which are then passed on to the customers.

Bar and restaurant operators argue, however, that laws concerning "obvious intoxication" are unfair and inconsistent, and that they are being singled-out. They question why liquor stores are not similarly penalized, for example. Restauranteurs claim economic ramifications as well. Their industry already operates at a significantly low profit margin, which is further strained by the trend toward less alcohol consumption; some establishments charge over $3.00 for nonalcoholic drinks and have raised menu prices 10–20% a year to bolster shrinking margins from lost liquor revenues. Increased insurance premiums only worsen their situation, they claim.

Nevertheless, the retail sector of the beverage alcohol industry has responded in several ways: it is increasingly promoting low and nonalcoholic beverages; it is providing alternative transportation for patrons; and it is using server training programs, many available from national and state trade associations.

Server intervention programs have three components:

*Training:* educational programs for those who serve alcoholic beverages, to teach them how to reduce the risk of intoxication among those served and to prevent those who are intoxicated from harming themselves and others.

*Environment:* to evaluate the interior design of the premises and its relationship to transportation facilities both public and private.

*Legal:* to become aware of state and local regulation of commercial alcohol outlets and understand what business practices must be followed; and to become familiarized with "dram shop" liability coverage and provisions (10).

### Taxation

Alcohol products are taxed at the federal level through federal excise taxes (FET), and at most state levels. The FET is not equally distributed, however, as it is based on alcohol content: distilled spirits are currently taxed at a rate nearly four times that of beer or wine. The FET was most recently raised in 1986, so that the rate for distilled spirits is currently $12.50/proof gallon, which translates to an effective 60¢ increase per 750 ml bottle. The Congressional Budget Office (CBO) has suggested further increases, to $21/proof gallon, which could raise $7.5 billion between 1986 and 1990. It also recommends doubling the FET on wine and beer, which could raise an additional $5.5 billion during the same period. Lobbyists for the American Bar Association are pushing for raising federal and state taxes on liquor and for equalizing the tax on beer and wine.

Increased taxation is based not only on the desire to increase revenues to state and federal treasuries but on a presumed correlation between price and consumption. The Miller Brewing Company, for example, has found that a 1% increase in the price of beer results in a 1% decrease in consumption. But decreased consumption could also result in lower employment at breweries, which currently employ about 42,000 people on an annual payroll of about $1.4 billion (11). Arguments for increased taxation also include the possibility of using the money to fund alcohol and drug treatment programs for minors.

## Public Interest Groups

According to the National Safety Council, approximately one-half of the 46,500 traffic deaths in 1985 were drinking-related, a statistic that has encouraged further efforts by existing public interest groups, prompted the formation of others, and in general focused public attention on issues of alcohol (and drug) abuse. Two well-known organizations are Mothers Against Drunk Driving (MADD) and Students Against Drunk Driving (SADD). These groups, and others, have lobbied vigorously for such laws as the National Minimum Drinking Act of 1984, which precludes allocation of federal highway funds to any state with a minimum legal drinking age below 21. Such groups on local and state levels have been instrumental in banning "happy hours," which offer discounted drinks at specified times, and in effecting the numerous state statutes concerning server liability.

Public interest groups were also active in congressional subcommittee hearings held in 1985 on banning radio and television advertising of beer and wine products. Producers argued that the removal of such ads would not necessarily reduce alcohol consumption and that the ban would be unconstitutional. The producers' position held, but brewers were admonished to curtail promotional efforts on college campuses. The public interest groups did, however, receive federal endorsement of counter-advertising. Such a law would require public service messages equal in time to beer and wine ads, which would warn of the dangers and consequences of alcohol abuse. The status of this proposed legislation is not certain at this time.

## THE INDUSTRY TODAY

### Distilled Spirits

Spirits manufacturers, as indicated, have carried the brunt of changing consumer tastes, and even those who maintain a preference for these products have increased their demand for varieties perceived as having a milder taste and presumably less potent effects. Hence, "white" products (gin, vodka, rum) have gained for the first time over "dark," with, in 1984, the former having a 42% market share and the latter only 39%. Spirits manufacturers were also hit by the FET rise and face further tax increases both federally and locally. Specialty liquors (premixed cocktails, brandy, cordials), however, have been increasing in market share, gaining 16% over the past six years.

Major liquor companies are diversifying, thus making an assessment of industry earnings difficult. For many companies, distilling provides a relatively stable influx or earnings and cash flow, with other operations experiencing volatility and perhaps growth. The Seagram Company, for example, derived more than two-thirds of its 1986 income from a 22.5% interest in Du Pont; National Distillers & Chemical Corporation generated nearly 80% of its 1985 profits from nonalcohol operations; Hiram Walker Resources' natural resources and gas utility businesses accounted for almost 60% of its 1985 earnings. Brown-Forman, Inc., was the last "pure" spirits and wine company until mid-1983, when it acquired Lenox, Inc., a maker of china, crystal, and other such products, which represented 15% of company profits in fiscal 1985.

It is unlikely that consumption levels for many traditional distilled spirits will rebound in the foreseeable future. Distillers, instead, will consider consolidating product lines and introducing new offerings. Hiram Walker is planning a new flavored schnapps, as an example. Seagram and Heublein are seeking a kind of low-proof designation, although others in the industry argue that changing the proof on the bottle will not put the industry back on the growth track: with fewer new drinkers and with existing drinkers consuming less, companies face a battle for market share.

### Beer

Per capita beer consumption declined 0.8% in 1985, for the fourth consecutive year, although total consumption was 0.1% higher (12). In the face of adverse social and legal pressures, the brewing companies have responded in several ways:

- Citing studies that purport to demonstrate beneficial effects of moderate alcohol consumption.
- Citing a 1985 study that contends that drunk driving is not ameliorated by raising the minimum drinking age to 21.
- Responding to the distilled spirits industry, which equates the effects of beer, wine, and hard liquor: brewers maintain that, based on chemical considerations, beer is a more "favorable" drink than distilled spirits.
- Launching advertising campaigns that advocate moderate consumption and dispensing free soft drinks to the driver of a group in a bar.
- "Building-in" moderation: Anheuser-Busch was the first to introduce a lowered alcohol content beer, named "LA."

Overall, brewers were quick to respond to consumer perceptions of health and fitness, by developing "light" beer. Public acceptance was far from instantaneous, but persistent efforts by Miller Brewing Company eventually propelled its product into the second-best-selling beer in the country. Light beers should continue to prosper in view of ongoing health and fitness concerns.

Imported beers have proven increasingly formidable competition for market share, growing 72% from 1980 to 1985, a gain that dwarfs the mere 1% growth for domestic brands and 2.9% of the total market. Upper income individuals who perceived superior quality in the imports helped drive their growth, as did a strengthened U.S. dollar.

## Wine

Wine sales increased 5.3% in 1985, the largest rise in five years, and rapid growth is projected in the premium domestic wine segment, with 10–12% increases forecast (13). A weakened U.S. dollar has helped curtail the growth of imports, a change that has of course adversely affected wine importers. In fact, the major obstacle to past domestic production increases has been the favorable performance of imported wines.

The stellar performers in the wine market, however, have been wine coolers, mixtures of wine and fruit juice whose alcohol content is approximately 50% of a typical wine. *Impact* noted that coolers currently occupy 15% of the total wine market, having experienced a 2,500% growth since 1983. The perceived wholesome character of the product has been most advantageous in a health-conscious consumer market. Some of this growth has apparently been at the expense of the table wine segment, however: in 1985, volume in that sector declined 7%, with present market share being 65%.

Favorable signs for future growth in wine sales include:

1  Increased personal income: demographic studies localize wine drinkers to higher-income categories.
2  Increased numbers in the over-40 group, who favor wine over beer.
3  Potential increase in per capita consumption: United States wine consumption is extremely low relative to other countries.
4  Preservation of wine consumption despite the possibility of more severe drunk-driving penalties: wine is consumed primarily in the home.
5  Improved exporting strategies by domestic wine manufacturers.
6  Relative price reduction compared to spirits, whose price has risen from increased federal excise taxes.

**REFERENCES**

1  "Prohibition and Its Repeal," *Brewers Digest,* December 1983, p. 14.
2  "Changing Habits in American Drinking," *Fortune* (October 1976), p. 156.
3  Ibid.

**4**   *The Economist,* December 22, 1984, p. 4.

**5**   Atkin, Charles, and Martin Block, "Content and Effect of Alcoholic Beverage Advertising," Michigan State University, 1980.

**6**   Breed, Warren, and James R. DeFoe, "Risk and Alcohol Lifestyle Advertising," *Abstracts and Reviews in Alcohol and Driving,* September 1981.

**7**   Pittman, David J., and Donald E. Strickland, "A Critical Evaluation of the Control of Consumption Policy," unpublished conference paper, September 1981. See also: Pittman and M. Dow Lambert, "Alcoholism Not Influenced by Media," *Modern Brewery Age,* January 1979.

**8**   Fleming, Alice, *Alcohol: The Delightful Poison,* New York: Delacorte Press, 1972, p. 56.

**9**   "Prohibition and Its Repeal," p. 12.

**10**   Mosher, James, "Server Intervention: Present Status and Future Prospects," Prevention Research Center, Pacific Institute for Research and Evaluation, May 1984.

**11**   Mosher, James, "New Strategies for the Prevention of Alcohol-Related Problems: Federal Regulatory and Safety Reforms." Paper presented to the American Psychological Association (August 27, 1982).

**12**   *Industry Surveys,* June 26, 1986.

**13**   Ibid.

## SPECIAL ACKNOWLEDGEMENT

The authors of this note wish to acknowledge with special emphasis the contribution of Mr. Curtis C. Christy, currently Program Director, LAST CALL, 3720 Anzo, San Francisco, CA 94121, and formerly associated with Prevention Research Center, Berkeley, CA. Mr. Christy's initiative, professional experience, and generosity were invaluable. He helped us to identify critical issues and resources on industry practices and public sector responses.

# EXHIBITS: Background on the U.S. Beverage Alcohol Industry

**EXHIBIT 1**
DISTILLED SPIRITS DISTRIBUTION AND MARKET SHARE

| Category | 1970 Million cases | 1970 % market share | 1975 Million cases | 1975 % market share | 1980 Million cases | 1980 % market share | 1981 Million cases | 1981 % market share | 1982 Million cases | 1982 % market share | 1983 Million cases | 1983 % market share | 1984 Million cases | 1984 % market share |
|---|---|---|---|---|---|---|---|---|---|---|---|---|---|---|
| Bourbon | 36 | 22.1 | 32 | 17.0 | 28 | 14.7 | 28 | 14.5 | 26 | 13.5 | 24 | 12.7 | 22 | 12.0 |
| Blends | 31 | 19.0 | 24 | 12.8 | 17 | 8.9 | 16 | 8.2 | 14 | 8.3 | 14 | 7.6 | 14 | 7.4 |
| Scotch | 22 | 13.5 | 24 | 12.8 | 20 | 10.5 | 20 | 10.5 | 19 | 10.2 | 19 | 10.3 | 17 | 9.4 |
| Canadian | 14 | 8.5 | 21 | 11.2 | 22 | 11.6 | 23 | 12.1 | 22 | 11.7 | 22 | 11.9 | 23 | 12.5 |
| Irish | * | ** | * | ** | * | ** | * | ** | * | ** | * | ** | * | ** |
| Total whiskey | 103 | 63.2 | 101 | 53.7 | 87 | 45.8 | 87 | 45.5 | 82 | 43.8 | 79 | 42.6 | 77 | 41.5 |
| Gin | 16 | 9.8 | 19 | 10.1 | 18 | 9.5 | 18 | 9.4 | 17 | 9.1 | 17 | 9.1 | 16 | 8.9 |
| Vodka | 21 | 12.9 | 37 | 19.7 | 41 | 21.6 | 41 | 21.5 | 35 | 22.5 | 42 | 22.6 | 42 | 22.6 |
| Rum | 6 | 3.7 | 8 | 4.3 | 13 | 8.8 | 13 | 6.9 | 13 | 7.3 | 14 | 7.8 | 15 | 8.0 |
| Tequila | NA | NA | 3 | 1.6 | 3 | 1.6 | 3 | 1.7 | 3 | 1.9 | 4 | 2.2 | 4 | 2.2 |
| Total white goods | 44 | 27.0 | 65 | 34.6 | 75 | 39.5 | 76 | 39.6 | 74 | 40.8 | 78 | 41.7 | 77 | 41.8 |
| Brandy | 6 | 3.7 | 6 | 3.2 | 8 | 4.2 | 8 | 4.5 | 8 | 4.7 | 9 | 5.0 | 9 | 5.1 |
| Cordials & liqueurs | NA | NA | 13 | 6.9 | 16 | 8.4 | 16 | 8.7 | 17 | 9.1 | 16 | 8.8 | 18 | 9.9 |
| Cocktails & mixed drinks | NA | NA | 2 | 1.1 | 4 | 2.1 | 3 | 1.8 | 3 | 1.7 | 3 | 1.9 | 3 | 1.7 |
| Total specialties | 16 | 9.8 | 21 | 11.2 | 28 | 14.7 | 29 | 14.9 | 28 | 15.4 | 29 | 15.7 | 30 | 16.6 |
| Total distilled spirits‡ | 163 | 100.0 | 188 | 100.0 | 190 | 100.0 | 191 | 100.0 | 183 | 100.0 | 186 | 100.0 | 185 | 100.0 |

*Less than 500,000 cases.
**Less than 0.05%.
‡Addition of columns may not agree due to rounding.
NA—Not available.
*Source: Impact* Databank. Industry Surveys, June 26, 1986.

**EXHIBIT 2**

WHAT AMERICA DRINKS
(Annual per capita consumption of beverages by type for
1985. Figures are measured in gallons.)

| | |
|---|---|
| Soft drinks | 43.3 |
| Beer | 24.8 |
| Fruit juices and drinks | 10.6 |
| Drink mixes | 5.1 |
| Bottled water | 3.8 |
| Wines | 2.4 |
| Spirits | 1.7 |

*Source:* Beverage Market Index, *Beverage World*, May 1986.

**EXHIBIT 3**

THE BEVERAGE WORLD TOP 20
(Based on overall beverage sales, these top companies worldwide are ranked according to
dollar volume. Also listed are principal beverage brands marketed.)

| Rank 1985 | Company | Sales ($000) | Principal beverage brands marketed |
|---|---|---|---|
| 1 | The Coca-Cola Company (Atlanta, GA) | 6,850,000 | Coca-Cola Classic, Coke, Cherry Coke, Sprite, Diet Sprite, Tab, Caffeine-Free Coke, Diet Coke and Tab, Fanta, Fresca, Mello Yello, Hi-C, Minute Maid, Five Alive, Bright & Early |
| 2 | Anheuser-Busch Companies, Inc. (St. Louis, MO) | 5,940,000 | Budweiser, Bud Light, Natural Light, Michelob, Michelob Light, Busch, Michelob Dark, LA, King Cobra, Carlsberg, Master Cellars, Baybry's |
| 3 | Philip Morris Companies, Inc. (New York, NY) | 3,592,000 | Miller, Lite, Lowenbrau, Milwaukee's Best, Meister Brau, Plank Road, Magnum, 7UP, Diet 7UP, Like, JuiceUp |
| 4 | PepsiCo, Inc. (Purchase, NY) | 3,128,500 | Pepsi-Cola, Diet Pepsi, Mountain Dew, Pepsi Free, Sugar Free Pepsi, Free, Slice, Diet Slice, Patio |

*(Continued)*

**EXHIBIT 3**
CONTINUED

| Rank 1985 | Company | Sales ($000) | Principal beverage brands marketed |
|---|---|---|---|
| 5 | The Seagram Company, Ltd. (Montreal, Quebec, Canada) | 2,970,000 | Seagram's, Paul Masson, Mumm's, B&G, Chivas Regal, Seagram's Cooler, Captain Morgan, Sterling Vineyards, Seagram's Mixers |
| 6 | Grand Metropolitan PLC (London, England) | 2,384,000 | J&B, Bailey's Irish Cream, Absolut, Bombay Gin, Budweiser, Watney's, Pepsi brands |
| 7 | Beatrice Companies, Inc. (Chicago, IL) | 2,200,000 | Tropicana, Arrowhead, Great Bear, Ozarka, Coca-Cola brands |
| 8 | The Stroh Brewery Company (Detroit, MI) | 1,500,000 | Stroh's, Schlitz, Schaefer, Old Milwaukee, Schlitz Malt, Old Milwaukee Light, Stroh Light, Schaefer Light |
| 9 | R. J. Reynolds Industries, Inc. (Winston-Salem, NC) | 1,400,000 | Sunkist, Canada Dry, Barrelhead, Hawaiian Punch, Del Monte, Smirnoff, Wild Turkey, Jose Cuervo, Heublein, Moosehead, Mouton Cadet |
| 10 | Guiness PLC (London, England) | 1,275,000 | Guinness Stout, Bass Ale, Harp Lager, Bell's, Kronenbourg, Furstenburg |
| 11 | John Labatt Ltd. (London, Ontario, Canada) | 1,152,000 | Labatt Blue 50 and Light, Budweiser, Canada Cooler, Everfresh, Alpenweiss, J.Z., Tree Ripe, Ssips |
| 12 | G. Helleman Brewing Company (LaCrosse, WI) | 1,129,132 | Old Style, Rainier, Blatz, Black Label, Colt 45, Red White & Blue, LaCroix, Country Cooler |

(*Continued*)

**EXHIBIT 3**
CONTINUED

| Rank 1985 | Company | Sales ($000) | Principal beverage brands marketed |
|---|---|---|---|
| 13 | Hiram Walker Resources, Ltd. (Toronto, Ontario, Canada) | 1,091,520 | Canadian Club, Kahlua, Courvoisier, Drambuie, Tia Maria, Haagen-Dazs |
| 14 | Adolph Coors Company (Golden, CO) | 1,077,880 | Coors, Coors Light, Herman Joseph's, George Killan's Irish Red, Golden Lager, Coors Extra Gold |
| 15 | McKesson Corporation (San Francisco, CA) | 1,037,084 | Ballantine's, Galliano, St. Pauli Girl, Sparkletts, Mount Gay, Emmetts, Folonari, San Miguel, Alhambra, Crystal |
| 16 | Cadbury-Schweppes PLC Ltd. Company (London, England) | 1,003,200 | Schweppes, Mott's |
| 17 | Brown-Forman, Inc. (Louisville, KY) | 904,600 | Jack Daniels, Early Times, Old Forester, Korbel, Cella, Bolla, Southern Comfort, Martell, Canadian Mist |
| 18 | General Foods Corporation (White Plains, NY) | 875,000 | Kool-Aid, Awake, Country Time, Tang, Crystal Light |
| 19 | JTL Corporation (Chattanooga, TN) | 850,000 | Coca-Cola, Dr. Pepper, Schweppes, Barq's and Sunkist brands |
| 20 | National Distillers and Chemical Corporation (New York, NY) | 680,000 | Windsor Canadian, Gilbey's, Almaden, Old Crow, Old Taylor, Old Grand-Dad, Dekuyper, Charles LeFranc, Sauza |

Source: *Beverage World*, 1986/87 Databank.

**EXHIBIT 4**

ALCOHOLIC BEVERAGE PRODUCERS AMONG THE TOP 100 LEADING
NATIONAL ADVERTISERS

| Company | Rank | 1982 ad budget (in millions) |
|---|---|---|
| Alcohol producer | | |
| Anheuser-Busch | 22 | $243.4 |
| Seagram | 44 | 150.0 |
| Brown-Forman Distillers | 76 | 74.0 |
| Stroh Brewing Co. | 90 | 55.5 |
| Hiram Walker Resources | 98 | 44.4 |
| E & J Gallo Winery | 99 | 42.9 |
| | | |
| Conglomerates and alcohol subsidiaries | | |
| R. J. Reynolds | | |
| Heublein, Inc. | 4 | $530.3 |
| Philip Morris | | |
| Miller Brewing Company | 5 | $501.7 |
| Norton Simon, Inc. | | |
| Somerset Importers | 33 | $191.2 |
| American Brands | | |
| Jim B. Beam Distilling | 78 | $72.3 |

Source: *Advertising Age,* September 8, 1983.


ALCOHOLIC BEVERAGE PRODUCERS AMONG TOP 25 ADVERTISERS
BY MEDIUM

Newspaper
  Seagram—23rd

Magazine
  Seagram—5th
  Hiram Walker—24th

Network radio
  Anheuser-Busch—13th

Spot radio
  Anheuser-Busch—1st
  Stroh—10th
  Adolph Coors Brewing—16th
  Van Munching—21st

Network TV
  Anheuser-Busch—11th

Outdoor
  Seagram—5th
  National Distillers—9th
  Hiram Walker—7th
  Brown-Forman—8th
  Anheuser-Busch—11th
  Bacardi—22nd
  G. Heileman Brewing Co.—23rd

Source: *Advertising Age,* September 8, 1983.

**EXHIBIT 4**
CONTINUED

TOP TEN BEER ADVERTISERS

| Company | 1982 ad budget (in millions)* |
|---|---|
| Anheuser-Busch | $193.9 |
| Miller (Philip Morris) | 137.9 |
| Stroh | 45.5 |
| Coors | 32.2 |
| G. Heileman | 21.9 |
| Van Munching | 21.9 |
| Olympia | 16.7 |
| Pabst | 14.3 |
| Martlet Importing | 11.0 |
| Genessee | 6.2 |

*These figures do not include nonadvertising forms of marketing, such as discount coupons, free beer parties, signs for taverns, and T-shirt sales.
*Source: Impact,* September 1983.

# Note on Product Safety

General managers readily admit today that we have entered an era of increased emphasis on safety in the design, production, and distribution of products. The problem of business's responsibility for its products and services is large in scope. According to government statistics, 20 million Americans are injured annually as a consequence of incidents involving consumer products, with 30 thousand of those killed. In addition, each year 5 million Americans are injured and 30 thousand killed as a result of automobile accidents. One safety engineer concluded: "The odds against escaping an injury at home, at work, or at the steering wheel are thus surprisingly low for the average American family of four—an injury every four years or so."[1]

Since the birth of the Industrial Revolution, a product-oriented philosophy has dictated that principles of efficiency should guide the design of industrial and consumer goods. This efficiency was reflected in lower operating expenses and lower per unit costs for finished goods. Obvious safety problems—ones impinging directly on the bottom line—were faced and many were solved. As the revolution matured, this product orientation gave way to a market orientation that "literally bombarded twentieth-century man with delights that an earlier age would have considered both miraculous and beyond the economic grasp of common people."[2] Consumers quickly grew accustomed to an economy that delivered innovative products capable of improving the buyer's lifestyle. Eventually, a conditioned public began to insist on infallibility in its products as well as availability.

The emphasis on product safety has been growing since World War II. Consumerism—a social movement that sought to augment the

[1] John Kolb and Steven S. Ross, *Product Safety and Liability* (New York: McGraw-Hill Book Company, 1980), p. 4.

[2] Ibid., p. 1.

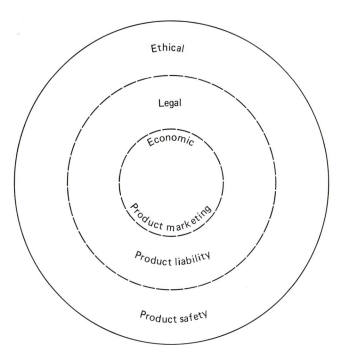

**FIGURE A**
General management's responsibilities.

rights and powers of buyers in relation to sellers—was born of a paradoxical market situation.[3] Although business had tried to pay full attention to the needs, wants, and satisfactions of its market, consumers began to raise their voices, exclaiming that business did not *care* about them. The problem in part for the general manager is philosophical: What constitutes a safe society, and what is a *safe* product for that society? While answers to such questions can be elusive, ignoring the spirit of such questions can lead to severe consequences not only for consumers but also for business and its managers.

Managing product safety requires that general management consider its economic, legal, and ethical responsibilities. As Figure A illustrates, these responsibilities are not mutually exclusive, nor are they arrayed on a continuum with economic concerns on one end and social concerns on the other. Rather, they are nested

[3]Philip Kotler,"What Consumerism Means for Marketers," *Harvard Business Review* (May–June 1972), p. 49.

domains—the economic within the legal and both of these within the ethical.

## ECONOMIC RESPONSIBILITIES

Business is expected to deliver desired goods and services at a profit. Although consumers usually accept some degree of risk with products they find necessary, most buyers assume that companies will be prudent in the design, production, and distribution of their products. While business can employ specialists (risk managers, insurers, lawyers) to weigh product risks against rewards (consumer benefit), it is the general manager who is held accountable. But the competitive dynamics of the "invisible hand" can often create tensions for general managers in the area of product safety.

## LEGAL RESPONSIBILITIES

Society expects business to operate within the laws and regulations society has laid down. Courts have moved toward a doctrine of strict liability, holding manufacturers responsible for any product defects that result in injury. Plaintiffs no longer need to prove manufacturer negligence to win a personal injury case. Increasingly, the courts and the regulatory agencies are placing the blame for corporate lawbreaking on the top manager, who is being held personally responsible and even jailed. The doctrine of "vicarious liability" holds that it is irrelevant whether the executive was directly involved in the illegal activity or whether he or she was simply informed of such activity. A "responsible manager" cannot always count on a corporate shield of protection. Nevertheless, this sue syndrome and the increasing frequency and size of court-ordered awards result in skyrocketing premiums for product liability insurance. *Caveat venditor* (let the seller beware) is replacing the old adage *caveat emptor* (let the buyer beware) as a watchword for business. Public policy, through the promulgation of numerous regulations, codifies many of management's responsibilities for product safety. In a world of rapidly emerging technologies, however, the "hand of government" does not always provide relevant guidance to the general manager.

## ETHICAL RESPONSIBILITIES

Society has expectations of business that transcend economic and legal requirements. Ethical responsibilities are difficult to define and consequently difficult for business to deal with. When the economic and political systems fail to provide guidance on product safety, however, the "hand of management" must fill the void.

Corporations have increasingly recognized the importance of social issues to their performance and success. At the same time, awareness of management's multidimensional responsibilities has not always been translated into meaningful action. A first step for managers who must deal with product safety controversies is to develop a philosophy to guide their future actions. As Figure B illustrates, companies that have been involved in product safety controversies can pass through several phases of social response.

Lacking adequate information and time for a complete analysis of the situation, managers must rapidly formulate some kind of public *reaction* in response to allegations that one of its products is not safe. If both the company and its critics believe there is time to discuss the safety controversy, a more thorough resolution is likely. This is seldom the case, however, especially when the public perceives a clear and present danger. When overwhelmed by public scrutiny and media attention, many business organizations—believing they have been unfairly attacked—will recoil in *defense*. The product safety crisis still remains in the public eye, however, thus further tarnishing the

**FIGURE B**
Corporate social response phases. (*Source:* Adapted from Archie B. Carroll, "A Three-Dimensional Conceptual Model of Corporate Performance," *Academy of Management Review,* vol. 4, no. 4., 1977, p. 502.)

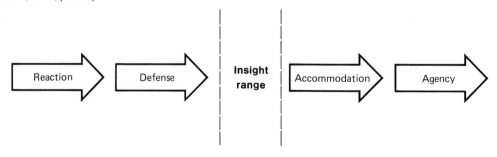

company's reputation. The *insight range* represents the most agonizing moment in the controversy. At this point, the company's stakes can be enormous and may involve its very survival. Management must remodel the situation in light of pressing external forces. *Accommodation* might consist of two different options: the company, still believing in its product, should refute the charges, if it can, that its product is not safe; otherwise, it must postpone its defense and withdraw the product to ameliorate public anxiety. *Agency* will involve actively researching the causes of the safety problem and then an education program to comfort or warn the public about the safety of the product in question.

A comprehensive understanding of the behavior of companies entangled in product safety controversies can help other general managers assess their own responsibilities and options. A company's social response strategy, if properly selected, can help it anticipate and confront difficult situations. Its reputation and future prosperity may hinge on its ability to gain insight into, and deal with, such crises.

The practical and philosophical issues raised in product safety controversies are profound. From a practical viewpoint, the management student is challenged to evaluate and compare specific responses to each product safety controversy. From a philosophical viewpoint, it is worth noting that the challenges involve more than product and safety considerations. In many ways, these issues cut to the core of the relationship between organizations and society. Goods and services of all kinds affect the physical and mental health of people both inside and outside the corporation. Safety is an issue that has both highly visible and subtle influences on the well-being of the community. The relationship among economic, legal, and ethical reasoning in the mind of an agent (either an individual or an organization) can become stressful as a particular controversy unfolds. Understanding how each crisis is handled sheds light on the values and beliefs that guide individuals and organizations involved in business activity. Although risk is inevitable in a society that considers innovation its economic bread and butter, the educated executive will be pressed to carefully balance the rewards of technology with the responsibilities of general management.

# Managing Product Safety: The McDonnell Douglas DC-10

On Thursday, March 21, 1974, John Brizendine, president of the Douglas Division of McDonnell Douglas, was handed a copy of *The New York Times* and carefully read the front page article under the headline "DC-10 MAKER BALKED AT A SAFETY ANALYSIS." This article, coming in the wake of a Turkish Airlines DC-10 crash, would undoubtedly add to the controversy that had surrounded the company's recently introduced jumbo jet.

The newspaper article, which cited company and government documents, suggested that the world's worst air disaster might have been avoided had McDonnell Douglas been more attentive to safety issues. Allegedly, the company had been unwilling to finance a study of new safety measures aimed at preventing the type of explosive decompression that most experts believed caused the DC-10 crash. All 346 aboard the Turkish Airlines jet were killed when it plunged into a forest shortly after takeoff from Paris on March 3, 1974. The recovery

of a cargo door—six miles from the airplane's point of impact—had reminded many aviation experts of a June 1972 emergency landing involving an American Airlines DC-10.

In this last-mentioned incident, the plane was in a climb over Windsor, Ontario when the rear cargo door flew off. The sudden loss of pressure in the cargo hold caused the rear floor of the pressurized passenger cabin to collapse, rupturing or jamming vital control cables from the cockpit to the plane's tail. A government investigation resulted in service bulletins being sent to DC-10 users that "recommended" improvements to the cargo-door latching mechanism. Federal aviation officials had been considering a number of additional changes to the door and had sought industry cooperation in further safety studies.

The tragedy of the DC-10 crash and the subsequent publicity that questioned the safety of the aircraft were viewed with grave concern by the company. McDonnell Douglas, like its competitors in the commercial aircraft industry, remained intimately involved with its products long after they had left the plant. It was alarming for the company to learn that one of its machines had become an occasion for so many deaths. And an airline crash was inevitably bad for business, particularly if the failure that caused it turned out to be mechanical rather than human. There would likely be massive publicity, recrimination, costly lawsuits and the possibility of expensive aircraft modification.

McDonnell Douglas believed speculation about the cause of the Paris crash was premature, since aviation investigators still had a great deal of evidence to examine before concluding their accident report. While the company was deeply concerned about the separation of the cargo door from the Turkish Airlines DC-10, it felt that earlier modifications—prompted by the Windsor incident—had made the latching mechanism safe. Government-approved changes in the locking system had been incorporated in all DC-10s used in commercial aviation. The company believed its plane, which had never been involved in a fatal accident, was "as safe as any aircraft flying."[1] By March 1974, the plane had "flown an estimated 45 million passengers nearly 54 billion passenger miles since the first aircraft entered service in August 1971."[2] The company believed that press accounts suggesting it could have prevented the tragedy were "irresponsible and malicious."[3] The air disaster, and the ongoing investigation of the crash, could play a large role in shaping the destiny of the company. McDonnell Douglas was pinning its hopes for prosperity on the DC-10 jumbo jet.

McDonnell Douglas maintained a cooperative relationship with federal aviation officials. The Federal Aviation Administration (FAA)—a regulatory agency in the U.S. Department of Transportation—was charged with oversight of commercial and general aviation and the public right of freedom of transportation through navigable air space. By act of Congress, the FAA had the dual responsibility to regulate the safety standards of American aviation and to promote its commercial success. All certifications and registrations of aircraft, as well as the prescription of safety rules and regulations, were under FAA control. The agency depended on manufacturers to cooperate with it on a voluntary basis and to bring forth any information which they thought was important for the safety of their aircraft designs. Since the FAA had neither the money nor the manpower to supervise its own comprehensive compliance program, it had to rely on "Designated Engineering Representatives" (DERs)—company engineers appointed, trained, and supervised by the FAA—to monitor compliance with government-mandated design specifications. Despite this heavy reliance on self-policing, there was a perception in aviation circles that the DERs were doing an adequate job.[4]

The National Transportation Safety Board (NTSB)—an investigatory agency in the U.S. Department of Transportation—was responsible for reviewing aircraft accidents and forwarding its recommendations to the FAA, which would then decide whether or not to act upon them. Relations between the FAA and the NTSB had recently deteriorated. Safety recommendations—usually carried out expeditiously—were now being turned down by the FAA. By 1972, the two agencies, which were supposed to be cooperative and complement each other's activities, were engaged in a public feud over the standards for airliner safety.[5] NTSB, apparently preoccupied with political attacks on its work, had been unaware that its recommendations relating to the DC-10 Windsor accident were largely disregarded. Nevertheless, many FAA officials had nagging con-

[1]McDonnell Douglas Corporation, *DC-10 Fact Sheet on Air Safety,* St. Louis, March 21, 1974, p. 1.
[2]Ibid., p. 1.
[3]McDonnell Douglas Corporation, *Press Release,* St. Louis, March 21, 1974, p. 1.

[4]"U.S. Safeguards Faulted As Plane Accidents Rise," *New York Times,* 19 June 1980, p. 1.
[5]Frank Burnham, *Cleared to Land—The FAA Story* (Fallbrook, California: Aero Publishers, Inc., 1977), p. 70.

cerns about the DC-10's cargo door and had been pressing jumbo jet builders to modify their designs.[6]

Despite the blitz of media attention and the fusillade of liability suits, the company was determined to defend the reputation of its airplane and the integrity of its organization. The company knew it would have to be prepared to answer questions about how it had dealt with the DC-10 cargo door following the Windsor incident. Congressional hearings had been scheduled for the coming weeks to investigate the actions of the FAA and McDonnell Douglas in light of the recent tragedy.

## COMPETITIVE ENVIRONMENT

The market for U.S. commercial aircraft had reached $5 billion a year by the early 1970s. The aircraft industry included three big plane makers that controlled most of American commercial manufacturing: Boeing (41% market share), McDonnell Douglas (27%) and Lockheed (20%). While all three manufacturers had relied heavily on defense contracts for their business during the Vietnam War, there had been a renewed interest in commercial aircraft as a result of new jet technologies and unprecedented demand for commercial air transportation. Aircraft orders were taken years in advance of actual delivery and usually resulted from aggressive marketing campaigns and complex sales agreements.

Competition in this industry could be fierce. All three companies were constantly seeking government contracts that would ensure a long-term earnings base and the opportunity to develop more advanced aerospace technologies. Government contracts were attractive because they operated on a "pay as you go" basis. This allowed each of the companies to avoid the risk of massive financial exposure that was required by the long period of time it took to develop commercial passenger aircraft.

In the mid-1960s, the development of a large military transport plane provided the technology that was to herald the age of the jumbo jet.

McDonnell Douglas was created in 1967 by a merger of Douglas Aircraft (an "unbankable" commercial aircraft company) and McDonnell Aircraft (a cash-rich military contractor). Although James McDonnell took over the management of the company, most Douglas Aircraft employees were retained to design and build the company's commercial airplanes. Since its founding in 1920, technological caution had always been part of the Douglas company's philosophy: "Be not the first by whom the new are tried, nor yet the last to lay the old aside."[7] McDonnell Douglas, which ranked 54th (in sales) on the 1974 *Fortune* 500 list of largest U.S. industrial corporations, believed it was the premier builder of commercial aircraft because it maintained a balance between traditional and innovative airplane design.

By the time the merger was consummated, the jumbo jet age had already begun. Boeing, thinking big, was the first to develop the new generation of passenger aircraft and had already committed most of its corporate resources to a four-engine 747 that could carry 350–490 passengers on long-haul air routes. It was also deeply involved in the government-sponsored supersonic transport (SST). The company was so heavily committed to these projects that it could not mount an effective campaign to compete for the contract to build the "all-purpose airplane."[8]

U.S. airline companies, reacting to an unprecedented boom in domestic air travel, quickly realized that they needed an aircraft that could carry 250+ passengers, would work economically on short- and medium-haul routes, and would not require a long-range runway. What were needed were fewer and larger

---

[6]"DC-10 Maker Balked at a Safety Analysis," *New York Times,* 21 March 1974, p. 82.

[7]Paul Eddy, Elaine Potter, and Bruce Page, *Destination Disaster—From the Tri-Motor to the DC-10: The Risk of Flying* (New York: New York Times Book Company), p. 98.

[8]John M. Mecklin, "Why Boeing Is Missing the Bus," *Fortune,* June 1, 1968, p. 80.

aircraft to replace the 130-seat Boeing 727s and 80-seat DC-9s. The 747 was too big for most municipal airfields and the large number of smaller craft in use had congested airports, placing a limit on the growth of commercial air service.

The idea of an "airbus" that could serve as the workhorse airliner of the 1970s was enthusiastically received by Lockheed, which was anxious to find a way back into the passenger business. As the primary builder of the large military transport, Lockheed was able to use its new fan-jet technology "to design an airplane from the inside out."[9] For the first time in aviation history, passenger seating—and not fuselage configuration—decided the design of a commercial aircraft. Lockheed was just about ready to take orders for its L-1011 when McDonnell Douglas joined the "airbus race." Its DC-10 was a billion-dollar gamble that the company "could not avoid, and could not afford to lose."[10] In order to catch up to the L-1011, McDonnell Douglas relied heavily on its subcontractors, General Dynamics and General Electric, for design assistance.

Most industry observers believed McDonnell Douglas and Lockheed were in a battle that only one could win—and that neither could afford to lose. The fate of the airbus would lie with the managements of four huge airlines—American, Eastern, TWA, and United. Although the U.S. airline industry consisted of some two hundred firms, the Big Four accounted for more than half of the passenger business. Experts assumed that the design which won the larger share of early orders would be the plane that was eventually produced. Lockheed, quickly followed by McDonnell Douglas, plunged into a rugged sales contest to win the crucial first airbus contract. Airline executives revelled in the leverage that

they could exercise. "It was great," said one airline CEO, "the longer the negotiations lasted, the more we got."[11] The airlines got all sorts of promises—higher payloads, more performance, better galleys, lower prices, and easier financing.

One apparently minor concession that American Airlines extracted from McDonnell Douglas concerned the operation of the rear cargo door in the DC-10. Douglas engineers had suggested hydraulic activators to close the door. They were thoroughly familiar with this technology, as were their subcontractors in General Dynamics, who were going to build the fuselage and its doors. American Airlines engineers thought a hydraulically operated door would be too complex in its working parts and persuaded McDonnell Douglas to change to electrically driven activators.

Despite a late start, McDonnell Douglas won the first airbus contract with an order for 25 DC-10s from American Airlines. According to American, "personal salesmanship" had made the difference because "the two planes were almost identical in price and design."[12] Lockheed, determined to win the next round, "slaughtered the price" of its L-1011 and soon made the largest sale in aviation history.[13] The fierce competition for airbus orders was to rage on for years. As each company cut its price, the break-even points on their respective commercial aircraft programs seemed to grow more and more distant.

On July 17, 1970, two and a half years after the first order was received, the prototype DC-10 was rolled out at Long Beach, California. The L-1011 was still in its hangar. McDonnell Douglas had won the "first leg" of the race and was comfortably ahead with 241 DC-10s on order (Lockheed had signed up customers for

[9]Paul Eddy, Elaine Potter, and Bruce Page, *Destination Disaster—From the Tri-Motor to the DC-10: The Risk of Flying* (New York: New York Times Book Company), p. 88.

[10]"McDonnell Douglas' Billion-Dollar Gamble," *Forbes,* August 1, 1969, p. 83.

[11]John M. Mecklin, "Why Boeing Is Missing the Bus," *Fortune,* June 1, 1968, p. 84.

[12]Paul Eddy, Elaine Potter, and Bruce Page, *Destination Disaster—From the Tri-Motor to the DC-10: The Risk of Flying* (New York: New York Times Book Company), p. 77.

[13]"McDonnell Douglas' Billion-Dollar Gamble," *Forbes,* August 1, 1969, p. 32.

173 L-1011s). It was becoming clear that the next great untapped market would lie overseas. Many foreign airlines had expressed an interest in joining the jumbo-jet club, and McDonnell Douglas and Lockheed were ready to oblige them. The early 1970s saw their respective sales teams crisscrossing the globe in an attempt to win more customers.

By 1974, the outlook for the airbus industry had turned gloomy. U.S. airlines, suffering from a sudden downturn in passenger traffic due to the energy crisis, had postponed many orders and even cancelled some aircraft purchases. Lockheed, which had not made a new L-1011 sale in over a year, was barely surviving despite winning sizable loan guarantees from the U.S. government. McDonnell Douglas revealed that it did "not expect to turn a profit on the DC-10 for at least five more years."[14]

## PRODUCT SAFETY CONTROVERSY (1968–1974)

In early 1968, McDonnell Douglas began to turn its "paper plane" into metal. The Convair Division of General Dynamics was awarded the subcontract to build and design parts of the DC-10 fuselage, including the system for the cargo doors. After studying the design that called for an electric system to close the cargo door (rather than the hydraulic system), Convair engineers had balked. They thought that such a system would necessitate a much more complicated locking mechanism to ensure that the doors stayed safely closed. After a lengthy technical debate, McDonnell Douglas was able to persuade Convair engineers to proceed with the specified design.

In June 1969, Convair engineers submitted a "Failure Mode and Effects Analysis" (FMEA) report that outlined nine possible failure sequences involving the cargo-door system. One of the sequences described a situation where the door would close and latch, but not safely lock, and the cockpit warning light would fail

to indicate that the door was unlocked. If this should happen, "the door would open in flight—resulting in sudden depressurization and possibly structural failure of the floor or damage to the aircraft due to expelled cargo and/or door."[15] Although Convair sent the report to McDonnell Douglas, later court testimony indicated that it was never forwarded to the FAA as required under airplane certification regulations. According to testimony by McDonnell Douglas, the company had been satisfied with a safety backup system that Convair designed to minimize the possibility of failure. Convair, unaware that McDonnell Douglas had not forwarded its FMEA, was, in any case, forbidden by the terms of its contract from reporting design problems directly to the FAA.

By May 1970, the first DC-10 (Ship 1) was undergoing ground tests to prepare for its maiden flight. As the air-conditioning system was being tested (a procedure which involved building up a pressure-differential inside the hull), the lower cargo door suddenly blew open, causing a section of the cabin floor to collapse into the cargo hold. McDonnell Douglas attributed the accident to the "human failure" of the mechanic who had closed the door. A "vent door" was added to prevent pressurization if a door was not safely closed and locked. Without cabin pressurization, a plane could not climb to a normal flying altitude and the pilot would return his craft to the airport for inspection. A new system of hand-driven door linkages was also employed as an extra safeguard.[16]

In April 1971, the Rijksluchtvaartdient (RLD)—the Dutch counterpart of the FAA—expressed concern about the vulnerability of the DC-10's floor to decompression. Unlike the 747, which had its control cables located above

[14]"Timetable Lengthens for Superjet Profits," *Industry Week,* January 14, 1976, p. 49.

[15]Evidence given by J. B. Hurt of Convair, *Hope* v. *McDonnell Douglas* et al.: Civ. No. 17631, Federal District Court, Los Angeles, California.
[16]Paul Eddy, Elaine Potter, and Bruce Page, *Destination Disaster—From the Tri-Motor to the DC-10: The Risk of Flying* (New York: New York Times Book Company), p. 179.

the passenger cabin, the DC-10's vital systems could be severed in the event of floor collapse during flight. The Dutch, who planned to operate the DC-10, wrote to the FAA and to McDonnell Douglas expressing their concern about this potential safety problem.

The FAA, believing that the likelihood of a door failure was "extremely remote,"[17] did not order any modifications. Certifying agents had tried to force the vent door (a backup safety system to the cargo door) shut and could not do it. They concluded that "it was not within the expected strength of ground-service personnel to force the vent-door handle closed when the door latch safety pins were blocked from proper placement."[18] In July 1971, the FAA certified the DC-10 and it took its place in world air fleets.

In June 1972, a baggage handler in Detroit had trouble closing the vent door on an American Airlines DC-10. He did what FAA inspectors could not do—forced it shut with his knee. As the lightly loaded plane climbed above Windsor, Ontario, the cargo door blew open and part of the passenger floor collapsed, jamming most, but not all, of the flight controls. The pilot was able to return to the airport, making an emergency landing that caused no serious passenger injuries.

NTSB accident investigators, alarmed at the failure of the locking mechanisms in the DC-10 cargo door, recommended immediate modifications. The FAA prepared an "Airworthiness Directive" (AD) that would have required two changes in the DC-10—installation of a small viewing window so that ground personnel could actually see whether the lock pins were engaged, and the addition of new parts to the mechanism so that the vent door could not be forced closed. Apparently, the baggage handler who had closed the door by force had bent a connecting rod in the latch mechanism which falsely indicated the position of the door. In

short, the overpowering of the backup system had obscured the failure of the cargo door's primary latching system.

McDonnell Douglas was preparing to leave on a round-the-world campaign (nicknamed "Friendship 72") to boost sales of its DC-10.[19] The company convinced the FAA to cancel the ADs—legally enforceable orders that are made public—allowing it to handle the problem through the issuance of private service bulletins. As part of a so-called "gentleman's agreement" with the government, McDonnell Douglas would "beef up the electric wiring and install a placard on each cargo door warning baggage handlers not to use more than fifty pounds of force when closing the latch handle."[20]

Shortly after the Windsor incident, Daniel Applegate, a Convair engineering director, wrote a lengthy memorandum to his superior, J. B. Hurt, in which he expressed his concern over the likelihood of a DC-10 crash due to a cargo-door design problem. Calling the DC-10 design modifications "more Band-Aids," he recommended "that overtures be made at the highest management level to persuade Douglas to . . . correct the fundamental cabin floor catastrophic failure mode." Upon reading the memo, J. B. Hurt consulted with upper echelons of his management and sent a memorandum in reply. In it, he said: "We have an interesting legal and moral problem" and concluded that Convair should not risk an approach to Douglas.[21]

In August 1972, Friendship 72 stopped in Istanbul, Turkey, as part of the DC-10 sales tour. Turkish Airlines (THY) had expressed an interest in purchasing 2 or 3 DC-10s, providing they could be in service to shuttle Turkey's migrant workers to and from Western Europe dur-

[17]"Jumbo Jet Jitters: Story of DC-10 Defects Raises Serious Doubts about Safety Policies," *Wall Street Journal,* 3 March 1975, p. 17.
[18]Ibid., p. 17.
[19]Paul Eddy, Elaine Potter, and Bruce Page, *Destination Disaster—From the Tri-Motor to the DC-10: The Risk of Flying* (New York: New York Times Book Company), p. 204.
[20]Ibid., 155.
[21]Evidence given by J. B. Hurt of Convair, *Hope* v. *McDonnell Douglas* et al.: Civ. No. 17631, Federal District Court, Los Angeles, California.

ing the Christmas holidays later that year. Court testimony indicates that when THY executives asked if the cargo door problem they had heard about was resolved, they were assured their DC-10s would be fully modified by the delivery date. The deal with THY meant that McDonnell Douglas could sell three unclaimed DC-10s. All Nippon Airways had cancelled an order, leaving several jumbo jets unsold. THY was to become the first non-American scheduled airline to operate the DC-10, which was a matter of great national pride.

This sale, however, was soon to be cause for some serious concern. As the training period progressed, it became apparent that a majority of the THY personnel were having difficulty fully understanding the complex operations of many critical systems of the huge aircraft. Despite the limited training time, Turkish authorities were anxious to get their new jets airborne and the two THY DC-10s (Ships 29 and 33) were put into service in mid-December 1972. During the following year, McDonnell Douglas personnel were gradually withdrawn, as THY management was unwilling to pay for any continuation of the support period unless a reduction in the charges could be negotiated. Despite a request from their own field personnel that recommended an extension of the support program "due to the deteriorating situation," McDonnell Douglas made it clear that it was not going to "subsidize a state-owned airline by making any further concessions."[22] Only a handful of McDonnell Douglas personnel were to remain in Turkey to monitor THY's spare parts program.

During the latter half of 1973, the FAA renewed its queries about jumbo jet floors. In letters to Boeing, Lockheed, and McDonnell Douglas, the FAA asked manufacturers to consider two alternative proposals: (1) the vital control systems could be rerouted away from the floor; or (2) the floor itself could be strengthened by reinforcing the supports and by adding vents which in the event of decompression would allow pressurized air in the passenger cabin to escape before its weight could collapse the floor. Boeing and Lockheed were plainly annoyed at being involved in the aftermath of Windsor. For its part, McDonnell Douglas replied that it thought the "present standard and levels of floor substantiation are adequate."[23] The FAA continued to press the issue of floor strength with little apparent success. Airbus Industries of France, upon learning of the FAA's concern, decided to strengthen the floor of its A300 European Airbus, which was then about to go into production.

In early February 1974, the FAA asked Lockheed and McDonnell Douglas to carry out a technical study of jumbo-jet floors. Lockheed replied that "the study called for would be expensive and time consuming and might be better done by the aviation industry as a whole, rather than by individual manufacturers." In late February 1974, McDonnell Douglas said much the same. "We do not have the manpower available at this time to undertake this study, nor are we in a position to accept this burden alone." It suggested that the government "consider paying for the study because of the magnitude of the effort required."[24]

At 12:31 P.M. on Sunday, March 3, 1974, THY #981, a DC-10 (Ship 29), took off from Orly Airport outside Paris on the last leg of a regularly scheduled flight from Istanbul to London. As the plane climbed through 11,500 feet on its ascent to a normal cruising altitude, the left rear cargo door separated from the aircraft, causing the plane's nose to pitch down violently into a dive. Within a minute, the DC-10 crashed into a forest located near the Paris suburb of Ermenonville, instantly killing all 337 passengers and 11 crew members on board. It had been the worst commercial aircraft disaster in history.

Initially, investigators on the scene at Ermenonville suspected the crash might have been caused by a saboteur's bomb. NTSB per-

[22]Hazell-McCabe Reports reprinted in Paul Eddy, Elaine Potter, and Bruce Page, *Destination Disaster—From the Tri-Motor to the DC-10: The Risk of Flying* (New York: New York Times Book Company), p. 387.

[23]Ibid., p. 163.
[24]"DC-10 Maker Balked at a Safety Analysis," *New York Times,* 21 March 1974, p. 1.

sonnel who had flown to Paris, however, soon learned that the tragedy might have been caused by the DC-10's cargo door. On March 7, McDonnell Douglas advised all operators of DC-10 aircraft "to review procedures and ensure that previously issued service instructions relating to cargo door latching are being strictly observed."[25] The FAA issued an Airworthiness Directive against the DC-10 that incorporated cargo-door modifications recommended by the McDonnell Douglas service bulletins. These bulletins had been sent to all DC-10 users. By March 9, investigators had tentatively concluded that a faulty latching mechanism in Ship 29 had caused the loss of the cargo door and the tragic crash. As the FAA began to review and investigate the history of the DC-10 cargo-door problem, McDonnell Douglas stood behind its aircraft: "The DC-10 meets all FAA regulations and we have complete confidence in its safety and airworthiness."[26]

## POSTSCRIPT

On March 22, McDonnell Douglas said in a news release that "preliminary evidence indicates the plane's rear cargo door did not incorporate all the approved changes" as prescribed in its 1972 service bulletins.[27] The THY DC-10 had been parked—lying unpurchased—at McDonnell Douglas facilities in Long Beach during the period that the cargo-door modifications were to have been completed. Although Ship 29 registration records indicate that the cargo door was checked by three company inspectors in July 1972, none of the three men, whose "quality stamps" appeared on company records, could ever recall having worked on the cargo door of Ship 29. Meanwhile, the FAA ordered four additional design changes to the DC-10 cargo door and mandated compliance within three months.

On March 27, McDonnell Douglas was blasted at congressional hearings as an FAA regional administrator revealed the events that had surrounded the "gentleman's agreement" following the Windsor accident. The company was further criticized when congressional investigators discovered that "long periods of time elapsed and millions of passenger miles were flown before modifications called for in the service bulletin were completed."[28] Only five of the 39 aircraft were modified (by airline companies) within 90 days of the issuance of the bulletin. Eighteen were not corrected until 1973, with some of these not completed until 11 months after issuance of the bulletin. One plane was not improved until two days after the Paris crash. When confronted with documents revealing its dispute with General Dynamics (Convair), McDonnell Douglas said it welcomed the opportunity "to present our company position and to state our complete and total confidence in the safety and airworthiness of our ... DC aircraft."[29] During these same hearings, the FAA came under fire and was accused of "bowing to industry pressure" to ease certification requirements.[30]

On April 8, French authorities confirmed what most aviation experts suspected and what McDonnell Douglas feared: that while several factors led to it, "a faulty cargo door was the sole reason for the crash" of THY #981.[31] As news of this finding spread around the world, damage suits totalling $134.5 million were mounted against McDonnell Douglas, General Dynamics, Turkish Airlines and the Federal Aviation Administration. Sales of American-made jumbo jets—the DC-10 and L-1011—came to a halt.

On April 17, McDonnell Douglas said the

[25]"McDonnell Douglas Asks Users to Review Procedures on DC-10 Door Latch," *Wall Street Journal,* 7 March 1974, p. 13.
[26]McDonnell Douglas Corporation, press release, St. Louis, March 21, 1974, p. 1.
[27]Ibid., p. 2.

[28]"House Panel Says DC-10s Flew without Change Vital to Safety," *New York Times,* 28 March 1974, p. 78.
[29]Hearings before the Subcommittee on Aviation of the Committee on Commerce (United States Senate, 93rd Congress), *Oversight Hearings on the DC-10 Aircraft,* Washington, D.C. (March 26–27) p. 1.
[30]"Shock Waves from the DC-10 Crash," *Business Week,* March 30, 1974, p. 26.
[31]"Paris Crash Laid to Faulty Door," *New York Times,* 9 April 1974, p. 25.

Paris crash had been "caused by human failure"—specifically by the failure of a baggage handler to close the cargo door properly.[32] The baggage handler could not read the cargo-door warning decals because they were printed in English. In addition, the company charged that THY had "improperly changed the door rigging after taking delivery of a properly-rigged plane."[33] THY denied all charges.

On April 19, the FAA released a report on its review of the DC-10 cargo-door problem. It amounted to a damning indictment of the DC-10 door and called it "an inelegant design worthy of Rube Goldberg."[34] The report also revealed airline reports to McDonnell Douglas of 1,000 problems that had been encountered with the DC-10 cargo door. Soon thereafter, McDonnell Douglas was ordered to pay for the installation of a floor vent system on all its DC-10s to prevent catastrophic failure of the cabin floor in the event of decompression in flight. It was estimated that this design modification would cost the company up to $40 million after taxes. During the previous year, McDonnell Douglas had earned a total of $107 million after taxes.

FAA administrator Alexander Butterfield said that the public would "see major improvements in the very near future. There's been a certain degree of complacency in the agency in the last five years. But there's plenty of blame for everybody in the DC-10 disaster."[35] A former FAA head, who presided over the DC-10 certification, said that he would never have "sat around, fat, dumb and happy" if he had been aware of the magnitude of the problem.[36]

In St. Louis, Missouri, McDonnell Douglas President John C. Brizendine said the company did not yet have an explanation for the apparent failure of the cargo door. He declared:

> We know that we have great responsibilities, and we take those responsibilities very seriously. . . . A Douglas aircraft is always a Douglas aircraft no matter who owns it, how long it remains in service, or what is done with it after it's beyond our control. Our planes are part of our lives and part of our identity; that's one reason why we develop and build them with such care.[37]

[32]McDonnell Douglas Corporation, press release, St. Louis, March 21, 1974, p. 1.

[33]"Design Negligence Alleged in Jet Crash Fatal to 346," *New York Times,* 31 October 1974, p. 37.

[34]"F.A.A. Is Criticized on DC-10 Changes," *New York Times,* 27 December 1974, p. 1.

[35]"The DC-10 and Safety: Changes Drafted," *New York Times,* 1 April 1974, p. 1.

[36]Paul Eddy, Elaine Potter, and Bruce Page, *Destination Disaster—From the Tri-Motor to the DC-10: The Risk of Flying* (New York: New York Times Book Company), p. 159.

[37]McDonnell Douglas Corporation, press release, St. Louis, 25 March 1974, p. 1.

# Managing Product Safety: The Ford Pinto

On Tuesday August 9, 1977, Herbert L. Misch, vice president of environmental and safety engineering at Ford Motor Company, picked up a copy of the magazine *Mother Jones* featuring an article entitled "Pinto Madness." This exclusive story would surely stir up a public controversy over the safety of the company's successful subcompact car, the Ford Pinto.

This self-styled radical magazine had cited Ford "secret documents" which, according to the author, proved the company had known for eight years that the Pinto was a "firetrap." The article claimed that preproduction rear-end crash tests had revealed the dangerous nature of the design and placement of the car's fuel tank. According to the author's investigation, Ford was so anxious to get the car on the market that it decided design changes would not be made— they would "take too much time and cost too much money." The article went on to charge that Ford had used "some blatant lies" to delay enactment of a government safety standard that would have forced the company to change the Pinto's "fire-prone" gas tank. The article concluded: "By conservative estimates, Pinto crashes have caused 500 burn deaths to people who would not have been seriously injured if the car had not burst into flames."[1]

Nothing in Ford's records supported the contentions made in the article. Nevertheless, Misch knew that the overall effect of this *Mother Jones* article—one that relied heavily on the testimony of a former Ford engineer—could be highly damaging to the company. It would sharpen consumer criticism of the U.S. auto industry in general and Ford in particular. Misch and his associates at Ford were angered by the allegations and were ready to denounce the article as "unfair and distorted."[2] They knew, however, that it would not be an easy task to counter such sensational charges with

[1] Mark Dowie, "Pinto Madness," *Mother Jones,* September/October 1977, p. 18.
[2] "Ford Is Recalling Some 1.5 Million Pintos, Bobcats," *Wall Street Journal,* 12 June 1978, p. 2.

their own statistical analyses of accident reports.

Ford believed that the source of this trouble, like so much of the criticism leveled at the auto industry, was external to its operation. The development of a large consumer movement, along with the enactment of the National Traffic and Motor Vehicle Safety Act of 1966, had revolutionized the car business. In the view of *Mother Jones,* the industry had been considered the "last great unregulated business" in the United States.[3] The industry now had to answer to many more people than just auto buyers. The multitude of often conflicting regulations had, according to auto executives, placed unreasonable burdens on domestic automakers. An exasperated company chairman, Henry Ford II, lamented, "It's the mess in which we live."[4]

The company had dealt with all of the major federal regulatory agencies in earlier controversies, some of which had involved the beleaguered Pinto. The National Highway Traffic Safety Administration (NHTSA)—a regulatory agency in the Department of Transportation—was considered the industry's chief antagonist. NHTSA investigations had led to previous Pinto recalls because of problems with engine fires and fuel-line hose construction. The appointment of Joan Claybrook—a Ralph Nader lobbyist—as NHTSA administrator had been strongly, but unsuccessfully, opposed by the auto industry. Claybrook was expected to press hard for increased safety and miles-per-gallon (MPG) features.

The Environmental Protection Agency (EPA)—a regulatory agency reporting directly to the U.S. president—had pressed the industry to reduce auto emissions in an effort to clean up air pollution. In 1973, after an internal audit, Ford volunteered it had withheld information from the EPA concerning unauthorized maintenance performed on emission test cars. The agency subsequently levied a $7 million fine on Ford. In one incident, a small number of Pintos had been recalled because of a flaw in the car's air pollution control equipment. The Federal Trade Commission (FTC)—a regulatory agency reporting directly to the U.S. Congress—had decided to become more involved in oversight activities in the industry. The FTC was mostly concerned that product performance features be candidly disclosed. It had charged that gas mileage claims made by Ford's Lincoln-Mercury division were inaccurate and exaggerated.

While relations between the government and the auto industry were often adversarial, each side realized that self-interest lay in maintaining a workable peace. Auto companies would often settle disputes by agreeing to a recall without admitting fault and without a flurry of negative publicity. The government preferred such voluntary actions because court battles were usually time-consuming and rarely resulted in an efficient resolution of a product controversy.

Another group that served as an industry watchdog was the Center for Auto Safety, a privately funded consumer advocate organization founded by Ralph Nader in 1970. The center had noticed in its records a larger-than-expected number of accident reports involving burn deaths in the Ford Pinto. In this, as in other cases, it forwarded the information to NHTSA in an effort to force the agency's hand in confronting the automobile companies. The center's director, Clarence M. Ditlow, who often pressed for auto recalls, had claimed that "the number of recalls and the (number of) cars involved would be high for several more years."[5] In the minds of some industry observers, the center had targeted the Pinto for special attention.

Ford was determined to fight hard for the Pinto. Since it was put into production in 1970, the subcompact had become one of the company's best selling cars and had allowed Ford to fight off some of the foreign competition. Fur-

[3]Dowie, "Pinto Madness," p. 23.
[4]Walter Guzzardi, Jr., "Ford: The Road Ahead," *Fortune,* September 11, 1978, p. 39.

[5]"Detroit Stunned by Recall Blitz," *New York Times,* 12 March 1978, Sec. 3, p. 1.

thermore, company executives knew that its next-generation small car would not be ready for introduction until 1980.

## COMPETITIVE ENVIRONMENT

The American automobile industry's fortune had historically been tied to the pattern of the nation's economic cycle. Three or four good years were inexorably followed by one or two poor years. There had been a shakeout of the weakest companies over the years, leaving four major U.S. automakers. In 1977 General Motors (46.4% market share), Ford (22.3%), Chrysler (11.1%), and American Motors (1.8%) shared the $100-plus-billion U.S. auto market. Imports, consisting mostly of subcompact cars, had captured 18.4% of this market. Car sales were made primarily through manufacturers' franchised dealers located across the country.[6]

Competition among the four U.S. firms was intense. Pricing, performance features, consumer financing, and advertising had always been important competitive weapons. With the arrival of stiffer foreign competition, however, pricing became an even more critical selling feature. Moreover, in the aftermath of the Arab oil embargo, good fuel economy became especially important, a trend that had favored foreign producers because they had adapted to high fuel costs in their home markets.

For domestic car companies profit margins on all vehicles had declined in the early 1970s, mostly reflecting poor recovery from inflation-related cost increases. Pricing was limited first by price controls, then by the 1974–1975 recession. According to industry experts, domestic labor costs had served significantly to disadvantage American automakers. Small car margins continued to decline after the recession as a result of reduced demand for small cars in general, heightened competition from imports, and cost increases to achieve safety, damagea-

bility, and emission requirements. Large cars, still in demand, fared much better.

Though auto companies were very secretive about new car designs and technologies, there were otherwise very few secrets in the car business. Auto company engineers could, and often would, tear apart a competitor's new car to glean details about a new design or production technique. If one firm changed its price structure or its financing rate, the competition would be able to adjust its strategy quickly. Because of its dominance in the American market, General Motors was considered the market leader and usually dictated the sales strategies for its smaller rivals.

Ford Motor Company was founded in 1903 and had been a family-owned and family-managed business until stock was first sold publicly in 1956. Family members still retained 40% of the voting power in the company, which ranked third (in sales) on the 1977 *Fortune* 500 list of the largest U.S. industrial corporations.

Much like its principal competitor, GM, Ford produced a complete range of cars and trucks. The company had scored some notable successes, however, in cultivating market segments ill-served by General Motors. Ford gained an early edge on its rival by producing the first American-made compact car, the Falcon, in 1960. Its luxury cars, the Thunderbird and Cougar, were also considered attractive by the American car buyer. The Mustang, designed and introduced in 1964 by Lee Iacocca (who later became Ford president), gained wide favor as the "sports car for the masses."[7]

Despite the successes of these specialty cars, Ford did not gain any ground on General Motors during the 1960s. Furthermore, some Ford executives believed that imports were posing a threat to Ford's traditionally strong position in the small car market. Though the company was ready with new compact cars (the Maverick was introduced in 1969), it still did

[6]"You're Damned If You Do . . . ," *Forbes,* January 9, 1978, p. 35.

[7]Mark B. Fuller and Malcolm S. Salter, "Ford Motor Company (A)" (Boston, Massachusetts: Harvard Business School, 1982), p. 4.

not have a subcompact to counter the import challenge effectively.

In June 1967 Ford management became embroiled in a protracted internal debate over the company's position on subcompacts. When it was over, Lee Iacocca had become Ford's president and the Pinto was born. Iacocca directed that the Pinto was to be in showrooms with 1971 models. Formal planning started immediately and the journey to production took less time than the prevailing industry average. In September 1970 the Pinto was introduced as a "carefree little American car," and it gained quick acceptance by the market.[8] After six years of production over 2 million Pintos had been sold, making it one of the company's all-time best-selling automobiles.

Between 1970 and 1977, the Pinto helped stabilize Ford's market position. The 1973–1974 Arab oil embargo hit Ford's major competitors (GM and Chrysler) particularly hard because neither had a large offering of small cars. The following year, Congress set mandatory fuel economy targets that encouraged auto makers to sell smaller cars. GM quickly responded with a massive downsizing program that helped it become more small car oriented. Chrysler, in bleak financial straits, belatedly followed with its own small car program. Ford undertook a program to convert its Wayne, Michigan, assembly plant from production of full-size cars to compact cars, completing this transition in only 51 days. By 1975 subcompact and compact cars glutted the market, however, as consumers shunned small cars. Burdened with high inventory levels, the industry began to offer rebates on most small cars. The Pinto, however, continued to outsell most competitive offerings in its size category. Consequently, Ford management decided to focus its new product development on a replacement for the compact-sized Maverick which had been introduced two years before the Pinto. The Pinto would have to hold the consumer's interest until the company was ready to make the investment in the next generation subcompact.

By mid-1977 the outlook for the auto industry was uncertain in the opinion of most industry analysts. While some predicted the coming year would bring record sales, others worried that shrinking consumer credit would reduce car buying. Apart from sales volume, several industry observers believed Detroit's profits would be hurt by declining margins and a "less rich" sales mix that included more small cars. Each company was scrambling to ensure that its fleet averaged the legally mandated 18 miles per gallon in 1978. This meant selling more models that were smaller and fuel-efficient but were also less profitable. Faced with intensified competition, most auto makers were placing a premium on innovative design and engineering.

## PRODUCT SAFETY CONTROVERSY (1970–1977)

To meet the competition from imported subcompacts, Ford accelerated the Pinto planning process. In June 1967 Ford commenced the design and development process; production of the Pinto began on August 10, 1970. Ford achieved this 38-month development time, 5 months under the average time of 43 months, by assembling a special team of engineers who directed their efforts entirely to the Pinto. Unlike the development cycles for most new car lines, Pinto start-up planning was simplified and included only a two-door sedan (hatchbacks and station wagons were added in later years). Pinto engineers were constrained by Iacocca's goal, known as "the limits of 2000"— the Pinto was not to weigh an ounce over 2,000 pounds and not to cost a cent over $2,000.[9] These limits, according to former Ford engineers, were strictly enforced. Even at this price and weight, the Pinto would still cost and weigh more than some imported subcompacts.

An early question during the car's design stage was where to safely put the gas tank. Although engineers were familiar with ways to move the gas tank away from the rear of the car—Ford had a patent for a saddle-type tank

---

[8]Lee Patrick Strobel, *Reckless Homicide?* (South Bend, Indiana: and books, 1980), p. 82.

[9]"Ford Ignored Pinto Fire Peril, Secret Memos Show," *Chicago Tribune,* 13 October 1979, Sec. 2, p. 12.

that could fit above and mostly forward of the car's rear axle—they opted for a strap-on tank arrangement located under the rear floorpan and behind the rear axle. At that time almost every American-made car had the fuel tank located in the same place. Late in the design process, however, an engineering study determined that "the safest place for a fuel tank is directly above the rear axle."[10] It was later determined by senior company engineers that such a design, while moving the tank farther away from a rear-end collision, actually increased the threat of ignition in the passenger compartment. The over-the-axle location of the fuel tank would also require a circuitous filler pipe more likely to be dislodged in an accident. Raising the height of the fuel tank by putting it above the axle would also raise the car's center of gravity, thereby diminishing its handling capabilities. In the opinion of Ford's senior engineers, this would undermine the car's general safety. Practical considerations also dictated the traditional location. The fuel tank could not be placed over the axle, for example, if a station wagon or a hatchback option was going to be offered. The over-axle location would also greatly reduce storage space and would make servicing more difficult.

When the Pinto was in the blueprint stage, the federal government had no standards concerning how safe a car must be from gas leakage in rear-end crashes. In January 1969, NHTSA proposed its first rear-end fuel system integrity standard, called Standard 301. The original standard required that a stationary vehicle should leak less than one ounce of fuel per minute after being hit by a 4,000 pound barrier moving at 20 mph. Ford supported such a standard in writing and voluntarily adopted the 20 mph standard as an internal design objective for its entire line of cars. In mid-1969 the company began a series of crash tests with preproduction Pinto prototypes, as well as with other car lines, in an attempt to meet this objective. Four tests were conducted on vehicles modified to simulate the Pinto's rear-end design. In three

of these tests, the leakage slightly exceeded the one-ounce-per-minute standard. In the other test, massive fuel leakage occurred because an improperly welded fuel tank split at the seams.[11] After these tests Ford altered the Pinto's fuel tank design and was able to incorporate these changes before production began. The first Pinto rolled off the assembly line on August 10, 1970. A month later the subcompact was introduced to the American consumer boasting a price tag of $1,919—about $170 less than GM's subcompact and within $80 of the best-selling Volkswagen Beetle.[12]

The 20 mph moving-barrier standard proposed by the government was never adopted. Just days after the manufacture of the first Pinto, NHTSA announced a proposal requiring all vehicles to meet a 20 mph fixed-barrier standard within 18 months. In a fixed-barrier test, the vehicle is towed backwards into a fixed barrier at the specified speed. NHTSA also indicated that its long-term objective for rear-end crashes included a 30 mph fixed-barrier standard. This new proposal caught auto makers by surprise and provoked universal industry opposition. Ford estimated that a 20 mph fixed-barrier test could, because of the laws of kinetic energy, be nearly twice as severe as a 20 mph moving-barrier test. Many auto engineers were quick to point out the unrealistic nature of fixed-barrier tests: in the real world, vehicles are not driven backwards into walls. Moreover, data available to Ford indicated that 85% of rear-end collisions occurred at speeds equivalent to or less than a 20 mph moving-barrier standard.[13] In addition, the available information indicated that only .45% of injury-producing accidents involved fire.[14] Preventing inju-

[10]Strobel, *Reckless Homicide?* p. 80.

[11]Ford Motor Company Crash Tests 1137, 1138, 1214; memorandum, H. P. Freers to T. J. Feaheny, January 31, 1969.
[12]Strobel, *Reckless Homicide?* p. 82.
[13]Fuel System Integrity Program, Percent of Rear Accidents Occurring at or below Equivalent Fixed (Movable) Barrier Speeds, Car Product Planning, March 14, 1971. (Accident data file from Accident Crash Injury Research [ACIR] Project at Cornell Aeronautical Laboratory.)
[14]"Observations on Fire in Automobile Accidents," Cornell Aeronautical Laboratory, Inc., February 1965.

ries from fires caused by rear-end impacts at very high speeds was beyond practical technology, according to many auto executives. Protection against fire at such high speeds would be of little benefit, it was argued, since the force of impact alone was likely to be fatal.

Ford considered it unlikely that the government would adopt fixed-barrier standards. Nevertheless, the company began to test its vehicles against this proposed requirement to determine what would have to be done to meet NHTSA's proposals. Subsequent fixed-barrier tests conducted with standard Pintos at 20 and 30 mph resulted in excessive leakage. To meet the more stringent fixed-barrier standards, a major tear up of all cars would be required to modify vehicle design. Because of the significant costs involved and doubts about the viability of the fixed-barrier standard, Ford management decided to continue with its own internal 20 mph moving-barrier standard. Engineering work on developing ways to meet a 30 mph moving-barrier standard—which Ford believed NHTSA would eventually adopt—continued.

In early 1971 a junior company engineer began to explore various ways to make the company's smaller cars capable of meeting the 30 mph moving-barrier standard. A 30-page study, called the "Pricor Report," listed several specific recommendations for how to make the car substantially safer from fuel leakage and fire in rear-end crashes. An over-the-axle gas tank, a repositioned spare tire, installation of body rails, a redesigned filler pipe, and an "inner-tank" rubber bladder were among major options for improving the Pinto's overall performance.[15] The first four suggestions were ruled out on the grounds that they would require extensive vehicle design changes. The rubber bladder—a tank liner with an estimated variable cost of $5.80—was seriously considered. On the basis of a crash test in which a bladder was hand placed inside a Pinto tank, a company en-

gineer concluded that the bladder tank "provided a substantial improvement in crashworthiness."[16] In cold weather, however, the bladders became stiff, making gas filling very difficult. And in very hot climates, the bladders failed under test conditions.

In August 1973, NHTSA announced a proposal for a 30 mph moving-barrier, rear-end fuel system integrity standard, effective September 1976 for all 1977 models. A prolonged debate ensued between government officials and industry executives over the appropriate test technique. NHTSA was a proponent of car-to-car testing, arguing that this was a closer approximation to actual accident situations. Auto representatives maintained that a standard moving barrier (which was towed along a track to the point of impact) was much more appropriate because it was repeatable and, therefore, a more reliable measurement of crashworthiness.

At the same time that NHTSA proposed the rear-end crash standard, it also adopted a fuel system integrity standard applicable to rollover accidents. Although Ford did not oppose the rear-end standard, it vigorously fought the rollover standard. Under provisions of the rollover test, minimal gasoline leakage would be permitted when a car was turned upside down in an accident. This presented auto makers with obvious problems as leakage would occur from the carburetor, fuel vents, and the gas cap air hole when a car was upside down; yet each of these openings was necessary for the normal functioning of the fuel intake. After extensive study Ford determined that the rollover requirement might be met by installing an $11 valve on each of its 12.5 million cars and trucks then on the road. Among the materials submitted was a cost-benefit analysis prepared according to NHTSA criteria and using government figures ($200,000 per death; $67,000 per injury). The values reflected only the economic loss to society resulting from injuries and

---

[15]A. J. Pricor, "197X Mustang/Maverick Program: Fuel Tank Integrity," Ford Motor Company.

[16]"Ford 157 Report—Bladder Fuel Tank Test," Ford Motor Company.

deaths, because the government had no estimate to place on human pain and suffering. The analysis, done by Ford personnel with no design responsibilities, presented the case that the $137 million in cost far outweighed the dollar values assigned for the loss of 180 burn deaths, 180 serious burn injuries, and 2,100 burned vehicles.[17] The rollover standard was eventually adopted with some minor modifications. The cost-benefit analysis on rollover accidents became the basis for countless media claims that Ford delayed *rear-end* fuel system integrity standards because "its internal cost-benefit analysis, which places a dollar value on human life, said it wasn't profitable to make the changes sooner."

The first notable public criticism of the Pinto's fuel tank design came in late 1973. Byron Bloch, an independent consultant in automobile safety design, warned a Department of Transportation conference that the Pinto's fuel system design was "very vulnerable . . . to even minor damage."[18] On a national television program, Bloch held up a model of a Pinto and pointed out what he saw as its fuel system hazards. When Ford announced it was recalling the Pinto for minor repairs, Bloch urged the government to require a recall that would improve the car's resistance to fires in rear-end crashes. Early in 1974 the Center for Auto Safety pressed NHTSA to investigate the fuel system integrity of the Ford Pinto and the Chevrolet Vega. The center cited concerns expressed by attorneys engaged in liability lawsuits, as well as its own research findings, in calling for a defect investigation. NHTSA reviewed these complaints and determined that there was no demonstrable safety problem.

NHTSA, still a relatively new federal agency in the mid-1970s, was seriously hampered in most of its investigatory work by a lack of relevant and meaningful statistical information. In early 1975 a study commissioned by the Insurance Institute for Highway Safety concluded that the number of fire-related incidents involving vehicles was growing more rapidly than the number of other incidents of fire. The study noted a striking difference between Ford's 20% national representation among domestic passenger cars and its 35% frequency in surveyed collision-ruptured fuel tanks.[19] The study's author cautioned, however, that it was not possible to draw definitive conclusions about causal relationships; nor was it possible to identify differences between car models. This study, and others like it, came at a time of growing public concern over motor vehicle fires. Between 1974 and 1976 consumer groups and Congress exerted considerable political pressure on NHTSA to finally implement all provisions of the fuel system integrity standard. In 1977 Standard 301 was fully enacted.

On August 10, 1977, the allegations contained in the *Mother Jones* article were first made public at a news conference in Washington, D.C. The charges against Ford appeared to have been based on quotes attributed to either past or present company engineers, along with a digest of confidential company memoranda. Ford executives took a dim view of the magazine, but they knew its editors had obtained some key sensitive documents that could easily be misinterpreted by the public. As far as the company knew, no government investigation was being conducted that concerned the Pinto's fuel system.

### POSTSCRIPT

On September 26, 1977, Ford officials publicly responded to the *Mother Jones* article—which had appeared seven weeks earlier—by issuing a news release aimed at refuting the magazine's allegations. The news release claimed: "There is no serious fire hazard in the fuel system of the Ford Pinto, nor are any Pinto models exceptionally vulnerable to rear-impact collision fires. [NHTSA] statistics establish that Ford

[17]"Fatalities Associated with Crash Induced Fuel Leakage and Fires," E. S. Grush and C. S. Saundby, Ford Motor Company, September 19, 1973.

[18]Strobel, *Reckless Homicide?* p. 145.

[19]Eugene M. Trisko, "Results of the 1973 National Survey of Motor Vehicle Fires," *Fire Journal* (March 1975), p. 23.

Pinto is involved in fewer fire-associated collisions than might be expected considering the total number of Pintos in operation." Ford cited government figures for the period 1975–1976 for which comprehensive information was available. These figures showed that Pintos were involved in about 1.9% of fire-accompanied passenger car fatalities in 1975–1976, years in which Pintos made up an average of about 1.9% of passenger cars. Ford explained that early experiments with its rubber bladder gas tank were conducted to see if the company could meet its own ambitious performance requirements. "The truth is that in every model year the Pinto has been tested and met or surpassed the federal fuel system integrity standards applicable to it."[20]

The company acknowledged that later model Pintos had an improved fuel system design, but argued that "it simply is unreasonable and unfair to contend that a car is somehow unsafe if it does not meet standards proposed for future years or embody the technological improvements that are introduced in later model years." The company denied that it had purposely delayed Standard 301 and said it had only "opposed . . . certain excessive testing requirements."[21]

In September 1977, NHTSA opened an investigation into the Pinto's fuel tank system and ran an engineering analysis of the pre-1977 Pinto. As reported by the *Wall Street Journal,* the agency found that "the fuel tank's location and the structural parts around it permitted easy crushing or puncturing of the tank in a crash. Officials also found that the short fuel tank filler pipe could easily pull away from the tank." There was "a real potential for trouble," said one government official.[22]

Ford's management was angered by NHTSA's inquiry and believed the basis for its examination to be unfounded. In a 1974 investigation of complaints, NHTSA had determined that no action concerning Pinto fuel system integrity was necessary. Indeed, by NHTSA's own admission, its action was in response to the enormous flood of mail demanding that it do something about the Pinto. The company was further incensed when the agency acknowledged that its accident statistics were "notoriously incomplete." NHTSA had only begun to develop a comprehensive accident reporting system.

By early 1978 the Pinto controversy began to attract national attention. The Center for Auto Safety had called for a national campaign to force Ford to recall the country's 2 million-odd Pintos and retrofit a safety bladder into the gas tank of *all* Pintos. The car's image was further tarnished by recalls due to piston scuffing and steering failures.

In February 1978 a California jury handed down a verdict that assessed $125 million in punitive damages against Ford in a case involving the rupture and explosion of the fuel tank on a 1972 Pinto. One person had died in the fiery Pinto crash, and the surviving passenger had undergone 60 different operations in the six years since the accident. It was testimony by Harley Copp, a former Ford senior engineer, that apparently convinced the court the Pinto was, in the words of one juror, "a lousy and unsafe product."[23] The massive amount of money awarded by the jury, easily the highest for such a suit in American history, led to heightened media interest in the Pinto issue. A judge later reduced punitive damages to $3.5 million.

During the same month as the California verdict, NHTSA conducted experimental crash tests of the Pinto as part of its ongoing investigation. A total of 11 rear-end crash tests of 1971–1976 Pintos were staged at speeds between 30 and 35 mph. Two cars tested at 35 mph caught fire, and the other tests at 30 mph resulted in "significant leakage."[24] When

[20]Ford Motor Company News Release (Dearborn, Michigan: Ford Motor Company, September 26, 1977), p. 1.
[21]Ibid, p. 1.
[22]"Car Trouble: Government Pressure Propels Auto Recalls toward A New High," *Wall Street Journal,* 16 August 1978, p. 1.

[23]"Why the Pinto Jury Felt Ford Deserved $125 Million Penalty," *Wall Street Journal,* 14 February 1978, p. 1.
[24]National Highway Traffic Safety Administration, *Report of Defects Investigation* (Washington, D.C., NHTSA, May 1978), p. 11.

NHTSA similarly tested GM's Chevrolet Vega, a larger and slightly heavier vehicle than the Pinto, minimal gasoline leakage was reported. Ford management believed these tests were unfair and inappropriate. Some of the tests were more severe than the government required even for later model vehicles, and this was apparently the first time the agency had ever used car-to-car crash tests to determine if there was a safety defect.

In March 1978 Pinto owners in Alabama and California filed class action suits, demanding that Ford recall all Pintos built from 1971 through 1976 and modify their fuel systems. The California civil complaint alleged that Ford "persistently and willfully failed and refused to remedy the design defect in the fuel tank." Around this time the head of the American Trial Lawyers Association, in an unprecedented step, had appealed to the company to "recall all of the cars in question."[25] Later that same month, NHTSA notified Ford that its 1976 Pintos had not passed a 30-mph *front-end* barrier test. This test result, which revealed occasional fuel leakage in the engine compartment, led to a recall of 300,000 Pintos.

On May 9, 1978, NHTSA announced that it had made an "initial determination" that a safety defect existed in the fuel systems of Ford Pintos for the 1971 through 1976 model years. This finding had been reached after eight months of analysis, testing, and review of pertinent company records. The government claimed that it was aware of 38 cases in which rear-end collisions of Pintos had resulted in fuel tank damage, leakage, and/or ensuing fires. Of those 38 cases, it said, there were 27 fatalities among occupants and 24 instances in which individuals suffered nonfatal burns. In its four-paragraph letter to Ford's President Iacocca, NHTSA informed the company that it could respond to the initial findings at a public hearing scheduled for mid-June.[26] During late May and early June, Ford officials met with NHTSA to discuss privately the government's findings and to consider possible remedies. A few days before the hearing date, the decision was made to recall the cars.

On June 9, 1978, after years of vigorously defending the safety of the Pinto's fuel system, Ford management announced the recall of 1.5 million of its subcompacts. In a press release issued on the day of the recall announcement, Ford management insisted "that it does not agree with the agency's initial determination ... that an unreasonable risk to safety is involved in the design of [the Pinto], and that it believes it can be demonstrated that the actual performance of the vehicles is comparable to that of other subcompact and compact cars manufactured during the same periods." The company did concede that "NHTSA had identified areas in which the risk of fuel leakage could be reduced significantly on a practical basis." Accordingly, Ford decided to offer the modifications to "end public concern that had resulted from criticism of the fuel system in these vehicles."[27] The company agreed to notify all Pinto owners that it was ready to replace the fuel filler pipe and install a polyethylene shield across the front of the fuel tank. Ford estimated this offer could cost the company as much as $20 million after taxes. During the previous year Ford had earned a total of $1.5 billion after taxes.[28]

NHTSA administrator Joan Claybrook said the government wanted to work out a voluntary agreement with Ford to avoid a long-drawn-out court battle. In response to Ford's recall, the government closed its investigation without making a final determination.

In Detroit, Michigan, Ford Chairman Henry Ford, II, said: "The lawyers would shoot me for saying this, but I think there's some cause for concern about the [Pinto]. I don't even listen to the cost figures—we've got to fix it."[29]

[25]"Class Action Suit Seeks Recall of 1971–76 Pintos," *Wall Street Journal,* 7 March 1978, p. 34.

[26]"U.S. Agency Suggests Ford Pintos Have a Fuel System Safety Defect," *New York Times,* 9 May 1978, p. 22.

[27]"Ford Orders Recall of 1.5 Million Pintos for Safety Changes," *New York Times,* 10 June 1978, p. 1.

[28]"Ford Is Recalling Some 1.5 Million Pintos, Bobcats," *Wall Street Journal,* 12 June 1978, p. 2.

[29]Guzzardi, "Ford: The Road Ahead," p. 42.

# Managing Product Safety:
# The Firestone 500

On Sunday, July 23, 1978, Mr. John Floberg, vice president and general counsel of the Firestone Tire and Rubber Company, picked up the Akron *Beacon Journal* and carefully read the front page article under the headline "FIRESTONE KNEW OF BAD TIRES." This article would only fuel the already raging public controversy that had surrounded the safety of the Firestone steel-belted radial 500 tire since the beginning of the year.

This newspaper's anonymous source within the Firestone company had supplied it with a 1975 company report marked "Proprietary" and "For Internal Use Only." The report showed that some Firestone steel-belted radial TPC tires—a version of the Firestone 500 made for General Motors—had failed a Department of Transportation (DOT) high speed test. Firestone's Research and Development Department conducted the DOT FMVSS No. 109 high speed test on 46 tires that had been in storage for about 18 months; 26 (56.5%) failed the test. Of another group of 34 tires, 16 failed a severe torture test much sooner than they should have.[1]

From Firestone's experience of the last six months, Mr. Floberg knew that the net effect of this revelation by "Deep Tread"—the name used by many to refer to the *Beacon Journal*'s inside source—could be highly damaging to the company. In the minds of the consuming public, this news would further tarnish the image of Firestone as a company that considered consumer safety of paramount importance. It would also serve to undermine the arguments Firestone had presented to the Congressional Subcommittee on Oversight and Investigations in defense of the 500's performance and safety record. Clearly, in this instance of media reporting, as in all others like it, Firestone's plain and stoic explanation would not impress the public as much as the sensational implications of the 1975 test results.

[1] "Firestone Knew of Bad Tires," *Akron Beacon Journal*, 23 July 1978, p. 1.

Floberg considered the NHTSA—a regulatory agency in the U.S. Department of Transportation—one of the externalities that promoted the current controversy. He and others at Firestone felt the company had enjoyed a positive relationship with the agency until legal skirmishes in the mid-1970s embarrassed agency directors. Firestone had voluntarily recalled tires it believed to be defective on about 50 different occasions, and NHTSA had alerted Firestone to a tire problem in only two of those instances. After a 1975 NHTSA recall order of Firestone tires was cancelled because the Justice Department said the government's case was too weak, the agency's bitterness was boldly demonstrated when they invited consumer complaints about the 500 steel-belted tire. Floberg thought that the political mood of the 1970s and the politics of those attacking the Firestone 500 helped explain the fervor of NHTSA and others.

Another group that fueled the controversy was the Center for Auto Safety, a privately funded consumer advocate organization founded by Ralph Nader in 1970. It was the Center that first brought the Firestone 500 to the attention of NHTSA and other consumer advocates in 1976. Since then, NHTSA and the Center had supplied each other with information. NHTSA, in fact, seemed to circumvent a federal court injunction by passing the results of a consumer survey to the Center, which then released them to the news media. The survey results did not cast the 500 tire in a favorable light. Firestone told the press that the Center's director, Clarence Ditlow, "appears to operate from an anti-automotive bias, . . . waging a campaign of verbal terrorism (in the media)."[2]

Last, but not least, there was the congressional subcommittee which had conducted hearings on the Firestone 500 case in May and July 1978. In Floberg's view, one prime purpose of many congressional hearings was to provide visibility and publicity for committee members. The subcommittee was chaired by Representative John E. Moss, a California Democrat with a reputation as an ardent consumerist and friend of the media. The special counsel to the subcommittee was Lowell Dodge, who was the Center's director before Mr. Ditlow took over.

Clarence Ditlow, Lowell Dodge and Joan Claybrook, the head of NHTSA since 1977, were all former associates of Ralph Nader. Mr. Floberg characterized this triumvirate as a consumerist clique or fraternity. He described the situation in the following way: "They scratch each others' backs. They get together and decide to play Ping-Pong or badminton with somebody."[3] In other words, in his view, Firestone was in its current predicament because it was chosen to be the ball or shuttlecock in this group's latest game.

## COMPETITIVE ENVIRONMENT

The American tire industry's growth and prosperity have paralleled that of the U.S auto industry. There had been a gradual shakeout of the weakest companies, which left the U.S. with five major firms (listed in order of size): Goodyear, Firestone, Goodrich, Uniroyal, and General. In 1977, Firestone had approximately a 23% share of the $5.6-billion U.S. automobile tire market. Goodyear's share was 33% for the same period.[4] Sales in this market are primarily to Detroit car manufacturers (the original equipment market—OEM) and to retail tire dealers (the replacement market).

Competition among the five U.S. firms had always been intense. With the ever-increasing interest in the U.S. market on the part of foreign producers, such as Michelin (France) and Bridgestone (Japan), competition had in-

---

[2]Anthony Cortizas, Jr., and Louis Banks, *Corporation v. Environment: The Case of the Firestone 500 Radial* (Cambridge, Massachusetts: Alfred P. Sloan School of Management, MIT [1979]), p. 4.

[3]Arthur M. Louis, "Lessons from the Firestone Fracas," *Fortune,* August 28, 1978, p. 47.

[4]Anthony Cortizas, Jr., and Louis Banks, *Corporation v. Environment: The Case of the Firestone 500 Radial* (Cambridge, Massachusetts: Alfred P. Sloan School of Management, MIT [1979]), p. 4.

creased. Pricing, warranty and adjustment terms, and advertising were key competitive weapons. High labor costs—one-third of tire production costs—and a slim pretax 10% profit were characteristic of the industry and made price cutting a heavy burden. In general, advertising and promotion expenditures were substantial. Firestone's recent annual expenditures in this area had been approximately $30 million, or 2.3% of annual tire sales revenues.[5]

While companies were very secretive about their tire adjustment rates—the percentage of tires sold that were returned for partial or full refunds—there were otherwise very few secrets in the tire business. If one firm discontinued or added a line of tires, or changed a price or warranty policy, the other firms knew about the change within a couple of hours. The tire retailers, especially retailers of more than one brand, were an excellent informal source of information about the competition. Firestone's belief that the adjustment rates of the 500 tire matched those of the competition's best steel-belted radial tire was in part based on what Firestone heard from friendly tire dealers.

The Firestone Tire and Rubber Company was founded in 1900 and had been a family-owned and family-managed business for most of its history. Family members still retained approximately 20% of the company, which ranked 46th (in sales) on the 1978 *Fortune* 500 list of the largest U.S. industrial corporations. Like other companies, Firestone produced numerous types of tires, many of which were sold under the private brand names of Montgomery Ward, Shell Oil, Atlas, and other large tire retailers. Firestone's sales in the replacement market were made by company-owned stores, independent Firestone dealers, and retailers that were not solely tire dealers.

Within the previous 10 years, consumer pressures along with the arrival of foreign tire producers in the U.S. market had created a scramble to develop better tire designs and technologies. In the late 1960s, the public's loss of confidence in the quality of the bias-ply tire forced American producers, led by Goodyear, to switch over to *bias-belted* tires. By 1970, these tires had become original equipment on a vast majority of new cars. Steel-belted radial (SBR) tires had a small (2.4%) but growing share of the U.S. market.[6]

In 1971, Michelin built a plant in Nova Scotia that would produce steel-belted radials for export to the U.S. (Michelin already was selling radials to Sears, which marketed the tire under a Sears brand name.) Bridgestone introduced the West Coast to its new steel-belted radial tire with a 40,000-mile guarantee. That same year Firestone won a race against its competitors by becoming the first American firm to produce radials for use in large numbers as original equipment on Detroit's new cars. By 1978, steel-belted radials were original equipment on more than 70% of all new cars and accounted for 40% to 45% of replacement market sales.[7] Before the 500 became controversial, it was the best-selling radial on the market. In all, 23.5 million 500s were produced by April 1978 when production ended.

Between 1972 and 1975, American tire producers greatly increased their capital spending to convert much of their capacity from bias tire to steel-belted radial (SBR) tire production. The threat of imports was not the only reason for the domestic industry's interest in SBRs. They were all quick to realize that a tire with steel in it was a tremendously marketable product. Even though a radial tire cost more than a conventional tire, it lasted 50% to 100% longer and improved gas mileage and certain aspects of a car's handling.

In mid-1978, the outlook for the tire industry was not very promising in the opinion of many industry analysts. The rising price of gasoline had Detroit producing more small, lightweight cars and fewer large cars. Smaller cars meant smaller tires. Auto makers had shrunk the spare tire into a miniature inflatable

---

[5]Ibid., p. 5.

[6]Ibid., p. 6
[7]Ibid., p. 7.

tire to be used only in emergencies. In the near future, new cars would not be equipped with any kind of fifth tire—a prospect that would reduce the original equipment market by 20%. In addition, replacement market sales were diminishing because SBRs did not need to be replaced as often as the non-steel-belted tires. Michelin had recently completed its second North American plant (in South Carolina) and, with its solid reputation for tire quality, was challenging American producers even more with a heavy price-cutting program. Faced with the possibility of near zero growth in the market until the 1980s, the other domestic companies were diversifying into nontire businesses.

## PRODUCT SAFETY CONTROVERSY (1972–1978)

In order to win the race to get the 500 tire into production before its competition, Firestone used modified bias-belted tire production equipment to manufacture its SBR tires. The switch-over saved time and money but turned out to be trouble-ridden. As company documents show, the Firestone 500 tire posed problems throughout its production life. A 1972 memo from a Firestone quality control manager warned of an "adhesion problem" and reported a tire test in which "the rubber peeled cleanly from the wire."[8] Company officials thought the problem was solved until another executive wrote in late 1972 about the "danger of being cut off by Chevrolet (a division of General Motors) because of belt separation failures."[9]

Firestone's problems with the Federal Trade Commission (FTC) began at this time. In its early customer leaflets on maintenance of the Firestone 500, the company warned against overinflation, but said nothing about *under*inflation. Firestone knew that inflation pressure affected a radial tire's performance more than that of a conventional tire and soon learned that underinflation led to irreversible damage within the tire. The FTC ordered Firestone to advertise the critical importance of radial tire inflation and the company agreed to settle the dispute by signing a consent decree. Ironically, Mr. Floberg would tell the Moss subcommittee six years later that the public's unfamiliarity with proper radial tire maintenance and its habit of driving on underinflated tires were major causes of radial tire failure.

A March 1973 memo from a quality assurance statistician said that customer warranty adjustments for the 500 showed the number of tread separations to be 2.5 times that of Firestone's glass-belted tires. "This indicates, we believe, a problem that needs attention," the statistician concluded. Referring to the fact that a better-adhering rubber compound was not yet being used, the chief of product development informed management that "it simply means that we are making an inferior quality radial tire which will subject us to belt edge separation failures at high mileage."[10]

Meanwhile, Firestone was receiving complaints from dealers, the Shell Oil Company, and the Atlas Tire Company (which would soon drop the Firestone 500 tire) about the increasing incidence of belt separation. This type of complaint, one that comes from the knowledgeable and sophisticated buyer, was the kind Firestone took seriously enough to investigate. According to Mr. Floberg, complaints from the individual consumer to Firestone had never been the original source of any Firestone tire recall. Some recalls had affected as few as 12 tires.

By the end of 1973, most of Firestone's plants had installed the ventilation equipment required by the use of a vaporous chemical (Resorcinol) that would improve the adhesion of the rubber to the tire's steel belt. In a few more months all the 500 tires produced contained this new rubber compound.

As 1974 began, General Motors and Ford continued to complain about the failure rates of original equipment tires. GM told Firestone that they were "the only supplier having this (adhesion) problem."[11] A Firestone field survey

[8]Ibid., p. 8.
[9]Ibid., p. 8.
[10]Ibid., p. 9.
[11]Ibid., p. 10.

made it evident that Resorcinol was not solving the adhesion problem. In this same year, a Firestone 500 tire blowout was blamed for a car accident for which Firestone was assessed $1.4 million in damages. When a California Firestone dealer visited Akron to report unusual problems with the 500 tire—adjustments 2–3 times above the normal rate—the company told him that his was a local and minor problem.

In 1975, Firestone conducted the secret high-speed tests the *Beacon Journal* would reveal three years later. Firestone did not report the test results to NHTSA, because the company did not consider the adhesion failures indicative of a defect. Referring to these tests, Firestone's outside attorney would later tell NHTSA that the tires "were not typical of tires being put into service."[12] These tests, coupled with further laboratory research, revealed that the presence of moisture in the rubber compound was the source of the adhesion problem. To solve the moisture problem, Firestone developed new and expensive production techniques. The installation of this "dry technology," however, was not completed until 1977.

Beginning in 1975, GM received a seven-ribbed radial 500 tire that had a stronger type of steel cord and thicker body plies than the old five-rib 500 tire. By April of that year, however, GM was already expressing its unhappiness with the "new 500." At this point Mr. Floberg's legal department was being deluged with product liability claims. In a memo to the company's chairman, Richard A. Riley, a quality control executive warned of the "extraordinary number of letters commenting on problems with this steel-belted radial 500 tire."[13]

In early 1976, Firestone settled what it considered "a commercial problem" by paying $500,000 to Montgomery Ward. Claiming it had been given a bad product, Montgomery Ward insisted that Firestone provide some financial compensation. Ward was a valuable customer, so Firestone obliged. Firestone's annual field surveys brought more bad news. The number of warranty adjustments on the seven-rib 500s had risen. The company's top management was told that tread distortion and separation continued to be a problem—and that field inspectors were finding few instances of tires failing because of underinflation.

In October 1976, a NHTSA press release announced the agency's ongoing investigation of the Firestone 500. Firestone claimed that consumer complaints about radials were industrywide and that "no significant safety-related defect trend existed in these complaints to NHTSA."

NHTSA then brought to Firestone's attention the fact that certain 500 tires produced in late 1973 and early 1974 did not fully comply with Department of Transportation standards. In February 1977, Firestone narrowed this problem to some 25,000 tires turned out by the Decatur, Illinois, plant during a temporary production problem. The company voluntarily recalled 400,000 tires in order to net the suspected defective tires. Such overkill in the number of tires recalled was a standard practice at Firestone. NHTSA's view of the recall was summed up by one NHTSA official: "It was a voluntary recall with some bloody-big arm twisting. The use of that wire (the wire cord in the tires was rusting due to moisture) shows a total disregard for the safety of their customers."[14]

The Center for Auto Safety took a close look at its consumer complaint file on tire failures and found that 50% of the file dealt with the Firestone 500. On November 28, 1977, Director Ditlow wrote a letter to Firestone's president, informing him of this fact and suggesting that Firestone spend less money on advertising and more on quality control. According to Mr. Ditlow, Firestone did not reply. (Firestone's version: the company sent a quality control executive to see Mr. Ditlow immediately after re-

---

[12]Ibid., p. 11.
[13]Ibid., p. 11.

[14]Ibid., p. 12.

ceiving the letter.) The following month NHTSA informed Firestone of the large numbers of complaints it was receiving and requested Firestone's own reports on accidents, injuries, and deaths involving the 500 tire.

In 1978, the Firestone 500 tire went from being primarily an issue of concern in the offices of Firestone and consumer agencies to being a sensational front-page controversy. By this time, Firestone had phased out production of its SBR 500, replacing it with its new 721 model. While Firestone preferred to consider the 500 tire a thing of the past, others would not let the safety issues disappear. The Center for Auto Safety said it "had reports of 35 accidents caused by Firestone steel-belted radial tires—accidents that claimed 15 lives and caused 12 injuries."[15]

In March 1978, NHTSA announced that it had begun a formal defect investigation of the Firestone 500. NHTSA sent to Firestone a "special order" requesting the answers to a list of 27 questions, and the surrender of certain documents. In a long and defiant reply, drafted by a Cleveland law firm, Firestone objected to practically every question. The company complained that the request for information was excessive and vague. Only "specific questions" would be answered. The company questioned the agency's authority to demand data about tires produced over three years earlier on the ground that such tires were exempt from agency control. According to news accounts, "Firestone upbraided the agency for asking it to send copies of certain documents when the company, under the law, only had to make documents available at (its) headquarters."[16] Firestone's refusal to cooperate did not please NHTSA. The prospect of a long court battle would eliminate any hope for a timely resolution of this product safety controversy.

In that same month, Firestone sought and obtained a restraining order in a U.S. District Court, preventing NHTSA from publishing the results of a survey on radial tire safety performance. During the previous year, the agency had mailed 87,000 survey cards to people who had bought new cars equipped with radial tires. Respondents were asked to indicate the brand of their tires and to tell whether they had experienced blowouts or other problems. At the time the survey was drafted, Firestone's lawyers complained that the survey's mailing list and its wording would prejudice recipients against Firestone's 500 SBR tire. (NHTSA later admitted that the survey was "statistically invalid.") They were unsuccessful, however, in preventing the survey from being mailed. Only 5,400 people—6.2% of those surveyed—bothered to respond, but within this group, Firestone received an overwhelming number of complaint citations.[17]

April was to be a catastrophic month for Firestone. On April 2, 1978, the NHTSA survey findings were leaked to the press and became front-page news. How the leak occurred was not clear, except for the fact that the survey got into the hands of the Center for Auto Safety, which made it public. The U.S. District Court judge who issued the restraining order was outraged that his injunction had been violated and promised that he would press criminal charges against whoever was responsible for the leak. Firestone was given authority to subpoena government officials and journalists in order to find out the source of the leak. The Center for Auto Safety protested that Firestone had proceeded to "harass investigators." Mr. Floberg considered the Center's statements typical: "When government agencies act as Firestone did, they say they are fulfilling a public obligation; but when a large corporation exercises its legal rights, these agencies and the press cry harassment and cite the First Amendment."[18] As of mid-1978, the source of the leak was still unknown.

---

[15]Ibid., p. 39.
[16]Arthur M. Louis, "Lessons from the Firestone Fracas," *Fortune,* August 28, 1978, p. 48.

[17]Ibid., p. 47.
[18]Anthony Cortizas, Jr., and Louis Banks, *Corporation v. Environment: The Case of the Firestone 500 Radial* (Cambridge, Massachusetts: Alfred P. Sloan School of Management, MIT [1979]), p. 15.

On April 13, the media reported that Firestone was selling the 500 tire at half-price in some southeastern states. Firestone explained publicly that the tire sale was not an attempt to unload a controversial product. It was an inventory clearance sale that had been scheduled since October 1977. Firestone's management considered this revelation—often coupled with news stories about Firestone's legal action against NHTSA's survey—the turning point in their thinking about the 500 tire issue. For the first time, top management acknowledged that the publicity about the 500 tire threatened the company's reputation for safe and high-quality products.

In May 1978, another bit of history caught up with Firestone. Two months earlier, a press report attributed to Firestone stated that production of the 500 tire had been stopped in 1976. But now, in a May 23 story, the *Miami Herald* reported that production of the 500 had ended only the previous month. Apparently, production of the 500 had been "phased out" over the past 18 months. While most factories had discontinued making 500 tires long ago, the last facility to close down its 500 line had done so only in the past month.

Concerned that the Firestone 500 investigation had been delayed by court proceedings, Representative Moss scheduled hearings before his subcommittee beginning in May. During the congressional hearings, Firestone's dual state of mind was evident. On an ideological level, Firestone management thought of itself as the industry's representative, its crusader for steel-belted radial tires. Firestone would educate congressional representatives as to the nature of radial tires, and thereby clear the 500 of all charges and create peace between government officials and the industry. On a more operational level, Firestone believed the 500 was an excellent tire, undeserving of the press it was getting, and was moved to argue every charge and admit nothing—damn the consequences.

John Floberg was assigned the most aggressive role in responding to the radial tire crisis and almost single-handedly represented Firestone at the Moss subcommittee hearings. Chairman Richard Riley limited his participation in the public debate but had approved the broad outline of Floberg's tactics in dealing with this controversy.

When Floberg appeared before the House subcommittee, he found himself in hostile surroundings. Under the glare of television lights, Moss denounced the company for "merchandising accidents, death, and destruction." Floberg had been preceded by seven witnesses—two police officers, two consumers, a Firestone dealer, a writer, and Clarence Ditlow—all of whom had testified against the 500 radial. Another congressman had cited warranty adjustment rates that, he said, were twice the tire industry average rate and 92 times that of the 721, the 500's successor. He continued, "Wherever we look and from whatever the source, the 500 has a terrible record."[19]

Firestone—in its own eyes—tried to explain itself in reasonable terms and had played the role of the stoic gentleman. When Firestone tried to blame motorists for dangerously underinflating the 500s, subcommittee members angrily reminded the company that the FTC had forced them to place informational advertisements in 1973 to address that very problem. Floberg had little success in convincing the subcommittee that Firestone's problems with the 500 were no more unusual than the problems experienced by the rest of the industry. Despite Floberg's hope, the hearings had not helped Firestone redeem itself in the public eye.

On July 7, 1978, NHTSA told Firestone that it had made an "initial determination" that the Firestone 500 tire had a safety-related defect. The agency did not pinpoint the defect but based its finding on the significantly higher failure rate of the 500 tire compared with other radial tire lines, and on the many accidents and fatalities involving the tire. It recommended that Firestone recall the 500 immediately, but refrained from issuing an order until Firestone had the opportunity to respond at an August hearing before the NHTSA.

To counteract adverse publicity about its SBR 500 tire, Firestone announced a program

[19]"Moss Denounces Firestone Attitude," *Automotive News,* May 29, 1979, p. 2.

for inspecting the tires free of charge. Meanwhile, the company prepared itself to pursue two different and divergent courses of action. The company had hired Clark Clifford, adviser to Democratic presidents and an expensive Washington lawyer noted for his ability to negotiate effectively with government agencies, to try to persuade Joan Claybrook to settle the dispute. One element of management wanted to clear the decks of the entire 500 controversy on the best terms possible, and concentrate on rebuilding with the new 721; this group was adamant in not wanting to generate any more publicity of the kind that came out of the May hearings. Concurrent with Mr. Clifford's efforts, however, Mr. Floberg and his staff were busily preparing to challenge in court the expected NHTSA order to recall the 500 tire.

The July 23 story in the Akron *Beacon Journal* that revealed the 1975 company report on the Department of Transportation speed tests would only further complicate a difficult situation for Firestone. As calls came in from the wire services and other news agencies during the week, Firestone confirmed the accuracy of the reported test results, but said the tests were "among thousands of research and development tests that are conducted each year (by Firestone) and general conclusions about the performance of the tires cannot be drawn from any one test or from a limited number of tests." Was Firestone's top management aware of these tests in 1975? "Test reports of this kind are for use within the development department, and that's as far as these particular tests went,"[20] replied a company spokesperson.

Firestone officials took great pains to explain the purpose of such safety tests. "The continuous testing of a tire model over its production life is a key part of the research always being done in pursuit of a better tire. To develop a better tire, researchers must first find and then understand the performance limits of existing tires. Consequently, most of the company reports on company or government-designed tests deal with tire failure. In most cases, tire failure is the intended result of the tests. And it is wrong to assume that tire failures which occur during tests necessarily indicate a safety-related problem."[21]

## POSTSCRIPT

On August 8, 1978, Firestone appeared before the NHTSA arguing that its steel-belted radial 500 was a safe tire despite public feelings to the contrary. On the second day of the hearings, however, the company made its first public gesture that it was interested in a speedy resolution of the safety dispute. Company representatives announced that they were "willing to take reasonable and appropriate action to allay public concern over the safety of its steel-belted radial 500 tires."[22] Firestone, however, was not yet ready to agree to a recall.

The willingness of Firestone to work cooperatively with the government was helped along by an August 15 court order that required the company to comply with NHTSA's "special order" of March 1978. The court dismissed arguments that Firestone was being singled out for harassment and disagreed with the company's contention that NHTSA lacked information-gathering power.

Meanwhile, Firestone's legal headaches were multiplying as a result of the controversy surrounding its SBR 500 tires. In addition to 250 civil suits alleging that defective 500s caused personal injury, five class action suits had been filed against the company within the past month. By this time, NHTSA had analyzed more than 6,000 reports from consumers alleging more than 14,000 individual tire failures—41 deaths and more than 65 injuries were linked to the Firestone 500.[23]

On September 8, 1978, the *Detroit News* reported that NHTSA would order a recall if

[20]Anthony Cortizas, Jr., and Louis Banks, *Corporation v. Environment: The Case of the Firestone 500 Radial* (Cambridge, Massachusetts: Alfred P. Sloan School of Management, MIT [1979]), p. 1.

[21]Ibid., p. 1.
[22]"Firestone, Calling Tire Safe, Says It May Try to Allay Public Doubt," *Wall Street Journal*, 9 August 1978, p. 11.
[23]*New York Times,* 1 September 1978, p. 110.

Firestone did not agree to one within three weeks. NHTSA and Firestone both denied the story. An NHTSA spokesperson said the agency was looking over extra data the company had provided under the court order. Apparently, the company was contending the agency could not order a recall because it had not proved there was a specific defect in the tire. The agency claimed that it could base a recall on customer complaints alone and accused Firestone of "stalling tactics."

On October 20, 1978, Firestone recalled approximately 10 million of its steel-belted radial 500 tires. The company agreed to replace, free of charge, every 500 tire manufactured between September 1975 and May 1976 that was still on the road. Firestone estimated that the recall would cost it up to $135 million after taxes. This would mean that the company would sink deeply into red ink for its fiscal year

1978. During the previous year, Firestone had earned a total of $110 million after taxes.

Secretary of Transportation Brock Adams said the government decided to work out a voluntary agreement with Firestone instead of going to court because "we wanted to get those tires off the road. . . . We can't measure lives against dollars."[24]

In Akron, Ohio, Firestone Chairman Richard A. Riley said the company agreed to the withdrawal not because it believed the tires were faulty, but because "there has been so much publicity. . . . The thought that there is a defect has been implanted so strongly that we have to convince our customers that we are interested in their welfare. So I think the best solution is to get this behind us."[25]

[24]*New York Times,* 21 October 1978, p. 4.
[25]*New York Times,* 21 October 1978, p. 4.

# Managing Product Safety: The Procter and Gamble Rely Tampon

On Thursday, September 18, 1980, Mr. Edward G. Harness, chairman of Procter & Gamble (P&G) leafed through a stack of newspaper clips that highlighted the health hazards associated with the company's Rely tampon. One newspaper carried the headline "RELY CAUSES 25 DEATHS" with an article citing conclusions from a just-released government report. The fact that another newspaper had just told the world that P&G had quietly halted production of Rely—which many people would take to indicate that the company knew something it wasn't telling—only made things more complicated. These articles would heighten the public controversy that had suddenly surrounded the safety of tampon usage since the beginning of the summer.

Harness and his associates at P&G believed that recent news accounts and allegations linking the Rely tampon to toxic shock syndrome (TSS)—a recently discovered disease that could result in death—were often inaccurate and misleading. Furthermore, P&G exec-utives felt this adverse publicity would only serve to alarm unduly an estimated 50 million American women that regularly used various brands of tampons. P&G had investigated TSS since the Center for Disease Control (CDC) first linked the rare disease to tampon use in a June 1980 study. This original CDC report had not implicated any particular brand of tampon with TSS.

In the September 1980 study, however, the Center said that "among women who develop the disease, the use of tampons generally and Rely in particular is more common than among comparable groups of healthy women."[1] CDC investigators had interviewed 50 women. Seventy percent reported using Rely tampons, about twice the percentage of users in a control group of 150 healthy women. The report did *not* conclude that Rely (or any other tampon) *caused* TSS; it simply concluded that there was

[1]Center for Disease Control, *Morbidity and Mortality Report,* Atlanta, Georgia (May 23, 1980), p. 230.

a "statistical association"[2] between the tampon and the disease.

P&G executives knew that they faced a major crisis. The allegations about Rely were the most serious charges against one of its products that the company had ever encountered in its 143-year history. The company had a reputation for reliability and was noted for its conscientious product testing. Now, in September 1980, the company found its recently introduced Rely tampon under a barrage of criticism. Some company executives were concerned that P&G was being tied to a "bad product" and worried that the publicity might blemish its other brands.

P&G had maintained a cooperative relationship with the Center for Disease Control—a *research* agency of the U.S. Department of Health and Human Services—since the time tampon use and TSS were first linked. The disease itself had been identified only two years earlier and little was known about its causes or symptoms. Intensive research efforts by tampon makers and CDC had so far failed to yield any new information beyond that established by the medical community. When one scientist publicly theorized—prior to concluding his investigation—that superabsorbent tampons, such as Rely, might be the trouble source, P&G executives expressed anger and dismay about the premature conclusion.[3] Despite an occasional disagreement, the company and the Center worked well together and kept each other fully informed of their research on TSS.

The Food and Drug Administration (FDA)—a *regulatory* agency in the U.S. Department of Health and Human Services—became involved with TSS research in midsummer 1980. P&G had dealt with the FDA on previous occasions in skirmishes over ingredients in peanut butter, detergent and deodorant products. Since the FDA had authority to issue consumer warnings and/or product recalls, its

relationship with P&G had been somewhat adversarial. Nevertheless, P&G and the FDA freely exchanged information pertaining to Rely tampons and TSS. The relationship had been chilled recently by FDA media tactics. Knowing P&G to be highly sensitive about bad publicity, the FDA aggressively used the media, some P&G insiders believed, to drive Rely off the market. The FDA claimed that it was critical to keep the public fully informed about "developments involving such an important health and safety issue."[4]

Despite the spate of public attention and the presence of a number of product liability lawsuits, P&G was "determined to fight for a brand, to keep an important brand from being hurt by insufficient data in the hands of a bureaucracy."[5]

## COMPETITIVE ENVIRONMENT

Menstrual products had become a $1 billion-a-year industry by mid-1980. Sales were evenly divided between tampons and sanitary napkins. The tampon business included five major competitors: Tampax (20.3% market share), Playtex (10.9%), P&G (8.4%), Johnson & Johnson (4.4%), and Kimberly Clark (2.9%).[6] The sanitary napkin business was dominated by Johnson & Johnson (29.0% market share) and Kimberly Clark (21.4%).[7] Menstrual products were usually sold in drug and grocery stores.

Competition in this industry was only a recent phenomenon. In 1936, Tampax pioneered the first commercially successful tampon and for the next 30 years it had the business to itself. By the 1960s, changing lifestyles converted more and more women to the advantages of internally worn protection and Tampax's busi-

[2]Ibid, p. 230.

[3]"Procter & Gamble Tampon is Withdrawn From Stores Because of Toxic-Shock Link," *Wall Street Journal,* September 23, 1980, p. 2.

[4]"The FDA and Rely," *Wall Street Journal,* November 11, 1980, p. 24.

[5]"Killing a Product: Taking Rely Off the Market Cost Procter & Gamble a Week of Agonizing," *Wall Street Journal,* November 3, 1980, p. 16.

[6]"Tampon Use Stays Strong Despite Scare, Though Some Women Alter Their Habits," *Wall Street Journal,* October 31, 1980, p. 31.

[7]Ibid., p. 31.

ness grew at an astonishing rate, return on equity reaching 40% in one year. The success of Tampax invited competition from some of the larger consumer goods companies. The marketing muscle of these bigger companies was released when a television advertising ban on menstrual products was lifted in 1972. Playtex quickly entered the market by introducing a new deodorant tampon and Johnson & Johnson soon followed with its own unique tampon design. Meanwhile, Procter & Gamble was preparing for its first product introduction in this market arena.

Procter & Gamble was founded as a partnership in 1837 and was initially engaged in the manufacture and sale of soap and candles in Cincinnati. From its very beginning, the company gained a reputation for being a "good listener"[8] that was responsive to consumer needs. The company, which ranked 23d (in sales) on the 1980 *Fortune* 500 list of largest U.S. industrial corporations, believed that close communication with consumers accounted for its success. The company's sales came from laundry cleansing, personal care, and food products.

The company first began work on menstrual products in the early 1950s but apparently did not succeed in developing a satisfactory product at that time. Following a 1957 acquisition of Charmin Paper Company, P&G researchers succeeded in overcoming the absorbency problems that had previously proved intractable. The research was first applied to such products as toilet tissue, paper towels and disposable diapers, all of which were introduced successfully. By 1968, P&G was convinced it had come up with "a revolutionary kind of tampon."[9] That design, which would later become Rely, consisted of a unique construction of superabsorbent cellulose material and foam rubber. It resulted in quick acceptance of the product by women who tried it.

In January 1974, Rely was test marketed for the first time and was vigorously promoted as being twice as absorbent as any other tampon then available. Rely surprised even P&G by quickly achieving a 30% market share in its trial cities. Early success was only briefly interrupted in 1975 by health-related publicity in the Rochester, N.Y., test market. P&G had conducted safety tests of the materials and clinical tests of the tampon by itself. At the time Rely was introduced, there were not any regulatory procedures in the law that pertained to government testing of medical devices such as tampons. Although P&G denied that Rely caused health problems—no specific health hazards had been cited—the company eventually reformulated Rely by removing polyurethane to quiet consumer complaints. Slowly, test market by test market, P&G expanded its distribution of Rely and gained skill in marketing the product.

Regional marketing began in August 1978. Rely's success was not lost on competitors, who had entered the "absorbency sweepstakes" by adding synthetic fibers to their own products. The competition became particularly intense in 1979. P&G filed a trademark suit against Johnson and Johnson's new superabsorbent tampon. The giant medical products company countered this action by claiming that P&G had "gone to great lengths to disrupt the test-marketing of its (Johnson and Johnson's) new tampon." (P&G's response: "It turned out, obviously, to be more a defensive effort than a business-building effort.")[10]

In February 1980, Rely finally went into national distribution and quickly captured a substantial share of the U.S. tampon market. To convince women to try Rely, P&G had mailed 60 million sample packages to reach 80% of the nation's households and had spent almost $10 million on advertising the product.[11] Even though Rely was gaining widespread

---

[8]"Good Listener: At Procter & Gamble, Success is Largely Due to Heeding Consumer," *Wall Street Journal*, April 29, 1980, p. 1.

[9]Pamela Sherrid, "Tampons after the Shock Wave," *Fortune* (August 10, 1981) p. 14.

[10]"Procter & Gamble Isn't Ready to Give Up on Tampon Market Despite Rely's Recall," *Wall Street Journal*, November 5, 1980, p. 3.

[11]"Tampon Alert Jeopardizes P&G's Rely," *Wall Street Journal*, September 19, 1980, p. 31.

attention, it still accounted for less than 1% of company sales.

Rely's success had cut deeply into the sales of its competitors. Tampax, the leading manufacturer, lost 8.2% of its market share and others suffered even larger proportional losses in their shares.[12] The competitive struggle further intensified with news that the tampon industry's unit sales growth had slowed. Two factors were cited to explain this phenomenon. Women were apparently finding that they did not have to change superabsorbent tampons as frequently and sanitary napkin makers had introduced a thinner and more absorbent product that had gained widespread acceptance. Faced with lower sales volume, many of the menstrual-products companies were rethinking their product and promotional strategies.

## PRODUCT SAFETY CONTROVERSY (1980)

The first known report concerning TSS was issued by a group of Denver pediatricians on November 25, 1978. In an article in a prestigious British medical publication, they reported finding common symptoms in a group of seven children (3 boys and 4 girls), which they postulated were caused by a new toxin produced by a *staphylococcus aureus* bacterium. No mention was made of menstruation or tampon use.

Searches of the medical literature, prompted by the appearance of this syndrome, uncovered a 1927 journal article that described a disease that resembled TSS but was also similar to scarlet fever. A 1942 medical report detailed a case of "clinical syndrome" indistinguishable from that of scarlet fever.[13] This disease, however, had not been specifically identified or named until the 1978 Denver study was released.

The next report of the disease came 15 months later. A March 28, 1980, letter to the editor of an American medical journal reported a disease characterized by high fever and fluid loss in three menstruating women. The letter suggested that herpes virus was a possible causative agent. There was no mention of tampon involvement.

A May 23, 1980, report from the Center for Disease Control (CDC) listed the symptoms of toxic shock syndrome (TSS). Most cases had occurred in women under 25 and had begun during the menstrual period. There were, however, some reports of TSS in men and children. As in earlier reports, no mention was made of tampons. In early June, at a hearing before Senator Edward Kennedy's Senate Committee on Labor and Human Resources, CDC described the symptoms of TSS and stated that "the cause was unknown."[14]

Procter & Gamble and other tampon makers first became involved with the CDC's investigative efforts in mid-June. On June 13, CDC contacted P&G to obtain data concerning tampon usage. CDC was organizing a new study of TSS cases involving menstruating women and was apparently exploring possible links to tampon use. In its telephone call to P&G, the CDC doctor mentioned speculation by a newspaper reporter that tampons might be associated with TSS, but indicated that there were "no data to suggest this."[15] P&G cooperation was pledged and CDC agreed to keep the company informed.

CDC telephoned P&G on June 19 and alluded to an apparent link between TSS in menstruating women and tampon use. A total of 93 women who had the disease were included in three studies, which were conducted by CDC and two state health agencies. All but one of the women regularly used tampons.

Representatives of all tampon manufacturers met with CDC on June 25–26, 1980, to discuss the preliminary research findings. At that

---

[12]"Toxic Shock and Tampax," *New York Times,* October 1, 1980, p. D8.

[13]"Mystery of Toxic Shock Cases Is Unfolding at Disease Center," *New York Times,* 9, October 1980, p. C6.

[14]U.S. Congress, Senate Committee on Labor and Human Resources, *Hearings Before a Senate Subcommittee on Health and Scientific Research,* Washington, D.C., June 6, 1980, p. 11.

[15]Procter & Gamble, "Current Knowledge Concerning TSS," Cincinnati, Ohio, 1980.

meeting, each of the tampon makers turned over product and market share data to the Center's researchers. P&G had been puzzled as to why CDC officials had specifically mentioned Rely (and no other brand) in their questioning at the meeting.

In a June 27 press release, CDC reported the apparent link between tampon use and TSS. It carefully noted, however, that "for the vast majority of women, the risk attributable to tampon use is so low that it seems unwarranted to recommend that use of tampons be discontinued."[16] CDC also noted that while 50 million American women used tampons, TSS was believed to occur in only about 3 of every 100,000 menstruating women. About 6% of those cases resulted in fatalities. Since 1978, according to the press release, 128 cases of toxic shock syndrome had been reported, with 10 resulting in death. A CDC spokesman reminded the public that the study had not implicated any particular brand of tampon.

According to the Center, TSS was characterized by high fever, vomiting, diarrhea, a sunburn-like rash and a rapid drop in blood pressure, which frequently resulted in shock. A CDC epidemiologist said they had not determined exactly how tampon use was related to the disease. If *staphylococcus aureus* was the cause, said CDC, "the use of tampons might favor growth of the bacterium in the vagina or absorption of the toxin from the vagina or uterus—but these possibilities have not been investigated."[17] Future tests were to be conducted in consultation with the Food and Drug Administration (FDA).

At this point, P&G began to collect information about the disease and any possible link between tampon usage in general and Rely in particular. P&G was prevented from obtaining access to patient lists used in the CDC study because of provisions in federal privacy laws. The company was able, however, to collect information from state health departments and individual physicians. This study found no correlation between any specific tampon brand and the toxic shock syndrome.

In July 1980, an FDA bulletin reported CDC's findings and also said that "no particular brand of tampons is associated with high risk."[18] The surgeon general said that women who have not had TSS "need not change their pattern of tampon use. . . ."[19]

During the summer months, P&G microbiologists continued testing the Rely tampon and each of its ingredients with particular reference to the growth of bacteria. Initial results from the program showed that the superabsorbent material in Rely did not encourage TSS and may have actually inhibited bacterial growth. During this time, the company also arranged to convene an outside advisory group, which included eminent scientists from around the country.

By the end of August, the Center for Disease Control had confirmed 213 cases of TSS across the country, of which 16 had been fatal. Public speculation about the cause of the disease began to focus on the superabsorbent tampons, such as Rely. One TSS victim filed a $5 million lawsuit against P&G. Other tampon-TSS suits quickly followed—three of every four TSS liability claims involved P&G's Rely tampon.

On Monday, September 15, CDC telephoned P&G's executive offices in Cincinnati, Ohio, to report that Rely was more frequently associated with TSS than any other tampon. CDC officials cited results from a just completed two-month survey of TSS victims. In the sample of 42 women who had suffered TSS, 71% had used Rely.[20] The results of CDC's second study prompted the scheduling of a meeting in Washington between P&G, the FDA and CDC officials. P&G prepared for this meeting

---

[16]Center for Disease Control, *Morbidity and Mortality Report,* Atlanta, Georgia (June 27, 1980), p. 2.
[17]"Tampons Are Linked to a Rare Disease," *New York Times,* June 28, 1980, p. 17.

[18]FDA, *FDA Drug Bulletin* (Washington, D.C.: July 1980), p. 11.
[19]Ibid., p. 11.
[20]Center for Disease Control, *Morbidity and Mortality Report,* Atlanta, Georgia, September 19, 1980, p. 1.

by quickly assembling a task force that included the vice president of the paper products division, a physician on P&G's staff, and members of the research and legal departments.

On Tuesday, September 16, thirteen P&G representatives met face to face with twelve FDA representatives and three CDC officials to exchange and review available data. P&G arrived ready to take issue with many parts of the CDC study. Company representatives argued that extensive news coverage of TSS may have biased the survey's results. They also challenged the study's interviewing techniques and claimed that CDC's data were "too limited and fragmentary for any conclusions to be drawn."[21] P&G was determined to fight for its product and felt it was being unfairly singled out for media attention.

According to one government representative, the FDA entered the meeting "very concerned about the data, . . . thinking that unless the company had a justification for keeping the product on the market, we would ask that it be withdrawn."[22] The FDA was convinced that Rely's superabsorbent ingredients were partly to blame for the incidence of TSS. They knew, however, that "P&G was not likely to roll over easily."[23] But, anticipating they might have to make some concessions, P&G managers had prepared a warning label that they were willing to put on their packages. The FDA's cool reception made it clear that warning labels would not be enough. The meeting ended with the government allowing P&G one week to study the CDC's findings and respond.

On Wednesday, September 17, P&G decided to halt production in the two plants that produced the Rely tampon. One P&G executive would later say that production was stopped because "it seemed likely that at the very least warning labels would be required on tampon packages, so we didn't want to fill more and more packages without labels."[24] At that time, the company had a one-month inventory of tampons on hand in its warehouses.

On Thursday, September 18, P&G was at a critical juncture in the Rely crisis. Media attention on its tampon was threatening to overwhelm the company. Earlier in the day, CDC released updated statistics on TSS and claimed 25 deaths had occurred since the syndrome was first identified. P&G was further jolted by the news that several of its major retailers had already pulled Rely off their shelves.

Without the abundance of information it normally compiled to make important marketing decisions, P&G had "excruciatingly little data" upon which to base its next move. Four days remained until the company would have to reappear in front of FDA and CDC investigators. P&G could continue its defense of Rely or it could begin to seek some kind of accommodation with the government.

## POSTSCRIPT

On Friday, September 19, the case for Rely weakened as the Utah Health Department reported results of its own study that seemed to confirm CDC's earlier linkage of Rely to TSS. As the weekend approached, P&G convened its previously recruited group of independent physicians, microbiologists, and epidemiologists to review all the studies that had linked Rely with TSS. This outside scientific advisory group reported that although the studies were inconclusive and fragmentary, and did not establish a scientific basis for a decision, they could not assure P&G that the data of the latest study could be safely ignored. One P&G executive later recalled that, "looking at the numbers, we couldn't tell if the TSS was already a major disease, with reported cases just a bare indicator, or whether it was still a small-scale disease but was spreading."[25] As Mr. Harness remembered,

---

[21]"P&G's Rely Tampon Found Implicated in Rare Disease by U.S. Disease Center," *Wall Street Journal,* September 18, 1980, p. 6.
[22]"Killing a Product: Taking Rely Off the Market Cost Procter & Gamble a Week of Agonizing," *Wall Street Journal,* November 3, 1980, p. 16.
[23]Ibid., p. 16.

[24]Ibid., p. 16.
[25]Ibid., p. 16.

"that was the turning point. . . . I knew what we had to do."[26]

On Monday, September 22, P&G announced that the company had suspended sale of Rely tampons. In a press release, the company said, "We are taking this action to remove Rely and the company from the controversy surrounding a new disease called toxic shock syndrome (TSS). This is being done despite the fact that we know of no defect in the Rely tampon and despite evidence that the withdrawal of Rely will not eliminate the occurrence of TSS. . . ."[27]

P&G estimated the voluntary suspension of sales would cost it $75 million after taxes. This would dampen earnings growth but would not place the company in severe financial difficulty. During the previous year, P&G had earned a total of $512 million after taxes.

The FDA viewed P&G's decision as a "preemptive strike" and, as such, a smart move. But at the September 23 meeting with the company, the FDA told the P&G delegation "it had to do more—much, much more."[28] P&G was concerned that the government might still ask the company to admit violation of safety standards. Such an admission would severely damage the company's defense in numerous product-liability suits being filed across the country. P&G did not want the word "recall" used because it might imply safety violations. P&G and the FDA hashed out the details

of the voluntary action for three days before finally reaching an agreement.

On Friday, September 26, P&G signed a consent agreement with the government. Under terms of the agreement P&G denied any violation of federal law or any product defect, but agreed to buy back any unused product the customer still had, including $10 million in introductory, promotional free samples. The company pledged its research expertise to CDC and agreed to finance and direct a large educational program about the disease. The company developed an informational advertising program of unprecedented scope that warned women not to use Rely and cautioned them on the use of other tampons. By deploying 3,000 members of its sales force, P&G removed Rely from retail stores within two weeks of the September 22 announcement.

Food and Drug Administration Commissioner Jere Goyan said, "The recent tampon recall showed how government and industry can act together in the public's interest and should reassure consumers about federal regulations."[29]

In Cincinnati, Ohio, P&G's Chairman Edward G. Harness said, "The company agreed to the withdrawal not because it believed the tampon was defective, but because we did not know enough about TSS to act, and yet we knew too much not to act. We did the right thing in suspending the brand."[30]

[26]Ibid., p. 16.
[27]Procter & Gamble, *Press Release,* Cincinnati, Ohio: Procter & Gamble Company, September 22, 1980, p. 1.
[28]"Killing a Product: Taking Rely Off the Market Cost Procter & Gamble a Week of Agonizing," *Wall Street Journal,* November 3, 1980, p. 16.

[29]"FDA Official Praises Tampon Recall," *Cincinnati Enquirer,* October 3, 1980, p. C11.
[30]Elizabeth Gatewood and Archie Carroll, "The Anatomy of Corporate Social Response," *Business Horizons* 24 (September/October 1980), p. 12.

# Collaborative Research, Inc.

John E. Donalds, the chief executive officer of Collaborative Research, Inc., a small biotechnology company in Lexington, Massachusetts, looked out the window of his spacious modern office and wondered what steps he should take to carry the firm through its current difficulties. As the fourth CEO in five years, Donalds had been brought in by the board of directors to give stability to the company. Donalds, 60, had been an executive at Dow Chemical for thirty-four years, the last eight of which as general manager of the Agricultural Chemical Department (the manufacturers of the controversial pesticide 2-4-5 T) and Director of Biotechnology.[1] He had served since 1981 on Collaborative's board and he had been persuaded to take the job of president to help the company survive the pressures that were squeezing all firms in the biotechnology industry: the heavy costs of financing a technology still in its infancy, the drying up of sources of capital, and the chronic lack of marketable products to generate adequate revenues. Collaborative had lost almost $8 million over the last two years and was continuing to lose money at a "burn rate" of $1 million a quarter.[2] With $16.5 million in liquid assets left over from a 1982 public offering, the firm could only survive for a few more years unless Donalds dramatically cut spending and raised revenues.

In addition to the immediate financial problems, Donalds had other considerations to weigh. One of the company's most promising new technologies was the development of a complete map of the human genome through a process known as RFLPs.[3] When complete, this technique would permit the diagnosis of up to three thousand genetic disorders during and in

[1]See "Note on the Export of Pesticides from the U.S. to Developing Countries," 9·384·097 [pp. 554–571 of this text.].

[2]"Burn rate" is industry slang for the speed of outward cash flow. For general background on the development and competitive environment of the biotechnology industry, see "A Note on the Biotechnology Industry," 9·384·214 [pp. 397–413 of this text].

[3]A genome is a collective term denoting all of the DNA found in human chromosomes.

some instances before pregnancy. The RFLPs project, however, was one of the few for which Collaborative had not found a pharmaceutical company to purchase a research contract, so the firm was financing the research itself. Furthermore the RFLPs project had at least two potentially ethically controversial applications: it could be used in conjunction with abortion to prevent the birth of children with genetic disorders and it could be used by employers to screen employees for potentially problematic (and expensive) diseases.

## COMPANY HISTORY

In 1961, Dr. Orrie Friedman, a 45-year-old professor of chemistry at Brandeis University, decided to leave academia and set up a company to perform biochemical research and to sell small volumes of specialized substances to laboratories to use in their research. Though the company's sales grew slowly (see Exhibit 1), it established a reputation as a high-quality producer of specialized products and an innovator in the emerging field of biotechnology.

In 1980, in the face of the tremendous excitement in the press and on Wall Street about the commercial potential for biotechnology, Friedman decided to build the firm into a leader in the new industry. He recruited the help of Dr. David Baltimore, a microbiologist who had been awarded the Nobel Prize in medicine. Baltimore became a member of the board of directors and assembled a group of leading scientists to form a prestigious Scientific Advisory Board to supervise the firm's research.

At the same time Friedman hired Modesto A. Maidique, a professor at the Harvard Business School and a specialist in the problems of high-tech start-up firms, as a consultant and two years later, in August 1982, Maidique assumed the position of interim president. Maidique set about converting the company from a privately held, entrepreneurial firm managed by the founder, to a publicly owned, professionally managed company that could survive in a rapidly expanding industry.

At first things seemed to go well. In 1981, Dow Chemical put up $5 million for a 5% share of the company and placed John Donalds, the Director of Biotechnology, on the board. On February 11, 1982 the firm went public and raised $17 million. In December of 1982, Orrie Friedman told a group of securities analysts in New York that the company was aiming at a five-year annual sales growth rate of 33 percent and hoped to have sales revenues of $60 to $70 million dollars by 1987.

In 1983, in preparation for the release of its new commercial products, the board approved the appointment of James Wimbush, formerly a division president at Johnson & Johnson, as the new chief executive officer. Wimbush arrived believing that it would be his job to introduce these new products into the marketplace and to begin building the company from a research firm into a small pharmaceutical company with its own manufacturing, distribution, and sales departments.

In 1983 it also became clear that the rosy predictions for the industry in general and Collaborative in particular had been unrealistic. The product which the board of Collaborative had hoped would generate the revenues to build the firm—a diagnostic technique known as EMIA—proved to be less effective and marketable than the board had thought. In an effort to resuscitate the project, Wimbush transferred some of the staff scientists, already disgruntled by Wimbush's completely market-oriented leadership, from their own projects to EMIA. After a year Wimbush realized that the firm was still a long way from bringing any products to market and in the spring of 1984 he quit.

The firm was in a difficult position: It had geared up to become a larger firm by adding staff and moving into new and expensive laboratory space, yet the only revenue the firm was receiving was the money from research contracts negotiated with large pharmaceutical companies and from certain licenses. Orrie Friedman, now seventy years old, briefly took control of the firm but this proved inadequate and the board persuaded John Donalds, who had been about to retire from Dow, to take over.

## INDUSTRY ENVIRONMENT

The problems faced by Collaborative were in part caused by an evolution in the structure of the industry which took place in 1983 and 1984. By 1984, though over two hundred small biotech start-up firms were active and the industry had invested more than $2.5 billion in research, no major products had reached the market in any of the three major areas to which biotechnology was being applied: pharmaceuticals, chemicals, and agriculture. This delay was partly the result of the normally long lead time—sometimes as much as eight or ten years—which was required to bring a new drug or chemical from the test tube through clinical tests, regulatory trials, and manufacturing scale-up to the market. As *Forbes* reported in December 1984, "investors are discouraged."

> The trouble is that the dream that promised a payoff in biotech contained a flaw not present in other high-tech fields. Unlike entrepreneurial companies in computers and semiconductors, the biotech start-ups had no products. Payoffs to investors come from profitable products, not from basic research. The fledgling companies are a long way from having such products.

In 1984 the major pharmaceutical and chemical firms also began moving into the field with enormous financial resources. In September DuPont dedicated a giant $85 million research facility and in October Monsanto opened its own $150 million dollar lab. As *Business Week* reported at the time:

> The large companies believe they will have the upper hand in the long run. Bringing a product from the lab to the marketplace requires large amounts of cash; just getting a drug through clinical testing can cost as much as $20 million. And it is becoming increasingly difficult for the start-ups to get additional funds.

The last point was particularly true—even the lead firms in the industry were having trouble raising money. Most of their stocks were selling below their initial prices (see Exhibit 2), and since the companies could not easily raise cash on the capital markets, they turned to seeking limited partnerships with some of the larger firms. These too proved elusive. In May of 1984 Biogen hoped to raise $60 million in a limited partnership but had to settle for $25 million. In April of the same year Collaborative tried to raise $45 million to fund the RFLPs project through a limited partnership but could find no takers. As Tom Oesterling, Collaborative's vice president for research and development, put it:

> Five years ago you could sell a research contract by walking into a big company and saying, "Hey, we know how to clone, we know how to make proteins; do you want to do a research contract?" And they'd say, "Sure, let's do a contract," because they didn't know anything about it then and they didn't have the internal staff. Now you can't do that. If you go to someone and say, "Hey, we're cloners," they say, "Big deal, so what? What can you do for us? Do you have some product you can show us?"

Despite these great difficulties, it was still widely believed that any firm that could hang on and survive a shake-out would benefit enormously from the boom in future sales, which industry analysts were estimating at between $24 and $60 billion by the year 2000.

## PRODUCTS

The most challenging task facing Collaborative in its effort to plan a successful strategy was to select a range of products to develop which fit with the abilities of the company, the needs of the market, and the activities of competitors. The ideal product was one which built on tested technology yet was protected by some kind of patent or exclusive license; represented a dramatic innovation yet was medically and politically uncontroversial; and met the needs of a population large enough to pay for the developmental costs.

In the fall of 1985, Collaborative Research had several projects under way.

## KPA

Under a joint contract with the Swiss pharmaceutical firm of Sandoz, AG, a research team of thirty-five persons was working on the development of Kidney Plasminogen Activator (KPA). KPA was a precursor to the enzyme urokinase which dissolves blood clots. In preliminary clinical trials KPA has been shown to seek out and dissolve blood clots without interfering with normal blood-clotting functions. Because it could be injected directly into the bloodstream, researchers at Collaborative hoped that it would be used to dissolve the clots blocking the arteries of heart attack and stroke victims.

According to a July 1985 article on the biotechnology industry in *Business Week,* four firms—Genentech, Biogen, Integrated Genetics, and Collaborative Research—were actively developing plasminogen activators, with Genentech's products already in large-scale human tests. All four firms were hoping to win approval from the Food and Drug Administration before the end of the decade and then to begin tapping an annual international market estimated at between $400 million and $1 billion.

## RFLPs

The second major research effort under way at Collaborative was staffed by thirteen people who were painstakingly using DNA probes to reveal Restriction Fragment Length Polymorphisms (or RFLPs, pronounced by everyone in the firm as "rif-ulps") as genetic markers. According to the firm's 1984 annual report:

> These markers result from normal variations in the size of DNA fragments generated by cleavage of DNA with special enzymes. Such RFLPs markers can be used to develop a unique "map" of human chromosomes.

When the RFLPs map was complete, the technology could then be used to develop diagnostic tests based on very small samples of blood or fetal cells for a wide range of genetic disorders such as cystic fibrosis, hemophilia, sickle cell anemia, and Duchenne muscular dystrophy. As the genetic element of other disorders is understood, the RFLPs map could also be used to test for a predisposition to schizophrenia, manic depression, heart disease, and certain forms of cancer.

The technology would also have several drawbacks. Because the technique works on comparing the genetic map of an afflicted member of the family to the genetic map of potential parents or of a fetus, the test initially would be used only in those families where the disorder had already been manifested. Parents with one child (or sibling) with cystic fibrosis, for example, would be able to establish conclusively whether a fetus had the disorder. The test would also be very expensive; current estimates ran from $1,000 to $2,000 for each family.

On the other hand, researchers at Collaborative felt that this work on RFLPs was extremely important. Since the techniques being used to develop the map were all well-known and unproblematic, the success of the project would depend on patience and persistence rather than brilliant innovation. When the map was complete, it would open doors to new research: for example, when the portion of the chromosome which was responsible for muscular dystrophy was located, it could then intensively be investigated to understand the precise genetic malfunction and thus possibly develop a cure. Indeed, the research scientists' only frustration with the project was that the lack of a research contract meant that Collaborative had to restrict the number of researchers to thirteen, thus slowing the work.

## Yeast Genetics

In September 1984, Collaborative Research was awarded the first patent on a genetically engineered form of rennin, the enzyme used in the coagulation of milk for commercial cheese production. Whereas in the past, the cheese industry had had to obtain rennin from a scarce source—the fourth stomach of an unweaned calf—the technique developed by Collaborative promised an abundant supply. Collaborative had licensed the initial technology to Dow Chemical and maintained a laboratory of eight people to continue to develop their expertise in yeast. Although the overall international market for genetically produced rennin was small (from $60 to $100 million a year) and the rennin licensing would be controlled by Dow, yeast genetics was one of the few areas where Collaborative had a clear technological lead; indeed, three of the four members of the Scientific Advisory Board were the world's preeminent experts on yeast genetics.

## Small Projects

Finally, Collaborative maintained a number of small research teams to work on more limited projects. These included four persons to work on the development of Interleukin-2, a product which enhanced the immune response system and was thought to be valuable in the treatment of immune suppression disorders such as AIDS; three persons to work on the antigen cloning project, which was developing a series of diagnostic tests for auto-immune diseases; and five persons to work on new product development.

Collaborative had also continued to produce small quantities of expensive and specialized research and diagnostic products for use by other laboratories.

In addition, Collaborative was developing the first commercial application of the RFLPs technology: a bone marrow test that would match bone marrow transplant donors and recipients. This test would be performed by two employees in a reference laboratory and was expected to generate revenues of $1–2 million a year beginning in the spring of 1986.

## ETHICAL ISSUES

Despite the general climate of dismay that companies were not bringing products to the market faster, scientists and executives in the genetics industry were still convinced that the major advances they had seen in the laboratory would eventually bring major changes to society. As Orrie Friedman said,

> The scientific techniques associated with biotechnology are the most powerful tools that molecular biologists have ever had. The rate at which our understanding of the most fundamental phenomena in biology are going to open up is just mind-boggling. It has all kinds of philosophical, moral, and ethical implications for society. . . .
>
> We can take evolution into our own hands now. Normally evolution proceeds by way of thousands of years of mutation, selection, survival, and so on, but now that we are able actually to manipulate the basic genetic materials—we can cut and stitch it. We can cut out pieces and move them and put them here and put new pieces in. You're dealing with the very essentials of the living person. That has all kinds of implications.

Yet while everyone at Collaborative spoke with similar enthusiasm about the enormous long-range potential of biotechnology, most suggested that such developments were so far in the future that their ethical dimensions did not need to be considered. Said John Donalds:

> I think the issues that you read about—the science fiction issues where people worry that genetic engineering companies like ours might develop projects where we are actually engineering human beings—that's frankly baloney. None of us is going to do it and it's an absolutely irrational thing for us to do.

Echoed Friedman:

> What curls people's hair is if you begin to try to make manipulations that actually change the genetic constitution of the individual in a way in which he will pass them on ad infinitum to his offspring. That brings up all the horrors of the master race and all these weird things. This is very difficult if not impossible for us to do now.
>
> The human genome consists of something like a trillion bases—it's enormous!—and no

one would even think about trying to understand the entire structure at the present state of the art. That is a much more difficult thing to do. So it's a nonproblem. I don't have to lay awake at night and think, "Jesus, should I change the human genome or should I not change the human genome?" It's not that I don't want to do it, I don't know how. It's a nonproblem.

In discussions between the case writer and the executives, board members, and scientists at Collaborative Research, the key question was to what extent, if at all, precursors of the long-range ethical problems raised by the emergent biotechnology could be discovered in the small, incremental decisions faced by a company struggling to survive under difficult business conditions. Over the course of several weeks of interviews, three general areas of ethical concern were defined: resource allocation, total product responsibility, and the proper place of ethical decision making.

## Resource Allocation

To be successful, a small firm such as Collaborative had to make two accurate predictions: that the technical problems posed by a potential product could be solved in the lab, and that a market existed for the product if and when it was produced. As several of the scientists at Collaborative noted, the number of products which could conceivably be manufactured by genetic means and which would be guaranteed a large market was relatively small: they included products such as human growth hormone, interferon, etc. At the same time, the number of laboratories (some of them backed or owned by large pharmaceutical companies) trying to produce these products was large.

Collaborative had several product strategies from which to choose. It could seek to be the technological innovator, such as in the case of yeast genetics. It could seek to be the high-quality producer, as in its development of KPA, which would almost certainly follow Genentech's plasminogen activator but which Collaborative hoped would prove medically superior. It could also try to carve out a niche for itself by working on more innovative and risky technologies or by seeking to produce products for markets deemed too small by the big competitors. This latter strategy was reflected in its pursuit of the minor industrial rennin market, in its development of the bone-marrow test, and perhaps in the case of RFLPs.

Because many of the potential markets for genetic products involved patients with severe medical problems, Collaborative routinely found itself trying to balance the estimated demand for a particular product against its limited financial resources. As Orrie Friedman put it:

> Say a certain individual lacks a certain enzyme through a genetic defect and as a result has the most horrible kinds of problems—he won't survive long and that sort of thing—it might be possible for us one way or another to insert the gene that is missing. Not many companies are going to do it because there's no money in it. These diseases are not that common and you do it once, and it's over with, so it's not a commercially viable thing. It isn't the thing that all the commercial companies are hungering to do because they'll go broke if they try to do it, but it may be socially useful. And you can do that. I am sure we will find ways.

In a few cases, Collaborative decided to pursue projects with limited promise of immediate financial return because they represented seminal developments, as illustrated in the following exchange:

*Casewriter:* Do you ever find yourself saying about a medical product "Well, we may not make a lot on this but it really needs to be made and it may have other positive long-term consequences?"

*Oesterling:* Yes. We have a project that fits that to a T: the Interleukin-2 project. Now if you look at these biotechnology products five years ago everybody was talking about interferon: it's going to cure cancer, it's going to be the new wonder drug. They're still studying interferons, but the bloom is off the rose. It's not looking so great anymore. I look upon this as an evolutionary product, and Interleukin-2 is the next generation interferon; it's an evolutionary product. I don't see it as ever being a gigantic product for anybody. But it's something you have to go through.

### Total Product Liability

A second area of ethical concern was the degree to which any biotechnology firm, by virtue of its role as the developer and distributor of a technology, should reflect upon and be considered responsible for the uses to which that technology might be put. In the case of KPA, a product which if successful would be likely to save thousands of lives, the responsibility was widely accepted within the company for making sure that Collaborative provided Sandoz with the purest KPA possible.

For the RFLPs project, the issues were more complex. On the one hand, the ability to detect genetic disorders at an early stage would allow parents and physicians to predict whether a parent carried a genetic defect, to terminate pregnancies, or to treat disorders long before their clinical symptoms appeared. By the time the project was complete, the scientists at Collaborative hoped to have identified gene sites for many of the more than three thousand genetic disorders, and such a map, though rudimentary in relation to the complexity of the gene, would inevitably lead to new discoveries. As John Donalds put it:

> RFLPs can truly revolutionize medicine and I am dedicated to making us one of the ones that are going to beat this revolution. If we don't, others will; it's absolutely inevitable. It's coming.

On the other hand, the RFLPs project also raised two potentially explosive ethical issues. The first was the issue of abortion. As board member and HBS finance professor Samuel Hayes put it:

> It doesn't bother me personally because I don't happen to be one of those who believes that

abortion is a moral issue. I certainly can see some ways that the use of a genetic map might lead to an abortion decision, but my guess is that you can probably get that information as easily from testing amniotic fluid as from a map. Abortion ... doesn't concern me as a moral issue, but I can see how it would for people for whom it was a question of morality.

The other issue was stated succinctly by Tom Oesterling:

> When RFLPs is finished you'll be able to measure any inherited trait, so of course the first target will be related to health care, starting out with any diseases that have genetic components and being able to provide diagnostic information to genetic counselors or whatever and that information is very sensitive. Some of the tests will be used to make family planning decisions; some will be used to make abortion decisions; and some of the information could play out in employment.
>
> Suppose you've been measured for what genes you carry and you go to an employer and the employer wants to know. And then the employer makes a decision on whether to hire you or not based on what he knows about your genes. Well, there's a lot of ethics involved in that—how's that going to be handled?

### Ethical Decision Making

Framed in general terms, the managers and board members all expressed a keen interest in considering ethical issues. Said board member Hayes:

> I don't hold the view that because we have a technology we also have the right to exploit it. Certainly I would be very sensitive to arguments that we were opening a Pandora's box. I feel very strongly about a board and a company acting responsibly.

Said John Donalds:

> If you're running an operation, you can't separate quality control and safety and housekeeping. If you're going to run a good plant, you have got to do them all. You can't do two out of three; it won't work. The same thing applies with morals and ethics. You really can't do a lit-

tle bit. I think you just have to try to do it all the way through your whole organization in every way.

In tracing product decisions through the levels of management, however, it became clear that social or ethical issues were rarely raised. Suggestions for new products were usually generated by the New Project Committee (comprised of staff scientists), reviewed with the Scientific Advisory Board, forwarded to Tom Oesterling, discussed at the Management Committee (made up of the VPs and John Donalds), and finally presented to the board of directors.

This is not to say that personal values did not influence decisions at all levels, as can be seen in one staff scientist's description of how the decision not to extend the RFLPs investigation into certain kinds of plant genetics was made.

> We realized that we could apply this technology to mapping traits in plants and we talked to this person who had done some marketing inquiries. She told us that corn was an obvious choice and she said, "Well, the other possibility is tobacco." And the other guy and I looked at each other and said, "We wouldn't do tobacco." We both hate smoking and smokers and everything about them. We just couldn't get excited about doing that kind of work to improve the tobacco crop.

Nonetheless, the almost unanimous opinion was that discussions of the ethical dimension of corporate decisions were extremely infrequent. Said Oesterling:

> We have many issues that come up but nothing that really smacks of an ethical issue; none that I can recall. We have lots of discussion about whether we take a contract or we continue to pursue a certain project or not, but not so much on the ethics.

Members of the board of directors offered similar observations:

> I don't know of any major ethical questions that have risen to the board level since I've been at Collaborative. (Hayes)

> We're breaking our butts trying to make a few products that might be of value and use to the public. We don't have great moral dilemmas; they are not options for us. (Friedman)

> In the year I've been out here most of the thought and conversations that I have heard about what products we should and shouldn't be working on has come from me and our Scientific Advisory Board and from Tom Oesterling. I've heard no thoughts whatever from my treasurers, my CFO, my operational people— it's as though they don't think about those issues. I'd have to say that if a company like this is going to operate in a proper, moral aspect, if the CEO doesn't blow the whistle probably nobody's going to do it. The responsibility has to come back to his shoulders. (Donalds)

## EXTERNAL CONTROLS ON ETHICAL DECISIONS

The executives at Collaborative seemed content with the relatively low level of discussion about the long-term implications of their product policy and of biotechnology because they felt that the external controls were adequate. Specifically they referred to the following forces which would control the behavior of the firm:

### Individual Decisions

In reference to the question of total product liability, the most common response was that the company was minimally responsible for the uses to which the product was put because the decision to market the product would be made by a larger pharmaceutical company and the decision to use it would be made by an individual physician and patient. Said John Donalds:

> How can we tell a doctor what is right and what is wrong morally in relation to his thoughts and his patient's feelings? I don't think we can.

### Market Forces (Collective Decisions)

Similarly, the managers felt that over time such individual decisions would aggregate into an expression of market will. Said Donalds:

> If you want to work on a new product you have to have a product that will fit society's needs

and will fit the moral and ethical requirements of society at the time you expect to bring it out. If you don't it's just an absolute waste of time and money. It's just poor business.

## REGULATIONS, LAWS, AND PUBLIC OPINION

Finally, the managers at Collaborative felt that the task of making moral judgments for the biotechnology industry belonged to the public expressing its will through the press and through the legislative system. As John Donalds put it:

> I feel that the ethical issues in biotechnology, at least in our society, will get debated. They will be discussed by people, they will be written up in the papers, in the Sunday supplements, and people will talk about it. If they get excited enough they will talk to their legislatures.
>
> When I speak to women's groups about biotechnology, I tell them this: you women should understand that you have every right to be heard, as much as any doctor, or as any scientist, or any politician, and don't let these other people tell you what is right and wrong.

Said Orrie Friedman simply:

> A businessman is a businessman. If something is allowed by law and you can make a profit doing it, good. I really don't think that a businessman should make such decisions; I'm not sure he would be free to make them.

## CONCLUSIONS

In September of 1985, John Donalds had many issues to untangle and decisions to make. In the immediate future he had to figure out a way to cut costs in order to decrease the burn rate. Over the longer term, he had to find a way to raise revenues through some combination of increasing research contracts, negotiating new joint ventures, or bringing products to market. Specifically he had to decide the future of the RFLPs project: should he continue to fund it on the chance that it would pay off or should he risk further dislocation of the company by discontinuing it? In what way should the ethical dimensions of the product be considered in his decision?

Donalds also had to give some long-range consideration to the identity of the firm. It had begun as a research project and diagnostic company and it had made a failed attempt to grow rapidly into a pharmaceutical company; what should it become in the future?

**EXHIBIT 1**
COLLABORATIVE RESEARCH, INC.

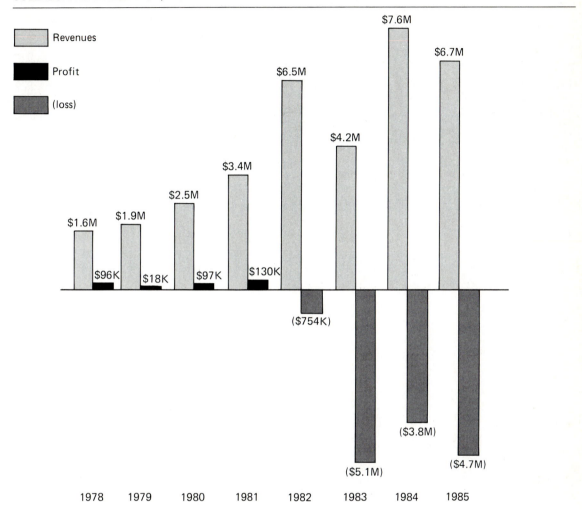

Source: Dr. Orrie Friedman

**EXHIBIT 2**

BIOTECH STOCK, INITIAL AND RECENT PRICES

| | Initial offering price | Recent price | Equity | Debt (in millions) | R&D limited partnership | R&D as % of Equity |
|---|---|---|---|---|---|---|
| Amgen | 18 | 4¼ | $ 59 | $8 | — | 0% |
| Cetus | 23 | 10 | 136 | 5 | $ 75 | 55 |
| Genentech | 35 | 50¼* | 96 | 5 | 120 | 125 |
| Genex | 9½ | 8⅛ | 49 | 9 | — | 0 |
| Centocor | 14 | 10¼ | 29 | — | — | 0 |
| Collaborative Research | 11 | 5¼ | 36 | — | — | 0 |
| Molecular Genetics | 9 | 6½ | 37 | — | 11 | 30 |
| Hybritech | 11 | 15½ | 125 | 3 | 77 | 126 |
| Biogen | 23 | 5¼ | 61 | 1 | 26 | 21 |
| California Biotechnology | 12 | 5¼ | 16 | — | 28 | 175 |

*Adjusted for splits.

*Source:* "Whale Securities," as quoted in *Forbes*.

**EXHIBIT 3**
CONSOLIDATED BALANCE SHEETS
As of August 31, 1984 and 1983

| | 1984 | 1983 |
|---|---|---|
| **Assets** | | |
| Current assets: | | |
| Cash and short-term investments ($18,720,000 in 1984 and $23,038,000 in 1983) | $18,974,121 | $23,448,734 |
| Receivables: | | |
| Trade (less allowance for doubtful accounts of $30,000 in 1984 and $48,000 in 1983) | 1,183,528 | 690,981 |
| Unbilled costs and fees | 26,523 | 90,530 |
| Interest | 678,868 | 594,539 |
| Inventories | 271,329 | 656,697 |
| Prepaid expenses | 87,866 | 75,788 |
| Total current assets | 21,222,235 | 25,557,269 |
| Equipment and leasehold improvements, at cost: | | |
| Laboratory and scientific equipment | 3,405,057 | 2,708,840 |
| Leasehold improvements | 4,135,283 | 3,550,181 |
| Office equipment, furniture, and vehicles | 354,943 | 276,793 |
| | 7,895,283 | 6,535,814 |
| Less—accumulated depreciation and amortization | 2,053,742 | 1,235,260 |
| | 5,841,541 | 5,300,554 |
| Other assets | 675,000 | 165,397 |
| Total | $27,738,776 | $31,023,220 |
| **Liabilities and Shareholders' Equity** | | |
| Current liabilities: | | |
| Accounts payable | 213,929 | 217,914 |
| Accrued expenses | 754,889 | 700,757 |
| Deferred contract revenue | | 27,474 |
| Total current liabilities | 968,818 | 946,145 |
| Deferred compensation | 337,608 | 251,820 |
| Shareholders' equity: | | |
| Common stock, $.10 par value—authorized—17,500,000; issued and outstanding—9,945,323 in 1984 and 9,887,212 in 1983 | 994,532 | 988,721 |
| Series B restricted stock, contingently convertible, $.10 par value—issued and outstanding—228,832 shares in 1984, and 408,112 shares in 1983 | 22,883 | 40,811 |
| Additional paid-in capital | 34,820,865 | 34,782,255 |
| Deficit | (9,003,405) | (5,251,930) |
| Installment receivable from sale of Series B restricted stock | (402,525) | (734,602) |
| Total shareholders' equity | 26,432,350 | 29,825,255 |
| Total | $27,738,776 | $31,023,220 |

**EXHIBIT 4**

CONSOLIDATED STATEMENTS OF OPERATIONS
For the Years Ended August 31, 1984, 1983, 1982

| | 1984 | 1983 | 1982 |
|---|---|---|---|
| Revenue | | | |
| Product sales | $3,450,661 | $1,984,700 | $2,034,708 |
| Contract revenue | 2,230,495 | 2,208,722 | 4,379,876 |
| Royalties | 1,925,000 | | 50,000 |
| Total revenue | 7,606,156 | 4,193,422 | 6,464,584 |
| Cost of revenue | | | |
| Cost of product sales | 3,215,441 | 1,556,105 | 1,206,129 |
| Cost of contract revenue | 1,822,052 | 1,532,084 | 3,217,972 |
| Cost of royalty revenue | 500,000 | | |
| Total cost of revenue | 5,537,493 | 3,098,189 | 4,424,101 |
| Gross profit | 2,068,663 | 1,095,233 | 2,040,483 |
| Operating expenses | | | |
| Research and development | 3,276,529 | 2,530,624 | 1,052,938 |
| Selling, general and administrative | 4,628,624 | 5,528,883 | 3,324,605 |
| Total operating expenses | 7,905,153 | 8,059,507 | 4,377,543 |
| Loss from operations | (5,836,490) | (6,964,274) | (2,337,060) |
| Interest income | 2,085,015 | 1,776,629 | 1,506,809 |
| Loss before income taxes | (3,751,475) | (5,187,645) | (830,251) |
| Credit for income taxes | | | 76,000 |
| Net loss | $(3,751,475) | $(5,187,645) | $ (754,251) |
| Net loss per common share | $(    .38) | $(    .60) | $(    .10) |
| Weighted average common shares outstanding | 9,930,501 | 8,713,374 | 7,423,447 |

# A Note on the Biotechnology Industry

*Science seldom proceeds in the straightforward logical manner imagined by outsiders. Instead its steps forward (and sometimes backward) are often very human events in which personalities and cultural traditions play major roles.*

—Dr. James D. Watson
*The Double Helix*

Watson's observation about the pioneering discovery of the structure of the DNA (deoxyribonucleic acid) molecule may offer a sign of what lies ahead for the industry that has sprouted in its wake—the esoteric, potentially lucrative, and somewhat intimidating business of biotechnology. The industry's birth had been anticipated for many years; it had become "the stuff of science fiction."[1] By the 1980s, the commercialization of recombinant DNA (rDNA) was a reality that attracted interest far beyond the laboratories of the scientific community.

Few technological advances had ever created as much excitement. According to some in the field, the commercial applications of rDNA would be "limited only by the imaginations of the scientists."[2] Genetic engineering opened up a new world of pharmaceuticals, industrial chemicals, plants, food products, energy sources, and pollution-control products. It was labeled by the mass media as the "industry of life" equipped with "gene machines." Some speculated that rDNA research might represent a scientific revolution with a potential impact greater than that of the industrial revolution.

By 1984, the commercial potential of genetic engineering had attracted a wide variety of firms from around the world—estimated to number more than 250—with well in excess of $2.5 billion in investment capital. With many rDNA products still years away from an introduction to the market, experts conservatively projected a $500 million market by 1985, climbing to $3 billion by 1990 and reaching $15 billion by 2000. Others cautioned that such numbers were "extremely tentative, since the situation is just too iffy at this stage."[3]

Despite the frenzy of investment activity,

[1]William Patterson, "The Rush to Put Biotechnology to Work," *Industry Week,* September 7, 1981, p. 65.
[2]Sheldon Krimsky, *Genetic Alchemy: The Social History of the Recombinant DNA Controversy* (Cambridge, MA: The MIT Press, 1982), p. 287.

[3]William Patterson, op. cit., p. 66.

few biotech firms had any big products to sell. For organizations with a large stockpile of cash, the lack of a product was not particularly bothersome; for smaller start-up ventures, however, the "burn rate" (industry slang for the speed of cash outflow) was a growing concern. As competition for capital and scientific expertise increased, rivalries intensified and the industry anticipated its first major shakeout.

The biotechnology industry faced a variety of challenges, including the murky areas of patents, the legal entanglements of licenses, the strained alliance with the academic community, and the much-debated prospect of biohazards. Government officials, while hailing the fast-breaking research, could not form a consensus on how to regulate biotechnology and took a "wait and see" attitude. Public concerns were abating, but there was still a general lack of understanding of biotechnology.

The industry was not without its skeptics and opponents. Declared social critic Jeremy Rifkind: "[This] marks the beginning of the genetic age and gives corporations the green light to begin engineering the gene pool. The *Brave New World* that Aldous Huxley warned of is now here."[4] Indeed, the commercialization of rDNA was certain to raise many important ethical, legal, economic, political, religious, and social questions for the biotechnology industry. As the CEO of Cetus Corporation (an established biotechnology firm) put it, "The crystal ball is still cloudy."[5]

## WHAT IS BIOTECHNOLOGY?

Biotechnology—"the use of living organisms or their components in industrial processes"—is possible because microorganisms naturally produce countless substances during their lives.[6] Some of these substances have proved commercially viable, and a number of different industries have already learned to use microorganisms as natural factories, cultivating populations of the best producers under conditions designed to enhance their abilities.

Applied genetics, the purposeful manipulation of genetic information within cells, could play a major role in improving the speed, efficiency, and productivity of biological systems. As practiced by ancient societies, applied genetics involved a minimum of human intervention. Alcohol and cheese fermentation and the recycling of wastes were undertaken by exposing the appropriate raw materials to the environment, whereupon a transformation of the substrates took place. Controlled animal and plant breeding was accomplished by placing prospective parents in proximity to one another.

Numerous important laboratory discoveries and scientific observations have led to the present-day boom in genetics. As early as the mid-1900s, Gregor Mendel was able to identify the rudimentary characteristics of the hereditary mechanisms—what was later to be called the gene. During the first few decades of the 20th century, scientists learned how to map genes by exchanging parts between chromosomes. In the early 1940s, a group of scientists led by Oswald Avery uncovered evidence that the gene was made of deoxyribonucleic acid (DNA), but many were reluctant to accept that such a simple molecule could determine genetic traits. It was not until 1953, when Francis Crick and James Watson uncovered a scientifically sound structure—the "double helix"—for DNA, that a major riddle of the gene was solved. Another important breakthrough took place in 1973, when Stanley Cohen and Herbert Boyer developed recombinant DNA methods that permitted scientists to move pieces of DNA from one cell to another. This "gene splicing" made possible the combination of the characteristics of one species of living organism with those of another—a process that normally does not occur in nature, since organisms of different species, with few exceptions, do not mate. With the Cohen-Boyer discovery, the "genetic age" had formally begun and was soon

---

[4]Ibid., p. 68.
[5]Ibid., p. 66.
[6]*Impacts of Applied Genetics,* Office of Technology Assessment, Congress of the United States (Washington, D.C.: U.S. Government Printing Office, 1981), p. 4.

to spark an unprecedented debate within the scientific community.

The central purpose of genetic engineering has been to harness the ability of cells to produce a desired chemical. Each cell, from the simplest bacterium to the most complex human cell, contains genes, i.e., instructions in the DNA molecule. The number and arrangement of the genes within a cell determine the nature of the instructions given. Genes instruct the productive mechanisms of the cell, which in turn facilitate the cell's chemical reactions. These reactions result in substances the cell requires for life, growth, and reproduction. In the reproduction process, a cell creates an identical set of DNA instructions and then divides. Genetic engineers control, by manipulation and alteration, the information coded in the genes in order to cause the cells to make substances useful to humans. Genetic engineering, therefore, is not in itself an industry—although many popularized it as such—but a *technique* that allows the researcher to modify the hereditary apparatus of the cells.

The modern technology of applied genetics encompasses a variety of procedures and processes. *Recombinant* DNA technology isolates fragments of DNA from separate sources and splices them together chemically to form a functional unit. The DNA fragments derive from the same organisms or from different organisms of the same species. There are six distinct phases in the *process* of rDNA technologies:

1   Isolation and purification of DNA
2   Fragmentation of DNA into reassociable segments
3   Sealing of DNA fragments together
4   Replication and maintenance of rDNA molecules
5   Selection of cells containing rDNA
6   Expression of rDNA into gene products

While the technology of recombinant DNA represents the most recently developed—and glamorous—form of genetic alteration, a number of *nonrecombinant* technologies have been available for many years. These include induced imitations (mutagenesis), cell fusion methods, conjugation, bioconversions, fermentation, gene therapy, and plant tissue culture techniques.

## THE QUESTION OF RISK

The announcement at the Gordon Conference on Nucleic Acids in June 1973, that segments of hereditary material from disparate organisms could be hooked together, provoked an immediate and dramatic response from assembled scientists. An urgent call was issued for wider discussion of this new-found ability to engineer genetic systems, and a flurry of papers on genetic engineering emphasized the public's right to know and decide the direction of science. As expressed by one commentator, "Scientists must assume the responsibility to tell society, in a forceful and persistent manner, what science is discovering and what the technological consequences are likely to be."[7]

In February 1975 the Asilomar II Conference, sponsored by the National Academy of Sciences and the National Institutes of Health, dealt with the controversy surrounding rDNA research. Scientists there agreed that most DNA research should proceed, but they called for a halt on several types of questionable projects until better guidelines for controlling safety in the lab could be available.

Despite the moratorium on certain genetic projects, public mistrust of scientists engaged in genetic engineering persisted. Many in the media painted "worst case" scenarios: epidemics caused by man-made virulent pathogenic bacteria escaping from laboratories; ecological imbalances; new tools for biological warfare and terrorism; and misuse of the power to control human genetic engineering.

Assessments of risk generally included at least two broad categories of hazards:

1   Hazards associated with organisms released, inadvertently or intentionally, from

[7]Sheldon Krimsky, op. cit., p. 340.

the laboratory and surrounding the physical plant in which experiments were conducted. (Internal Containment)

2 Hazards associated with evolutionary consequences of conducting particular genetic experiments. (External Consequences)

At the urging of the scientists at Asilomar II, the National Institutes of Health (NIH)—a research unit of the U.S. Department of Health and Human Services—took the first step to regulate the research on recombinant DNA. The NIH Guidelines contained descriptions of experiments that were prohibited and those that were allowed under defined conditions, as well as requirements for physical and biological containment.

Congressional attempts to give the NIH Guidelines the force of law—requiring *all* emerging biotech firms to comply—failed to produce a consensus. The NIH Guidelines were to remain "voluntary" for privately funded institutions engaged in developing rDNA applications. Nevertheless, these firms were required to establish an internal Institutional Biosafety Committee (IBC) to review projects for compliance with NIH Guidelines and to petition NIH about experiments that were not explicitly covered by the guidelines. Regulation of rDNA research remained a lively public topic as a wide range of options were discussed by legislators, bureaucrats, interest groups, and scientists. Options ranged from complete self-regulation by the community of scientists to complete government control of the research in federal laboratories.[8]

Within a period of three years, public concern over gene-splicing technology was to undergo a remarkable transformation, as reflected in the attention given the issues by the mass media. During the spring of 1977, when federal legislation seemed imminent, *Newsweek* magazine, in its cover story entitled "The DNA Furor: Tinkering with Life," warned of the perils of unbridled scientific research. In March 1980, *Time* magazine used its cover to trumpet "DNA's New Miracles." The scientific community had accomplished a significant feat—the issue of biohazards had been largely put to rest in the public mind. Attention was now almost exclusively directed toward commercial possibilities, patenting, and sources of venture capital.

By 1982 the NIH Guidelines were relaxed and made simpler. Experiments still under NIH control involved toxin genes, drug resistance genes, and the release of recombinant material into the environment. Overall, there was a belief that the NIH Guidelines had been observed by the organizations (and their scientists) in private industry. According to a scientist at one biotech firm, "there hasn't been anyone who has gotten so much as a cold from recombinant DNA."[9] Still, some remained unconvinced. One widely respected university scientist noted the opportunities for conflict of interest: "Most of the scientists have an industrial connection. It is not wise for them to raise issues of risk. An orthodoxy has now developed that rDNA is not risky. But what is the likelihood that we are going to get a free lunch out of this?"[10]

By 1984, there was no single federal government agency with specific responsibility to regulate the research on the commercial development of rDNA. Authority to regulate different aspects of commercial genetic engineering was dispersed among at least 10 federal statutes:

• The Federal Food, Drug, and Cosmetic Act and the Public Health Service Act gave the FDA authority over drugs, food products, and biologics.
• The Occupational Safety and Health Act gave OSHA and NIOSH authority over worker health and safety with specific re-

---

[8]Patrick J. Hennigan, *Regulating Biomedical Technology: The Case of Recombinant DNA Research* (New York: Columbia University, 1981), p. 5.

[9]Michael Wines, "Genetic Engineering—Who'll Regulate the Rapidly Growing Private Sector?" *National Journal,* October 15, 1983, p. 2098.
[10]William Patterson, op. cit., p. 70.

sponsibility to inspect federally funded rDNA laboratories.

- The Toxic Substances Control Act, the Marine Protection Research and Sanctuaries Act, the Federal Water Pollution Control Act, the Clean Air Act, the Hazardous Materials Transportation Act, the Solid Waste Disposal Act, and the Federal Insecticide, Fungicide, and Rodenticide Act all gave the EPA authority over environmental matters associated with rDNA.

Long-standing statutory duties also called for the cabinet-level involvement of the U.S. Department of Agriculture, Health and Human Services, and Labor. With no single government oversight mechanism, there was nothing to reduce the regulatory confusion caused by

conflicting interpretations of federal law. Federal interagency coordination of safety issues concerning the worker, the product, the laboratory, and the environment involved at least nine different federal agencies, as illustrated in the diagram on this page.

As rDNA research moved from the laboratory to the marketplace, concern about the effects of genetic material was very likely to keep regulatory agencies involved. In the laboratory, most research was limited to 10-liter batches or less. Moderate-scale facilities required fermenters in the 100–1,000 liter range, and larger facilities called for equipment in the range of 2,000–50,000 gallons. Scaling up the research and manufacturing processes required new procedures for production, transportation of materials, waste disposal, and pollution control.

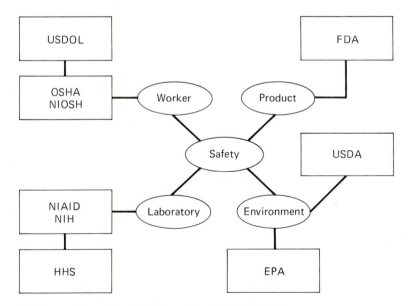

OSHA   — Occupational Safety and Health Administration
NIOSH  — National Institute of Occupational Safety and Health
NIAID  — National Institute of Allergy and Infectious Disease
NIH    — National Institutes of Health
FDA    — Food and Drug Administration
USDA   — U.S. Department of Agriculture
EPA    — U.S. Environmental Protection Agency
HHS    — U.S. Department of Health and Human Services
USDOL  — U.S. Department of Labor

Thus, in all likelihood, more companies would be affected by most or all of the federal statutes mentioned earlier. States like Maryland and New York had invoked their "police powers" to protect the health and safety of their citizens. A few local jurisdictions (Cambridge, MA; Princeton, NJ; Berkeley, CA) insisted that bio-tech firms comply with NIH's voluntary guidelines.

Although most experts believed from their experience that the immediate hazards posed by basic research were minimal, nobody could be certain about all the consequences of placing genetic characteristics in micro-organisms, plants, and animals that had never carried them before. There were at least three separate areas of concern:

- Genetically engineered microorganisms might have potentially deleterious effects on human health, other living organisms, or the environment in general. Unlike toxic chemicals, organisms reproduce and spread of their own accord; if released into the environment, they might be impossible to control.
- Evolution thus far has depended on genetic diversity; replacing in nature diverse inferior strains by genetically superior strains might increase the susceptibility of living things to disease and environmental insults.
- Engineering of genetic material requires understanding of life itself, affording the scientist unprecedented responsibility and power.

While the going had been slow for most biotechnology firms, a solid coalition within the scientific community worried about the time when the technical reach might exceed the public's grasp. "What you've got now is an extremely competitive industry," said one participant in the public policy debate. "There are lots of new products being developed and lots of pressure to be first on the market. You've just got this feeling that at some point, someone's going to say, 'We've got to move now.'

And right now, there are no regulations to stop that."[11] When plans to release modified bacteria into the environment with the approval of NIH were announced, a furor quickly ensued. One critic called it "ecological roulette" and predicted that industry would soon be conducting thousands of such tests. "All it takes," he said, "is for one of those experiments to go haywire."[12]

## THE PROMISE OF GENETICS

In the early stages of the DNA debate, scientists tried to balance risks against benefits of research. As the public gained a greater understanding of the risks associated with DNA research, scientists began focusing on the other side of the equation—the social benefits. They cited the opportunity costs to society should this research be restrained. These costs would take the form of delayed discoveries that might have resulted in cures for serious diseases or in developments of medically important products that the new technology was certain to spawn. Some scientists continued to believe that science should do no harm, which meant reducing risks to a negligible factor regardless of the anticipated benefits.

Congress's Office of Technology Assessment (OTA) pondered over the impact of the "genetic revolution":

> Interest in the industrial use of biological processes stems from a merging of two paths: the revolution in scientific understanding of the nature of genetics; and the accelerated search for a sustainable society in which most industrial processes are based on the use of renewable resources. The new genetic technologies will spur that search in three ways: they will provide a means of doing something biologically—with renewable raw materials—that previously required chemical processes using nonrenewable resources; they will offer more efficient, more economical, less polluting ways for producing both old and new products; and they will in-

[11]Michael Wines, op. cit., p. 2097.
[12]"Biotech Comes of Age," *Business Week,* January 23, 1984, p. 90.

crease the yield of the plant and animal resources that are responsible for providing the world's supplies of food, fibers, and some fuels.[13]

OTA contended that the market value of key genetic products in six basic areas where rDNA might have its greatest impact—pharmaceuticals, chemicals, agriculture, food, energy, and pollution control—could reach $27 billion by the end of the century.

### Pharmaceuticals

Gene splicing represented a fundamental shift in the research and development being done in the $15 billion pharmaceutical industry. Instead of testing one chemical after another to arrive at a useful drug, scientists will be able to identify the substances that form the body's natural defenses and biotech firms will be able to manufacture them genetically. Some products—an anticancer agent (interferon), a clotting agent for hemophiliacs, insulin, and a human growth hormone—were all close to receiving regulatory approval for commercial marketing.

A broad variety of faster, more accurate diagnostic tests were already reaching the market to facilitate treatment of difficult-to-diagnose diseases such as prostate cancer. Less costly, more effective, and safer vaccines were being developed for such diseases as hepatitis, herpes, and sickle-cell anemia. OTA estimated that the market for genetically produced pharmaceuticals could reach $1.2 billion by the year 2000.

### Chemicals

Nearly $50 billion worth of products were sold annually by the chemical industry, and all but a small fraction were derived from oil, which was in limited supply. Many chemicals could be made—and produced less expensively—with the water-based chemistry of living organisms. Biomass held particular promise as an en-

ergy source for the industry. Indigo dye, a finished product, was being made experimentally by genetic manipulation rather than through the normal synthetic process. Many experts believed that high-volume chemical feedstocks such as ethylene, a critical ingredient in plastics, could be made commercially through biotechnology. OTA estimated that the market for genetically produced chemicals could reach $7.0 billion by the year 2000.

### Agriculture

Growth hormones for cows, products that promised significant increases in milk production, were already being field-tested. Research was under way to develop technologies for such animal applications as hoof and mouth vaccines, swine dysentery vaccines, synthesis of animal hormones to increase livestock yields, improved animal breeding techniques, and the development of a bovine interferon that could treat a wide variety of diseases. The potential benefit of any one of these breakthroughs was very significant, as worldwide losses from hoof and mouth disease exceeded $1 billion annually.

In plant genetics, scientists were developing new crop varieties that were resistant to herbicides, could grow in drought conditions, or could thrive in high-salinity soil. These "super" plants were also being given enhanced nutritional value. OTA estimated the market for genetically produced agricultural products at anywhere from $10 billion to $100 billion by the year 2000.

### Food Processing

Genetics could be used in food processing in two ways: to design microorganisms that transform inedible biomass into food for human consumption or animal feed; and to design organisms that aid in food processing, either by acting directly on the food itself or by providing materials that can be added to food. Aspartame sweetener for soft drinks was being produced by genetically engineered bacterial enzymes.

[13]*Impacts of Applied Genetics*, p. 43.

OTA provided no estimate of market potential for this category.

## Energy

Bacteria have been used to leach metals such as uranium and copper from low-grade ores. Enhanced oil recovery techniques made possible by genetics could help gain access to 300 billion barrels of U.S. oil reserves. There was also the prospect of a fuel-producing bacterium. OTA provided no estimate of market potential for this category.

## Pollution Control

Genetically engineered microbes and bacteria could eventually compete with natural microbes in isolated "clean-up" applications. The first patented genetic product was capable of digesting oil slicks but had yet to be put into commercial production. OTA provided no estimate of market potential for this category.

As with any new technology, the commercial prospects were mostly framed by the competitive environment. Genetics offered many substitutes for old product lines and had to contend with many established firms operating in concentrated industries. Furthermore, like many of these firms, biotech needed to gain government approval of its products—in a timely fashion—before marketing them. The stakes were surely high and the competitive risks were large, but there was no denying that biotechnology was a business that had come of age.

## COMPETITIVE ENVIRONMENT

"We're definitely looking at a biological revolution. The decade of the 1980s is going to be the age of biology,"[14] said the president of the Cetus Corporation, the oldest and largest of the genetic engineering firms. Unlike the industrial revolution or the more recent computer up-

surge, biotechnology was a particularly academic sort of industrial revolution. Most breakthroughs had come not from research departments of large companies but from America's most prestigious universities, and it was there that the foundations for the biotech industry had been laid in the 1970s. Now, many of these academics had left the university, joining together with venture capitalists, private investors, and research scientists at large diversified companies.

By early 1984, biotech had attracted a crowded field of competitors. Participants included dozens of small entrepreneurial start-up ventures—many had developed into relatively large, well-financed, and well-managed organizations—as well as internal rDNA laboratories of larger established corporations. With such high profit potential, industry structure was changing rapidly and rivalries were beginning to emerge.

## Entry

According to a well-placed chemical engineer, the typical biotechnologist had usually developed impeccable scientific skills in the academic environment. Translating those skills to a business environment, however, posed an entirely new set of challenges. It was apparent that the path from laboratory to marketplace was long and tortuous. Some observers thought biotechnologists could be blind to some of the practical problems that fell between discovery and commercial exploitation. These included any of the following:[15]

1   *The economics of production.* Many schemes to produce bulk chemicals or biotechnology fuel could not compete on a cost basis with traditional processes using hydrocarbon feedstocks.
2   *The problems of scale-up.* It was a huge step from the laboratory flask to the industrial

---

[14]Interview with Dr. Peter Farley, "MacNeil/Lehrer Report," WGBH TV, March 10, 1980.

[15]Marshall Sittig and Robert Noyes, *Directory of Genetic Engineering and Biotechnology Firms/USA* (Kingston, NJ: Sittig and Noyes, 1983), p. A-2.

fermentation tank; many apparently promising developments would never make this transition.

3  *The delays inherent in the commercialization of new processes,* particularly in the case of human health products, even if regulatory authorities generally appeared to be taking a more relaxed view.

There were also some serious questions about how to stay in the field. According to the Chicago-based Policy Research Corporation, there were several ways to enter the biotech business—each with its own price tag.[16]

| Possible corporate moves | Estimated cost |
| --- | --- |
| Establish some sort of access to a molecular biologist consultant. | $20,000–$30,000/year |
| Employ at least two molecular geneticists for in-house research and development. Build modest laboratory facility. | $2.0–2.5 million |
| Obtain an equity option from a biotechnology firm. | $1.0–5.0 million |
| Establish a joint venture with a biotechnology firm in a product segment where the firm has position and market knowledge. | $2.0+ million |
| Participate in a parallel project: specific university research grant with exclusive commercial rights. | $.1–50 million |

One way to get in and stay in (without legal entanglement) was to license the basic Cohen-Boyer patent(s) from Stanford University and the University of California. This nonexclusive patent covered the gene splicing and cloning methods developed in the universities' laboratories and had an initial price tag of $10,000. Under the Stanford–U. Cal. license plan, companies would funnel a small percentage of sales to the university once commercial marketing

was under way. The universities stood to gain well in excess of $1 million annually under these arrangements. Over 80 firms have signed this license/royalty agreement.

Economics and a variety of vested interests—namely, those holding control of profitable old-line technologies—were certain to play a part in the unfolding of genetic technologies. Costs for bringing a large-scale rDNA plant on line were estimated to be in the range of $40 million to $100 million. Expensive marketing programs would be needed to position and sell rDNA products. An investment house specializing in biotechnology offered a prescription for survival—and success:[17]

- Biotech firms must have a staff of proven scientific excellence.
- Biotech firms should not have all their eggs in speculative baskets. They should either be active across a wide biotechnological front or specialize in a particularly promising subfield.
- Biotech firms should have links with a wide range of industrial companies that can act as customers to the technology, help finance projects, and assist with commercial development.
- Biotech firms should pay particular attention to the scaling up of commercial projects.

So, while the entry barriers were not prohibitive, the requirements for maintaining a viable presence in the industry—large inflows of capital and scientific expertise—pressed the industry toward consolidation.

### Suppliers

Several factors would affect the future development of genetic engineering. Of these, two particularly critical issues concerned the limited supply of capital funding and the shortage of first-rate scientific talent. In the face of these constraints, many biotech firms had developed

[16]Ibid., p. A-3.

[17]Ibid., p. A-3.

creative relationships with customers and universities.

Most specialized biotech firms were founded with privately placed investment money long before any genetic products were expected to reach the marketplace. Genentech, considered by many to be best positioned to offer the first rDNA products, was the first firm to go to the public capital markets. In late 1980 the firm offered 1.1 million shares at $35 each that were gobbled up in a frenzy with the price bid up to $89 on the first day alone. Genentech's earnings in the previous year had totaled $116,000, or a mere 2¢ a share. While some other biotech firms initially had "big plays" on Wall Street, investors were less sanguine about subsequent offerings. In the words of one stock analyst, "The 100-yard dash that investors expected has turned into a marathon."[18]

Wall Street's lack of enthusiasm for biotech stock effectively capped the growth of start-ups, and many existing companies shelved plans to go public. Large pharmaceutical and chemical companies that once had been slow to recognize the potential of biotechnology were now picking up the slack and taking a position with direct investments in biotechnology companies. Schering-Plough Corporation owned an 11% interest in Biogen; American Cyanamid owned 8.6% of Molecular Genetics; Standard Oil of Indiana owned 21% of Cetus; and Koppers owned 25% of Genex. Eli Lilly was involved in joint ventures with Genentech and had announced a long-term agreement with the International Plant Research Institute to improve crop yields. In effect, the specialized rDNA companies had been surrounded and infiltrated by large established firms.

The initial outpouring of venture capital established the U.S. as the world leader in gene splicing. Biotechnology was not, however, an American monopoly. Competition from Japan and Europe was growing rapidly, and this served two purposes: it allowed foreign companies to catch up to U.S. research through the purchase of technology transfer agreements, and it provided a vital infusion of cash for American ventures that found a closed window on the stock market.

U.S. companies already had signed about 15 trade agreements giving the Japanese marketing rights in return for royalties. For example, Shionogi & Company was to get gamma-type interferon technology from Biogen. Genentech had a similar contract with Torroy Industries Inc. and Daiichi Seiyaku Company of Japan. International Nickel of Canada had invested in Plant Genetics, which was largely occupied with rDNA agricultural applications. Elf-Aquitaine of France had also invested in U.S. companies engaged primarily in biomedical projects. The list of well-funded corporate partners was certain to grow as the specialized biotech firms moved their research closer to commercial development.

Paralleling the growing role of large companies was the declining role of venture capital. The big rash of start-ups had passed. "The major players have already staked out the territory," one biotech venture capitalist flatly stated.[19] What little venture capital activity remained was being aimed at highly specialized and narrowly focused companies. "You have to go out there [now] with a rifle, not a shotgun," said a financial manager of one biotech company.[20]

Even more problematic than the shortage of cash was the shortage of top-notch scientific expertise. The guidance of researchers with national or international reputations was considered essential if a company was to operate at the leading edge of the new technology. According to one industry analyst " . . . most of them [molecular scientists] . . . were grabbed up long ago by the small venture capital companies, where they now hold equity interests and are reluctant to leave."[21] This work force shortage initially frustrated many of the larger compa-

[18]"Biotechnology's Drive for New Products," *Chemical Week,* February 24, 1982, p. 4.

[19]"Biotech Comes of Age," p. 89.
[20]Ibid., p. 89.
[21]"Genetic Engineering's Manpower Problem," *Dun's Review,* January 1982, p. 93.

nies that had the marketing expertise and financial resources to capitalize on genetic engineering. As more trained graduates enter the work place, larger organizations can expand their laboratories and be less beholden to small firms.

Still to be resolved was the uneasy alliance between the academic and the business communities. Before the advent of rDNA research, most universities relied heavily if not exclusively on the federal government for funding of scientific research. This arrangement permitted universities to take a "pure" approach toward basic research. Reductions in federal support mandated by government budget cuts and accompanied by a renewed private-sector interest in funding science had fundamentally changed the relationship between academia and business. The growing ties between corporations and universities raised many questions about ethics, objectivity, and academic freedom.

As many highly regarded biochemists became aligned with DNA companies, some argued that there would be a slowing of the information exchange among scientists and that the emphasis would be limited to experiments that were commercially justified—that is, patentable. Some argued for the maintenance of a detached and free academic research community that would not exist solely to serve the interests of any one industry. David Baltimore, a leading figure in the DNA debate, argued that society had much to gain from a marriage of academic and industrial interests. But he stipulated three provisos:[22]

- Scientists should be entirely open about their industrial affiliations.
- University laboratories should not be turned into "factories for the solution of industrial problems."
- Students should be allowed to work on problems that arise from their intellectual interests rather than predefined needs.

The real sticking point centered on the sanctity of open scientific inquiry. Many foresaw a time when profit-oriented scientists would keep secrets for corporate advantage, thus actually retarding science. In testimony before Congress, Jonathan King, professor of microbiology at MIT, worried aloud about the fate of scientific research because of the involvement of scientists and universities in commercial gene-splicing companies.

I can tell you that the atmosphere around biology department coffeepots has changed in the last two years. I know scientists who have asked other scientists for a strain of a particular organism and either their requests have been ignored or they have been told that it is not being given out, because the university is applying for a patent.

At a recent meeting of the American Society of Microbiology, an official of an oil company told one session, "In the future, when you come to a scientific meeting, you should consider getting the material you are presenting notarized and consider not telling your colleagues certain things." I thought this was tongue-in-cheek, but then I realized it wasn't.[23]

Others worried about "faculty raiding" and the loss of crucial scientific talent from the university setting. Said Nobel Laureate Dr. Paul Berg of Stanford:

The universities cannot compete on financial or even on other grounds. It raises a concern in my mind that we may lose the better part of a generation of molecular biologists, cell biologists, and geneticists. Who will then achieve the breakthroughs of tomorrow?[24]

The commercial world had tempted not only scientists but universities as well. A good many, including Harvard and Stanford, considered forming their own rDNA companies. The complexities of the marketplace combined with faculty and public uproar to quash the idea, but the universities were allowed to proceed with

---

[22]Sheldon Krimsky, op. cit., p. 287.

[23]Jonathan King, "Testimony before House of Representatives Committee on Science and Technology, *U.S. Government Printing Office,* June 8, 1981.
[24]William Patterson, op. cit., p. 69.

licensing their patents to outside companies. Stanford, Harvard, and MIT were among the first to collect royalties from research conducted on their campuses.

### Substitutes

In many cases, genetically produced materials were aimed at supplanting naturally produced materials. The acceptance of rDNA products would be a function of two factors: price reduction and performance improvement. Of course, in many cases rDNA would result in new products and market acceptance would proceed rapidly. It was of particular note that many of the specialized biotech firms were concentrating their initial efforts on drug products. The pharmaceutical industry was relatively concentrated, relatively protected by patents, and accustomed to earning high profits from portfolios of rather risky investments. Therefore, the commercial introduction of some substitutes—rDNA drugs—would largely depend on the ability to leapfrog economically the naturally occurring technology employed by most pharmaceutical concerns.

The insulin case was particularly interesting in this respect. Once produced in bacteria, its payoff to society was widely acknowledged and believed to be immediate. Estimates of the number of diabetics in the United States ranged from 5 to 6 million; approximately one quarter of a million Americans received insulin. Most of the insulin taken by diabetics was extracted from cattle and swine. To produce a bacterium with a human insulin-producing gene resulted in a purer product and one that was an exact copy of human insulin. It promised to be of enormous benefit to people who reacted poorly to animal insulin (estimated to be about 5 percent). It was quite possible, according to some experts, that the supply of insulin might exceed demand. For DNA companies, the questions of market size and regulatory approval would weigh heavily on scale-up decisions, while pharmaceutical companies selling conventionally produced insulin would need to consider the cost of switching production technologies.

A drug that competed with insulin to be the first "blockbuster" product of rDNA technology was interferon. Discovered in 1957, interferon was a natural substance produced by the body's cells that interfered with virus production and appeared to inhibit the growth of certain cancer cells. One of the methods of producing the substance explained its scarcity: it required 65,000 pints of blood to generate 100 milligrams of the material. Since cancer was the second major cause of death in the United States, there was no lack of support for interferon's development and clinical use. It was understandable that the race to be first with an rDNA interferon product had drawn many contestants, but there remained the question of how quickly it could be developed and how the spoils of rDNA research would be divided.

Beyond questions of genetic substitution for "natural" materials, there was a growing debate about the substitution of one rDNA product for another. The issue of patent protection was both controversial and extremely important to commercial enterprises. In 1980 two rulings established the much-awaited precedent of patent protection for the biotech industry. In the minds of many, these decisions effectively christened the commercialization of recombinant DNA technology.

On June 16, 1980, the U.S. Supreme Court ruled in a narrow 5-4 decision that the General Electric Company should not be denied patent protection on an "oil eating" microorganism developed eight years earlier. In his majority opinion, Chief Justice Berger wrote: "We must determine whether [this] microorganism constitutes a 'manufacture' or 'composition of matter' within the meaning of the [patent] statute."[25] The court determined that the principal criteria upon which an invention was deemed patentable (namely, that it be new, useful, and nonobvious) were in no way infringed by the fact that the invention was alive. The court as a whole declared that Congress should take up

---

[25] *Diamond v. Chakravarty,* 100 Supreme Court, 2204, 2207 (1980).

the policy issue of patentability for living organisms.

On December 2, 1980, Stanford University and the University of California were jointly awarded a patent dealing with gene cloning techniques used in rDNA experiments. The techniques, developed by Stanley Cohen and Herbert Boyer, had become the basis for virtually all rDNA experimentation to date. Both universities were allowed to license the patent and proceeded to do so on condition that licensees adhere to the NIH Guidelines. Because part of the research had been published abroad, however, the Cohen-Boyer patent was applicable only in the United States. Furthermore, there remained a nagging legal question about whether the patent could withstand a challenge if it was deemed to inhibit the commercial development of rDNA technology. These events made it clear that the promise of genetics was both real, and—what was of greatest relevance to commercial enterprises—could be proprietary.

### Buyers

As the products of gene-splicing technology were beginning to enter the marketplace, the major unresolved issue centered upon the structure of the marketing and distribution system. Given rDNA's potential benefits in pharmaceuticals, chemicals, and agriculture—industries dominated by large firms—it was quite clear that they would be very influential buyers. The superior financial, production, marketing, and distribution capabilities of major corporations in applied genetics made them formidable competitors for small research firms attempting to launch their own fully integrated enterprises.

One way small firms could remain relatively independent and still gain access to the marketing and manufacturing expertise they lacked was to form a joint venture with a large drug or chemical company. In fact, many of the start-ups had long ago licensed their first products to provide sufficient financing to keep them solvent. Joint ventures allowed the small companies to retain a larger share of revenues

than did licensing, a popular approach for some when new ventures were cash-constrained. Genentech had licensed its human insulin to Eli Lilly & Company but had also recently set up several joint ventures. Another large firm had undertaken a joint venture with American Hospital Supply to develop, manufacture, and market medical diagnostic tests. In the face of what some believed to be long odds, a few small firms signed long-term research contracts with larger organizations. Other biotech companies, realizing that overseas marketing was difficult even under the best of circumstances, had profitably ceded the marketing rights for certain territories, allowing them to retain domestic markets for themselves. While the giants may have made good partners for many start-ups, it was clear that they were becoming increasingly determined competitors as well.

### Rivalry

An intriguing collection of companies and organizational relationships had developed in the biotechnology industry. These included small-to-medium-sized specialized research companies, major corporations with internal research capability, and foreign firms and international consortiums with specific scientific expertise. Many firms had research relationships with one another and many employed scientists still tied to major universities. Now that some of the fruits of scientific research was beginning to be harvested, there was mounting speculation about the future structure of the industry and the strategy of some key players.

The relatively young, specialized firms had certainly been the most visible actors in the industry thus far, partly because of the flurry of attention given to their early equity issues. The five leading firms—Biogen, Cetus, Genex, Genentech, and Molecular Genetics—were all direct spin-offs from universities and had a combined "war chest" of $700 million. Biogen and Genentech were considered models in their field, and their emerging rivalry was a sign of what was in store for biotechnology. Recognizing that they had to manage "a controlled eating into capital," both firms mapped a long-term product marketing strategy long before their research was commercialized.[26] The plan was to maximize much-needed short-term cash inflows in the form of license fees, without giving away too much of the expected long-term rewards. Biogen, utilizing license agreements on its animal growth hormone, was thus able to sustain a broad range of research projects. Similarly, foreign marketing rights for its diagnostic kit for hepatitis were negotiated, but the firm retained the lucrative domestic market for itself.

For its early move into alpha interferon (the interferon produced by white blood cells in a defensive response to viruses), Biogen teamed up with Schering-Plough. Biogen announced in early 1980 that it had produced a few molecules of interferon, which had an explosive effect on business executives and scientists: the stock of Schering-Plough, which at the time owned 16% of Biogen, shot up eight points for a nifty paper gain of $426 million. It also resulted in negative comments about scientific presentations at press conferences and failure to give full credit to earlier researchers. Meanwhile, Genentech had secretly entered into a rival partnership with Hoffman LaRoche to work on the same substance. The two teams were neck and neck in their race through clinical trials to gain FDA approval—and get to substantial royalties.[27]

Both Biogen and Genentech were trying to underwrite themselves, as a possible ticket to corporate independence, through work on gamma interferon, a natural product of cells of the lymph system that was thought to have the most promise for cancer treatment. Since the research required an enormous cash reserve, both Genentech and Biogen sought further capitalization. In Biogen's case, this meant using one of its last unplayed financial aces: making a public stock offering. While some limited licenses were sold for gamma interferon, both companies were careful to keep the rich Western markets for themselves. The rewards were

believed to be substantial: industry observers estimated that gamma interferon could be a $1 billion-a-year blockbuster. Biogen's president spoke of the stakes: "We are in a race, and we feel the pressure. The key is the technology, and we will stay on the cutting edge."[28]

The rapid pace of the industry's development had favored the expansion of small firms, whose flexibility and quick decision making provided an R&D edge over more ponderous corporations. The heavy reliance of these smaller start-ups on research contracts, production processes, and marketing arrangements with corporate partners was viewed as a serious problem for their future growth. Independence would require that they remain content with being a small service enterprise—providing research skill on demand—or that they develop a specialized market niche where they could hold a long-term proprietary (patent) advantage. Most anticipated that there would be some "shakeout" of small firms that had exhausted their financial resources. Mergers within the ranks of the specialized companies were foreseen in cases where combining research initiatives might have a synergistic effect. Acquisitions of floundering biotech firms by larger diversified concerns were also widely anticipated in cases where the larger companies wanted to bolster their own research capabilities. To date, only a handful of firms had failed, but more burnouts were likely to occur. In those instances, the scientific talent—which was still relatively scarce—would in all likelihood be quickly re-employed elsewhere. Since many of the specialized firms were publicly owned, consolidation was likely in many cases where cash flow was not even a major issue. Many small firms could become attractive takeover candidates on the basis of their successful scientific inquiry.

Large companies—representing agriculture, food, forestry, petrochemical, pollution control and process engineering industries—had long ago stopped thinking of biotech as too speculative for their involvement. Few companies whose businesses might be affected by

[26]"Can Biotech's Biogen Cut It?" *Boston Globe,* November 16, 1982, p. 45.
[27]Ibid., p. 45.

[28]"Biotech Comes of Age," p. 90.

genetic engineering were willing to stand idly by on the sidelines. In the words of one pharmaceutical chief, "It is risky *not* to be in the [biotech] business."[29]

Many of these firms had research efforts under way that rivaled the specialized firms. Du Pont was exploring a broad range of projects from pharmaceuticals and improved plant varieties to pesticides and chemical stocks. Monsanto was just completing a huge research lab that would eventually house 1,000 scientists. Eli Lilly and Schering-Plough had established large, well-staffed, in-house labs. In agriculture, several large seed companies were conducting joint research and testing on genetically manipulated materials. Food processing giants like Kroger, General Foods, and CPC International were already using biotechnology to improve their products and develop new processes.

There were several reasons why experts believed these corporate "giants" would eventually dominate biotechnology. The larger firms were more able to handle the cost of getting products through the lengthy regulatory process and were not nearly so dependent on a single product as were some of the specialized ventures. Corporations with a large internal R&D staff were also more likely to achieve a "critical mass" of talent that would allow for an open and useful sharing of scientific discovery. Grafting a production line to their research labs was a costly and in many cases prohibitive proposition for small companies. Pharmaceutical companies, with their solid experience in fermentation technologies—an important process in commercializing biotechnology—held a significant advantage in the production area. Lastly, larger organizations held a supreme market position and were much farther along in understanding potential applications for genetic research. Their wide product lines and carefully cultivated relationships with customers made these industrial corporations formidable rivals.

Stiff competition from overseas was also expected. The European and Japanese governments had each taken up biotechnology as an important "industry of the future" and provided funding in excess of $100 million a year each for genetic engineering projects. In contrast, the U.S. government had been spending approximately $20 million on such research.[30] The powerful French state-owned energy company, Elf-Aquitaine, had substantial investments in European biotechnology as well as smaller investments in many American ventures. Hoechst, the West German chemical giant, had a $50 million contract with Massachusetts General Hospital to develop genetic capabilities. Japanese firms, many of them substantial trading companies, had pooled their efforts through a government-sponsored "Biotechnology Council," and many had invested in American R&D activities. Even though Japan was a latecomer in the rush to biotechnology, by capitalizing upon their expertise in fermentation technology, they were expected to be big players in the global biotech market. Because the Japanese had historically demonstrated tremendous talent in applying technology commercially, there was a growing fear that they could dominate the industry. The increasing collaboration between American and Japanese biotech companies was particularly alarming to some in Washington. "We ought to take a more hard-nosed attitude toward protecting the enormous investment we make in biotechnology," exclaimed one biotech watchdog in Congress, "otherwise we will not remain leaders in this field for long."[31]

## SOCIAL AND ETHICAL ISSUES

While the political, public, and scientific debate had focused on the issue of biohazards, it became apparent that the implications of gene splicing were much more far-reaching. The consequences of mistakes or failures in laboratories had received a great deal of attention, but success in learning how to manipulate genes was often thought to have enormous societal bene-

---

[29]Ibid., p. 86.

[30]"A Government Boost for the Biotechnology Industry," *Business Week*, December 14, 1981, p. 110.

[31]Ibid., p. 114.

fits. Nevertheless, this new knowledge carried an anxiety over applied genetics focused on the "Frankenstein factor," according to a major U.S. government study, and this raised troubling questions about human beings assuming the role of creator.[32]

Some scientists were quite unsettled by the prospects and had grave reservations:

> Do we want to assume the basic responsibility for life on this planet—to develop new living forms for our own purposes? Shall we take into our hands our own future evolution? . . . Perverse as it may, initially, seem to the scientist, we must face the fact that there can be unwanted knowledge.[33]

The Frankenstein story also seemed appropriate because of the scientist's search to control his monster, calling to mind the concerns raised about the distribution of power and control associated with gene splicing. "Each new power won by man is a power over man as well."[34] Of equal or greater concern was the view, expressed by some scientists, that even they might be unable to control the "monster." As one leading scientist remarked, "You can stop splitting the atom; you can stop visiting the moon; you can stop using aerosols . . . but you cannot recall a new form of life."[35] If an organism could find a suitable niche, it might survive—and even evolve.

Concerned testimony from religious leaders, philosophers, scientists, and public policy makers led to the formation in 1980 of a U.S. presidential commission to study the social and ethical issues of genetic engineering. After two years of study and debate, the commission concluded that many of the public's concerns were unfounded and exaggerated. In fact, the group of commissioners, representing a diverse cross-

section of American society, thought the new knowledge to be "a celebration of human creativity."[36] They also concluded, however, that there was a need for a more coordinated approach to regulation and urged those engaged in biotechnology to communicate regularly with the public. New issues were certain to arise, and the industry should be prepared to maintain a dialogue with all concerned parties to ensure an appropriate standard of responsibility.

The commission considered both religious and secular views in addressing two basic issues: concerns about "playing God" and concerns about consequences. The idea that research in genetics might lead someday to the ability to direct human evolution had caused particularly strong reactions. Some believed that such capability brought with it responsibility for retaining the genetic integrity of people and of the species as a whole, a responsibility that challenged many of society's deeply held values. Others, however, found the idea of directing evolution to be exciting. They viewed the development of genetics and the opportunities to change things as a natural part of evolution. The commission was unable to define criteria for the oft-repeated charge that genetics was an arrogant interference with nature. In one sense, the commission observed, *all* human activity interferes with nature. And, indeed, it was "quite nice to fool Mother Nature if it meant countering melanoma or wiping out smallpox."[37]

### Concerns about Consequences

Some critics warned against the dangers of attempting to control or interfere with the "wisdom of evolution" in order to satisfy scientific curiosity. Those who held this view objected to crossing species lines by gene splicing because they believed that the inability of different species to produce fertile offspring by sexual repro-

[32]*Splicing Life: The Social and Ethical Issues of Genetic Engineering with Human Beings,* by the President's Commission for the Study of Ethical Problems in Medicine and Biomedical and Behavioral Research (Washington, D.C.: U.S. Government Printing Office, 1982), p. 14.
[33]Ibid., p. 15.
[34]Ibid., p. 15.
[35]Ibid., p. 16.

[36]C. Keith Boone, "Splicing Life, with Scalpel and Scythe," *The Hastings Center Report,* April 1983, p. 10.
[37]Ibid., p. 9.

duction was an adaptive feature that conferred significant survival advantages. They viewed species lines as natural protective barriers that human beings could circumvent only at their own peril.

Current attitudes toward human reproductive activity have derived from several important assumptions, among them that becoming a parent required a willingness, within very broad limits, to accept the child to which the woman gives birth, that parents' basic duties to children were more or less clear and settled, and that reproduction and parenting were and should remain largely private and autonomous spheres of people's lives. The doors that genetic engineering could open were almost sure to challenge all three of these assumptions.

Society's obligation to protect or enhance the health of children and future generations had usually rested on some notion of an adequate minimum of health care. That benchmark, in turn, came from assumptions about normal functioning and adequate health. As technological capabilities grew, these assumptions would probably undergo change affecting people's views about what a society owes to its children and future generations.

Since the application of rDNA technology would bring benefits as well as costs, and since it would be funded at least in part by public resources, several other questions arose. Who would benefit from the new technology? And how would the benefits and costs be distributed equitably? The public had seen how technology affected the distribution of benefits in society; it could have unequal impacts, and those who could pay, or who were most in need, were not necessarily always the ones who received the benefits. The possibilities presented by genetics called into question the scope and limits of a central element of democratic theory and practice: the commitment to equality of opportu-

nity. It also was a challenge to the capitalistic economies: to meet and fulfill basic human needs.

Beyond any fear of the malevolent use of gene splicing, there was a need for attention to a more basic question about the distribution of power: Who would decide which lines of genetic engineering research ought to be pursued and which applications of the technology ought to be promoted? These questions revived doubts about the private enterprise system's ability to deliver new products in a timely fashion. While patent protection clearly motivated commercial development, many wondered if competing parochial interests could deliver science to society at the same rate as could "open" academic inquiry. Commercial decisions would likely be based more on expected financial return than on pure scientific merit. The debate over "orphan products" (drugs or chemicals with undeniable medical benefit that served an insignificant market size) was likely to be renewed. It was foreseeable that some breakthroughs that might have a significant impact in the Third World (a more effective smallpox vaccine or a drought-resistant crop) would never be commercially developed simply because market conditions would not allow an adequate return on investment. This was not a new issue to the scientific community, but it was one that the biotech business would have to consider when developing its corporate strategies.

Concern about the consequences of biotechnology was unlikely to abate. Even the leading experts in the field conceded that "the most predictable aspect of this technology may be its very unpredictability."[38] As Dr. Watson wrote, "This science is not likely to develop in the most straightforward and logical manner."

[38]*Splicing Life: Social and Ethical Issues*, p. 19.

# Environmental Pressures: The Pollution Problem

A prominent politician commented in 1970 that "ecology has become the political substitute for the word 'mother.'"[1] Since the publication of Rachel Carson's *Silent Spring* in 1962, ecology had become a political issue of increasing salience. By 1970, environmental protection had carved out a niche in the federal bureaucracy with 26 quasi-government bodies, 14 interagency committees, and 90 separate federal programs dealing with the environment. Federal spending on maintaining or improving the quality of the environment had risen from less than $5 million in the mid-fifties to several hundred million dollars by 1970.

More significant than federal spending were the new regulations and standards legislated for industry. It had been estimated that business would have to spend approximately $22 billion to meet the air and water pollution standards in effect as of January 1, 1973.[2] Industries which would have to spend the most were:

| Total investment required | |
|---|---|
| Electric utilities | $ 3.9 billion |
| Petroleum | 2.7 billion |
| Chemicals | 2.3 billion |
| Iron and steel | 1.7 billion |
| All manufacturing | 16.1 billion |
| All business | 22.3 billion |

This case and the one that follows focus on the effects of government pollution regulations and their enforcement on one alleged industrial polluter, Reserve Mining Company. This company's situation was chosen because of the importance of the issues to the parties involved and the accessibility of relevant information. It

[1]Jesse Unruh as quoted in *Newsweek*, 1/26/70, p. 31.

[2]*Business Week*, 5/19/73, p. 78.

is not intended to illustrate "right" or "wrong," "wise" or "unwise" actions by any of the parties involved. That is for the reader to consider, bearing in mind that the information herein was drawn from a variety of published material as well as almost 20,000 pages of public court records. A great deal of material was of necessity omitted, and these cases represent the casewriter's attempt to present fairly, in a highly condensed form, some of the major issues involved in a long and complex controversy.

Because the issues were still in litigation at the time of the writing of the case, neither the plaintiffs nor the defendants were given the opportunity to modify the selection of material presented herein, all of which was drawn from publicly available sources.

## RESERVE MINING COMPANY

### The Situation in April 1974

On April 20, 1974, Judge Miles Lord of the Federal District Court in Minneapolis handed down a decision ordering the Reserve Mining Company to halt the discharge of taconite tailings (or wastes) into Lake Superior. The company's plant, the largest in the world, was ordered to close down for an indefinite period of time.

This order climaxed the biggest pollution case ever, "The Classic Pollution Case," according to *Time* magazine. The trial had lasted 8½ months, and had generated almost 20,000 pages of testimony and more than 800 exhibits. The stakes involved dwarfed all previous environmental cases. The Reserve plant produced about 10,000,000 tons of iron ore annually (15% of total United States ore production), valued at close to $150 million. It supplied between half and three-quarters of the ore needs of its parent companies, Republic and Armco Steel, which were two of the country's five largest steel companies. Three thousand jobs were directly at stake, and an estimated 8,000 more were indirectly involved. It was alleged that Reserve's daily discharge of 67,000 tons of taconite tailings threatened the ecological balance of the world's largest freshwater body, and in addition created a significant health hazard to the communities which drew their drinking water from the lake.

Two days after Judge Lord's decision, an Appeals Court granted a 70-day stay on the order. The plant was allowed to reopen, but Reserve and its parent firms were given 25 days in which to present plans for abatement of the discharges into the lake.

### Reserve's Early History

Reserve Mining Company was organized on March 24, 1939, with ownership divided among Armco Steel, Wheeling Steel, Montreal Mining Co. and Cleveland Cliffs Iron Co. Later that year, the company obtained leases on land near Babbitt, Minnesota, in the Mesabi Range. The land contained a deposit of magnetic taconite 9 miles long, an average of 2,800 feet wide, and as thick as 175 feet, with an estimated two billion tons of ore.

Although about 95% of the Mesabi Range iron formation was taconite, it was not commercially mined until the 1950s. High-grade ores (up to 70% iron oxides compared with 30% or less for taconite), were more economical to mine, as they could be shipped directly to steel mills without processing.

The Babbitt property was considered a long-term investment, to be mined if and when taconite became competitive with direct shipment ores. Steel production expanded greatly during World War II, and by the late forties the high-grade ores in the Mesabi Range were largely gone. The economy of northern Minnesota declined sharply, unemployment soared, and the Mesabi Range appeared to be becoming another Appalachia.

In 1942, however, Reserve personnel and Dr. E. W. Davis, Director of the Mines Experiment Station at the University of Minnesota, had begun research into processes for transforming taconite into usable form. By 1947 their work had yielded results: a method of refining and concentrating taconite into small pellets of iron ore, usable as blast furnace feed. The decision was made to build a beneficiation[3] plant to process taconite mined at Babbitt. The estimated reserves were enough to yield up to 650 million tons of ore, sufficient to keep the plant in operation for 75 years. Since the beneficiation process required large amounts of water, a plant site was selected at Silver Bay, on the north shore of Lake Superior.

In 1950 Republic Steel purchased 42½% ownership of Reserve, and the following year, Armco and Republic acquired the remaining interest, bringing their shares up to 50% each.

In late 1955, five years after construction began, the Reserve Mining Company plant at Silver Bay was completed, and by the middle of 1956, a million tons of iron ore had been produced.

The new plant played a key role in revitalizing the economy of northeastern Minnesota. Congressman John Blatnik, who represented the area, said:

> Reserve Mining was not just another industry in Silver Bay, Minnesota. It was the forerunner of a dramatic revolution in the entire economy of northeastern Minnesota and a pacesetter for the iron ore industry. Reserve Mining Company initiated the taconite industry with an investment that eventually totalled $350 million.[4]

By 1972, total investment in taconite plants and facilities in the Mesabi Range had amounted to well over a billion dollars.

The Silver Bay plant was hailed as a technological breakthrough of major importance to the American economy. Estimates of future sources of iron ore showed taconite filling the gap caused by depletion of available direct shipping iron ore. *Engineering and Mining Journal,* in a 1956 article, commented:

> The Reserve taconite project is one of the most impressive in mining history, not only because of its size, but also because of the numerous

technical headaches involved in large-scale mining, concentrating, and pelletizing concentrates from one of the hardest, toughest, abrasive ores known to man.[5]

The Reserve plant employed the world's largest crusher and the world's strongest conveyor belt. It required construction of a 47-mile railroad (to haul the ore from Babbitt to Silver Bay) with specially constructed railroad cars, which allowed rotation of 180 degrees without uncoupling, to facilitate unloading, and included numerous other innovations in material handling and processing.

### Processing Taconite

The process used by Reserve was essentially the same as that developed by Dr. Davis in the forties. First, at the mine in Babbitt, rocks and earth were stripped away to expose the taconite. Jet piercers, invented for this purpose, used a 4,250°F flame to drill 40-foot-deep holes in the hard rock. Explosives were loaded into the holes and detonated to break the taconite into pieces. The rocks were hauled by truck to crushing plants where they were reduced to pieces 4 inches or less in diameter, and then loaded on rail cars to be carried the 47 miles to Silver Bay.

At Silver Bay another crushing plant further reduced the taconite to less than ¾-inch size. The taconite was then conveyed to the concentrator plant, where beneficiation or separation of the mineral was performed in three stages of grinding and five steps of separation. In this process, the taconite was reduced to a powder finer than flour. Large magnets were used to separate particles rich in iron oxide from those that were lean or barren. The latter were called "tailings." Hydraulic separation, a process in which heavier iron-rich particles were permitted to sink in a pool of water while lighter, low-iron-content particles overflowed as tailings, was also employed. The grinding and separation steps were performed with the

---

[3]The process of extracting usable ore from taconite.
[4]*National Journal Reports,* 3/2/74, p. 310.

[5]*Engineering and Mining Journal,* December 1956, p. 75.

solid material suspended in water. Finally, the tailings from each step of separation were joined together and transported down a system of troughs and discharged into Lake Superior. When the discharge entered the lake, it was a slurry (mixture of water and suspended solids) of approximately 1.5% solids. In the lake, the slurry formed a "heavy density current" (the solid material suspended in water made it heavier than the surrounding water) which flowed to the bottom of the lake. Over the years, the coarser tailings discharged from the troughs had settled offshore and formed a delta. . . .

The iron ore concentrate from which the tailings had been separated was conveyed to a pelletizing plant where it was rolled into ⅜-inch pellets and hardened by heating to 2,350°F. Approximately 3 tons of taconite were required to produce 1 ton of pellets.

## Importance of Water

Water was vital in taconite processing. Edward Furness, the President of Reserve, explained the importance of water to the company's operations as follows:

> A substantial part of the success of Reserve's taconite operations is the availability of large quantities of water. The grinding and the following magnetic separation stages—where the magnetic iron ore is recovered from the waste sand—is done with the material suspended in water. It requires 50 tons of water to make 1 ton of finished iron ore concentrate—about 12,000 gallons! We use about 350,000 gallons of water a minute.
>
> On the subject of water use in taconite processing, let me point out one thing—water is used, but it is not lost. The separation process uses no heat; therefore, there is no evaporation except what would occur naturally. Thus, after the water is used and the tailings settle out, the water again becomes part of the existing water supply.
>
> Reserve's earliest studies showed that it wasn't possible to conduct its concentration process at Babbitt, the site of our mine. There

simply was no water available in Babbitt. The only solution, engineering studies made clear, was to locate the processing plant at Silver Bay and bring the crude taconite there by rail from Babbitt.

It's very expensive to haul that crude rock down to Silver Bay. We had to build a 47-mile, double-tracked railroad through muskeg and rock—the worst kind of terrain. And, since we mine 3 tons of taconite for every ton of pellets we make, two-thirds of all the material we haul is unusable.

After thorough study, then, engineers agreed that the only possible site for our processing plant was on the north shore of Lake Superior at what is now Silver Bay. The site was suitable both because of the existence of nearby islands to which breakwaters could be built forming a harbor and, directly offshore from the plant, there is a very deep area of Lake Superior.

This deep area—a great depression extending for many miles parallel to the shore—is 600 to 900 feet deep. Its proportions are immense; up to 8 miles wide, 59 miles long, big enough to hold our entire Babbitt ore body without raising the bottom more than a few feet. It is here our tailings settle. From a conservation standpoint, Reserve's use of Lake Superior is sound. There is no waste water and no injury to water. Reserve's method of disposal of the sand left over from processing taconite incorporates harmless, permanent deep-water deposition of an inert material—tailings.[6]

## Permits for the Plant

Certain federal and state permits were required to either withdraw water from or discharge into a public body of water. In 1947 Reserve applied to the Minnesota Department of Conservation and the Water Pollution Control Commission for permits to use Lake Superior water and discharge taconite tailings into the lake. Hearings were held, and in December 1947, Reserve received the desired permits, subject to certain conditions. In 1956 the permit was amended, increasing allowable water usage from 130,000

[6]Digest of Statements presented by Reserve Mining Co. to Conference on Pollution of the Interstate Waters of the Lake Superior Basin—May 13, 14, 15, 1969, pp. 2–3.

gallons per minute (GPM) to 260,000 GPM. In 1960, it was further increased to 502,000 GPM.

In 1947 Reserve also applied to the Army Corps of Engineers for a permit. They routinely issued thousands of permits a year, applying the sole criterion of whether the discharge would obstruct navigation. This permit was granted and periodically revised and renewed until 1960, when Reserve was given an indefinite extension.

The Corps of Engineers permit became a problem to Reserve in 1966, however, when President Johnson issued an executive order providing that the Secretary of the Interior give assistance to other departments in carrying out their responsibilities under the Federal Water Pollution Control Act. The next year, this policy became operational as the regulations of the Corps were altered so that in granting permits consideration would be given to the "effects of permitted activities on the public interest, including effects upon water quality, recreation, fish and wildlife, pollution, our natural resources, as well as effects on navigation."[7] Indefinitely extended permits such as Reserve's were to be periodically reexamined, applying the new criteria.

### Stoddard Report

Thus in November 1967, revalidation proceedings were begun for Reserve's permit and Charles Stoddard, the Interior Department's Regional Coordinator, was assigned the task of compiling and consolidating the various reports which could pertain to Reserve's impact on the environment. Studies and reports from the Bureau of Commercial Fisheries, the Bureau of Mines, the Bureau of Sport Fisheries and Wildlife, the Federal Water Pollution Control Administration, the Minnesota Department of Conservation, the Minnesota Pollution Control Agency (PCA), and the Reserve Mining Company were among those considered.

In December 1968, after about a year of preparation, the Stoddard Report was completed but not officially released. Its conclusions [some of which are included in Appendix A] and the recommendation that Reserve be required to dispose its tailings on land after three years posed a serious problem to Reserve. The report, written for Interior Department officials and the Corps of Engineers, was leaked to the press, and soon became embroiled in controversy. Reserve attacked the report, claiming that it contained serious errors and jeopardized thousands of jobs. It was alleged that pressure was applied on the Johnson Administration and that the Interior Department reacted by claiming the report was only preliminary, classifying it as "unofficial" (thus keeping it out of circulation) and rewriting the conclusions and recommendations.[8] An "official" report issued later recommended continuing surveillance of Reserve, but little action to halt the discharge.

### Enforcement Conference

On January 16, 1969, Secretary of the Interior Udall called for an Enforcement Conference on the pollution of Lake Superior. Under the terms of the Federal Water Pollution Control Act, the Secretary of the Interior could initiate enforcement proceedings if it was believed that the health and welfare of persons in one state were endangered by pollution originating in another state. The first step in this process was an Enforcement Conference, to be followed by public hearings and court action if the pollution persisted.

The first session of the Enforcement Conference began in mid-1969 and lasted for several months. It provided a forum for politicians, company officials, and environmentalists. Technical consultants for Reserve and the environmentalists gave conflicting testimony, and the final recommendation called for

> ... further engineering and economic studies relating to possible ways and means of reducing

[7]Stanley Ulrich et al., *Superior Polluter* (Duluth, Save Lake Superior Association and Northern Environmental Council, 1972), p. 30.

[8]David Zwick et al., *Water Wasteland,* Ralph Nader's Study Group report on water pollution (New York: Grossman, 1971), pp. 144–9. *Superior Polluter,* pp. 40–43.

to the maximum practicable extent the discharge of tailings to Lake Superior and . . . a report on progress to the Minnesota PCA and the conference within six months of the date of release of these recommendations.[9]

In December 1969, Reserve filed a suit against the Minnesota PCA seeking exemption from a state water pollution regulation (WPC-15) as it related to their disposition of tailings. Two months later, the state filed a countersuit to force compliance with the regulation. The effect of these suits was to force a delay in hearings scheduled to consider alleged permit violations by Reserve. The hearings, requested by the Sierra Club,[10] could have led to immediate revocation of Reserve's dumping permit.

The trial was held at the Lake County District Court, only 20 miles from Silver Bay. As in the past, contradictory evidence was presented by each side. In December 1970, the District Court found that WPC-15 was not applicable to Reserve, but Reserve was ordered to alter its method of disposition so that the tailings would be confined to a small section of the lake. The PCA appealed the District Court ruling to the State Supreme Court. In August 1972, a decision was handed down ordering Reserve to apply to the PCA for a variance from WPC-15, reestablishing the legal position which had existed three years earlier.

Meanwhile, the focus had shifted back to the Federal Government. A second session of the Enforcement Conference was convened during 1970. Most notable of its findings was that there was interstate pollution, thereby conferring jurisdiction on the conference. In April 1971, a third session was held. A Reserve proposal to pipe tailings to the bottom of the lake was rejected, and the EPA served notice on Reserve that it was in violation of established federal water quality standards. The company was given 180 days to submit an acceptable plan for tailings disposal. This laid the foundation for future court action.

## "THE CLASSIC POLLUTION CASE"

In January 1972, EPA chief Ruckelshaus asked the Justice Department to take Reserve to court to force abatement of its discharge. The government suit, filed a month later, claimed Reserve violated Minnesota water quality standards and the Refuse Act of 1899, created a public nuisance, had an invalid permit to discharge, and polluted the waters of other states.

The trial promised to be important, complex, and lengthy. Intervenors entered the case on both sides, and the final lineup pitted the Justice Department; the states of Minnesota, Wisconsin and Michigan; the Minnesota PCA; the cities of Duluth, Minnesota, and Superior, Wisconsin; and five environmentalist groups against Reserve, Armco, Republic Steel, and 11 towns, counties, and civic associations in northeastern Minnesota. Highly technical determinations had to be made, especially regarding the taconite tailings and their ecological impact. The two sides were at odds over basic questions such as the quantity of tailings being discharged, their movement in the lake, the amount which remained suspended, and their size. The plaintiffs charged that the Reserve discharge adversely affected the lake by:

1 Increasing turbidity and reducing water clarity by 25% or more over an area of more than 600 square miles
2 Causing a "green water" phenomenon in which sections of the lake reflected a muddy green color
3 Assisting algae growth and accelerating a process which has severely damaged the other Great Lakes (eutrophication)
4 Being ingested by fish, altering their feeding habits, and killing trout sac fry

The most significant controversy centered on the movement of the tailings once they entered the lake. Reserve contended that the slurry which flowed off the delta in front of the plant formed a "heavy density current" which flowed down to the lake bottom, where the tailings were deposited. The environmentalists did not dispute the existence of this current, but claimed that a variety of phenomena caused a

---

[9]*Superior Polluter,* p. 87.
[10]A nationwide environmental and educational organization with more than 140,000 members.

significant portion of the tailings to become suspended and dispersed over more than 2,000 square miles of the lake. To support their position, Reserve presented an inventory allegedly accounting for 99.6% of their tailings within a small area directly offshore from the plant. Environmentalists then pointed out that even if the Reserve inventory were accepted, over one million tons of tailings were still unaccounted for.

## Consequences of a Shutdown

To some observers it appeared that the esthetic benefits of keeping Lake Superior pure would have to be weighed against the economic hardship which would be created by closing, or forcing on-land disposal. But Verna Mize,[11] a leading opponent of Reserve, pointed to the economic impact of the company's discharge:

> You can't put a price tag on one of the world's largest and cleanest bodies of fresh water, the one lake responsible for flushing the other already polluted Great Lakes. If you want to argue dollars, Lake Superior was conservatively estimated to be worth $1.3 trillion for pure drinking water alone. We may soon know whether that value has been reduced to zero.[12]

On the other hand, if Reserve were to shut down, it appeared the consequences would be far more tangible and immediate.

There would clearly be an economic effect on the economy of northeastern Minnesota. Reserve had 3,000 employees on its payroll. In 1973 Reserve had purchased $44,000,000 of supplies from 530 Minnesota businesses. It had been estimated that indirectly each Minnesota mining job supported about nine people; thus 27,000 people could be affected.

Reserve contributed a significant portion of the revenues for six taxing districts. A total of $6,500,000 in state and local taxes was paid in 1973. Hardest hit by the loss of revenues

would be the towns of Babbitt (80% of revenues from Reserve) and Silver Bay (64%) and Lake County (57%). Babbitt and Silver Bay had issued bonds secured by revenues from Reserve, and these probably would go into default. The threat of a Reserve shutdown had already made financing difficult for Silver Bay; a recent attempted bond issue was withdrawn when there were no bidders to underwrite it.

The towns of Babbitt, Silver Bay, Ely, and Two Harbors were those most dependent on Reserve. More than 70% of the company's employees resided in these towns. Their relative dependence on Reserve is shown in Table A.

Silver Bay and Babbitt had been carved out of the wilderness and built entirely by Reserve in the early fifties. In 1974, they remained "company towns."

Silver Bay's dependence on Reserve had been stated with obvious pride in a Chamber of Commerce brochure:

> The area's industry is Reserve Mining Company. Due to its tremendous tonnage of taconite pellets, Reserve has earned for the village the slogan "Taconite Capital of the World." To produce this tonnage, the village affords a population of 3,800 people.

In the center of town, a 7-foot figure of a taconite man stood on a pedestal of taconite ore. Most local merchants provided visitors with free sample packets of taconite ore and pellets, and the Chamber of Commerce actively distributed bumper stickers proclaiming "Silver Bay—Taconite Capital of the World." . . . Even the altar and baptismal font of the Catholic church were made of taconite. Few would disagree with the mayor, who said the loss of Reserve "would effectively terminate the village."[13]

The people who lived in Silver Bay had come in two migrations, one associated with the opening of the plant in the mid-fifties and the other with its later expansion. Their homes were built by Reserve and sold to them with lit-

---

[11]A housewife and secretary from Potomac, Maryland (and a former Michigan resident), who had lobbied in Washington against Reserve for seven years.
[12]*National Journal Reports*, 3/2/74, p. 312.

[13]*U.S.A. et al.* v. *Reserve Mining Co. et. al.*, U.S. District Court, District of Minnesota, Fifth Dist. Civil Action, No. 5—72, Civ. 19, Offer of Proof, pp. 12–13.

**TABLE A**
DEPENDENCE ON RESERVE

|  | Number of Reserve employees (8/73) | Estimated population directly dependent on Reserve (@4 per employee) | Estimated total population |
|---|---|---|---|
| Silver Bay | 930 | 3,720 | 3,800 |
| Babbitt | 665 | 2,660 | 3,076 |
| Ely | 500 | 2,000 | 4,904 |
| Two Harbors | 249 | 996 | 4,437 |

tle or no down payments. Their children attended one of three schools built by Reserve at a cost of over $6,000,000. The threat of a Reserve shutdown had shaken the community, however:

> The problem of their homes is the thorn that keeps awakening in the workers the dimensions of their possible fate. If the company goes, the town goes. No one believes there will be any buyers for the wood frame residences that line the streets of Silver Bay.[14]

Babbitt was haunted by a similar episode in its past. In the early twenties, the Mesabi Iron Company had attempted a pioneering venture in mining taconite. A town was constructed at Babbitt and 300 workers were employed there until 1924. Unable to compete with direct shipping ore, Mesabi abandoned the mine and the town. In 1954, when Reserve arrived, there was only one family remaining. Four miles from the abandoned town, Reserve built the new Babbitt. The houses at first were rented to employees, but had since been sold on what were believed to be excellent terms. By all accounts, Reserve had been a good benefactor, and Babbitt residents were grateful.

> They like the company. They don't think of it as patronizing; they think it's just good to its workers. When the men talk of Iron Range jobs, they say Reserve is the best employer of the bunch. The key reason is few layoffs—and perhaps more important, they like Babbitt and its environment of lakes and forest. Talk with a Babbitt resident for all of three minutes, and he'll start the pitch about Babbitt being a great place to raise kids and to hunt and fish.[15]

The effects of a Reserve shutdown would extend beyond Minnesota. There were reports that parent firms Republic and Armco could be forced to shut down some operations at least temporarily. Senior officials of the Steelworkers Union (USW) estimated that as many as 50,000 jobs could be affected. Reserve's stockpile of 3,000,000 tons of taconite would be sufficient to keep the furnaces operating for only four months. Republic obtained 55% of its ore supply from Reserve, and four of its six domestic mills relied primarily on Reserve ore. Armco would likely be hit harder, as 75% of its ore came from Reserve. Alternative sources of that magnitude were not believed to be presently available. The University of Minnesota's School of Mineral and Metallurgical Engineering, in 1970, saw the following consequences of a Reserve shutdown:

> A loss of such tonnage would have severe impact on the abilities of the steel producers (particularly Armco and Republic) to meet their demands. It would force the reopening of abandoned mines that are incapable of providing the high-grade pellet feed so essential to the economic operation of blast furnaces today. More likely the companies would attempt to purchase on the world market where the supply is already short, tending to increase prices and causing a further deterioration in our balance of

[14]*Minneapolis Star*, 4/22/74, p. 4A.

[15]*Minneapolis Tribune*, 5/5/74, p. 13B.

payments. A compounding factor is the real and present possibility of long strikes or expropriation of foreign producing mines, causing further disruptions. The loss of some 10 million tons of Canadian production in 1969 due to strikes is a case in point.[16]

### The Outlook in Early 1973

In early 1973, despite the magnitude of the stakes involved, the upcoming trial appeared to some observers to be just another step in the long history of unsuccessful attempts to halt Reserve's alleged pollution. Previous suits and hearings had bogged down in contradictory and inconclusive testimony, and had resulted in weak court orders and calls for further study. The case against Reserve did not appear to warrant immediate action, and the economic consequences of a shutdown all but ruled out that path. In 1973, one environmentalist commented:

> How much more time will Reserve Mining gain to continue its dumping? Five years have gone by since Charles Stoddard organized Interior's study, and nearly four years have passed since that first Enforcement Conference in Duluth. If the Federal Court finds against the firm, there are always appeals.[17]

Another predicted that "the case could drag on for years in the courts."[18]

### The Asbestos Issue

On June 15, 1973, a totally new factor was introduced into the controversy. The EPA released a report revealing that high concentrations of asbestos fibers, which were alleged to be from Reserve's discharge, were present in the drinking water of four Minnesota communities which depended on Lake Superior for their supply. Asbestos was believed to be a cancer-pro-

ducing agent (carcinogen) when inhaled. Ingestion of asbestos had not been studied extensively, but it also was believed to cause cancer.

The EPA warning recommended that "while there is no conclusive evidence to show the present drinking water supply is unfit for human consumption, prudence dictates an [alternative] source of drinking water be found for young children."[19] The rationale for suggesting the alternative source for only young people was that even if the water were dangerous, the damage had already been done to those people who had drunk the contaminated water for years.

The asbestos fibers were believed to have originated in Reserve's ore body at Babbitt. It was claimed that at least 25% of the ore consisted of minerals closely related to asbestos, and an undetermined portion of those were identical to amosite asbestos,[20] that which was believed to cause cancer. It was also alleged that in processing the ore at Silver Bay, Reserve emitted asbestos fibers into the air, as well as discharging them into the lake in their tailings.

Although the EPA warning dealt only with the contamination of drinking water, it also served to focus attention on the potential hazards from emission of asbestos into the air.

### Reaction to the EPA Warning

Reserve reacted immediately to the EPA warning. Mr. Edward Schmid, assistant to the president, stated:

> We know of no indications to support the charge that there is any present or future hazard to drinking water supplies due to tailings. It is unfortunate that this unfounded charge has been made public without testing its validity. . . . (There is no) more substance to this charge than there was to similar claims involving arsenic and mercury in Reserve's tailings

---

[16]*U.S.A. et al.* v. *Reserve Mining Co. et al.,* Defendant Reserve Mining Co.'s Opening Statement, p. 12.
[17]*Audubon* magazine, March 1973, p. 121.
[18]*Minneapolis Tribune,* 6/16/73, p. 1A.

[19]Ibid.
[20]Most of the other ore in the Mesabi Range was believed to be free of asbestos.

which created mild sensations before they were disproved and abandoned.[21]

In Duluth, the largest city affected, residents were scared by the EPA warning. Bottled water sales took off. In the words of one merchant, it was "selling to beat hell and people don't care about price."[22] State and local officials, working with the EPA, attempted to locate available alternative water supplies. Thirty EPA staff members were brought in from other states to set up water monitoring operations with the PCA. Meanwhile, well water from the Superior, Wisconsin, municipal system was trucked into Duluth, bottled, and sold through food stores.

Political leaders looked to the Federal Government and Reserve to bear the costs. Within a month

- The Army Corps of Engineers brought in portable filtration units to test their effectiveness in removing the tiny asbestos fibers.
- Duluth received a $100,000 federal grant to purchase bottled water for low-income families.
- The mayor of Duluth proposed a city water filtration system to be paid for mainly with federal funds.
- A state senator urged that Reserve be forced either to close or to provide pure drinking water to the affected communities for at least 18 months.

In Silver Bay, where asbestos allegedly contaminated both the air and the water, there was little visible reaction. Most of the bottled water sold continued to go into car batteries and irons, as the average person dismissed the EPA warning. One woman commented, "We've lived here for 16 years. Our children are perfectly healthy. If I worried about this with all these kids, I wouldn't be here today. . . .

I just don't believe there's any danger."[23] An accountant for Reserve complained that "since 1965, everybody has been gunning for us. Let's get these people off our backs. . . . They're just trying to take our jobs away."[24]

Asbestos soon became the subject of local jokes. Dr. Selikoff, the asbestos expert who had expressed strong concern for the health hazard, became "Dr. Silly Cough." Asbestos was adopted as a synonym for water, and people spoke of a Silver Bay man who died recently, and when they tried to cremate him, his body wouldn't burn. Clearly, in this town where Reserve's plant and offices were located, people felt there were more serious things to be concerned about than a little asbestos in the air and water.

**The Trial**

On August 1, 1973, the trial began in the Federal District Court in Minneapolis. The dominant issue had now become the potential health hazard created by Reserve's discharge. During the course of the trial evidence was taken from nearly all of the world's experts on asbestos. Judge Miles Lord, who presided, commented that "the scope and depth of the review of the literature and scientific knowledge in this area which was presented to this court [have] not been approached either in the field of science, or in law.[25] Weeks of testimony by experts representing both sides was often contradictory. Judge Lord relentlessly cross-examined the experts, and finally reached the following conclusions:

1 There probably would be a consensus of opinion that there is a level of exposure below which there is no detectable increase in asbestos-related diseases—a so-called threshold. Unfortunately, no one can state with any authority what this level of exposure is.
2 The state of the art at present is so limited, as

---

[21]*Minneapolis Tribune*, 6/16/73, p. 1A.
[22]*Minneapolis Tribune*, 6/19/73, p. 1A.

[23]*Minneapolis Star*, 6/19/73, p. 1A.
[24]Ibid., p. 4A.
[25]*U.S.A. et al.* v. *Reserve Mining Co. et al.,* Supplemental Memorandum, p. 53.

indicated by the various studies in this case, that man's ability to quantify the amount of particles in the air and water is subject to substantial error. Hence, we are faced with a situation where too much exposure to these particles results in fatal disease, and yet nobody knows how much is too much.

3 The asbestosis and various cancers associated with asbestos exposure are generally irreversible and often fatal.

4 There is a significant burden of amphibole (asbestos) fibers from Reserve's discharge in the air of Silver Bay, a burden that is commensurate with the burden that was found in areas in which there had been a proven health hazard.

5 The evidence in this case clearly indicates that the ingestion of amphibole, or asbestos fibers, creates a hazard to human health. . . . When asbestos workers inhale asbestos, approximately 50% of what they inhale is coughed up or brought by ciliary action into the back of the throat and then travels to the stomach. Furthermore, once fibers are ingested, they have the ability to pass through membranes and find their way to various parts of the body.

6 It is virtually uncontradicted that there is an extensive latency period before asbestos-related diseases are manifested. Generally, it is not until 20 or 30 years have elapsed from the initial date of exposure to a population that there is a detectable increase in disease. The Reserve plant has been in operation for only 17 years, and it was only in 1960, after a major plant expansion, that present levels of taconite discharge were achieved. Because of these factors, it would be highly unlikely that the public health effects from the discharge would be noticed for some years to come. . . . It should be pointed out that Duluth residents do not at this time enjoy a fortunate position with respect to the cancer experience for the entire state of Minnesota. There is at this time a statistically significant excess of rectal cancer with an increasing trend. . . . Consistent with past experience of populations exposed to asbestos, the actual health effects of Reserve's discharge on the people in Duluth will not be known for many years.[26]

In ordering the plant closed, Judge Lord concluded:

> The court has no other alternative but to order an immediate halt to the discharge which threatens the lives of thousands. In that defendants have no plan to make the necessary modifications, there is no reason to delay any further the issuance of the injunction.[27]

## ALTERNATIVE METHODS OF DISPOSAL

During the course of the controversy over Reserve's pollution the company and its opponents had proposed numerous alternatives to reduce or eliminate the environmental damage resulting from the tailings discharge.

### Reserve's Deep Pipe Plan

In 1971 Reserve had proposed extending a pipe from the Silver Bay plant to the bottom of Lake Superior. The taconite tailings would thus be discharged directly into the lower depths. It was claimed that this "deep pipe" would ensure that the tailings would fall harmlessly to the bottom. Originally, capital costs were estimated to be $14 million, with $2.4 million added to annual operating costs. By 1972, the estimates had nearly doubled to $27 million of capital costs and $4.7 million in annual operating costs, or about 3% of the value of ore shipped.

Numerous disadvantages to the "deep pipe" concept were raised. It increased operating costs but produced no improvement in plant efficiency or product quality. There was little chance that it would eliminate pressure from the environmentalists, since the tailings were still entering the lake, and future legislation could make this "solution" obsolete.

### EPA Proposals

The EPA, recognizing the need for alternatives other than simply closing the plant down, com-

[26] *U.S.A. et al.* v. *Reserve Mining Co. et al.,* Supplemental Memorandum, pp. 53–74.

[27] *U.S.A. et al.* v. *Reserve Mining Co. et al.* Memorandum and Order, p. 12.

missioned independent studies of Reserve's options.

The most important of these was an International Engineering Company analysis (IECO Plan) of the costs and feasibility of constructing a new concentrator, tailings disposal pond, and related facilities at Babbitt. This alternative would involve moving beneficiating operations from Silver Bay to Babbitt, but leaving the pelletizing plant in Silver Bay. This plan was strongly endorsed by the state and by the environmentalists, who saw several advantages in this setup. The health hazard would be removed far from Lake Superior. The area had a favorable topography, dam construction materials were close by, and there was ample room for expansion of the tailings disposal pond. In addition, savings would probably be realized in transportation costs, as the tonnage hauled to Silver Bay would be reduced by two-thirds because concentrated ore rather than taconite would be carried. There was also the possibility of improvements in pellet quality which could not be achieved if tailings were pumped into the lake. By decreasing silica content of the pellets, the parent companies could recognize savings in coke costs and blast furnace lining wear. The silica reduction would increase the iron content of the pellets, resulting in further savings by increasing the amount of iron obtained from one operation of the blast furnace. Total capital costs were estimated at $188–$211 million.

## Reserve's Palisades Plan

In April 1974 Reserve advanced a new proposal which provided for total on-land disposal in the Palisades Creek area near Silver Bay. Reserve Chairman William Verity made the following offer:

> Reserve and its shareholders are prepared to authorize commencement of engineering on April 22, 1974, and to recommend to the respective Boards of Directors the construction of facilities which would eliminate the discharge of taconite tailings to Lake Superior and place those tailings in a total on-land system in the Palisades Creek area as modified near Silver Bay. . . . The new facilities will be so designed as to provide for some improvement in the finished pellets in an effort to make the pellets competitive and improve Reserve's posture among similar producers.

The Palisades Creek total tailings plan is estimated to cost approximately $172,000,000. The expenditure of such sums would substantially reduce the rate of return on the Reserve investment.

This additional large investment would not result in any economic benefit to the shareholders, even taking into consideration product improvement. Integral parts of this offer are the following would-be conditions:

1 Continued operation during construction is required so as to be in a position to generate the coarse tailings essential for dam building.

2 Appropriate permits to be issued by all affected regulatory agencies ensuring that the operation of Reserve will be permitted to continue for the anticipated mine life.

3 A satisfactory court resolution of the alleged health hazard issues, thus permitting a reasonable operating lifetime for the properties and helping make possible the financing of the project.

4 Inasmuch as the existing facilities were constructed and operated in accordance with state and federal permits, it is believed that any change now required constitutes a violation of Reserve's rights to so operate for the life of the permits. Under these circumstances, we believe it appropriate that governmental financial assistance be extended as may be legally available, including assistance with industrial revenue bonds and a satisfactory mechanism be established for assistance in pledges for repayment of bonds. Consistent with the foregoing, it is the intent that the new facilities would be financed and paid for by Reserve with, however, assistance in bonding requirements so as to secure a lower interest rate on the substantial indebtedness.[28]

---

[28]*U.S.A. et al.* v. *Reserve Mining Co. et al.,* Transcript, pp. 19, 075–19, 078.

### Reaction to Palisades Plan

The state rejected Verity's offer, and continued to reject modifications of the Palisades concept, for the following reasons:

1  The site of the tailings basin was only a few miles from Lake Superior. It was possible that asbestos particles could flow from there into the lake.
2  The dams would be visible from North Shore scenic and recreational areas. One dam would be 7,000 feet long and 450 feet high or more than twice as long as, and only 100 feet lower than, the Grand Coulee Dam.
3  The dam, constructed from earthen materials, would present a potential hazard to the people and area below it.
4  Any plan must provide for use of asbestos-free ore during the switch-over to land disposal.

Judge Lord also found the plan unacceptable. He stated:

The chief executive officers of both Armco and Republic have proposed a plan for an on-land disposal site in the Palisades Creek area adjacent to the Silver Bay plant. Although this particular plan was in existence for several years, it was not brought forward until the latest stages of this proceeding. The plan, which has been rejected by the plaintiffs because it is not environmentally sound, is totally unacceptable to the court because of the conditions imposed with it. In the first place implementation of the proposal fails to effectively deal with the problem caused by the discharge of amphibole fibers into the air. Secondly, the plan contemplates that the discharge into the water will continue for five more years. In light of the very real threat to public health caused by the existing discharge, this time period for abatement is totally unacceptable. Third, it is suggested that the court order all appropriate state and federal agencies to grant permits that would immunize Reserve's operations from ever complying with future environmental regulations as they might be promulgated. The court seriously doubts that it has the power for such an order and states flatly that if it had the power it would not grant such an order. Reserve in this case has argued that certain state and federal permits granted years ago sanction their noncompliance with existing regulations and should preclude the court from abating the discharge of human carcinogens into the air and water. Such a claim is preposterous and the court will have no part in perpetuating such claims. The proposal is further conditioned on obtaining compensation from the federal and state governments. The court has previously discussed the lack of necessity for such a subsidy and finds the suggestion absurd. Finally, the proposal was conditioned upon favorable findings by the court as to the public health issues The court finds this condition to be shocking and unbecoming in a court of law. To suggest that this or any other court would make a finding of fact without regard to the weight of the evidence is to ask that judge to violate the oath of his office and to disregard the responsibility that he has not only to the people but also to himself.

Defendants have the economic and engineering capability to carry out an on-land disposal system that satisfies the health and environmental considerations raised. For reasons unknown to this court, they have chosen not to implement such a plan.[29]

## RESERVE STRATEGY

Both the plaintiffs and the court were interested in Reserve's strategy for dealing with the pollution issue. Midway through the trial, the court subpoenaed internal company documents. Boxes of reports and correspondence, including confidential memoranda and handwritten notes, were made available to the judge and plaintiffs. Some of these entered into the public domain by being quoted or offered as exhibits in the trial. The documents available to the public and accounts by various observers can be used to sketch a tentative picture of Reserve's responses at various times. Because the issues were still in litigation as of the writing of the case, the casewriter did not discuss Reserve's strategy with company officials.

[29]*U.S.A. et al.* v. *Reserve Mining Co. et al.,* Memorandum and Order, pp. 10–11.

## Political

The Stoddard Report, completed in December 1968, appeared to have posed the first serious threat to Reserve.[30] It was alleged that when company officials heard about the report and its recommendation that Reserve be forced to switch to on-land disposal within three years, their response was to contact Congressman John Blatnik, whose district included Reserve's operations.

It was claimed that Blatnik was a good friend of Reserve President Edward Furness, and that he had worked closely with company officials to obtain passage of a 1964 amendment to the Minnesota Constitution which provided for favorable tax treatment of the taconite industry. An aide to Blatnik had commented that the congressmen and Reserve people "have a real support." The report prepared by Ralph Nader's task force described their view of Reserve's actions in response to the Stoddard Report:

> It was only natural when the Stoddard Report came out on December 31, 1968, with its recommendation that Reserve's dumping permit be terminated in three years, that Ed Schmid, Assistant to the President of Reserve Mining for Public Relations, should telephone Blatnik's Washington office immediately to express his outrage at the findings. Schmid's call signaled the beginning of an all-out attempt by Reserve to quash or at least discredit Stoddard's work.... Another government official contacted by Reserve was Max Edwards, the Assistant Secretary of Interior for Water Research and Pollution Control.... Edwards was leaving government to become an industrial pollution control consultant and presumably wouldn't

have minded lining up a future customer—Reserve Mining.

> Edwards went right to work. He ordered all Interior copies of the Stoddard Report held in his office for "review" and refused to release the study or its findings to inquiring newsmen.... When asked by newsmen about the Stoddard study, Edwards described it as not an official document and full of inaccuracies.... Congressman Blatnik, who had been in touch with Assistant Secretary Edwards (for fact-finding) as well as Udall, echoed for the press what Edwards was saying about the report. The study, according to Blatnik, had no official status, was only a preliminary report ... (and) was completely false.[31]

The Federal Enforcement Conference on the Pollution of Lake Superior became the next hurdle for Reserve. In April, 1969, a month before the conference began, Harry Holiday, Executive Vice President of Armco, wrote a memorandum which appears to lay out an organizational structure to deal with Reserve's pollution problems. Seven committees were set up "to ensure proper coordination and decisive action in the various areas of concern regarding the Reserve tailing disposal problem." One of the seven, the Public Affairs Committee, was instructed to

> meet immediately to determine (1) the identity of those individuals in federal, state, or local governments who should be contacted, (2) the identity of those individuals who should make the contacts, and (3) the type of information that should be supplied.... Preparation for and carrying out of the presentation for the May 13 conference has priority in the activities of all committees, but it should be clearly understood that the tailings disposal problem will be a continuing one. Such being the case, all committees will be prepared to continue their efforts in the indefinite future.[32]

According to the Nader report, by the time the Enforcement Conference opened in May

---

[30]This account of the events that transpired was drawn primarily from two sources: *Superior Polluter,* a book published by two environmentalist groups, and *Water Wasteland,* written by a Ralph Nader task force. No information was available on the authors of *Superior Polluter.* David Zwick, the editor of *Water Wasteland,* was a third-year law student and graduate student in Public Policy at Harvard University. The members of the task force were mainly graduate students.

It should be noted that other Nader reports had drawn both praise and criticism and had been quite controversial.

[31]*Water Wasteland,* pp. 144–9.
[32]*U.S.A. et al.* v. *Reserve Mining Co. et al.,* Exhibit, Memorandum from Harry Holiday, April 24, 1969.

1969, Max Edwards, the first public official to criticize the report, was out of government and on retainer as a consultant to Reserve Mining. The Nader report continued:

> The government was still walking a shaky tightrope between Congressman Blatnik and Lake Superior. The political sensitivity of the proceedings was underscored by Secretary Hickel's unusual choice for conference chairman. Assistant Secretary of Interior Carl Klein headed the gathering, the first time in 46 federal enforcement actions that FWQA's Murray Stein had not been in charge. If Klein's performance at the conference is any indication, he had been brought there for one reason: to repudiate the Stoddard Report. The Assistant Secretary stayed only one day, just long enough to run through what appeared to be a well-rehearsed routine with Congressman Blatnik.
>
> *Mr. Blatnik:* . . . I ask you for a brief comment at this point, Mr. Secretary. Do you or any of your administrators or officials under your jurisdiction to your knowledge, know of any federal report that has been suppressed?
>
> *Mr. Klein:* Congressman Blatnik, you give me a chance to lay the ghost to rest. . . . the official report and the only official report of the Department of the Interior . . . was issued about a week ago. There has been no attempt at suppression by any congressman or any other federal official. There is in existence a report put out by an individual who used to be employed by the Department of the Interior shortly before he left and that is his report, despite the fact it bears the words "Department of Interior." *The Department of the Interior did not authorize it* and is not bound by the report. The only report that was put out officially by the Department of the Interior is this one put out a week ago.[33]

In October 1969, after the first session of the Enforcement Conference had been completed, Armco's manager of Air and Water Pollution Control, in a memo to Harry Holiday, laid out the action alternatives to be considered:

> With a limited amount of time to evaluate this problem, it appears there are several alterna-

tives that must be weighed and considered. Some of these are:

**a** The recommendations made at the conference are not "official" until they have been approved and issued by the Secretary of the Interior.

By vigorous political activity, primarily in Washington, D.C., it may be possible to amend or modify the "conclusions" and "recommendations."

**b** While I do not claim to have a detailed knowledge of the legal aspects involved, it appears to me that the federal case of "interstate pollution" is very weak. The facts presented both in May and September 1969 have not demonstrated a significant danger to the "health and welfare."

I would assume that if we (Reserve-Armco-Republic) were to fight this issue in the courts that the "public image" would suffer somewhat from the "robber baron" concept. Nevertheless, I believe this approach must be carefully studied.

**c** A careful study should be made of the present processing techniques to determine if the production of "superfine tailings" can be reduced by changes in processing—even perhaps if it involves a decrease in product quality. This may be a way to satisfy, at least temporarily, the recommendations of the conference.

**d** The engineering committee can prepare a "broad brush"-type concept of several alternative ideas to present at the next meeting of the conference, which will probably be in April or May 1970. I would suggest that if this is the desired approach that we present several schemes that have been studied but without indicating that we have sufficient detailed knowledge to recommend any given scheme or that we are prepared to designate a timetable for completion. We should indicate to the conference members to realize the magnitude of the problem, the complexities involved, and the tremendous impact on the economy of the region.

I suggest that we should also offer some "pilot" schemes that we believe may have merit in reducing the problem. By this technique we may be able to gain a few years' time.

**e** Another obvious alternative that is available to management is to close down the existing

[33] *Water Wasteland*, pp. 144–9.

facilities, which eliminates the reported water pollution problem. If the Federal Government will assume a major part of the cost (equity) involved in this decision it may have some merit for consideration. After all, they were involved in the original hearings that granted the permits which led to the establishment of this particular process.[34]

Lobbying efforts in Washington were conducted by Reserve, Armco and Republic in late 1971. In April, the Federal Enforcement Conference had rejected the "deep pipe" plan and federal action against Reserve appeared likely. Top officers from Armco and Republic went to Washington to sell key congressmen on the "deep pipe" plan, although it had been claimed that this plan had already been found impractical. In court testimony, Mr. William Verity, Armco President, explained:

> We felt it would be very advisable to inform various people as to the problem at Reserve Mining, and so a presentation was prepared to take this information to various people who might have an interest in the Reserve Mining situation. So that this was a joint effort by Republic and Armco to do as good a job as we could in describing the underwater system and why we felt this system of deposition was the best. . . . There [were] Senator Muskie, Senator Humphrey, various congressmen like Mr. Blatnik and others who were very interested in this problem. There [were] a great number of people which we felt were entitled to know our view on the situation. . . . They were mostly in charge of the various committees of the Senate. We did meet with Republicans. We showed this to Mr. Taft, Jennings Randolph. . . . I can't recall the whole list, but we presented this to quite a few different people.[35]

The plaintiffs and the court were also interested in the political activities and relationships of the companies and their executives with the Nixon Administration. Portions of the trial proceedings relating to this are shown in Appendix B.

During several days of intense questioning, no evidence of illegal activity emerged.

### Charges of Delay

Reserve was accused of attempting to delay resolution of the pollution problems and the associated investments as long as possible. One alleged tactic was to continue to offer variations of the "deep pipe" plan after an internal Engineering Task Force had advised against it. In June 1972, this internal task force had reported:

> Information recently obtained from the Colorado School of Mines study indicates that the required pipe flow velocity and related line pressure loss and pipe wear will be far greater than assumed initially. This may make it impossible to move the tailings the distance required underwater from a delta pumping station. A second question is raised by the extreme difficulty anticipated in replacing and extending pipe under all weather conditions in the open and unprotected reaches of Lake Superior. . . . For these reasons, the Engineering Task Force does not recommend pursuing this concept any further.[36]

Although environmentalists, state officials, and the EPA had opposed the "deep pipe" concept from the start, and the Task Force had found it infeasible, Reserve repeatedly revised and resubmitted it until February 1974, when it was finally abandoned.

The value of the numerous exhibits and data supplied by Reserve was openly questioned by Judge Lord. At a point near the end of the trial, he asked Reserve for cost estimates which were "not padded" and then added:

> I might suggest to you that the reason that I make this statement that I just made about padding figures, and so forth, is based on the nine months of experience in looking at Reserve's exhibits, which have, by and large, not been worth the paper they're written on. And I deter-

---

[34] *U.S.A. et al.* v. *Reserve Mining Co. et al.,* State of Minnesota, Exhibit 74.

[35] *U.S.A. et al.* v. *Reserve Mining Co. et al.,* Transcript, pp. 18,879–18,882.

[36] *U.S.A. et al.* v. *Reserve Mining Co. et al.,* U.S. Exhibit 430.

mine that, well, the profits are at the rate of sixty thousand dollars a day. Every time they can keep the judge looking at an exhibit all day, it's worth sixty thousand dollars, even though the exhibit is useless in its final analysis.[37]

In April 1974, as the trial was drawing to a conclusion, Judge Lord recounted Reserve's alleged tactics of delay:

When the case was started, Mr. Sheran asked me if I could help to negotiate a settlement of this case. I started to negotiate toward a settlement of this case. And my first utterances were "Is there any plan? Can you bring any sort of skeleton plan forward which would provide for on-land disposal?"

Mr. Fride (a lawyer for Reserve) said "No, judge, that's not fair to me. You have prejudged the matter by even asking the question. We have an underwater disposal plan which we— the so-called 'deep pipe,'—we want you to consider that."

All discussions—I withdrew from discussions then, waiting anxiously to hear about the underwater pipe. About six months later, the underwater pipe was brought forward. That's six months later and ten million dollars' profit later and fifty billion fibers later down the throats of the children in Duluth, after I applied every bit of judiciousness and dedication and study and patience that I could to the problems created here, I found that the six months that I had spent—not the total six months, but a good portion of it—the six months I had spent waiting to hear about "deep pipe," and the week or two that we spent hearing about it were just another presentation by Armco and Republic to delay that which I now found you then knew to be the inevitable day when that discharge would be taken out of the lake.

We've now gone on about four months past that time. We had a judge named Eckman who about three years ago in a state trial, who heard all the ecology said, "This must come out of the lake. We must change the charge." They were then talking to him. They were feeding him the "deep pipe."

All of this delay—now you're talking— when we talk about the time from Judge Eckman's trial forward, the total profits to Reserve are somewhere in the vicinity of fifty to sixty million dollars. The total damage to the people of Duluth I cannot equate.

Now, as soon as I saw that "deep pipe" was no longer an alternative method of disposal, when I myself decided it was a joke, I then ordered you into negotiations. The negotiations have gone on.

What you're arguing about is a question of some twenty or thirty million dollars. No matter what I write here, if I appeal—you appeal it, you can have your cake and eat it, too. You can have the time within which to make another twenty million dollars and pay in your profits the cost that you will here argue about.

The cost to the people of Duluth I cannot calculate. I don't wish to alarm anybody. All I can say is I don't know. Dr. Brown, whom I retained as a court witness at the suggestion of Reserve, says it should come out. He can't calculate it.

Now, what I want to ask you is there any prospect that you—and I know what the pressures are here and you know what they are. The court here is faced with the prospect of a stranded population, hostages of the Reserve Mining Company, with a whole economic segment standing almost in arms ready to march on the State Capitol or the Federal Government in Washington. They're doing it because Armco and Republic have seen fit to hold out for the last dollar of profit and to the last point of time.

If I indicate to you that you have turn-around time, you will immediately take the indication to the Court of Appeals and say the judge found there was no health hazard. He gave us turnaround time. We want the time for the Court of Appeals to minutely examine this record of some eighteen thousand pages, several thousand exhibits, with all the briefing that goes with it, the people of Duluth for another year will have that unwelcomed addition to their diet. Your own internal documents indicate the game you have been playing with the court.[38]

---

[37] *U.S.A. et al.* v. *Reserve Mining Co. et al.,* Transcript, p. 19,387.

[38] *U.S.A. et al.* v. *Reserve Mining Co. et al.,* Transcript, 19,069–19,072.

## Appeals Court Decision

After Judge Lord's order closing the plant, Reserve immediately appealed to the U.S. Court of Appeals for a stay of the ruling. Two days later, on April 22, 1974, a 70-day stay was granted and the Reserve plant reopened. The Appeals Court, in its limited review, stated:

> We have reviewed the testimony on the health issue. . . . While not called upon at this stage to reach any final conclusion, our review suggests that this evidence does not support a finding of substantial danger and that, indeed, the testimony indicates that such a finding should not be made. . . . We believe that Judge Lord carried his analysis one step beyond the evidence. Since testimony clearly established that an as-

sessment of the risk was made impossible by the absence of medical knowledge, Judge Lord apparently took the position that all uncertainties should be resolved in favor of health safety.[39]

The Court also instructed Reserve and the plaintiffs to attempt to reach a settlement within the 70-day period. Otherwise, the Appeals Court would review the status of the stay order based on plans, comments and recommendations of Reserve, the plaintiffs and Judge Lord, and decide to either continue it, or let the plant close down.

[39]*Reserve Mining Co. et al.* v. *U.S.A. et al.,* U.S. Court of Appeals, Eighth Circuit, No. 74-1291, pp. 9, 24.

## APPENDIX A: Stoddard Report, Excerpted Conclusions*

The following [are some of the] conclusions derived from the investigations and analysis of findings of the Interior Taconite Study Group on the effects of taconite waste disposal in Lake Superior:

- Slightly less than half of the tailings waste discharged between 1956 and 1967 was deposited on the delta above the deep trough in Lake Superior; evidence indicates that some of the remainder moves downshore with lake currents.
- Turbidity is commonly three to five times greater in the area near and southwest of the plant. Turbidity values in bottom water over the tailings deposit are ten to sixty times greater than at the surface.
- Tailings suspended in the water cause "green water" for distances at least 18 miles southwest from the point of discharge.

- Tailing are dispersed on the lake bottom at least 10 miles offshore and 18 miles southwest of the plant.
- Net lake current velocities are sufficient to keep micron-size particles in suspension for long periods and carry them long distances and to carry such particles across State boundaries.
- Federal-state water quality standards for iron, lead, and copper are violated as a result of tailings discharge.
- The water quality criteria recommended by the National Technical Advisory Committee for zinc and cadmium for aquatic life production are exceeded.
- The widely accepted criteria of 0.01 mg/l of phosphorus to limit algal growth is exceeded.
- Bottom fauna, especially one species important as a fish food, show progressive reduction in numbers southwest of the plant.
- In laboratory tests, tailings less than 0.45 microns stimulated additional algal growth in Lake Superior waters.
- Taconite tailings discharged from the effluent were found to be lethal to rainbow trout sac fry in a few days.

*Source: An alleged copy of the original (but unofficial and unreleased) Stoddard Report provided to the casewriter by Northern Environmental Council. The above conclusions are reproduced here because of their impact at the time of their circulation. Some of the above conclusions still remain unsubstantiated and have been dropped from subsequent actions against Reserve, and thus their validity is open to question.

# APPENDIX B: Political Activities of Companies and Executives, Selected Excerpts

Testimony indicated that William Verity had served on the National Industrial Pollution Control Commission Subcouncil on Steel and had been chairman of a region of the Ohio Republican Finance Group. Along with other Armco executives he had taken a $10,000 table at a "Victory Dinner" for the 1972 Nixon campaign.

It was also brought out that both Armco and Republic encouraged employees to make political contributions. In fact, the two companies had adopted similar plans which allowed employees to have a portion of their salary withheld and put into a trust. When the employee decided to make a political contribution, he notified the trust and a check was sent to the individual or party specified.

Mr. Verity's relationship with the Nixon Administration was also of particular interest to the plaintiffs and Judge Lord. The following exchange took place during the trial:

*Q.:* Did you call anyone on the telephone at the Department of Justice between September 1, 1971, and October 5, 1971?

*Verity:* Not to my recollection.

*Q.:* Did you call anyone at the Department of Justice on the telephone between October 5, 1971, and March 1, 1972?

*Verity:* Not to my recollection.

*Q.:* Did you meet with any official of the Justice Department during the period October 5, 1971 to March 1, 1972?

*Verity:* Not to my recollection.

*Judge Lord:* Now, let us stop here. We will take a recess. You have answered the last four questions not to your recollection, which are in effect nonanswers. You should, in matters as important as this, be able to have a yes or no answer. You think that over.

We will recess for ten minutes.

(Recess)

*Judge Lord:* You see, Mr. Verity, one of the problems that I have here is that in your work as president of the company apparently you have such a remarkable memory that it is not necessary for you to take any notes or memoranda, because none are in existence, as you say, so you must be doing your work by memory. Now, what has happened to that memory this morning?

*Mr. White (defense lawyer):* I am sorry, Your Honor, I am not clear on just what the question is.

*Judge Lord:* He doesn't remember any meetings and he has no records of them. You see, ordinarily a corporate president would get memoranda from his underlings, he would get summaries, he would get notes, he would have notes of meetings and summaries of meetings, and position papers. Now, absent the existence of those papers you must assume that in order for the corporation to stay on the black side, that the people have remarkable memories. Now, when you ask him about what happened, he doesn't remember. How does this work? If you have neither a memory nor a piece of paper, what happens to the company?

*Mr. White:* Your Honor, I respectfully submit that if there are memoranda relative to that, they would be in the documents of some five boxes that we have presented.

*Judge Lord:* Well, that may be. Let me ask a question about that. Do you keep a diary? Does your secretary keep a diary for you?

*Verity:* I keep an appointment book, if that is what you are referring to.

*Judge Lord:* All right. Is your appointment book a part of the papers that have been sent here this morning?

*Verity:* No, sir.

*Judge Lord:* Well, you may examine further.*

Mr. Verity's appointment book was finally produced and gave a picture of his relationship with administration officials. For example, between February 7, 1974 and April 23, 1974, he attended dinners for Alexander Haig and Secretary of Commerce Dent, met with Dent and attended a White House dinner for the Russian Trade Delegation.

Mr. Verity claimed that Reserve was not discussed with members of the Committee to Re-Elect

---

*\**U.S.A. et al.* v. *Reserve Mining Co. et al.*, Transcript, pp. 18,891–3.

the President, although he did discuss it with Interior Secretary Morton.

The purpose of the conversation was to tell him that it appeared that there might be a requirement to do something on land and that this would be such a financial burden to the company that we were wondering if it was possible under any legal or government grant to get help to finance whatever might be required.†

†*U.S.A. et al.* v. *Reserve Mining Co. et al.*, Transcript, p. 18,902.

# Du Pont Freon Products Division

"Evidence of Ozone Depletion Found over Big Urban Areas; Pattern Widens; Severity Surprises Experts," ran a front-page headline in *The Washington Post* on March 16, 1988. The day before, atmospheric scientists from an interagency government research team headed by the National Aeronautics and Space Administration (NASA) had made public new information linking chlorofluorocarbons (CFCs) to the destruction of stratospheric ozone. Ozone depletion, the scientists reported, was considerably more severe and widespread than had previously been anticipated. Furthermore, there was now hard evidence that CFCs had already contributed to ozone depletion over Antarctica. Since stratospheric ozone shielded the earth from ultraviolet radiation, the depletion of the ozone layer was allowing increased levels of radiation to reach the earth's surface. Eventually, this was likely to cause increases in skin cancer rates and could cause damage to crops and fisheries.

CFCs, invented in the 1930s, were now widely used in a variety of industries because they were chemically stable, low in toxicity,

and nonflammable. CFCs were the leading heat transfer agent in refrigeration equipment and air conditioning systems for buildings and vehicles. They were used in the manufacture of various kinds of foam, including building insulation. And they were used as solvents and cleaning agents in semiconductor manufacturing and other businesses. In Europe and Japan, they were still widely used as propellants in aerosol containers, although this use had long since been banned in the United States.

Even though no substitutes existed for many of these uses, concern for stratospheric ozone had led, in September 1987, to an international accord under which each country would hold production of CFCs at its 1986 level, and cut production in half by 1999. But the newest scientific evidence cast doubt on whether even these reductions would suffice to protect the ozone layer.

For Joe Glas, who ran the Freon Products Division of E. I. Du Pont de Nemours and Company, these new findings posed an extraordinary challenge. Du Pont, the world's largest manufacturer of CFCs, received $600 million in revenues from this business in 1987. Citing the uncertainty of the science until the early 1980s, Du Pont had led producers and users in opposing CFC regulation. Recently, though, it had taken the opposite tack, pushing the industry to change its position from opposition to any regulation to support for the international regulatory accord.

Despite this change in position, Du Pont was severely criticized in the press and in Congress for not doing even more. A New York University physician, testifying at a House of Representatives hearing on ozone depletion, had recently described a "near epidemic" increase in skin cancer rates. Senate hearings on the issue were scheduled for March 30, and Du Pont officials would have to testify. Joe Glas now needed to decide whether the Freon Products Division should let the regulatory process run its course (do nothing), take an active role in support of or in opposition to further controls, or take some unilateral action such as cutting back on its own production.

### THE CFC BUSINESS

CFCs were a class of chemical compounds containing carbon, fluorine, and chlorine. Each of the CFCs was suited to one or two industrial applications; although some applications could use any of several CFCs, substitutability across CFCs tended to be limited. There were two main classes of CFCs: chlorofluoromethanes and chlorofluoroethanes. The Du Pont Company, which had invented most CFCs, marketed them under the trademark "Freon."

The first group, chlorofluoromethanes, consisted of two commercially important variations. CFC-11 was used, in the United States, primarily as a blowing agent for foams. The end products ranged from the soft foams used in mattresses, furniture, and car seats (about 20% of blown foam applications), to foams used in food packaging and as the insulation in refrigerators (about 20%), to the rigid foams used as insulation in the construction of new buildings (60%). CFC-11 was also used in the U.S. in special, unregulated aerosols.

CFC-12 was used primarily as the coolant in refrigeration systems, including home refrigerators and air conditioners for buildings, cars, and trucks. Its secondary uses included foam blowing. In Europe and Japan, CFC-11 and CFC-12 were also widely used as aerosol propellants.

The other major class of CFCs, the chlorofluoroethanes, consisted of CFC-113, CFC-114, and CFC-115. CFC-113 accounted for more than 95% of the total use of chlorofluoroethanes. They were used primarily as solvents in the electronics and defense industries to clean high-value electronic components like printed circuit boards. In the United States, this use accounted for about half of CFC-113 demand; other applications included metal degreasing, dry cleaning, and cleaning medical implants and guidance systems.

A similar class of compounds, HCFCs, was composed of carbon, chlorine, fluorine, and also hydrogen: although not strictly CFCs, these were sometimes lumped into the same category. The most important HCFC was HCFC-22. About a third of HCFC-22 production was used as raw material in the manufacture of polytetrafluoroethylene (better known under its Du Pont trademark "Teflon") and other polymers. Significant end uses of HCFC-22 included air conditioning for buildings (but not for vehicles) and commercial refrigeration equipment.

In addition to CFCs and HCFCs, a third class of compounds, called Halons, shared many of the same properties (including the propensity to deplete stratospheric ozone). Halons were similar to the chlorofluoromethanes but included bromine as well as chlorine and fluorine. Production of Halons, however, was small relative to that of CFCs. They were used mainly in commercial and military fire protection systems.

### Production

CFCs were produced by reacting simple chlorinated organic compounds (called "chlorocarbons") with hydrofluoric acid (HF). The principal chlorocarbons used in CFC manufacture were all basic commodity chemicals produced by several firms in the United States. In 1988, no American CFC producer was integrated backward into chlorocarbons because buying them cost less than producing them in-house. But in Europe and Japan, most CFC manufacturers also produced their own chlorocarbons.

HF was produced by reacting calcium fluoride (fluorospar) with sulfuric acid. Firms varied in degree of vertical integration. Du Pont mined its own fluorospar and made HF, but also bought some HF under long-term contracts. Most firms purchased fluorospar and used it to make HF. HF was highly acidic and reactive, and was thus expensive and somewhat dangerous to transport.

CFC-11 and CFC-12 were produced by reacting HF with carbon tetrachloride in the presence of a catalyst. The process was relatively simple. CFC-11 and CFC-12 were typically produced together, since their raw materials were the same, and then the resultant mixture was distilled to separate the two compounds. The plants used to produce these products averaged 50 million pounds of capacity per year.

In the CFC-113 process, perchloroethylene was combined with chlorine to produce hexachloroethane, which was then reacted with HF in the presence of a catalyst to make CFC-113. This two-step process was substantially more difficult to manage than the one-step process used for CFC-11 and CFC-12. Chemical engineering expertise in the manufacture of 11 and 12 was not transferable to 113 production, and it was beyond the technical capability of many of the smaller American firms to make CFC-113 cost-effectively. "Every time they try it, they screw up," said one plant manager. CFC-113 manufacture also required dedicated plants: Facilities designed to produce CFC-11 and CFC-12 could not be used economically. Plants for CFC-113 tended to be smaller than CFC-11/12 plants. The average plant had a capacity of 30 million pounds per year.

To produce HCFC-22, chloroform was reacted with HF. This, too, required dedicated plants. More difficult to make than CFC-11 and

CFC-12, it was somewhat easier than CFC-113. HCFC-22 plants tended to be about the same size as CFC-113 plants. An average-sized plant designed to make CFC-11 and CFC-12 could be retrofitted to produce HCFC-22 for about 20% of the original investment and a 50% reduction in production volume.

Hydrochloric acid (HCl) was produced in large quantities as a byproduct of CFC manufacture. If the acid were not sold as a chemical, it had to be neutralized with caustic soda before disposal (unless dumped in the ocean where dilution would mitigate its effects). Allied-Signal was the only American CFC maker with a permit, valid through 1991, for ocean disposal of HCl.

CFC manufacturers used several measures to lower their costs. The most important technical factor was the yield, the ratio of actual production to the level that could theoretically be achieved. Increasing yields required incremental tinkering with the production process; the slope of the learning curve was difficult to estimate. Manufacturers also attempted to avail themselves of scale economies in raw materials purchasing and in capital costs. Investment in CFC-11 and 12 plants at an efficient scale cost 50 to 60 cents per pound of annual capacity.

### Marketing

CFC-11 and CFC-12 were commodity chemicals sold through elaborate distribution channels. While large purchasers like General Motors and General Electric bought their supplies directly from manufacturers, most of the production in the United States was sold through a network of independent distributors who typically dealt in more than one company's products. Sales of CFC-113, by contrast, were typically handled by distributors dedicated to the products of a single firm.

In Europe, the channels were somewhat different. Each manufacturer had a dedicated distributor network that did not handle other firms' CFCs. Further, in each of the larger Western European countries, one firm had traditionally dominated the market. In Japan, distributors also tended to be dedicated to a single manufacturer.

### Competitors

Only one firm—Du Pont—produced CFCs in all three major CFC markets: North America, Europe, and Japan. Value to transportation cost ratios were low. CFC-12 had to be shipped under pressure in steel containers, and a 20,000-pound container cost $40,000. CFC-11 and CFC-113 could be shipped in drums, but even for these compounds it cost 7 to 10 cents per pound in freight and handling for a transoceanic shipment. For this reason, trade among regional markets was small in proportion to overall production. In 1986, only 8% of U.S. consumption was imported from Europe (mostly from Britain by ICI), but only small quantities were moved between Europe and Japan or Japan and America.

Most of the major CFC producers manufactured a full line of products, but there were a few exceptions. Du Pont Nederland, for instance, made only chlorofluoroethanes and HCFC-22, and bought CFC-11 and CFC-12 for resale. Outside purchases to round out product lines were standard practice, since distributors wanted to be able to offer a full line to their customers.

Shares of 1985 capacity in each of the three markets are shown in Exhibit 4. The figures are aggregated to show total CFC production and capacity, but the shares within each major segment (CFC-11 and 12, HCFC-22, and CFC-113, 114, and 115) tended to be similar. The major exception was in the American market, where Du Pont and Allied were the only producers of CFC-113.

### CFCs AND OZONE DEPLETION

CFCs were used widely because of their chemical stability and other distinctive properties. They did not react readily with other materials during the manufacture of final products or while those final products (like refrigerators)

were being used. This stability also meant that, once released to the atmosphere, CFCs would not react with other effluents to form smog. Nor were CFCs toxic to humans.

CFCs could be released to the atmosphere immediately upon use (if, for example, they were used as solvents and then allowed to evaporate), or they might remain locked into a final product (a rigid foam, for example, or a refrigerator) for several years after manufacture. But sooner or later, all CFCs created were released to the environment.

What happened to these released CFCs was long thought to be a matter of little concern, because of their stability. An industry consortium to study the environmental fate of CFCs was formed in 1972. Then, in 1974, Mario Molina and Sherry Rowland, two chemists at the University of California at Irvine, postulated that the CFCs could be responsible for widespread destruction of stratospheric ozone. According to this theory, CFCs tended to migrate slowly to the stratosphere, the upper level of the atmosphere between 15 and 30 miles above the earth's surface. There, they were broken into their constituent elements by ultraviolet radiation from the sun. The chlorine atoms released could then act as a catalyst in a series of reactions that converted ozone ($O_3$) into oxygen ($O_2$). Because the chlorine acted as a catalyst rather than as a reagent, a single chlorine atom could destroy large numbers of ozone molecules. And because CFCs persisted for long periods before breaking down to form free chlorine, the effects of today's use of CFCs would not be felt for decades or even centuries.

In the lower atmosphere (the troposphere), ozone was an artificial pollutant, one of the characteristic and most unhealthy constituents of "smog." Societies spent billions of dollars trying to control its levels. In the stratosphere, however, ozone blocked out some of the ultraviolet radiation from the sun and prevented it from reaching the surface of the earth. Depletion of stratospheric ozone would thus allow higher levels of ultraviolet radiation to reach the earth. Higher rates of skin cancer in humans, as well as damage to crops and fisheries,

**CHART 1**

SOME PHYSICAL AND CHEMICAL PROCESSES INFLUENCING THE OZONE LAYER AND CLIMATE

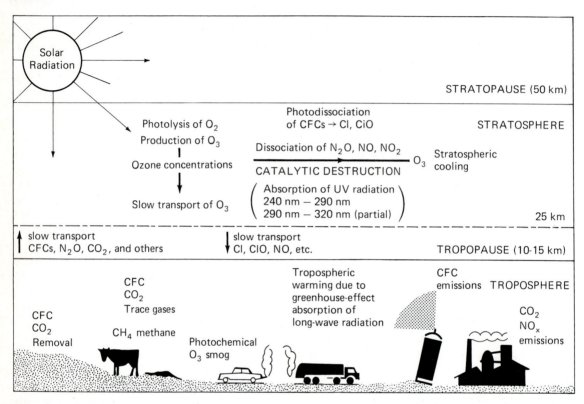

Major Ozone Modifying Substances Released by Human Activities

| Chemical | Source |
|---|---|
| CFC-11 ($CFCl_3$) | Used in aerosol propellants, refrigeration, foam blowing, |
| CFC-12 ($CF_2Cl_2$) | and solvents |
| CFC-22 ($CHClF_2$) | Refrigeration |
| CFC-113 ($C_2Cl_3F_3$) | Solvents |
| Methyl Chloroform ($CH_3CCl_3$) | Solvent |
| Carbon Tetrachloride ($CCl_4$) | CFC production and grain fumigation |
| Halon 1301 ($CB_rF_3$) | Fire extinguishant |
| Halon 1211 ($CF_2ClB_r$) | |
| Nitrous Oxides ($NO_x$) | By-product of industrial activity |
| Carbon Dioxides ($CO_2$) | By-product of fossil fuel combustion |
| Methane ($CH_4$) | By-product of agricultural, industrial, and mining activities |

*Source:* World Resources Institute, "The Sky Is the Limit: Strategies for Protecting the Ozone Layer" (Washington: November 1986).

were likely to result. A 1% decrease in stratospheric ozone concentrations could result in a 2% increase in the amount of ultraviolet radiation reaching the earth's surface. In turn, a 1% increase in cumulative exposure to ultraviolet radiation was expected to result in a 2% increase in the incidence of skin cancer. (See the Appendix for a summary of these environmental concerns.)

The ozone depletion mechanism postulated by Rowland and Molina was, as CFC manufacturers and users were quick to point out, only a theory. Empirical verification was unavailable in 1974, and could not be expected for years because of the difficulties in measuring actual levels of stratospheric ozone. Some 300 million tons of ozone were created and destroyed each day in a dynamic stratospheric equilibrium. Ozone levels in the stratosphere varied widely, for natural reasons, over the course of each day, each year, and each multi-year sunspot cycle. Further, even if a trend toward lower ozone concentrations could be detected, it would be difficult to be sure that CFCs were responsible.

Government agencies, academic institutions, and industry groups built computer models to simulate the chemical and physical processes that determine ozone levels in the stratosphere. The models used data on estimated chlorine-ozone reaction rates, the persistence of chlorine in the stratosphere, the effects of other stratospheric contaminants, and global meteorological patterns as inputs, and used the data to assess the effects of various levels of CFC loadings.

The ultimate scientific goal was a confirmation of modeling results by the empirical data. Ozone concentrations were affected not only by CFCs but by a host of other natural and man-made gases, including carbon dioxide, oxides of nitrogen, and methane. Thus, the problem of matching observations to models was significant. It was compounded by the "one-dimensional" nature of the models. Actual ozone concentrations over time were different not only at different altitudes but at different latitudes as well: since the models predicted only averages across all latitudes, they were difficult to verify using empirical data. In response, scientists tried to develop "two-dimensional" models that predicted ozone concentrations at different latitudes and altitudes over time.[1] But two-dimensional models were more difficult to

[1]Because both kinds of models also had a temporal element, the "one-dimensional" models were actually two-dimensional and the "two-dimensional" models really three-dimensional. In counting the dimensions of a model, however, the temporal dimension was ignored.

create, more expensive to run, and even more sensitive to scientific uncertainty.

Almost as soon as the news of Rowland and Molina's work reached the popular press, American consumers began switching to non-aerosol packaging for common household products like deodorants. U.S. sales of CFCs peaked in 1973. The U.S. Environmental Protection Agency, with other government departments, considered it prudent to ban certain "nonessential" uses of CFCs. The ban took effect in 1978; its main impact was to stop the use of CFCs as an aerosol propellant, except for essential medical and military uses. At the time, the U.S. consumed about half of all CFCs manufactured worldwide, and aerosol uses accounted for about half of this consumption. Manufacturers of personal care products and of aerosol containers used in industry switched to other propellants, including carbon dioxide and simple aliphatic hydrocarbons like propane and butane.

With a few exceptions—Canada, Norway, and Sweden—other OECD governments did not impose comparable bans on aerosol uses of CFCs. The European Economic Community did promulgate voluntary, nonbinding guidelines for CFC aerosol uses in 1980, and this led to gradual reductions in these uses over time. These reductions were not enough, however, to offset Western European and Japanese trends toward increasing CFC use. CFC use grew apace in the developing world. In the United States, consumption of CFCs fell by 50% when aerosols were banned, but began climbing slowly back toward its mid-1970s level as demand in the nonaerosol sectors grew.

Shortly before the presidential election in 1980, EPA announced that it was investigating the need for further restrictions on CFCs. Following the Reagan victory, with "regulatory relief" an important item on the new administration's domestic agenda, this investigation was curtailed, although never formally terminated.

During the early 1980s, refinements of the computer models led many scientists to believe that Rowland and Molina had overstated the problem, and that ozone depletion from CFCs was likely to be less than the 1974 predictions.

For example, the National Academy of Sciences (NAS), using a one-dimensional model, had predicted in 1979 that continued growth in CFC use would lead to a loss of 16.5% of the stratospheric ozone by the time a new equilibrium was reached (perhaps 100 years later). But in 1982, NAS revised this estimate to a depletion level of 5% to 9%. Two years later, the estimate fell again, to between 2% and 4%. At the same time, actual monitoring of stratospheric ozone levels produced no hard evidence that any depletion was occurring. Finally, CFC production during this period was flat because of restrictions on aerosols and the worldwide recession in the early 1980s.

Then, in 1985, with CFC production once again on the rise as the world economy recovered, British scientists working in Antarctica reported a dramatic decrease in springtime stratospheric ozone concentrations above that continent. The presence of this "hole" in the ozone layer called into question a whole generation of scientific models. The new findings hinted that the model results had been too optimistic, and raised the possibility that ozone depletion might be occurring more rapidly than even Molina and Rowland had predicted.

Reactions to this new information varied widely. The Natural Resources Defense Council (NRDC) and other environmental groups called for a worldwide production ban. Congress held hearings, and *The New Yorker* published an article by Paul Brodeur that was highly critical of the CFC industry and especially Du Pont. Interior Secretary Donald Hodel drew some ridicule for appearing to suggest that ozone depletion problems could be mitigated through the use of suntan lotion and sunglasses.

Government and industry scientists hurried to update their models, while diplomats held a series of meetings designed to bring about an international consensus on the ozone problem. A report by NASA and the United Nations World Meteorological Organization said that, based on new model calculations, it might be possible to allow CFC production to increase by 1.5% per year without any deleterious effects on the ozone. In the prevailing political climate, though, some controls tighter than a mere cap on the growth rate were inevitable. In Montreal in September 1987, virtually all of the world's industrial nations, under the auspices of the United Nations Environment Programme, pledged to cap production of CFC-11, 12, 113, 114, and 115 in their respective countries at its 1986 levels by 1989. Total production levels were to be cut back to 80% of 1986 levels by 1994 and to 50% of 1986 levels by 1999. Halon production was to be capped in 1993. The Montreal Protocol allowed certain exemptions for developing countries. It also provided for amendment should the scientific conclusions about the effects of CFCs change.

The Protocol was to take effect when countries responsible for two-thirds of global production had ratified it, possibly in 1988. Individual countries could decide how to allocate production among CFCs and among producers, subject to an overall ceiling for each country that was expressed in terms of ozone depletion potential. (Different CFCs had differing potencies as depleters of ozone; the Protocol accounted for this. For instance, 1 pound of CFC-11 was thought to have the same potential to deplete ozone as 1.25 pounds of CFC-113.)

Even before the treaty was negotiated, a suit by the Natural Resources Defense Council had forced EPA to resume its investigation into further regulatory controls on CFCs. After the Protocol, EPA proposed mandatory cutbacks of production on the same schedule as the international protocol.

According to EPA, failure to make such cutbacks could lead to an increase of about 150,000,000 in the number of nonmelanoma skin cancers among the current population of the U.S. and future populations born before the year 2075, and an increase of about 3,000,000 in premature deaths from skin cancer among those populations. EPA also predicted large increases in the number of cases of cataracts (a debilitating eye condition) as a result of increased exposure to ultraviolet radiation. Damages to crops and aquatic organisms, including

**CHART 2**
GLOBAL OZONE DEPLETION FOR ALTERNATIVE CONTROL OPTIONS CASES

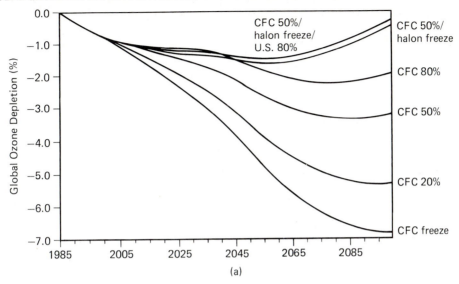

(a)

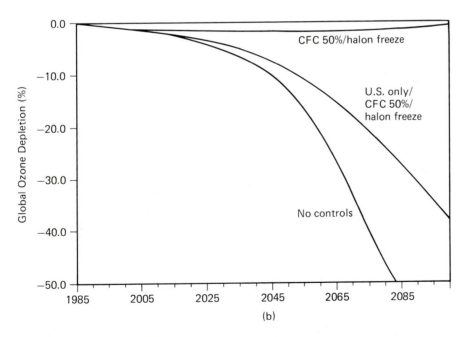

(b)

*Note:* The charts show projected changes on stratospheric ozone over time under various reductions of CFC production. For example, "CFC 50%" shows the ozone levels EPA expected if CFC production were cut by 50%.
*Source:* EPA Regulatory Impact Analysis.

several commercially important fish species, were also predicted. CFCs also, according to EPA, played a small role in the trend toward global warming. So although the costs of mandatory substitution would be significant, EPA concluded that the costs of doing nothing were substantially greater.

EPA's regulations for implementing the Protocol, proposed in December 1987, would set limits on the amount of CFCs each firm could sell in the American market. The limit for each firm would be based on the firm's 1986 production, weighted according to the ozone depletion potential of each compound. Under that limit, firms could choose how much of each CFC to produce; a firm with permits to make 1,000 tons of CFC-11 could produce 1,250 tons of CFC-113 instead (or 250 tons of CFC-11, 250 of CFC-12, and 625 of CFC-113). Firms could also transfer production and sales rights among themselves to take advantage of scale economies in production.

The regulations would establish both production and consumption rights. Production rights would be allocated among producers according to their 1986 production. Consumption rights would be allocated to producers and importers. In order to manufacture and sell a pound of CFCs, a firm would need to have both production and consumption rights for that amount. Only consumption rights were required for importing CFCs. Consumption rights were not allocated to the actual users of CFCs.

In the absence of regulation, CFC use was expected to grow at about the level of GNP in the industrialized world, and somewhat faster in developing countries. Capping production, much less cutting production, could lead to substantial price increases, particularly in the short run when users had not yet switched to other substances or otherwise curtailed their consumptions of CFCs.

EPA also expressed concern about the large "windfall profit" that could accrue to CFC producers as regulatory shortages drove prices upward. This regulatory economic rent might be as high as $600 million per year for the first few years after the Protocol took effect, with a discounted value of $9 billion over the period 1990–2010. EPA was considering some sort of fee or tax to capture these rents for the U.S. Treasury instead of allowing them to fall to CFC producers; however, its statutory authority to do so was unclear.

## DU PONT'S BUSINESS STRATEGY

E. I. Du Pont de Nemours and Company was founded in the early 1800s as an explosives manufacturer. One hundred years later, Du Pont was the first firm in the world to adopt the divisional structure which became standard for large corporations; it also pioneered the development of modern management techniques for analyzing and controlling decision making in a large, decentralized operation. By 1987, Du Pont ranked ninth in the Fortune 500, with over $30 billion in revenues. Its products ranged from gasoline, plastics, and pesticides to sophisticated biomedical equipment.

In addition to modern management, Du Pont's name has historically been synonymous with science, and with the harnessing of science for commercial ends. Nylon and "Teflon" were invented in the firm's laboratories in 1938. Later "Orlon" and "Dacron" fabrics, "Lycra" spandex fiber, "Tyvek" packaging materials, and "Kevlar" for bulletproof vests were developed by Du Pont chemists. The influence of science on the company extended beyond the product line, pervading the corporate culture. Du Pont managers routinely spoke of the firm as being "science-driven" and were unimpressed with companies that could not be described that way. Du Pont did not ignore the marketplace, as its $30 billion in sales attested. But its middle managers saw themselves fundamentally as scientific problem solvers with the right tools to serve an increasingly technological society.

Joe Glas embodied this scientific culture. An Iowa native, he earned a Ph.D. in chemical engineering from the University of Illinois and joined Du Pont in 1964 as a research engineer. After holding nine positions in five states, he became the director of the Freon Products Division in 1985. At important meetings, Glas listened not only to his business managers but to Ph.D. chemists Mack McFarland, who was hired to appraise and develop ozone science, and Joe Steed, who headed the team responsible for the division's scientific, government relations, and public affairs policies.

The Freon Products Division, with 1,200 employees involved in the production and sales of CFCs, was a microcosm of the Du Pont scientific and managerial culture. It was a self-contained profit center with its own production, marketing, and R&D staffs. Virtually all of its revenue came from the sale of CFC-11, 12, 113, 114, and 115, and HCFC-22.

Du Pont enjoyed international patent protection on CFCs through the late 1940s. Just as the patents expired, demand for CFCs skyrocketed as building and vehicular air conditioning and household aerosols became common. Du Pont did not begin manufacturing CFCs in Europe and Japan until after indigenous firms had already become entrenched. Still, by virtue of its early scientific leadership in CFCs, it was by far the world's largest producer, and the only firm with a significant worldwide presence.

**Manufacturing and Marketing**

Du Pont had historically maintained the largest CFC manufacturing facilities in the world. In 1987, it operated eleven plants, including six in Europe, Japan, and Latin America, and five in the United States. Du Pont made CFC-11 and CFC-12 in New Jersey and California, HCFC-22 in Kentucky and Michigan, and CFC-113 in Texas. The Michigan plant could produce any of the CFCs, although costs there were higher than at the dedicated plants. The Freon Products Division accounted for 2% of Du Pont revenues in 1987 (the figures for the preceding years were 2.2%, 1.7%, and 1.8%), about 2% of corporate assets, and about 0.9% of Du Pont's employees.

Profitability in the CFC business resembled that of other oligopolistic organic chemicals businesses, at least until Rowland and Mo-

lina ignited concern about effects on the ozone. The drastic decline in aerosol demand left all American producers with substantial overcapacity in CFC-11 and CFC-12. The same thing happened to feedstock suppliers; CFC manufacture, for example, accounted for over 90% of carbon tetrachloride sales. Du Pont lost a third of its CFC business. The losses were even heavier for the smaller American producers that did not make HCFC-22 or CFC-113 nor have significant international operations.

Du Pont, Allied, and Pennwalt each closed a CFC-11/12 plant after the aerosol ban, but still too little rationalization occurred. Only one of six producers left the market. Real list prices fell by about 20% during the late 1970s; actual prices, which reflected discounts given by manufacturers, fell even further. Aftertax operating income for the Freon Division was only 1.6% of sales during 1974–79, and during the first four years of the eighties had recovered only slightly, to about 3%. Efforts by Du Pont to lead CFC-11 and CFC-12 prices upward met with failure. Small producers were willing to cut price to achieve higher capacity utilization and thereby offset Du Pont's scale economies. As a result, Du Pont's capacity utilization was the most cyclical in the industry.

CFC-11 and 12 varied widely in their ultimate value to different customers. For example, CFCs accounted for 20% of the raw material costs of blown foams. By contrast, a refrigerator costing $800 might contain half a pound of CFCs (at $.60 per pound), and a $6,000 air conditioning system might contain no more than $10 worth of CFCs. Makers of CFC-11 and 12, however, had allowed their customers to capture essentially all of this surplus through their failure to rationalize after the aerosol ban.

Du Pont sold hundreds of blends of CFCs, each tailored to a specific application, in an attempt to escape from this price war. It also marketed its auxiliary services aggressively: It worked with consumers on new applications, offered training and education programs, and tried to provide better service than its competitors. As a result, Du Pont was able to command a slight price premium over other producers. Despite all these efforts, however, CFC-11 and 12 remained commodities, and companies fundamentally competed on price.

In the early 1980s, when Du Pont management concluded that costs were too high and that the CFC business was "not earning its keep," it made a concerted effort to slash costs. At a cost of some $75 million, Du Pont extended the scope of its backward integration into chlorocarbon production so that it could make chloroform as well as perchloroethylene and carbon tetrachloride at its Texas facility. Total annual capital expenditures peaked in 1984, at $68 million. The chloroform capacity was never used. Du Pont's chlorocarbon suppliers scrambled to accommodate Du Pont, offering to sell it chlorocarbons at a lower price than Du Pont could offer itself. The suppliers also agreed to take back the hydrochloric acid byproducts of CFC manufacture, so that Du Pont was no longer burdened with neutralization costs. Although the $75 million investment was written off, Du Pont's operating profits improved somewhat as a result of its improved raw materials cost position, averaging 4% in 1984–87 even after the writeoff was accounted for. Since 1984, the Freon Division's annual capital expenditures had declined at a rate of about 30% a year through 1987. Du Pont continued the efforts to cut costs after the mixed success of the backward integration effort. Most of the cost-cutting efforts centered on incremental improvement of yields and on continuing reductions in operating and maintenance costs. Du Pont managers felt that this effort enabled them to become the low-cost CFC producer in the U.S. by 1987.

The picture was brighter for CFC-113. Du Pont and Allied were the only American producers; the smaller makers of CFC-11/12 could not meet the engineering requirements of 113 production. Many CFC-113 users were quite price-insensitive; the cost of CFC-113 to clean a printed circuit board was trivial compared to the price of the board itself. CFC-113 buyers were also more willing than CFC-11 and 12 consumers to regard the chemical as part of a more broadly defined service that included troubleshooting and training. With weak currencies in the early 1980s, some Japanese and European firms had been trying to invade the American 113 market, but the Japanese manufacturers were capacity constrained at home so that only the imports from Britain and France were significant. Pretax operating profit for Du Pont and Allied in CFC-113 were thought to exceed 20% of sales.

During the Montreal Protocol negotiations and after the Protocol was passed, Du Pont eschewed a short-term profit maximization strategy in favor of one that mitigated the regulatory effects in order not to drive price-sensitive customers completely out of the market. "If we raise price to the market clearing price, we may drive some of the low-value consumers out of business," said one Du Pont official; "then they won't be around when we introduce substitutes. We might, instead, want to maximize the number of current customers so we can switch them to other products later."

"We now see the ozone/regulatory situation as a marketing opportunity for substitutes," another manager remarked. "If we can show them [customers] we have a leadership position in alternatives, then they see that as a contribution to their current business." Some other CFC makers, however, were managing their businesses for maximum short-run cash flow, knowing the usefulness of the plants was limited.

### Substitute Development

Du Pont and other manufacturers were working to synthesize less stable HCFCs (and similar substances containing no chlorine) that would not reach the stratospheric ozone layer. Du Pont had invested more heavily in developing such chemicals than any of its competitors. This investment had varied as scientific concern over ozone depletion waxed, waned, and then exploded again. In the late 1970s, during the initial furor over ozone depletion, Du Pont spent $3 to $4 million per year in attempts to identify substitutes. During 1981–85, however, Du Pont spent practically nothing on substitute development because it doubted that further regulatory restrictions on CFCs were forthcoming, and because the substitutes were uniformly more expensive. "There was obviously no interest in the marketplace to go to alternatives at three times the price" of existing compounds, said one Du Pont manager. In 1986 research on substitutes jumped to $5 million, and doubled again the following year; in 1988, Du Pont planned to spend more than $30 million.

Testing potential substitutes for toxicity, which was required by EPA before the products could be brought to market, was time-consuming and expensive. For a standard two-year toxicity study (in which laboratory animals inhaled high concentrations of the chemical and were checked for tumors and other problems), 100,000 pounds of chemical might be required at a cost of perhaps $20 per pound.[2]

In 1987, Du Pont estimated that the alternative HCFCs, if they passed the toxicity and other tests, might be produced at full commercial scale at costs two to five times higher than existing CFCs; raw material costs would be higher, and the new chemical processes used easily to make the substitutes were more complicated. Old CFC plants could not easily be retrofitted to produce the new compounds. Further, the new manufacturing processes were sufficiently different that yields were expected to be low for the first several years.

In addition to completely new products, manufacturers were interested in expanding the use of HCFC-22. HCFC-22 was not regulated under the Montreal Protocol or by EPA because it was less stable than other CFCs and was thought not to reach the stratosphere.

As of late 1987, the status of substitute development in each of the major CFC applications was as follows: for foam blowing, HCFC-22 could be substituted for CFC-11 and CFC-12 in some applications. Chlorocarbons like methylene chloride could be used for foam blowing as well, and were widely available. (Du Pont did not produce them.) But many chlorocarbons were thought to be carcinogenic, and some were ozone precursors (i.e., they led to higher ozone levels in the lower atmosphere, and contributed to the health problems caused by smog).

Du Pont was ahead of its competitors in efforts to develop other chemicals that could be used in foam blowing. Attempts had focused on two substances, HCFC-141b and HCFC-123. These were chemically similar to CFCs, but reacted faster upon release to the environment and thus did not reach the stratosphere. No viable large-scale manufacturing process had been devised, however. In the case of HCFC-123, the Freon Division was still searching for an effective catalyst for production. The substances were estimated to cost from 1.5 to 4 times as much to produce as CFC-11.

In some of the solvent markets currently served by CFCs, chlorocarbons could be substituted, but presented the same problems in this application as in foam blowing. Chlorocarbons did not meet the technical specifications of the electronics manufacturers, and no substitutes for these uses had been identified.

Chlorocarbons could not be used in air conditioning systems. HCFC-22 was a possible substitute, but its application to automobile air conditioning was problematic. The automobile industry had estimated that it would take a billion dollars in research money and from five to seven years to redesign mobile (vehicular) air conditioning systems to use HCFC-22 rather than CFC-12. Du Pont and ICI were both testing a possible substitute, HFC-134a, which was likely to cost 3 to 5 times as much as CFC-12. It contained no chlorine and hence would not effect stratospheric ozone. As with HCFC-123, production difficulties centered on the lack of a catalyst and on the need for multistep manufacturing processes.

In the refrigeration market, no substitutes for CFCs were commercially available in 1988, although ICI and Du Pont were optimistic that HFC-134a could serve this market as well.

Finally, numerous substitutes existed for the remaining aerosol applications of CFCs. In 1978, most American makers of aerosol pack-

---

[2]The manufacture of chemicals for testing was typically contracted out to specialty chemical firms. Costs were much higher even than the projected prices of the substitutes, because the amounts required were small and no firm had significant experience in making the new chemicals.

aging had switched to simple compounds like propane and butane rather than more expensive propellants made by Du Pont. Because of the short time between the aerosol ban's promulgation and its effective date, aerosol producers had had little time to test other products. Propane and butane were flammable, an undesirable characteristic for a propellant. Du Pont hoped that the longer lead times of the Montreal Protocol would allow European and Japanese aerosol producers to try Du Pont's more sophisticated and less flammable (and expensive) substitutes.

## DU PONT'S POLITICAL STRATEGY

Du Pont had long subscribed to a companywide "Safety, Health, and Environmental Quality Policy" which read, in part, that the company "will comply with all applicable laws and regulations" and "will determine that each product can be made, used, handled, and disposed of safely and consistent with appropriate safety, health, and environmental quality criteria." Adopted in 1971 at a time when Earth Day and tough new pollution control legislation were focusing public attention on industrial pollution, the environmental parts of this policy were part of an attempt to formalize what Du Pont managers had always seen as an ethos of corporate responsibility. In the Freon Products Division, this policy was paraphrased, "If we can't make it safely, we won't make it at all." In practice, the policy meant that Du Pont would comply with government regulations or with its own standards, whichever were stricter.

When the ozone depletion issue first came to light in 1974, Du Pont felt that the science was too weak to justify the widespread regulation of a whole class of demonstrably useful chemicals. At the same time, Du Pont made a public promise to change its position if the scientific case against CFCs solidified. In advertisements in newspapers and magazines, Du Pont's chairman, Irving Shapiro, said that "should reputable evidence show that some fluorocarbons cause a health hazard through de-

pletion of the ozone layer, we are prepared to stop production of these compounds." Dr. Raymond McCarthy, a Du Pont scientist, testified in Congress to the same effect: "If credible scientific data . . . show that any chlorofluorocarbons cannot be used without a threat to health, Du Pont will stop production of these compounds."

Beginning in 1972, Du Pont had invested in basic ozone science. Along with other CFC makers, it formed the Fluorocarbon Program Panel (FPP) under the auspices of the Chemical Manufacturers Association to pool funds for science and to oversee industry research on ozone depletion. Total Du Pont expenditures on atmospheric science, aimed at a better understanding of the ozone depletion problem rather than at any immediate commercial advantage, had averaged $1 million per year through the ensuing decade.

After aerosols were banned in the United States, Du Pont, like other American CFC manufacturers, continued to sell CFCs for use as aerosols in non-American markets. These sales were not precluded by American or foreign regulation, and the company felt that the science did not warrant the elimination of aerosol uses. Thus, continued sales were seen as consistent with Du Pont's environmental policy. But as one manager put it, "We don't actually chase that kind of business very hard."

In 1980, when EPA was threatening further restrictions, Du Pont was instrumental in forming the Alliance for Responsible CFC Policy. This trade association, which was unusual in that it included both CFC producers and consumers, lobbied Congress and EPA for what it deemed a measured response to the ozone issue. In 1980, for example, the Alliance orchestrated a flood of 2,000 letters to EPA opposing further regulation. Alliance literature placed great emphasis on the essential nature of CFC uses—electronics manufacture, energy conservation, and air conditioning—and on the high cost and relative unattractiveness of substitutes. One Du Pont executive estimated that Du Pont spent several million dollars per year on research for alternatives, responses to

EPA proposals, contributions to Alliance expenditures, and other expenditures related to CFC policy.

From 1980 to 1986, Du Pont led industry opposition to further CFC controls. Du Pont felt that if any more regulatory action were taken it should be international: American industry had suffered from their government's unilateral restrictions on aerosols. While ozone depletion was on the back burner at EPA and internationally, the basic science underwritten by Du Pont bore some fruit when the firm developed the first credible two-dimensional model of stratospheric ozone.

By mid-1986, the two-dimensional scientific models of ozone depletion showed that significant sustained increases in CFC emissions were likely to decrease ozone eventually. These new model results, combined with the disturbing new evidence of the Antarctic "hole," were sufficiently worrisome that Du Pont changed its position. According to a press release written by Steed's ozone policy team, "It would be prudent to limit worldwide emissions of CFCs while science continues to work to provide better guidance to policymakers." But only international action would be effective, Du Pont felt, so the company supported "the development and adoption of a protocol under the United Nations Vienna Convention for the Protection of the Ozone Layer to limit worldwide CFC emissions." Du Pont worried that further unilateral action by the United States would provide a convenient excuse for other nations to delay regulating their own producers, as had occurred with the aerosol ban.

Other corporate members of the Alliance at first resisted this change in policy. Most thought that restrictions on the rate of growth of CFC production, not on the actual levels of production, would be sufficient. As scientific and public concern over ozone depletion continued to mount, however, the Alliance acknowledged the need for production caps. The Alliance, like Du Pont, was emphatic in its support for international action. It supported an international accord partly out of fear of the competitive disadvantages that could arise if

the U.S. acted alone, and partly, according to some observers, because some members felt that once the issue reached the international negotiating table the Europeans and Japanese would reject any measures stronger than a production cap. By the time the Montreal Protocol was enacted, however, it went far beyond the cap that most observers had anticipated, with reductions in total output scheduled for the 1990s. Nonetheless, Du Pont and the Alliance supported its ratification. Du Pont's reading of the science available at the time was that the Protocol's measures would protect the ozone layer with a significant safety factor.

## THE IDES OF MARCH

In late February of 1988, three senators from the Environment and Public Works Committee—two Republicans and a Democrat—wrote to the Du Pont CEO, Richard Heckert, to remind him of the promises Du Pont had made in the 1970s to stop production should reputable evidence show that fluorocarbons cause a health hazard. Senators Stafford, Durenberger, and Baucus suggested, not too delicately, that the time had come. "We request and urge," they wrote, "that within the next twelve months, the Du Pont Corporation cease all further production and sale of chlorofluorocarbons 11, 12, 113, 114, and 115," unilaterally if necessary.

Heckert took the opportunity to restate Du Pont's position on the ozone issue. "Du Pont stands by its commitment," he wrote back in a letter drafted by the Freon Division staff, but "at the moment, scientific evidence does not point to the need for dramatic CFC emission reductions." The Freon Division thought it would be bad policy to buckle under pressure if the pressure had no scientific basis, so the letter they wrote for Heckert emphasized the continuing uncertainty of the science. The letter pointed out that there was no certain linkage between CFCs and ozone depletion, that recent empirical studies had shown decreases in ultraviolet radiation at the earth's surface, and that the health effects of ozone depletion were also uncertain. Because of the importance of many CFC uses, Heckert went on, the senators' proposal for a unilateral Du Pont cutback was "both unwarranted and counterproductive." CFC markets needed time to develop and adapt to improved substitutes. To interfere with a smooth transition through drastic production cutbacks would be "irresponsible," Heckert wrote.

Ten days after Heckert sent his letter, the United States became the first major nation to ratify the Montreal Protocol. The Senate vote was 83–0 in favor of ratification.

The next day, March 15, scientists on the interagency Ozone Trends Panel headed by NASA issued the Executive Summary of their report. While couched in careful language, the report described a fundamental change in the

scientific understanding of the CFC-ozone connection. First, there was hard empirical evidence of reductions in stratospheric ozone concentrations, not just over Antarctica but over temperate, populated regions as well. (See Chart 3.) The model had predicted a 0.5% decline in ozone at these latitudes, but the measured depletion was 2.5%. Second, the causal link between CFCs and ozone depletion over Antarctica was finally established: The spatial patterns of ozone depletion strongly indicated that CFCs were responsible for the ozone "hole." Third, ozone levels over Antarctica were lower not just during the Antarctic spring, but year-round. Fourth, while previous model results had suggested that the Protocol would result in little net depletion of ozone, improved two-dimensional models forecast continuing

**CHART 3**
OBSERVED CHANGES IN OZONE AT TEMPERATE LATITUDES, 1969–1986

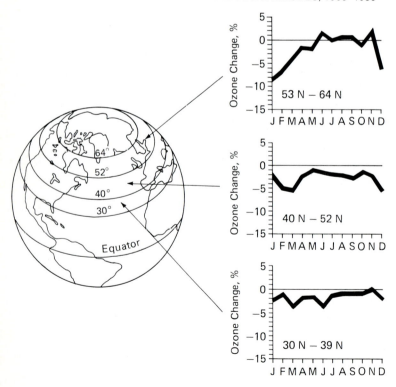

*Source:* NASA, March 1988.

ozone decreases even if the Protocol were implemented.

The model results were doubtful, mainly because the mechanisms responsible for the Antarctic "hole" might not affect the ozone of temperate latitudes in exactly the same way. At least one panel member, though, called the new evidence the long-awaited "smoking gun." Further, stratospheric chlorine from CFCs would continue to increase if no further measures than the Protocol were taken. (See Chart 4.) Only a nearly complete phase-out of CFCs appeared to offer any margin of safety for the ozone layer, according to this evidence.

Steed and McFarland attended the Ozone Trends Panel press conference on March 15 and conferred with other team members immediately afterward. McFarland, a member of

**CHART 4**
EFFECT OF CFC REDUCTION RATES

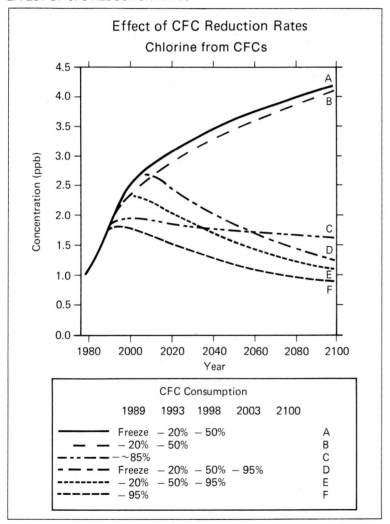

*Source:* Du Pont, "Fluorocarbon/Ozone Update," July 1988.

the Ozone Trends Panel, had been prohibited from revealing data from the panel's investigations prior to the public release. As the only industry representative on the panel, however, he had read the entire draft report, not only the Executive Summary. The two men phoned Glas and other Du Pont executives in Wilmington with an assessment that the findings were accurate. This appeared to mean that several of the statements Heckert had just made to the Senate about ozone science had been overtaken by events.

Joe Glas heard national coverage of the report on the evening of March 15. He summoned Steed and McFarland to his office early the next morning. They presented the more detailed analysis they had prepared after arriving home the night before, including the plot shown in Chart 4.

Glas needed to decide whether Du Pont should now change its strategy—and he needed to decide quickly. Heckert had called, and wanted to know *that day* what the Freon Products Division intended to do.

# EXHIBITS: Du Pont Freon Products Division

**EXHIBIT 1**
TOTAL WORLD PRODUCTION OF CFCs OVER TIME

| | Millions of pounds of production | | | | Changes on previous year | | | | Share of total | | | |
|------|-----|-----|-----|-------|--------|--------|-------|--------|------|------|------|-------|
| Year | 11 | 12 | 113 | Total | 11 | 12 | 113 | Total | 11 | 12 | 113 | Total |
| 1970 | 537 | 660 | 102 | 1,299 | | | | | 41% | 51% | 8% | 100% |
| 1971 | 583 | 712 | 111 | 1,406 | 8.6% | 7.9% | 8.8% | 8.2% | 41% | 51% | 8% | 100% |
| 1972 | 659 | 801 | 125 | 1,585 | 13.0% | 12.5% | 12.6% | 12.7% | 42% | 51% | 8% | 100% |
| 1973 | 733 | 901 | 147 | 1,781 | 11.2% | 12.5% | 17.6% | 12.4% | 41% | 51% | 8% | 100% |
| 1974 | 755 | 940 | 158 | 1,853 | 3.0% | 4.3% | 7.5% | 4.0% | 41% | 51% | 9% | 100% |
| 1975 | 654 | 821 | 150 | 1,625 | −13.4% | −12.7% | −5.1% | −12.3% | 40% | 51% | 9% | 100% |
| 1976 | 692 | 878 | 180 | 1,750 | 5.8% | 6.9% | 20.0% | 7.7% | 40% | 50% | 10% | 100% |
| 1977 | 657 | 839 | 202 | 1,698 | −5.1% | −4.4% | 12.2% | −3.0% | 39% | 49% | 12% | 100% |
| 1978 | 652 | 822 | 234 | 1,708 | −0.8% | −2.0% | 15.8% | 0.6% | 38% | 48% | 14% | 100% |
| 1979 | 650 | 815 | 256 | 1,721 | −0.3% | −0.9% | 9.4% | 0.8% | 38% | 47% | 15% | 100% |
| 1980 | 642 | 819 | 272 | 1,733 | −1.2% | 0.5% | 6.3% | 0.7% | 37% | 47% | 16% | 100% |
| 1981 | 641 | 838 | 311 | 1,790 | −0.2% | 2.3% | 14.3% | 3.3% | 36% | 47% | 17% | 100% |
| 1982 | 595 | 727 | 339 | 1,661 | −7.2% | −13.2% | 9.0% | −7.2% | 36% | 44% | 20% | 100% |
| 1983 | 637 | 748 | 386 | 1,771 | 7.1% | 2.9% | 13.9% | 6.6% | 36% | 42% | 22% | 100% |
| 1984 | 677 | 808 | 498 | 1,983 | 6.3% | 8.0% | 29.0% | 12.0% | 34% | 41% | 25% | 100% |
| 1985 | 688 | 809 | 545 | 2,042 | 1.6% | 0.1% | 9.4% | 3.0% | 34% | 40% | 27% | 100% |
| 1986 | 720 | 859 | 591 | 2,170 | 4.7% | 6.2% | 8.4% | 6.3% | 33% | 40% | 27% | 100% |
| 1987 | 745 | 898 | 650 | 2,293 | 3.5% | 4.5% | 10.0% | 5.7% | 32% | 39% | 28% | 100% |

*Source:* Du Pont estimates.

**EXHIBIT 2**
UNITED STATES PRODUCTION
(Millions of pounds)

| Year | CFC number | | | | |
|------|-----|-----|-----|-----|-----|
|      | 11  | 12  | 113 | 114 | 115 |
| 1980 | 158 | 295 | 126 | 4 | 5 |
| 1981 | 163 | 326 | 126 | 5 | 6 |
| 1982 | 140 | 258 | 126 | 6 | 7 |
| 1983 | 161 | 299 | 126 | 7 | 8 |
| 1984 | 185 | 337 | 150 | 8 | 9 |
| 1985 | 176 | 302 | 161 | 9 | 10 |
| 1986 | 202 | 322 | 175 | 9 | 10 |
| 1987 | 223 | 368 | 189 | 9 | 10 |

*Source:* Testimony by Elwood Blanchard, Executive Vice President, E. I. Du Pont de Nemours and Company, before the Senate Environment and Public Works Committee, March 30, 1988.

**EXHIBIT 3**
SUMMARY OF USES OF REGULATED CFCs
(Millions of pounds)

|  | Aerosol | Foam | Refrigerant | Other | Total |
|--|---------|------|-------------|-------|-------|
| **1975** | | | | | |
| United States | 413 | 113 | 150 | 75 | 750 |
| Rest of world | 633 | 230 | 230 | 58 | 1,150 |
| World total | 1,045 | 343 | 380 | 133 | 1,900 |
| **1985** | | | | | |
| United States | 43 | 255 | 383 | 170 | 850 |
| Rest of world | 438 | 313 | 250 | 250 | 1,250 |
| World total | 480 | 568 | 633 | 420 | 2,100 |

*Source:* Case writer estimates.

**EXHIBIT 4**

PRODUCTION CAPACITY FOR CFCs AND HCFC-22
UNITED STATES, EUROPE, AND JAPAN

|  | Plants | Capacity* |
|---|---|---|
| **United States** | | |
| Du Pont | 5 | 706 |
| Allied-Signal | 4 | 364 |
| Pennwalt | 1 | 143 |
| Essex | 1 | 99 |
| Kaiser | 1 | 77 |
| **Europe** | | |
| ATOCHEM (France) | 2 | 375 |
| ICI (UK) | 1 | 276 |
| Hoechst (Germany) | 1 | 194 |
| Montefluos (Italy) | 2 | 190 |
| Du Pont (Netherlands) | 1 | 110 |
| Kali (Germany) | 2 | 88 |
| Akzo (Netherlands) | 1 | 60 |
| ATOCHEM Espana (Spain) | 1 | 55 |
| ISC (UK) | 1 | 55 |
| SICNG (Greece) | 2 | 33 |
| Hoechst Iberia (Spain) | 1 | 15 |
| Kali-Chemi Iberia (Spain) | 1 | 11 |
| **Japan** | | |
| Daikin Kogyo | 2 | 143 |
| Asahi Glass | 1 | 132 |
| Du Pont—Mitsui** | 1 | 66 |
| Showa Denko | 1 | 26 |
| Central Glass | 1 | 11 |

*Figures are in millions of pounds per year annual capacity as of 1985; they include CFCs 11, 12, 113, 114, 115, and HCFC-22.
**Du Pont and Mitsui each own half of the plant.
*Source:* Maria Geigel, ''CEH Product Review: Fluorocarbons,'' *Chemical Economics Handbook* (SRI International, 1985).

**EXHIBIT 5**

AVERAGE PRODUCTION COST DATA FOR CFCs, 1985
(Cents per pound)

|  | CFC-11 | CFC-12 | CFC-113 |
|---|---|---|---|
| List price | 60 | 71 | 92 |
| Discount | 16 | 6 | 5 |
| Selling price | 44 | 65 | 87 |
| Costs of production | | | |
| Raw materials | 26.7 | 39.4 | 33.5 |
| Freight | 4.4 | 6.5 | 6.1 |
| Labor | 2.8 | 4.1 | 4.8 |
| Depreciation | 4.4 | 6.5 | 8.7 |
| Overhead | 4.4 | 6.5 | 8.7 |
| Research | 0.7 | 1.1 | 1.7 |
| Total | 43.4 | 64.1 | 63.5 |
| Earnings (pretax) | 0.6 | 0.9 | 23.5 |

*Source:* Case writer estimates.

**EXHIBIT 6**
SUMMARY OF EPA's ESTIMATES OF THE COSTS AND BENEFITS OF THE MONTREAL
PROTOCOL

Benefits and costs are expressed in 1985 dollars, and are for the United States only.

Health benefits (avoided deaths and avoided cases) are counted for all people who will be born before 2075.

Other benefits, and all costs, are those that will be realized before 2075.

- Value of avoided premature death from skin cancer: $6,349 billion. [To derive this number, EPA compared the number of deaths from skin cancer expected to occur under a "no controls" scenario with the number expected if the protocol were implemented. An analogous procedure was used to calculate the other benefits. EPA used a value of $3 million per life saved; this figure increases over time as GNP increases, which offsets the effects of discounting for the future.]
- Value of avoided cases of skin cancer and cataracts: $65 billion. [This figure includes avoided medical and social costs of illness.]
- Avoided damage to crops from ultraviolet (UV) radiation: $23.4 billion. [Highly uncertain.]

- Avoided damage from increased tropospheric ozone: $12.4 billion. [Increased UV radiation may increase the rate at which ozone forms in the troposphere, leading to increased severity of health and environmental problems caused by tropospheric ozone.]
- Avoided damage to fish from UV radiation: $5.5 billion. [Highly uncertain.]
- Avoided damage from sea level rise from global warming: $4.3 billion. [This figure reflects only the relatively small anticipated contribution of CFCs to global warming, with numerous assumptions about the releases of other "greenhouse" gases and their interactions.]
- Avoided damage to polymers from UV radiation: $3.1 billion. [Increased UV radiation is projected to lead to premature deterioration of polymers used in paints, siding, window glazing, and other applications.]
- Total benefits of regulation: $6,462.7 billion (of which 98.2% is from the avoided premature deaths from skin cancer).
- Costs of regulation: $27 billion.

*Source:* U.S. EPA, "Regulatory Impact Analysis: Protection of Stratospheric Ozone," chap. 4 (Washington, D.C., 1987).

**EXHIBIT 7**
ORGANIZATION CHART

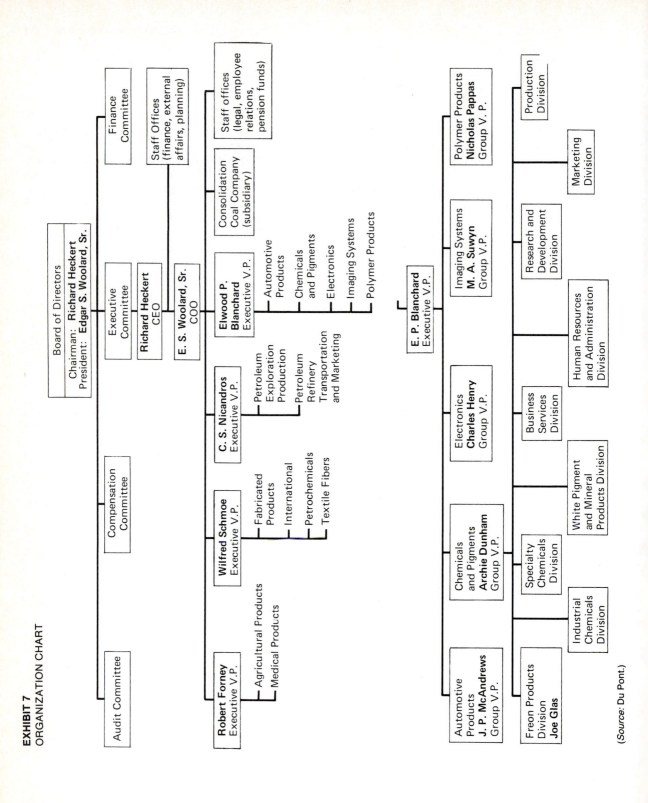

(*Source:* Du Pont.)

**EXHIBIT 8**
RESEARCH AND DEVELOPMENT EXPENDITURES
(Millions of dollars)

|  | 1978 | 1979 | 1980 | 1981 | 1982 | 1983 | 1984 | 1985 | 1986 | 1987 | 1988 |
|---|---|---|---|---|---|---|---|---|---|---|---|
| **Du Pont Company** | | | | | | | | | | | |
| R&D | 461 | 509 | 591 | 718 | 879 | 966 | 1,097 | 1,144 | 1,156 | 1,223 | |
| Revenue | 10,646 | 12,650 | 13,744 | 21,600 | 29,061 | 28,798 | 30,559 | 29,483 | 27,148 | 30,468 | |
| **Ratios of R&D to** | | | | | | | | | | | |
| **total revenue** | | | | | | | | | | | |
| Du Pont | 4.3% | 4.0% | 4.3% | 3.3% | 3.0% | 3.4% | 3.6% | 3.9% | 4.3% | 4.0% | |
| Freon Division | 2.4% | 2.2% | 2.0% | 1.4% | 1.4% | 1.3% | 2.0% | 2.0% | 1.4% | 1.6% | 5.0% |

**APPENDIX:**
ORGANIC CHEMICALS

The use of organic chemicals (i.e., chemicals containing carbon) can be environmentally worrisome for several reasons. First, some are acutely *toxic* to humans or are thought to cause cancer. EPA requires firms that wish to manufacture a newly invented compound to test it to determine its toxicity. Based on the results of these tests, EPA can preclude the substance's use in commerce. Many chlorocarbons are toxins, suspect carcinogens, or both; the CFCs in widespread use in 1988 (CFC-11, 12, 113, 114, and 115 and HCFC-22) are thought to be neither.

Second, organic compounds with short atmospheric lives (measured in hours or days) are called *ozone precursors* because they react with other pollutants in the presence of ultraviolet radiation from the sun to increase the levels of ozone in the troposphere. Ozone in the troposphere causes adverse health effects (mostly respiratory problems) and damages both manmade materials and ecosystems. EPA and the states regulate the emissions of ozone precursors. The majority of them come from cars and trucks; oil refineries and petrochemical plants are also important sources.

Third, chlorinated organics with very long atmospheric lifetimes (measured in decades) can reach the stratosphere and contribute to *ozone depletion*. This is the primary basis for the concern about CFCs. Most HCFCs are thought to have atmospheric lifetimes too short for them to reach the stratosphere and thus to be negligible contributors to ozone depletion; on the other hand, their lifetimes are long enough that they are not expected to be significant ozone precursors. Another group of possible CFC substitutes contains no chlorine, and thus can not deplete the ozone.

Finally, CFCs are one of many gases thought to contribute to *global warming* (the "greenhouse effect"). The amounts of CFCs produced, however, are small compared to the amounts of carbon dioxide produced by the combustion of fossil fuels. Reducing CFCs is expected to mitigate global warming to some extent, but will not by itself reverse any trend toward global warming that exists.

Depletion of stratospheric ozone may increase tropospheric ozone levels by allowing more ultraviolet radiation into the troposphere and speeding the reactions that create ozone there. Increases in tropospheric ozone will not significantly enhance levels of stratospheric ozone because ozone concentrations in the troposphere are generally much lower than in the stratosphere.

# Ashland Oil, Inc.: Trouble at Floreffe

On Saturday, January 2, 1988, at 5:02 P.M., a 4-million-gallon storage tank at the Floreffe terminal outside of Pittsburgh, Pennsylvania, collapsed while being filled, releasing a 3.9-million-gallon wave of diesel fuel. As the fuel gushed, it slammed into an empty tank nearby and surged over containment dikes onto the surrounding properties, creating the first major oil pollution accident for Ashland Oil, Inc. (AOI) in its 64-year history. By nightfall, nearly three quarters of a million gallons of oil had spilled into the Monongahela River, threatening the drinking water supply of communities in Pennsylvania, Ohio, and West Virginia, as well as the safety of nearby residents.

Over the next three days nearly 200 people participated in the clean-up, including AOI employees; the Coast Guard and its Gulf Coast emergency strike force; O. H. Materials Co. of Ohio, a professional hazardous material clean-up company hired by AOI; the Red Cross; and the Audubon Society.

On Tuesday, January 5, at 10:00 A.M., John Hall, CEO and chairman of the board of AOI,

as well as other officers and executives boarded two of six corporate Cessna aircraft to address the media in Pittsburgh at a press conference scheduled for 2:00 P.M. that afternoon. Accompanying Hall were Robert Yancey, Jr., president of Ashland Petroleum Company (APC), H. M. Zachem, senior vice president, External Affairs, and J. Dan Lacy, vice president, Corporate Communications, AOI. For security reasons Charles J. Luellen, president, AOI, flew to Pittsburgh on a separate plane. With him were Richard W. Spears, senior vice president, Human Resources and Law; and metallurgist Vern Ragle. (See Exhibits 1 and 2 for organizational charts.) During the past three days the circumstances surrounding the spill had gone from bad to worse. Initial reports, which indicated no oil had entered the river, had soon proved false, and a number of discrepancies concerning the construction of the tank were making headlines in the local and national press. As Hall entered the aircraft he reflected on the events that had transpired over the last few days and thought about how he should respond to the issues that would confront him at Floreffe. The news conference would be the first time Hall had spoken publicly on the disaster, and he knew his every word would be intensely scrutinized.

## COMPANY BACKGROUND

Ashland Oil, Inc., with revenues exceeding $7 billion in FY 1987, was the sixtieth largest company in the country and the nation's largest independent oil refiner. The company employed over 42,000 people worldwide and had refining capacity of 346,000 barrels of oil per day. Key oil supplies came from the Middle East and Nigeria, where Ashland Oil had a long-term production contract. To reduce its dependence on the volatile refining industry, AOI had diversified into other energy-related activities such as petroleum product transportation and marketing; chemicals; coal; engineering and highway construction services; as well as oil and gas exploration and production operations. Oil refining remained the backbone of the business, however, with Ashland Petroleum Company (APC) representing about 30% of sales in 1987. (See Exhibit 3 for sales and profit information of key business units.)

Sales of $7,189,000,000 in 1987 reflected a modest decline from sales of $7,283,000,000 in 1986. However, margins and profitability were even more volatile. A severe crude oil margin squeeze in 1987 caused APC's record-high operating income of $252 million in 1986 to drop to only $10 million. Record profits occurred in 1986 because crude oil prices declined, widening the gap between crude oil and product prices. In 1987, however, the table turned. As APC's refineries and other refineries throughout the industry built product inventories, OPEC returned to its official pricing system, increasing crude oil prices. Unable to pass through the price increases due to its high inventory levels, APC margins suffered serious erosion. In fact, Ashland's average margin on a barrel of oil dropped by $2.17.

Ashland Oil, Inc. produced a range of petroleum products which it sold primarily to re-

sellers and consumers in the East, South, and Upper Midwest. In addition to its refining business, key business units included: SuperAmerica, a chain of more than 450 combined gasoline and convenience stores; Valvoline, the number three marketer of branded motor oil and related automotive chemicals such as coolants and rust preventatives, and an operator of 100 quick-lube outlets; Ashland Chemical, a growing division in chemical distribution and specialty chemical products; Engineering and Construction Division, whose APAC group was a leading highway contractor in the South and Southwest; as well as several other coal, oil and gas interests.

The SuperAmerica stores and Valvoline Division represented cornerstones of AOI's strategy, which relied on key distribution channels and specialty products as well as large volume fuel production to provide earnings strength and stability. In addition to its SuperAmerica outlets, Ashland sold gasoline products to over 1,500 other company or dealer-operated outlets. As part of its terminal/distribution infrastructure, Ashland Oil operated the largest private tank barge fleet on the inland waterways and had recently expanded this system by acquiring terminal locations at Cincinnati, Ohio, and Midland, Pennsylvania. At the time of the spill, Ashland operated 32 terminals in nine states. At these terminals the various products resulting from the oil refining process—like diesel fuel—were stored in holding tanks, awaiting further distribution.

## RECENT EVENTS

Ashland Oil grew from a relatively small $448 million company in 1965 to a $9.5 billion conglomerate in 1981, enabling the company to compete more effectively with major oil companies. Growth was achieved primarily through acquisitions under the "wheeling and dealing"[1] guidance of former chief executive

---

[1]"Ashland Just Can't Seem to Leave Its Checkered Past Behind," Zachary Schiller, *Business Week,* October 31, 1988, p. 122.

Orin Atkins. As one former officer described him, "For a number of years, Atkins was just God around [the] company."[2] However, some executives felt that Atkins' aggressive acquisition strategy and loose deal-making style strained other corporate resources. As a result, some business units were sold when new management took power in the early 1980s.

Ashland's rapid growth and diversification was not without a few adverse moments in the public eye. Ashland received its first public reprimand in 1975, when the Securities and Exchange Commission (SEC) fined AOI for making $717,000 in illegal political contributions. Ashland, along with several other companies, was also cited by the Justice Department for rigging construction bids in the Southeast.

From 1979–1981, senior executives became divided over a series of questionable payments to Middle Eastern middlemen, some of whom were foreign government officials. (The Foreign Corrupt Practices Act barred U.S. firms from bribing foreign officials.) While Ashland wasn't publicly reprimanded, the eventual shake-up changed the management team at Ashland and brought in John Hall as CEO. These difficulties aside, Ashland Oil fended off a takeover bid by the Canadian-based Belzberg family in 1986. The Belzbergs were later charged with violating federal disclosure laws.

As management entered the latter part of the decade, it was optimistic over the core strengths and capabilities of the firm, feeling it was well positioned to deal with the uncertainties and instability inherent in global petroleum and financial markets. It also embarked on a large-scale technology systems program to improve the quality, safety, and efficiency of its operations and renewed its commitment to employee involvement and innovation programs.

## THE FLOREFFE SPILL

### Saturday

Within seconds, storage tank No. 1338 ripped open after being filled to 45 feet, 10¼ inches

with diesel fuel at 5:02 P.M., January 2, 1988. Immediately Ashland personnel shut off all pumps, called the National Response Center as required by the Clean Water Act, and turned off all electrical power in the terminal.

In a second call from the Floreffe terminal manager to the National Response Center, at about 7:00 P.M., the agency informed him that the U.S. Coast Guard and the U.S. Environmental Protection Agency (EPA) had also been notified of the accident. By this time, local authorities including the Floreffe fire department, Jefferson Borough police, and various hazardous materials teams had already arrived on the scene.

By late evening, the confusion, darkness, and lack of electrical power made it difficult to assess the full scope of the spill. However, fire officials at the scene eventually discovered that the spilled oil had crossed Ashland property lines onto nearby highway 837 and surrounding wetlands, as well as flowed onto the adjoining property of Duquesne Light Company. Upon entering the utility property, the oil seeped into an open storm sewer, which then carried over 700,000 gallons of oil undetected into the Monongahela River.

Clean-up of the spill began around 9:00 P.M. when the Coast Guard and hazardous materials removal experts stretched booms, absorbent pads, and air-filled fire hoses across the river to contain and absorb the oil. Since oil is lighter than water, officials hoped to skim the oil off the river's surface. To help clean-up efforts the Coast Guard closed river traffic on the Monongahela from the spill site to the Lock and Dam No. 2 in Braddock, a few miles downstream. By 10:00 P.M. the West Pennsylvania Water Co. and the West View Water Co., the nearest water companies downstream of the spill, were notified of the accident.

Clean-up efforts were halted later Saturday night due to unusually swift river currents (moving at twice their normal speed), and sub-zero temperatures. To avoid any injuries the Coast Guard recalled clean-up crews from the river until daylight the next morning.

As these activities transpired, AOI man-

[2]Ibid., p. 123.

agement tried to assess the severity of the situation. Bob West, director of Surface Transportation and Facilities at Floreffe, walked down to the dock where oil had been pumped from barges to the storage tanks to determine if any oil had spilled into the river. Shining his flashlight onto the river to detect any sheen that would indicate oil on the surface and checking the aroma in the air, he decided no oil had reached the river. At 6:30 P.M. he communicated this information initially to his boss Bob Keifer, group vice president, Supply and Transportation for APC. However, unbeknownst to West, oil was pouring into the river at the rate of 250 gallons per minute from a storm drain on the adjacent utility property. In addition, as the oil moved downstream through the series of locks and dams it began emulsifying. By 8:30 Keifer received a second telephone call from West confirming that oil was definitely in the river. At that time Bob Yancey, Jr., Richard Thomas, then vice president and division counsel of APC, and Roger Schrum, manager of corporate media relations, at corporate headquarters in Ashland, Kentucky, were informed of the spill. At headquarters, management began forming a crisis team to fly to Floreffe first thing Sunday morning. The task force included Thomas, Schrum, Keifer, as well as an environmental engineer, a metallurgist, and the project engineer who had constructed the tank.

By 11:00 P.M. Saturday night, Ashland employees living near Pittsburgh had set up a command post at the spill site to delegate action and organize activities. But with the EPA, fire department, Coast Guard, and the Pennsylvania Department of Environmental Resources (DER) as well as other agencies trying to direct activities, the situation was more chaotic than organized.

During the night (around 1:00 A.M.) emergency personnel believed that an undisclosed amount of gasoline had leaked from a pipeline connected to a storage tank near the spill area. Unsure of the amount of gasoline spilled and concerned over the resulting risk of fire and explosion, local emergency personnel evacuated 1,200 people from communities surrounding the Floreffe terminal. The evacuation order was eventually lifted by 12 noon once authorities plugged the leak and closed the sewer drain from which the oil was leaking.

## ASHLAND'S RESPONSE

### Sunday Morning

On the way to Floreffe, the crisis management team asked their pilot to fly over the Floreffe terminal facility so they could get a better view of the spill. Roger Schrum recalled that as the pilot made several passes over the facility, everyone in the plane fell deadly silent.

> We could see the spill in the river. We could see the collapsed tank. Our first impression was, "Oh, my God! This is absolutely beyond what we ever dreamed had happened." We thought maybe the tank was still upright, and had just split or something. The tank was ripped open and thrown back a hundred yards from where it had been sitting. [See Exhibit 4 for a picture of the collapsed tank.]

The AOI crisis management team was greeted by police when it arrived at the terminal gates and escorted to the volunteer fire station being used as the command center. According to Schrum:

> There were literally hundreds of emergency people all over the place. Some were sleeping; some were doing television interviews; complete bedlam. . . . I got ushered into a meeting with the head of Allegheny County's disaster emergency service. I was worried for a while. We had a lot of police around us, and I thought they were going to arrest us or something. Police were literally circling us. Finally, they let us into the terminal. We had one or two hours to understand the nature of the situation before waves of press and politicians began showing up.

About noon, U.S. Senator Arlen Specter arrived from Philadelphia with an entourage of press and cameramen to examine the spill site.

Diesel fuel was in pools waist deep. Concerned about safety, Schrum offered to guide Senator Specter on a tour of the facility and discussed what had occurred. Schrum then offered to join the senator in a meeting with the press following the tour. During the half-hour tour, the senator met with AOI personnel, the EPA representative, and the Coast Guard representative. Similar situations occurred with Lt. Governor Mark Singel, who flew in by helicopter, and local Congressman Doug Walgren. Meanwhile, AOI employees continued the clean-up effort, siphoning the oil from the retention dike to prevent ground water contamination.

Later that afternoon, the first of an ongoing series of joint news conferences took place. The news conference panel, moderated by a representative of the EPA, included representatives from AOI and all other participating agencies. These panel-like news conferences continued to be held twice daily over the next several days.

Initially, authorities felt that the residential and commercial water supplies would not be adversely affected, since the river intakes were from 16 to 20 feet below the river's surface. With the oil floating on top, it was not expected to enter the water supply system.

**2:00 P.M.**

When John Hall was first informed of the spill at about 9:00 Sunday morning, he knew he had a major environmental problem on his hands. However, he believed the immediate logistical problems could be controlled by on-site AOI personnel. As a result, he decided not to go to the site. Rather, Hall spent early Sunday morning in his office with Charles Luellen keeping in touch with his people at the site via speaker phone, gathering information, and authorizing expenditures to hasten clean-up activities. His immediate goal was to determine an overall company response that would minimize the spill's impact.

At Floreffe, however, the situation continued to worsen. Authorities estimated that the slick was nearly 33 miles long and moving downriver at 10 to 20 miles per hour. Emergency crews continued to place containment booms around the perimeter of the spill to control the floating oil. Vacuum trucks, pumper trucks, and skimming barges stationed offshore attempted to skim the oil off the water as the slick moved downriver. However, as the fuel oil emulsified with water, it flowed past the booms, making containment and clean-up extremely difficult.

Hall soon learned that the Western Pennsylvania Water Co., which supplied part of suburban Pittsburgh, had shut down one of its facilities whose water intake was downriver from the spill. Suddenly the problem took on a whole new dimension: water shortages. To prevent a threat to the water supply of greater Pittsburgh, Hall directed AOI to pay for a temporary pipe to be laid across the affected area to secure fresh water from the Allegheny River. (The Allegheny and Monongahela Rivers merged downriver from the terminal, forming the Ohio River. See Exhibit 5 for map.) To expedite clean-up, Hall authorized flying in the Coast Guard Strike Force on TC5A planes. Attention at Floreffe focused more sharply on working with various agencies to offset water shortages.

That evening Hall telephoned Governor Casey of Pennsylvania and Governor Moore of West Virginia to apologize for the situation and to assure them that the company was making every possible effort to improve it.

**Monday Morning 6:30 A.M.**

Hall arrived at his office a half hour earlier than usual. Believing the crisis management team at the terminal and other Ashland management at headquarters were controlling problems associated with the spill, Hall took advantage of his three-hour Monday morning meeting with his top executives to discuss other business issues in addition to the spill. However, by midmorning the situation had seriously escalated.

At a Monday morning news conference at the terminal, the national press began increasing its coverage and investigation of the spill. The media expanded its original story from the details of the collapsed tank and began investigating the potential water crisis and issues related to the tank construction, quality, and testing. The press began quizzing AOI representatives on such matters as the age of the tank, whether it had been properly tested before it was filled, and whether the company had received a proper permit allowing its construction.

Unable to respond immediately, Ashland representatives began investigating these issues. Sources at Floreffe indicated that Ashland had indeed followed proper procedures. At the time, the project engineer and his staff produced a document at the spill site as proof of a permit for the tank. Other crew members stated that the tank was newly constructed in 1986 and that it had been tested before it was filled.

By early afternoon, however, as the press questions continued, it became clear to the media, Ashland management, and Hall that the information AOI provided was inaccurate. One member of the press contacted the local Fire Marshal's office where a written permit would have been filed. No permit or request for a permit was on file for the tank in question. Further investigation revealed that the documentation provided by Ashland personnel was actually a statement from a different agency acknowledging that construction was underway.

Another member of the press, armed with a copy of American Petroleum Industry (API) standard 650 (the industry guideline for proper testing of oil tanks), began asking whether the tank had been properly tested by the hydrostatic (water) method specified by API 650. (Hydrostatic testing was a process that required new tanks be filled with water in order to settle their foundations and test their welds for strength.)

**2:00 P.M.**

As Hall dug deeper into the situation discrepancies became greater. He found that the tank had not been hydrostatically tested as directed by API 650, but was tested by an alternative method. Oil was sprayed on the welds inside the tank and then vacuum suction was applied from the outside to determine if any oil could be pulled through possible leaks in the welds. Additionally, the tank had been filled with only three feet of water to settle the foundation. Apparently, this alternative testing method, while specified by API 650, was intended for desolate locations where water was scarce.

As to the age of the tank, Hall learned that it was indeed newly constructed, but that it had been rebuilt from 40-year-old steel, which was moved from a tank at the Cleveland terminal. Reconstructing tanks from used steel was not uncommon within the industry, since steel did not deteriorate with age, but to Hall this had the ring of a bad decision.

As Hall forced a deeper investigation into the issues the press was probing, he continued to uncover "bad facts." Apparently, employees closely involved with construction of the collapsed tank had wrongly communicated to management that AOI had received a construction permit for the tank. What became clear was that while an application for a permit had been made, construction started based on verbal communication only. Furthermore, the permit application did not mention that the tank would be constructed of used steel.

Meanwhile, 15,000 residents of Pittsburgh were without water and authorities asked the remainder of the city to ration water supplies. That evening, Hall watched TV network news anchors describe to the nation the effects of Ashland's oil spill.

The print press also continued to push the tank construction issue. News stories reported discrepancies between what AOI was claiming as fact and what other sources were claiming as fact. For example:

> Ashland spokesmen, in discussing the accident, made no mention of the tank's age until asked by *The Pittsburgh Press*.... "The tank's supposed to be brand new. That's what we were told ... [on] Sunday," [claimed Jacobs, Allegheny County Fire Marshal, in a live interview] ... Jacobs [added that] the age of the tank was likely to become a factor in a joint local, state, and federal investigation into what caused the tank to burst Saturday night.[3]

---

[3]"Failed Storage Tank Was Used in Ohio," Dennis B. Roddy, *The Pittsburgh Press*, January 4, 1988.

As the climate intensified, the growing sentiment among Ashland's crisis management team was that Hall needed to come to Floreffe.

Later that night Hall himself began thinking he should go to the site to survey the situation, see how things were going, and be visible there.

> By this time we had part of the city of Pittsburgh with no water. We've got everybody downriver wondering whether they will have water or not. We don't know if it will cause the water problems for Ashland, Kentucky, next week. We have the press all over us, we don't have a permit for the tank. It's old steel. What's the long-term environmental impact going to be? Who's going to pay for all this? What's the financial impact on the company going to be? All of this is brewing.

Repercussions from the financial community also concerned Hall. Monday morning, AOI stock fell one point to 57¾ "amid nervous speculation about Ashland's financial liability resulting from . . . [the] massive oil spill."[4] News sources quoted William Hyler of Oppenheimer and Co. as saying, "Whenever you hear about a spill, investors get a little scared."[5] To protect against speculators taking advantage of the adverse circumstances and buying undervalued AOI stock, management initiated an immediate buy-back strategy through an existing board resolution.

To get an outside impression of the situation, that night Hall telephoned a close personal friend, a fellow CEO who lived in Pittsburgh. After asking him what he was hearing about the accident, Hall's friend replied, "It's pretty damn bad. . . . Ashland is not getting its story through." That conversation convinced Hall to go to Pittsburgh.

## CANDOR VS. LIABILITY

### Monday Evening—Pittsburgh

Members of the crisis management team met with AOI's outside legal counsel in Pittsburgh.

[4]Reuters News Service, January 4, 1988.
[5]Ibid.

They knew that legal action would result from the spill, but tensions heightened amid growing concern that communicating inaccurate information—although unknowingly—could have legal implications as well. To minimize future litigation, AOI lawyers advised caution and prudence in responses to future questions by the press. They advised Ashland to respond to inquiries by replying that the company was trying to investigate the matter as quickly as possible and that the firm would cooperate with all authorities.

### Tuesday Morning—Ashland

Hall announced he was going to make a public statement at the accident site. Dan Lacy initially made arrangements to hold the news conference at 11:00 A.M. at the Pittsburgh press club. However, Lacy later learned that Governor Casey planned to give his assessment of the accident in another news conference in downtown Pittsburgh at noon. Knowing that competing news conferences would not work in AOI's favor, Lacy postponed the news conference until 2:00 P.M.

Drafting the company's statement became the next challenge. Many people contributed ideas and concerns for the statement including Hall, Lacy, Luellen, Yancey, and Spears. As Lacy related:

> That statement was very important on a lot of different levels. Obviously there were legal ramifications but additionally we knew that this was the first time the Boss had spoken directly. So what he said was critical. The tone was critical and we felt the statement would position all future actions for the company. We also wanted it to come across as factual as possible. We knew it would be the basis for a lot of responses to press inquiries during the next few days. So it was important from a communications point of view as well.

When Spears learned from Luellen that the tank had been built without a written permit, he knew that whether or not it turned out to be a violation of law, the press and the public would interpret it as such. As a result, Spears believed Hall needed to address the issue. On the other hand, Spears was keenly aware that an openly admissive statement by Hall could have far-reaching legal implications.

Paramount on Spears' mind was the risk of jeopardizing the attorney-client privilege. The privilege protected clients, and of course lawyers, from revealing conversations, documents or other forms of communication from open courtroom proceedings in both civil and criminal cases. Trial and practice lawyers zealously guarded the privilege. Once an issue, which might be privileged, was revealed, every matter associated with it was open to inquiry. If Hall, as CEO and spokesman for the company, publicly admitted any wrongdoing, including whether AOI had a permit, he could open the issue to further public scrutiny and possibly risk the privilege. The client privilege in this situation applied to AOI as a corporation as well as to individuals in the company.

Spears was also aware of other issues that might hover over the company. Class action lawsuits were likely, as well as possible criminal exposure. The increasingly nasty situation regarding the lack of a permit and reconstruction of the tank out of 40-year-old steel could also leave individuals open to criminal indictment. Ashland's legal staff was deeply concerned that whatever was said in the press conference would have legal—if not criminal—repercussions.

## THE TRIP TO PITTSBURGH

### Tuesday 10:00

After spending the morning discussing latest developments with staff, Hall drafted a public statement for the afternoon news conference. But, from the time Hall wrote the draft until he addressed the media, the statement was in perpetual change. As Lacy recalled,

> I remember taking with me Scotch tape, scissors, and a black marker. On the flight up to Pittsburgh, on the way to the terminal so Mr. Hall could survey the damage and speak to our team, and in the car on the way to the press conference, I was cutting and pasting and changing it.

Throughout the flight, the pros and cons of the various responses to issues resulting from the spill were debated. To prepare Hall for any questions the press might ask, Yancey and Lacy frequently played devil's advocates, ferreting out any angles they had not considered.

Once everyone reached Floreffe, they received word that Governor Casey's news conference had been postponed until 2:00 P.M. In response, Lacy rescheduled Hall's press conference for 4:00 P.M.

As Hall toured the terminal he expressed genuine thanks to everyone who had been working 18-hour days in cold, wet, and miserable conditions to clean up the spill. During the entire week temperatures never reached above 10 degrees and the wind chill factor frequently pushed temperatures below zero. As the Ashland team surveyed the terminal, they met with EPA officials from Philadelphia and various emergency clean-up crews. They attempted to get current on new developments, particularly the water shortages, and to demonstrate the company's responsiveness to do whatever they could to improve the situation. One representative from a local agency informed Luellen that in the next day or so they would need towboats and barges to go upriver to bring fresh water to communities whose water supplies were in danger of contamination. Concerned that time was of the essence, Luellen ordered the vessels to be sent immediately.

Climbing into the car that would take him and his group to the press conference, Hall pondered the situation confronting him. Regardless of which course he took in his statement—publicly admitting "wrongdoing" or being somewhat circumspect on issues like the permit and the used steel—he was in for tough questioning by the press. Furthermore, he would undoubtedly be queried on the wisdom of the actions the company had taken so far. He himself was unsure about this. Should others who had been more closely associated with the clean-up also participate in the press conference? The trip from the terminal to the press conference site was short, and Hall knew he had to resolve his mind finally on these points before he met reporters.

# EXHIBITS: Ashland Oil, Inc.

**EXHIBIT 1**
ASHLAND OIL, INC.—JANUARY 2, 1988

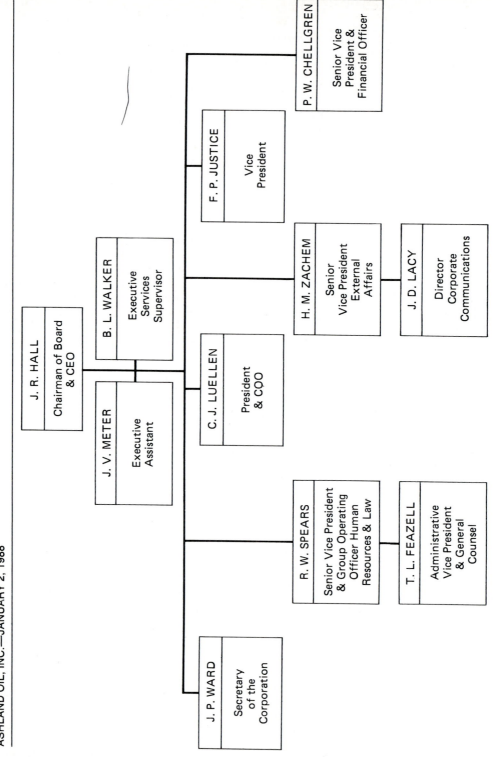

**EXHIBIT 2**
ASHLAND PETROLEUM COMPANY—JANUARY 2, 1988

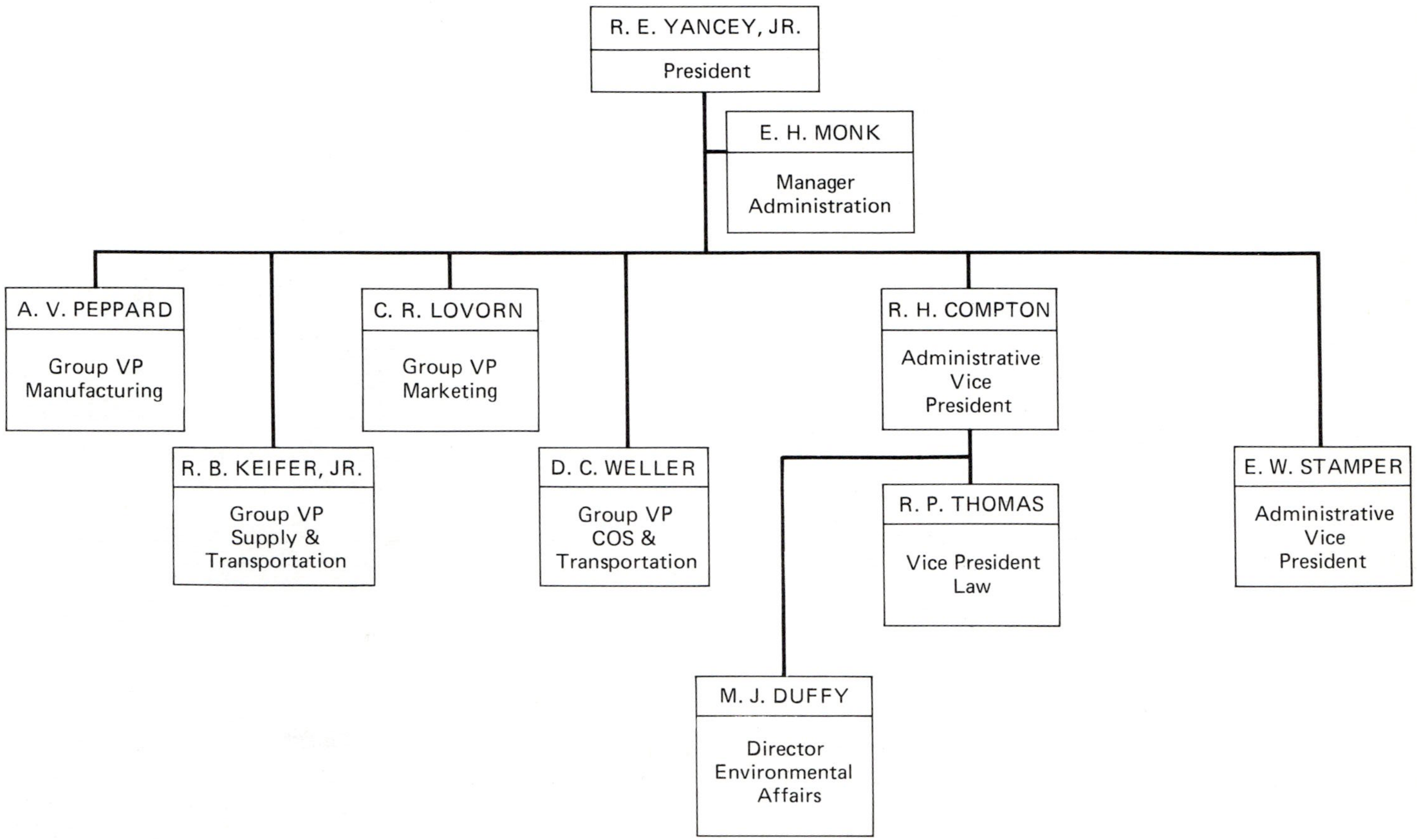

**EXHIBIT 3**

ASHLAND OIL, INC.—KEY BUSINESS UNITS
Fiscal year revenue and income (in millions)

|  | 1987 | 1986 |
|---|---|---|
| Petroleum | | |
| Sales and operating revenues | $2,919 | $3,366 |
| Operating income | 10 | 252 |
| SuperAmerica | 1,364 | 1,365 |
| | 16 | 37 |
| Valvoline | 552 | 529 |
| | 48 | 37 |
| Chemical | 1,643 | 1,477 |
| | 90 | 71 |
| Coal | 199 | 190 |
| | 31 | 14 |
| Engineer construction | 1,317 | 1,185 |
| | 72 | 86 |
| Exploration | 248 | 232 |
| | 1 | (23) |
| Intersegment sales | | |
| Ashland Petroleum | (813) | (851) |
| Exploration | (213) | (184) |
| Other | (27) | (26) |

*Source:* 1987 company annual report.

**EXHIBIT 4**

COLLAPSED STORAGE TANK NO. 1338

**EXHIBIT 5**
MAP OF SPILL AREA

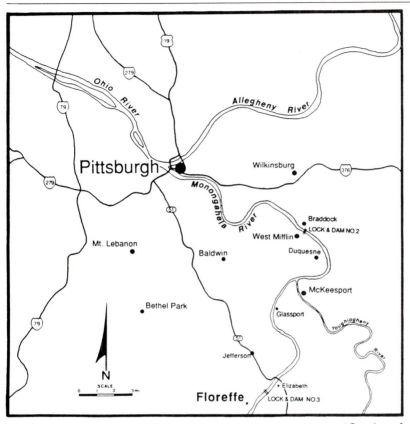

(*Continued*)

**EXHIBIT 5**
CONTINUED

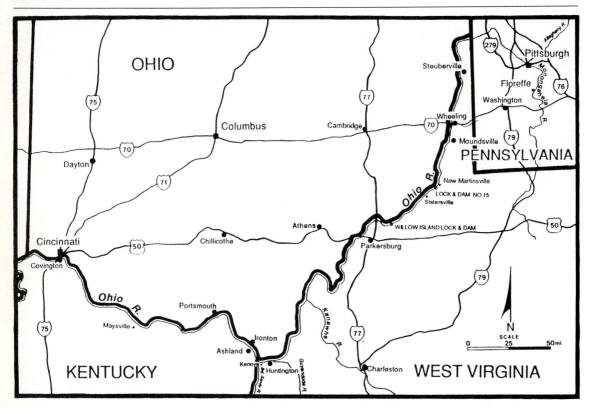

# Braniff International: The Ethics of Bankruptcy

On Friday, May 7, 1982, Howard Putnam, chief executive officer of Braniff International (BI), walked to his car after another long week. The day before he had spoken at the annual stockholders' meeting and then chaired a board meeting. The company had been on the verge of bankruptcy since he took charge on September 22, 1981. For the next seven months, he and Phil Guthrie, his chief financial officer (CFO), had lived constantly on razor's edge trying to get through the next cash crisis. At that point BI owed $439 million to 39 senior-secured creditors. Despite a cash infusion from a deal in which Eastern Airlines had leased BI's South American routes, Putnam did not know if Braniff would have enough cash to meet its payroll on Thursday, May 13.

Suggestions were made that BI have another 2-for-1 sale like the highly successful one held in February 1982, when passengers received one free ticket for every one purchased. But Putnam was concerned about whether or not the public would view it as a last-ditch attempt to raise cash. He and Guthrie had also been invited to make a BI presentation to institutional investors on Wall Street but had declined the offer. With Braniff's future uncertain, they believed the timing was inappropriate. Too much talk about bankruptcy could be a self-fulfilling prophecy. If bankruptcy was under consideration, however, didn't people have a right to know ahead of time? The ultimate question was when to file; if BI had to file, then Putnam wanted to file under Chapter XI to preserve Braniff's assets and reorganize. There was always the danger—especially with rumors of impending bankruptcy—that BI would be placed in involuntary bankruptcy by a creditor and thus be forced to liquidate all of its assets.

## IF YOU'VE GOT IT, FLAUNT IT

BI was founded in 1928 by Tom Braniff in Tulsa, Oklahoma. In 1942 the airline moved to Dallas and served the Midwest until 1946, when it began flights to Latin America. In 1965 Harding Lawrence, who had been in charge of daily operations at Continental Airlines, became CEO and president of BI. Under Lawrence, Braniff gained a reputation for innovation. Shortly after his arrival, he announced his dream for a new airline, including an all-jet fleet. With the encouragement of advertising executive Mary Wells, whom Lawrence later married, he declared the end of "the plain plane," had BI's fleet painted in bright colors, and adopted the slogan "If you've got it, flaunt it." He paid artist Alexander Calder $100,000 for his design ideas and had the stewardesses wear Pucci-designed uniforms.

From 1965 to 1977 BI grew rapidly and enjoyed strong returns. In 1973, for example, the company earned $17 million on revenues of $372 million, a 99% increase in earnings over 1972. In November 1977 the airline began construction of its lavish $70 million world headquarters at the Dallas–Ft. Worth (DFW) airport.

In October 1978 the Airline Deregulation Act was passed. Lawrence seized the opportunity to expand aggressively, fearing that Congress might soon reverse its decision. Within six months BI had obtained the authority to serve—if it desired—437 of the 1,300 new routes offered by the Civil Aeronautics Board (CAB). In this time span the company opened new routes to Europe, Asia, and the Middle East. In a single day—December 15, 1978—BI began flying to 16 new cities. By comparison, United Airlines, the largest carrier in the industry, added only one new route.

Braniff increased capacity to service its new routes. It bought 41 new Boeing planes over a three-year period, including three 747s, and it took options on 44 other aircraft for a total cost of $925 million. From 1978 to 1979 BI increased its available seat miles by 32%,

and its breakeven load factor changed from 50.2% to 59.9%.[1]

The gods of the airline industry, however, did not smile upon Lawrence's hubris. In 1979 the economy entered a severe recession and passenger traffic plummeted; at the same time, the cost of fuel doubled. With rate setting by the CAB eliminated, airlines began competing by offering discount fares that reduced yields per revenue mile (the amount passengers paid per mile of flight). A $45 million net income in 1978 turned into a $44 million loss in 1979 and a $131 million loss in 1980. (Exhibits 1 and 2 document the dramatic change in BI's financial fortunes.) In December 1980 Lawrence resigned under pressure, it was reported, from BI's lenders and board of directors.

Lawrence was replaced by John J. Casey, who had been Braniff's vice chairman. Casey started a major turnaround effort that included streamlining management, dropping unprofitable routes, selling unneeded aircraft, and gaining salary and productivity concessions from employees. In February 1981, nonetheless, the company's creditors refused to grant BI additional credit, thus putting it on a cash-in-advance basis for such major operating expenses as fuel. In March 1981 Casey was successful in persuading BI's employees to accept an across-the-board 10% paycut. In July of that year Casey negotiated a postponement of the interest and principal due on BI's $653 million debt until February 1, 1982. By then, Braniff was supposed to have a financial restructuring plan acceptable to all 39 major lenders; if not, all of its debt would be declared in default and therefore immediately due in full.

BI was not alone in these dire straits. In

---

[1] Because costs in the airline industry were more directly related to the number of seats flown over a given distance than to the number of passengers, the unit of production was the *available seat mile*, or one passenger seat flown one mile. The product of the number of passengers carried and how far they flew gave *revenue passenger miles* (RPMs). *Load factor* was a measure of how full an airline's planes were, expressed as the ratio of revenue passenger miles to available seat miles.

1980 there was a net operating loss for U.S. airlines of $225 million, with losses for 1981 expected to be even greater because of the sluggish economy. The firing of air traffic controllers on August 3, 1981, caused an even further decline in traffic for the entire industry. It was estimated that 15,000 domestic airline employees had been laid off in 1981 before the controllers' strike and that another 15,000 would be laid off by the end of that year.

## LEAVING PROFITS FOR PROBLEMS

When Putnam was in his early forties, he asked his son to join him in parachuting from a small plane at 3,000 feet. His son replied, "Why on earth would anyone want to jump out of a perfectly good airplane?" Yet, for Putnam, who had soloed at 16 from a pasture near the family farm in Iowa, it was something he had always wanted to do. Accompanied by his daughter as he prepared to jump, Putnam thought, "This is the scariest thing I've ever done." Although he acknowledged that it was fun, he did not think he would do it again, "but sometimes in life, there are challenges you must attempt."

When Putnam was asked by Casey to become Braniff's president, he had been CEO at Southwest Airlines from 1978–1981. Southwest was the most profitable airline in the industry, and Putnam and Guthrie, his CFO there, were credited with much of its success. During their term Southwest had nearly tripled its revenues, earnings, and route size. Putnam insisted on bringing Guthrie with him to BI.

Industry experts lauded the choice of Putnam to try to turn Braniff around. One airline analyst said: "He obviously looked over Braniff's books. And a man of Mr. Putnam's caliber would not take the position if he didn't think there was hope to turn Braniff around." Putnam was also known for his interest in people and had built a reputation for working with employees, characterizing himself at one time as the "head cheerleader" for Southwest's employees.

To avoid any conflict of interest, Putnam and Guthrie restricted themselves to learning about BI's financial condition from published sources and information generally available from its management. In discussing the possibility of bankruptcy with BI's executive committee, he said: "If you are expecting me to go for a government bailout, I am not your guy. I will not do that. If we can make it live on its own, fine, and if we can't, it will die." No one dissented.

On arriving at BI, Putnam and Guthrie found an airline that had no free assets—all had been pledged; in addition, it had no borrowing capability and had a negative net worth. Although the company was marginally cash positive, advance bookings were decreasing dramatically. There was no coherent marketing strategy. According to one observer, the atmosphere was one of a continuing cash crisis. Because BI's employees had frequently been told that BI was in trouble, crisis comments were "starting to run off everybody's back like water off your raincoat."

Within a week after Putnam started, he learned that both Lawrence and Casey had discussed retaining bankruptcy counsel with the board of directors. He was also shocked to learn that there was only enough cash on hand to cover 10 days of operations. This was particularly alarming because every Thursday BI had to pay $7 million in cash for the next week's fuel, and every other Thursday there was a $12 million payroll due. What was more, Guthrie told Putnam that there would be a severe cash crunch from February to April, 1982. Putnam also learned that BI's top management believed American Airlines was competing unfairly; he was advised not to talk with American's executives without clearance from counsel.

On September 30 BI reported a third quarter net loss of $20.3 million, bringing its losses through September to $85 million. Load factors had dropped from 62% for the third quarter of 1980 to just under 58% for the third quarter of 1981.

Shortly after his arrival Putnam sent out questionnaires to employees to find out what was on their minds. The first page began, "Dear Mr. Putnam, Braniff can be improved by . . . " with the rest of the page blank and an option for the person's signature. Putnam had stated that he would personally respond to every questionnaire received, and although it took several months, he did handwrite a note to each of the 3,000 or so respondents. Putnam later stated, "That effort by employees and management opened up communications and improved productivity immediately."

Putnam and other senior officers began having three or four meetings with employees per week to field questions and get suggestions. Putnam once showed up unannounced and dressed in coveralls to load bags for a morning to find out what was on the minds of the employees. He commonly found several employees outside his door at 5:00 P.M. waiting to talk. Sometimes he went to DFW on Saturday mornings and spent about an hour going from gate to gate talking with employees. When he was asked if Braniff was going to make it, his answer was a contingent one: "Folks, our future rests on the following points." He then would summarize what was happening, what the risks were, what he wanted to happen, and what the unions and employees could do to help.

### FOURTH QUARTER, 1981

Putnam quickly announced a turnaround plan that he hoped to have in place by Christmas 1981. First, he wanted to restructure BI's $591 million debt. Second, he wanted to find a niche in the marketplace. "There may not be one. If not, we have to find a way to create one," he said. Third, he wanted to increase the productivity of BI's employees, although he did not plan to ask for another pay cut. Putnam also wanted to reshape the organization from top to bottom with an emphasis on achieving efficiency through simplicity. Finally, he planned to reduce costs as soon as possible. On October 22, BI offered to sublet all or part of its headquarters building, which cost about $500,000 in monthly payments.

As part of its new marketing strategy, BI announced on November 4 the start of "Texas Class" beginning November 24. BI had previously offered 582 different fares, but in a move described by Putnam as going "back to basics," the airline would now have only 15 fares nationwide. Prices were also lowered 45–55% from the previous full fare levels. Braniff's one-way full fare between Dallas and Los Angeles, for example, was lowered from $248 to $135. In addition, all first-class seats were replaced by coach seating with extra leg room, thus expanding capacity on most planes from 134 to 146. Putnam explained: "Texas Class had several purposes. It simplified fares and employee work load, increasing productivity. It meant a higher quality of service, all the same class. Since 80% of all airline passengers were already traveling on discounted fares, the overall yield dilution was only 10–12%. It was also an excellent marketing tool to show fare comparisons to the old, full fares."

As Putnam expected, BI's new fares were immediately matched by American, which competed with Braniff on almost all of its domestic routes. An American spokesperson said: "There will be no route on which Braniff and American compete where there will be a fare offered lower than American's." Delta Airlines soon lowered its fares in the "cutthroat madness," as it was called by Wall Street. The Atlanta-based airline said that its planes would have to fly 105% full for it to break even in the Dallas market.

Although the new fares caused BI's break-even load factor to rise from 59% to mid-60%, Putnam was optimistic that the increase in traffic would more than offset the low fares. He also reasoned that because operating costs were rapidly being trimmed, the new fare structure would be profitable in the long run.

BI's creditors had given the airline until February 1, 1982, to restructure its debt. A second deadline was March 31, when the plan had to be presented in writing. Putnam and Guthrie immediately began meeting with the 39 senior-secured creditors to work out a plan, but were hampered because every issue and covenant had to be unanimously approved.

They usually met with a committee that represented the principal banks and insurance companies. Small meetings had 30–40 people and the larger ones up to 150. Within the secured creditor committee there were specialty committees that looked at such things as asset values and aircraft maintenance. Some of the large creditor institutions had full-time staff members whose only job was to monitor how well Braniff was doing and to look after the creditor's interests. Starting in October, there were large formal meetings at least twice a month, more frequent meetings of smaller groups, and daily telephone contacts with at least 10 of the major lenders. Aside from the 39 senior-secured creditors, there were about 3,000 bondholders and 40,000 small, unsecured creditors—principally employees and ticketholders.

In plotting the flow of cash receipts for an airline, the results would be not a smooth line but a series of spikes representing three major points for settling receipts. Cash from the sale of tickets by travel agents came through the Area Settlement Plan (ASP) and occurred weekly or monthly depending on the travel agency's size. Each agency reported its ticket sales and sent a check to the area settlement bank which then broke out the portion owed each airline and sent it a draft for that amount. Thus, an airline would not know until it received this draft how much it would get from the ASP. A monthly receipt of cash also came through the Airline Clearing House (ACH). Carriers would send tickets that they had written, but which included travel on other carriers, to the ACH for collection or payment. The ACH would take all of these tickets and derive a total for each airline. The third important receipt was the settlement of credit card travel, which usually occurred on a weekly basis. The uncertainty about the amounts of these receipts meant that if one overlaid the flow of receipts on disbursements, BI was vulnerable to cash shortages.

Putnam found negotiating with the creditors and unions frustrating. Typically, one group would say that it was in favor of what he was proposing, but that it would not cooperate until another group conceded something as well. Some of the creditors told him that they would agree to certain proposals only if the unions made concessions. But the unions did not take seriously the creditors' statements that they would neither provide additional cash nor continue to defer debt repayment.

There were five unions at BI: The International Association of Machinists (IAM), the Association of Flight Attendants (AFA), the Airline Pilots Association (ALPA), the Teamsters, and the dispatchers' union. In November Putnam was negotiating with the IAM for productivity increases in return for profit sharing when L. T. Faircloth, the union's representative, told him, "I would rather see Braniff go under than give you anything."

In a move to halt big cash "bleeders," BI stopped serving Canada on November 1; this move saved half a million dollars a month. Although BI had already reduced its work force by 1,100 after the air traffic controllers' strike, the suspension of service to Canada resulted in the additional furlough of 132 pilots and 88 flight attendants.

On December 5 it was announced that ALPA had ratified a two-year contract with BI, increasing each pilot's maximum flying time from 75 hours to 85 hours per month. Putnam stated, "Our pilots have given us the opportunity to increase our aircraft utilization up to 16% over current levels without incurring additional pilot expense. We are delighted with the agreement and the constructive attitude demonstrated by our pilots." He also said that because of this new contract BI would begin 21 new flights from DFW to 11 cities.

## JANUARY 1982

By the beginning of January, the results of Texas Class were starting to come in. For the month of December, Braniff's load factor of 60.7% was the highest in the industry. Advanced bookings had also risen sharply.

This infusion of cash enabled Putnam and Guthrie to negotiate a financial restructuring from a stronger position. This was finally accomplished on January 22. As part of the restructuring, BI was forgiven interest and principal payments until October 1, 1982. Summertime was typically a period of high traffic for airlines, thus the new deadline would enable BI to improve its financial position from the hoped-for good season. Not having a restructuring in place until only eight days before the deadline, however, had sparked numerous rumors of bankruptcy and had adversely affected bookings.

On January 26, BI's board named Putnam CEO and president. Casey retained the title of chairman and, according to one source, would be "spending a lot of time in employee communications."

Despite the initial success of Texas Class, BI showed a negative cash flow for the first time in January and Putnam and Guthrie agreed that the only prudent thing to do was to retain bankruptcy counsel. The board also agreed that if it did not bring in bankruptcy counsel at this point, it would not be doing the right thing.

### FEBRUARY 1982

Braniff chose the law firm of Levin and Weintraub and Crames in New York, and the president, Michael Crames, agreed to take on the case himself. Putnam invited him to the February 4 board meeting to begin educating all of them about the bankruptcy process. At that meeting Crames reviewed the bankruptcy law and the mechanics of filing. He emphasized that if they planned to file under Chapter XI of the bankruptcy law and attempt to reorganize, they had to protect their assets (see Exhibit 3). He stressed that the only way that this could be accomplished was through surprise. BI should not reveal that it was considering filing, because assets might be impounded and not available for reorganization. Advance notice could also cause a creditor to file for involuntary bankruptcy and result in a liquidation. In addition, who would want to fly on an airline that might go bankrupt? From this point on, there was almost daily telephone contact between Crames and either Putnam or Guthrie.

Considering the concrete details of bankruptcy was difficult for Putnam. He had grown up in a small town in Iowa with only *one* bankrupt person. His father had told him, "Son, when you get out in the real world, watch out for that bankrupt guy. That's bad. You want to pay your bills."

On February 11, BI announced that for every ticket purchased at full fare during a 48-hour period, it would sell a second ticket of equal or lesser value for $1. Within hours American matched the offer without the $1 charge; Delta followed suit the next day. Ticket sales skyrocketed. One BI sales office that usually sold 700 tickets per day by mail sold more than 6,000 by noon the next day. Some people stayed up all night in long lines to make sure they got a ticket.

Denying that BI had initiated the 2-for-1 sale out of financial desperation, Sam Coats, vice president in charge of public relations, stated, "We didn't have a two-day sale to save the airline. It was intended to boost sagging traffic levels during a slow period." Remarking on how the sale enabled many people to visit places they would not ordinarily have gone to, Coats mentioned that BI was trying to promote goodwill with the sale. Putnam also stated that the overall intent of the sale was "to generate cash and yet to try to retain public confidence."

That same week Putnam and Guthrie went to a New York meeting with major creditors. When they asked for the right to proceed with accounts receivable financing, they were refused. One lender said the employees should make more concessions and proposed a 50% pay cut for six months. On that visit, Putnam and Guthrie tried to sell the airline's accounts receivable to commercial credit lenders. This had never been done before in the airline industry, and the proposal was turned down every place they tried.

On February 20 BI furloughed an additional 825 employees and announced that more layoffs would be made in 90 days. It also stated that it had sold 21 airplanes during the past three months, thereby reducing its fleet to 75 planes, down from 116 at the end of 1979.

At the end of February Braniff reported a record $160.6 million loss for 1981. It was expected that Braniff's accountants would once again include in the annual report, as they did in 1980, the statement: "There are conditions which indicate that the company may be unable to continue as a going concern."

## MARCH 1982

"Braniff Move Called Last Resort" was the headline on a March 3 article in the *Dallas Morning News,* reporting the airline's decision to defer for a week 50% of that week's payroll. The article reported that BI told its employees they would receive half their paycheck that week and the remainder the next week; subsequent paychecks would be postponed a week. It was estimated that this would free up about $8 million in short-term cash. Guthrie said, "I wouldn't characterize this action as desperate. This should not be looked on as a last-ditch effort. We are in an obvious cash flow slump." Commenting on the pay deferral, Marvin Schlenke, president of Teamster's Local 19, said, "It was get paid 50% or nothing at all. We don't want to see 10,000 people without jobs. I don't think anyone likes it. But nothing can be done."

On March 4 the headline on the front page of the *Dallas Morning News* read, "Braniff Chief Uncertain If Firm Can Survive." Putnam was quoted in an interview: "A women called on the phone today and asked if her ticket to Honolulu would be good in May. I told her I didn't know. She probably went right out and traded the ticket in for one on another airline." He continued, "I can't just name a date and say I know we have enough cash to operate until then. It's not that easy. We certainly have no current plans to cease operations, but I can't guarantee we won't."

At that point Putnam began to suspect that travel agents were diverting traffic from BI because bookings from agents were down consid-

erably. When individual agents were asked, however, they denied it. One Dallas travel agency did state that "increasing numbers of potential Braniff passengers are requesting other airlines." It was learned that BI's load factor for February was 51.9%, down from last February's 57.6%, and well below the break-even load factor of 65%. BI announced another 2-for-1 sale on March 5, but it was limited to flights in Texas and Oklahoma. American again immediately matched the offer.

On March 6 the CAB approved a plan that provided for other airlines honoring tickets on any airline that went bankrupt, including tickets issued by travel agencies. When he returned from the CAB meeting in Washington, Putnam was met at the airport by several hundred cheering Braniff employees. He told them the airline had a "more than 50% chance" of survival.

It became apparent at this time that there was no White House support for a rescue if BI failed. David Kirstein, general counsel for the CAB, said, "The view is that it's tough out there and there are some people who are not going to make it." Drew Lewis, secretary of transportation, stated, "We would like for it [Braniff] to survive. It would be in the best interest of the nation. But we will not provide any subsidy. We won't provide a bailout of the type Chrysler received."

Around mid-March Putnam received a letter from Lanny Rogers, president of District 146 of the IAM, citing the union's labor contract. He said: "We have seen the contract openly and flagrantly violated almost daily and almost always with the excuse from management that 'We can't help it. We must save the airline.'" The letter went on to accuse BI of using "fear and scare tactics"; it stated: "The most flagrant example of this is the company's garnishment of one-half of the employee's pay. This must be regarded as one of the most cavalier acts I have ever witnessed by any chief executive." Rogers ended by asking Putnam to restore normal paydays, to cease labor contract violations, and to negotiate with the union. Commenting on the letter, Putnam said that it was "obvious that Rogers had not recognized the seriousness of the situation."

On March 16 John Casey resigned and accepted a position in operations at Pan American World Airways (Pan Am). One New York analyst said: "I don't blame John for taking the job. He had been stripped of one job after another at Braniff. He is a strong, capable operations man. And I can't say I am surprised that he accepted the Pan Am offer."

Although no airline had ever leased its routes before, Putnam began negotiating in March with Ed Acker, chairman of Pan Am, to lease its South American routes on which it had lost $15 million the previous year. Putnam's plan was to lease the routes for a few years and then get them back when BI was healthy. A major reason for leasing the routes was that BI's South American fleet had to be replaced shortly because of new federal noise regulations, and BI could not purchase or lease new aircraft. Furthermore, Putnam sought to lease the South American routes because BI was the designated carrier for the State Department and Department of Defense, and he wanted to make sure these services would not be interrupted if BI filed for bankruptcy.

Putnam and Acker arranged a deal in which Pan Am paid BI $7 million in cash immediately, would pay another $13 million later in the spring, and a final $10 million in 1983. BI's petition to the CAB to approve the agreement asked that a decision be made by April 13. If approved, Pan Am would have a monopoly on service to South America and BI would lay off 1,100 domestic employees. On March 27 Putnam and Guthrie flew to Miami, where most of BI's South American flights originated, and explained to a group of 200 somber and hostile Miami employees why they would be losing their jobs if the CAB approved the Pan Am venture.

## APRIL 1982

During the first week of April, Braniff reported that its 2-for-1 ticket sale had boosted traffic for the month of March. Traffic for what was nor-

mally a slow month increased 7.6%, and load factor increased by .7% to 60.3%. On domestic routes, passenger traffic was up 19.4% and load factor was up to 61.8% from 57.2% in March 1981. On South American flights, the company reported a 20.8% decline in revenue passenger miles, and a drop in load factor from 66.2% to 55.5%.

Rumors traveled quickly in the airline industry. Sometimes a rumor would work its way to London after being killed in the United States, and then after being killed there, would resurface in New York, only to have the cycle begin again. Conventional wisdom was that if a company was going to file for bankruptcy, it would be done on a Friday. From mid-February on, a Friday did not pass without inquiries from the press or creditors as to whether or not BI would be filing that day. To cope with the rumor mill, Putnam began to send out daily messages to employees briefing them on what was happening. He had decided that only he, Guthrie, and Coats could speak for the corporation. He also made himself accessible to the press, granting numerous interviews.

During the first part of April, Putnam and Acker made the rounds in Washington to drum up support for the proposal to lease BI's South American routes to Pan Am. Both Texas senators and 10 of its congressional representatives wrote the CAB to support the plan. The Department of Transportation also publicly supported it, and the State Department said that the South American routes were an important foreign policy concern and asked that the CAB act quickly.

Citing "broad competitive reasons," the CAB turned down BI's request on April 15 to lease its South American routes to Pan Am. The board invited Braniff to find another carrier as a partner in the venture.

A few days later, a local comedy club hosted a roast for Putnam. The capacity crowd gave Putnam a standing ovation and booed loudly whenever American was mentioned. Putnam was introduced as "a man who took a shaky, financially troubled airline and turned it into a shaky, financially troubled airline dependent on Pan American." Some of the other jokes were: "If God had intended us to fly, He would not have invented Braniff Airlines" and "Braniff is so poor, the meals are catered by Goodwill."

During this time the Justice Department began inquiries into allegations that American was illegally trying to force BI out of business, including the following charges: (1) dumping tickets on the industry clearing house to create a cash shortage for Braniff; (2) encouraging ticket agents to urge customers to fly American instead of Braniff; (3) holding meetings to discuss ways to hurt Braniff; (4) American pilots causing unnecessary delays on runways; and (5) fabricating technical problems on its own planes, thus causing BI to make costly preparations to accommodate displaced passengers that never showed up. Denying these allegations, American's president Robert Crandall said, "American's ethical standards are as high as its service standards. The company has done nothing and will do nothing to compromise those standards."

On April 23, Braniff filed an emergency request with the CAB asking it to reconsider its Pan Am proposal. President Reagan, the State Department, and the Department of Transportation sent letters to the CAB asking it to decide quickly. That night Frank Borman, chairman of Eastern, called and said he was interested in the South American routes. Putnam and Guthrie flew to New York and met Borman and his staff Sunday night, and working until 3:00 A.M. they put together a deal. On April 26 the CAB kept its office open later than usual to receive Braniff's documents; at about 11:00 P.M. that night Putnam was called by Dan McKinnon, CAB chairman, and told that the leases to Eastern were approved. Under the arrangement, Eastern would immediately pay Braniff $11 million, another $7 million when the relevant South American countries approved the venture, and a final $12 million in monthly payments to begin in 1983. Eastern agreed to take about 1,200 of BI's South American personnel, but BI would still lay off about 1,100 of its domestic employees. Braniff used the cash, ob-

tained on Wednesday, to meet its Thursday payroll. Putnam was hopeful that the Eastern agreement would help with the next restructuring of the company's debt.

Pan Am's Acker was furious when Putnam called to say he was sorry. It was part of the original agreement that the $7 million paid by Pan Am to Braniff was unreturnable, although BI had guaranteed the transaction with collateral of five of its gates at Houston's Intercontinental Airport. Acker sued Braniff for $107 million—$100 million for damages and the rest was to get back what Pan Am had already paid. Putnam said he was flattered that Pan Am thought Braniff had even close to $100 million.

## MAY 1982

On May 1 Braniff announced it lost $41.4 million during the first quarter of 1982; other airlines were reporting similar losses. Putnam said, "We believe the appeal of Texas Class service to the traveling public and the increased productivity that we are receiving from our physical and personnel resources have postured Braniff in a unique position to reap the benefits that an upturn in the economy will have on airline passenger traffic." Putnam also mentioned that he was pleased with the size and cost reductions the airline had made. BI's cost per available seat mile was 7.24 cents in March, down from 8.6 cents in the first quarter of 1981. Its yield per revenue mile was only 10.10 cents, however, far below the industry rule of thumb that yield had to be double unit cost to have a profitable airline. Braniff would have 7,900 employees after the layoffs from the Eastern deal, and it hoped to be down to 6,800 by the summer. Load factors in April had declined, at times being in the low 30s. Domestic travel agency sales were down 40–50% from the previous year.

On May 3 Braniff began a 3-for-2 sale. This "Great Escape Sale" allowed customers over a nine-day period to purchase two full-fare tickets to any of eight destinations to be used that summer and receive a free roundtrip anywhere in the continental United States for use in the off-season that fall. American immediately made a similar offer with fewer restrictions. In contrast to the 2-for-1 sale, there was little response this time. A disappointed Putnam said, "We gave a party and nobody came."

At the stockholders' meeting on May 6 Putnam reviewed the financial condition of BI when he had started, and the changes he had made; he then stated:

> We have proven to ourselves, to the industry, and to our lenders that on the operating cost side, we have a viable entity. We now have to generate revenue to make this airline successful for the long term. The shadow of doubt that hangs over our future creates a "chicken-and-egg" dilemma as we approach financial restructuring. We need to remove the cloud to get results. The lenders want to see results before they remove the cloud.
>
> The company continues to evaluate all possible alternatives including, but not limited to, continuing new marketing innovations, pricing promotions, new infusions of capital from outside investors, potential combinations with other entities, operating agreements with other airlines and, as a last resort, seeking protection under the federal bankruptcy statutes. This last alternative is obviously a last resort after all other alternatives have been exhausted.

Putnam concluded by praising the support of Braniff's employees and the community but added, "All the moral support in the world will not replace the monetary support needed to keep your company and your investment alive." When Putnam finished, a stockholder stood up and said, "Let's have a hip, hip, hooray for management," and the crowd cheered and applauded. He was amazed that his remarks about bankruptcy had such little impact

and told his secretary, "They didn't even listen."

Putnam then met with the board. First, he and Guthrie reviewed the cash flow. Because load factors were running in the low 30s and advanced bookings were very low, it was clear that the hoped-for increase in summer traffic would not happen. The settlement of the ACH and travel card receipts on May 11 would be critical. Putnam also told the board that he would be in New York the following week to testify in a suit brought by ALPA over the dismissal of pilots as a result of the Eastern deal. Although previous company attempts and those of its investment banker, Lazard Freres, had not uncovered any parties that might be interested in a merger or joint marketing venture, Putnam received permission to contact other airline presidents to explore such arrangements.

In the next few days, Putnam explored these possibilities with several airlines and financiers but had no success. He asked Bill Huskins, executive vice president of operations, to put together a plan over the weekend to see how small an airline they could possibly run under Chapter XI, even though no airline had ever continued flying while under Chapter XI.

Driving home exhausted late that night from an interminably long day of appointments, anxious faces, and ringing telephones, Putnam relaxed in the darkness of his car with the lights from the dashboard softly glowing like a cockpit. He thought of all the people whose lives depended on his decisions—employees, families, pensioners, creditors, stockholders, travelers, travel agents, and still others. He wondered who would be harmed the most if the company went under and if there was a right and a wrong way to go bankrupt. Perhaps the only remaining option was to file for Chapter XI.

**Note**: Exhibits 1 to 3 appear on pages 479–481.

# EXHIBITS: Braniff International—The Ethics of Bankruptcy

## EXHIBIT 1

FIVE-YEAR REVIEW OF SELECTED FINANCIAL DATA, 1977–1981

($ Thousands Except Per Share Amounts)

| | 1981 | 1980 | 1979 | 1978 | 1977 |
|---|---|---|---|---|---|
| **Operating revenues** | | | | | |
| Airline: | | | | | |
| Passenger | $1,097,232 | $1,305,305 | $1,200,329 | $845,353 | $678,177 |
| Revision of prior years' revenue estimates | (25,200) | — | | | |
| Other transport revenues | 80,422 | 104,893 | 107,824 | 95,161 | 84,062 |
| Transport related | 28,510 | 31,595 | 28,213 | 24,789 | 21,795 |
| Nonairline subsidiaries | 8,011 | 10,337 | 9,909 | 6,805 | 7,123 |
| Total operating revenues | 1,188,975 | 1,452,130 | 1,346,275 | 972,108 | 791,157 |
| **Operating expenses** | | | | | |
| Airline flying, maintenance and ground operations | 974,943 | 1,215,171 | 1,106,167 | 682,013 | 543,925 |
| Nonairline subsidiaries | 5,066 | 2,488 | 3,271 | 2,992 | 2,965 |
| Sales and advertising | 172,785 | 198,906 | 158,659 | 108,737 | 83,416 |
| Depreciation and amortization | 83,551 | 89,296 | 75,343 | 60,980 | 55,593 |
| General and administrative | 47,430 | 53,762 | 41,273 | 37,227 | 36,230 |
| Total operating expenses | 1,283,775 | 1,559,623 | 1,384,713 | 891,949 | 722,129 |
| **Operating income (loss)** | (94,800) | (107,493) | (38,438) | 80,159 | 69,028 |
| Nonoperating expenses (income) | | | | | |
| Interest expense | 62,396 | 92,101 | 55,919 | 34,201 | 28,275 |
| Interest capitalized | (6) | (3,398) | (6,265) | (4,992) | (2,278) |
| Other nonoperating income—net | (691) | (60,613) | (6,362) | (4,285) | (6,428) |
| Total nonoperating expenses | 61,699 | 28,090 | 43,292 | 24,924 | 19,569 |
| Income (loss) before income taxes and preferred dividends | (156,499) | (135,583) | (81,730) | 55,235 | 49,459 |
| Provision (credit) for income taxes | — | (7,072) | (37,400) | 10,005 | 12,767 |
| Income (loss) before preferred dividends of subsidiary | (156,499) | (128,511) | (44,330) | 45,230 | 36,692 |
| Preferred dividends of subsidiary | 4,112 | 2,925 | — | — | — |
| Net income (loss) | $ (160,611) | $ (131,436) | $ (44,330) | $ 45,230 | $ 36,692 |
| Net income (loss) per common share | $ (8.02) | $ (6.57) | $ (2.21) | $ 2.26 | $ 1.83 |
| Weighted average number of common shares outstanding | 20,019 | 20,019 | 20,019 | 20,016 | 20,008 |
| Cash dividends declared per common share | $ — | $ .05 | .36 | $ .345 | $ .285 |
| **Selected balance sheet items** | | | | | |
| Current assets | $ 200,237 | $ 197,790 | $ 211,041 | $156,519 | $134,028 |
| Current liabilities | 405,077 | 341,032 | 276,330 | 170,543 | 124,008 |
| Working capital (deficiency) | $ (204,840) | $ (143,242)) | $ (65,289) | $ (14,024) | $ 10,020 |
| Property and equipment—net | $ 777,471 | $ 868,443 | $ 863,429 | $612,189 | $493,319 |
| Total assets | $1,008,297 | $1,107,368 | $1,157,901 | $870,165 | $699,523 |
| Senior debt | $ 438,980 | $ 488,600 | $ 507,912 | $320,985 | $235,312 |
| Subordinated debt | 80,250 | 95,002 | 70,286 | 27,692 | 37,307 |
| Noncurrent liabilities under capital leases | 71,782 | 69,473 | 87,047 | 49,393 | 47,988 |
| Total long-term obligations, less current maturities | $ 591,012 | $ 653,075 | $ 665,245 | $398,070 | $320,607 |
| Redeemable preferred stock of subsidiary | $ 39,455 | $ 35,343 | $ — | $ — | $ — |
| Common stock and paid-in capital | $ 56,795 | $ 56,795 | $ 56,795 | $ 56,792 | $ 56,732 |
| Retained earnings (deficit) | (151,226) | 9,385 | 141,822 | 193,359 | 155,035 |
| Total common shareholders' equity (deficiency) | $ (94,431) | $ 66,180 | $ 198,617 | $250,151 | $211,767 |

*Source:* Braniff International annual report, 1981.

**EXHIBIT 2**
FIVE-YEAR STATISTICAL REVIEW, 1977–1981

| Revenue passenger miles (in thousands) | 1981 | 1980 | 1979 | 1978 | 1977 |
|---|---|---|---|---|---|
| Continental U.S. | 5,612,863 | 6,597,957 | 8,216,145 | 6,402,163 | 5,399,563 |
| Hawaii | 643,680 | 738,442 | 1,272,529 | 771,207 | 557,283 |
| Mexico | 336,470 | 354,390 | 367,882 | 332,858 | 247,620 |
| South America | 1,781,707 | 1,950,520 | 1,888,128 | 1,535,289 | 1,307,053 |
| Atlantic | 463,152 | 1,731,072 | 1,445,106 | 562,908 | — |
| Pacific | — | 527,586 | 230,549 | | |
| Total scheduled | 8,837,872 | 11,899,967 | 13,420,339 | 9,604,425 | 7,511,519 |
| Charter | 52,521 | 98,344 | 266,265 | 395,562 | 353,948 |
| Total | 8,890,393 | 11,998,311 | 13,686,604 | 9,999,987 | 7,865,467 |
| **Available seat miles (in thousands)** | | | | | |
| Continental U.S. | 10,112,406 | 12,002,065 | 15,486,324 | 12,477,921 | 10,877,174 |
| Hawaii | 1,089,998 | 1,075,519 | 1,759,381 | 1,192,125 | 975,527 |
| Mexico | 570,596 | 549,555 | 572,613 | 565,124 | 550,096 |
| South America | 2,912,705 | 3,079,151 | 2,991,437 | 2,652,514 | 2,392,957 |
| Atlantic | 839,127 | 2,724,932 | 2,523,879 | 951,144 | — |
| Pacific | — | 929,533 | 511,822 | | |
| Total scheduled | 15,524,832 | 20,360,755 | 23,845,456 | 17,838,828 | 14,795,754 |
| Charter | 74,595 | 136,774 | 339,801 | 491,557 | 452,642 |
| Total | 15,599,427 | 20,497,529 | 24,185,247 | 18,330,385 | 15,248,396 |
| **Revenue passengers enplaned (in thousands)** | | | | | |
| Scheduled | 10,453 | 12,153 | 14,354 | 11,550 | 9,814 |
| Charter | 42 | 71 | 154 | 194 | 169 |
| Total | 10,495 | 12,224 | 14,508 | 11,744 | 9,983 |
| System scheduled passenger load factor (%) | 56.9 | 58.4 | 56.3 | 53.8 | 50.8 |
| Breakeven passenger load factor before income tax (%) | 63.6 | 64.5 | 59.9 | 50.2 | 46.8 |
| **Revenue plane miles (in thousands)** | | | | | |
| Scheduled | 103,737 | 132,422 | 161,803 | 131,014 | 114,259 |
| Charter | 488 | 947 | 2,306 | 3,366 | 3,058 |
| Total | 104,225 | 133,369 | 164,109 | 134,380 | 117,317 |
| Revenue block hours flown | 279,063 | 349,518 | 435,621 | 362,154 | 316,779 |
| Average segment length in scheduled service (miles) | 637 | 665 | 648 | 583 | 554 |
| Average daily aircraft utilization (block hours) | 8:07 | 8:23 | 10:42 | 10:16 | 9:45 |
| Yield per revenue passenger mile | 12.42¢ | 10.97¢ | 8.94¢ | 8.80¢ | 9.03¢ |
| **Operating jet fleet (at December 31)** | | | | | |
| Owned Aircraft: | | | | | |
| Boeing 747-200 | 1 | 1 | 1 | — | — |
| Boeing 747SP | 1 | 2 | 1 | — | — |
| Boeing 727-100* | 3 | 10 | 14 | 15 | 17 |
| Boeing 727-200 | 58† | 58† | 66 | 59 | 49 |
| Douglas DC-8-62 | 8 | 8 | 8 | 7 | 1 |
| Douglas DC-8-51 | — | — | 4 | 4 | 4 |
| Total owned | 71 | 79 | 94 | 85 | 71 |
| Leased Aircraft: | | | | | |
| Boeing 747-100 | 1 | 2 | 3 | 3 | 1 |
| Boeing 747-200 | 1 | 2 | 2 | — | — |
| Boeing 727-100* | 6 | 7 | 8 | 6 | 6 |
| Boeing 727-200 | 4 | 5 | 5 | 5 | 5 |
| Douglas DC-8-62 | — | 2 | 2 | 2 | 7 |
| Douglas DC-8-51 | — | — | 2 | 2 | 2 |
| Total leased | 12 | 18 | 22 | 18 | 21 |
| Total | 83 | 97 | 16 | 103 | 92 |

*B727-100 aircraft were removed from operating fleet in January 1982.
†Includes seven aircraft owned by Braniff Realty Company which are leased to Braniff Airways.
*Source:* Braniff International annual report, 1981.

**EXHIBIT 3**
CHAPTER VII AND CHAPTER XI, BANKRUPTCY REFORM ACT, 1978*

---

Bankruptcy legislation served, first, to effect an equitable distribution of the debtor's property among his creditors and, second, to discharge the debtor from his debts and enable him to rehabilitate himself and start afresh.

Chapter VII of the Bankruptcy Reform Act of 1978 provided for the liquidation and termination of the business of the debtor, distribution of his assets, and usually a discharge of all dischargeable debts. Under Chapter VII there could be either a voluntary or an involuntary petition. In a voluntary bankruptcy, the debtor filed a petition with the courts asking to be declared a bankrupt. In the involuntary case, the debtor is forced into bankruptcy by creditors who file a petition requesting that the debtor be judged a bankrupt.

After secured creditor claims were satisfied, proceeds from the liquidation of assets were distributed according to a priority of claims: (1) expenses of administering the estate, (2) unsecured claims incurred after the filing of the petition and before either the appointment of a trustee to administer the estate or the judge's ruling, (3) wage, salary, and commission claims up to $2,000 earned within 90 days before the filing or the cessation of the debtor's business, (4) claims for contributions to employee benefit plans for services rendered 180 days before filing or the cessation of business and up to $2,000 per employee, (5) unsecured claims up to $900 for monies deposited in connection with the purchase, lease or rental of property or the purchase of services, for personal, family, or household use, (6) specified taxes owed to governmental units for certain income, property, employment, or excise taxes. Remaining unsecured creditors shared proportionately in any remaining assets.

Chapter XI had as its goal the rehabilitation of debtors by allowing them to reorganize and restructure their debt while assets were protected from creditors' claims. To be confirmed by the courts and be binding upon all parties, several conditions had to be met, including *feasibility*. This meant that the reorganized debtor must have adequate working capital, sufficient earning power to meet fixed lien charges, reasonably good credit prospects, ability to retire or refund its proposed debt over the period of extended maturity, must be soundly capitalized with no disproportionate ratio of debt to total value of assets, and have assurance of competent management. Before confirmation, it also had to be established that each holder of a claim or interest either accepted the plan or would receive as much under the reorganization plan as would be received in liquidation proceedings. For secured creditors, this meant that they would receive the value of their security either by payment or by delivery of the property. After a plan was confirmed, the reorganized entity began life anew with only those obligations imposed on it by the plan.

*Note: Adapted from L. Y. Smith et al., *Business Law,* 5th ed. (St. Paul, Minn.: West Publishing Co., 1982), p. 792. On June 28, 1982, the U.S. Supreme Court ruled that provisions of the Bankruptcy Reform Act of 1978 concerning the jurisdiction of judges were unconstitutional and gave Congress until October 4, 1982, to make appropriate changes. As of June 1984, this had not been done, leaving the status of the Act itself in limbo. See *Northern Pipeline Construction Co.* v. *Marathon Pipe Line Co. and United States,* 458 U.S. 50 (1982).

## PART FOUR

# Corporate Values: International Business

As we have seen in the cases studied so far, solutions to problems that have ethical dimensions do not come easily. In Part 4, we move to a series of cases, indeed complex, that deal with international business activity. The complexity arises, in the context of this book, from two basic problems. One is the obvious factor that other countries may have customs and values which are or seem to be different from our own—and the distinction between "are" and "seem" can be substantial and important. For the businessperson, understanding and assessing whether and how these cultural and ethical conflicts should be taken into account is often most difficult.

The second major problem stems, ironically, from attempts by the United States government to establish legal guidelines for some of the difficulties mentioned above, through the enactment of the Foreign Corrupt Practices Act (FCPA) in 1977. As the introductory note in this section ("The Foreign Corrupt Practices Act: A Reconsideration") indicates, the application of that law has appeared to many to be as ambiguous as the dilemmas that it presumably set out to resolve. This book does not purport to treat that law exhaustively, but students concerned with business ethics should know of its existence and understand its intent and implications; it is a universal concern to American firms that do business in international markets. We think those objectives will be achieved by the introductory note and the case that begin Part 4.

Philosophers, whose intellectual concerns are typically at a higher level of generality, have similar difficulty with cross-cultural differences. There is debate as to whether the differences are real and, if so, how important they are and how they can be dealt with in moral thinking. One well-known British philosopher, Philippa Foot, describes this problem in a seeming paradox: "Granted that it is wrong to assume identity of aim between people of different cultures; nevertheless there is a great deal that all men have in common."*

*Philippa Foot, *Moral Relativism* (Lawrence, KS: University of Kansas, 1979), Lindley Lecture.

While this is undoubtedly true, the generality of the statement stands in sharp contrast to the highly specific decisions which American business executives are forced to make against the twin backdrops of the real or presumed differences in ethical standards between countries and the constraints of the FCPA.

"The Foreign Corrupt Practices Act: A Reconsideration" and "Two Cases of Questionable Payments" have to do with the legal and moral implications of bribery and extortion. The introductory note discusses the background and objectives of the act; presents its text; describes the results of surveys regarding its impact; and presents the main points of a revised bill, introduced in 1981, that has not been passed as this book is being written. "Two Cases of Questionable Payments" describes the efforts made by a company to investigate its own practices in two specific instances, one taking place overseas and one in the United States. In each instance the investigatory group found it difficult to reach a conclusion as to the propriety of the actions described.

Next, "The IBM-Fujitsu Dispute" presents another apparent cultural difference, this time over the ethics of intellectual property. Do American and Japanese values differ, as they seem to, over whether software can be "owned"?

The next case, "The ICCR and the Debate over South African Disinvestment," takes a close look at how companies are responding to external pressure from church groups and shareholders regarding their presence in South Africa. The Sullivan Principles used to be thought of as the creative response, but perhaps no longer. This case familiarizes us with apartheid and challenges us to consider whether American companies should continue to do business in South Africa, and if so, how they should conduct themselves.

The next case in Part 4 is "Smoking and Health: United States Tobacco Companies—National and International Operations." The smoking and health controversy is so well known in the United States that it needs no elaboration here. In addition to raising that issue, the case goes beyond the boundaries of the United States and raises important and interesting issues about the activities of American tobacco companies in other nations, especially in third world countries.

The "Note on the Export of Pesticides from the United States to Developing Countries" presents an overview of a problem that is not specific to just one industry: Is it proper to sell in other countries materials which cannot be sold in the United States or whose sale and use in the United States is carefully restricted? "Velsicol Chemical Corporation" places the issues described in the note on the desk of the corporate manager. Should Velsicol proceed with the development of what appears to be a promising safety labeling program for exports? Can it, if competitors do not also participate?

Part 4 concludes with "Dow Corning Corporation: Business Conduct and Global Values (A)" and "(B)." This case series provides effective closure not only to Part 4 but also to the casebook as a whole. The presenting issue is how to formulate and implement a consistent corporate value system on a worldwide basis—even when different business practices prevail in different geographical areas. But the case also includes the themes we have traced throughout: personal values, corporate values looking inward and outward, and the special challenges of international business activity.

# The Foreign Corrupt Practices Act: A Reconsideration

As a result of the "Watergate" and similar investigations, it came to light in the mid-1970's that a large number of publicly owned U.S. corporations had engaged in illegal or "questionable" payments to political figures both in the U.S. and abroad, and that many of these payments had been falsified on company books and records, or were not disclosed at all. At that time the Securities and Exchange Commission (SEC) had no legal power to prosecute cases of directly illegal payments to foreign officials or altered records of such payments, but it could take action against "corporate coverups," i.e., a corporation's failure to disclose these kinds of transactions in its reports to the SEC. In adjudicating such cases, the SEC argued that the traditional legal standard of financial materiality (i.e., importance) was not the exclusive criterion for judging a case, but rather that materiality also consisted of *managerial integrity*—regardless of the dollar amounts involved—because this factor was material to investors and stockholders.

This same position had been asserted by the SEC in 1964 *(in re Franchard Corp.),* but had not been utilized or enforced in subsequent cases. However, after the extensive disclosures of questionable payments during and after the Watergate hearings, the SEC was able to force a considerable number of companies to conduct inquiries into their own activities, and to submit their findings to the SEC. It became clear that many companies had engaged in illegal payments and/or questionable activities, and that they had interpreted the federal disclosure laws to mean disclosure of illegal acts only when they involved material amounts of money. As a result of these investigations, the U.S. Congress passed the Foreign Corrupt Practices Act in December 1977.[1] The act made it a criminal offense for an American company or its executives to bribe foreign officials and pol-

[1] This explanation of the FCPA is derived from an article by Hurd Baruch, "The Foreign Corrupt Practices Act," *Harvard Business Review,* Jan.–Feb. 1979.

iticians; it also contained accounting provisions that applied to all business firms.

Debate on the effects and effectiveness of the FCPA began immediately and continues today. Critics claimed that the law unduly restricts overseas business activity. "The anxieties created by the act among men and women of utmost good faith have been, in my experience, without equal," said Harold Williams, former chairman of the SEC. Many businesses claim to be losing deals to competitors operating without restrictions. Critics felt the accounting provision of "reasonable detail" was unnecessarily perplexing and that the more common "materiality" standard should have been adopted. Critics also claimed that the law was too vague, leaving too much discretion in the hands of the enforcement agencies.

Prosecutions under the Act have not been frequent. The SEC has brought seven cases and the Justice Department two or three. No jail sentences have resulted. One $50,000 fine was levied. The remaining cases resulted only in injunctions or are pending.

Nevertheless, the FCPA has apparently had substantial impact. A recent General Accounting Office survey indicates that, of 185 U.S. companies, 84% have initiated or toughened antipayment policies and 80% have strengthened their auditing since the passage of FCPA. Over 70% reported believing the law has been effective in reducing questionable foreign payments.

Claims of lost business have been disputed. U.S. exports have boomed since the passage of the FCPA. A 1977–78 study of 65 major U.S. corporations showed that business losses attributable to FCPA are small.[2] Only 16 firms reported lost business exceeding $1 million in sales, and only 15% of these cases exceeded .5% of corporate sales. Only 25% of the cases exceeded 1% of foreign sales. This study concluded that the amount of business attributed to past payment practices has been overesti-

mated, and that payments were often unnecessary. The study concluded:

> . . . It is unwise and unsound, from both an ethical and a long-term economic standpoint, for U.S. corporations to continue to engage in questionable foreign payments and practices. The immediate economic gains that might be derived from engaging in them can be greatly offset by future losses, costs, and penalties. It is far wiser, from an opportunity cost standpoint, for companies to focus on strengthening their legitimate competitive advantages internationally, rather than to drain off considerable time, energy, creativity, and resources in deciding whether or not, and how, to engage in questionable acts without getting caught.

A 1981 survey of 58 Fortune 500 companies showed that 66% do not feel that stopping illegal payments has given them a competitive disadvantage. 62% stated that they had lost no business as a result of FCPA.[3]

However, a 1978 report of the White House Export Disincentives Task Force cited the FCPA as significantly contributing to economic losses by constricting American business.[4] The overseas construction business has been particularly hard hit, according to the National Constructors Association.[5] In 1976, the U.S. ranked #1 in market share, but it trailed Japan, Korea, West Germany and Italy in 1978. The problem, according to some is that foreign companies operate under no similar restrictions. One article stated:

> The value of a law like the FCPA will be diminished unless other industrialized countries can be persuaded to adopt and enforce a similar law on their own multinational firms. . . . In Germany, for example, tax manuals confirm that

[2]Richman, Barry, "Can We Prevent Questionable Foreign Payments?" *Business Horizons,* June, 1979, pp. 14–19.

[3]Tipgos, Manual A., "Compliance with the Foreign Corrupt Practices Act" *Financial Executive,* August, 1981, pp. 38–48.
[4]Pastin, Mark, and Hooker, Michael, "Ethics and the Foreign Corrupt Practices Act," *Business Horizons,* December, 1980, p. 44.
[5]"U.S. Firms Say '77 Ban on Foreign Payoffs Hurts Overseas Sales," *Wall Street Journal,* August 2, 1979, p. 1, 19.

although bribes to domestic officials are not deductible as business expenses, bribes to foreign officials are. . . . Canadian law stipulates that firms should comply with the laws of the countries in which they operate. . . . No matter how strictly American laws on the subject are written, the temptation for American firms to avoid them is much greater if their competitors based abroad are able to capture major contracts by meeting the payoff demands that the American firms must reject.[6]

A 1978 Peat, Marwick, Mitchell & Co., survey showed that a majority of executives of multinational corporations thought the FCPA to be an inappropriate response to corporate governance. 79% surveyed said the law would not stop bribery of foreign officials by U.S. companies, and 71% thought the FCPA would cause a significant loss of business to foreign competitors.[7]

## A PROPOSAL

In 1981, Senator John Chafee (R, RI) introduced a bill which would revamp the FCPA, renaming it the Business Practices and Records Act.[8] The proposed act would amend both major portions of the FCPA.

The accounting standards requirement would be changed to provide that records be compiled accurately in all *material* respects so that financial statements might be prepared in conformity with generally accepted accounting principles. In addition, persons would be liable for violating the accounting standards provisions only when they knowingly falsified books, accounts, or records.

It would be unlawful to offer a bribe to a foreign official in order to induce him to act in violation of his legal duties. Customary payments, and payments to expedite performance, would be excluded, as would gifts given as a courtesy, as a token of regard or esteem, or in return for hospitality, or gifts related to marketing or product demonstration activities.

The bill also provides that:

1   Sole enforcement of antibribery prohibitions would rest with the Justice Department.
2   A review procedure would be established through which the Justice Department would provide binding responses to specific inquiries on enforcement intentions.
3   An interagency task force would be formed to review further clarifications of the Act and to issue guidelines and general precautionary procedures.

The proposed changes drew mixed reviews.[9] William Brock, the President's special trade representative, agreed that the FCPA "needs major surgery." Senator Proxmire (D, WI) called the amendments "a disaster."

Controversy attended both portions of the new bill. The materiality standard in the Chafee bill "will gut the law," said John Burton, former chief accountant of the SEC. He said that Exxon's $60 million payments in the 60s and 70s would not have been material, and would be legal under the proposed law. Harold Williams, quoted earlier, said materiality is "totally inadequate as a standard for an internal control system."

Changes in the bribery provisions were also criticized. Deletion of the "having reason to know" language regarding bribes by agents drew most of the criticism. It would be replaced by language requiring an official to "corruptly direct or authorize" a bribe. Peter Fishbein, a New York attorney, characterized the Chafee Bill as stating: "If you aren't sophisticated and pay a bribe, then you're fined $1 million, but if you get an agent, then you're okay."

---

[6]Kaitati, Jack G., and Label, Wayne A., "American Bribery Legislation: An Obstacle to International Marketing," *Journal of Marketing,* Fall, 1980, p. 40.
[7]Peat, Marwick, Mitchell & Co., "Survey of Business Attitudes toward the Foreign Corrupt Practices Act," January 16, 1979.
[8]*U.S. Code Congressional and Administrative News,* No. 3, May, 1981, p. ix.

[9]*Wall Street Journal,* May 20, 1981.

# APPENDIX: Public Law 95-213 [S.305]; Dec. 19, 1977
# Foreign Corrupt Practices Act of 1977

An Act to amend the Securities Exchange Act of 1934 to make it unlawful for an issuer of securities registered pursuant to section 12 of such Act or an issuer required to file reports pursuant to section 15(d) of such Act to make certain payments to foreign officials and other foreign persons, to require such issuers to maintain accurate records, and for other purposes.

*Be it enacted by the Senate and House of Representatives of the United States of America in Congress assembled,*

**Securities Exchange Act of 1934, amendment. Foreign Corrupt Practices Act of 1977. 15 USC 78a note.**

## TITLE I—FOREIGN CORRUPT PRACTICES

**Short Title**

**Sec. 101**   This title may be cited as the "Foreign Corrupt Practices Act of 1977".

**Assets, transactions and dispositions. 15 USC 78m.**

## Accounting Standards

**Sec. 102**   Section 13(b) of the Securities Exchange Act of 1934 (15 U.S.C. 78q(b)) is amended by inserting "(1)" after "(b)" and by adding at the end thereof the following:

"(2) Every issuer which has a class of securities registered pursuant to section 12 of this title and every issuer which is required to file reports pursuant to section 15(d) of this title shall—

**15 USC 78***l***. Post, p. 1500. Records, maintenance.**

"(A) make and keep books, records, and accounts, which, in reasonable detail, accurately and fairly reflect the transactions and dispositions of the assets of the issuer: and

**Internal accounting controls, establishment.**

"(B) devise and maintain a system of internal accounting controls sufficient to provide reasonable assurances that—

"(i) transactions are executed in accordance with management's general or specific authorization;

"(ii) transactions are recorded as necessary (I) to permit preparation of financial statements in conformity with generally accepted accounting principles or any other criteria applicable to such statements, and (II) to maintain accounting ability for assets;

"(iii) access to assets is permitted only in accordance with management's general or specific authorization; and

"(iv) the recorded accountability for assets is compared with the existing assets at reasonable intervals and appropriate action is taken with respect to any differences.

**Exemption directive, issuance and expiration.**

"(3) (A) With respect to matters concerning the national security of the United States, no duty or liability under paragraph (2) of this subsection shall be imposed upon any person acting in cooperation with the head of any Federal department or agency responsible for such matters if such act in cooperation with such head of a department or agency was done upon the specific, written directive of the head of such department or agency pursuant to Presidential authority to issue such directives. Each directive issued under this paragraph shall set forth the specific facts and circumstances with respect to which the provisions of this paragraph are to be invoked. Each such directive shall, unless renewed in writing, expire one year after the date of issuance.

**File maintenance. Annual summary, transmittal to congressional committees.**

"(B) Each head of a Federal department or agency of the United States who issues a directive pursuant to this paragraph shall maintain a complete file of all such directives and shall, on October 1 of each year, transmit a summary of matters covered by such directives in force at any time during the previous year to the Permanent Select Committee on Intelligence of the House of Representatives and the Select Committee on Intelligence of the Senate.

### Foreign Corrupt Practices by Issuers

**Sec. 103**   (a) The Securities Exchange Act of 1934 is amended by inserting after section 30 the following new section:

"FOREIGN CORRUPT PRACTICES BY ISSUERS

**15 USC 78dd-1.**
**15 USC 78l** *Post,* **p. 1500**

"Sec. 30A. (a) It shall be unlawful for any issuer which has a class of securities registered pursuant to section 12 of this title or which is required to file reports under section 15(d) of this title, or for any officer, director, employee, or agent of such issuer or any stockholder thereof acting on behalf of such issuer, to make use of the mails or any means or instrumentality of interstate commerce corruptly in furtherance of an offer, payment, promise to pay, or authorization of the payment of any money, or offer, gift, promise to give, or authorization of the giving of anything of value to—

"(1) any foreign official for purpose of—

"(A) influencing any act or decision of such foreign official in his official capacity, including a decision to fail to perform his official functions; or

"(B) inducing such foreign official to use his influence with a foreign government or instrumentality thereof to affect or influence any act or decision of such government or instrumentality,

in order to assist such issuer in obtaining or retaining business for or with, or directing business to, any person:

"(2) any foreign political party or official thereof or any candidate for foreign political office for purposes of—

"(A) influencing any act or decision of such party, official, or candidate in its or his official capacity, including a decision to fail to perform its or his official functions: or

"(B) inducing such party, official, or candidate to use its or his influence with a foreign government or instrumentality thereof to affect or influence any act or decision of such government or instrumentality,

in order to assist such issuer in obtaining or retaining business for or with, or directing business to, any person: or

"(3) any person, while knowing or having reason to know that all or a portion of such money or thing of value will be offered, given, or promised, directly or indirectly, to any foreign official, to any foreign political party or official thereof, or to any candidate for foreign political office, for purposes of—

"(A) influencing any act or decision of such foreign official, political party, party official, or candidate in his or its official capacity, including a decision to fail to perform his or its official functions: or

"(B) inducing such foreign official, political party, party official, or candidate to use his or its influence with a foreign government or instrumentality thereof to affect or influence any act or decision of such government or instrumentality, in order to assist such issuer in obtaining or retaining business for or with, or directing business to, any person.

**"Foreign official."** "(b) As used in this section, the term 'foreign official' means any officer or employee of a foreign government or any department, agency, or instrumentality thereof, or any person acting in an official capacity for or on behalf of such government or department, agency, or instrumentality. Such term does not include any employee of a foreign government or any department, agency, or instrumentality thereof whose duties are essentially ministerial or clerical.".

**Penalties.** *Ante*, p. 1495. (b)(1) Section 32(a) of the Securities Exchange Act of 1934 (15 U.S.C. 78ff(a)) is amended by inserting "(other than section 30A)" immediately after "title" the first place it appears.

(2) Section 32 of the Securities Exchange Act of 1934 (15 U.S.C. 78ff) is amended by adding at the end thereof the following new subsection:

"(c) (1) Any issuer which violates section 30A(a) of this title shall, upon conviction, be fined not more than $1,000,000.

"(2) Any officer or director of an issuer, or any stockholder acting on behalf of such issuer, who willfully violates section 30A(a) of this title shall, upon conviction, be fined not more than $10,000, or imprisoned not more than five years, or both.

"(3) Whenever an issuer is found to have violated section 30A(a) of this title, any employee or agent of such issuer who is a United States citizen, national, or resident or is otherwise subject to the jurisdiction of the United States (other than an officer, director, or stockholder of such issuer), and who willfully carried out the act or practice constituting such violation shall, upon conviction, be fined not more than $10,000, or imprisoned not more than five years, or both.

"(4) Whenever a fine is imposed under paragraph (2) or (3) of this subsection upon any officer, director, stockholder, employee, or agent of an issuer, such fine shall not be paid, directly or indirectly, by such issuer."

### Foreign Corrupt Practices by Domestic Concerns

**15 USC 78dd-2.** **Sec. 104** (a) It shall be unlawful for any domestic concern, other than an issuer which is subject to section 30A of the Securities Exchange Act of 1934, or any officer, director, employee, or agent of such domestic concern or any stockholder thereof acting on behalf of such domestic concern, to make use of the mails or any means or instrumentality of interstate commerce corruptly in furtherance of an offer, payment, promise to pay, or authorization of the payment of any money, or offer, gift, promise to give, or authorization of the giving of anything of value to—

(1) any foreign official for purposes of—

(A) influencing any act or decision of such foreign official in his official capacity, including a decision to fail to perform his official functions: or

(B) inducing such foreign official to use his influence with a foreign government or instrumentality thereof to affect or influence any act or decision of such government or instrumentality,

in order to assist such domestic concern in obtaining or retaining business for or with, or directing business to, any person;

(2) any foreign political party or official thereof or any candidate for foreign political office for purposes of—

(A) influencing any act or decision of such party, official, or candidate in its or his official capacity, including a decision to fail to perform its or his official functions; or

(B) inducing such party, official, or candidate to use its or his influence with a foreign government or instrumentality thereof to affect or influence any act or decision of such government or instrumentality,

in order to assist such domestic concern in obtaining or retaining business for or with, or directing business to, any person: or

(3) any person, while knowing or having reason to know that all or a portion of such money or thing of value will be offered, given, or promised, directly or indirectly, to any foreign official, to any foreign political party or official thereof, or to any candidate for foreign political office, for purposes of—

(A) influencing any act or decision of such foreign official, political party, party official, or candidate in his or its official capacity, including a decision to fail to perform his or its official functions; or

(B) inducing such foreign official, political party, party official, or candidate to use his or its influence with a foreign government or instrumentality thereof to affect or influence any act or decision of such government or instrumentality,

in order to assist such domestic concern in obtaining or retaining business for or with, or directing business to any person.

**Penalties.**

(b) (1) (A) Except as provided in subparagraph (B), any domestic concern which violates subsection (a) shall, upon conviction, be fined not more than $1,000,000.

(B) Any individual who is a domestic concern and who willfully violates subsection (a) shall, upon conviction, be fined not more than $10,000, or imprisoned not more than five years, or both.

(2) Any officer or director of a domestic concern, or stockholder acting on behalf of such domestic concern, who willfully violates subsection (a) shall, upon conviction, be fined not more than $10,000, or imprisoned not more than five years, or both.

(3) Whenever a domestic concern is found to have violated subsection (a) of this section, any employee or agent of such domestic concern who is a United States citizen, national, or resident or is otherwise subject to the jurisdiction of the United States (other than an officer, director, or stockholder acting on behalf of such domestic concern), and who willfully carried out the act or practice constituting such violation shall, upon conviction, be fined not more than $10,000, or imprisoned not more than five years, or both.

(4) Whenever a fine is imposed under paragraph (2) or (3) of this subsection upon any officer, director, stockholder, employee, or agent of a domestic concern, such fine shall not be paid, directly or indirectly, by such domestic concern.

**Civil action.**

(c) Whenever it appears to the Attorney General that any domestic concern, or officer, director, employee, agent, or stockholder thereof, is engaged, or is about to engage, in any act or practice constituting a violation of subsection (a) of this section, the Attorney General may, in his discretion, bring a civil action in an appropriate district court of the United States to enjoin such act or practice, and upon a proper showing a permanent or temporary injunction or a temporary restraining order shall be granted without bond.

# Two Cases of Questionable Payments

The passage of the Foreign Corrupt Practices Act in 1977 (see "The Foreign Corrupt Practices Act: A Reconsideration," which precedes this case) came about as a result of various governmental investigations of business activities in the U.S. and abroad. The investigations continued after passage of the act. In March, 1978, one U.S. firm, which is here called the Corporation, found itself the target of three separate Federal investigations, by the SEC, the Internal Revenue Service and the Department of Justice. It had as yet initiated no comprehensive internal survey of its own. In May of the same year, the Corporation's Board of Directors appointed a special committee to inquire into all aspects of Corporation operations which might have involved questionable payments or related improper accounting practices. This case presents two illustrations of the kinds of practices which the Committee's investigations revealed. Both events occurred in the same division (here called the Company) of the

Corporation; the first case occurred abroad and the second within the U.S., and both indirectly or directly involved high-ranking officials of foreign governments. The materials presented in Case A and Case B have been derived from the Special Committee's report to the Corporation's Board of Directors in 1979, now in the public record. Names, dates, and figures have been disguised, but where quotations have been used they are so indicated.

## CHARACTER OF THE CORPORATION AND THE COMPANY DIVISION

In 1978, after many years of diversification and internal growth, the Corporation consisted of five major market groups (including one having to do with aerospace and related products) and approximately 30 divisions. Most of the divisions were located in the United States, but several divisions also maintained offices and plants overseas. In 1970, the Corporation had begun to increase its international activities at a rapid pace—none more rapidly than the Company in question—so that in 1978 fully 30% of the Coproration's sales of several billions of dollars consisted of export sales or sales from operations located outside the U.S.

Repeatedly asserting its belief in decentralized authority, the Corporation maintained a relatively small Corporate Office staff. This staff included the group controllers and five group vice presidents, whose chief responsibility was to monitor the divisions in their groups and act as two-way interpreters between the Corporate Office and the divisions in activities such as planning, product and market development, and capital programs. Each division operated as a "complete, self-sufficient enterprise conducting business under its own name with its own operating officers and management."

Up until 1969, the Company involved in Cases A and B had operated almost exclusively in the United States, and the majority of its products (which served the aerospace industry) were bought by the United States military. Its few foreign markets were serviced by independent companies which acted as agent representatives on a commission basis and maintained service facilities and inventories of spare parts.

After 1969, declining military sales in the U.S. forced the Company to expand its international sales market and to hire an experienced international salesman, Mr. Ed Jones, to head its newly created International Marketing Department. Mr. Jones' aggressive sales campaign and streamlining of the Company's international distribution system rapidly built up international sales to a point where in 1978 they accounted for 50% of the Company's sales (as compared with 10% in 1969).

In the course of these transactions, periodic episodes occurred in which foreign government officials required personal payments before approving of or securing contracts with the countries which they represented. No formal policy for such payments had been devised by Mr. Jones or the Company's senior managers, but there was a general understanding that the Company should not make questionable payments. The agent dealers, however, as independent businessmen, could distribute their commissions as they wished. It was latter revealed in the Special Committee's investigations that numerous Company personnel had in fact either specifically arranged with a dealer to assign commissions in advance to a third party (which in some cases clearly included government offficials), or personally negotiated with such officials. In one instance a Company person carried cash out of the U.S. to make a payment directly to a foreign government official.

At the same time, however, certain Company policies were enacted to prevent questionable payments: the Company would not sell products at prices above the Company's standard price, nor would it pay additional or excessive commissions to local representatives.

In the summer of 1976 the Corporation's Chairman issued a general statement regarding standards of conduct for Corporation employees, representatives, agents, and consultants. He expressed the opinion that the head office knew of no unlawful or improper payments within the Corporation, but that the number of other companies which had made such payments suggested that it would be appropriate to reassert the Corporation's position in these matters. In December of the same year, key executives were asked to sign a statement as part of the annual audit to confirm that no illegal, improper, or questionable payments had occurred "anywhere within the Corporation family." On the evidence of these statements the Chairman asserted in the spring of 1977 that the absence of such activities had been "verified." Company involvement in payments to foreign officials remained officially isolated from the Corporate Office until a careful review of the 1976 Corporation audit suggested that several divisions, and the Company in particular, were or had been making questionable payments at home and abroad. This evidence, along with the initial findings of the federal investigations of the Corporation and the subsequent passage of the FCPA in December 1977, motivated the Board of Directors to initiate its own investigation into Corporation activities.

## THE INVESTIGATION

In May of 1978 a Special Committee was formed consisting of several nonemployee directors to investigate "possible questionable payments" and related improper accounting practices, which were defined as "payments to government officials or political candidates; off-balance sheet funds or accounts; incomplete, false or misleading recording of entries on the books and records of the Corporation; commercial bribery; improper receipt of payments or gratuities by Corporation employees; and overbilling, accommodation payments and other practices which were contrary to Corporation policies." Among the Committee members were a lawyer, a professional scientist with extensive experience in international legislation regarding certain experiments within his field, and a professional accounting consultant. All members held directorships in other companies having international dealings.

The Committee began by meeting with the Corporation's internal and independent auditors, as well as the Audit Committee of the Board of Directors, to establish the most effective channels for its inquiry and the best ways to obtain cooperation from all parties. The Corporation's legal and financial departments were employed in gathering and collecting documents, and the SEC investigating staff was frequently consulted to determine appropriate areas of inquiry and to review the Committee's findings. In addition to various document searches, a 30-item questionnaire, circulated to approximately 2000 employees from all divisions, surveyed the employees' personal participation in and knowledge or suspicions of all kinds of questionable payments and activities. After the results of the initial questionnaire were reviewed, the Committee conducted special interviews, at division level, with the managers and senior executives responsible for divisional marketing, accounting, and personnel activities. One division (which this case calls the Company) immediately came under especially close scrutiny, and for over four weeks the Committee examined documents and conducted over 50 interviews at the Company's headquarters.

Former employees of the Company as well as nonemployees who had had dealings with the Company were also questioned. In a few cases employees denied requests for interviews and claimed Fifth Amendment rights. Mr. Ed Jones (Vice President International Marketing) and several members of his staff agreed only to limited interviews under conditions agreed upon with their counsel, and responded to supplemental questions only through counsel. Wherever practicable, the Committee sought confirmation of its conclusions from more than one witness or participant.

The Committee recognized the difficulties of adjudicating such a complicated tangle of affairs, many of which occurred five or six years earlier, and it assessed its duty as follows:

It must be recognized that the Committee is not a governmental agency and does not have the power to compel testimony or the production of documents. The Committee's interviews were not taken under oath and were not stenographically recorded, although counsel prepared memoranda following each interview. . . . the Committee believes these relatively informal procedures, supplemented by the opportunity to review the transcripts of formal testimony of employee witnesses before the SEC staff and by access to all subpoenaed documents, were the most efficacious method of gathering all possible relevant information within reasonable constraints of cost and time. . . .

The Committee's findings are based on a weighing of the evidence obtained by the Committee as a result of its investigations. . . . In reading its findings the Committee has had to resolve conflicts in the evidence, including the testimony of witnesses, and to make the other choices inherent in any fact-finding process. . . . The Committee's findings are set forth without noting, except here, that they are of necessity the product of judgment.

In the cases where the Committee found it particularly difficult to reach a conclusion, it summarized conflicting evidence within its report. The following two cases are derived from the Committee's summaries.

## CASE *A*: A Commission in Xanadu

### HISTORY OF THE COMPANY'S DEALER IN XANADU

From 1965–77 the Company had been represented in Xanadu by Chai, Inc., a dealership headed by one Mr. E. Grey. Sales to Xanadu had always been quite small, and by the time of the Special Committee's investigation, Chai's contract had already been terminated and a larger dealer in the region had absorbed Xanadu into its sales territory.

### THE SALE IN QUESTION

In 1972 the Company was negotiating to sell five large pieces of military equipment to the U.S. Government, which would in turn sell them to Xanadu under the U.S. Grant-in-Aid Program. As part of the deal, the Company was required to submit in writing an assurance to the U.S. Department of Defense that no commissions were being paid on the sale, in accordance with DOD regulations forbidding the payment of commissions on Grant-in-Aid sales. The company complied with the proviso and gave its written assurance to the DOD.

Prior to the final agreement, Mr. Grey had made great efforts within Xanadu to promote the sale, and personnel in the Company's International Marketing division felt an obligation to reimburse him for his work. They proposed to set up a consulting agreement with Mr. Grey to conduct an in-depth study of some of Xanadu's military requirements. His compensation would be $40,000—about 20% lower than the normal dealer's commissions on the five pieces of equipment. When the proposal reached the Finance Department, it refused to make payment until the study was completed. International Marketing then asked Mr. Waters, Senior Vice President of the Company, to approve a consultancy agreement with Mr. Grey by which he would receive $40,000 in advance for providing "certain future services" which were enumerated in the agreement. A Company manager later testified to the Special Committee that Mr. Waters was informed at that time that the $40,000 would actually be a method of compensating Mr. Grey for his services in helping to secure the Xanadu equipment contract. Mr. Waters approved the consultancy agreement.

Mr. Grey's efforts in the deal appear to have been considerable. He had several contacts with Xanadu's Commander of the Air Force, Michael Tumen, and sent a series of memoranda regarding the negotiations back to International Marketing at Company headquarters in the U.S. The first memo originated in the office of Cdr. Tumen. A handwritten note, labeled "in strict confidence," indicated that Grey had made financial arrangements with one or more government officials in Xanadu:

> I have made a promise to Commander Tumen which I must keep to the letter. Until I write again to give definite instructions on this please request Jack Mason [the Company's head of Accounts Payable] to withhold the credit documentation. . . . And, in any case, please ask him to address all Credit Memos on this deal *personally* to me and not merely marked for my attention [emphasis in original].

Several months later Mr. Grey indicated to the same personnel that he had to act "most discreetly" with respect to commissions since he was accommodating the "personal interests of top officials" in Xanadu to "sustain their continued interest in Company products." He then forwarded a third memorandum to the effect that the U.S. Military Attaché in Xanadu, who apparently had assisted Mr. Grey in the course of the sale, would be leaving the country shortly and that he (the Attaché) expected Mr. Grey to "honor his promise" before that time. When the U.S. Attaché was about to leave Xanadu, Mr. Grey hosted a farewell party for him and his wife, and also sent the wife a gift "of modest value."

Mr. Grey also requested several accommodation payments, "which Mr. Grey characterized as travel expenses" to private individuals in Europe and Asia to be used by Xanadu's military officers and technicians. Subsequent analyses of dealer commission accounts indicated that the company had disbursed approximately $22,000 in accommodation payments on Mr. Grey's initiative.

When the Special Committee interviewed Mr. Grey and informed personnel at the Company's International Marketing division, Mr. Grey claimed to have made no payments to Cdr. Tumen other than to cover his travel expenses, which came to about $5000 over eight years. Personnel in International Marketing expressed the opinion that Mr. Grey's arrangements with Cdr. Tumen probably referred to Mr. Grey's previous commitments to provide funds to train some of Xanadu's military personnel, and they felt that there was no indication of questionable payments in any of Mr. Grey's dealings.

Mr. Waters, the senior vice president who had approved the consultancy agreement, could not recall the specific details of the transaction when questioned by the Special Committee, and testified that he was not aware of Mr. Grey's memos to International Marketing, nor of the expense reimbursements through individuals outside Xanadu. The special committee concluded:

> Although Mr. Waters approved of the consulting agreement, there is no evidence that any Company officer or any Corporation officer was aware of the highly suspicious references to questionable payments in the correspondence from the dealer or of the expense reimbursements and gift which the dealer's employee has stated were made.

## CASE *B*: A Grant to a Medical Foundation

In July 1973, Samuel Ahrdad began a rotating general internship at Hospital X. Early that same fall he decided to specialize on Obstetrics-Gynecology and subsequently put his application in at Hospitals X and Y for a residency in that field. Both hospitals, however, rejected his application because their OB-GYN residencies were reserved for interns already specializing in this area. Samuel called Mr. Jasper Adams, president of the Company, whom he knew socially, and asked for his help on the application to Hospital Y, which was located in the same city as Company headquarters.

Samuel's acquaintance with Mr. Adams originated through the president's association with his father, General Carleton Ahrdad, Secretary of War in a Near Eastern country (here called Burrisia), which happened to be the Company's largest overseas customer. Gen. Ahrdad was the instrumental figure in procuring aircraft for his country. From 1971–73 Mr. Adams had sought "frequent and direct contact" with Gen. Ahrdad to the end that almost 500 Company aircraft were sold to Burrisia in 1972. During the final negotiations of the 1972 sale there was some question over a commission which a local Burrisian dealer expected, and although it was finally agreed to pay the dealer $3 million, Gen. Ahrdad informed Mr. Adams that the Company needed no such agent in dealing with Burrisia's military. Thereafter subsequent sales of over $800 million were arranged between the Company and the Burrisian Army through Gen. Ahrdad.

After Ahrdad's son requested aid on his medical residency application, Mr. Adams contacted Mr. Herbert Brown, president of the medical foundation which supported the medical school with which Hospital Y was associated. Mr. Adams indicated that he would appreciate Mr. Brown's help in support of Samuel's application, and explained that Samuel's father was a very important customer with whom he had had personal contact on many occasions. Adams assured Brown that he would be willing to vouch for Sam's integrity and character. Although careful to point out that he had nothing to do with the admissions process and that his call would have little or no effect, Mr. Brown agreed to do what he could.

A month after a series of calls between Mr. Brown, the president of the medical school, and the chairman of Hospital Y's OB-GYN department, Mr. Adams was informed by Mr. Brown that Samuel would be a strong candidate if any opening developed at Hospital Y. Mr. Brown added that he was raising funds for the medical foundation, which, he pointed out, benefited Company employees, and expressed the hope that the Company would make a contribution. He emphasized, however, that there was absolutely no connection between his personal assistance on Samuel's application and a Company contribution. Mr. Adams later told the Special Committee that he advised the Corporation's chairman of his efforts to help Gen. Ahrdad's son secure a residency, and that in a second conversation when the application was pending and likely to be accepted, he suggested that the Corporation "might want to consider making a contribution to the medical foundation." According to Mr. Adams, the chairman indicated that "the possible contribution should be handled on its own merits and kept separate from the subject of Ahrdad's residency." The chairman later recalled the first conversation about Adams' help, but could not remember ever discussing a possible contribution to the medical foundation.

Samuel Ahrdad was found to be "the only

## EXHIBIT 1

### CONTRIBUTION PROGRAM OF THE CORPORATION CHARITABLE TRUST

| | |
|---|---|
| 1974 | $1.5 million |
| 1975 | $2+ million |
| 1976 | $2− million |

Largest single compounded donation (1970–1976): $100,000*

*The Special Committee's report carried the following sentence: ". . . The $100,000 pledge was the largest pledge made by the Corporation to a single charitable organization during the period under review, although annual contributions equal to or exceeding the annual payments on that pledge have been made to other charities."

qualified applicant who had not made other arrangements by that time," and the hospital accepted him into its residency program, which Samuel subsequently completed to the hospital's satisfaction. Both Samuel and his father "were aware of Mr. Adams' assistance in providing a personal recommendation."

In March 1974, Mr. Adams requested in a formal application that the Corporation's Charitable Trust approve a $100,000 donation to the medical foundation in the form of three annual installments (see Exhibit 1 for a record of the Trust's Giving Program). The Contribution Committee was advised by the senior vice president of the Corporation responsible for the Company's affairs that Gen. Ahrdad's son held a residency at one of the teaching hospitals supported by the foundation. Adams' request was approved by the Committee without any extended discussion, and the donation was subsequently approved by the Corporation's Board, which was presented with the Committee's minutes in which no reference to Ahrdad or Hospital Y was made.

It was part of the Special Committee's task to determine whether the medical foundation donation was an inappropriate or questionable payment. The following presents the Special Committee's decision:

> The Committee examined the charitable contributions made during the period under review by the Corporation Charitable Foundation

Trust, the Corporation's vehicle for making all substantial charitable contributions. The Committee found no evidence that any charitable contribution was used as a vehicle for a questionable payment and found no evidence of any other impropriety in connection with charitable contributions.

The Committee did, however, examine in great detail the circumstances surrounding a $100,000 contribution made at the request of the Company to a medical foundation, a well-established charitable organization affiliated with a medical school. This inquiry was made because of a possible relationship between the contribution and the admission of the son of a high military official of an important government customer of the Company to the school's medical residency program. The Committee found no impropriety in connection with the contribution.

# The IBM–Fujitsu Dispute

In November 1988, after more than three years of negotiations, two arbitrators issued a 43-page agreement settling a long, bitter dispute between IBM and Fujitsu, its largest Japanese rival. The pact ended the battle over IBM's claim that Fujitsu had extensively copied the operating system software that controlled the inner workings of IBM mainframe computers. Fujitsu vigorously rejected this charge, arguing that it had carefully respected IBM's intellectual property rights. The conflict was so acrimonious that one of the arbitrators later commented, "These two parties have hardly been able to agree what color a stoplight is." Observers of the dispute explained its bitterness by noting that the two companies were fierce competitors, each governed by different legal systems and responsive to disparate business norms and cultural values.

The settlement governed Fujitsu's future use of material developed from existing IBM materials as well as from new IBM products. Under strict procedures, Fujitsu could inspect strategically crucial IBM materials, but only in a secured facility. It could also develop new products derived from IBM materials. Fujitsu customers who used such products would no longer need fear that IBM would prosecute them. In exchange for access, permission for past and future use, and immunity from liability, Fujitsu agreed to pay IBM a total of $833,251,000, an amount more than double its 1988 net income. Fujitsu would also make additional payments of $25 million or more each year depending upon the IBM materials it used in the future. The arbitrators' decision involved no findings of wrongdoing by Fujitsu.

The arbitrators' decision was designed to resolve the parties' dispute completely, binding them outside of U.S., Japanese, or universal copyright law. The agreement required that IBM and Fujitsu maintain the confidentiality of all their proceedings, both during and after the arbitration. The two arbitrators who created the agreement were chosen by the parties' law firms. IBM's law firm chose John L. Jones, a retired executive vice president of Norfolk Southern Corporation. Fujitsu's law firm in the United States chose Robert H. Mnookin, the Adelbert H. Sweet Professor of Law at Stanford Law School and the director of the Stanford Center on Conflict and Negotiation.

Like the arbitration process itself, the agreement gave Jones and Mnookin substantial long-term power over IBM and Fujitsu. For the next 15 years, the two would supervise all disputes arising from the agreement. For the next five to ten years, they could set the prices and terms of any agreement between IBM and Fujitsu over mainframe operating software. Their decisions, unlike judicial decisions, would be final and unreviewable.

## THE PARTIES

### IBM

During the 1980s, IBM earned 70–75% of world mainframe revenues, and these provided roughly two thirds of IBM's profits. By the end of the decade, annual worldwide mainframe revenues were roughly $30 billion. Vast R&D expenditures, a global organization, a large, highly trained sales force, and customer relationships built up over decades had all helped IBM dominate the worldwide mainframe business. (See Exhibit 1 for IBM financial data.) IBM's dominance of the mainframe business originated in the revolutionary System/360 computers it introduced in the early 1960s.

IBM had also litigated actively, extensively, and frequently to protect its rights. *Business Week* said IBM had a history "as one of the world's most ferocious legal combatants." Throughout the 1970s, the company fought a massive antitrust case brought by the U.S. Justice Department, and the government ultimately dropped the case. In 1983, after Hitachi pleaded guilty in federal court to criminal charges that it conspired to transport stolen IBM technical documents to Japan, IBM filed its own civil damages suit against Hitachi for stealing the technology. Hitachi settled the civil suit in 1983, agreed to pay IBM about $300 million, and allowed IBM to inspect future Hitachi products.

IBM's case against Hitachi resulted from a complex "sting" operation devised by IBM and the Federal Bureau of Investigation. The climax of the effort was a payment of more than $500,000 made by a senior Hitachi engineer to a Silicon Valley consultant for IBM technology. The consultant was actually working for IBM and the FBI. IBM's efforts led one observer to write that "the scale of the operation and the publicity it drew were more reminiscent of a high-security Soviet counterespionage program than a mere effort to protect trade secrets."[1]

IBM dominated the world market for operating systems software for mainframes. During the 1980s, the price of IBM systems software products grew at an annual compound rate of 28%. This software was among the most complex programs in existence, with millions of lines of code, and IBM had thousands of programmers working continuously to develop it. Cloning this software or developing alternative products was extremely difficult: Amdahl spent six years and $10 million in such an effort and then gave up in 1988 because it concluded customers would not want to risk an alternative to IBM systems software, especially when they already had millions of dollars of customized software written for IBM mainframes and operating systems software.

During the 1980s, IBM's market had begun to change. The computer industry shifted from emphasis on single, large, central processing units, typically mainframes, to networks of computers. Mainframe sales slowed; some forecasts showed them growing only 3% a year between 1986 and 1996. Analysts also predicted that the personal computer market would soon surpass the mainframe market in sales volume. Moreover, hardware revenues were expected to grow at only slightly more than a third of the 20% annual rate of growth predicted for software revenues in the late 1980s and 1990s. IBM was moving into these new areas, but it faced much greater competition there than in mainframes.

[1]Marie Anchordoguy, *Computers Incorporated* (Cambridge. MA: Council on East Asian Studies, Harvard University, 1989), p. 1.

## Fujitsu

Fujitsu, Japan's largest computer maker and the third largest in the world, made IBM-compatible computers. In the early 1970s, when the Japanese government targeted computers as a strategic industry, Fujitsu and Hitachi were charged with entering the mainframe business. At the time, IBM's stunning success with the System/370 was driving rivals like GE and RCA out of the computer industry. (By the early 1970s, IBM's position in the U.S. computer market was so strong that its American competitors were referred to as "the seven dwarfs" or "the bunch," and one of its rivals observed that "IBM is not the competition; it's the environment.")

Fujitsu and Hitachi both chose a plug-compatibility strategy. In effect, they cloned the 370's hardware and the operating system software that controlled it. Fujitsu's efforts benefited from a strategic alliance with Amdahl Corporation, a California-based manufacturer of mainframes founded by Gene Amdahl, the engineer who designed the IBM 360. In 1972, Fujitsu paid $54 million to purchase a 49.5% stake in Amdahl, and thereby secured access to its technology. Fujitsu's customers could buy its mainframes and then run IBM applications software—programs for payroll, data processing, and other functions—on these machines. Fujitsu could also begin selling mainframes to IBM customers, and they could run their libraries of applications software on Fujitsu machines. The strategy succeeded: By 1979 Fujitsu sales in Japan outstripped IBM Japan's.

Nevertheless, Fujitsu viewed itself, as did many outside observers, as an underdog in its contest with IBM. Even after the success of Fujitsu's plug-compatibility strategy, the sales of IBM's Japanese subsidiary alone were almost as large as Fujitsu's. In the minds of the Japanese, the IBM–Hitachi conflict "symbolized the ever-present threat of an IBM so powerful it could squash its competitors."[2] (See Exhibit 2 for recent Fujitsu financial results.)

By the early 1980s, some Fujitsu main-

[2]Marie Anchordoguy, *Computers Incorporated*, p. 2.

frames outperformed comparable IBM products on a price-performance basis. Like IBM, Fujitsu depended heavily on mainframe sales (which accounted for more than 60% of its profits and 70% of its sales), it built most of the parts it used, and its culture was said to be a Japanese version of IBM's stern, no-nonsense approach. Fujitsu distributed internationally but had limited influence outside Japan. Its overseas sales amounted to only 23% of total revenues (about half of IBM's comparable figures), and its profit margins were less than half of IBM's 9.7%. Fujitsu products were sold in the United States by Amdahl.

While Fujitsu's domestic sales were growing very strongly, its foreign sales had suffered from IBM's allegations about Fujitsu's behavior and their protracted dispute. Fujitsu's European distributor, Siemens-AG, stopped selling Fujitsu equipment in 1986 after IBM alleged infringement. According to one press report, some Siemens customers were embarrassed by surprise visits from auditors sent by IBM to determine the type of software they were using. Fujitsu executives were angered by these tactics and charged that IBM was continuing a practice that industry observers had nicknamed "FUD": ways of spreading *f*ear, *u*ncertainty, and *d*oubt among computer buyers thinking of buying non-IBM products.

## THE DISPUTE

Operating system software stood at the center of the two companies' dispute. An operating system is a collection of software used to assist and in part control the operations of a computer. Operating systems generally manage the computer's internal functions and facilitate the use of applications software. They coordinate the reading and writing of data between the internal memory and such peripheral devices as disk drives, keyboard, and printer; perform basic housekeeping functions for the computer system; and prepare the computer to execute applications programs.

System software is like the phonograph stylus that turns the grooves on a record into music.[3] The better the operating system's design, the more efficiently applications software runs on it. Moreover, the operating system of a mainframe determines whether competitors' products such as disk drives, personal computers, and other software can be used with the mainframe. According to some computer experts, operating systems are the principal products of the industry and are critical to securing hardware orders.

Operating system software contains two kinds of information. One type tells what a computer does. Customers and others get this information so they can determine what peripheral equipment will be compatible with the computer or so they can write applications programs the computer can run. The second kind of information tells how the computer does what it does. Fujitsu had sought the second, more sensitive information because it believed it was necessary for designing IBM-compatible mainframes.

Fujitsu used IBM programming material to create their early operating system programs, including the M-series operating system released in 1976. Fujitsu acknowledged that some of its other early programs reflected substantial use of copyrighted IBM material, as did the successor versions of these early programs Fujitsu released between 1982 to 1987.[4]

IBM objected to Fujitsu's use of this information. It argued Fujitsu should have relied only upon "reasonable and adequate" interface information. This information is like the specifications for plugs and holes in the back of a stereo amplifier that users need to plug in compatible components. It is not information about the internal design of the amplifier. But before the 1988 agreement, IBM did not differentiate

its interface information from internal design information. IBM began to copyright its basic systems software in 1978.

## THE 1988 AGREEMENT

In October 1982, IBM alleged that Fujitsu operating system programs and manuals contained IBM programming material in violation of IBM's intellectual property rights. Eight months of negotiations followed. In July 1983 IBM and Fujitsu reached a settlement that required Fujitsu to make substantial payments to IBM, even though Fujitsu did not admit to being guilty of copyright infringement. The settlement also contained procedures for resolving future disputes.

But these arrangements soon unraveled. Critics said the agreement was poorly drafted, and new disputes arose about infringement of IBM's intellectual property rights. At issue were the "successor versions" of early Fujitsu programs. IBM claimed that these involved extensive copying of IBM's system software. IBM filed a demand for arbitration in July 1985 with the American Arbitration Association (AAA), a private, nonprofit entity. Arbitration hearings on the IBM–Fujitsu dispute over intellectual property rights began in December 1985. Considering the complexity of the dispute, the initial agreement providing for arbitration was relatively short. One of the two arbitrators later commented, "It didn't take long to write down what these two parties agreed on. . . . The two parties have never agreed on anything, other than to agree that the only way to resolve this was to get us to solve it."

Three years later the two arbitrators produced an agreement to define what information was protected, govern future use of existing programs, permit each firm to inspect some of the other's technology, and provide fair compensation for its use. The agreement created three arrangements: a paid-up license, a secured facility regime, and a way to define protected information.

[3]Michael Miller, "Fujitsu Can Legally Clone IBM Software: The Question Now, Will It Be Able To?" *Wall Street Journal,* December 1, 1988, p. B1.
[4]*International Business Machines Corporation v. Fujitsu Limited,* American Arbitration Association, Commercial Arbitration Tribunal Opinion, Case No. 13T-117-0636-85, November 29, 1988, p. 8.

## The Paid-up License

IBM agreed to give Fujitsu the right to continue using and selling products based upon IBM intellectual property. Because the parties disagreed on the value of the material, the arbitrators heard extended testimony from experts representing both parties and then established their own valuation. In the end, Fujitsu had to make a final payment of $237 million to IBM, bringing its total outlay since 1983 to $833 million.

## The Secured Facility Regime

To provide each party with access to the other's interface information, the arbitrators created a secured facility regime. Under this system, either party could examine without restriction the other's unlicensed system software material. In contrast, examination of licensed materials was carefully controlled. Fujitsu had to set up a special building in Tokyo in which it could scrutinize IBM system software, once it reached the market. Inside the facility, Fujitsu personnel could inspect and analyze IBM system software as it evolved over the 1990s, but only for the purpose of its own independent software development.

The arbitrators established strict, detailed procedures for the building's security. They would decide what documents could leave the building and how much Fujitsu would pay for the information it used. IBM did not plan to establish a secured facility in which to examine Fujitsu material.

## Defining Protected Information

The agreement emphasized the parties' obligation to differentiate between licensed and unlicensed material, and it stipulated criteria for identifying the interface information the other party could use. Under the agreement, IBM had to give Fujitsu enough interface information that it could offer its customers application program compatibility. This meant customers could run the same applications programs on either IBM or Fujitsu equipment.[5] The huge investment in applications programs written for IBM operating systems made such compatibility essential to Fujitsu's existing customers.

The agreement also ensured that customers could communicate and share a reasonable amount of data between IBM and Fujitsu systems. In general, the goal was to permit "any to any connections."[6] This meant any terminal or application in a network managed by Fujitsu operating systems would be able to efficiently and reliably access any terminal or application in an IBM-managed network or vice versa.

Some industry analysts viewed the agreement as a victory—and perhaps a vindication—for Fujitsu. One Japanese analyst said that "Fujitsu got off with a very light sentence." *Business Week* reported that "There were broad smiles at [Fujitsu's] staid yellow headquarters building in Marunouchi, the heart of Tokyo's business district."[7] Analysts in the United States stressed that the resolution might provide IBM with a vigorous rival in a critical part of the mainframe business.

## INTELLECTUAL PROPERTY BATTLES

The IBM–Fujitsu dispute was only the most prominent in a long series of commercial and trade battles over technology during the 1980s. Increasingly, these international and domestic controversies focused on protection of intellectual property rights, particularly for software and patents. Conflicting laws on the international protection of investors' and authors' rights created so much ambiguity that they failed to deter, and sometimes even fostered, infringement of those rights. Exacerbating the problem were the increasing costs of developing new

[5]American Arbitration Association, *Summary of Opinion, International Business Machines Corporation v. Fujitsu Limited*, p. 7.
[6]American Arbitration Association, *Summary of Opinion, International Business Machines Corporation v. Fujitsu Limited*, p. 11.
[7]Neil Gross and John Verity, "Can Fujitsu Break Big Blue's Grip?" *Business Week*, December 19, 1988, p. 102.

products and the increasing ease of copying,[8] cloning, and improvement engineering.

Large-scale, institutional efforts had been made to address the problem of intellectual property generally, but not for computer software specifically. Trade negotiation organizations such as the General Agreement on Tariffs and Trade (GATT) and the U.N.-based World Intellectual Property Organization (WIPO) were focusing on the discrepancies among countries' protection of foreign intellectual property rights.

The most recent round of GATT talks, the Uruguay Round that began in September 1968, emphasized the work of the Committee on Trade-Related Aspects of Intellectual Property Rights (TRIPS). GATT's objective, however, was not to harmonize the laws but to establish three things: "(1) minimum substantive standards for protection of intellectual property rights; (2) measures for the effective enforcement of these rights both internally and at the border; and (3) a dispute settlement mechanism."[9]

Some countries had enacted new legislation to redress infringement. In the United States, for example, the 1988 trade bill made it easier to control and penalize imports of products that infringed upon American patents. Before this legislation, patent holders had to prove that someone had infringed on their patent *and* that the infringement had damaged them financially. The new law made proof of patent violation sufficient.

Not all countries endorsed stronger protection for intellectual property rights. Developing nations, such as Brazil, often opposed these measures. They held that protecting intellectual property was a way to keep them dependent on the technology and creativity of the industrialized world and stop them from developing local capabilities to invent and create. Believing "knowledge was the heritage of all mankind," these countries viewed protection as "denying them the educational and instructional tools available from copyrighted works and the social and industrial contributions of patented products." Protection, they believed, made these tools and contributions too expensive for developing countries and available only under conditions that "violate the sovereignty of those countries."[10]

Disputes between developed nations, particularly between American and Japanese companies, over infringement of intellectual property were numerous, and many resulted in litigation. Some industry observers have suggested that the United States and Japan had established roles in intellectual property development: The United States researches and develops the property, then licenses or sells it to Japan, and Japan then uses and perfects the technology.

Recent disputes included Fusion Systems Corporation's battle with Mitsubishi Electric over patent rights for a microwave lamp; IBM, Intel, and Texas Instruments' litigation against Japanese competitors over patent and copyright infringement; Corning Glass's suit against Sumitomo Electric for infringement of fiber-optic patents; and Texas Instruments' suit against nine companies, including NEC, Matsushita, Fujitsu, and Mitsubishi Electric, for patent infringement after the defendants refused to pay the increase in royalties that Texas Instruments demanded on its microchips. Despite their efforts, American companies lost some of these legal battles. Intel, for example, lost its suit alleging that NEC had stolen ideas, specifically Intel's microcode, for Intel's microprocessors. NEC argued successfully that it developed the

---

[8]Statement of National Planning Association's committee on Changing International Realities, as cited in Helena Stalson, *Intellectual Property Rights and United States Competitiveness in Trade* (Washington, D.C.: National Planning Association, Committee on Changing International Realities, 1987), p. v.

[9]"U.S.–Japan Friction Remains on Patent Issues," *Background Bulletin* (Press Office, United States Information Service, March 2, 1989), text of statement of Michael Kirk (Assistant Commissioner for External Affairs at the U.S. Department of Commerce), testimony before Senate Subcommittee on Foreign Commerce and Tourism delivered February 28, 1989.

[10]Stalson, *Intellectual Property Rights and U.S. Competitiveness in Trade*, p. 48.

product in question, not by infringement but by completely legal reverse engineering.

American computer companies have also fought each other, often over complex reverse-engineering issues and accusations that one company's user-interface software had stolen the "look and feel" of another's. When IBM refused to buy a license for Berkeley Limited Partnership's patent, which Berkeley said covered some basic software operations found in almost all personal computers and word-processing programs, Berkeley sued IBM for infringement. In response, IBM countersued Berkeley for racketeering and extortion, but the court dismissed the countersuit. IBM then settled Berkeley's suit.[11]

Despite these legal efforts, borrowing, copying, and cloning software remained common, in part because companies have grown more adept at crossing legal mine fields. For example, IBM did not sue Phoenix Technologies, Ltd. when it cloned IBM's BIOS software for personal computers, in part because Phoenix's reverse engineering divided its programmers into separate groups: those who dissected IBM's product to determine its tasks and those who took a list of tasks IBM's products perform and developed a new product to do those tasks.[12]

## LEGAL PROTECTION OF INTELLECTUAL PROPERTY IN AMERICA AND JAPAN

Legal protection for intellectual property differs between the United States and Japan. Copyright, patent, and trade secret laws in the countries differ, as do the legal theories justifying the protection. Under these laws, protection for computer software is particularly ambiguous.

A 1983 American appeals court decision, which ruled that American copyright law extended to operating system software, was one of a very few legal decisions that had begun to reduce uncertainties about the scope of protection for operating system software under American law. In 1984 Japan considered enacting a Computer Program Rights Law to end ambiguities about computer programs in its copyright law. It would have required binding arbitration to resolve copyright infringement suits involving computer programs. But Japan rejected the Program Rights Law proposal under pressure from the United States. Instead, it chose to amend its copyright law in 1985, leaving the ambiguities for computer programs in place and changing only items such as the duration of copyright protection.

### Copyrights

**Subject Matter.** American and Japanese copyright systems both protect the form of expression, but not the underlying idea, of an author's work. Under both systems, the work must be original and may be within the broad realms of literature, science, fine art, or music to be eligible for protection. Computer programs and databases were within the general statutory definition of protected literary works under the American Copyright Act of 1976. Whether software falls under the Japanese law remained a matter of interpretation.

**Duration.** Until 1985 American and Japanese systems' copyright protection differed in duration. Generally, U.S. law gave works created on or after January 1, 1978, copyright protection for life of the author, plus 50 years after the author's death. Japan formerly protected the work for only 20 years from the date of granting of the copyright, but in 1985 it adopted provisions like those in the United States.

**Protection from Infringement.** Copyright infringement is the violation of any of the copyright owner's exclusive rights. Both systems allow for use of copyrighted works without infringement in situations involving teaching, scholarship, and research. But Japan permits uses of copyrighted material that American law would scrutinize more carefully. For example, under Japanese law a user of a copyrighted computer program may debug and upgrade it, and even modify it for the purpose of replacement.

[11]"Will Software Patents Cramp Creativity?" *Wall Street Journal*, March 14, 1989, p. B-1.
[12]*The Economist,* December 23, 1989, pp. 101–102.

Its copyright law also leaves ambiguous the distinction between upgrading and revising a computer program.

**Remedies.** When a copyright infringement occurs, the holder of the copyright can take legal action against the infringer. Both American and Japanese legal systems provide for injunctive relief (this requires the infringer to stop the offending conduct), for damages that compensate for lost profits or royalties, and for criminal sanctions.

### Patents

**Subject Matter.** American and Japanese patent-law systems both require that patentable inventions be novel or contain an inventive step, and be nonobvious or useful. Both include processes as well as products, and improvements to either. Japan's patent law defines an invention as "the highly advanced creation of technical ideas utilizing natural laws," a definition that depends on how the terms "natural laws" and "technical ideas" are interpreted.

Japan and most industrialized countries give priority to the first of competing patent applicants to file an application for the patent on the technology. The United States grants the patent to the first to invent the technology.

In general, a Japanese patent covers a single claim or novel advance. American patents, in contrast, often list several independently valid claims. This compels Japanese inventors to file more patents to cover a single technology. In 1983, for example, about 100,000 patent applications were filed in the United States, while more than 250,000 were filed in Japan.[13]

Explanations for these differences vary. The scope of a patent—a single claim versus multiple claims—is one. Another is Japan's "first to file" system. Still another factor is that Japanese law, unlike the United States, permits the government to grant other parties the right to use an invention if an inventor fails to do so or if work-

ing the patent serves the public interest. This creates incentives to make a patent as *narrow* as possible to maintain its exclusivity and, hence, its economic value. Multiple, narrow patents are each more likely to be worked sufficiently, and a narrow patent has more limited economic consequences than one encompassing a class of related inventions. Finally, Japan requires that patent applications cover only specific and proven inventions. Under U.S. law, patents could describe an invention more broadly and cover multiple variations of the invention. To cover the possible variations, inventors in Japan had to file multiple applications.

The application process in the two countries also differs. The U.S. system examines all patents in the order in which applicants file them. Japan examines applications only at the patent applicant's request and may defer examination as long as seven years. Confidentiality of the patent application is absolute in the United States; publication follows the grant of the patent, at which time the patentee can take legal action for copying and other infringement on his technology. But patent applications in Japan are published or "laid open" after 18 months, often before the patent is granted, if granted at all. Opponents of the grant of a patent may oppose it during the three months after examination is requested and before the patent is granted in Japan. In the United States, opponents must wait until the patent is granted.

Some analysts believe that Japan's "laying open" of patent applications promotes a practice called "patent flooding" because competitors can file multiple improvement patents to force the inventor to cross-license its technology rather than defend the patent in litigation. Protection of rights in the technology also depends on the length of time between filing a patent application and the issuing of a patent on the technology. That period in Japan averages six years, compared to a 20-month average in the United States.

**Remedies.** As with copyright infringement, the remedies of injunctive relief, damages, and criminal sanctions are available in both

---

[13]Krista McQuade and Professor Gomes-Casseres, "Fusion Systems Corporation," HBS case 390·021, 1990.

countries for patent infringements. Injunctive relief in Japan includes the right to demand not only destruction of the resulting product of the infringement, but also removal and destruction of the equipment involved in and contributing to the infringement. Japan also allows for measures to restore the patentee's business goodwill.

## Trade Secrets

**Subject Matter.**   Most U.S. states define trade secrets as any "formula, pattern, device, or compilation of information used in one's business and which gives him an opportunity to obtain an advantage over competitors who do not know or use it."[14] Examples include chemical formulas, manufacturing processes, machine patterns, and customer lists. Japan does not identify any such trade secrets by statute, but it does protect trade secrets covered by contract. Both systems rely on contract terms to set the duration of the restriction on use of, disclosure of, or access to another's trade secrets.

**Protection from Infringement.**   U.S. law provides several ways of protecting trade secrets: trade secret and criminal statutes, explicit contracts such as postemployment noncompetition agreements and nondisclosure agreements, and implied contracts, created by special relationships such as licensor/licensee. Japan relies only on contracts, such as nondisclosure agreements. Japan's strictly contractual approach precludes protection against third parties that wrongfully acquire trade secrets. Protection against third parties is possible in the American system if the third party knows that it is a trade secret and the information is disclosed to it through a breach of duty.

**Remedies.**   Generally, damages and criminal sanctions are available in both systems, but the scope of those remedies and the underlying

---

[14]Restatement of Torts §757, comment (b)(1939) as cited in Michael A. Epstein, *Modern Intellectual Property* (New York: Law & Business, Inc./Harcourt Brace Jovanovich, 1989), p. 3, n. 3.

legal theories differ in America and Japan. Injunctive relief against competitive employment is available in the United States and may be permanent; in Japan, the commercial nature of the rights in question makes injunctions unlikely, but not impossible.

Damages are available in both systems. In the United States, one can get attorney's fees, punitive damages (which are discretionary with the judge), and actual damages based upon the trade secret owner's loss, the misappropriator's gain, and/or a reasonable royalty. State and federal criminal sanctions may apply in the United States, under general criminal laws and the Federal Trade Secrets Acts. Japan has no criminal law specifically prohibiting unauthorized disclosure of, or access to, trade secrets. But its criminal code may punish the use of unlawful means such as threat, fraud, bribery, or theft of tangible data.

## IMITATION IN JAPANESE CULTURE

The many, heated intellectual-property disputes between American and Japanese companies led some observers to seek cultural perspectives on the issues. The most controversial of these, and perhaps the most common, was the view that Japanese culture sanctioned imitation to a greater degree than the American.

Proponents of this view emphasized that Japan has borrowed extensively from foreign cultures. Through contacts with China, for example, Japan imitated elements of Chinese culture, adopting a Chinese-style legal code (Ritsuryò) as the basis for the criminal and administrative codes of its legal system. During the nineteenth century, Japan emulated European and American technology. Meiji Japan consciously imitated European and American organizational models in developing its postal and police systems and its newspapers. Japan selected its parliamentary system of government from among American and European models, and Germanic law informed Japan's civil law system, as did Anglo-American influences during the postwar occupation period.

Japanese artists have traditionally studied

their crafts in apprenticeships and learned technique by copying that of the master. Between 1750 and 1850, Japanese artists, particularly Hokusai and Hiroshige, learned by imitating: Their works and sketches originated in the drawings of seventh-century Buddhist figures. Masters generated schools of artists, whose followers produced works in particular style. Japanese artists did not begin to sign their works until the sixteenth century. The Zen tradition of repetition of a task or skill to yield mastery or perfection also greatly influenced and informed the arts, as well as other aspects of Japanese culture.

Scholars who have studied the history of Japanese fine arts have acknowledged a tendency toward imitation. One wrote, for example:

> It has been remarked that a pupil's training consists in copying and recopying his master's works and that there are model-books which show the proper method of painting various subjects. So much stress upon tradition, at once a safeguard against radicalism and an obstacle to free development, naturally gave birth to pronounced school mannerisms and to restrictions which extend even to choice of subject and result in inevitable repetition. . . . It is probable, however, that the special references in the "Six Canons" [a classic guide to Japanese painting] to copying old masters was not intended to mean mere copying; rather it should be interpreted as emphasizing the importance of preserving that part of tradition which ever lives as an eternal principle and of transmitting it to the next generation.[15]

Explanations of Japan's alleged tendency to emulation are diverse. Some suggest it is Japanese openness to other cultures. The Dutch journalist Karel Van Wolferen, a long-time resident of Japan, asserts that Japanese culture is based on "the notion that there is a perfect way of doing things . . . that mastery is reached by the removal of the obstacles between the self and the perfect model, embodied by the teacher, a view which emphasizes great technical skill with a lack of personal expression; there is no room for the idiosyncratic individual."[16] In this view, imitation of aspects of Chinese, European, or American civilizations is part of Japan's "catching-up disposition," emulation deriving not merely from pursuit of perfection, but also from a self-perception of "falling short."

In contrast, other writers attribute cultural emulation, and particularly its innovative applications and expressions in Japan, to Japanese self-assertion. Some argue that Japanese emulation is an effort to make Japan respected internationally. In other instances, Japan's imitation may have reinforced an even more aggressive strategy. In Meiji Japan, according to this argument, widespread emulation occurred to prevent any one nation from becoming indispensable to Japan's modernization. Japan sought not only to hold its own but ultimately to grow dominant.

The view of Japan as a peculiarly imitative nation is often criticized for cultural bias, dubious methodology, and general offensiveness. Cultural emulation and imitation are hardly unique to Japan. Many other nations have looked to other nations' cultures and civilizations when developing their own. For example, British industrialists were horrified at the quality of the American guns on display at the Great Exhibition in London in 1851. They believed the Americans had unfairly appropriated British designs. In later decades, the British made similar complaints about German and American efforts in synthetic dyes, metals, armaments, penicillin, radar, and computerized tomography. Moreover, by 1986 Japan had a higher percentage of its population engaged in R&D than America, and by the mid-1980s it accounted for 20% of new patents in ceramics, 26% in communication equipment, and 33% in office-computing and accounting machines.

Historical studies also point to Japanese creativity. Japan's postal and police systems and

---

[15]Kojiro Tomita, "Art—Far Eastern Methods," in *Japanese Art: A Selection from the Encyclopedia Britannica* (New York: Encyclopedia Britannica, 1933), p. 34.

[16]Karel Van Wolferen, *The Enigma of Japanese Power: People and Politics in a Stateless Nation* (Knopf, 1989), pp. 378–379.

newspapers, according to some studies, are actually examples of rapid, innovative adaptations of overseas models to Japanese circumstances. Numerous schools of artists existed in Japan, often at the same time; new masters often emerged, establishing new schools and traditions. Unique painting often embellished or individualized otherwise identical pottery forms. Even Zen acts of repetition can be viewed differently. The former Harvard professor and ambassador to Japan, Edwin Reischauer, sees these acts as triumphs of individualism and innovation—the application of one's whole being to a task and a reliance on individual will, self-discovery, and self-discipline to master a practice or an idea.

While some debated these cultural tendencies and their effects on Japanese laws and company behavior, others speculated on the longer-term consequences of the IBM–Fujitsu arbitration. Would IBM and Fujitsu somehow learn to collaborate, now that they were joined in this peculiar, coerced strategic alliance? Would Fujitsu now bring serious competition to the system software market? Would IBM prevent this by rapidly changing its systems software or by moving functions from software to hard circuitry, which Fujitsu could not inspect? Would Fujitsu continue its efforts to develop non-IBM systems software or even team up with AT&T in an alliance against IBM? Would other companies use it as a model for managing international intellectual property disputes?

## NOTE ON SOURCES

In addition to the documents cited in the footnotes, the data in this case was based upon articles in the general business press and more specialized publications covering the computer industry.

The discussion of Japanese culture and emulation draws, in part, upon D. Elanor Westney, *Imitation and Innovation: The Transfer of Western Organizational Patterns to Meiji Japan* (Cambridge, Mass.: Harvard University Press,

1987); William Watson, ed., *Artistic Personality and Decorative Style in Japanese Art* (London: University of London Colloquies on Art and Archeology in Asia, no. 6, 1976); and Henry P. Bowie, *On the Laws of Japanese Painting* (New York: Dover Publications, 1951).

The section on intellectual property laws in the United States and Japan is intended for background information only and should not be construed as legal advice. This section drew upon the following sources: Jay Dratler, Jr., "Trade Secrets in the United States and Japan: A Comparison and Prognosis," 14 *Yale Journal of International Law* 68 (1989); Michael A. Epstein, *Modern Intellectual Property* (New York: Law & Business Inc./Harcourt Brace Jovanovich, 1989); Tohru Nakajima, "Legal Protection of Computer Programs in Japan: The Conflict Between Economic and Artistic Goals," *Columbia Journal of Transnational Law* 143 (1988), p. 27; Robert P. Benko, *Protecting Intellectual Property Rights: Issues and Controversies* (Washington, D.C.: American Enterprise Institute for Public Policy Research, 1987); Mary Ann Glendon, Michael Wallace Gordon, and Christopher Osakwe, *Comparative Legal Traditions: Text, Materials and Cases* (St. Paul, Minn.: West Publishing Co., 1985); Robert W. Russell, compiler, *Patents and Trademarks in Japan (A Handy Book)* (Tokyo, Japan, 1984); Fenwick, Stone, Davis & West, "Legal Protection of Computer Software in Japan," in Miles R. Gilburne, [symposium] chairman, *Intellectual Property Rights in High-Technology Products and Sensitive Business Information* (New York: Law and Business, Inc./Harcourt Brace Jovanovich, 1982); Earl W. Kitner and Jack Lahr, *An Intellectual Property Law Printer: A Survey of the Law of Patents, Trade Secrets, Trademarks, Franchises, Copyrights, and Personality and Entertainment Rights* (New York: Clark Boardman Company Ltd., 1982); and Tervo Doi, *The Intellectual Property Law of Japan* (Alphen aan den Rijn, Germantown, Nd.: Sijthoff and Noordhoff, 1980).

# EXHIBITS: The IBM–Fujitsu Dispute

**EXHIBIT 1**
IBM: SELECTED FINANCIAL DATA
Five-Year Comparison* (in millions of dollars)

|  | 1988 | 1987 | 1986 | 1985 | 1984 |
|---|---|---|---|---|---|
| **For the year** | | | | | |
| Revenue | 59,681 | 55,256 | 52,160 | 50,718 | 46,309 |
| Net earnings | 5,806 | 5,258 | 4,789 | 6,555 | 6,582 |
| Investment in plant, rental machines, and other property | 5,431 | 4,312 | 4,644 | 6,434 | 5,507 |
| Return on stockholders' equity | 14.9% | 14.5% | 14.4% | 22.4% | 26.5% |
| **At end of year** | | | | | |
| Total assets | 73,037 | 70,029 | 63,020 | 56,983 | 44,989 |
| Net investment in plant, rental machines, and other property | 23,426 | 22,967 | 21,310 | 19,713 | 16,396 |
| Long-term debt | 8,518 | 7,108 | 6,923 | 6,368 | 4,232 |
| Stockholders' equity | 39,509 | 38,263 | 34,374 | 31,990 | 26,489 |

Lines of Business Revenue (in millions of dollars)

|  | 1988 | 1987 |
|---|---|---|
| Sales | $39,959 | $36,424 |
| Support services | 9,285 | 9,297 |
| Software | 7,927 | 6,836 |
| Rentals and financing | 2,510 | 2,699 |

Number of employees, 12/31/88: 387,112

*IBM financial statement, *Annual Report,* 1989, p. 43. *Moody's Industrial Manual,* 1989, p. 463.

**EXHIBIT 2**
FUJITSU: SELECTED FINANCIAL DATA
Five-Year Comparison* (in millions of U.S. dollars)

|  | 1988 | 1987 | 1986 | 1985 | 1984 |
|---|---|---|---|---|---|
| **For the year** | | | | | |
| Net sales | 16,374.4 | 12,256.3 | 9,399.0 | 6,174.9 | 5,401.2 |
| Net income | 336.9 | 148.0 | 216.3 | 351.9 | 297.6 |
| Return on stockholders' equity† | 6.2% | 3.4% | 6.4% | 20.5% | 19.0% |
| **At end of year** | | | | | |
| Total assets | 18,532.8 | 13,686.2 | 10,398.5 | 6,801.0 | 5,699.3 |
| Net investment in plant, rental machines, and other property | 4,735.4 | 3,741.3 | 3,078.2 | 1,996.2 | 1,466.5 |
| Long-term debt | 2,412.9 | 2,312.7 | 1,978.1 | 998.0 | 914.8 |
| Common equity | 6,616.2 | 4,660.3 | 3,535.2 | 2,405.0 | 1,934.8 |

Net Sales by Main Product Category* (in millions of U.S. dollars)

|  | 1988 | 1987 | 1986 | 1985 | 1984 |
|---|---|---|---|---|---|
| Computers and data processing systems | 10,976.1 | 8,291.9 | 6,202.8 | 3,711.3 | 3,247.2 |
| Communications systems | 2,598.2 | 1,851.2 | 1,412.0 | 833.2 | 830.7 |
| Electronic devices (semiconductors and electronic components) | 2,048.8 | 1,520.6 | 1,253.2 | 1,288.7 | 972.5 |
| Total other | 751.3 | 592.6 | 531.1 | 341.7 | 350.8 |
| Car audio (and car electronics) | 496.6 | 387.9 | 366.1 | 231.3 | 241.2 |
| Others | 254.7 | 204.7 | 165.0 | 110.4 | 109.6 |

*All financial data are from Fujitsu's annual reports for current year. The exchange rate used in Fujitsu conversion from yen to dollars in current year ranged from ¥125 = US$1 in 1988 to ¥253 = US$1 in 1985 and ¥224 = US$1 in 1984.
†Each year's return on equity is from *Worldscope® Industries Company Profiles*, 1989.

# The Interfaith Center on Corporate Responsibility and the Debate over South African Disinvestment[1]

*We, the following Protestant denominations, Roman Catholic orders, religious organizations, and institutions, working through the Interfaith Center on Corporate Responsibility, have now entered a new phase in our effort to break the bonds of economic oppression that make United States corporations partners in apartheid, the abhorrent policy of racial oppression by the Government of South Africa.*

With these words, the representatives of fifty-four Christian organizations and churches announced at a press conference in New York City on May 20, 1985, a new campaign directed at twelve American firms which allegedly supported the South African government "through products and services used by the police and military, by the size of their assets in the country, by their sales and number of employees, and by the strategic nature of their involvement or financial services rendered." The church organizations demanded that the corporations inform the government of South Africa that it must take specific actions as necessary precon-ditions for the firms' remaining in that country. Those actions included abandoning officially the "homelands policy," ending the various apartheid laws such as influx control and the Group Areas Act, restoring full political rights, and releasing unconditionally all political prisoners. (For the complete text of and signatories to the statement, see Exhibit 1.)

The twelve corporations were Burroughs, Chevron, Citicorp, Control Data, Fluor, Ford, General Electric, General Motors, IBM, Mobil, Newmont Mining, and Texaco.

## HISTORY OF ICCR

*The churches have been involved from the early 1970s in raising questions with companies about their involvement in South Africa. Some of these compa-*

[1]"Disinvestment" generally refers to the withdrawal of U.S. firms from the South African economy, and "divestment" refers to the sale of stocks in businesses which operate in South Africa; some use the terms interchangeably.

*nies we have talked to since the beginning—Mobil,*
*Citibank, and General Motors, for example. The ex-*
*pansion of the campaign is a logical extension of the*
*work we have been doing for fifteen years and can be*
*seen as a mirror of the expanded concern and debate*
*that is occurring in this country.*

—Timothy Smith

Sitting in his unair-conditioned office on
the fifth floor of the New York headquarters of
the National Council of Churches—a square,
modern building known as the "God Box"—
Tim Smith did not look or sound like a man
who had been challenging the largest corporations in the world for more than a decade.
Smith, 43, had a rounded face and curly black
hair streaked with gray; his voice was consistently soft-spoken and friendly. His words,
however, revealed both his exhaustive familiarity with the history of church-corporate relations and his deep determination.

> We have put a very specific request before the
> companies. We're giving them time to answer,
> and we are seeking a meeting between the chief
> executives and top-level church representatives
> to discuss the issue. If the companies will not
> stop sales to the government or state that as a
> precondition for staying in South Africa apart-
> heid must be dismantled, then the churches will
> move to a full-fledged campaign to achieve their
> goal.

The Christian Church's involvement in
economic issues can be traced back to the time
of Jesus of Nazareth, whose egalitarian pro-
nouncements and critical statements on wealth
("You cannot serve both God and Mammon,"
Matthew 6:24) have inspired and troubled generations of his followers. Since the early centuries of the church, Christians have been involved in social justice issues which often
brought them in conflict with political and economic power. In 1833, for example, British
evangelical Christians such as William Wilber-
force opposed commercial interests and successfully persuaded Parliament to ban the slave
trade.

In the past century, as corporations grew
and spread across national boundaries,

churches—themselves multinational in scope
and membership—became increasingly vocal
about economic issues. In 1954, the General
Board of the National Council of the Churches
of Christ in the United States, an ecumenical
organization made up of Protestant, Orthodox,
and Episcopal churches, announced that
"Christians should be guided by their ethic to
seek such adjustments of economic institutions
as will serve most fully the three positive values
of justice and order and freedom."[2] According
to a report put out by the Washington-based Investor Responsibility Research Center, "In
1963 the United Presbyterian Church linked investment policies with the church's policy on
equal employment opportunity; four years later
the Episcopal Church called attention to the
'moral dilemma' presented by investments in
South Africa and called upon church officials to
'exercise responsible stewardship over the
funds entrusted to their care.'"

Because of a rising interest in corporate responsibility generated simultaneously by national opposition to the Vietnam War, criticism
of apartheid in South Africa, concern for domestic civil rights, and increased consumer activism, the National Council of Churches established the Corporate Information Center in
1969 to collect information on the social aspect
of business activities. Several denominations
set up "Committees on Social Criteria in Investments" and adopted statements such as
the following from the United Presbyterian
Church:

> Church investment policy involves not only
> sound economic, but theological consider-
> ations. Its central goal should match effective
> investment management with imaginative and
> efficient allocation of resources to programs that
> contribute positively to a Christian concept of
> humanity's spiritual and material well-being.[3]

In the spring of 1971, six major Protestant
denominations decided to pool their efforts and

[2]For a short history of church involvement in shareholder
resolutions, see Lauren Talner, *The Origins of Shareholder
Activism* (Washington, D.C.: Investor Responsibility Research Center, 1983).
[3]Ibid., p. 30.

form the Interfaith Committee on Social Responsibility in Investments. Within a few years, this was combined with the Corporate Information Center to form the Interfaith Center on Corporate Responsibility. Timothy Smith was hired as project director in 1972 and executive director in 1976.

## CURRENT STRUCTURE AND EFFORTS

According to its fiscal 1984 annual report, the Interfaith Center exists to

> . . . assist its member boards, agencies and instrumentalities (composed of thirteen Protestant denominations, two ecumenical organizations, and over two hundred Roman Catholic groups) to express social responsibility with their investments. Members of ICCR agree that as investors in companies they are also part owners with the right and obligation to monitor the social responsibility of corporations, and act where necessary to prevent or correct corporate policies or practices causing social injury.

As a clearinghouse for information and a coordinator of church investment efforts, ICCR was involved in a wide range of social issues. In 1984–85 the group created an alternative investment clearinghouse, coordinated the filing of dozens of shareholder resolutions on issues ranging from plant closings and nuclear weapons construction to equal employment opportunity, brought the seven-year-old international boycott of Nestlé products to a successful conclusion, drew attention to the burden on the world's poor created by the international debt crisis, and initiated the "intensive focus campaign" on companies that were doing business in South Africa.

Even though its budget for 1984 and 1985 hovered at less than $500,000 (see Exhibits 2 and 3 for membership and financial statements), ICCR could accomplish such extensive and diverse activities because it coordinated the substantial resources of the member denominations, many of whom had offices in the same building as ICCR. For example, the leaders and bishops of the United Methodist Church could theoretically disseminate ICCR

material through local churches to all 9,500,000 United States members of the denomination. Member churches also had extensive international contacts with whom multinational activities could be exchanged. The total investment funds of member churches—from operating budgets, retirement and pension funds, trusts and other investments—which could be used to vote for shareholder resolutions or to support a divestment campaign, totaled more than $12 billion.

## APARTHEID IN SOUTH AFRICA

The origins of apartheid can be traced to the early history of the country, which was originally colonized by Dutch, German, and French Huguenot settlers and then seized by the British in 1795. The British denied many political rights to the non-English-speaking "Afrikaners" who migrated in 1836 to the interior of South Africa on what became known as the "Great Trek." Isolated from contact with Europe, fighting with the nomadic black natives who also lived in the area, the Afrikaners (also known as Boers) developed the trait of fierce and narrow-minded independence for which they are still famous. Such traits were strengthened by their religious convictions. In 1838, for example, on the evening before a battle with the Zulu tribe, a group of Afrikaners promised God that they would make the day a Sabbath if they survived. The next day the Afrikaners successfully resisted attacks by 15,000 Zulu warriors, and the anniversary of that event is still celebrated as the Day of the Covenant on December 16.[4]

After the Anglo-Boer War of 1899–1902, the British asserted final control and in 1910

---

[4]Material on the origins of apartheid and U.S. corporate involvement in South Africa was drawn from Desaix Myers, *U.S. Business in South Africa* (Bloomington: Indiana University Press, 1980); publications of the Investor Responsibility Research Center, Washington, D.C.; *United States Private Investment in South Africa,* Hearings before the U.S. House of Representatives Subcommittee on Africa (1978); J. Matthews, K. Goodpaster, and L. Nash, *Policies and Persons* (New York: McGraw-Hill, 1985); and published press accounts in *Business Week,* the *New York Times, Wall Street Journal,* and *Boston Globe.*

the previously separate Afrikaner and English-speaking states were combined to establish the Union of South Africa. The Afrikaners maintained their cultural independence and language and attempted to gain political control of the nation. They succeeded in 1948 when the Nationalist Party came to power.

A cornerstone of the Nationalist ideology and program was "apartheid"—an Afrikaner word meaning "separateness." Over thirty years, more than 200 pieces of legislation were enacted to erect barriers between racial groups such as whites, blacks, and so-called coloreds (South Africans of mixed race, Indian, or Asian ancestry). The three principal components of apartheid were:

1. *Petty apartheid:* This refers to the practice, as in the American South prior to the civil rights movement, of requiring different races to use different bathrooms, transportation, beaches, restaurants, and theaters. Other apartheid laws also prohibited intermarriage between races, although President P. W. Botha relaxed this ban in 1985 and amended others as evidence of reform.
2. *Homelands policy:* The South African government believed that because integration of the heterogeneous population of 30 million was not possible, the country should be divided into separate "states"—ten African, and one white. To this end, the white government set aside ten reservations or "bantustans" to serve as tribal homelands for South African blacks. The homelands, which comprise 13% of the area of South Africa and include some of its most arid territory, are completely surrounded by the white republic, and are expected to support 24.9 million blacks who represent 70% of the population.

   Because the South African economy depended on the availability of black labor, some blacks were permitted to live near urban areas though they were often separated from their families who had to remain in the arid homelands. Under the Group Areas Act, blacks were required to live in special zones or townships which had minimal medical, educational, or recreational facilities. Soweto, for example, was a township outside of Johannesburg with a population of approximately 1.5 million.
3. *Influx control:* To control the movement of black labor between the rural and urban communities, the South African government instituted the "pass laws" which required blacks over the age of 16 to carry passbooks at all times. Blacks were also not permitted to remain in white areas without a special permit. In the mid-1970s, an average of more than 1,000 blacks a day were arrested for pass law violations.*

## U.S. CORPORATE ACTIVITY IN SOUTH AFRICA

U.S. corporate involvement in the Republic of South Africa began shortly after World War II when South Africa began a major industrial expansion effort. Aggregate U.S. private investment grew from $286 million in 1960 to $964 million by 1970, $1.99 billion by 1978, and $2.75 billion by 1985. Fifty-five of the *Fortune* top 100 companies had subsidiaries in South Africa, and six thousand more did business indirectly through sales agents and distributors.

Within the South African economy, the U.S. firms provided 14.4% of total foreign direct private investment which constituted in turn 24% of all private investment in South Africa. American companies controlled about 40% of the petroleum market, 23% of auto sales, and 65% of computer sales. Out of a labor force of eight million, American firms employed approximately 100,000 people of whom 70,000 were black (about 1% of the black labor pool).

## THE SULLIVAN PRINCIPLES

In 1970, the Rev. Leon Sullivan, a black pastor from the Zion Baptist Church in Philadelphia, was appointed to the board of directors of Gen-

*Since the writing of this case, the "pass laws" have been repealed.

eral Motors. He attracted national attention when at his first annual meeting in January 1971 he voted for a shareholder resolution that called on General Motors to withdraw from South Africa.

According to Sullivan's testimony before Congress in 1978:

> In the summer of 1975 I made a trip to Central and Southern Africa. Over and over again I was asked to see what I could do to make American businesses truly a positive force for change in that country.

In January 1976, Sullivan, together with Thomas K. Murphy (CEO of GM) and Frank Cary (CEO of IBM), met with leaders from fifteen U.S. corporations to discuss how they could become constructive agents for change in South Africa. The participants decided that the most effective tactic would be to draft a statement of principles governing corporate conduct and then get as many corporations as possible to sign. On May 1, 1977, Sullivan released a statement of six principles to which twelve of the companies had agreed. These principles covered such areas as nonsegregation of all facilities, equal pay for equal work, equal employment practices, initiation of training programs for nonwhites in managerial positions and improved quality of life for employees outside of work in areas such as housing, education, and health. By May 1985, over 150 companies had signed the principles; compliance was monitored and rated by Arthur D. Little, a Boston-based management consulting firm.

## GROWING DISSATISFACTION IN THE UNITED STATES

In the year preceding ICCR's press conference, a number of events had contributed to a sense of growing urgency and crisis over the South African issue. These included:

1   The selection of Anglican Archbishop Desmond Tutu as the recipient of the 1984 Nobel Peace Prize.

2   A sharply renewed interest in divestment on college campuses, including demonstrations and sit-ins at Columbia, the University of Michigan, and many others.

3   The partially successful attempt to pressure institutional investors, universities and state and municipal pension funds to sell off their South African stocks. For example, the New York City Council voted to purge its $8-billion-dollar pension fund of such holdings. State legislators in Michigan, Massachusetts, New Jersey, and elsewhere also ordered their pension and other state funds to divest.

4   A congressional loss of patience with the Reagan Administration's assurances that the policy of "constructive engagement" (in which the South African government was privately encouraged to make improvements) would lead to substantive reform.

5   The daily picketing of the South African embassy, including the arrest of 23 members of the U.S. House of Representatives.

6   Sustained outbreaks of violence between blacks and police in South Africa that led to the death of more than 500 blacks over a nine-month period.

7   Increased public appeals for assistance from South Africans, particularly from members of South Africa's Council of Churches. (See Exhibits 4 and 5.)

In response to criticism of their activities in South Africa, many companies pointed to their adherence to the Sullivan Principles as proof of their good faith and intentions. However, on May 7, 1985, in an article in the *Philadelphia Inquirer,* Leon Sullivan called on companies to take steps very similar to those recommended by ICCR:

> There must be a moratorium on all American economic expansion in South Africa until apartheid is ended officially. A timetable is needed for conclusive action in South Africa. Lives are being lost daily and the nation is on the threshold of a revolution. If apartheid is not

legally and actually ended within twenty-four months, there should be a total U.S. economic embargo against South Africa, including the withdrawal of all U.S. companies.

## ICCR's NEW CAMPAIGN

In an interview in July 1985, Timothy Smith described the origins of the most recent campaign:

> We believe that U.S. business is unable to be the force for change it desires to be in South Africa, because the South African government has no desire to share political and economic power with the black majority. Despite the earnest appeals of many U.S. business leaders, the Botha government has maintained white supremacy and only allowed minimal reforms. In addition, many American companies provide products—whether it be petroleum from Mobil or Texaco or computers from IBM—that help the South African government maintain apartheid. We agree with Dr. Sullivan that there must be a tough timeline; the South African government must know that if apartheid is not dismantled, U.S. business will withdraw.
>
> A number of factors contributed to our decision to focus on these twelve companies. We wanted to exercise significant pressure on specific companies. The idea of focusing on twelve came from a number of churches who said that they planned to look at specific companies who played a strategic role in South Africa as they implemented their divestment programs.
>
> The fifty-five church bodies who made the announcement each made the decision individually. They had to say, "Yes, we are willing to join this campaign and we are willing to do it ecumenically." The plan that brought the fifty-five church groups together was worked out at one of ICCR's meetings that dealt with South Africa. That meeting established a steering committee that prepared an implementation plan for action by the church.

When asked from where the churches derived the authority and right to question the activities of major corporations, Smith pointed to three factors: first, the religious authority drawn from Christian scripture to speak out on issues of human justice; second, the legal authority derived from the status of churches as shareholders, and thus part owners of the major corporations; and third, the representative authority granted by (in most instances) democratically elected representatives of local churches who expressed their opinions in annual conference and diocesan meetings, and who had given their support to ICCR's effort. Moreover, Smith commented:

> . . . with regard to South Africa, the church is particularly important, because South Africa defines itself as part of the white, Christian, anti-Communist West, and uses Christian beliefs to legitimize apartheid. The churches here thus feel a very special obligation to challenge that as blasphemy.

Smith and the steering committee of the campaign saw the May 20 press conference as a first step which would be followed by meetings with senior executives of some of the companies. If companies refused to respond to the church request, the members of the coalition would select additional steps. Their options included filing shareholder resolutions, holding additional press conferences to bring media pressure, organizing consumer boycotts, holding demonstrations and distributing materials outside company headquarters or regional offices, and divesting their shares. As Smith pointed out, such actions might not be limited to the United States:

> The South African Council of Churches has just passed a resolution calling for disinvestment from South Africa, which is a very brave thing to do, since they may have broken several laws by doing so. . . . Whereas a couple of years ago we were getting quiet signals from South African church leaders to go ahead on these issues, now it's a ringing call. It's done on CBS News every night and it's done in phone calls and in visits and letters. Bishop Tutu said, "For God's sake, please exert as much pressure as you can on South Africa to prevent a racial bloodbath."

One of the hopes I would entertain is that some of the pressures are going to come from South Africa. Three or four months ago there was a sit-in at Citibank in South Africa. The names of these companies are known in South Africa as some of the chief supporters of apartheid.

In discussing the strategy of the campaign, Smith noted that in the past, churches and corporations had sometimes become entrenched in their positions, and had found it almost impossible to negotiate a settlement. This was no longer the case, he suggested, because their extensive negotiating experience had taught the members of ICCR to look for mutually beneficial solutions.

There is always the concern on the part of the company to avoid being perceived as caving in to pressure. The churches are sophisticated enough that if a company does respond to our requests, we do not have to wave flags and shout, "We won! We won!" We know how to make those situations "win-win" just as the companies do.

If a company said, "We are concerned about giving into pressure, but we think your idea is a good one," I would be more than willing to say they invented the idea. They could tell us they made the decision six months ago and just happened to tell us now. Our goal is to get companies to be responsive to what we think is a reasonable request to put pressure on South Africa.

ICCR's position on specific companies was detailed in information sheets which were distributed at the press conference; the IBM sheet is reproduced as Exhibit 6.

Over the summer, ICCR began receiving letters from the companies in response to their campaign (letters from Mobil and IBM are in Exhibit 7). Meanwhile, in South Africa, the crisis seemed to be accelerating in speed and intensity (a selected chronology of events between July 20 and August 15 can be found in Exhibit 8).

## CASE IN POINT: IBM IN SOUTH AFRICA

*The debate over whether American companies should do business in South Africa has taken on new urgency. This is fueled by South Africa's continued resistance to all but the most limited reforms of apartheid and the continued suffering of blacks and other nonwhites. Some individuals say American firms there must now oppose apartheid more directly and publicly; others are pressuring them to withdraw fully. As a result, IBM has again reexamined its practice of doing business in South Africa. We have concluded we should remain there.*

> —John F. Akers
> President and CEO of IBM,
> writing on the Op Ed page of
> *The New York Times,* March
> 1985

International Business Machines first began business in South Africa in 1952 and by December 31, 1984, had 1,914 employees there. Though IBM had repeatedly refused to make information on its total sales and assets public, company statements suggested that "revenues from the South African affiliate are less that 1% of IBM's total annual gross revenues," which, in 1984, were $45.9 billion dollars.

According to industry observers, however, IBM played a prominent role in the South African computer industry.[5] It sold a product line comparable to that in the United States; that is, everything from typewriters to its largest mainframe, the 3084. In 1983, the company expanded its line by introducing the personal computer which, according to the December 16, 1983, *Financial Mail,* almost instantly captured 20% of the market and threatened to dominate.

The South African economy and system of apartheid depended on the use of computers to coordinate its pass law and military and security data. Under the Carter Administration,

[5]Information for this section of the case was drawn from IBM publications such as "IBM Operations in South Africa" (1983, 1984, 1985); from reports issued by the Investor Responsibility Research Center; and from articles in the national press.

trade restrictions were imposed that prohibited the export of all U.S. goods, including computers, to the South African police and military. These restrictions were relaxed by President Reagan in his first term to bar only equipment which would contribute "significantly" to police and military functions. Products such as word processors, personal computers, hand-held calculators, and copying machines were considered legitimate for export.

In its public document on "IBM in South Africa," issued in 1983 and again in 1984, IBM stated:

> Government accounts yield a small portion of IBM's revenues in South Africa. IBM computer applications, in both public and private sectors of South Africa, are those usually found in commerce elsewhere.
>
> It is IBM's policy not to bid for business where it believes its equipment would be used to abridge human rights for repressive purposes. We know of no case where it is so used. However, it would be misleading to suggest that any manufacturer can control how its products are used. To our knowledge, no IBM equipment or people are involved in the issuance and monitoring of the passbooks that South African blacks are required by law to possess.

## IBM EMPLOYMENT PRACTICES

In 1977 IBM became one of the first signatories of the Sullivan Principles and had been consistently rated by Arthur D. Little as "making good progress," the top category.

A 1984 article in IBM's corporate magazine *Think* stated that "IBM South Africa spends nearly three times as much of its yearly gross earnings on corporate responsibility as the company's worldwide average." This is because

> ... the business community [in South Africa] largely agrees on an imperative that cuts across racial, political, and economic ground: in the longer term, the economy's success, if not its survival, is possible only with better training and education of blacks along with improved

living conditions and their equal treatment as employees.

It is this hard economic fact, more than altruism, that prompts so many influential business and civic leaders of all colors to support peaceable attempts at broadening the sharing of material and political privilege.

Accordingly, IBM affirmed a strong commitment to equal employment practices. Though they would not provide wage information, they stated that they paid significantly more than 30% above the minimum living level (MLL) for an African family of six (the 30% standard had been required of all Sullivan signatories). In 1983, the MLL for an African family of six was 312 rand per month, or approximately $265 at 1983 exchange rates.

IBM maintained a formal job classification procedure and a single wage curve to assure equal pay for equal work. It also continued to increase its black and nonwhite work force percentages (see Exhibit 9).

## EFFORTS TO IMPROVE EDUCATION

"Because IBM's operations in South Africa are largely concentrated in sales and technical service," stated a company document in 1984, "many of the jobs require high-level technical skills." Faced with the limited number of university-educated blacks (less than .05% of a black population of 20 million), IBM had chosen to invest in educational programs. These included:

- A $2.7 million program to videotape lessons in mathematics, physical science, and biology for use in black high schools.
- The construction of a library for the Funda educational and cultural center in the black township of Soweto at a cost of R1.2 million.
- A contribution of R325,000 to the PACE commercial high school in Soweto.
- A gift of books to libraries in ten black schools in Soweto, Durban, and Port Elizabeth; and typewriters to a secretarial school near Durban.

In April of 1985 IBM announced a five-year program to "enhance reading and writing skills among South African children." The company planned to provide 250 South African schools with computer-assisted education programs that would reach 37,000 elementary school children each year. In a statement released at the time, John Akers said, "We believe one of the most important things we can do to promote change in South Africa is to advance the educational development of black South Africans. We believe this program can help accelerate the process of peaceful and meaningful change."

Writing in *The New York Times,* Akers summed up his company's arguments for opposing divestment:

> For some critics, the conduct of American companies in South Africa is not the issue. They argue that only a small percentage of nonwhites have jobs with American firms, and that whatever benefits they receive cannot outweigh the need to take a symbolic stand against racism by withdrawing completely.
>
> I believe that people who hold this view tend to overestimate the economic and political impact such action would have on the government. Moreover, they often underestimate how economic activity can generate social change. Business people are not social reformers in disguise; but economic activity does have profound social effects, direct and indirect, that enhance the climate for change. . . .
>
> IBM could depart with very little financial sacrifice. IBM South Africa generates less than one percent of IBM's worldwide revenues. But we believe the right thing to do is to remain and to redouble our efforts to advance social equality. IBM urges other companies to do the same—many already are. Pressure on apartheid will be increased by more corporate involvement, not less. . . .
>
> Corporations have a choice. We can view South Africa as a tragedy, wash our hands of it, and wait for the explosion that may or may not come. Or we can do business in ways that provide a model for a society in which black, white, Asian, and colored might someday enjoy peace and freedom. It may be an impossible dream. But I'm not ready to give up on it.

## THE MAY 20 PRESS CONFERENCE: STATEMENTS BY ICCR MEMBERS

At the press conference on May 20, various church leaders read statements in support of the new campaign. Randolph Nugent, general secretary of the General Board of Global Ministries of the United Methodist Church, said:

> The United Methodist Church has been actively involved in opposition to apartheid for over twenty-five years. . . . In the early 1970s, our church participated with others in both persuasion and pressure, conversing with top management and participating in the first round of church-sponsored shareholder resolutions. For a time we hoped that the actions by U.S. companies in lessening racial discrimination in the workplace would spill over in South African society and assist in a transition toward full rights of all races. Unfortunately, while U.S. investments grew in the 1970s and 1980s, the basic system of apartheid remained firmly in place. U.S. corporations flourished and built a partnership with the South African government.
>
> Many of these companies will immediately defend their record by pointing to their reforms in the plant under the Sullivan Principles. That is increasingly an argument of convenience.

Audrey Smock, chairperson of the Interfaith Center on Corporate Responsibility, said:

> It is true that many of these twelve corporations have admirable workplace conditions and have made worthwhile educational and charitable contributions in South Africa. Such measures, however, cannot compensate for the major structural support and assistance these corporations either inadvertently or advertently have rendered to the apartheid system.
>
> Time is running out on the more gradualist strategies which the religiously based corporate social responsibility movement has employed during the past fifteen years. More and more, time and time again, we are hearing the voice of South African church leaders with whom we are in partnership telling us that massive economic pressure is the only nonviolent strategy remaining which may avert the bloodbath into which South Africa is degenerating.

# EXHIBITS: The Interfaith Center on Corporate Responsibility and the Debate over South African Disinvestment

### EXHIBIT 1
ICCR PRESS RELEASE

---

*Office of Communication*
*United Church of Christ*
*105 Madison Avenue*
*New York, NY 10016*
*(212) 683-5656*
*William C. Winslow, Press Contact*

### STATEMENT ON AMERICAN CORPORATIONS
### WHICH ARE KEY TO APARTHEID

We, the following Protestant denominations, Roman Catholic orders, religious organizations and institutions, working through the Interfaith Center on Corporate Responsibility, have now entered a new phase in our effort to break the bonds of economic oppression that make United States corporations partners in apartheid, the abhorrent policy of racial oppression by the Government of South Africa.

We believe that conditions in South Africa, marked by increased violence against blacks demanding their basic rights, require a new strategic approach toward U.S. corporations whose presence in South Africa undergirds the South African Government's ability to enforce its policy. We have chosen to concentrate on the following 12 corporations with which we have a history of interaction, because they are key investors in apartheid. All support the South African Government through products and services used by the police and military, by the size of their assets in the country, by their sales and number of employees, and by the strategic nature of their involvement or financial services rendered.

The companies are: Burroughs, Chevron, Citicorp, Control Data, Fluor, Ford, General Electric, General Motors, International Business Machines, Mobil, Newmont Mining, and Texaco.

Our new strategic approach will focus special attention on these companies by:

1 Calling upon them to cease immediately all sales and service relationships with the South African Government and government-owned corporations.
2 Demanding that they make clear to the South African Government that the following changes in government policies are a necessary precondition for their remaining in South Africa:
   a. Abandon officially the "homelands" policy.
   b. End the various apartheid laws, such as influx control and the Group Areas Act.
   c. Restore full political rights—such as freedom of speech, freedom of assembly and voting—to all peoples.
   d. Cease forced removals and population relocations.
   e. Guarantee the right of all people to own land.
   f. Release, unconditionally, all political prisoners, detainees, and those charged with treason.
   g. End the banning of organizations and individuals.
   h. Increase public funding of education, health care, social services, etc., for the black majority.

We believe that if there has not been significant progress toward achievement of these goals by the end of 1986, these corporations' continued presence in South Africa cannot be justified.

Additional aspects and goals of this new approach will be elaborated in the future.

To affect the targeted corporations' policies, we will press forward with a coordinated campaign utilizing a variety of our traditional approaches such as shareholder resolutions and meetings with corporate leaderships. In addition, we are prepared to take new steps—such as more extensive acts of public witness, calls for the firms' withdrawal from South Africa, launching of selective buying campaigns, and divestment of their securities—if these companies fail to respond.

Besides these 12 corporations, we will conduct an ongoing review and evaluation of other firms involved in South Africa which may be subject to special attention in the future. When they have been identified, we will issue a new list.

We have agreed that our goal is not to encourage U.S. corporations to ameliorate the efforts of apartheid, but to play their part in dismantling that system. We are committed to an ecumenical effort to break up such economic patterns of support, and will continue until apartheid is ended.

May 20, 1985

### Signatories to the ICCR Press Release

Adrian Dominican Sisters
African Methodist Episcopal Church
American Central Province of the Xaverian Brothers, Inc.
Brothers of the Christian Schools of the St. Louis Province, Corporate Responsibility Committee
Christian Church (Disciples of Christ)
Christian Methodist Episcopal Church
Church Women United, Inc.
Committee on Social Responsibility in Investments of the Episcopal Church
Commission for Racial Justice, United Church of Christ
Dominican Sisters (Sparkill, NY)
Franciscan Sisters of Allegany, Inc.
General Board of Church and Society, United Methodist Church
General Board of Global Ministries, United Methodist Church
Grey Nuns of the Sacred Heart
Holy Name Province, Franciscans, Corporate Responsibility Committee
Justice and Peace Office, Maryknoll Fathers and Brothers
Leadership of Missionary Oblates of Mary Emaculate, Southern U.S. Province
Marianist Office of Justice and Peace
Missionary Servants of the Most Blessed Trinity
Missionary Servants of the Most Holy Trinity
National Baptist Convention, U.S.A., Inc.
National Council of Churches of Christ in the U.S.A.
Priests of the Holy Cross, Southern Providence
Presbyterian Church (U.S.A.)
National Ministries, American Baptist Churches, U.S.A.
National Office of the Jesuit Social Ministries
New York Conference, Board of Trustees, United Methodist Church
Sisters of the Blessed Sacrament
Reformed Church in America
Religious of the Sacred Heart of Mary
Roman Catholic Archdiocese of Milwaukee

Sisters of Mercy of Rochester Council
School Sisters of Notre Dame of St. Louis
Sisters of Charity of Cincinnati
Sisters of Charity of Halifax, Nova Scotia
Sisters of Charity of Mount St. Vincent, NY
Sisters of Charity of New Jersey, Ethics in Investment Committee
Sisters of Divine Province
Sisters of Notre Dame de Namur
Sisters of St. Francis of Holy Name Province
Sisters of St. Francis of Philadelphia
Sisters of St. Joseph of Brentwood, NY
Sisters of St. Joseph of Buffalo, NY
Sisters of St. Ursula of the Blessed Virgin Mary of NY
Society of Saint Suplice (The Suplicans)
Spiritans of Western Province
The Central Administration of the Sisters of St. Joseph of Rochester, NY
The Ministers and Missionaries Benefit Board of the American Baptist Churches, U.S.A.
The General Council of the Sisters of St. Dominic
Unitarian Universalist Association
Unitarian Universalist Service Committee
United Church Board for World Ministries, United Church of Christ
Ursuline Sisters of Tildonk

**EXHIBIT 2**
ICCR ANNUAL REPORT—1984
ICCR Income and Expenditures, Fund Balances and Reserves—December 31, 1984

| Income | | Expenditures | |
|---|---|---|---|
| Members | $182,560 | Salaries & related costs | $301,141 |
| Special church giving | 30,300 | Rent | 41,405 |
| Foundations | 27,000 | Equipment | 5,699 |
| Individuals/others | 11,703 | Supplies | 4,187 |
| Sales | 7,819 | Telephone and telegraph | 18,644 |
| Subscriptions | 13,227 | Postage | 11,750 |
| Subscriber service | 24,352 | Duplication | 16,293 |
| Meeting registration | 7,176 | Publications | 18,425 |
| Honoraria | 1,053 | Travel | 14,252 |
| Reimbursements | 11,500 | Meetings | 7,805 |
| Earnings on reserves | 736 | Miscellaneous | 158 |
| Designated income | 157,973 | Consultants | 6,297 |
| Total Income | $475,399 | Literature | 1,390 |
| | | Research | 7,483 |
| TOTAL Income | $475,399 | Legal fees | 8,390 |
| TOTAL Expenditures | 491,859 | Common services | 28,540 |
| Balance 1984 | ($16,460) | Total Expenditures | $491,859 |
| | | | |
| Cash on hand 1/1/84 | $ 20,848 | Available funds 1984 | $496,247 |
| Income 1984 | 475,399 | Expenditures 1984 | 491,859 |
| Available funds 1984 | $496,247 | Cash on hand 12/31/84 | $ 4,388 |
| | | | |
| ICCR fund balances: | | ICCR reserves: | |
| Advance contributions 1985 | ($59,833) | Salary contingency | |
| Cash on hand 12/31/85 | 4,388 | (invested) | $ 8,342 |
| ICCR fund balance 1/1/85 | ($55,445) | | |

**EXHIBIT 3**
ANNUAL REPORT 1984–1985

## GOVERNING BOARD OFFICERS

Any religious denomination or organization can become a member of ICCR by contributing a minimum of $1,500. Each ICCR member agency may name up to four representatives to the ICCR governing board. The officers of the board, serving one-year terms beginning June 1984, were:

- *Chairperson:* Dr. Audrey Smock, world issues secretary, United Church Board for World Ministries, United Church of Christ.
- *Vice chairperson:* Vernon S. Broyles, director, Office of Corporate Witness in Public Affairs, Division of Corporate and Social Mission, General Assembly Mission Board, Presbyterian Church, U.S.A.
- *Treasurer:* Sr. Barbara Aires, SC, assistant provincial, Sisters of Charity of St. Elizabeth of New Jersey.

In addition to its formal members, ICCR provides information on corporate responsibility, proxy resolutions, and church advocacy to over one hundred major institutional investors. ICCR also reaches out to and works with nonprofit institutions such as universities on specific issues and campaigns.

## Staff

Full-time staff as of June 30, 1984, included twelve persons: nine women (four of whom are minorities) and three men: Timothy H. Smith, executive director; Valerie Heinonen, RU, program associate; Dara Gardner Demmings, program associate; Diane Bratcher, manager of publications and budget; Keith Rolland, program associate; Carol Somplatsky-Jarman, program associate; Phyllis Gabriel, program associate, made up the program staff. Marcia Grange, administrative clerk; Evelyn Rodriguez, secretary; Maureen Dwyer, secretary; Patricia Burkett, secretary; and Sarah Saavedra, part-time circulation manager, made up the administrative staff. Herb Gunn was a full-time program intern. ICCR is an equal opportunity employer whose employees are members of the Staff Association of the National Council of Churches of Christ in the United States, an independent employees' union.

## Membership (January 1, 1984 through December 31, 1984)

The American Baptist Home Mission Society
American Friends Service Committee
American Lutheran Church
Archdiocese of Milwaukee
Atonement Friars
Catholic Foreign Mission Society of America
Church of the Brethren General Board
Church of the Brethren Pension Board
Church Women United in the U.S.A., Inc.
Conference on Corporate Responsibility of Indiana-Michigan
The Domestic and Foreign Missionary Society of the Protestant Episcopal Church in the United States of America
The Episcopal Church Publishing Company
Illinois Committee for Responsible Investment
Iowa Coalition for Responsible Investment

Lutheran Church in America
Marianist Society, Inc.
Mid-Atlantic Coalition for Responsible Investment
Midwest Coalition for Responsible Investment
National Office of Jesuit Social Ministries
New England Coalition for Responsible Investment
Philadelphia Area Coalition for Responsible Investment
Presbyterian Church (U.S.A.), General Assembly Mission Board
Presbyterian Church (U.S.A.), Program Agency
Reformed Church in America
Region VI Coalition for Responsible Investment
Sisters of Charity of St. Elizabeth of New Jersey
Sisters of Charity of St. Vincent de Paul of Halifax, Nova Scotia
Sisters of Charity of St. Vincent de Paul of N.Y., Inc.
Sisters of Mercy Health Corporation, a Michigan nonprofit organization
Society of Catholic Medical Missionaries, Inc.
Texas Coalition for Responsible Investment
Tri-State Coalition for Responsible Investment
The United Christian Missionary Society
Unitarian Universalist Association
Unitarian Universalist Service Committee
United Church Board for World Ministries, United Church of Christ
United Methodist Church, General Board of Church and Society
United Methodist Church, General Board of Global Ministries, National Division
United Methodist Church, General Board of Global Ministries, World Division
Urban and Rural Ministries Office, World Council of Churches
Western New York Coalition for Responsible Investment
Western Pennsylvania Coalition for Responsible Investment
Wisconsin Coalition for Responsible Investment

**EXHIBIT 4**
SOUTH AFRICA: LAND OF CONTRASTS

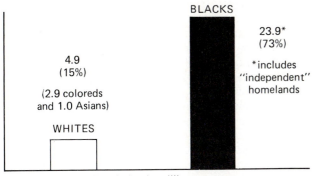

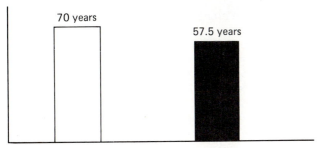

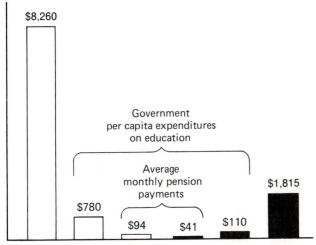

Source: Time magazine, August 5, 1985.

**EXHIBIT 5**
SACC STATEMENT ON DISINVESTMENT ISSUED ON JUNE 28, 1985

This *National Conference of the South African Council of Churches,* being deeply concerned at the violent conflict in which the people of South Africa are now embroiled,

1    Reiterates the statement which the Council has made in the past that foreign investment and loans have been used to support prevailing patterns of power and privilege in South Africa.

2    Recognizes that many church leaders and Christian people in South Africa are in favour of (selective) disinvestment and economic sanctions because they believe that the situation is now so serious that economic action must be taken to strengthen political and diplomatic pressures on South Africa to force the South African government to take seriously the need for fundamental change in South Africa.

3    Is agreed that fundamental change would include the dismantling of apartheid and the democratic involvement of all South Africans in the planning of new political, economic, and social structures which would seek to guarantee for all people justice, development, freedom, and peace.

4    Welcomes the concern and support of our fellow Christians in other countries who are working to assist us in finding nonviolent ways in which fundamental change can be brought about in South Africa.

5    Believes that the pressure in western countries for disinvestment and divestment has been most effective in moving white South Africans into a more serious consideration of the cause of the political conflict in this country.

6    Concludes from the evidence placed before it that foreign investment does not necessarily create new jobs, and that the contrary is often the case because new investment is frequently in the form of sophisticated technological equipment.

7    Draws attention to the fact that the churches have, for many years, tried to address the problem of structural unemployment in black communities and has not been aware of any serious concern being shown by the business sector, foreign or South African, or by government until recent months when economic sanctions have become a legislative probability in the United States.

8    Confesses that in the churches there has been no proper debate and consideration of the disinvestment question, because we have allowed ourselves to be restrained by the severity of laws designed to prevent open discussion of economic sanctions. This has meant that the only arguments being heard in South Africa are those in opposition to disinvestment.

This Conference therefore resolves:

a    To express our belief that disinvestment and similar economic pressures are now called for as a peaceful and effective means of putting pressure on the South African government to bring about these fundamental changes this country needs.

b    To ask our partner churches in other countries to continue with their efforts to identify and promote effective economic pressures to influence the situation in South Africa toward achieving justice and peace in this country and minimizing the violence of the conflict.

c    To promote fuller consideration of the issues by placing the case for the imposition of economic sanctions and disinvestment before the Executive Committees of the SACC and the Regional Councils, and the Councils of our member churches and organizations with the request that they encourage congregations to study and debate them.

d    To ask the Executive to appoint, in consultation with the director of Justice and Reconciliation, a task force to examine the whole question of economic justice as well as issues of disinvestment and economic sanctions, to review and coordinate the responses from the churches, and to assist the church leaders by making available to them information and analyses.

**EXHIBIT 6**

PROFILE OF INTERNATIONAL BUSINESS MACHINES CORPORATION

| | | |
|---|---|---|
| Year operations in South Africa began: | 1952 | |
| Number of employees: | White | 1,419 |
| | African | 265 |
| | Asian/colored | 109 |
| | Total | 1,793 |

| | |
|---|---|
| Total assets: | $88.6 million |
| Total sales: | less than $230 million |
| Number of subsidiaries/affiliates: | 2 |
| Names of major subsidiaries: | International Business Machines SA (Pty.) Ltd. |
| | IBM South Africa Product Distribution (Pty.) Ltd. |

### Description of Operations

Markets, installs, supports, and services full line of IBM computers and business equipment. Computers include mainframes, minicomputers, personal computers, and word processing systems, plus disk and tape storage devices, terminals, printers, and other peripheral equipment. Also sells typewriters, computer-aided design systems, copiers, electronic typesetters, encoders and automatic teller machines (ATMs). Sells software and provides maintenance, consulting, user training, and computer bureau services.

### Strategic Importance

Computers have become crucial for the maintenance of apartheid because they have made possible the concentration of administrative, coercive, and economic power that the small white minority needs to maintain such absolute control over the great majority. IBM dominates the South African market with an estimated 40–50 percent of the installed computer base. About 17 percent of IBM's South African revenue comes from the central and provincial governments, according to the company. However, a large but unspecified additional percentage comes from municipal governments and parastatal corporations. IBM computers are found in almost every important government department and agency, including the departments of the Prime Minister, Inland Revenue, and Education; The Atomic Energy Board; Human Science Research Council (which coordinates national social research as the government sees fit); Industrial Development Corporation; SA Railways; SA Airways; Vecor Heavy Engineering; and other parastatals.

Most crucial for the enforcement of apartheid, IBM computers are at the SA Defense Force (including command and control and logistics services); and, with Control Data, the government's Council for Scientific and Industrial Research (CSIR), the key provider of military, nuclear, electronic, and industrial R&D.

All sectors of the South African economy—finance, manufacturing, distribution, services—depend on computers. This is especially true of companies using high technology, such as military contractors. IBM computers dominate this South African business market. Among IBM customers are AECI (largest chemicals company), Leyland–South Africa, and Barclays and Standard, South Africa's two biggest banks, to whom IBM is selling automatic teller machines (ATMs). IBM is also taking over the South African personal computer market and automatic teller machines in competition with Apple.

## HISTORY OF INSTITUTIONAL SHAREHOLDER ACTION

| Year | Description of Resolution Submitted to Company |
|------|------------------------------------------------|
| 1975 | Sales to South Africa |
| 1976 | Report on sales to South Africa |
| 1980 | Sales to South Africa |
| 1981 | Sales to South Africa |
| 1982 | Withdrawal from South Africa |
| 1983 | Human rights |

### Company Position

IBM states that it complies with U.S. government restrictions (as revised in 1982) on computer exports to the South African police and military, to the SA Atomic Energy Board, and to the South African government departments of Interior, Cooperation and Development, Community Development, Justice, and Manpower, and to homeland agencies carrying out similar functions. The restrictions prevent not all sales to these agencies and departments, but only those sales that help enforce apartheid. However, these restrictions do not prevent computers that have already been sold to these agencies and departments from being used to enforce apartheid. The restrictions also allow the continued servicing of computer contracts that predate the regulations.

As the largest computer company in South Africa, IBM assumes a high-profile stance in favor of continued U.S. business there. It cites its internal policy of not selling equipment and services that might be used to support a repressive society. It also cites its good reports under the Sullivan Principles, its activities to further black education, the progressive impact of business on South Africa, and its expression of its "thoughts" about social concerns both directly to the government and indirectly through business groups. In a recent *New York Times* column, IBM chairman John Akers quoted the company's South African managing director as calling for "bringing blacks into the constitutional framework." Mr. Akers cited this as an example of IBM's progressive impact, but did not say whether this statement meant support for "one person, one vote" or for the South African government's ideas for limited rights for urban blacks.

### Church Position

In spite of the fact IBM officials have stated that the company will not make sales that assist in repression or abridge human rights, IBM has refused to stop sales to the South African government or to place a moratorium on further investment in South Africa. In addition, IBM has refused to meet with church shareholders.

IBM is one of the U.S. companies most active in information efforts and lobbying against the divestment movement. IBM management often testifies in Congress against proposed legislation to increase pressures on South Africa.

*Source:* Prepared from information gathered by the Investor Responsibility Research Center

**EXHIBIT 7**
RESPONSES TO THE ICCR CAMPAIGN

---

*Mobil Corporation*

*150 East 42nd Street*
*New York, New York 10017*

*Rawleigh Warner, Jr.*
*Chairman of the Board*

July 15, 1985

Audrey C. Smock
World Issue Secretary
United Church Board for Women Ministries
Interfaith Center on Corporate Responsibility
475 Riverside Drive
Room 566
New York, New York 10115

Dear Ms. Smock:

This will respond to your letter of May 20, 1985.

We deeply regret that you have seen fit to take an action which reflects, in our judgment, so little appreciation of the realities of life in South Africa and the desires of the segment of the population you wish to help. It is also regrettable that you would propose to use as your whipping boys those very companies which have for many years publicly deplored apartheid and made bona fide attempts to change it by assuming leadership roles in carrying out Sullivan programs and activities including the adoption by the companies of the Fourth Amplification in November 1984, which calls for the dismantling of apartheid through peaceful, legal methods. It is reassuring to us that other church groups have advised us that they deplore your action and have urged us to continue our vigorous leadership in the Sullivan effort.

We repeat what we have said to you before on many occasions. We do not agree with your methods even though we share the same ultimate goal: the ending of apartheid. Rather than curse the darkness we have chosen to help accelerate the process of change in South Africa through fair and equal employment practices, assistance to employee housing, education, community development and health. We have also joined with others to protest the very conditions about which you write. There is a long way to go in South Africa before full equality exists, but it is not the same country it was ten years ago. Changes are taking place, changes which are beginning significantly to undermine the structure of apartheid. We must, each of us, decide whether to assist in that process or leave it to those who seek violent confrontation which will benefit no one—black or white. It would seem unconstructive, if one believes in constructive and peaceful change, to remove oneself from that process as you suggest.

We regard our presence in South Africa as a moral affirmative for change. We disagree not only with your analysis but, also, with your conclusions although we respect your right to state both. We intend to continue to work with other companies and other groups (American, South African, European) to help bring about a free and open society for all South Africans. Only South Africans are going to change their country. You are not going to change it, nor are we. We can only help.

Mobil as a company is committed to equal opportunity in all areas of the world where it operates. We have publicly stated both in the United States and in South Africa that we are opposed to any form of discrimination, that apartheid must be eliminated. Our commitment remains firm and will not change.

We would like to make sure that all the other signatories to your letter and to your May 20th press release are familiar with our anti-apartheid efforts and those of the other Sullivan companies. To that end I would appreciate your providing us with their addresses so we may forward each full information about our involvement in South Africa.

We recognize your commitment to change in South Africa, and regret that you do not recognize ours despite many meetings in the past few years. Under these circumstances we don't believe another meeting would serve any useful purpose.

Sincerely,

Rawleigh Warner, Jr.

*International Business Machines Corporation*

*Office of the President and Chief Executive Officer*                          *Armonk, New York 10504*

June 6, 1985

Ms. Joyce D. Sohl
Treasurer, Women's Division
General Board of Global Ministries
The United Methodist Church
475 Riverside Drive
New York, New York 10115

Dear Ms. Sohl:

No one is more opposed to apartheid, or any other form of racial discrimination, than IBM. We have chosen to remain in South Africa and confront apartheid on a day-to-day basis—in the work place, in the marketplace, and in public discussion.

Our actions bear witness to our beliefs. IBM practices nondiscrimination; we give equal pay for equal work and employ blacks in all major activities, including management. We comply fully with the United States export regulations and do not sell products and services used by the police and military in South Africa. Economic activity has profound social effects, direct and indirect, which enhance the climate for change. We believe the presence of IBM and other enlightened companies can have a positive effect on South Africa. As I stated in *The New York Times,* we may be pursuing an impossible dream, but I am not ready to give up.

Enclosed is additional information regarding our activities in South Africa and a description of our new social responsibility initiatives.* I hope you will give thoughtful review to IBM's record in South Africa and conclude that our activities in that country ought to be supported, not terminated.

Sincerely,

John F. Akers

JFA:lr
Enclosures

*These materials are summarized on pp. 519–521 of the case.

**EXHIBIT 8**
A SELECTED CHRONOLOGY OF EVENTS RELATING TO THE CRISIS IN SOUTH AFRICA
(JULY 20–AUGUST 15, 1985)

### Saturday, July 20

The South African government in Pretoria imposes an emergency decree in 36 black districts. The decree gives police "near absolute powers to arrest people, search homes, seize property, and order people to move from one area to another. Their powers are bolstered by an exemption from any legal action against them for carrying out their duties." (*New York Times*, 7/24)

"Under emergency powers, police can detain anyone for 14 days and hold them indefinitely after that period with ministerial approval. Political or other organizations can be suspended without notice and property can be searched and seized without warrant." (*Boston Globe*, 7/22)

### Monday, July 22

200 primarily black community leaders—including members of the United Democratic Front, members of the clergy and labor unions—are detained in predawn raids, bringing to a total of 350 the number of people in detention. (*BG*, 7/23)

### Tuesday, July 23

White activist Molly Blackburn is arrested immediately prior to meeting with Robert McNamara and Donald McHenry, who are visiting from the United States. (*BG*, 7/24)

### Wednesday, July 24

The French government suspends all new investment in South Africa and recalls its ambassador. France currently has $1.6 billion in investments in South Africa. It also receives 25 percent of its uranium and most of its coal from the country. South Africa also is France's largest electronics goods customer. (*NYT*, 7/25)

### Thursday, July 25

South African police shoot five to death and wound nineteen as a crowd of 4,000 mourners is leaving a funeral in the black township of Daveyton, 25 miles east of Johannesburg. (*BG*, 7/26)

Bishop Desmond Tutu criticizes the Reagan Administration in an interview, saying:

> We will not forget what has happened to our people and where the American administration stood at a time when we needed them desperately. We feel basically hurt, very deeply hurt because we have fought to bring about change in South Africa by peaceful means, and this great country America aids and abets one of the most racist systems since Nazism and Communism. What would Mr. Reagan's reaction have been if it was not black people who, 500 or more of them, were killed since last August? What would be his reaction if those casualties were whites? (*BG*, 7/26)

In Washington, White House spokesman Larry Speakes urges talks between whites and blacks, while Secretary of State George Schultz tells reporters in an airborne interview that there is no need for a ban on investments, since "the political instability and turmoil will be enough to discourage investors." (*NYT*, 7/26)

### Friday, July 26

The U.N. Security Council votes to urge member governments to suspend all new investments; the U.S. and British representatives abstain. Earlier in the day, U.S. and G.B. vetoed an amendment that would have required the council to consider mandatory economic and political sanctions if the South African government failed to end apartheid. (*NYT*, 7/27)

### Saturday, July 27

White House spokesman Larry Speakes urges the Pretoria government to lift its emergency decrees, saying, "The real cause of violence in South Africa is apartheid." Speakes also tells the press that President Reagan is opposed to economic sanctions, since they "could lead to more bloodshed." (*NYT*, 7/27)

### Monday, July 29

South African President P. W. Botha refuses to meet with Bishop Tutu to discuss means of ending the violence, arguing that his schedule is too tight. (*NYT*, 7/30)

### Tuesday, July 30

Financial dealers around the world report the widespread selling of shares in S.A. gold-mining companies. (*NYT*, 7/31)

### Wednesday, July 31

House and Senate conferees reach agreement on a bill that would impose economic sanctions on South Africa. South Africa announces sweeping restrictions on attendance at funerals for the victims of black unrest. Such funerals had become, according to the *New York Times,* "an opportunity for mass rallies addressed by a multitude of speakers and attended by thousands of black activists carrying anti-apartheid banners and chanting the songs and slogans of dissent." The new government orders include a ban on outdoor funerals for people who die of "unnatural causes" and prohibit against any but ordained clergy speaking to the gathering. (*NYT*, 8/1)

### Thursday, August 1

The House of Representatives votes 380–48 in favor of economic sanctions against South Africa, but a Senate vote is stalled by threat of a filibuster by eight senators until after the August recess. (*NYT*, 8/2)

Following France's example, ten more European Economic Community nations recall their ambassadors in protest over South African apartheid. (*NYT*, 8/2)

Top civil rights lawyer Victoria Mxenge, 43, is shot to death as she steps from her car outside her home in Umlazi, a black township outside of Durban. Members of the African National Congress charge that a death squad sent by the Botha government is responsible. 1,000 students march through Durban to protest the murder, but are dispersed by police using attack dogs and clubs. (*NYT*, 8/2)

### Friday, August 2

An article in the business section of the *New York Times* reports:

> Many of the 300 American companies operating in South Africa are increasingly uncomfortable with their presence there and some are looking for ways to retreat or reduce their involvement, according to interviews yesterday with executives at dozens of these companies. Virtually all the major American concerns say they plan to remain there. But they are closely following the growing unrest in that country. And companies that can pull out easily, such as banks, are beginning to do so. . . . Almost all of the executives who were interviewed said their companies' doubts were a result of deteriorating business conditions in South Africa, which has suffered a severe drought and recession for the last three years, and not a result of mounting pressure from American activists to sell off South African holdings. But the pressure of the divestment movement—"the hassle factor" as it is sometimes called—takes a toll, some executives acknowledge. (*NYT*, 8/2, p. D1)

### Tuesday, August 6

Police in the small town of Brandfort raid the home of Winnie Mandela, though Mrs. Mandela was in Johannesburg at the time. The police fire tear gas into the home, arrest thirty people, confiscate belongings, and smear a clinic connected to Mrs. Mandela's home with blood. (*NYT*, 8/8)

### Thursday, August 8

National Security Adviser Robert McFarlane travels to Vienna to warn South African officials that President Reagan would not be able to sustain a veto of economic sanctions unless there is "accelerated movement" away from apartheid. U.S. officials express optimism that Prime Minister Pieter W. Botha will announce major changes when he addresses a conference of the ruling National Party on Thursday, August 15. (*BG,* 8/11, *NYT,* 8/10)

Rioting in Durban claims lives of sixteen as black members of the Zulu tribe attacked South African Indians. (*NYT,* 8/9)

### Saturday, August 10

The Rev. Allan Boesak, a leading antiapartheid campaigner and the president of the World Alliance of Reformed Churches, is arrested for civil disobedience as he tried, in defiance of police orders, to attend the Capetown funeral of a teenager who had been shot by police on July 29. (*NYT,* 8/11)

Black-Indian violence in Durban continues; death toll rises to 56.

### Sunday, August 11

At the funeral of Victoria Mxenge, a black soldier is run down and stoned to death by an angry mob. After his murder, his body is doused with gasoline and burned. (*NYT,* 8/12)

On a trip to Cameroon, Pope John Paul II publicly denounces apartheid. (*BG, NYT,* 8/12)

### Monday, August 12

South African police shoot and kill a twelve-year-old girl in a demonstration of students in a township near Pretoria. (*NYT,* 8/13)

### Tuesday, August 13

Winnie Mandela's home is firebombed. Mrs. Mandela, who had remained in Johannesburg, charges the fire was set by the "security branch directed by the government in Pretoria." (*NYT,* 8/14)

The United Nations announces that it has completed divestment of all holdings in companies doing business in South Africa from its $4 billion pension fund portfolio. University of Minnesota announces that it has sold 17 percent of all similar holdings. (*NYT,* 8/14)

### Wednesday, August 14

Blacks riot in thirteen townships. One off-duty black policeman is stoned to death by a mob. (*BG,* 8/15)

### Thursday, August 15

In a speech to 2,500 delegates of the National Party's Natal Conference, President Botha vows not to "lead white South Africans and other minority groups on the road to abdication and suicide." Despite strong prior expectations and hints to the contrary, Botha makes no concessions to the country's black majority, and promises he would continue reforms at his own pace. Botha also castigates the outside world for meddling in the internal affairs of his country.

In the United States, lawmakers express strong disappointment over the absence of any concrete proposals or reforms, and ten U.S. senators each contribute $500 to a fund to be given to Winnie Mandela for the reconstruction of her home. (*BG,* 8/16)

**EXHIBIT 9**
IBM EMPLOYMENT BY RACE AND JOB CATEGORY, 1980–1983

| | Number of Employees, 1980 | | | | Number of Employees, 1983 | | | |
|---|---|---|---|---|---|---|---|---|
| | **Blacks** | **Coloreds** | **Whites** | **% Nonwhite** | **Blacks** | **Coloreds** | **Whites** | **% Nonwhite** |
| Managers | 4 | 2 | 246 | 2.4 | 4 | 4 | 343 | 2.3 |
| Professionals | 3 | — | 193 | 1.5 | 8 | 23 | 211 | 12.8 |
| Sales/systems engineers | 33 | 10 | 357 | 10.8 | 60 | 19 | 426 | 15.6 |
| Customer engineers/ technicians | 41 | 13 | 296 | 15.4 | 49 | 16 | 371 | 14.9 |
| Administrative | 95 | 47 | 117 | 54.8 | 116 | 38 | 43 | 78.2 |
| Information systems and office machine operators | 27 | 6 | 17 | 66.0 | 28 | 9 | 25 | 59.7 |
| Total | 203 | 78 | 1,226 | | 265 | 109 | 1,419 | |

*Source:* Investor Responsibility Research Center.

# Smoking and Health: United States Tobacco Companies—National and International Operations

On January 11, 1979, Dr. Julius Richmond, the Surgeon General of the United States, issued a mammoth 1,200-page report on tobacco use in which he declared that there was "overwhelming proof" that cigarette smoking was a causal factor in lung cancer. The document, whose release marked the fifteenth anniversary of former Surgeon General Luther Terry's landmark report (wherein cigarettes were first designated by the U.S. Department of Health, Education, and Welfare as being extremely hazardous to health), drew on the results of 30,000 research papers to demonstrate links between cigarette smoking and a host of diseases which included lung cancer, heart disease, chronic bronchitis, and emphysema. On the basis of this research, Richmond cited cigarette smoking as "the largest preventable cause of death in the United States." Secretary of HEW Joseph A. Califano announced that the report revealed that smoking was "far more dangerous than was supposed in 1964," and he restated his support of HEW's antismoking campaign, which was budgeted to receive $22 million that year (up from $6 million in 1978).

The tobacco industry labeled the new report "more rehash than research," and criticized it for demonstrating statistical relationships for which science could not as yet provide any definitive clinical explanation. The Tobacco Institute, which was the chief spokesman for the industry, repeated its previous charge that although cancerous cell changes had been induced in animals, no production with smoke of human-type lung cancer, heart disease, or emphysema had ever been verified in laboratory experiments.

The chief antismoking lobby, Action on Smoking and Health (ASH), also scored the report, claiming that it was "criminally deficient and misleading," and that it had not gone far enough in demonstrating the health hazards of smoking, which—according to ASH—were really comparable to heroin addiction.

A tobacco farmer interviewed by *The New York Times* said in response to Califano's cam-

**TABLE 1**

OCCURRENCE OF FIVE MAJOR TYPES OF LUNG CANCERS
IN SMOKERS AND NONSMOKERS

| Type | Total | Male | | Female | |
|---|---|---|---|---|---|
| | | Smoker | Never-smoker | Smoker | Never-smoker |
| Epidermoid | 992 | 892 | 7 | 80 | 13 |
| Small cell | 640 | 533 | 4 | 100 | 3 |
| Adenocarcinoma | 760 | 492 | 39 | 128 | 101 |
| Large cell | 466 | 389 | 16 | 46 | 15 |
| Bronchioloalveolar cell | 68 | 35 | 4 | 13 | 16 |
| Total | 2,926 | 2,341 | 70 | 367 | 148 |

*Source:* Edward C. Rosenow III and David T. Carr, "Bronchogenic Carcinoma," *Ca—A Cancer Journal for Clinicians,* 29(4), 1979, pp. 233–245.

paign, "A man's smoking is his own damn business."[1]

## CIGARETTE SMOKING AND DISEASE

In 1900 the death rate in the United States was 17 per 1,000 persons per year; in 1979 that figure had dropped to fewer than 9 per 1,000. While mortality rates from communicable diseases had been vastly reduced, degenerative diseases such as heart ailments, stroke, and cancer had increased dramatically to account for 75% of all deaths in the U.S. A July 1979 report by the Surgeon General concluded that while Americans were generally healthier than ever, they were killing themselves needlessly through smoking, drinking, poor diet, and preventable accidents. Of these, cigarette smoking was deemed the single most preventable cause of death. Many attempts had been made to calculate the economic cost of smoking-related health care, and one estimate in 1976 placed the figure at $8 billion plus $19 billion in lost productivity.[2]

[1] "Cigarette Smoking and Disease" *The New York Times,* January 14, 1978, p. A11.
[2] "Smoking, Tobacco, and Health," U.S. Dept. of Health and Human Services, Washington, D.C., 1981, p. 15.

Although the precise numbers varied between studies, the general figure cited by the Public Health Service for overall mortality rates was 17 deaths for smokers to every 10 nonsmoker deaths. For many of the smoking-related diseases, death rates were clearly associated with how many cigarettes were smoked daily, how long a person smoked, the pattern of inhalation, and length of butt. The disease most clearly associated with smoking was lung cancer; comparison studies, such as those listed in Table 1, and cohort studies which attempted to sort out various other causal factors such as behavioral, genetic, or environmental conditions, confirmed that smokers had a much higher risk of developing and dying from cancers of the lung. Despite the fact that the precise human carcinogenic mechanism in smoke had never been isolated clinically, Richmond's report concluded that causal relationships between lung cancer and emphysema had now been substantially documented, and that the broader category of coronary heart disease was less specifically but nonetheless generally associated with smoking as well.

These findings were not startling in the sense that they confirmed previous studies, but other parts of the 1979 report revealed additional trends and relationships between smoking and personal health that had not been previously known. Two new categories of smokers which appeared to be particularly susceptible to the harmful health effects from smoking were especially singled out: (1) workers exposed to particular or chemical hazards, and (2) pregnant women. For example, it had been discovered that uranium miners as a group showed a higher-than-average rate of respiratory cancers than the general population (up to 90 times higher than nonsmokers) but that uranium miners who smoked displayed a mortality rate six times higher than nonsmoking uranium miners (see Table 2). From figures such as these some researchers suspected that cigarette smoke might be acting synergistically with toxic agents in the workplace to produce a greater effect on health than the two would separately.

Richmond's report also revealed that women who were pregnant and smoked took much greater chances of having spontaneous abortion, complications of pregnancy, and pre-term deliveries than comparable nonsmokers. Babies born to women who smoked in pregnancy were on the average seven ounces lighter than babies born to comparable nonsmoking women. Moreover, the incidence of lung cancer among women was rising sharply, a finding which reversed past assumptions about women smokers, who until recently had displayed relatively low lung cancer rates, from which it had been thought that women might have some genetic immunological mechanism which pro-

tected them from smoking-related cancers of the lung.

In 1980 Richmond announced that the first signs of an epidemic of smoking-related diseases among women were appearing and that within three years the lung cancer rate was expected to surpass that of breast cancer. What was most dramatic about the report was the rapid acceleration of lung cancer in women during the past 15 years (see Table 3). "Cigarette smoking," said Richmond, "an early sign of woman's social emancipation, is now a major threat to her personal health and her ability to bear healthy children."

## U.S. CONSUMPTION OF CIGARETTES

Although the medical significance of the Surgeon General's 1979 and 1980 reports on smoking and health were widely debated by scientists and laypeople, the studies did demonstrate beyond a doubt that American consumption patterns for cigarettes had changed substantially. Both men and women were smoking in fewer numbers than in the 1960s: in 1955, the first year in which the government began measuring smoking rates, 52% of adult males and 24.5% of adult women smoked; in 1965 the rate among men was nearly the same as ten years earlier (51%) while the number of women smokers had jumped to 32%. But in 1979 the figures had dropped to 36.9% and 28.2%, respectively, or a 32% overall rate (down from 33.7% total adult consumption in 1966; for demographic breakdown see Exhibit 1). Annual per capita consumption, which had peaked in 1963 at an average rate of 4,345 cigarettes per adult per year, had dropped to approximately 3,900 in 1979, which was the lowest figure since 1957.[3] Translated in total numbers of cigarettes, approximately two billion fewer ciga-

**TABLE 2**
COMPARISON OF RESPIRATORY CANCER RATES AMONG URANIUM MINERS AND NONMINERS*

| Demographic group | Rate per 100,000 person years |
|---|---|
| White males, never smoked | 1.1 |
| White males who smoked two or more packs a day | 8.9 |
| Uranium miners, never smoked | 7.1 |
| Uranium miners, smoked | 42.2 |

*1979 Surgeon General's Report on Smoking and Health.

[3]*Farm Paper Letter,* U.S. Dept. of Agriculture, Oct. 15, 1979. Per capita smoking figures are statistical guides rather than direct indications of actual smoking habits, and nonsmokers are included in the data base. Another estimate, cited in *Farmline,* August 1980, p. 10, put per capita consumption at its lowest since 1898.

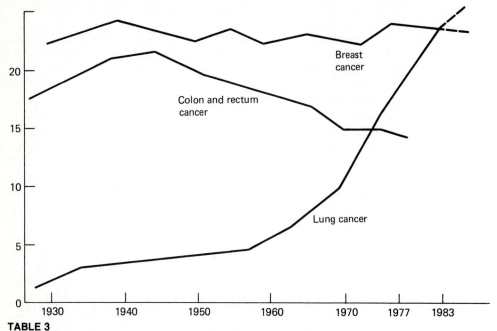

**TABLE 3**
Age-adjusted cancer death rates for females for selected sites, 1930–1983 (rate per 100,000).
Data for 1983 are estimated. (*Source:* National Center for Health Statistics.)

rettes were consumed domestically in 1979 than in 1978. In 1980 the steady decline since 1966 had again reversed, and unit sales of cigarettes had risen after adjustments by approximately 1.5–2% in the United States, which was the cigarette industry's best performance in five years.

Even teenagers, whose smoking habits were a chief concern in Richmond's 1979 report, were smoking less. A study by the University of Michigan's Institute for Social Research for the National Institute of Drug Abuse revealed that of 17,000 high school seniors who were surveyed in April 1980, 21% reported smoking daily as against 29% in 1977. The Michigan results indicated that the increasing trend in teenage smoking (between 1968–1974 smoking among girls age 12–14 had increased eightfold) had peaked in 1977, and the decline in number of high school smokers was accelerating rapidly. Girls still outnumbered boys as

heavy smokers, but they were also giving up smoking more rapidly than the boys were.

Demographic studies revealed that the greatest declines in consumption were occurring among the white, educated, upper and upper middle class populations.

**RESPONSES TO THE HEALTH ISSUE: ADVERTISING, PRODUCT, LEGISLATION, RESEARCH**

In 1979 tobacco—and cigarettes in particular—was still a highly active part of the American life-style, and various groups worked in various ways at reducing the potential hazards of that product.

**1 Advertising**

Perhaps the most visible change in the industry was the way in which cigarettes were advertised and marketed. As of July 27, 1965, a year and a half after Surgeon General Terry's report on smoking, all cigarettes sold in the U.S. were required to carry the warning: "Caution: Cigarette Smoking May Be Hazardous to Your Health." The warning label was revised by an Act of Congress on January 1, 1971, to read: "Warning: The Surgeon General Has Determined That Cigarette Smoking Is Dangerous to Your Health," and its use was extended to include all newspaper, magazine, billboard and other advertising. The previous year cigarette manufacturers had announced that they would voluntarily disclose the Federal Trade Commission's "tar" and nicotine content test results in all advertising; flavor additives, however, which had increased with the reduction of tar content, were not revealed.

There was also general agreement in the tobacco industry that cigarette advertising and promotion should not be directed toward young people. In 1963 a number of tobacco companies discontinued advertising in school and college publications and also ceased to distribute sample cigarettes or engage in promotional efforts on school and college campuses. The Public Health Cigarette Smoking Act of January 1, 1971, made it illegal to advertise cigarettes on television or radio, after which time cigarette companies became heavy users of newspapers, magazines, and outdoor advertising. In 1981 the industry spent approximately $900 million on cigarette advertising and promotion, as opposed to $361 million ten years earlier.

Both the tobacco industry and the Surgeon General characterized cigarette advertising as the promotion of one brand over another rather than as a direct appeal to begin or continue smoking. In 1980 cigarettes were viewed as the ultimate self-image product and evoked more brand loyalty than any other product in the U.S. (35mm film had the second strongest loyalty, followed by laxatives and cold remedies). Over 160 brands directed toward highly specific sociological groups could be found on retail shelves in 1980 as opposed to 1950, when there were only three popular cigarette brands in the country. U.S. packages and advertising of cigarettes were designed to convey very specific images of life style and personality such as rugged frontier individuality, urban modernity, or youthful flamboyancy.

In the Surgeon General's opinion (1979 report), the influence of such mass media efforts on smoking behavior was "relatively unclear." Moreover, studies of countries where cigarette advertising was restricted (France, Italy, U.S.) showed no reduction of consumption after restrictions had been imposed. In Norway there was a drop in consumption immediately after a complete cigarette advertising ban and a substantial tax increase, but the slowdown was only temporary and shortly reversed itself again.[4]

## 2  Product Changes

Accompanying the change in advertising was a change in cigarette content as well. In 1955 less than one percent of cigarettes were filter-tipped, but by 1977 this percentage had increased to 90. The most radical and influential change on the cigarette market in the late 1970s, however, was the dynamic rise in consumer preference for "low tar"[5] cigarettes, which had arisen in part out of a concern for the health hazards of tar and nicotine. In 1975 low-tar cigarettes represented less than 10% of total cigarette sales, but as the public became more aware that tar and nicotine had been indicted as prime factors in the health hazards of smoking, low-tar cigarettes gained a dramatic increase in share— about 43% in 1980, according to John C. Maxwell, Jr., a well-known industry analyst for Lehman Brother Kuhn Loeb.[6] This trend to low tar sparked what was variously called a "tar war" or "tar derby" within the U.S. industry, and by 1980 tobacco companies were competing on tar

---

[4]References to these studies cited in "Tobacco in the Developing Nations," The Tobacco Institute, Inc., November 1980, p. 5.
[5]FTC definition: any cigarette whose tar content is 15 milligrams or less. The highest tar contents in the U.S. in 1980 were approximately 25 mg.
[6]*The New York Times,* January 25, 1979, p. D1.

and nicotine levels to the point where several "ultra-low-tars," whose contents were as low as less than one-tenth, began to appear. Average tar content fell by 32% between 1968 and 1981, and nicotine by 26%. As a result of these efforts to drive tar levels down, less tobacco was being used in American cigarettes.

The low tars were not able, however, to overcome the health risks of smoking. Rates of smoking-related diseases were still higher for low-tar smokers than for nonsmokers, and in 1980 some researchers were suggesting that low-tar smokers tended to adopt changed smoking habits to compensate for the reduction in tar content (such as taking longer and deeper puffs or smoking more cigarettes per day) and that these changes were likely to offset the health advantages which an initial reduction of tar and nicotine might achieve.[7] Moreover, reduced tar had no effect on the amount of carbon monoxide inhaled during smoking, a factor which some scientists felt was potentially as harmful to health as nicotine or tar.

## 3  Legislation

In addition to federal advertising and promotion restrictions, there were various legislative attempts to control smoking in public places, the most notable of which was Proposition 5— a proposal initiated in 1977 by the Clean Indoor Air Committee and included on the November 1978 California state ballot to limit smoking to specially assigned areas in all buildings open to the public (with the exception of bars and a few other places), all places of employment, and all educational and health facilities. After an initial positive response by more than 600,000 voters who signed petitions to put Proposition 5 on the ballot and a late August survey which revealed 58% of the voters in favor of the legislation, a widespread campaign against the proposal was launched by Californians for Common Sense (CCS). Proposition 5 was subsequently defeated, 54 to 46 percent.

The Clean Indoor Air Committee had raised $658,422 in campaign funds while CCS had spent $6,002,333—over $6 million of which had been contributed by R. J. Reynolds Co., Philip Morris Co., Brown and Williamson, and P. Lorillard.[8]

## 4  Research

Not surprisingly, the chief challenge to the Surgeon General's reports on smoking came from the tobacco industry itself, whose chief representative was the Tobacco Institute. Its objections to the Surgeon General's conclusions and to consequent antismoking programs were based on scientific, sociological, and economic grounds. Past statistical studies were faulted for inconsistencies of reporting and for failing to isolate all the factors which posed special problems in the study of health consequences in relation to smoking such as the tremendous variety of tobacco use, strength, texture, composition, additives, smoking habits, and various behavioral, environmental, and genetic traits. In its opinion, smoking would not be "proved" harmful to health until science isolated clinically the human disease-causing agents in cigarette smoke. To further such research problems the industry formed the Council for Tobacco Research–USA Inc. in 1954 to award research grants to independent scientists working on questions of tobacco use and health. As of 1979 the Council had awarded more than $58 million for 398 investigations, and many of these projects also received support from other nonindustry organizations such as the National Cancer Institute, the American Clean Cancer Society (which in 1979 allocated $55,550,000 or 34% of its funds to research) and the U.S. Public Health Service. The U.S. Department of Agriculture sponsored a host of agronomic research projects including experiments to develop a tobacco foodstuff.

Historical and sociological studies on the use of tobacco were utilized by the industry to

---

[7]*The New York Times,* June 15, 1980, p. D1.

[8]*The New York Times,* February 4, 1979, p. 4.

corroborate its claim that cigarette companies were responding to a preexisting consumer demand rather than creating a new one. For example, a study conducted by cultural anthropologist Sherwin Feinhandler,[9] revealed that out of 183 societies worldwide under examination, 112 used tobacco as a trade or sale item, and that the product—introduced into the Old World in the sixteenth century—had played an important social, material, medical, and ceremonial function in these societies. Among the score of behavioral and social roles which Feinhandler associated with tobacco in modern society were personal pleasure and solace, presentation of self, mood enhancement or suppression, aid to concentration, boundary mediation, event marking, and time filling.

Or as Ross Millhiser, vice chairman of Philip Morris, put it,

> I love cigarettes. It's one of the things that make life really worth living. . . . Cigarettes supply some desire, some need of the fundamental human equation. The human equation is always trying to balance itself, and cigarettes play some part in that.[10]

## THE U.S. TOBACCO INDUSTRY

Cigarettes also played an integral part in the American economy. As the sixth largest cash crop—worth $2.6 billion in 1979[11]—tobacco products generated approximately $57.6 billion toward the nation's Gross National Product and accounted directly and indirectly for 2.5% of the private sector labor force (c. 2 million jobs) with $30 billion in wages and earnings. Americans spend approximately $21.3 billion over the counter for tobacco products (93% of which went toward cigarettes) which generated approximately $6.3 billion in federal, state, and local tax revenue (cigarette taxes represented 98.8%).

Tobacco was a particularly attractive crop for its return, $2,124 per acre, which was the highest yielding crop per acre in America (as compared to wheat at $71 and soybeans at $162). Moreover, because it was labor intensive with a relatively stable production and price level, tobacco was a profitable undertaking for the small farmer, and of the total 276,000 tobacco farms in the U.S., the average acreage was 3 acres. Cigarette manufacturers did not grow tobacco but rather purchased it from farmers primarily at auction.

Government assistance to tobacco growers took three basic forms: the maintenance by the U.S. Dept. of Agriculture of marketing quotas, a price support loan to farmers by the Commodity Credit Corporation with unsold tobacco as collateral, and grading standards which supplied the basis for CCC loans. Costs of these programs were difficult to assess, but over the 44 years of price support, the loans advanced to farmers minus interest paid, and minus revenue from sales of tobacco collateral, had yielded a net loss of approximately $50 million. In 1977 no tobacco loans were charged off as unpayable. In 1979, government inspection and market news service costs were $6.6 million.

## U.S. TOBACCO COMPANIES

Six companies (see Table 4) manufactured over 99% of the cigarettes in the United States in 1980, with R. J. Reynolds and Philip Morris

**TABLE 4**
SHARE OF U.S. CIGARETTE MARKET*

| Company | 1980 | 1970 |
|---|---|---|
| R. J. Reynolds | 32.6% | 31.7% |
| Philip Morris | 30.9 | 16.5 |
| Brown and Williamson | 13.7 | 16.7 |
| Lorillard | 9.7 | 8.7 |
| American Brands | 10.8 | 19.6 |
| Liggett Group | 2.2 | 6.8 |

*John Maxwell, Jr., Lehman Brothers Kuhn Loeb Research, reprinted in *The New York Times,* April 12, 1981, Ill, 1.

[9]Social Systems Analysts, Watertown, Mass.
[10]Interview, "Tobacco: Profit Despite Attacks," by Peter T. Kilborn, *The New York Times,* January 25, 1979, D1.
[11]Unless otherwise indicated, all figures are for 1979.

(the Big Two) dominating the market both for overall share and in the top ten brands. Marlboro (P. Morris) was the #1 cigarette brand in the U.S. (17.7%) and in the world, followed by Winston (R. J. Reynolds, 13% in the U.S.).

Ever since the mid-1960s, the tobacco companies had adopted a policy of unrelated diversification, and in 1980 the Big Two were highly diversified (see Exhibit 2). At the Philip Morris Co., for example, tobacco contributed approximately 60% of the company's revenues in 1980 as compared with 85.1% ten years earlier; R. J. Reynolds had similarly reduced tobacco revenue to 54% (down from 74% in 1970). As a cash generator, however, tobacco still dominated the cigarette companies' net earnings (73% of R. J. Reynolds' 1980 earnings), and despite their diversification strategies the Big Two were fully committed to remain in the tobacco business. Reynolds had recently unveiled a $1 billion ten-year program to expand and modernize its cigarette-making facilities, while Philip Morris was constructing a new cigarette manufacturing plant in North Carolina and a new Operations Center in Richmond, VA, to support both its U.S. and its international tobacco operations.

## U.S. INTERNATIONAL TOBACCO OPERATIONS

Although 1980 had marked a five-year high for the U.S. tobacco industry in domestic cigarette sales, the real growth area was overseas: worldwide consumption of cigarettes (unit sales) averaged a 3.1% annual rate of increase between 1970 and 1980, with developing countries increasing at a 5% rate. Latin America had the highest rate of tobacco use and Africa the lowest, due in part to differences in levels of money available for discretionary spending.

Some U.S. tobacco companies responded to these worldwide trends in cigarette consumption by substantially increasing their activities abroad. In 1979 U.S. exports of leaf tobacco and manufactured products totalled a record $2.2 billion, or about one-third of the U.S. crop and a 15% increase over 1978. Imports totalled $463 million, up 12.2% as the cheaper foreign tobacco began to be used more and more as "filler," which made a $1.7 billion positive contribution to the U.S. balance of payments. In Europe the European Community offered duty-free access for tobacco from associate members in Africa and a preferential tariff quota for imports from developing countries in Asia and Latin America.

In the U.S. the Big Two were particularly active in developing their international tobacco operations: both companies had international tobacco divisions and were investing substantially in expanding overseas operations. In 1980 Philip Morris International's share of the 3.8 trillion unit cigarette market outside of the United States rose to about 6.2% (from 6.0% in 1979 with a 10-year average compounded growth rate in unit sales of 10.3%) and was substantially higher in many other countries (see Exhibit 3); operating revenues from its international cigarette sales rose 24.2% and income increased 26% (after absorbing a LIFO charge of $6.9 million). The company was the nation's No. 1 exporter of consumer products in 1980 and 18th largest of all U.S. exporters. R. J. Reynold's International tobacco operations had a five-year annually compounded growth rate in sales and earnings of 16% and 32% respectively, and in 1980 its international tobacco sales reached $2.09 billion. Both companies had struck trade agreements with China (the world's largest tobacco-producing nation) to manufacture cigarettes in that country. Philip Morris' annual report for 1980 summarized the company's international tobacco operations as follows:

> We manufacture cigarettes in 24 countries. These operations are welcomed by the host countries. They provide jobs, not only in the factories but on farms, in the distribution network, and in stores. They stimulate local economies. They generate taxes that can be used by governments for social purposes. Of our 72,000 employees at the end of 1980, 31,000, or 43%, were based abroad. And with few exceptions, all were nationals of the countries where these facilities are located. We have no hesitancy in saying that all of the countries where we operate

benefit economically and socially from the Philip Morris presence.

In May 1981 Philip Morris also announced a partial merger with Rothman's International, the British-based tobacco company whose Dunhill and Peter Stuyvesant brands were known worldwide. At R. J. Reynolds, chairman and CEO J. Paul Sticht predicted that his company's "international business in cigarettes could match our domestic business in the next ten years."[12]

As already noted, the fastest growing segment of the international market was in the developing countries. With the exception of China, most developing countries were increasing their allotments of tobacco acreage to meet an increasing demand both domestically and for export, and of the 500,000 metric tons of tobacco produced by these nations in 1977, one-third was exported and the rest used for domestic markets.[13] While it is difficult to generalize about the international tobacco market in developing countries as a whole, certain conditions and aspects of consumption, promotion, and marketing distinguished it from the U.S. domestic market.

Contrary to consumption patterns in America, in developing countries the smoking of Western-style cigarettes was most prevalent among the wealthy educated classes and could be characterized as the habit of college and university students rather than of nonstudents and the unemployed. As a symbol of affluence and modernism, cigarettes were one of the first items which newly solvent people tended to buy, and some cigarette brands (such as "Varsity," "Graduate," or "Embassy") appealed to this perception of smoking as a sophisticated activity.[14] In many of the countries cigarettes could be purchased by the pack or by individual cigarette at local tobacco shops. The rate of women who smoked varied tremendously from country to country, but in general the women smokers in developing nations tended to favor the traditional local forms of tobacco more than men did.

Although there was some indication that tobacco use might be related to the same diseases as it was in the U.S., the health effects of these smoking trends in developing countries were not well documented as of 1981. Few data on disease and tobacco use were available nor were life expectancies high enough to exhibit, for example, lung cancer rates among smokers and nonsmokers which could be compared with U.S. statistical patterns. One case comparison study in India, however, found that cigarette smokers there compared with nonsmokers had a relative risk of lung cancer of 2.36, while other research revealed that traditional forms of tobacco in India created even higher risks of bronchial cancer.[15] Moreover, population-specific variations in other predisposing factors such as a lower incidence of circulatory system diseases or increased nutritional deficiencies suggested that the health effects of tobacco use might be quite different between developing countries.[16]

Advertising and promotion restrictions generally appeared with less frequency in developing as compared with developed countries, although there were notable exceptions. In Kenya the nation's only cigarette company was its fourth largest advertiser, but Singapore had had an almost complete ban on media advertising since 1970 (foreign periodicals were exempted).[17] Requirements concerning warning labels also varied tremendously (see Exhibit 4), while for the most part public health education efforts were directed against more prevalent disease and nutritional problems than against smoking. Transnational companies observed the local advertising and promotion

[12]Interview, *The New York Times,* April 12, 1981, p. III, 22.
[13]USDA Foreign Agricultural Service, "World Tobacco Supply and Distribution 1959–1977," Washington, D.C., June 1978.
[14]"Tobacco in Developing Nations," p. 5.

[15]"Tobacco—Hazards to Health and Human Reproduction," *Population Reports—Issues in World Health,* Johns Hopkins University, March 1979.
[16]Population Report, p. L-9.
[17]Ibid., p. L-31.

1 not offer additional information ing labels or FTC tar and nicotine levels when they were not required. A paper by the Tobacco Institute justified this policy on the grounds that tobacco manufacturers were respecting the right of health officials to offer opinions on matters relating to public health, that the imposition of the U.S. code would be "neocolonialistic," and that so-called "league tables" regarding tar and nicotine content were likely to mislead the consumer by suggesting that levels of certain ingredients had proven health significance when "despite all the research that has been done over the years here and abroad, no one has demonstrated that these milligram numbers do indeed have any significance."[18]

Cigarettes for sale overseas were manufactured both in the U.S. and by licensed producers in some of the countries where they were sold. In Brazil, for example, high import tariffs precluded the use of anything but local manufacturing equipment for almost every stage of the cigarette manufacturing process, and international tobacco operations in the southeastern portion of the country had generated a relatively high degree of industrial development there including facilities capable of processing the leaf to the point of consumption/export transport and an all-weather road from Santa Cruz to the state capital of Porto Alegre.

In some countries local tobacco was much stronger than the American flue-cured and burley which made up a large portion of the American cigarette, and the international tobacco companies responded to these established local preferences by offering a similar range of yields on the assumption that people tend to smoke what they are used to.[19] Western style tobaccos such as Virginia leaf, which required artificial heat for the curing process, were being cultivated increasingly in South America, Africa and Asia with the agronomic assistance of the transnational tobacco companies. Government regulations which in some instances required that a certain percentage of locally grown tobaccos be included in the product blend further altered the tar and nicotine yields of a given brand. It was alleged, for example, that Marlboro, Kent, Kool and Chesterfield cigarettes averaged 17.5 mg. tar in the U.S., but 31.75 mg. tar in the Philippines.[20]

## STUDY BY THE ECONOMIC INTELLIGENCE UNIT LTD.[21]

Tobacco companies described these product differences as a response to an already existing market, and argued that if they were to make rapid reductions in the yields which were geared to the market's current preferences, "the remaining higher yield brands would undoubtedly become the consumers' choice."[22] A study by the Economic Intelligence Unit Limited, however, suggested that in two-thirds of the world the economic pressures to use local tobacco sharply influenced the availability of tobacco product tastes, and that what appeared to be a dominant home market taste preference was more a function of what consumers were offered than what they wanted.[23]

This same study undertook to develop in great detail an understanding of the economic contribution of tobacco growing to Third World countries, to assess the effect of tobacco production on Third World farmers, communities, and nations, and also to evaluate the role of the international tobacco companies in this process. Five Third World countries (Brazil, India, Nigeria, Costa Rica, and Malaysia) with widely varying tobacco markets and methods of cultivation and sale, and in different stages of development, were chosen for the study, and

---

[18]"Tobacco in Developing Nations," p. 7.
[19]"Tobacco in the Developing Nations," p. 8.

[20]Unreferenced study cited by Walter S. Ross, "Let's Stop Exporting the Smoking Epidemic," *Reader's Digest,* May 1980, pp. 144–5.
[21]An independent economic research organization located in Great Britain.
[22]"Tobacco in Developing Nations," p. 8.
[23]"Leaf Tobacco: Its Contribution to the Economic and Social Development of the Third World," The EIUL, London, 1980, pp. 32–35.

the casewriter's summary of EIU's conclusions is offered below.

Despite the small scale of many tobacco farmers' operations, the tobacco farmers displayed a high degree of sophistication concerning cultivating techniques, due in large part to extensive instruction programs, seed, and technical assistance which the transnational tobacco companies offered their potential suppliers. Tobacco offered stability and in many instances the only opportunity for the farmer to improve his income—hence the tobacco grower tended to rank among the elite in his community. Big companies tended to be associated with wealth and rarely did the farmer feel that he had been "robbed by the multinationals."

The same did not hold true for some governments, however. While President Ferdinand E. Marcos of the Philippines, for example, and his Minister of Agriculture gave their support to current tobacco production, they also criticized the transnational firms for withholding certain technology in order to prevent the Philippines from exporting finished products rather than leaf, and objected to their own citizens' preference for foreign cigarettes which had led to the licensed production of foreign cigarettes within the country.[24] On the other hand, the EIU study found no deliberate manipulation of the host countries to suit the transnationals' own ends:

> The impression gained is one of the companies undertaking a purely commercial activity with only limited awareness of its overall development consequences (broader socioeconomic matters only require consideration to maximize the cost effectiveness of the operation): as a matter of sound business principle, a company will endeavor to pay the grower the perceived minimum consistent with maintaining adequate and continuing supplies of leaf and provide the perceived minimum assistance to achieve this end. In order to accomplish this, of

course, the companies must offer the farmer a satisfactory return for tobacco in comparison with other possible alternative crops (p. 9).

EIU's main economic reservation was the high risk which was associated with the high investment needed to grow tobacco, and most farmers had to take on large loans to finance their operations, which in turn tied them to tobacco crops for a number of years.

While on an absolute level any tobacco cultivation could be said to compete with the production of food, in no area of the EIU study did any food product offer the same return or stability to the farmer as did tobacco, and frequently the most likely foods for growing were already in local surplus due to vagaries in supply and demand. In some countries, such as Malaysia, government policies required that tobacco not compete with food crops, but when rice and tobacco crops were planted in rotation, farmers had achieved noticeably higher rice yields subsequent to tobacco cultivation, and were at the same time fulfilling a government objective of crop diversification to alleviate rural poverty. Of crucial importance to development, however, was that per capita income levels rise at a rate high enough to outpace rises in the population stemming from immediate increases in per capita income—a cycle commonly termed the "poverty trap." Estimates of the rate of annual per capita growth in income required to escape the poverty trap ranged from 3% to 20%.

Tobacco's effect on local development varied extensively in proportion to its ultimate use (export vs. local), overall percentage of the nation's agricultural activity, and reallocation of tax revenues. In the Santa Cruz area of Brazil the economic "spinoffs" from tobacco growing were considerable, and ancillary economic activities included:

1 Retail outlets for consumer durables purchased by farmers, instructors and processing plant employees
2 Agricultural equipment stores
3 Brick making (for barn construction)

[24]"It Was One of CORESTA's Quieter Congresses," *World Tobacco,* Jan. 1981, p. 70.

4 Timber growing (for fueling barn operation)
5 Transportation of tobacco and agricultural inputs
6 Extension services
7 Motor vehicle servicing facilities: for trucks; for instructors' Volkswagens, Jeeps or motorcycles; for farmers' cars and tractors; etc.
8 Tobacco grading, redrying, threshing, etc., plants and associated infrastructure and employee provisions
9 Accomodation for international tobacco buyers
10 The design and fabrication of processing equipment to point of consumption/export transport and associated infrastructure

These, in turn, generated medical services, legal services, a newspaper and radio station, and rural electrification.

Not all countries experienced the same results or benefits from tobacco production and a brief summary regarding three of the five countries studied illustrates the major economic aspects of tobacco cultivation in each country. R. J. Reynolds was one company associated with the first example, and Philip Morris was associated with all three.

1 **Brazil** Without tobacco the small landholder would be confined largely to subsistence-type agriculture centering on maize. The instructor system was highly efficient and effective in controlling agronomic problems. Problems in the industry included a scarcity of labor and of wood for flue curing (some transnationals were supplying seedlings for reforestation), intense competition for supply of leaf, inflation, increase in sharecropping, and diversion of tobacco-generated revenue to uses of little direct benefit to the tobacco growing region.

2 **Costa Rica** Tobacco was of minor importance and grown principally for domestic consumption. The independent Junta de Defensa del Tobaco regulated every step of production and sought to maintain an equitable balance between the farmers and the companies. In Parrita, the area studied, tobacco had been introduced relatively recently along with rice, and had succeeded in achieving some crop diversification (the dominant crop was palm oil), in producing a greater number of independent farmers, and in providing a local economic stimulus which included an inflow of farm laborers from other areas. Competition for new farming land had inflated farm prices, but the local banks were readily providing financial support to tobacco farmers based on the above-average yields which the region had been producing. The latter achievement was due in large part to the assistance offered by the tobacco companies, although it was feared that their encouragement of mechanization might lead to future problems of finance and organization.

3 **Nigeria** The Shinkafe-Sabon Birni district of Sokoto State in the extreme northwest of Nigeria was chosen for the study although tobacco was grown in widely spread areas throughout the country. As in Brazil, rural/urban migration was a major problem for Nigeria. Sokoto was hot and harsh: seven months of the year it suffers a drought. The Hausa population there was primarily engaged in subsistence agriculture and was only partially cash-oriented. Those who grew tobacco had access to the only good soil in the region near tributaries of the Rima River, and the air-cured tobacco which they produced was low in yield (700 kg per hectare with potential of 1,000 kg). Few were willing to adopt the extra agronomic practices which would increase yield, but by regulating tobacco sales the farmers were able to obtain cash even during the dry season, and were associated with the highest social and economic class in the area. Despite an undersupply of leaf, prices were low and tobacco was not attracting further interest. In some instances

following the development of tobacco cultivation farmers were stimulated to produce food crops for cash sale and if tobacco prices remained the same, some food crops might even be more rewarding to the farmers.

EIU's report summarized tobacco growing in the Third World as follows:

The key to the success of tobacco growing is the community of interests between the farmer and the purchaser of his leaf. If the leaf company creates an environment in which the farmer can, if he works well, earn a reasonable income, this in its turn almost inevitably creates an environment for the production of good quality leaf to meet local demand. Support for the farmer centers upon extension services, backed by tobacco research. Significantly, with just a few exceptions, tobacco research and extension for the benefit of farmers are taken most seriously, and are most fruitful, in countries where the international tobacco manufacturing companies are active. Ironically, the very success and effectiveness of the best of these private operations are liable to reduce any incentive that governments may have to provide adequate research and extension services themselves. Moreover, where the government has assumed responsiblity it is not always able to successfully emulate the companies' performance.

Farmers who have mastered the disciplines of tobacco growing have become technically sophisticated and thus, in theory, receptive to the cultivation of other crops if so desired.

## ACTIVITIES AND COMMENTS OF OTHER ORGANIZATIONS

Third World efforts at tobacco cultivation received assistance from such international agencies as the World Bank and the U.N. Development Program. At one time tobacco was included as a commodity in the U.S. Dept. of Agriculture's Food for Peace program and was offered at the receiving country's request as long as it was not in competition with food. In 1980 tobacco was discontinued as an available

commodity in the program. Another U.N. agency, the World Health Organization at its Fourth World Conference on Smoking and Health (Stockholm, June 1979), urged that the increasing consumption of tobacco in the Third World be fought by all governments with increased public antismoking campaigns. In 1979 and 1980 several articles appeared in newspapers and periodicals scoring the U.S. tobacco companies for their increased activities in developing nations. While the facts presented in those articles are already summarized within this case, the opinions expressed therein are not, and a few examples here follow:

### Let's stop exporting the smoking epidemic

Tobacco companies—helped by government—are pushing their lethal product on the unsuspecting Third World. Result: As taxpayers, we have become accomplices in the barter of people's health for profit. (Walter S. Ross, *Reader's Digest,* May 1980.)

"Try Winston, the great taste of America"—this advertising slogan exemplifies the marketing effort that transnational tobacco conglomerates have made to create an appetite for cigarettes among the hungry of the third world.

Our government, using tax dollars, has helped by making tobacco products and technology a major American export.

As a result, at a time when they are striving for political and economic independence, the developing nations are entering into a new form of life-threatening bondage—addiction to cigarette smoking.

Faced with the prospect of diminishing sales in North America and Europe, the tobacco industry identified the third world as a vast untapped market. An aggressive advertising campaign was developed to create the new demand. The effort in most cases unhindered by regulations or health-education programs, has been tragically effective. (Margaret J. Sheridan, *The New York Times,* Editorial Page, 4/13/80.)

The best test for a scientific hypothesis is its repeatability in further experiments. The Third World is becoming a vast laboratory to show, once again, that smoking kills. How can this be happening? What is the smoke screen that prevents people from seeing the hazardous reality?

While a public health doctor in parts of Africa, I witnessed how people are lured into the habit. (Emile Wennen, "The Smoke Screen in Africa," *World Smoking and Health,* Autumn 1979.)

Governments have found it difficult to adopt vigorous, health-oriented tobacco policies partly because of the substantial export and tax revenues derived from tobacco. Nevertheless, health professionals should be aware of the full range of risks associated with tobacco. Especially those who work in maternal and child health and family planning should understand the dangers that tobacco poses for the reproductive process and for infants and children so that they can educate prospective parents to these dangers. (*Population Reports,* p. L-1.)

## EXHIBITS: Smoking and Health—United States Tobacco Companies, National and International Operations

**EXHIBIT 1**
DEMOGRAPHIC CHARACTERISTICS OF SMOKERS 20 YEARS AND OLDER, 1976

| | Percent smoking | |
|---|---|---|
| | Male | Female |
| **Family income** | | |
| Under $5,000 | 42.5 | 28.3 |
| $5,000 to 9,999 | 45.5 | 33.5 |
| $10,000 to 14,999 | 45.5 | 32.5 |
| $15,000 to 24,999 | 40.4 | 33.0 |
| $25,000 or more | 34.7 | 35.1 |
| **Occupation** | | |
| White collar (total) | 36.6 | 34.3 |
| Professional, technical, etc. | 30.0 | 29.1 |
| Managers and administrative (nonfarm) | 41.0 | 41.6 |
| Sales | 39.9 | 38.1 |
| Clerical and related | 40.4 | 34.8 |
| Blue collar | 50.4 | 39.0 |
| Farm | 36.9 | 31.3 |
| Currently unemployed | 56.8 | 40.0 |
| Not in labor force | 32.9 | 28.2 |
| **Marital status** | | |
| Never married | 40.1 | 28.3 |
| Currently married | 41.1 | 32.4 |
| Widowed | 32.6 | 20.4 |
| Separated | 63.3 | 45.1 |
| Divorced | 59.9 | 54.8 |
| **Education** | | |
| Grade school or less | 37.4 | 18.2 |
| Some high school | 47.8 | 33.2 |
| High school graduate | 45.6 | 31.9 |
| Some college | 36.1 | 32.2 |
| College students | 28.1 | 21.1 |

*1975 data.
*Source:* 1980 Surgeon General's Report.

**EXHIBIT 2**
DIVERSIFICATION IN THE TOP TWO U.S. TOBACCO COMPANIES
(Dollars in Millions)

| | 1980 | | 1976 | |
|---|---|---|---|---|
| **R. J. Reynolds Industries, Inc.** | **Operating revenues** | **Operating income*** | **Operating revenues** | **Operating income*** |
| Domestic tobacco | $ 3,521.2 | $ 800.8 | $2,550.0 | $ 545.3 |
| International tobacco | 2,087.7 | 177.2 | 1,221.1 | 64.4 |
| Foods and beverages | 2,265.3 | 94.3 | 264.5 | 20.5 |
| Transportation | 1,413.7 | 65.8 | 920.7 | 123.2 |
| Energy | 985.0 | 182.9 | 741.8 | 36.2 |
| Packaging products | | | | |
|   Outside | 104.5 | | 114.4 | |
|   Intersegment | 100.3 | | 61.5 | |
| Other (principally intersegment eliminations or corporate expense) | (123.6) | (62.4) | (61.9) | (23.8) |
|   Total | $10,354.1 | $1,269.4 | $5,812.1 | $ 779.6 |
| **Philip Morris Company** | **Operating revenues** | **Operating income*** | **Operating revenues** | **Operating income*** |
| Domestic tobacco | $ 3,272.1 | $ 786.1 | $1,963.1 | $ 401.4 |
| Philip Morris International† | 3,205.4 | 328.5 | 1,084.0 | 130.1 |
| Miller Brewing Company | 2,542.3 | 144.7 | 982.8 | 76.1 |
| The Seven-Up Company | 353.2 | (7.1) | — | — |
| Philip Morris Industrial (paper and chemical products) | 276.5 | 16.9 | 169.1 | 10.6 |
| Mission Viejo Company (preplanned community development) | 172.8 | 30.6 | 94.8 | 16.3 |
|   Total | $9,822.3 | $1,299.7 | $4,293.8 | $ 634.5 |

*For R. J. Reynolds the operating income data are before interest and debt expense, foreign currency gains (losses), general corporate expenses, nonrecurring items and provision for income taxes. The operating income figures for Philip Morris may not be directly comparable.
†In 1980 includes operations of Seven-Up International.
*Source:* 1980 annual reports of the companies except for parenthetical additions by the casewriter to Philip Morris' operating divisions.

**EXHIBIT 3**

PHILIP MORRIS INTERNATIONAL, OPERATING RESULTS, 1980

| | $ in millions | Percentage increase (decrease) over 1979 |
|---|---|---|
| Operating revenues | $3,205.4 | 24.2% |
| Operating income | 328.5 | 26.0 |
| Overall sales volume | 238 billion units | 6.1 |
| Export sales from U.S. | 43.1 billion units | 10.4 |
| **Unit sales** | | |
| Selected Brands or Total Philip Morris Operations in Region | | |
| Marlboro—total region Middle East/Africa/Europe | | 11.0% |
| Marlboro—West Germany | | 23.0* |
| Marlboro—France | | 54.0 |
| Marlboro—Belgium | | 51.7 |
| Merit—Italy | | 42.8 |
| Philip Morris U.K. | | 21.0 |
| Philip Morris Eastern Europe | | 9.8 |
| Philip Morris Middle East/Africa | | 17.8 |
| Latin America/Iberia | | NA |
| Australia/New Zealand/Asia | | NA |

*Total West German cigarette industry growth in 1980 was 2.8%.

**EXHIBIT 4**
NATIONAL POLICIES TO CONTROL PROMOTION AND USE OF TOBACCO, 1978

| Developed | Restrictions on advertising | Health warning on packages | Restrictions on sales to minors | Restrictions on smoking | Antismoking education |
|---|---|---|---|---|---|
| Australia | ✓ | | | | |
| Austria | ✓ | ✓ | | | |
| Belgium | ✓ | ✓ | | | |
| Bulgaria | ✓ | ✓ | ✓ | ✓ | |
| Canada | ✓ | ✓ | ✓ | ✓ | ✓ |
| Czechoslovakia | ✓ | ✓ | | | |
| Denmark | ✓ | ✓ | | | |
| Finland | ✓ | ✓ | ✓ | ✓ | ✓ |
| France | ✓ | ✓ | ✓ | | ✓ |
| Germany, F.R. | ✓ | ✓ | | | |
| Iceland | ✓ | ✓ | | | |
| Ireland | ✓ | ✓ | | | |
| Italy | ✓ | ✓ | ✓ | ✓ | ✓ |
| Japan | ✓ | ✓ | | ✓ | |
| Malta | ✓ | ✓ | ✓ | ✓ | |
| Netherlands | ✓* | * | ✓ | | |
| New Zealand | ✓ | ✓ | ✓ | | |
| Norway | ✓ | ✓ | ✓ | ✓ | |
| Poland | ✓ | ✓ | ✓ | ✓ | |
| Soviet Union | ✓ | ✓ | ✓ | ✓ | ✓ |
| Sweden | ✓ | ✓ | ✓ | | |
| Switzerland | ✓ | ✓ | ✓ | | |
| United Kingdom | ✓ | ✓ | ✓ | | |
| United States | | | | | |
| by state | | | 45 | 30‡ | 34¶ |
| Total | 23 | 13 | 10 | 7 | 6 |

| Developing | Restrictions on advertising | Health warning on packages | Restrictions on sales to minors | Restrictions on smoking | Antismoking education |
|---|---|---|---|---|---|
| Burma | ✓ | | | | |
| Colombia | ✓ | ✓ | | | |
| Costa Rica | | ✓ | | | |
| Ecuador | ✓ | | | | |
| Egypt | ✓ | | | | |
| Greece | | | | | ✓ |
| India | † | ✓ | | | |
| Iraq | | | | | |
| Korea, South | ✓ | ✓ | | | |
| Malaysia | ✓ | | | | |
| Mexico | ✓ | ✓ | | | |
| Morocco | ✓ | ✓ | | ✓ | |
| Mozambique | ✓ | | | | |
| Panama | † | ✓ | | | |
| Peru | † | ✓ | | | |
| Romania | ✓ | | | | |
| Saudi Arabia | ✓ | | | | |
| Singapore | ✓ | | | ✓ | |
| Spain | ✓ | | | | |
| Thailand | | ✓ | | ✓ | |
| Turkey | | | ✓ | | |
| Venezuela | ✓ | | | | |
| Zambia | | | | | |
| Total | 12 | 9 | 1 | 3 | 1 |

*Restrictions on a voluntary basis.
†Warnings required in advertising.
‡Of these, 22 are considered relatively stringent or extensive.
¶Mandatory drug, alcohol and tobacco education programs.
*Source:* US Office on Smoking and Health (225), World Tobacco (5).

# Note on the Export of Pesticides from the United States to Developing Countries

The sale or distribution of any pesticide within the United States was prohibited by law unless it was registered with the Environmental Protection Agency (EPA). Registration required the submission of toxicity data showing that intended use of the pesticide posed no unreasonable risk to people or the environment. Each year, however, U.S. companies exported to developing countries millions of pounds of unregistered pesticides and pesticides whose registration had been canceled or restricted. In 1976, for example, 25% of U.S. exports, or 140 million pounds, were unregistered and another 31 million pounds were pesticides whose registrations had been canceled.[1] This practice was legal as long as these pesticides were manufactured only for export.

As concern about the environment increased in the 1970s, the morality of this prac-

tice, what to do about it, and who was responsible for changing it became widely debated. In *Circle of Poison,* David Weir and Mark Schapiro claimed that the export of these pesticides resulted in tens of thousands of poisonings and scores of fatalities in developing countries each year. Referring to the practice as an international scandal, they blamed the pesticide industry for dumping these pesticides in developing countries and argued that Americans were also harmed because imports treated with these pesticides contained toxic residues. The *Christian Science Monitor* called the situation morally indefensible and urged government intervention.[2] A main charge of critics was that the practice was based on a double standard—the lives of people in developing countries were less valuable than the lives of Americans. Phillip Leakey, assistant minister of the environment in Kenya, asserted: "There is no question that

[1] *Better Regulation of Pesticide Exports and Pesticide Residues in Imported Foods is Essential* (Washington, DC: General Accounting Office, 1979), p. 3.

[2] "Exporting Poisons," *Christian Science Monitor,* February 13, 1980, p. 12.

KEY TO ACRONYMS

| | |
|---|---|
| ADI | Acceptable daily intake |
| AID | Agency for International Development |
| Amvac | American Vanguard Corporation |
| EPA | Environmental Protection Agency |
| FAO | Food and Agricultural Organization |
| FDA | Food and Drug Administration |
| FFDCA | Federal Food, Drug, and Cosmetic Act |
| FIFRA | Federal Insecticide, Fungicide, and Rodenticide Act |
| GAO | General Accounting Office |
| GIFAP | Groupement International des Associations Nationales de Fabricants de Produit Agrochimiques |
| IPM | Integrated pest management |
| NACA | National Agricultural Chemicals Association |
| OSHA | Occupational Safety and Health Administration |
| OXFAM | Oxford Committee for the Relief of Famine |
| WHO | World Health Organization |

the industrial nations and the companies which are manufacturing these things are guilty of promoting and sponsoring dangerous chemicals in countries where they think people don't care."[3] "What is at stake here is the integrity of the label *Made in U.S.A.,*" argued Rep. Michael D. Barnes (D—Md.), who introduced legislation in 1980 to limit the export of dangerous pesticides abroad.[4]

The U.S. pesticide industry was opposed to more government regulation and countered that it, too, was concerned about the harm done by pesticides, but that this was largely a result of misuse. Spokespeople for the industry argued that they were making significant attempts on their own to reduce harm through education and by developing safer promotional and advertising methods. A principal argument of the industry was that each country had the right to make up its own mind about the risks and benefits of using a particular pesticide. Dr. Jack Early, president of the National Agricultural Chemicals Association (NACA), accused critics of elitism and asked: "Should we tell other countries on the basis of our affluent standards where the appropriate balance of benefits and risks should lie for them? What does the EPA know—or care, for that matter—about the strength of Brazil's desire to obtain a particular pesticide that has some undesirable ecological effect?"[5]

## SOME EXAMPLES OF MANUFACTURERS AND PESTICIDES

### Velsicol and Phosvel

In 1971 Velsicol Chemical Company of Chicago began U.S. production of Phosvel, its trade name for the pesticide leptophos. The WHO classified leptophos as extremely hazardous due to its delayed neurotoxic effects—it could cause paralysis for some time after exposure. Phosvel was not approved for sale in the U.S. by the EPA, although it was granted a temporary registration. Velsicol however, sold it to developing countries where there were no restrictions on its importation.

There were reports in 1971 that Phosvel was involved in the deaths of water buffalo in Egypt.[6] Velsicol contended, citing the report of the U.S. Pesticide Tolerance Commission, that a conclusive determination of Phosvel's role in the incident could not be made because of incomplete facts. In 1973 and 1974 there were additional accounts of poisonings of animals and people.[7]

[3]"Kenya tries to put cap on imports of hazardous chemicals," *Christian Science Monitor,* May 3, 1983, p. 13.
[4]"Hazards for Export," *Newsday,* December 1981, reprint, p. 14R.

[5]Ibid., p. 13R.
[6]Cited by Jacob Scherr, *Proceedings of the U.S. Strategy Conference on Pesticide Management* (Silver Springs, Maryland: Teknekron Research, Inc., 1979), p. 33.
[7]David Bull, *A Growing Problem* (Oxford, England: OXFAM, 1982), p. 40.

In 1976 OSHA revealed that workers at Velsicol's Bayport, Texas plant that manufactured Phosvel had developed serious disorders of the nervous system. They vomited, complained of impotence, were fatigued and disoriented and became paralyzed. Workers sued Velsicol, and EPA sued for pollution violations, and OSHA levelled fines. The company then withdrew its application for registration of Phosvel and closed the Bayport plant.

From 1971 to 1976, when Velsicol stopped manufacturing Phosvel, estimates were that it exported $10–18 million worth of Phosvel to developing counties. After the Bayport incident, several countries banned the import of Phosvel. Claiming that when used properly, Phosvel was safe, Velsicol tried to sell remaining stocks of Phosvel in developing countries.[8]

In 1978 Velsicol began reforms to change its environmental image. Responding to criticisms of the company, Richard Blewitt, vice president of corporate affairs, stated: "I'm sorry to say we don't have control over worldwide inventories of Phosvel. Velsicol has made an attempt . . . to secure at our cost those inventories and make sure thay are properly disposed of, . . . which far exceeds our obligation."[9] He observed, however, that some distributors were resisting the efforts to buy back inventories of Phosvel.

As of 1984, Velsicol sold heptachlor, chlordane, and endrin to developing countries. Use of these pesticides had been canceled or restricted in the U.S. because they were suspected of being carcinogenic or mutagenic, although Velsicol claimed there was no medical evidence that exposure to these chemicals had caused any case of cancer or birth defects in man.

## Amvac and DBCP

After workers at an Occidental plant in California were found to be sterile in 1977, the state canceled the use of another pesticide, DBCP. At that time Dow, Occidental, and Shell stopped producing it. In 1979 the EPA canceled all uses of DBCP except for use on Hawaiian pineapples because it was suspected of being carcinogenic.

After the ban the American Vanguard Corporation (Amvac) could no longer sell DBCP directly to American companies, but it did continue exporting it. The company's 1979 10-K report stated: "Management believes that because of the extensive publicity and notoriety that has arisen over the sterility of workers and the suspected mutagenic and carcinogenic nature of DBCP, the principal manufacturers and distributors of the product (Dow, Occidental, and Shell Chemical) have, temporarily at least, decided to remove themselves from the domestic marketplace and possibly from the world marketplace." The report continued: "Notwithstanding all the publicity and notoriety surrounding DBCP it was [our] opinion that a vacuum existed in the marketplace that [we] could temporarily occupy. [We] further believed that with the addition of DBCP, sales might be sufficient to reach a profitable level." According to Weir and Schapiro, a former executive had stated: "Quite frankly, without DBCP, Amvac would go bankrupt."[10]

## Dow Chemical and 2,4-D and 2,4,5-T

2,4-D and 2,4,5-T were herbicides that often contained dioxin as a contaminant. These herbicides were probably best known as components of Agent Orange, one of the herbicides used as a defoliant by the United States during the war in Vietnam. A study done by Dr. Marco Micolta, director of the San Antonio Central Hospital in rural Colombia, claimed that 2,4-D and 2,4,5-T were responsible for the many miscarriages and birth defects—usually harelip and cleft palate or both—that occurred in the region.[11] In the United States 2,4-D and 2,4,5-T

[8]David Weir and Mark Schapiro, *Circle of Poison* (San Francisco, CA: Institute for Food and Development Policy, 1981), p. 23.
[9]*Newsday*, p. 11R.

[10]Weir and Schapiro, p. 22.
[11]*Newsday*, p. 11R.

were manufactured and sold abroad by several companies, including Dow Chemical Company. All uses of these pesticides containing dioxin were illegal in the United States, and use of them without dioxin was restricted.

"Dioxin Reportedly Worst Cancer Causer" read the headline of an article in the *Boston Globe*. The article summarized a report by scientists for the EPA which concluded that dioxin was "the most potent cancer causing substance they have ever studied." It was further stated that dioxin probably caused cancer in humans and presented an unacceptable cancer risk when found in water in parts per quintillion. A trillionth of a gram of dioxin in a cubic meter of air would produce about nine additional cases of cancer for each 100,000 people, it was reported. The article pointed out that the conclusions in the report contrasted sharply with industry claims that "the most serious health effect caused by exposure to dioxin is a serious skin rash called chloracne."[12]

In testimony to Congress, a Dow vice president and toxicologist, Perry Gehring, stated that dioxin had "only mild effects on humans." Consistent with its policy of maintaining that 2,4-D and 2,4,5-T were safe when properly used, Dow had been lobbying to have restrictions of these pesticides eased. Robert Lundeen, chairman, said that Dow was trying to reverse the 1979 suspension of 2,4,5-T because "it was patently unsound and had no scientific merit. If we caved in on this one, we might lose the next one, when it was important." One study of the herbicide followed 121 workers in a Monsanto plant that produced 2,4,5-T. They had been accidentally exposed to dioxin in 1949 and developed chloracne and other temporary symptoms. After 30 years of observation, the University of Cincinnati's Institute of Environmental Health reported that their death rate was below average and rates of cancer and other chronic disease was at or below normal.[13]

## WHAT IS A PESTICIDE?

Most pesticides were synthetic organic chemicals that were able to kill pests, including insects, weeds, fungi, rodents, and worms. (Clearly, people had different ideas as to what counted as a pest. One survey in the Philippines found that the farmers studied believed that any insect found in their fields should be killed by insecticides.) Pesticides were classified either by use or by chemical makeup. The three major kinds of pesticides by use were herbicides, insecticides, and fungicides. Classification by chemical makeup produced four major categories: organochlorines, organophosphates, carbamates, and pyrethroids. In addition to the generic names of the active ingredients (e.g., paraquat) pesticides also had been given brand names by the companies that produced them (e.g., Gramoxone).

In assessing the risks or hazards of using a pesticide, it was common to distinguish between the intrinsic properties of the chemical and aspects of risk that were under human control. Toxicity, persistence, and fat solubility were important innate characteristics to consider. Toxicity was measured in terms of the lethal dose ($LD_{50}$) required to kill 50% of the test animals—usually rats. Acute toxic effects included nausea, dizziness, sweating, salivation, shortness of breath, unconsciousness, and possibly death. Some commonly used pesticides, like parathion, could cause death by swallowing only a few drops or by skin contact with a teaspoon of the chemical. Chronic toxicity was produced by long-term, low-level exposure and was evidenced by infertility, nervous disorders, tumors, blood disorders, or abnormal offspring. A pesticide was considered persistent if it did not break down easily. Since persistent chemicals remained in the environment longer, they were more likely to affect organisms other than the target pest. The persistence of a chemical varied according to its interaction with the environment. For example, DDT had a half-life of 20 years in temperate climates but was reported in some studies to have a half-life of less than a year in the tropics as a result of increased

---

[12]The *Boston Globe*, July 24, 1983, p. 19.
[13]"Dow vs. the Dioxin Monster," *Fortune*, May 30, 1983, pp. 84–85.

sunlight, warmth, and moisture.[14] If a pesticide was fat soluble, it could bioaccumulate in the body and remain there. This accumulation might result in long-term harm. Although not acutely toxic, DDT was considered hazardous because of its persistence and fat solubility.

Controllable risk factors included the precautions taken in the manufacture, storage, and transport of a pesticide; the nature of the formulation of the active ingredients; the manner of application; the place used; and the amount of chemical applied.

## THE PESTICIDE INDUSTRY

The first step in producing a pesticide was synthesizing or creating thousands of chemicals and testing them for useful biological activity—in this instance, the ability to kill pests. If the chemical passed this initial screen (and only 1% did in the first stage of development) then laboratory tests for acute toxicity began, along with a patent application. In the second stage of development, laboratory and greenhouse tests continued. The chemical was tested for specificity of action—did it kill only a few pests or a wide variety? An experimental permit was also applied for. In the final stage testing continued, full registration was applied for, and final preparations for manufacturing and marketing began. (Figure A shows the process in more detail.) In 1981 it took six to seven years from the time of discovery of a chemical with biological efficacy to final registration with the EPA. A company might have screened 12,000–30,000 chemicals before it brought one to market. It was estimated that the research and development costs for a single pesticide averaged $20 million.

Major pesticide companies synthesized active ingredients and formulated them, or combined the active ingredients with inert substances to make them ready for application. U.S. production moved from the pesticide

[14]Ram S. Hamsagar, "Petrochemicals and the Environment." Paper published by *Groupement International des Associations Nationales de Fabricants de Produit Agrochimiques* (GIFAP), September 23, 1983, p. 4.

manufacturer to distributor to dealer to the farmer. Production in developing countries was similar, except that dealers in the United States were often trained by pesticide companies and were knowledgeable about pesticide use, whereas in developing countries the user often bought pesticides from a small shopkeeper who was not well informed about pesticide use and toxicity. In addition, some large companies had established plants in developing countries that formulated the basic toxicants, which were then imported by the parent company. This enabled companies to decrease production costs due to lower labor costs and less government regulation. They also were able to take advantage of tax incentives offered to foreign investors in these countries. (Table A lists the top 10 producers of pesticides in 1980.)

From the 1940s to the late 1970s the pesticide industry, driven by the frequent introduction of new products, experienced rapid growth. Investment of R&D was high to sustain innovation and cheaper manufacturing processes. In 1981 R&D budgets were 8% of sales. The industry also required high capital investment because of the rapid obsolescence of plant and equipment; thus, capital expenditures were 7.2% of sales. These high technology costs, as well as high regulation and marketing costs, posed significant barriers to entry.

Sales of U.S. producers steadily increased from $1.2 billion dollars in 1972 to $5.4 billion in 1982. (Figure B shows the increase in sales and exports of pesticides from 1960 to 1980.) Exports steadily rose from $220 million in 1970 to about $1.2 billion in 1980. Production of pesticides in the U.S. rose from 675 million pounds in 1960 to a peak of 1.7 billion pounds in 1975 and declined to 1.3 billion pounds in 1980.

Prices and profits for pesticides depended largely on whether or not patents were involved. Pretax profit margins on proprietary products that had a market niche were about 48%. Older products, like DDT and 2,4-D, functioned more like commodities and returned considerably less on investment. Even though a product was patented, competing

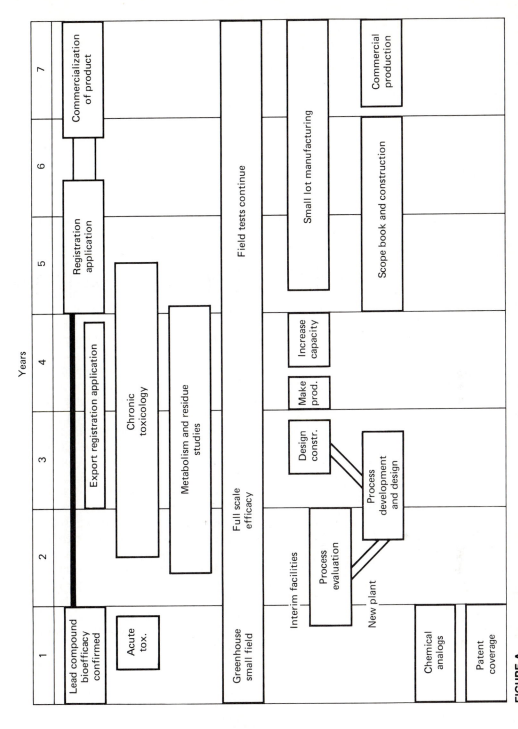

**FIGURE A**
Pesticide R&D process: activities and timing. (*Source:* Data gathered by casewriter.)

559

**TABLE A**
TOP 10 PRODUCERS OF PESTICIDES, 1980

| Company | Value ($ mil.) | Production (mil. lb.) | % market share by value | % cumulative market share |
|---------|---------------|----------------------|------------------------|---------------------------|
| Monsanto | $552–580 | 169–173 | 20% | 20% |
| Ciba-Geigy | 354–358 | 142–147 | 13 | 33 |
| Stauffer | 330 | 150–117 | 12 | 45 |
| Eli Lilly | 285–300 | 72–82 | 10 | 55 |
| DuPont | 220 | 75–99 | 8 | 63 |
| Cyanamid | 220 | 82 | 8 | 71 |
| Union Carbide | 150–160 | 57–63 | 6 | 77 |
| Shell | 132–155 | 40–55 | 5 | 82 |
| FMC | 135–140 | 55 | 5 | 87 |
| Mobay | 125–135 | 40–45 | 5 | 92 |

Source: *U.S. Pesticides Market* (New York: Frost and Sullivan, Inc., 1981), p. 126.

**FIGURE B**
U. S. sales of pesticides, 1960–1980.
(*Source:* Data gathered by casewriter.)

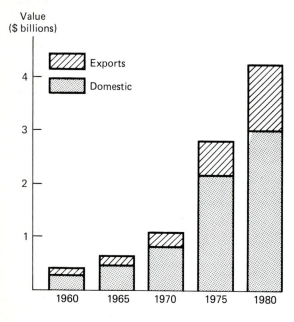

companies often developed similar products not covered by the original patent. Prices of pesticides tripled between 1970 and 1980; in 1981 herbicides had the highest price and accounted for 60% of sales.

The pesticide industry was a mature industry and U.S. markets had become saturated. As demand in the U.S. slowed, exports increased. In 1978 exports were 621 million pounds and were 36% of total shipments. In 1990, it was predicted, exports would be 855 million pounds and would be 43% of total pesticide shipments. Dollar volume of U.S. exports was projected to reach $2.6 billion by 1990.[15]

Industry analysts agreed that exports would provide the fastest growth for U.S. producers, since the U.S. markets were saturated. Farmers were also using fewer pesticides because of increased costs, declining acreage under cultivation, a slowing of growth in farm income, and increased use of integrated pest management (IPM) techniques which relied more on cultural and biological controls and less on pesticides.

There were 35 producers of pesticides worldwide with sales of more than $100 million per year. In 1982 total worldwide sales were

[15]"Pesticides: $6 Billion by 1990," *Chemical Week,* May 7, 1980, p. 45.

$13.3 billion, up from $2.8 billion in 1972. Six countries—United States, West Germany, France, Brazil, the USSR, and Japan—accounted for 63% of worldwide sales. All of the developing countries combined accounted for 15% of the worldwide market in dollar volume. A report by the U.S. General Accounting Office (GAO) estimated that pesticide requirements in dollar value for these countries were expected to increase fivefold from 1979 to 1985.[16]

## THE BENEFITS OF PESTICIDES

The pesticide industry and many agricultural scientists defended the sale of pesticides to developing countries, declaring that pesticides were necessary to feed an ever-increasing world population, most of it poor, and that pesticides were of great value in fighting diseases which primarily affected the poor. They also argued that there were important secondary benefits.

In 1979 the world population reached approximately 4.4 billion people. Using a minimum-intake level for survival, with no allowance for physical activity, the Food and Agricultural Organization (FAO) of the United Nations estimated that there were 450 million chronically malnourished people in the world. Using a higher standard, the International Food Policy Research Institute put the figure at 1.3 billion.[17]

World population doubled from A.D. 1 to A.D. 1650; a second doubling occurred after 200 years; the next took 80 years; and the last doubling took place in 1975, requiring only 45 years. Given the 1980 worldwide average birthrate of 2.05%, according to Norman Borlaug the next doubling would occur in 2015, when world population would total 8 billion. At that birthrate, 172 people would be born every minute, resulting in an additional 90 million people

each year. David Hopper of the World Bank stated that developing countries accounted for 90% of this increase.[18]

In 1977, Borlaug noted, world food production totaled 3.5 billion tons, 98% of which came directly or indirectly from plants. On the basis of rates of population growth and projected income elasticities for food, Hopper emphasized the necessity for an increase in food availability of about 3% per year, requiring a doubling of world food production to 6.6 billion tons by 2015. Increasing demand for food by developing countries was reflected in the fact that imports of grains to these countries rose from 10 million tons in 1961 to 52 million tons in 1977, according to Maurice Williams, and food shortages were projected to reach 145 million tons by 1990, of which 80 million tons would be for the low-income countries of Asia and Africa.[19]

A major cause of these shortages was that food production in developing countries had not kept pace with the increased demand for food. While per capita production of food for developed countries had steadily increased since 1970, per capita production in developing countries *decreased* by an average of 50%, with the economies of Africa and Latin America showing the greatest drop.

Although experts agreed that it was important to attack the world food problem by lessening demand, they also concurred that deliberate efforts to slow population growth would not produce any significant decline in demand for food for the next decade or so. It was argued, then, that ameliorating the world food problem depended on increasing the food supply. Norman Borlaug, recipient of the 1971 Nobel Peace Prize for the development of the high-yield seeds that were the basis for the Green Revolution, argued that developed

[16]*Better Regulation,* p. 1.
[17]Maurice J. Williams, "The Nature of the World Food and Population Problem," in *Future Dimensions of World Food and Population,* ed. by R. G. Woods (Boulder, Colorado: Westview Press, 1981), p. 20.

[18]Norman Borlaug, "Using Plants to Meet World Food Needs," *Future Dimensions,* p. 180; David Hopper, "Recent Trends in World Food and Population," *Future Dimensions,* p. 37.
[19]Borlaug, pp. 118, 128; Hopper, p. 39; and Williams, p. 11.

countries would not make significant additional increases in yields per acre and that developing countries had to increase their per capita food production. Due to the scarcity of easily developed new land, Borlaug concluded that increases in world food supply could come only from increased yields per acre in these countries, and that this required the widespread use of pesticides.[20]

There was little argument, even from critics, that pesticides increased food production. The technology of the Green Revolution, which depended on pesticides, had enabled scientists in the tropics to obtain yields of 440 bushels of corn per acre versus an average yield of 30 bushels per acre by traditional methods.[21] The International Rice Research Institute in the Philippines had shown that rice plots protected by insecticides yielded an average of 2.7 tons per hectare (2.47 acres) more than unprotected plots, an increase of almost 100%. They also found that the use of rodenticides resulted in rice yields up to three times higher than those of untreated plots.[22] (*Only* producing more food would not end world hunger. What kinds of foods people eat and the quantity are correlated with income. Thus, many experts maintain that economic development is equally important in eliminating world hunger.)

Even with the use of pesticides, worldwide crop losses because of pests before harvest averaged about 25% in developed countries and around 40% in undeveloped countries. In 1982, GIFAP estimated that total crop losses due to pests for rice, corn, wheat, sugar cane, and cotton were about $204 billion. Most experts (quoted in Ennis et al.) estimated an additional loss of 20–25% of food crops if pesticides were not used.[23]

Pesticides also contributed to reducing losses after harvesting. A National Academy of Sciences study identified most postharvest loss resulting from pests and observed that "conservative estimates indicate that a minimum of 107 million tons of food were lost in 1976; the amounts lost in cereal grains and legumes alone could produce more than the annual minimum caloric requirements of 168 million people." Postharvest losses of crops and perishables through pests were estimated to range from 10% to 40%. Insects were a major problem, especially in the tropics, because environmental conditions produced rapid breeding. The National Academy of Sciences noted that "50 insects at harvest could multiply to become more than 312 million after four months." In India, in 1963 and 1964, insects and rodents attacked grain in the field and in storage and caused losses of 13 million tons. According to Ennis et al., this amount of wheat would have supplied 77 million families with one loaf of bread per day for a year.[24]

Many developing countries also relied on the sale of agricultural products for foreign exchange that they needed for development or to buy the commodities they could not produce. Cotton, for example, was an important cash crop for many of these countries. Several experimental studies in the United States had shown that untreated plots produced about 10 pounds of seed cotton per acre, but over 1,000 pounds were produced when insecticides were used.[25] It was estimated that 50% of the cotton produced by developing countries would be destroyed if pesticides were not used.

It was also argued that major indirect benefits resulted from the use of an agricultural technology that had pesticide use as an essen-

[20]Borlaug, p. 114 and pp. 129–134.
[21]Hopper, p. 49.
[22]Bull, p. 5.
[23]*GIFAP Directory* 1982–1983, p. 19; W. B. Ennis, W. M. Dowler, W. Klassen, "Crop Protection to Increase Food Supplies," in *Food: Politics, Economics, Nutrition, and Research*, ed. P. Abelson (Washington, DC: American Association for the Advancement of Science, 1975), p. 113.

[24]E. R. Pariser et al., *Post-Harvest Food Losses in Developing Countries* (Washington, DC: National Academy of Sciences, 1978), pp. 7, 53; Ennis, p. 110.
[25]William Hollis, "The Realism of Integrated Pest Management as a Concept and in Practice—with Social Overtures," paper presented at Annual Meeting of Entomological Society of America, in Washington, DC, December 1, 1977, p. 7.

tial component. This "package" was more efficient not only because it increased yields per acre, but also because it decreased the amount of land and labor needed for food production. In 1970 American food production, for example, required 281 million acres. At 1940 yields per acre, which were generally less than half of 1970 yields, it would have taken 573 million acres to produce the 1970 crop. This was a savings of 292 million acres through increased crop yields.[26] The estimated 300% increase in per capita agricultural production from 1960 to 1980 also meant that labor resources could be used for other activities. Other experts estimated that without the use of pesticides in the United States, the price of farm products would probably increase by at least 50% and we would be forced to spend 25% or more of our income on food.[27] It was held that many of these same secondary benefits would accrue to developing countries through the use of pesticides.

Pesticides also contributed both directly and indirectly to combating disease; because of this, their use in developing countries had increased. Pesticides had been highly effective in reducing such diseases as malaria, yellow fever, elephantiasis, dengue, and filariasis. Malaria was a good example. In 1955, WHO initiated a global malaria eradication campaign based on the spraying of DDT. This effort greatly reduced the incidence of malaria. For example, in India there were approximately 75 million cases in the early 1950s. But in 1961 there were only 49,000 cases. David Bull estimated that by 1970 the campaign had prevented 2 billion cases and had saved 15 million lives. In 1979 Freed estimated that one-sixth of the world's population had some type of pest-borne disease.[28]

### RISKS TO HUMANS

Reliable estimates of the number of pesticide poisonings worldwide were difficult to obtain because many countries did not gather such statistics. Using figures from WHO, Bull of the Oxford Committee for the Relief of Famine (OXFAM) calculated that in 1981 there were 750,000 cases of pesticide poisoning and about 14,000 deaths worldwide, with over half of the fatalities being children. OXFAM estimated that in developing countries there were 375,000 cases of poisoning with 10,000 deaths a year. Thus, developing countries, with 15% of pesticide consumption, suffered half of the accidental poisonings and three-fourths of the deaths. Another survey by Davies et al. estimated that in 1977, the annual worldwide mortality rate was over 20,000.[29]

Experts agreed that these estimates contained large margins for error, and they believed that the actual number of cases was substantially higher. Many countries did not collect statistics on pesticide poisonings. In addition, pesticides were often used in remote areas that lacked easy access to clinics or had physicians who were not trained to recognize the symptoms of pesticide poisoning.

### CAUSES OF PESTICIDE POISONING IN DEVELOPING COUNTRIES

Pesticide poisoning resulted from many causes in developing countries. Workers would remain in the fields when planes were spraying crops; they might not have left for fear that they would lose their jobs, or they might not have understood the risk. Much of the spray drifted through the area to cover homes, utensils, clothes hanging on lines, children playing, irrigation ditches, and animals. Sometimes workers too quickly entered a newly sprayed field; the pesticide, then still moist on the plant, rubbed off on their skin and clothing. Later, when they washed, they did so with what was available—the pesticide-contaminated water in the irrigation ditches. This may also have been the source of their drinking water. Reports also

[26]Borlaug, p. 106.
[27]Ennis, p. 113.
[28]Bull, p. 30; Virgil Freed, *Proceedings,* p. 21.

[29]Bull, p. 38; John Davies, et al., *An Agromedical Approach to Pesticide Management* (Miami, FL: University of Miami, 1982), p. 9.

surfaced of pilots dumping excess pesticide into lakes or rivers that were often vital food and water sources.

Another cause of pesticide misuse was the lack of education—many of the people who used pesticides in developing countries were illiterate. In addition, they knew little or nothing about the dangers of pesticides and how they interacted with the environment. Developing countries did not have the elaborate agricultural extension services that existed in industrialized countries, especially in the United States. The farmers and laborers often did not know safe or effective methods for transporting, mixing, applying, storing, and disposing of pesticides.

Consider the example of one village on the shore of Lake Volta in Ghana. The fishermen began using Gammalin 20 (lindane) to catch fish. They would pour the pesticide into the lake and wait for the poisoned fish to float to the surface. The village depended on the lake for its food, income, drinking water, and water for cooking and washing. Soon the people around the lake complained of blurred vision, dizziness, and vomiting—all symptoms of lindane poisoning. The number of fish in the lake declined 10–20% a year. The villagers initially did not connect their symptoms with the declining fish population. They believed that both were due to natural causes. When they did become aware that the fish were poisoned, they believed the poison remained in the fish's head and that cutting off the head made the fish safe to eat.[30]

Sometimes poisoning resulted because proper safety precautions were not taken when chemicals were mixed and applied. Often workers mixed the pesticides with their hands, or, if in granular form, they sprinkled pesticides on the plants with their hands. The director of the National Biological Control Research Center in Thailand reported: "When mixing the formulation for spraying, the farmer may dip his finger into the mix and taste it by dabbing his fin-

ger to his tongue. If it gets numb it indicates the right concentration." Frequently, workers were not supplied with protective clothing, could not afford it, or chose not to wear it because of the heat. They also often had faulty equipment. If sprayers were carried on their backs, leaky valves allowed the pesticide to run down their shoulders. One survey done in the Philippines indicated that none of the farmers studied knew that a leaky valve could be fatal. Another survey in Gujarat, India, showed that none of the farm workers had face masks, only 50% covered their noses and mouths with a cloth, and 20% did not wash after spraying.[31]

Distribution methods in developing countries also caused problems. Pesticides were shipped in bulk containers and were then repackaged in smaller containers. Local merchants customarily sold the products in unlabeled bottles and kept them on shelves with other foodstuffs. Farmers relied on the local shop owner, often untrained, to advise them about what pesticide to use and how. For example, paraquat, which was dark in color, caused numerous poisonings because it was mistaken for coke, wine, or coffee.

The large drums in which pesticides were shipped were frequently used to hold drinking water and store food. Few understood that the residues of the pesticide on the walls of a drum might still be toxic. In one case 124 people were poisoned, eight fatally, after eating food prepared in recycled pesticide drums.[32]

Critics contended that labels often failed to give the detailed information necessary for safety precautions and were sometimes not written in the language of the area in which they were to be distributed. Even when they were, however, many of the users could not read them, because they were illiterate. According to Dr. Fred Whittemore, pest management specialist for AID, a check in Mexico found that 50% of the pesticides sold were incorrectly labeled. Labels usually did not state first-aid recommendations or contained recommenda-

[30]Ruth Norris, ed., *Pills, Pesticides and Profits* (Croton-on-Hudson, NY: North River Press, 1982), p. 13.

[31]Bull, p. 49.
[32]Davies, p. 88.

tions that were unrealistic. In a remote part of India one pesticide label specified calling a physician and using the substances atropine and 2 PAM as an antidote; however, the local clinic was hours away and when checked, had never heard of 2 PAM.[33]

Critics charged that through promotion and advertising, companies encouraged farmers to view pesticides as panaceas. They emphasized that frequently the advertisements failed to mention the dangers of pesticides and created the impression that pesticides were safe to use. Critics also argued that companies occasionally encouraged overuse by advocating calendar spraying rather than spraying on the basis of the number of pests attacking a crop. They pointed out that many in developing countries trusted the goodwill of American companies. As Dr. Harold Alvo Nunez, former Colombian Minister of Health, put it: "You know, the label 'Made in U.S.A.' is very powerful here."[34]

### RISKS TO THE ENVIRONMENT

Problems with pesticide overuse were particularly severe in developing countries. For example, Weir and Schapiro estimated that pesticide use was 40% higher in Central America than necessary to achieve optimal production. In 1975 El Salvador, with a population of 4.5 million people, was using 20% of the world production of parathion. This averaged out to 2,940 pounds per square mile, according to Wolterding.[35]

In *A Growing Problem,* David Bull described the process by which farmers became hooked on using greater and greater quantities and more and more varieties of pesticides. He called this the *pesticide treadmill.* When an insecticide was used, for example, it killed not only the targeted insect but also other insects that were its natural enemies. These natural controls also kept in check other insects that potentially could become pests. Once the natural controls were killed, there could be not only an increase in the original target pests but also an increase in these secondary pests. Faced with an unexpected increase in pests, the farmer's typical response was to spray even more. Another result of repeated pesticide use was that pests developed a genetic resistance to them. Once this happened, the usual response again was to spray in larger quantities and then to try another kind of pesticide. An additional reason for overuse was that formulation and methods of application for many chemicals had been developed for use in temperate climates. The more rapid breakdown of chemicals in tropical climates, however, required more frequent and larger applications.

The cultivation of cotton in Central America illustrated the pesticide treadmill at work. At the turn of the century, Central American farmers began growing cotton, which was native to the region, on a commercial scale. At that time, the boll weevil was cotton's only major pest and it was controlled by natural enemies and by hand removal from the cotton plants.

In the 1950s, as the amount of acreage under cultivation increased, mechanization and intensive use of pesticides began. Initially, insecticides were applied about eight times a year and resulted in improved yields. By the mid-1950s, three new pests were attacking cotton. During the 1960s insecticide use increased; as many as 50 different pesticides became available for a single pest. The number of applications increased to 28 per season. By 1970 there were eight pests causing serious damage to cotton. As new pests appeared the old ones became more resistant, and farmers applied more and more pesticides. By 1974, Central American growers were spraying up to 40 times a season. An average of 3,380 pounds of pesticide was being applied for every square mile.[36]

Food crops as well as cash crops were affected. Rice was the staple crop for hundreds of

---

[33]Bull, p. 89.
[34]*Newsday,* p. 11R.
[35]Weir and Schapiro, p. 6; Martin Wolterding, "The Poisoning of Central America," *Sierra,* September–October 1981, p. 64.

[36]Wolterding, p. 64.

millions of people in Southeast Asia. One study reported that 8 rice pests were resistant to at least one insecticide in 1965; 14 pests were resistant to pesticides by 1975.[37]

Pests worldwide have rapidly developed resistances to pesticides. In 1951 there were 6 species of pests of either medical or agricultural importance that were resistant. By 1961 Davies estimated that the number was 137 and in 1980 resistant pests increased to 414 species. An exacerbating factor was that sometimes pests developed multiple resistance to a whole group of chemicals in the same class. An example was the diamondback moth, which attacked cabbage in one region of the Malay peninsula. The moths had become so resistant that farmers now sprayed three times a week, often using a "cocktail" made up of several insecticides. The diamondback moth, in turn, developed some degree of resistance to at least 11 insecticides. Bull estimated that in 1978 insecticides accounted for one-third of the production costs of cabbages. It was believed that soon it would no longer be profitable to grow cabbage in the region.[38]

In the 1970s a resurgence occurred in the incidence of malaria. For example, in India, although the number of cases dropped from 75 million in the 1950s to 49,000 in 1961, the figure rose to 6.5 million in 1976. In Haiti there were 2,500 cases in 1968 but 26,000 in 1972. Worldwide the number of cases increased by over 230% between 1972 and 1976.[39] This increase was attributed to the disease-carrying mosquito's resistance to pesticides. (As Figure C indicates, the rate of introduction of new pesticides had not kept up with the rate at which pests were developing resistance.)

**INDUSTRY RESPONSE**

The pesticide industry argued that each country had the right to set its own policy based on its individual estimate of the risk/benefit ratio of using a particular pesticide, and that the risk/

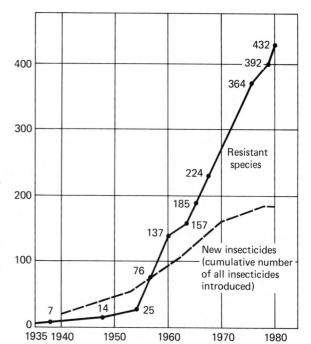

**FIGURE C**
Resistant species of arthropods and new insecticides, 1938–1980. (*Source:* David Bull, *A Growing Problem,* OXFAM, Oxford, England, 1982, p. 24.)

benefit ratio for developing countries varied with economic and social conditions. A country with widespread malnutrition or insect-borne disease might be more willing to risk using a pesticide whose use had been canceled or restricted in the United States. Dr. William Upholt, consultant to the U.S. National Committee for Man and the Biosphere, stated: "Less industrial countries may consider a few cases of cancer in older people a small price to pay for increased yield of food crops. So it is reasonable to conclude that all nations do not need the same pesticide. There is an old saying that one man's food is another man's poison, and I guess that could be reversed."[40]

DDT was cited as an example of a pesticide whose registration had been canceled for use on food crops, but which was still produced

[37]Bull, p. 13.
[38]Davies, p. 65; Bull, p. 18.
[39]Bull, p. 30.

[40]Upholt, p. 35.

in India and used by several developing countries. Robert Oldford, president of Union Carbide's Agricultural Products Division, said:

> How do some of the developing countries consider chemicals that have been banned or restricted here? Burma, for example, has stated that, "In many other countries the use of chlorinated hydrocarbons is being restricted because of their persistent nature. The official position here is that these insecticides are effective, cheap, and, if used properly, ... no more hazardous than other newer and more expensive insecticides."[41]

In developing the risk/benefit argument, Frederick J. Rarig, vice president and associate general counsel of Rohm and Haas Company, stated:

> Margaret Mead taught us that morality is a relative, cultural concept. I have learned in 35 years of work in the field of hazard analysis that safety is similarly a relative, cultural concept. Safety is never an absolute. It is *not* an *absence* of hazard. Safety is an *acceptable* level of hazard.
>
> Men will not forgo shelter simply because the only shelter they can build is combustible. Mothers will not leave their children naked and exposed to the elements because the only available cloth with which to clothe them is combustible cotton.... Men will not starve while insects and rodents flourish simply because there are risks connected with the poisoning of insects and rodents.[42]

Dr. William Hollis, science coordinator of NACA, also pointed out the toxicological risks from crops damaged by pests. He observed: "In this light, the risk versus benefit concept to evaluate pesticides is inappropriate. The ultimate evaluation to be made must consider risk versus risk. That is, the risk of using the pesticide versus the risk of not having optimum production and protection of food, thereby not preventing unnecessary human health hazards. Such health hazards include exposure to pest-induced toxins, carcinogens, mutagens, and allergens."[43]

NACA claimed that sometimes the EPA was out of step with other countries in its interpretation of toxicological data. For example, NACA pointed out that whereas the EPA suspended on-food uses of 2,4,5-T on the basis of study of its health effects, other countries—including the United Kingdom, Canada, New Zealand, and Australia—reviewed the same data and concluded it was acceptable to continue using the herbicide for such purposes.[44]

In trying to place the toxicity of certain pesticides in perspective, Dr. Ram Hamsager, chairman of Hindustan Insecticides Limited, compared the $LD_{50}$ of DDT with nicotine. He indicated the $LD_{50}$ for DDT was about 118 mg. per kilogram of body weight while the $LD_{50}$ for nicotine was about 60 mg. per kilogram of body weight. He asserted: "This proves that nicotine is twice as poisonous as DDT. The toxicity levels of some of the other naturally occurring chemicals which form part of our daily intake, like caffeine found in coffee and thiobromine found in tea, are comparable to safe pesticides like DDT, and BHC."[45]

Defending the export of pesticides that were not approved for use in the United States, Robert Oldford stated: "There are two fundamental reasons why such exports occur. First, products are not usually registered in the U.S. for an agricultural pest crop use which does not exist here—coffee or bananas, for example. Second, developing countries have approval agen-

[41]Robert Oldford, Statement to the Subcommittee on Department Operations Research, and Foreign Agriculture of the Committee on Agriculture, U.S. House of Representatives, June 9, 1983, p. 13.

[42]*Proceedings*, p. 29.

[43]Hollis, p. 11. See Wendell Kilgore et al., "Toxic Plants as Possible Human Teratogens," *California Agriculture*, November–December 1981, p. 6; Garnett Wood, "Stress Metabolites of White Potatoes," *Advances in Chemistry*, p. 149, 1976, pp. 369–386; Bruce Ames, "Dietary Carcinogens and Anticarcinogens, *Science*, September 23, 1983, pp. 1256–1262.

[44]*Food, Health, Agricultural Chemicals and Developing Countries*, published by NACA, May 1983, p. 4.

[45]Hamsagar, p. 8.

cies that typically will require valid evidence of registration in a developed country in addition to other information needed to make a decision in the best interest of their citizens."[46]

The industry was trying to minimize pesticide misuse through education and had cooperated with several international organizations such as the FAO, AID, WHO, and the World Bank. Dow Chemical conducted over 400 agricultural chemicals meetings in South America in 1981, and Monsanto brought union officials of one developing country to the company's U.S. plants to learn of the safety procedures used there. Since 1978 NACA sponsored a series of international conferences between representatives of importing countries and U.S. manufacturers to harmonize registration requirements and develop safety training programs. As a result of a two-year consultation process with industry, consumer, church, and environmental representatives, NACA had adopted a product stewardship code containing voluntary guidelines for its 115 member companies.

It was also argued that 1978 amendments to U.S. law greatly reduced the possibility of inadequate labeling, but that the industry on its own was also trying to develop better labeling procedures. For example, Velsicol had developed a "One World Communication System," using pictographs adapted to different cultures to instruct users in safe handling techniques, supplementing the labels required by U.S. law. Manufacturers, however, had little control over how distributors in developing countries repackaged and labeled pesticides after removing them from bulk shipping containers.

The U.S. pesticide industry showed concern over the rise of thousands of small "pirate" manufacturers of chemicals that were imitations of proprietary pesticides produced in the United States. These companies, usually not closely regulated, sold products in developing countries that were less effective and more dangerous because of contaminants. They were often cheaper, however, than pesticides sold by quality-conscious U.S. companies.

## REGULATING PESTICIDES

Jacob Scherr of the Natural Resources Defense Council commented at the 1979 U.S. Strategy Conference on Pesticide Management: "Some developing countries have enacted virtually no legislation to govern the importation, domestic use, and disposal of potentially toxic chemicals. Few maintain any facilities for monitoring the effects of the products on health or the environment. Even where decent laws are on the books, many governments lack the technical and administrative capacity to implement them."[47]

### Regulation in Developing Countries

*An Agromedical Approach to Pesticide Management* asserted that "a number of developing countries already have strong pesticide laws on their books, but in many cases efforts aimed at enforcing the laws are either negligible or nonexistent."[48] Few countries, it was reported, had the necessary regulatory infrastructure for monitoring, testing, setting residue limits, enforcement, and so forth.

The FAO studied the extent of pesticide control among members. Of 144 countries surveyed, 31 had well-developed procedures and enforcement; 26 had well-developed procedures but the degree of enforcement was unknown; 6 were developing control procedures; and 81 had no control procedures or gave no information.[49]

Many developing countries asked the United States and other industrialized countries to help them develop adequate legislation, monitoring, and enforcement mechanisms. In particular, they requested the United States to share its knowledge of the harmful effects of the many chemicals already tested by the U.S. government or corporations. Many also wanted to

[46]Oldford, p. 13.

[47]*Proceedings,* p. 32.
[48]Davies, p. 238.
[49]Bull, p. 144.

be kept informed of changes in the status of pesticides registered in the United States.

The following comments made by Samuel Gitonga, agriculture expert for the National Irrigation Board of Kenya, were typical:

> We do not have the necessary machinery to go through an entire testing program to determine whether the product is safe or not. For these reasons, I believe that the U.S. and other developed countries have a responsibility to ensure that the information they have painfully gathered is made available to as many people as possible in the developing world. I certainly reject the idea that the developing countries always know what they want or which pesticides are best to use. Information that a product is not allowed for use in a particular country would be a very useful starting point. The less developed countries must be made aware that there is a problem with using a particular product. These very real dangers of incompletely tested or banned products being used in the less developed countries should be strongly condemned by the international community.[50]

### Regulation in the United States

A 1979 report by the General Accounting Office to Congress, entitled *Better Regulation of Pesticide Exports and Pesticide Residues in Imported Food is Essential,* contained the following passage: "The Food and Drug Administration does not analyze imported food for many potential residues. It allows food to be marketed before testing it for illegal residues. Importers are not penalized if their imports later are determined to contain illegal residues. The safety and appropriateness of some residues allowed on imported food has not been determined." In 1977 the United States imported $13.4 billion of agricultural products. Most of these imports were from developing countries with less effective regulatory mechanisms than those in the U.S.—28% of U.S. pesticide exports went to Central American countries from which we obtain 38% of our imported agricultural commodities. The United States imported approximately 600 different food commodities from over 150 countries in 1979.[51]

U.S. pesticide exports and imports were regulated by the Federal Insecticide, Fungicide, and Rodenticide Act of 1947, as amended, and the Federal Food, Drug, and Cosmetic Act of 1938, as amended.

FIFRA required the EPA to register all pesticides before they were distributed, sold, or used in the United States. The EPA registered a pesticide when it determined that the pesticide, when used according to commonly recognized practice, could safely and effectively perform its intended function without unreasonable risk to humans or the environment. If a pesticide was produced for export only, however, it was not required to be registered by the EPA and could be exported regardless of its regulatory status or its intended use. FIFRA required that domestic producers maintain records of shipments and purchasers' specifications for packaging. Amendments made in 1978 required that unregistered pesticides produced solely for export be labeled "Not Registered for Use in the United States of America." Foreign purchasers of unregistered chemicals had to sign statements acknowledging their understanding that these pesticides were not allowed for U.S. use. Copies of foreign purchaser acknowledgments were then sent to the government officials of the importing countries. Labels for exports had to contain the same information as products intended for U.S. use. Among those requirements were the display of a skull and crossbones if highly toxic and a statement of practical treatment, warning or caution statements, and no false representations.

FFDCA required that tolerances be established for pesticide residues. Any food was considered adulterated if it contained residues in excess of these tolerances or if it contained a residue for which the EPA had not established a tolerance.

The EPA and the Food and Drug Administration (FDA) administered these laws. The EPA established tolerances on the basis of the

---

[50] *Proceedings,* p. 41.

[51] *Better Regulation,* cover page.

nature, amount, and toxicity of the residue of a pesticide. The FDA was responsible for ensuring that all food marketed in the United States, either domestic or imported, met FFDCA residue requirements. The FDA monitored imported food for conformance with these requirements by chemically analyzing samples collected from individual shipments received at various U.S. entry points. Food that was adulterated was required to be denied entry and reexported or destroyed.

In its report, the GAO stated that "pesticide use patterns in foreign countries clearly indicate that a large portion of food imported into the United States may in fact contain unsafe pesticide residues."[52] For example, a 1978 study of coffee imported to the United States showed that 45% (25 out of 55) of the samples contained illegal residues. All of these residues were from pesticides whose use had been canceled or severely restricted in the United States. The cycle of food contaminated by U.S. pesticide exports being imported into the Unied States was referred to as the *boomerang effect*.

The FDA estimated that approximately one-tenth of the food imported into the United States contained illegal residues. However, the GAO argued that this estimate was probably too low due to inadequacies in the FDA's analytical and sampling procedures. The two multiresidue tests used by the FDA could detect residues of only 73 of the 268 pesticides that had U.S. tolerances. The GAO studied the pesticides allowed, recommended, or used in developing countries on 10 major commodities: bananas, coffee, sugar, tomatoes, tea, cocoa, tapioca, strawberries, peppers, and olives. It found that an additional 130 pesticides used on these foods had no U.S. tolerances and could not be detected by the FDA's tests. Since the FDA did not know which pesticides were used by other countries on food imported into the United States, it did not know which analytical test to use. This was one reason why the FDA used only *two* of the six multiresidue tests available and *no* single residue test. Without this knowledge, use of other tests would be too

costly in terms of time and money. The GAO further concluded that the "anomalies" it found "do not inspire confidence in the validity of the FDA's sampling program."[53]

The report also pointed out that "even when the pesticide residues on imported food are identified as being violative, the food will probably be marketed and consumed rather than detained or destroyed." For example, in Dallas, Texas, Department of Agriculture personnel complained of an insecticide-like smell coming from a shipment of imported cabbage. Despite this complaint and the fact that the importer had a history of shipping adulterated products, the cabbage was allowed to be marketed. The GAO found that "half of the imported food that the Food and Drug Administration found to be adulterated during a 15-month period was marketed without penalty to importers and consumed by an unsuspecting American public."[54]

The Department of Health, Education and Welfare criticized the methodology of the GAO report and disagreed with several of its conclusions and recommendations:

> We believe this draft report neither accurately nor fairly reflects either the degree to which pesticide residues pose a risk to the U.S. consumer or the Food and Drug Administration's (FDA) program for identifying and detaining violative imported products. We recognize the need for improvements in FDA's coverage of imported food for pesticide residues, and several actions are well under way to accomplish these improvements. However, many of the criticisms of FDA programs and professional competence are based upon unsubstantiated conclusions. GAO has posed hypothetical situations without citing sufficient evidence to substantiate their occurrence and thereby may create unfounded apprehensions about the food supply and those charged with assuring its safety.[55]

NACA argued that the safety factor built into the setting of tolerance levels and the Market Basket Surveys carried out by the FDA

---

[52]Ibid., p. 6.

[53]Ibid., p. 14.
[54]Ibid., pp. 39–40.
[55]Ibid., p. 70.

since 1965 provided adequate safeguards for the American consumer. Tolerances were established by first determining a no-toxic-effect level for a pesticide on test animals and then increasing that many times over, usually by a factor of 100, to set the legal maximum for humans. As part of its yearly surveillance programs, the FDA examined 30 samples, each composed of 117 food items, from different regions and representing the diets of adults and children to determine the average daily intake of pesticide residues. These results were then compared with acceptable daily intake levels. Several studies had consistently shown that acual daily intake was less than ADI levels. For example, the average daily intake of parathion consumed in 1977 was 1/5,000–1/1,000 of the ADI. In no instance was the actual intake of a pesticide as high as the ADI.[56]

NACA asserted that "we are being indicted in the so-called 'circle of poison issue' in spite of the basic fact that, according to the best experts, no one anywhere in the world has suffered illness from pesticide residues in or on food commodities."[57]

The pesticide industry was not in favor of increased government regulation of pesticide exports to alleviate the risks of pesticide use in developing countries and, indirectly, in the United States. About such a proposed change in 1980, Earl Spurrier, director of government relations for Monsanto, said that "the extra restrictions are unduly stringent and they are going to throw much of the export business to foreign competitors, who are not similarly restricted."[58] Instead, the industry favored voluntary efforts by companies to alter the pattern of pesticide misuse that existed worldwide.

---

[56]See the ongoing study of the dietary intake of pesticides in the United States in *Pesticide Monitoring Journal,* in Vols. 5, 8, and 9. See, also, J. Frawley and R. Duggan, "Techniques for Deriving Realistic Estimates of Pesticide Intakes," in *Advances in Pesticide Science,* Part III, ed., H. Geissbuhler (New York: Pergammon Press, 1979).

[57]Jack Early, Remarks of the National Agricultural Chemicals Association before the Latin American Forum, May 4, 1982, p. 6.
[58]"The Unpopular Curbs on Hazardous Exports," *Business Week,* September 1980.

# Velsicol Chemical Corporation

Early in the morning of June 16, 1983, Michael Moskow, chief executive officer of Velsicol Chemical Corporation, was debating whether to continue funding for the company's One World Communication System (OWCS). OWCS had been invented to address the problem of pesticide misuse in developing countries. It used labels that contained simple, easily understood pictograms to convey information on the safe use of pesticides, and was designed especially for the small farmer who was illiterate or could not understand the precautionary information on current labels.

Velsicol was scheduled to present OWCS at a conference in Washington, D.C., next week to a large group of representatives from other agricultural chemical companies, government agencies, and environmental and public interest groups. Moskow needed to reach a decision on the project before the conference in order to present a clear, coherent, and uniform position.

At 3:30 P.M. today, he was to meet with those who had developed OWCS as well as with other senior executives and Velsicol's chairman, Paul Hoffman, to announce his decision.

## THE OLD VELSICOL

Velsicol was founded in 1931 by Joseph Regenstein Sr. to develop, manufacture, and sell products derived from hydrocarbon polymers, mainly resins and solvents. These were sold to manufacturers of paints, varnishes, can coatings, drying and core oils, and saturants. Although sales rose from $1 million in 1932 to over $4 million in 1945, the company turned a profit in only a few of those years.

In 1942, DDT was marketed commercially and its success as an insecticide was spectacular, particularly against the malaria-carrying mosquito. Because DDT was a chlorinated hydrocarbon, Hyman began experimenting with chlorinating other compounds. In 1945, Velsicol applied for a patent on chlordane, one of the earliest synthetic chlorinated hydrocarbon molecules to be marketed in the U.S. Patents for aldrin, dieldrin, heptachlor, and endrin soon followed. Population increases after World War II put greater demand on agriculture, and sales of these pesticides soared; Velsicol's sales from 1950 to 1960 increased fivefold, to over $30 million. In 1961, the company patented Banvel, a popular herbicide used to protect corn, sorghum, and other major crops, and was able during this period to expand its production facilities and acquire two other chemical companies. By 1964, sales had increased to $64 million.

In 1965, Joseph Regenstein, Jr. sold Velsicol to the Chicago and Northwestern Railway Company, reorganized in 1967 under Northwest Industries, Inc. By the mid-1960s, Velsicol had moved to its new headquarters in downtown Chicago, owned extensive research facilities and five production plants, employing over a thousand people. During the remainder of the decade, however, sales and profits generally declined as the entire chemical industry experienced overcapacity, increased costs and rising prices, and felt the effect of numerous new environmental regulations. These new standards called for expensive pollution control equipment, costly testing of new products, and increased time for commercialization.

The 1970s were particularly difficult years for Velsicol. A series of environmental accidents with attendant publicized litigation along with insensitivity to the country's rapidly growing concern over the environment created a widely held negative image of the company. An Environmental Defense Fund (EDF) lawyer in 1978 described Velsicol as a "corporate renegade that seems totally lacking in public responsibility." A February 13, 1978, *Wall Street Journal* front-page story entitled "Small Chemical Firm Has Massive Problems with Toxic Products" cited an EPA spokesperson: "Velsicol's record of compliance with environmental statutes is one of the worst of any company."

In 1973, it was learned that Michigan Chemical Corporation (a sister company which was merged into Velsicol late in 1976) had accidentally substituted an undetermined amount of a toxic flame retardant PBB for an

animal feed supplement. The Farm Services Bureau, a Michigan cooperative, then sold the supplement to farmers. This mistake resulted in what the *Wall Street Journal* called "one of the worst agricultural disasters in U.S. history." Over two million farm animals and millions of pounds of dairy products were destroyed, over 650 civil property damage claims were eventually paid, and over 250 families filed lawsuits claiming personal injury from eating PBB-contaminated food. Velsicol and the Farm Services Bureau finally settled nearly all claims for over $40 million.

From 1971 to 1976 Velsicol produced the pesticide Phosvel at its Bayport, Texas, plant. "Phosvel" was the trade name for leptophos, an insecticide which was classified as "extremely hazardous" by the World Health Organization (WHO) and was never registered in the U.S.; leptophos was manufactured by Velsicol for export only. It was learned in 1976, as a result of inquiries by federal agencies, that workers at the plant were suffering from such neurological complaints as dizziness, vomiting, weakness, and loss of muscular control. The Occupational Safety and Health Administration recommended fines against Velsicol for 44 alleged workplace safety violations, and a U.S. Senate committee criticized the company for permitting the manufacture of leptophos to continue even after it had been warned by its own medical consultants that health complaints by workers might be related to leptophos production. Although the company had notified EPA in the fall of 1975 that there might be effects on workers from Phosvel exposure, it was also alleged that Velsicol withheld information concerning employee neurological disorders from government agencies. In addition, there were allegations that in 1972 and 1974, Phosvel had been involved in the poisonings of water buffalo and humans in Egypt. In January 1976, Velsicol ceased production of Phosvel.

The Environmental Protection Agency (EPA) also recommended fines in 1976 for water pollution violations at the Bayport and Memphis, Tennessee, plants. And the state of Michigan sought to have the company's St.

Louis, Michigan, plant closed because of water pollution complaints.

In addition, Velsicol became a major producer of tris-BP, a chemical flame retardant that was banned for use in children's nightwear in 1977 after studies showed it could cause cancer in laboratory animals. During this time, chlordane and heptachlor, two of Velsicol's major products, also came under suspicion as carcinogens. There was laboratory evidence, for example, that chlordane caused cancer in mice, although epidemiological studies of workers at chlordane production plants and of pest control operators had shown no carcinogenic effects on humans.

Velsicol encouraged a bad press by its aggressive antimedia and antiregulation stance. The CEO during this period, Robert K. Morris, was philosophically opposed to government regulation and disagreed with environmentalists' concern over toxic chemicals. Discussing Velsicol's environmental problems in 1978, Northwest Industries President Ben Heineman said:

> When Bob Morris was making speeches personally attacking the administrator of EPA, I did take a position that I was not going to interfere in the chief executive's activities in connection with his own company—even though based on many, many years of government experience I thought they were extremely foolish. . . . I probably made a significant mistake in applying our decentralization policy to anything that sensitive.[1]

## THE NEW VELSICOL

In 1978 Velsicol was told to clean up its act. At a meeting of all of the company's managers, Heineman described Velsicol as a "beleaguered company" and stated:

> Were Velsicol to have another disastrous occurrence it would destroy the company. And accordingly, our first priority in the allocation of capital is not for its expansion, but to make the plants and its products environmentally secure and safe for its employees to manufacture—and hopefully, subject to proper instructions, safe in their application. This is the first priority, and this priority for allocation of capital to Velsicol takes place before profit, before growth—Velsicol must be made reasonably secure.[2]

The major step in this turnaround was the appointment of Heineman's personal assistant, 31-year-old W. Howard Beasley III, as vice chairman of Velsicol. Beasley was given the task of restructuring Velsicol, with Heineman's directive to "clean it up, spend whatever is necessary, but don't gold-plate it." Beasley, who became president in 1980, replaced more than half of the company's directors and vice presidents and brought in a younger management team. He also hired high-ranking EPA engineer John Rademacher as vice president of environmental, health, and regulatory affairs and gave him line authority to veto new projects on environmental grounds. The company adopted a more conciliatory posture in dealing with regulatory officials and groups claiming environmental damage, with Beasley sometimes handling these negotiations personally. The company also instituted a new worker health and safety program. In addition, Richard Blewitt, who had been hired as director of public affairs, built new internal and external communications programs that included a faster response to the press, more civic activity, sending company speakers out into the community, and providing more information to customers and government officials.

The turnaround also included a new business strategy. The company decided to concentrate in agricultural chemicals, which at that time constituted 90% of sales, and sold its flame-retardant business in 1981. In order to shorten the development process for new products, Velsicol also acquired products from other companies, believing this would make full use of existing distribution and marketing

[1]"Velsicol: The Challenge and the Choice," *Chemical Week* (August 23, 1978), p. 51.

[2]Ibid.

systems as well as reduce the company's reliance on existing products.

By 1982, many observers felt that the "reincarnated" company had overcome its environmental and health problems. In 1982 and 1984 the company won the Lammot duPont Safety Award given by the Chemical Manufacturer's Association for the best injury reduction rate among major producers over a five-year period. In 1984, Velsicol had operated for nearly two years without a lost-time injury. Kristine Hall, EDF attorney and co-chair of its toxic chemicals program, said of Velsicol:

> It has gone from a renegade to one of the better models of how a corporation should act. It's hard for me to come out and praise a company in an industry, but there is a real responsiveness in Velsicol's upper echelon.

In the spring of 1983, a considerable amount of Velsicol's time and money went to prepare for hearings held by the State Pesticide Board of Massachusetts on whether or not to ban sales of chlordane. In fact, Velsicol spent more on these hearings than its gross sales in Massachusetts in that year. CBS was doing a program on the controversy and attended the hearings, televising part of them on April 10, 1983, on "60 Minutes." To show that chlordane did not pose a risk when instructions on the label were followed properly, Velsicol paid hefty consulting fees to independent researchers who had studied the effects of chlordane on humans to testify at these hearings. Ultimately, the State Pesticide Board decided not to ban sales of chlordane but did limit its use to licensed applicators. In the fall of 1983, the state of New York began similar hearings.

By 1984, Velsicol had almost 2000 employees, six manufacturing sites in the U.S., one in Mexico, and another in Brazil. The company focused on three markets: herbicides, insecticides and rodenticides, and specialty chemicals used primarily as intermediates in the agricultural chemical, plastics, and cosmetics industry. Banvel continued to be the backbone of its agricultural chemicals business and

captured 35% of its market. Although the EPA had cancelled the U.S. registration of chlordane for crop use and restricted its application to certified pest control operators, the company continued to be the only producer of chlordane in the world, with annual sales of over one million gallons. With heptachlor and chlordane, Velsicol controlled about 80% of the termiticide market in the U.S. In 1981, net sales were $208.7 million with operating earnings of $10.9 million. Exports accounted for 40% of total sales.

## PESTICIDE MISUSE

Using World Health Organization (WHO) data, in 1981 the Oxford Committee for the Relief of Famine (OXFAM) estimated that there were 750,000 cases of pesticide poisoning and 14,000 deaths worldwide. More than half of these fatalities were children. Although developing countries accounted for only 15% of worldwide pesticide use, they suffered half of the accidental poisonings and three-fourths of the deaths. Another survey put the annual worldwide mortality rate in 1977 at over 20,000. Experts agreed, however, that the actual number of poisonings was probably much higher because many countries did not collect such statistics, most poisonings occurred in remote areas, and often doctors in rural areas could not distinguish symptoms of pesticide poisoning from other diseases.

A major cause of these poisonings was pesticide misuse. Many of the end users in developing countries were illiterate and ignorant of the dangers or safe use of pesticides; most did not have sophisticated pesticide training programs like those in the U.S. or Japan. At every step of the delivery and use of pesticides, including transporting, mixing, applying, storing, and disposing of used containers, there was great potential for harm to humans, wildlife, and the environment.

The distribution system was a major problem. Pesticides were exported in bulk and then repackaged on arrival into smaller containers which often were unlabeled. In small shops in rural areas throughout the Third World, pesticides were frequently sold in unmarked coke or beer bottles and placed on shelves next to foodstuffs. In addition, the end user, often a small farmer with a few acres or less, relied upon the local shopkeeper, himself untrained, for advice on pesticide use.

Critics also charged that labels often contained misleading or inadequate safety and first-aid information and were sometimes not written in the language of the country where used. However, even when labels were adequate, there was misuse because much of the population was illiterate or could not understand the technical information.

Much of the discussion about pesticides focused on the morality of exporting to developing countries pesticides whose use had been cancelled or restricted in the U.S. A major question in this debate was who had the responsibility for doing something about the misuse of pesticides: the pesticide companies, the U.S. government, the governments of developing countries, international bodies like the UN or WHO, the end users? Many environmentalists and public interest groups charged that it was the responsibility of the companies to prevent misuse and that the U.S. government should enact new monitoring regulations. The agricultural chemical industry, however, claimed it was making progress on its own and was opposed to further government intervention.[3]

## THE DEVELOPMENT OF THE ONE WORLD COMMUNICATION SYSTEM

In December 1980, Charles H. Frommer, director–regulatory affairs at Velsicol, attended a conference in Jamaica on pesticide training sponsored by the Department of State. As a result of this trip, Frommer recalled, "I got the opportunity to see how pesticides were used in a developing country and how great a potential

there was for mishandling them out of ignorance. Where the end user is buying a pesticide in an unlabeled brown paper bag, this potential is absolutely fantastic." Seeing that much of the misuse of pesticides came from the user's inability to comprehend the precautionary information contained on labels, Frommer also began thinking about using pictograms to convey safe handling techniques and the potential role that Velsicol could have in addressing this problem.

Upon returning to Velsicol, he spoke with his boss, Jack Rademacher, Rich Blewitt, vice president–corporate affairs, and Bill Cunnea, manager of communications, about helping the governments of developing countries teach people to handle pesticides more safely and, in particular, about creating a system of simple pictograms that could be understood by illiterate end users in diverse cultures. The group discussed these ideas with Beasley, then CEO of Velsicol, who gave them his blessing and asked Blewitt to coordinate the project. At this point, in early 1981, the group decided to approach the National Agricultural Chemicals Association (NACA), the industry trade and lobby group, believing that NACA would be the most effective sponsor because it could enlist the resources of its 115 member companies. Over the next several months, Frommer spoke to Dr. William Hollis, NACA's coordinator of scientific affairs, about the project, and Paul Hoffman, chairman of Velsicol, presented the proposal to NACA's board of directors.

According to Frommer, however, this "quickly became an exercise in futility"; after a year, NACA still had not acted on the idea. He speculated about inevitable bureaucratic resistance in trying to move such a large group and NACA's preoccupation with related projects. For example, Hollis himself was spearheading efforts to develop worldwide, uniform pesticide registration requirements.

Cunnea, who knew of General Motors' use of "rational graphics" to train new, "nonacademically oriented" repairmen in automobile diagnosis and repair, was also aware of the controversy over pesticide companies dumping

---

[3]For a fuller discussion of these issues, see *A Note on the Export of Pesticides from the U.S. to Developing Countries,* Harvard Case Services 9·384·097.

banned products in Third World countries. He welcomed the challenge and led the creative effort to develop prototypes of cross-cultural labels that could convey to an illiterate user necessary precautionary information. In February 1982 he wrote Blewitt and Beasley a memo stating: "If GM can do this for a car, we can do it for a pesticide label." They both agreed.

Cunnea hired a local design firm to help. After research on cross-cultural communication and the efforts made by other companies to use pictograms on a limited basis, they developed prototypes to convey the information contained in a Banvel label. Exhibit 1 shows a traditional label used in Latin America.

In January 1982, Beasley became an executive vice president of Northwest Industries, and in June 1982, Michael H. Moskow became the new chief executive of Velsicol. Moskow had begun his career as an academic economist, then served during the Nixon and Ford administrations in high-level appointments in the Council of Economic Advisers, the labor department, HUD, and the Council on Wage and Price Stability. After that, he worked for the multibillion-dollar Esmark Corporation as vice president for corporate development and planning, and when picked to be CEO of Velsicol, was executive vice president of Estronics, a division of Esmark that manufactured high-fidelity loudspeakers and industrial products, and distributed dental and electrical supplies. Cunnea presented the project to Moskow in August 1982 and the CEO told Blewitt at that meeting to continue with it, but not to spend any more than $50,000 without further approval.

In January 1983, Cunnea, Rademacher, and Frommer flew to Washington, D.C., where they presented the concept and the prototypes to Albert Printz of the Agency for International Development (AID) and Bill Hollis of NACA. They were surprised and pleased when Printz suggested that AID, NACA, and the Department of State sponsor a conference at which Velsicol could present its One World Communication System, as the project was now called.

At this meeting, they also learned that NACA had just begun participating in the Ag-

ricultural Chemicals Dialogue Group, a small number of representatives from industry, environmentalist, church, and public interest groups who were meeting to formulate voluntary guidelines for advertising practices in developing countries.

## THE CONFERENCE

The Workshop on Training for Safe Pesticide Use in the Less Developed Countries was scheduled for June 20–21, 1983, in Washington, D.C. Over 250 people were invited, representing agricultural chemical companies, environmental and public interest groups, churches, government agencies, university and medical schools, representatives from governments of developing countries, and concerned private citizens. According to Printz, the conference was the first of its kind, never before had such a large number gathered in such a cooperative atmosphere to discuss this subject.

Cunnea prepared a summary of his presentation for participants (Exhibit 2) and he planned to emphasize that the system was only a prototype which had not yet been field-tested (although Velsicol planned to do so in August). Velsicol's major objective was to get feedback on the system from conference participants, especially from large companies like Monsanto, Eli Lilly, and Ciba-Geigy. No one knew what the response would be. "They might think we're right on the money or 180° off," thought Cunnea.

Cunnea, who was to be the lead speaker at the conference, planned to end his presentation with:

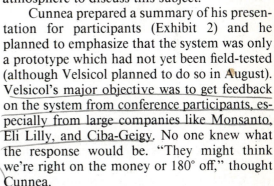

We need to somehow do everything in our power to get information on how to safely use pesticides to these societies because I believe—and the people for whom I work at Velsicol believe—that we're there to help, and every abuse of a pesticide is going to create a problem that we do not want to take the responsibility for. We will do what we can beyond the legalities to try to prevent this abuse.

I'd like to ask each one of you in this room to take whatever information we're able to gather over the next few days and go back to your individual areas of responsibility and dream about what would happen—not only in the circle of influence each of you has but as citizens of this world—if we were able to implement a program . . . to effectively prevent the misuse of pesticides.

I'll end with my favorite quote, which is by Lawrence of Arabia: "All people dream but not equally. They who dream by night in the dark recesses of their mind awake in the day to find it is but vanity. But the dreamers of the day are dangerous people, for they live their dreams with open eyes to make it possible." Ladies and gentlemen, I think we can make it possible.

## DIFFERENT POINTS OF VIEW

To prepare for the afternoon meeting, Moskow was reviewing notes he had taken on informal, individual conversations with members of the ad hoc group that had developed OWCS. He reviewed his sense of each person's attitude toward the project.

It was clear that Cunnea had done an excellent job in putting the system together and in presenting it. Moskow recalled Cunnea wondering how anyone could *not* be interested in the project because it was such a "mom and apple pie" issue—preventing millions of people who are hungry and who need to use pesticides from being harmed. Yet Cunnea believed that for the project to succeed, it would need the blessing of some developing countries. Further, the implementation and distribution of the system would have to come from the industry itself—if they felt it was in their own interest to develop and use such a system. Cunnea thought that the system would be a wonderful marketing and public relations tool. He also believed that the industry would "have to get there before Ralph Nader does." Ever-increasing public concern over corporate accountability would eventually result in companies' being required to use such a system, regardless of whether or not they agreed with it.

As one of those who endorsed the idea of using pictograms, Charlie Frommer had a strong personal investment in OWCS. He had sent Moskow a memo outlining a pilot program for testing and refining and had included in his budget for 1984 about $60,000 for this purpose. The first stage would be to design a training program in consultation with the government of Jamaica. The next step would be a safety training conference sponsored by the Ministry of Agriculture of Costa Rica and attended by the ministries of agriculture from other Central American and South American governments as well as regional representatives from Velsicol.

Frommer had also suggested as one way of refining the system the use of general pictogram labels, product specific labels, and geographic labels. Thus, in addition to the general or pesticide safety labels, there would be a specific label for each product; for each product, there would be a different label for each cultural region. He recognized, however, that such a total program would be costly. Frommer considered the pictograms only one part of a safety training program. An adequate program, he believed, would also include native trainers in developing countries to explain the pictograms to end users.

Moskow saw in his notes that Frommer had indicated that Velsicol's regional sales managers, who were primarily nationals, had a hard time appreciating the company's concern over environmental issues and had not been enthusiastic about OWCS, even though it was an effort to reduce the suffering caused by pesticides in their own countries. Frommer believed this was because these nationals either did not understand the pressures for corporate environmental responsibility exerted by special interest groups in the U.S. or Velsicol's own interest in assuring proper use of its products worldwide. Even some of the U.S. sales and marketing staff were reluctant to modify existing labels because of the increased costs.

Heinrich Stepnizcka, vice president–international, was responsible for Velsicol's foreign operations and also supported the project but was concerned about how much additional work would be required to implement it. He was skeptical about how host countries would respond because it had been his experience in developing international standards for flame retardants that "many countries resented being told what to do." The attitude, he thought, was "We can develop our own standards, thank you." Stepnizcka was proud, however, that Velsicol had instituted a voluntary training program on the safe use of chlordane for pest control applicators in Japan. To date, over 11,000 of Japan's 19,000 applicators had gone through the program.

Jack Rademacher had emphasized to Moskow that since pesticide labels were legal documents with their contents specified by U.S. law, Velsicol could not just begin on its own using new labels to replace the old ones. Rademacher thought developing countries had a lot of responsibility for safety training programs and that the EPA would probably agree to allow the use of pictogram labels if the importing countries made them part of their importation requirements. He was particularly interested in seeing what the response of the large companies would be at the conference. He believed that there was a status issue involved—the larger companies might pooh-pooh OWCS because Velsicol was small by their standards. He wondered aloud to Moskow what might happen if one of the "biggies" like Monsanto decided to sponsor the project.

Blewitt thought that the project was good but expressed reservations about the cost necessary for longer-term reliability and effectiveness. Stressing that Velsicol was "only a fly in the land of the giants," he still thought that the best hope for the project would be to have it sponsored by NACA.

*gov backing*

Finally, there was the disquieting point that someone had raised: It was not clear how concerned certain governments were about protecting the lives of the poor, illiterate farmers in their own countries.

To date, OWCS had cost Velsicol about $100,000. About $18,000 of that had been for travel, consulting fees, and printing costs, and the rest for time the group had spent on developing and promoting the system.

Two considerations seemed particularly important to Moskow. After reading Cunnea's materials, he was struck by the difficulty of trying to create a set of pictograms that would convey the necessary precautionary information yet be simple and easily understood by people who were illiterate, in diverse cultures. After all, people had been trying to develop universal languages like Esperanto for many years without much success. Research to develop an effective program could involve psychologists, linguists, and anthropologists as well as pesticide experts, and would probably be very expensive.

Finally, he imagined a small supermarket chain deciding on its own to implement bar code checkout labels. Real effectiveness and efficiency for such an undertaking would make no sense unless the effort was industrywide. He wondered if the use of OWCS wasn't the same.

Balanced on the other side, however, was the indisputable fact that the misuse of pesticides was a major problem in developing countries. It would be good for Velsicol to be in the vanguard of efforts to solve this problem.

## EXHIBITS: Velsicol Chemical Corporation

**EXHIBIT 1**
HERBICIDE LABEL FOR LATIN AMERICA

---

# FOR EXPORT ONLY
# PARA EXPORTACIÓN SOLAMENTE
## ALTO LEA LA ETIQUETA ANTES DE USAR EL PRODUCTO

**VELSICOL**

# Monvel™
# HERBICIDA

**VENENO**

**NO ALMACENAR EN CASA DE HABITACIÓN.**

**MANTENGASE FUERA DEL ALCANCE DE LOS NIÑOS, ANIMALES DOMESTICOS Y DE LOS ALIMENTOS.**

E.P.A. Est. No. 37507-MT-01

**CONTENIDO NETO:**

No. Lote _____

Fecha vercimiento _____

Manufacturado y distribuido por
**VELSICOL CHEMICAL CORPORATION** 341 East Ohio Street, Chicago, Illinois 60611
IMPORTADOR: VELSICOL DE CENTRO AMERICA S.A. Guatemala City, Guatemala

07253-530AB

**INGREDIENTES ACTIVOS:**

| | |
|---|---|
| Sal Dimetilamina de Dicamba (Acido 3,6-Dicloro O-Anisico) | 16.0% |
| Acidos relacionados de sal Dimetilamina | 2.8% |
| Sal Dimetilamina del ácido 2-Metil-4-Cloro fenoxiacético | 31.7% |
| Ingredientes Inertes | 49.5% |
| TOTAL | 100.0% |

Contiene: 1.25 Libras de Dicamba y 2.50 libras de MCPA por galón

**PRECAUCIONES — TRATAMIENTO PRACTICO**

Evite el contacto con la piel, ojos y ropa. Trata sintomaticamente.
**Si ingerido:** Tómese 1 to 2 vasos de agua y induzca al vómito tocándose la parete interna de la garganta con un dedo o un objecto romo. No inducir vómito ni de algo por la boca a una persona inconciente.
**Si inhalado:** Ubique a la victima donde haya aire fresco. Aplique respiración artificial si es indicado.
**Si en contacto con la piel:** Lave con un jabón suave y agua.
**Si en los ojos:** Enjuague los ojos por lo menos durante 15 minutos con agua. **LLAME A UN MÉDICO** inmediatamente!

**ENVASE Y ALMACENAMIENTO**

No contamine el agua de uso doméstico o irrigación por el almacenamiento. Evite el almacenamiento cerca de semillas, fertilizantes, insecticidas o fungicidas. Mantane en un area apropiado para pesticidas.
**Despues de utilizados, los envases vacios deben ser lavados y destruidos.**

**IMPORTANTE:**

No aplique el herbicida Monvel directamente y/o permita que los vapores asperjados se pongan en contacto con plantas tales como vegetales, flores, uvas, tomates, papas, remolachas, habichuelas u otras plantas sensibles. (Aspersiones pesadas son menos susceptible de arrastre por el viento). Para evitar daños a plantas sensibles, el equipo usado en Monvel debe ser lavado con algún limpiador químico antes de usarse para otro propósito. No aplique (excepto como se recomiénda) o limpie el equipo en o cerca de árboles u otras plantas deseables o en áreas donde las raíces puedan extenderse o donde el químico pueda ser lavado y arrastrado hacia sus raíces.

**INDICACIONES PAR SU USO**

| ALGUNAS DE LAS MALEZAS CONTROLADAS POR MONVEL™ | CULTIVO | DOSIS, USO Y APLICACIÓN |
|---|---|---|
| Amania: Ammania coccinea | **ARROZ** | POSTEMERGENTE: MONVEL |
| Bledo: Amaranthus sp | | —0.4—0.6 Litro (400-600 cc) por acre o 1—1.5 Litro por hectárea. |
| Batatillo: Ipomoea sp | | MONVEL MAS PROPANIL: |
| Bruscas: Cassia sp | | —0.4 Litro (400 cc) Monvel más 0.5—6.0 Litros Propanil 3 EC por acre o |
| Celedonia: Chenopodium album | | 1 Litro Monvel—8—14 Litros Propanil 3 EC por Hectárea. |
| Caperonia: Caperonia palustris | | |
| Caguey de agua: Cyperus odoratus | | Aplicar a los 21 dias después de siembra y/o trasplante cuando las malezas estén pequeñas (2-3 hojas) y activamente creciendo. |
| Culantrillo: Ludwigia erecta | | |
| Clavito: Jussiaea suffruticosa | | |
| Escoba: Sida sp | | |
| Fogaraté: Mucuna pruriens | | |
| Juana la blanca: Borreria laevis | **CAÑA DE AZUCAR** | PRE—POSTEMERGENTE TEMPRANO: RENOVACION O FOMENTO: |
| Junquillos: Eleocharis sp | | —0.5 Litro (500 cc) más 3 libras de Ametrina 80WP y/o 2 Litros Ametrina 50 FW por acre. |
| Molinillo: Leonotis nepetaefolia | | |
| Malcasada: Euphorbia spp | | —POSTEMERGENTE: RETOÑO: |
| Morivivi: Mimosa pudica | | 0.5—0.75 Litro (500-750 cc) por acre |
| Moco de pavo: Heliotropium indicum | | Aplicar cuando las malezas estén pequeñas y activamente creciendo. |
| Pato de laguna: Linmocharis flava | | |
| Pelo de mico: Fimbristylis miliacea | | |
| Quininito: Helianthus annuus | | |
| Rabo de zorra: Acalipha alopecuroides | **PASTOS** | POSTEMERGENTE: APLICACIÓN FOLIAR: |
| Siempreviva: Eclipta alba | | MALEZAS ANUALES Y BEJUCOS |
| Sanguinaria: Alternanthera sessilis | | Solución: 0.5—1% (½-1 galón de Monvel en 100 galones de agua). |
| Suelda consuelda: Commelina sp | | |
| Tabaquillo: Cleome viscosa | | Aplicar cuando las malezas estén pequeñas y creciendo activamente. |
| Verdolaga: Portulaca oleracea | | |
| Yerba de chivo: Ageratum conyzoides | | Use la dosis minima para las malezas anuales en estado de crecimiento activo; la dosis media en malezas desarrolladas (antes de la floración) y la dosis máxima para bejucos y malezas semileñosas. |
| Yerba de leche: Euphorbia heterophylla | | |
| Yerba de plato: Heteranthera reniformis | | |

# MODERADAMENTE TÓXICO

**EXHIBIT 2**
SUMMARY OF VELSICOL PRESENTATION

# Velsicol Chemical Corporation's Communication Alternatives for Pesticide Handling in Developing Countries

# A Proposed One World Communication System

(*Continued*)

**EXHIBIT 2**
CONTINUED

## Introduction

As citizens of the world, we have a problem. In our roles as producers, regulators, and members of concerned environmental organizations, we have a major concern.

The concern which all of us share — each from our unique viewpoint — is the uses and abuses of pesticides.

Now we ask that you tolerate, if not accept, certain premises — premises which were factors in the development of a communication program for our world — the world in which we now live and the world in which our children will live.

The premises are:

1) Developed countries do now and will continue to export pesticides to developing countries — often by request.

2) Both developed and developing countries have this problem of pesticide misuse and abuse.

3) Even the most sophisticated and well-educated individuals frequently do not read label instructions.

4) Food production in less developed countries is severely affected by insect and weed pests.

5) Imported pesticides are often technical grade products—by importing government mandate — in order for local formulators to generate an industry within the society.

6) Products exported have very specific, detailed labels — identifying the product, its target, its appropriate use, its hazards, and precautions for use and disposal of the containers. Remedies for exposure are also articulated.

However — that label — in all its detail

1) Is written

2) Is affixed to the drum of the product — a drum which is emptied as soon as it arrives at the formulators for the introduction of the product into the country's distribution system.

So much for the premises — now for the problem —

products are misused

products are abused

In many cases, humans suffer profoundly.

Articles which address the problems of pesticide misuse and abuse mention that 500 million people around our world don't get enough to eat.

The abuses and misuses of pesticides are our problem — as are the 500 million hungry people.

*(Continued)*

**EXHIBIT 2**
CONTINUED

## Development Considerations

The development of a communication program which would be effective on a global basis, necessitated the consideration of a universal language. Programs of this type have been attempted over many years, yet all have required the inclusion of a long learning period. Naturally, this condition precluded the implementation of any of these forms, some of which were highly sophisticated and developed with extensive research.

Obviously, a **written** language would present enormous educational problems. A language that relied on abstractions would necessitate that the abstractions be universally understood. Some symbology or illustration seemed to be the most appropriate and fundamental form for developing a global communication system — a one world communication system.

However, the symbology concept required extensive cross checking because of the vast cultural differences in developed and developing countries. For instance, the skull and crossbones or "death's-head" symbol, which has been used extensively in the United States as a sign of poison or of dangerous substances, is considered a sign of "macho" or machismo in some Latin countries.

Similarly, in the very sophisticated and communication-intensive environment of the United States, the death's head is being removed from many poisonous labelings because children in the United States do not equate it with death, but rather with a pirate ship flag or the "Jolly Rodger." A substitute for the skull and crossbones in the United States has been developed, and is finding its way into societal use. This image is a circular face with a simple eye and nose depiction with the tongue extending out indicating a grimace. The image is printed in a putrid green and is referred to as "Mr. Yuck."

In addition, various cultures put heavy emphasis on certain aspects of life which are irrelevant or inconsequential to other cultures. Gestures which may be greetings or salutations in one culture, could well be interpreted as profound and deadly insults in another.

Ultimately, the research which Velsicol Chemical Corporation did evolved down to that most fundamental of human methodology for communication — facial expressions and the human form. While the interest has abated to a certain extent recently, the concept of body language or communication through gesture — however subtle, however subconscious — was the subject of many popular

(*Continued*)

**EXHIBIT 2**
CONTINUED

books. Recently, a best-selling fictional account of the evolution of society, *The Clan of the Cave Bear*, by Jean Auel, dealt with Cro-Magnon's ability to communicate with very little spoken language, but a great deal of gesture and facial expression to depict not only general messages, but subtleties and nuances which flesh out the overall message.

Some of the abstract communication devices or pictograms which are used in more sophisticated societies  are such that the individual viewing them **needs to know what they mean** in order to understand what they mean.

That is, a silhouette of a phone, or an elevator in an international airport, is an excellent way to communicate to individuals from many different language backgrounds and cultures. However, if you have never seen a phone nor ever ridden in a box that goes up and down, you would have very little understanding of what these images meant. Thus, even as we attempt to become most fundamental in our communication, we are extraordinarily sophisticated.

Ultimately Velsicol's research indicated that the most effective and most fundamental of conveyance systems for information had to be the human form. Additionally, we investigated and determined that photographic representation would present too much information in many societies, be very non-selective in its depiction, and could present inordinate expense.

We chose to use illustration as the format which would selectively present information. In addition to this, consideration was given to the fact that some cultures read from right to left, and others read from left to right.

In language we use sounds which are grouped into words which are then grouped into sentences — through sentences we communicate. In a non-verbal communication technique we look at elements which contribute to an overall scene, which grouped together, contribute to a pattern. In the development of a program such as a one world communication program for pesticide handling, the pattern was decided to be effect and cause.

Silhouettes of human form were an initial consideration, because it would reduce racial characteristics and dress variations to a minimum. However, the very fact that the silhouettes would reduce facial characteristics to a minimum, would do a disservice to the effectiveness of the

(*Continued*)

**EXHIBIT 2**
CONTINUED

communication, since human beings look first to another human's eyes and face for information, and then to their hands for information. Thus, we humans establish some awareness of what type of relationship we will have.

We resolved the discussion to the point of having simple pictograms (or drawings) to be used as a communication technique to illustrate the hazards, precautions and disposal techniques for pesticides in developing countries.

Illustrations can create some difficulty, for certain cultures use illustrative art to depict actual situations in their life. The relationship in size determines the status of the individual depicted in that society. This was a common technique in Egyptian drawings, where the rulers of the society were depicted as being very large, the nobles of society being of somewhat smaller stature, and the servants being miniscule in proportion to the leaders of the society. This was not a matter of perspective in terms of vision, but of perspective in terms of social rank.

Some movements, gestures or facial expressions become universal. The concept of a person standing up while others are seated, indicates some preeminence over the others.

This is true whether it is a sophisticated society or a primitive one in which one person wants to get all the others' attention.

The shaking of hands or the opening of a palm as a greeting is viewed as a universal expression of friendship. (At least, no weapon is contained within that hand.)

Affection or intimacy, shown by people who lean very close to one another, is also a universal expression of trust and affection.

The next step was to view what illustration would most efficiently indicate the pesticide itself, whether it was in the original container or in various stages along the distribution chain through formulation and repackaging. The result of this investigation showed that the larval stage of insects, whether flying or crawling was almost universal. In addition, most pesticides are herbicides and insecticides. The herbicides are segregated into grassy weed pests and broadleaf weed pests. These were simply illustrated.

When an insect is depicted as lying on its back, it is perceived as dead. So in the larval, the winged insect and the crawling insect depictions were all drawn on their backs.

The weed pests were identified with drooping leaves.

However, we then had to determine what would be the effective way to indicate that these symbols on containers would eliminate either the insect or the weed pest. Our first conception was that an "X"

(*Continued*)

**EXHIBIT 2**
CONTINUED

through the target would be sufficient. However, we have found that in some countries with high illiteracy, symbology is used by political parties to indicate their various political positions. In order to indicate espousal of these political parties, a red "X" is shown on billboards and on posters indicating a vote **for** this posture, rather than an elimination of it.

Since many of the compounds are used in a liquid form, depiction was made of a puddle surrounding the insect or weed pest, with droplets falling upon it. While this can be effective, it restricts the format of the pesticide being applied. As a consequence, the as yet untested, but preferred depiction, shows a granular product being dropped on either the **target insect or the target weed. This** granular effect works because it can be viewed as droplets or as powder.

Due to the vast differences in physiognomy in humans, a decision was made to take the illustrations showing effect and cause, and put them into various racial characteristics. Since the program is yet untested, only three general characteristics were specified: Asian or Eurasian, Hispanic and Negroid. In each case, the scene was shown in precise detail, utilizing specific characteristics, while keeping in mind the vast differences within even one culture.

Finally, we needed to determine how to announce the intention of the cause and effect relationship. The resolution was to use the human face as literally a "head"-line with the "body" copy following, showing cause and effect. Because of the differences in cultures in reading direction, redundancy was built in to show the direction in which the panel should be interpreted. First, arrows indicating a left-to-right direction were put on the pictograms. Next, the first panel had one dot, the second had two dots, and the third having three dots placed in the arrows. Finally, human foot prints, with the toes pointing in the direction which the pictogram should be read, were put beneath the picture to further emphasize and create a redundancy.

(*Continued*)

**EXHIBIT 2**
CONTINUED

7A Do not drink this liquid, it is hazardous.

7B Do not use this material near water supplies, it is hazardous.

7C Do not rinse this container in water supplies, it is hazardous.

*(Continued)*

**EXHIBIT 2**
CONTINUED

## Societal Information Delivery Systems

The program utilizing the pictograms—the One World Communication program developed by Velsicol—cannot replace the label that is required and applied to products which are exported. However, used as a supplemental educational device, it can serve to advise and forewarn individuals who are not literate (albeit they may be very sophisticated within their own given area of expertise) of the dangers, hazards and precautions. The development of a pictographic communication system however, is not sufficient unto itself, for should it remain in Velsicol or even in the United States, we would be doing ourselves a great disservice. Somehow this information has to infiltrate a culture and reach the most isolated citizens, who could be impacted by the use or abuse of pesticides.

The company continued its investigation into how a society learns and through what systems information is delivered or distributed. While we may not have included all available data, we have identified some major and minor delivery systems into a society. Those systems which we identified had as their charge contact with the society on various levels, ranging from religious or church leadership, to hospital or paramedic training, to media work and government agencies of information.

In our opinion, none of these should be viewed as a better or a worse choice for delivery for the information. Rather, all should be viewed as instruments to be used in concert to deliver the communication system to the society. By utilizing this multi-faceted approach to distributing information to a society, the advantage of adding on to the information base of the individual in that society, is enhanced.

We have a message which we believe is not merely convenient, but absolutely essential. Only through constant application of the message, the symbology, and the pictogram can we attempt to guarantee the initiation of a program for protecting a society against the misuse and abuse of pesticides.

## One World Delivery Systems

1. Governmental Agencies
2. Educational Systems
3. Public Media
4. Hospitals/clinics
5. Private Industry:
    A. Formulators
    B. Farming Associations
    C. Farmers
6. Importers
7. Chautauqua — traveling entertainment and educational shows
8. Churches
9. Armed Services
10. Village Leaders

*(Continued)*

**EXHIBIT 2**
CONTINUED

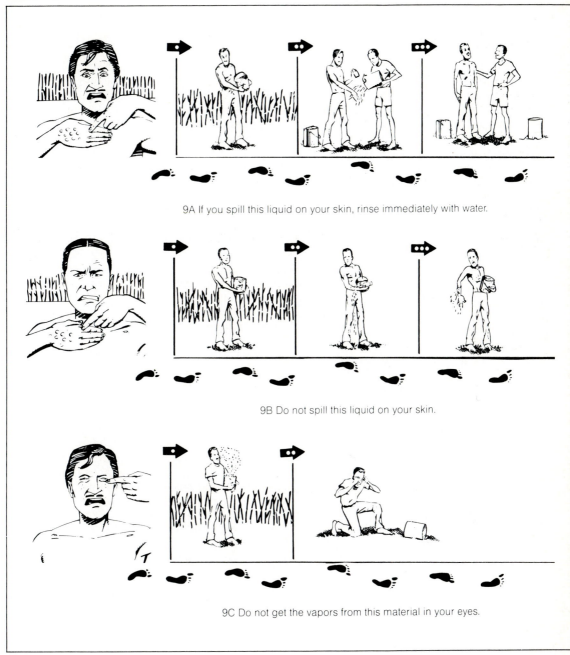

9A If you spill this liquid on your skin, rinse immediately with water.

9B Do not spill this liquid on your skin.

9C Do not get the vapors from this material in your eyes.

*(Continued)*

**EXHIBIT 2**
CONTINUED

## Societal Information Media

The selection of media to distribute information in a society is wide-ranging. Certainly in developed countries, the major problem is the super-abundance of communication, rather than the selection of channels which will provide information. However, in developing countries, many of the communication techniques, which citizens of more sophisticated societies presume to be commonplace, have never been implemented.

Consequently, with the same concept of redundancy, a selection of 16 communication media were identified which could be used individually, but preferably in concert, to make the society aware on a recurring basis of this system of warnings, hazards and precautions. While each has its role and all work well in tandem, perhaps that which would be of primary importance to implement throughout the various distribution systems, would be a teaching unit.

This teaching unit is not merely a subject to be covered, but a comprehensive package which would include points to be made; teaching techniques to be utilized; feedback mechanisms from the class to have them restate the solutions and the problems in their own words; to firmly cement the concepts in their minds; and follow-up testing techniques to reinforce the information.

In addition, a teaching unit could be developed for this communication system (or for any other system that might be implemented). Most certainly a teaching unit, once established, would work well within the educational network of a society, certainly within some government agencies whose charge it is to inform the society. The public media could modify it to present their information, hospitals and clinics could hold small teaching classes in their various areas of influence and private industry formulators could also serve. Farming associations could use it to train their workers, as could major landowners. In addition, importers, through various marketing and sales functions, could hold teaching sessions with the people with whom they are in contact. Church groups, who have as their charge the spiritual well-being of members of a society, could certainly use this type of information to enhance the health and well-being of their members. Armed service representatives, who are wide spread throughout every culture, could use this teaching unit to inform the members of society with the additional advantage that they are frequently drawn from the immediate locale and have a local reputation or circle of influence in that society. Village leaders could use this in their positions of authority to help educate their members for the well-being of that local society.

(*Continued*)

**EXHIBIT 2**
CONTINUED

# One World Communication Media

1. Labels
2. Stickers
3. Posters
4. Booklets/Magazines
5. Flip charts
6. Teaching Units (can be modified for various distribution systems).
7. Flash cards/Games
8. Copy and artwork for newspapers
9. Flyers
10. Puppet Shows
11. Film Strips
12. Slide Shows
13. Movies
14. Speeches
15. Radio
16. Television

(Continued)

**EXHIBIT 2**
CONTINUED

12A Do not reuse this container, dispose of it properly.

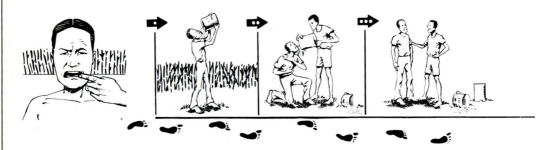

12B Do not drink this liquid. Flush with water if you do so.

12C Do not use a pesticide container for cooking. It is hazardous.

**Velsicol's proposed One World Communication System does not purport to be comprehensive nor definitive. Please feel free to use it for testing, to modify it to make it more effective, and to suggest improvements to more fully meet the important need which it attempts to address.**

**All comments are welcome. Please direct them to Corporate Affairs, Velsicol Chemical Corporation, 341 E. Ohio, Chicago, IL 60611, U.S.A.**

# Dow Corning Corporation: Business Conduct and Global Values (A)

In the early 1970s, both the aftermath of Watergate and disclosures by the Lockheed Corporation that it had spent millions bribing Japanese officials produced a mood of cynicism regarding large organizations, especially multinational corporations. It was expected that Congress would enact legislation prohibiting the use of bribes to obtain business (which it eventually did with the passage of the Foreign Corrupt Practices Act in 1977, see Exhibit 1). In response to this mood, the IRS asked the heads of U.S. corporations to answer eleven questions concerning bribes, gifts, slush funds, and "grease payments."

Considering how to answer these questions forced Jack Ludington, the CEO of Dow Corning Corporation (DCC), to think about the company's way of doing business. Ludington believed the company already deserved high marks for corporate responsibility, but he thought that more could be done. Ludington was keenly aware of how quickly DCC had expanded overseas and the problems of doing business in other cultures. In the early 1960s, less than 3% of its employees were in foreign operations; by the 1970s, about one-third of its work force was based in other countries.

Ludington was confident that his corporate managers would not intentionally do anything questionable and would even blow the whistle if they learned of any actual wrongdoing within the company. But with so many new employees from other cultures, where values and ways of doing business were different, he wanted to feel confident that everyone would live up to the same high ethical standards.

In March 1976 Dow Corning's board of directors appointed a three-person Audit and Social Responsibility Committee (ASRC) to oversee certain aspects of the company's internal as well as external activities. In May of that year four senior managers were appointed by Ludington to the first corporate Business Conduct Committee (BCC), which would report to the ASRC.

The Business Conduct Committee was charged with the following tasks:

- Learning more about how the company really operated outside this country.
- Developing guidelines that would be the basis for communicating legal and ethical standards of business conduct around the world.
- Developing a workable process for monitoring and reporting the company's business practices.[1]
- Recommending ways to correct questionable practices as they became known.

In order to prepare a code of conduct, the BCC studied codes of other companies and learned of efforts to develop an international code by such groups as the International Chamber of Commerce and the Organization for Economic Cooperation and Development (OECD). The committee also examined existing and proposed legislation and surveyed area managers to learn what issues they thought a code should cover.

## THE COMPANY

Dow Corning Corporation was founded in 1943 as a 50/50 joint venture of Dow Chemical Company and Corning Glass Works. The corporation's charter was to develop, manufacture, and market silicone-based products. Silicones were made by combining the element silicon with organic compounds. They could be formulated to possess unique physical characteristics, such as electrical insulating properties, maintenance of physical properties at extreme temperatures, water repellency, resistance to aging, lubricating characteristics, and chemical and physiological inertness. Because of these

properties, silicone-based products had a multitude of uses. In 1984, DCC sold over 2,000 different silicone products to more than 40,000 customers in every major industry, including automobiles, health care, construction, aerospace, pharmaceuticals, cosmetics, petroleum, electronics, and textiles.

Dow Corning was a multinational company with headquarters in Midland, Michigan. In 1983, it employed 6,000 people and had twelve manufacturing locations in the U.S. and thirteen abroad, with offices in thirty-five countries. Approximately 50% of sales came from foreign operations, primarily Europe and the Pacific. DCC depended on distributors for over one-third of its total business.

In 1983 DCC had a record $763 million in sales, up 15% over 1982, and had net income of $68 million, a 30% improvement over the previous year. The company was ranked 355th in sales among *Fortune* 500 companies and 183rd in net income. Exhibit 2 shows the company's 1983 consolidated balance sheets and statements of income and retained earnings.

DCC was technology-driven and, in 1983, invested $57 million in R&D (7% of sales). The company held well over 4,000 silicone patents, and one out of ten employees was involved in new product development.

Initially, Dow Corning's expertise in silicones had made it the sole producer of many products. Within the past fifteen years, however, competition at home and abroad had increased dramatically, and DCC's market share for many products declined. Companies competed on the basis of product quality, performance, price, and technical service and delivery, and there were now thirteen major competitors worldwide.

In 1967, DCC reorganized from a conventional divisionalized structure into a global matrix form of organization, which the company called "multidimensional." Along one dimension were the different businesses, defined by product lines. Along a second dimension were the traditional functions, such as marketing, R&D, and manufacturing. The third dimension comprised the five geographic areas of the U.S.,

---

[1]Dow Corning considered the pros and cons of the commonly used sign-off procedure whereby employees, on a selected level of management, annually attest in writing that they have not participated in illegal or unethical practices during the preceding year. In view of its decision to use face-to-face audits, Dow Corning decided against the use of sign-offs.

Europe, the Pacific, Canada, and InterAmerica (Latin America and South America). Exhibit 3 illustrates the multidimensional structure.

While retaining the basic matrix structure, in 1981 DCC reduced its businesses to five: Fluids, Resins, and Process Industries; Elastomers and Engineering Industries; Basic Materials Business; Health Care; and New Ventures. In that year Dow Corning recommitted its efforts to strengthen its ties to the marketplace and to concentrate on value-added growth.

For each business, there was a business board, with a manager responsible for the profits for that business as the only full-time member. The other members of the board were representatives from the various functions. Thus, dual-authority relationships existed for professional personnel. Functional staff reported directly to their functional group heads, such as the vice president–sales and marketing, but also had a dotted line relationship to a business manager.

The effect of this structure was to decentralize authority and push decision making as far down as practical. The structure put a premium on communication, planning, teamwork, and trust. DCC believed the structure was particularly valuable in providing flexibility to respond to a rapidly changing and competitive environment.

DCC's culture therefore was open, informal, and relaxed; there was little emphasis on official status or a traditional organizational chart with clear-cut reporting relationships. Exhibit 3, however, does indicate some of the reporting relationships in 1984 when the formal designation of a U.S. area was eliminated, and the executive vice president became responsible for business in the U.S. and for maintaining the balance between U.S. resources and the other areas.

## WRITING THE CODE OF BUSINESS CONDUCT

Not everyone was enthusiastic about developing a corporate code of conduct in 1976. In a lengthy memo to Ludington, the Pacific area manager expressed the views that DCC was "clean" and that a code should only be for internal use. He also pinpointed some issues in the Pacific area that should be addressed in such a code. Portions of that memo are included as Exhibit 4.

Once the corporate code was drafted, it was sent to area managers with instructions that they develop their own codes, paying particular attention to their unique concerns. The only constraint was that area codes not conflict with the corporate code.

Writing the several area codes was a lengthy process and involved many revisions, with contributors often debating whether or not a phrase captured exactly what was meant and whether it was liable to misinterpretation. A recurring dilemma was producing a code general enough to be relevant to a variety of cultures and business practices and, at the same time, specific enough to be a useful guide for action.

In 1977, DCC published its first corporate code, *A Matter of Integrity* (see Exhibit 5) along with five separate area codes for the Pacific, Latin America, Canada, Europe, and the U.S. It was distributed to employees accompanied by a letter from Ludington encouraging them to read it. Emphasizing that one of DCC's "most valued assets is our reputation for quality and integrity," he stated: "Our aim should be to continually build commitment to the highest standards possible throughout the organization. . . . I personally believe the integrity of Dow Corning's people is exceedingly high. As of now, we can all consider our business conduct to be as subject to accountability as anything we do." Ludington closed with "If you have any questions, please let me know."

DCC revised the code in 1981. This time there was one corporate code and each area manager wrote a message on a panel of the code brochure which would be distributed in his area. In keeping with what was now the company's goal of reviewing the code every two years, it was again revised in 1983, and sent to all employees, accompanied by a letter from Ludington emphasizing the company's commitment (see Exhibit 6).

## COMMUNICATING THE CODE AND MONITORING COMPLIANCE

To communicate the code to employees and to monitor compliance, the Business Conduct Committee began conducting annual audits in 1977. In that year audits were held at the area level in Mexico City, Toronto, Brussels, Hong Kong, Tokyo, and Midland. In 1979, seventeen audits were held worldwide, and they began to include regional personnel, one or two levels below area management. It was thought that this would allow input from those closest to day-to-day operations. Since 1979, approximately twenty audits per year have been conducted by the BCC.

Prior to each audit, a worksheet containing a list of questions or issues was sent to the managers at the audit site in order to guide—but not restrict—the discussions. Exhibit 7 contains the worksheets sent to managers in preparation for the 1980 audits. (Not all questions and issues listed on the worksheets pertained to every location audited.) Audits included five to fifteen people and lasted 5 to 8 hours. At least one representative of the Business Conduct Committee was present and sometimes two or more. A written record of each audit was kept in the files of the BCC at corporate headquarters. Each year, the committee summarized the results of all of the year's audits in a report to the Audit and Social Responsibility Committee of the Board of Directors. The annual report on business conduct was also presented to Dow Corning's global management at a regular meeting in August.

Each summer, the BCC discussed the results of the previous year's audits (it operated on a split year which ended in June), and with suggestions from area and regional managers, decided where and when audits would be held for the year ahead. In the fall, the auditing process began anew.

A typical audit opened with a summary of objectives; a review of the BCC's activities; a discussion of "gray areas" of business practices, such as what constitutes a questionable payment; and a briefing by the committee on issues related to the code of conduct, such as interpretations of the FCPA, progress on international codes, etc. The remainder of the meeting was then spent discussing such topics as competitor, government, and customer relations; distributor practices; pricing; entertainment; questionable payments; conflicts of interest; importing procedures; employee concerns; purchasing practices; and product and environmental stewardship.

Since its inception, the BCC had asked Dow Corning managers in key locations to keep a file of code-related incidents. By 1980, a more systematic approach was developed to document such incidents. A copy of the Business Conduct Reporting Procedures is included as Exhibit 8. This form helped assure that (1) only relevant incidents were kept on file, and (2) that a uniform method was used by Dow Corning worldwide.

The company used the audits to clarify questions of interpretation regarding the code of conduct and to get suggestions for revisions. For example, in 1981 the code had stated: "We will also respect information belonging to others, and will not condone any attempt to secure proprietary information belonging to others." At one U.S. audit, it was learned that a salesman had been offered a competitor's price list by a customer. Not being sure if this was allowed by the code, he refused it. Learning that an opportunity was lost to obtain valuable competitive information in a legal way, the vice president–sales and marketing suggested changing the code. The 1984 code read: "We will respect proprietary information belonging to others."

In reflecting on his seven-year tenure as a member of the Business Conduct Committee, John Swanson, manager–business communications, observed that audits were generally spirited and informal. He believed the key to their success was face-to-face interaction and that committee members were supportive, open-minded, and listened a lot. He did point out, though, that at first there was some anxiety because people did not know what to expect and many employees, even those in top management, were not sure how serious the company was about its increased emphasis on corporate responsibility and ethics. Jerry Griffin, DCC's treasurer in 1977, admitted wondering early on whether or not it was just going to be a short-lived response to media issues.

Although audits were the most significant way in which the message and commitment to the code was communicated to employees, several other channels were used. The code was framed and hung in conspicuous places in all offices around the world. DCC also used videotapes of the annual reviews of audits as well as videotaped discussions of current audit topics by BCC members in order to keep employees informed. These videotapes were often sent ahead to sites where audits were being held for the first time. Business conduct updates were occasionally included in the six annual management reports to employees. In addition, two of the company's training programs included modules on the code. And in the semiannual employee opinion survey, there was a section on business ethics. The survey indicated that employee attitudes toward the company's ethical posture had improved every year since the code was developed.

## THE U.S. BUSINESS ETHICS COMMITTEE

While the scope of the corporate BCC was global, the president of the U.S. area appointed a separate U.S. Business Ethics Committee in 1978. At first, this committee did audits also, but in 1979 it functioned more like an ombudsman, studying various issues brought to its attention by employees. For example, in 1982 the committee responded to employee concerns over the privacy of personnel records. Working with the Personnel Policy Committee, it reviewed the recordkeeping process and formulated guidelines for what should be in company files and when these files should be purged. Some of the issues that the U.S. Business Ethics Committee was examining in 1983–84 were: the company's forced ranking performance review system, how to deal with the older employee, sexual harassment, and restric-

tions on accepting gifts and gratuities by salesmen.

The BCC and the U.S. Business Ethics Committee had been different in that the BCC was responsible for making policy, revising the code, and monitoring compliance, whereas the U.S. committee responded primarily to issues as they "bubbled up" from the ranks. Relationships between the two committees had been informal, and they met only as needed.

Beginning in 1982, the BCC began conducting an increasing number of audits within the United States. By mid-1984, it was determined that there was no need for a separate U.S. committee and it was disbanded.

## THE FUTURE

In discussing the future, Swanson pointed to both general and specific concerns. He wondered about the effect of the anticipated amendment to the FCPA, for example. How would less stringent legal requirements impact future revision of the company's code of conduct? Another concern was an increasingly competitive marketplace and its potential effect on Dow Corning's process of monitoring global business conduct.

Speaking of future code revisions, Swanson said, "We stress to our people that the code of conduct is a 'living' statement, one that can change as accepted business practices change. A few statements in the code probably will not change: (a) All relations with employees will be guided by our belief that the dignity of the individual is primary and, (b) Dow Corning will be responsible for the impact of its technology upon the environment. Other positions are subject to continuing review. The recognition (not endorsement) of facilitating payments in our current code is one example."

The BCC also planned to look more closely at health care business practices. DCC had only recently decided to expand into this market and believed there were some questionable but common practices here. For example, it was well known that medical suppliers sometimes entertained doctors in a more lavish manner than was customary in the industrial segment of Dow Corning's business. The committee wanted to make recommendations as to what DCC's policy should be with regard to these practices.

Other items on the agenda were: transborder data flow, developing duty classification guidelines, discriminatory practices, the security of the company's information systems, ex-amining purchasing practices, and whether or not foreign subsidiaries and joint ventures should be expected to abide by the code of conduct. Swanson was also certain that Dow Corning's current strong concern over the protection of proprietary information would continue to receive high priority as competition for markets increased.

## EXHIBITS: Dow Corning Corporation: Business Conduct and Global Values (A)

### EXHIBIT 1
BACKGROUND ON THE FOREIGN CORRUPT PRACTICES ACT

In response to disclosures in 1976 that 450 U.S. companies reported over $300 million in questionable payments, on December 19, 1977, Congress passed the Foreign Corrupt Practices Act (FCPA). The FCPA covered all issuers of securities subject to the jurisdiction of the SEC under the Securities Exchange Act of 1934 and any other "domestic concerns." Put simply, the intent of the act was to prohibit the use of bribes to obtain business. Using some of the key language of the act, the following summarizes the major provisions: The FCPA prohibited the offer or payment of anything of value, directly or indirectly, to foreign officials, political parties, or candidates for foreign political office for the purpose of influencing an act or decision of such person(s) or to induce such person(s) to influence or affect an act of a government, or instrumentality thereof, where such influencing is intended for the purpose of retaining or obtaining business for the U.S. concern.

Companies and their managers were also liable if they knew or had reason to know that their agents used the payments received from the U.S. concern to pay a foreign official for a prohibited purpose. The law also applied to a foreign subsidiary of a U.S. company if it was using the subsidiary as a conduit for illegal payments.

Violations of the act carried fines of up to $1,000,000 for companies and up to $10,000 or five years in prison for individuals. If an individual was fined, his/her company could not pay the fine for the employee.

The act intended to exclude facilitating or "grease payments" by distinguishing "foreign officials," who acted in an official capacity, from those whose duties were "essentially ministerial or clerical." Payments to the latter were legal, although such transactions had to be recorded according to the act's accounting standards.

Although the U.S. business community praised the overall intent of the FCPA, there was widespread criticism of it on the grounds that portions of the act were ambiguous and unduly restrictive. Much criticism was directed at the section which held a company liable if it "had reason to know" an agent was making questionable payments. It was claimed that "reason to know" was too vague and that U.S. companies should not be held liable for an agent's actions, particularly if those actions were legal in the agent's country.

Many in the business community claimed that the FCPA had resulted in significant and widespread loss of business for U.S. companies. Others, however, disputed this. For a discussion of this debate, see "The Foreign Corrupt Practices Act: A Reconsideration," 1981, HBS Case Services 9·382·032.

**EXHIBIT 2**
DOW CORNING CORPORATION AND SUBSIDIARY COMPANIES

| Consolidated balance sheets (thousands of dollars) | | | Consolidated statements of income and retained earnings (thousands of dollars) | | |
|---|---|---|---|---|---|
| | **December 31** | | | **Year ended December 31** | |
| | **1983** | **1982** | | **1983** | **1982** |
| **Assets** | | | | | |
| Current assets | $364,163 | $322,512 | Net sales | $763,063 | $662,755 |
| Property, plant and equipment | 479,178 | 492,372 | Interests, royalties, and other income | 15,939 | 8,811 |
| Other assets | 22,620 | 22,979 | Net revenues | 779,002 | 671,566 |
| Total assets | $865,961 | $838,547 | Costs and expenses | 664,264 | 587,896 |
| | | | Income from operations | 114,738 | 83,670 |
| | | | Provision for income taxes | 44,405 | 29,062 |
| | | | Minority interests' share in income | 1,933 | 1,823 |
| | | | Net income | 68,400 | 52,785 |
| | | | Net income per share (in dollars) | $27.36 | $21.11 |
| | **December 31** | | | | |
| | **1983** | **1982** | | | |
| **Liabilities and stockholder's equity** | | | | | |
| Current liabilities | $154,046 | $133,622 | | | |
| Long-term debt | 125,734 | 153,907 | | | |
| Deferred credits and other liabilities | 109,941 | 97,040 | | | |
| Minority interest in subsidiary companies | 13,759 | 11,955 | | | |
| Stockholders' equity | 462,481 | 442,023 | | | |
| Total liabilities and equities | $865,961 | $838,547 | | | |

*(Continued)*

**EXHIBIT 2**
CONTINUED

### Industry segment and foreign operations
(thousands of dollars)
The company's operations are classified as a single industry segment. The following table summarizes information regarding the company's geographical operations.

| | Year ended December 31, 1983 | | | | | |
|---|---|---|---|---|---|---|
| | United States | Europe | Pacific | Other | Eliminations | Consolidated |
| Sales to customers | $390,152 | $182,696 | $137,267 | $52,948 | $ | $763,063 |
| Transfers between geographic areas | 101,314 | 4,409 | 254 | — | (105,977) | — |
| Total sales | $492,466 | $187,105 | $137,521 | $52,948 | ($105,977) | $763,063 |
| Operating profit | $133,934 | $ 9,915 | $ 18,002 | $ 7,200 | ($ 7,515) | $161,536 |
| General corporate expense | | | | | | (44,374) |
| Interest expense, net | | | | | | (2,424) |
| Income from operations | | | | | | $114,738 |
| Identifiable assets | $474,415 | $195,025 | $156,290 | $34,628 | ($102,684) | $757,674 |
| Corporate assets | | | | | | 108,287 |
| Total assets | | | | | | 865,961 |

*Source:* Dow Corning Corporation Form 10k for fiscal year ended December 31, 1983.

**EXHIBIT 3**
THE MULTIDIMENSIONAL ORGANIZATION

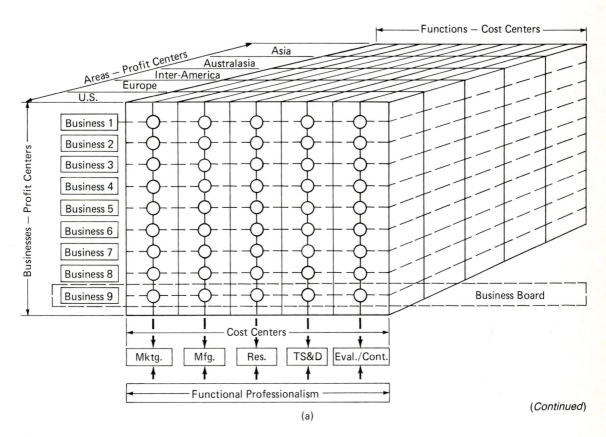

(a)

*(Continued)*

*Source:* "How the Multidimensional Structure Works at Dow Corning," *Harvard Business Review* (January–February 1974), p. 57.

**EXHIBIT 3**
CONTINUED

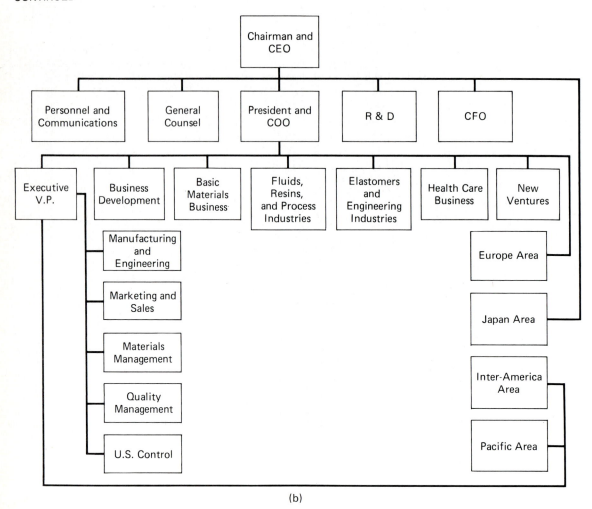

(b)

*Source:* Dow Corning Corporation, 1984.

**EXHIBIT 4**
MEMO FROM PACIFIC AREA MANAGER

April 1, 1976

*To:*      J. S. Ludington

*From:*    [Pacific area manager]

*Subject:*   **Corporate Code of Business Conduct**

First of all let me say that I don't think Dow Corning has a problem and that our house doesn't need putting in order. Therefore, we need to agree on the purpose of any code and that purpose must arise from some need. What is the need if we already believe (as I do) that we are morally, legally, and ethically correct in all aspects of our business conduct?

I think the need arises from inflation by the news media (and some social-conscience mongers) of some malpractices by some companies—often MNCs [multinational corporations]—over the past several years. The fact that such stories have so much credibility to the general public, besides a sad commentary on the abuse of their power by the media, also means that public denials or public statements of corporate codes are bound to misfire and be considered self-serving. Thus I believe the purpose of any code should be primarily internal—a means of listing those company standards which represent the minimum acceptable performance in conducting business. Every member of management then has the responsibility to see that his subordinates understand the code and are working properly within it. The outside world will become convinced only by consistent demonstration, in practice, of the agreed principles.

So I am fully in favor of a Dow Corning Code of Business Conduct to be used as an internal management and operating tool. Such a code must not only embrace parochial Dow Corning and U.S. moral, legal, and social requirements, but must also have pertinence and value in the rest of the world. If we are to do business successfully in such diverse places as U.S.A., Latin America, Japan, Italy, Korea, and India, we have also to operate in accordance with each local country's set of laws, customs, and prerogatives.

● ● ●

Now to the Asian Area. We do have some problem areas, of course, and some downright conflicts. I'll try to indicate some of the issues where I think we'll need to modify or expand the general principles in a Code of Conduct.

**Equal Pay**

The aggressive "equality of the sexes lobby" in the U.S. might lead Dow Corning to declare adherence to the principle of equal pay. In most, if not all, Asian countries, such a concept is laughable at the present time. Thus we would need to write something like: "Dow Corning will pay its employees fairly and competitively in each country and in accordance with legal and social practices."

**Sex Discrimination**

Again, I'm sure our corporate code would want to point out that our policy is to have none. But in many countries in Asia, the roles of male and female are still severely and vehemently separated. I'm sure there are places where we would not be allowed to promote a woman rather than a man or to have a female manager or supervisor. So we would need a qualifying clause here too.

## Job Security

The two-way commitment between company and employee varies enormously from the one extreme of the lifelong contract in Japan to the laissez-faire attitude existing in Hong Kong and other places. Therefore, we would need to be very careful that any policy statement did not overcommit the company or place an unwarranted restriction on the employee. We'd need to say something like: "It is Dow Corning's policy to establish a stable and lasting employment situation for its employees consistent with the need for the company to meet its overall business and social objectives and with the need for the employee to develop his full career potential."

## Bribery and Special Payments

As you know, various forms of commissions, finder's fees, or whatever you want to call them, are the norm in several countries out here and such payments are considered normal business expenses. This situation is not going to change overnight because it has been going on for many years and is endemic in the system. We are careful not to get directly involved but we know that it goes on and will continue. Therefore our statement should be pretty general, something like: "Dow Corning will not pay bribes, illegal political contributions, or any form of nonstandard commission or business expense, in an attempt to influence customers to do business with Dow Corning."

## Pricing

In view of the laws in the U.S., we may decide to say something pretty specific about fair pricing. But if such a policy is applied rigidly here, it may deny us necessary flexibility. We need something like: "Dow Corning will price its goods in the marketplace according to the value of the goods as determined by the market forces. It will not seek to offer unfair and unilateral advantages to some customers on a selective basis."

**EXHIBIT 5**
CORPORATE CODE OF BUSINESS CONDUCT, 1977

## A Matter of Integrity

Dow Corning believes in private enterprise. We will seek to establish an atmosphere of trust and respect between business and members of society, an atmosphere where business and the public understand, accept, and recognize the values and needs of each other.

To establish and promote this atmosphere of mutual trust and respect, Dow Corning accepts as our responsibility a recognition, evaluation and sensitivity to social needs. We will meet this responsibility by utilizing our technological and management skills to develop products and services that will further the development of society.

The watchword of Dow Corning worldwide activities is integrity. We recognize that due to local differences in custom and law, business practice differs throughout the world. We believe that business is best conducted and society best served within each country when business practice is based on the universal principles of honesty and integrity.

We recognize that our social responsibilities must be maintained at the high standards which lead to respect and trust by society. A clear definition of our social responsibilities should be an integral part of our corporate objectives and be clearly communicated to every employee.

## Statement of General Conduct

We shall not tolerate payments in any illegal or questionable form, or nonstandard commissions or other compensation, given or received, that may influence business decisions.

We shall not make any political contribution nor participate in partisan political activity as a company, recognizing however the rights of employees to participate in legal political processes as private citizens.

We shall be knowledgeable of local laws and customs and operate within them. On the other hand, when we are not being treated legally or ethically we will pursue whatever legitimate recourses are available to us.

## Responsibilities to Our Employees

Relations with employees are based on the understanding that attracting and retaining talented and dedicated employees is vital to the accomplishment of financial and social objectives.

### Our responsibilities to our employees are:

To manage our activities in such a way as to provide security and opportunities for our productive employees.

To hire, train, evaluate, and advance on the basis of individual ability, contribution, potential, interest, and company needs without distinction as to nationality, sex, age, color, or religion.

To compensate in accordance with local, national, or industry practice.

To provide a safe and healthy work environment that at least meets the applicable government laws and regulations.

To provide a work environment that encourages individual self-fulfillment, open communication, and free interchange of information and ideas.

## Responsibilities to Host Countries in Which We Operate

Activities in host countries are based on the premise that we can and wish to contribute to the economic objectives of the host government while concurrently meeting our corporate objectives.

### Our responsibilities to host countries are:

To preserve and, where possible, enhance the environment through elimination or control of pollution.

To conserve natural resources.

To design and modify facilities which meet or exceed current and anticipated environmental and safety laws and regulations.

To hire, train, and qualify host country nationals for positions of responsibility consistent with their demonstrated capabilities.

To pay our required share of taxes and duties but resist inequitable or double taxation between countries.

To resolve any government relations problems or conflicts among overlapping jurisdictions through prompt, direct and open discussions with responsible government officials.

To follow responsible monetary and credit practices and conduct foreign exchange operations not for speculative purposes, but in accordance with normal business requirements and to protect our exposure fluctuations.

To encourage the flow of our technology across borders to the extent needed and appropriate in our local operations and markets, and to receive adequate compensation and protection of this technology.

**EXHIBIT 6**
CORPORATE CODE OF BUSINESS CONDUCT, 1983

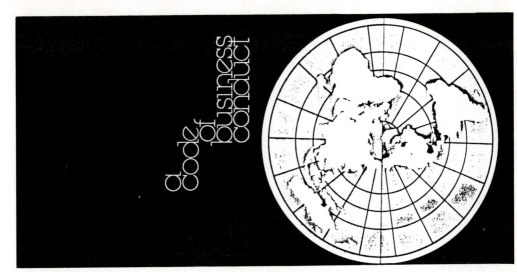

DOW CORNING CORPORATION

**Dow Corning
Area Headquarters**

United States
Midland Center
P.O. Box 1767
Midland, MI 48640

Europe
154 Chaussee de la Hulpe
1170 Brussels, Belgium

Inter-America
Midland Center
P.O. Box 1767
Midland, MI 48640

Pacific
21 Tattersall Road
Blacktown
New South Wales 2148
Australia

Japan
15-1, Nishi Shimbashi 1-chome
Minato-Ku, Tokyo, 105, Japan

DOW CORNING

Dow Corning Corporation
Midland, Michigan 48640 U.S.A.

## To Dow Corning Employees:

At the top of the list of our corporate objectives is this statement: "Dow Corning's actions shall be guided by its Corporate Code of Business Conduct." Dow Corning places an exceedingly high value on corporate integrity. A sense of fair play, honesty and ethical business practice has always been the foundation of Dow Corning's operating philosophy.

Since 1976 we have extended our efforts to formalize Dow Corning's approach to business conduct. The Code itself is regularly reviewed and updated; a top level Corporate Committee monitors and audits our worldwide compliance with Code principles; we report on business conduct practices annually to the Audit and Social Responsibility Committee of the Board of Directors.

Our intent goes beyond compliance with the law, although that is quite fundamental. Throughout the organization we are developing a sense, or attitude, of personal integrity among our employees. Each employee plays a part in maintaining the integrity of the organization in all its business activities.

I assure you the management of Dow Corning places top priority on fair, legal and ethical business conduct. As an employee of Dow Corning, I ask that you continue to share this key commitment.

Sincerely,

John S. Ludington
Chairman and Chief Executive Officer

(Continued)

**EXHIBIT 6**
CONTINUED

## Our Standards of Business Conduct

Fair, legal and ethical business practice has been the cornerstone of Dow Corning's operating philosophy since the company was founded in 1943. We believe that business is best conducted and society best served when business practice is based on the principles of honesty and integrity.

The Code of Business Conduct provides guidelines, but can not cover every situation you may encounter. Should you become aware of — or involved in — a questionable practice, bring it to the attention of your supervisor or a member of the Business Conduct Committee at any time.

## Dow Corning's Responsibilities to Employees:

All relations with employees will be guided by our belief that the dignity of the individual is primary.

Opportunity without bias will be afforded each employee in relation to demonstrated ability, initiative and potential.

Business decisions will be consistent with our intent to provide long-term stability and opportunity to all productive employees.

Qualified citizens of countries where we do business will be hired and trained for available positions consistent with their capabilities.

The work environment will encourage individual self-fulfillment, the maximization of skills and talents, open communication and the free exchange of information and ideas.

A safe, clean and pleasant work environment that at minimum meets all applicable laws and regulations will be provided.

The privacy of an individual's personal records will be respected; employees may participate in a review of their personnel records upon request.

## Employee's Responsibilities to Dow Corning

Employees will regard proprietary information as a valuable corporate asset and will avoid the unauthorized disclosure of Dow Corning's business activities, future plans, technology or other proprietary information. We will respect proprietary information belonging to others.

Employees must be free of conflicting interests which could inhibit or detract from their on-the-job performance or with Dow Corning's business interests.

Employees will not engage in bribery, price fixing, kickbacks, collusion, or any practice which might give the appearance of being illegal or unethical.

Employees will avoid discussions with competitors that could be construed as unfair competition or the restriction of free trade. Relations with our competitors will be limited to buyer-seller agreements, licensing agreements or matters of general concern to the industry or society. All such discussions will be documented.

## Relations with Customers, Distributors, Suppliers:

Dow Corning will provide on time products and services that meet the requirements of our customers. We will provide information and support necessary to maximize the use and effectiveness of our products.

Dow Corning expects and encourages its agents, representatives and distributors to conduct business in a legal and ethical manner.

The purchase of supplies, materials and services will be based on quality, price, service, ability to supply and the vendor's adherence to legal and ethical business practices. Fees paid for business services must be reasonable and in line with customary local rates.

## Conservation, Environmental and Product Stewardship Practices:

Dow Corning will be responsible for the impact of its technology upon the environment. We will protect the natural environment by continually seeking reasonable ways to eliminate or minimize discharges of potentially harmful waste materials.

All waste will be recycled when possible and economical. Non-recyclable waste will be disposed of in accordance with applicable standards.

New facilities will be designed to optimize the efficient use of natural resources and to conserve energy. Existing facilities will be modified to meet current and anticipated environmental laws and regulations.

We will continually strive to assure that our products and services are safe, efficacious and accurately represented in our literature, advertising and package identification.

Product characteristics, including toxicity and potential hazards, will be made known to those who produce, package, transport, use and dispose of Dow Corning products.

## International Business Guidelines

Dow Corning endeavors to be a productive and cooperative corporate citizen wherever we do business. We recognize,

however, that laws, business practices and customs differ from country to country and may occasionally inhibit rather than foster open competition. Such practices could include boycotts, information requests, tax systems, duty classification procedures, labor standards and property protection, among others. If there is a conflict with U.S. law or a Dow Corning standard of business conduct, we will seek reasonable ways to resolve the difference. Failing resolution, Dow Corning will remove itself from the particular business situation.

Dow Corning personnel will not authorize or give payments or gifts to government employees or their beneficiaries in order to obtain or retain business. We will strongly discourage facilitating payments to expedite the performance of routine services. Where the practice is common and there is no reasonable alternative, a minimum payment may be considered. Such payments will be accurately documented and recorded.

No payment, contribution or service will be offered by Dow Corning to a political party or a candidate, even in countries where such payments are legal.

While encouraging the transborder transfer of technology necessary to support its subsidiaries and joint ventures, Dow Corning expects to receive fair compensation for, and protection of, its technology.

Dow Corning will strive to establish intercompany prices at a level that would prevail in arm's length transactions. The intent of this approach to pricing is to assure each country a fair valuation of goods and services transferred.

## Financial Responsibilities:

Dow Corning funds will be used only for purposes that are legal and ethical. All transactions will be properly and accurately recorded.

Dow Corning will maintain a system of internal accounting controls and assure that all involved employees are fully apprised of that system.

Dow Corning encourages the free flow of funds for investment, borrowing, dividending and the return of capital throughout the world.

### We Are Committed...

...to the letter and spirit of this Code of Business Conduct. The character and conduct of Dow Corning Corporation depend on the actions of its employees. As a Dow Corning employee, you are expected to know these standards and live up to them.

*©1984 Dow Corning Corporation

**EXHIBIT 7**
WORKSHEETS—CODE OF BUSINESS CONDUCT AUDITS

## "ISSUES" TO BE EMPHASIZED IN AUDITS AT AREA OR REGIONAL HEADQUARTERS

### I. Customers, Distributors, and Competitors

a. Dow Corning encourages competition in the open market and will avoid all association with competitors that could be construed as unfair competition or the restriction of free trade. Competitor relations will be limited to buyer-seller agreements, licensing agreements, or matters of general concern to the industry or society. *Dow Corning personnel do not participate in discussions on the pricing of our products with our competitors.*

b. *No bribe, payoff, rebate, kickback, or other form of remuneration will be given to secure or retain business. This applies to all Dow Corning officers and employees as well as agents, consultants, distributors, or any third party authorized to represent Dow Corning.* It precludes the use of agreements, arrangements, or devices intended to compensate government employees (including agencies and commissions) or shareholders of private customers for decisions or actions that would give Dow Corning Corporation an unfair competitive advantage.

  1. Has Dow Corning ever found it necessary to provide "grease payments" in order to get products evaluated or qualified as an approved source in government facilities or in commercial operations?

  2. Have we ever used any distributor or agents to make questionable payments or accept kickbacks on behalf of Dow Corning or any of our employees?

  3. Do the improper payments that are reported in the local papers generally occur in (1) public companies, (2) private companies, (3) government-managed manufacturing, or (4) government agencies?

c. Dow Corning does not use reciprocity in any form in obtaining orders from our customers.

d. Dow Corning personnel are being practical and judicious in their offering or accepting of gifts and entertainment in their relationships with customers, distributors, suppliers, and government employees.

  1. Are there any examples of business that Dow Corning has lost because of our refusing to provide "gifts" or other incentives to government officials or various personnel at our customer's facilities?

  2. Payment of travel expenses for government officials, consultants, or employees of customers or prospective customers who visit a facility of Dow Corning, or a Dow Corning-sponsored event is permissible under certain conditions. First, there must be a legitimate business reason for the trip. Second, the expenses must be reasonable and properly recorded and accounted for by Dow Corning.

e. Dow Corning employees are not involved by investment, consulting, or employment in any situations that could be considered a conflict of interest.

  1. Do any of our employees have any ownership or financial interest in any of our distributors?

  2. In any other organization that supplies services to Dow Corning?

f. Procedures have been established in all areas to provide *appropriate controls* on any requests for terms beyond 30 days to 60 days.

  1. What use is made of special arrangements involving items such as extended terms, rebates, discounts, allowances, etc.?

g. Dow Corning distributors, sales representatives, and agents have received copies of our Code of Business Conduct. They have acknowledged that they have read the code, understand it, and will abide by it. In addition, our 1981 contracts with distributors, agents, and representatives require adherence to the Dow Corning Code of Business Conduct.

1. What do distributors think about our Code of Business Conduct Program? Do they fully understand our Business Conduct brochures?
2. Have our salesmen been able to conduct the Business Conduct discussions with our distributors in such a manner as to actually strengthen our ties and relationship with them?
3. Do we find it necessary to employ any distributors with questionable character or integrity or those who are highly political?
4. Has Dow Corning been forced to terminate any distributors because of their "Business Conduct" practices?
5. Do you believe that our distributors are in "regular" contact with their competitors? If so, why?
6. Are any customers invoiced by our distributors at a price higher than the "established local market" price? Are these invoiced amounts over market price rebated to anyone?
7. Have we received any customer lists or other proprietary information from our distributors? How is this information protected?
8. Are our distributors asking for or expecting any "gifts" or special arrangements?
9. Have we paid any expediting fees or travel expenses for our distributors?
10. Have any of our employees been exposed to extensive entertainment by any of our distributors? Are our employees able to remain objective in their dealings with competitive distributors?
11. Are any of our distributors involved in any programs that will involve the relabeling or repackaging of our products? Have they been authorized by Dow Corning to do this? Does their repackaging and relabeling meet Dow Corning's standards?

h. Sales representatives should only be compensated in the country in which they operate and in the currency or currencies in which they are doing business.
i. Product characteristics, including toxicity and potential hazards, are being made known to customers and distributors who use, package, transport, or dispose of Dow Corning products.
    1. Is Dow Corning able to provide adequate "Emergency Response" in the event that a major spill or other crisis develops in the transportation or use of our product?
j. Dow Corning personnel—with considered judgment and guidance from their country and/or regional manager—document all definite, illegal, or improper incidents involving customers, distributors, government representatives, suppliers or consultants.
k. The changes that Dow Corning has initiated in order to comply with the Code of Business Conduct have added some expense; also, a few significant orders may have been lost. However, the overall program is definitely leading to a stronger, healthier relationship with our customers, distributors, and employees.

## II. Host Country Relationships

a. Qualified citizens of countries where we have facilities will be hired and trained for available positions consistent with their capabilities.
b. Dow Corning will provide a work environment that encourages individual self-fulfillment, the maximization of skills and talents, open communication, and the free exchange of information and ideas.
c. Dow Corning will establish a safe, clean, and pleasant working environment that at a minimum meets all applicable laws and regulations.
d. Dow Corning will abide by the applicable United States laws in all its worldwide operations. Dow Corning will also obey the laws of those countries where we do business. If there is a conflict, Dow Corning

must follow the dictates of the U.S. law. Have any problems resulted from this position? How have they been resolved?

e. Dow Corning appreciates that *business practices and customs* differ from country to country and occasionally tend to inhibit, rather than foster, open communication. When a host country practice restricts free trade or conflicts *with a Dow Corning policy or guideline, we will seek reasonable ways to resolve the difference.* Lacking appropriate resolutions, *Dow Corning will remove itself from the particular business situation.*

1. In what countries will we experience major conflicts with the "Dow Corning policies"?
2. Which specific "Dow Corning policies" conflict with local practices?
3. Can these differences be resolved or will Dow Corning be forced to discontinue seeking specific pieces of business in certain countries?

f. *No funds or services of the Dow Corning Corporation, its subsidiaries, and joint ventures will be contributed to political parties, politicians, or office holders—even in countries where such payments are legal.* However, employees may make individual political contributions through legal and company-approved programs, e.g., a Political Action Committee in the United States.

1. In what countries is it difficult for Dow Corning to do business without making political contributions?
2. What percentage of the silicone business could be affected?

g. Dow Corning employees do make necessary "expediting payments" for the company, but they are not considered to be excessive or improper in consideration of the services being performed. Accurate records of such payments are kept.

1. How are the "expediting payments" being documented?
2. Is the need for "expediting payments" increasing or decreasing?

h. Dow Corning is maintaining a comprehensive system of internal accounting controls and is taking steps to assure that all employees having access to our funds or other resources are fully aware of the existence of these controls.

1. Do you feel our financial controls are adequate to prevent funds being accumulated to make improper payments?
2. If you do not feel our controls are adequate, how would it be possible to work around them?
3. Are any of Dow Corning's procedures exposing any of our employees to inappropriate temptations?

i. Dow Corning will *not make any payments, other than approved payrolls and documented petty cash, in currency.* No payments shall be made into numbered bank accounts or any other Dow Corning account by any means that is not clearly identifiable. Any form of payment that could be viewed suspiciously is to be avoided.

j. *The use of "false" invoices or other misleading or fictitious documentation for any purpose is prohibited.* This applies to the invention of any false entities such as sales, purchases, services, loans, and other financial arrangements.

k. Dow Corning does not provide any inaccurate or incomplete memos, pro-forma invoices, or other documents that could assist distributors or customers in arranging for lower duties on indent shipments of our products.

1. Do our distributors pay the appropriate import duty on their indent shipments?
2. Do you believe it should be a Dow Corning concern if the distributor "arranges" for a lower, questionable duty on his indent shipments, provided Dow Corning support is not used in making the arrangement?

l. Dow Corning does not support or participate in any boycotts involving the selling or distribution of our products.

## ADDITIONAL ISSUES

1　Are we *inappropriately* favoring any customers or distributors with allocated products, large samples, low prices, bargain off-spec material, credit terms and allowances, or excessive gifts and entertainment?

2　Are "Competitive Activity Reports" being completed and filed on specific customers to support our selling below book price? Do we frequently review these situations to determine if below book prices are still being offered at this account by the competition?

3 How much notice do local companies expect and offer on price increases when inflation is running 10 percent to 20 percent?

4 Have we been approached by individuals affiliated with competitors, distributors, sales agents, or any other contacts with offers to purchase proprietary information—such as customer lists, technical information, etc.? Have others been approached?

5 Is Dow Corning putting adequate emphasis on the protection of our employees from international or national terrorism and local crime?

6 Do any of our business practices expose our personnel to any improper temptations (i.e., cash collections without proper controls)?

7 Of the countries within this area or region, list those in which you believe the majority (80 percent) of U.S. companies could operate within the general guidelines of the Dow Corning Code of Business Conduct.

8 Also list the countries that you believe would fall far short of this target.

9 In what cities are your people experiencing requests for grease money in amounts that definitely exceed the usual requests for tips or "expediting payments"?

10 What is the status of the Code of Business Conduct file? Does it need to be cleaned up? Does it contain sufficient information to adequately describe questionable experiences and their resolution?

11 Do you believe the region's business conduct standards have been improved significantly, slightly, or not at all by the programs of the past four years?

12 What comments have you heard from companies that use "a sign off procedure" with their regional management rather than a business conduct audit? What do you think of this approach?

13 What have you heard about the practices other U.S.-based companies are following in their business conduct audits?

14 Do you have any suggestions to make the Dow Corning Business Conduct Program more productive?

15 What is the most significant weakness in the Dow Corning Code of Business Conduct program?

16 What type of questionable business conduct do we miss in our present business conduct audit program? What additional specific questions should be asked?

**EXHIBIT 8**
BUSINESS CONDUCT REPORTING PROCEDURES

### Purpose

The nine questions listed below were developed to facilitate the accurate and uniform reporting of improper and illegal situations in which Dow Corning personnel could be implicated. A reportable situation could involve customers, distributors, government officials, suppliers, consultants or Dow Corning employees. Examples of reportable incidents could include: conflicts of interest; requests for questionable payments or kickbacks; misleading or deceptive product classifications intended to affect import duties. The Corporate Code of Business Conduct describes several additional situations that, if violated, would be reportable incidents.

### Reporting

The resolution of a business conduct problem is expedited when the details of the incident, and the subsequent action(s), are immediately reported and recorded. *The question should include only that information believed to be accurate.* The reporting steps are as follows:

1   Complete the questionnaire as completely as possible.
2   Send the questionnaire to the department manager or regional manager for review, judgment, and, if possible, resolution.
3   If the manager determines that area headquarters' attention is required, copies should be sent to the area manager and to the chairman, Business Conduct Committee.

### Disposition

Business conduct files in regional offices should be purged every six months and completely cleaned at the end of 12 months. Area headquarters will retain a business conduct file containing reports of incidents for the current year. That file should be destroyed in December of the following year.

### DOCUMENTATION OF ILLEGAL, UNETHICAL, AND/OR QUESTIONABLE BUSINESS PRACTICES

1   List name(s) and title(s) of individual(s) and their organization(s) who offered, or were a party to, the questionable business practice or proposition.
2   Specify by name, title, and organization others outside Dow Corning who were directly or indirectly involved.
3   List other Dow Corning employees who have first-hand knowledge of the proposition or who have helped you resolve the proposition.
4   If the questionable business practice could possibly damage Dow Corning or its reputation—or involve us in any way—but was not presented directly to Dow Corning, please explain how you learned about it (i.e., distributor and customer, distributor and government agent, etc.).
5   Briefly describe the proposition itself and what, in your opinion, it was expected to accomplish.
6   What form of remuneration was to be used: cash, gifts, entertainment, extraordinarily high fees or payments, reciprocity, other?
7   Describe actions taken or being considered to resolve the situation by you and/or others?
8   Did our response or action have any effect, positive or negative, on Dow Corning's operations (i.e., customer relations, sales, relationship with distributor, relationship with a supplier, etc.)?
9   What suggestions do you have that might prevent, or reduce, the possibility of this type of questionable business practice occurring another time from a different source?

# Dow Corning Corporation: Business Conduct and Global Values (B)

"When in Rome, some do as the Romans do," thought Bill Hargreaves. Hargreaves was a senior vice president assigned to special projects, one of which was chairmanship of the BCC. He was contemplating the report he was about to present to Dow Corning's Audit and Social Responsibility Committee (ASRC). This report would summarize the results of the BCC's most recent audit cycle, indicating that on a global basis, Dow Corning was complying with its Corporate Code of Conduct. There were, however, two situations that required tough decisions. Both were considered "accepted practices" in the countries where they occurred. While the details of how the problems were resolved would not be presented to the ASRC, Hargreaves was thinking about how he would handle specific questions if they should come up.

## COUNTRY X

The first situation involved a major distributor for DCC's products in Country X. The owner had a reputation for reliability and efficiency, but the most recent audit suggested that he was bribing customs officials in order to obtain lower duty rates for DCC products. DCC's Business Code of Conduct prohibited the company from using distributors who engaged in bribery. Also, under the Foreign Corrupt Practices Act of 1977, DCC would be in violation of the law if it had reason to know one of its agents was bribing officials to obtain business.

Following the procedure used since the adoption of the Business Code of Conduct, DCC had asked the distributor to agree in writing to abide by the code but he had refused to do so. At the time there was no evidence suggesting bribery. When the company's suspicions increased due to last year's audits, the area manager discussed the issue with the distributor, who argued that the payments were customary in Country X, and that he could not compete effectively without them. A year had passed and he still had not agreed to the code. His contract was up for renewal this year and the suggestion had been made that DCC should refuse to renew it unless he agreed to abide by the code.

The Country X distributor had represented Dow Corning for many years, and was doing close to a million dollars per year in business with DCC at that time. Hargreaves was also aware that his major competitor was paying duty rates as low—and possibly as illegal. Could DCC ask its distributor not to use bribery if the company knew the competition would continue the practice? How "morally imperialistic" could the corporation be? And what about the three other distributors in Country X, each doing over $500,000 per year in business with Dow Corning? If one contract were terminated because of a refusal to live by the code, what would happen with these other distributors?

## COUNTRY Y

The second situation involved one of Dow Corning's legal entities in Country Y. The country manager, a national, had made contributions to the political campaigns of high-ranking government officials. Not only was this practice legal in Country Y, but often considered exemplary for corporations. U.S. companies were prohibited by law from making political contributions, and Dow Corning Corporation's Code of Conduct also prohibited such contributions from company funds anywhere in the world.

Did Dow Corning have the right to insist that this particular country operation stop doing what was legal in Country Y and do business according to U.S. corporate standards? What if it were the other way around, and a company from Country Y insisted that one of its American branches follow Country Y's norms and laws? Who would have to give in?

Although Hargreaves knew it would be difficult to resolve these problems, he welcomed the opportunity to test DCC's commitment to its values and to learn how to make them even more operational. He also wanted to test a belief he knew some of his business colleagues held: that maintaining a strong commitment to a global set of values would significantly harm DCC's financial fortunes. In a 1979 memo to Hargreaves, the Pacific area manager questioned the adoption of this policy in Asia:

> We may find, this time next year, that we either do business the way some American companies and the Europeans and Japanese do or we forget the Philippines market. We know we are already losing business in Korea and India by adopting a rigorous attitude to local agents' commissions. How much we can lose in Korea and still have a meaningful long-term strategy, including perhaps manufacturing investment, is an open question. But it is one we had better ask ourselves pretty quickly. If the corporation wishes to continue to put Dow Corning at a competitive market disadvantage because of some ethical (not legal) concern, that is its prerogative. But to pressure area management, at the same time, to increase market share and leadership ... seems inconsistent to say the least.

## THE COSTS OF CONSCIENCE

It was difficult to quantify the costs and benefits of Dow Corning's business conduct program. Inevitably, one heard through the grapevine about specific incidents. One incident in particular had received considerable attention in the corporation's offices worldwide. It involved an Asian distributor who had been with Dow Corning before it developed its code of conduct. The country involved was well known as a difficult place for Western firms to do business, partly because of the widespread use of questionable payments. A BCC audit had suggested that the distributor was bribing customers to obtain their business. When first asked to sign the code, he said he could not do business that way. After representatives from Dow Corning met with him several times to press for his cooperation, he left to represent another manufacturer. Losing this distributor cost the corporation about $600,000 that year. At the end of the year, however, he asked to represent DCC again, this time agreeing in writing to do business according to the code.

The company had also lost business opportunities in Central and South America, where bribes and "facilitating payments" were frequent. In September 1977 a DCC sales agent for Dow Corning Mexico met with a purchasing agent for a large, state-owned utility. They discussed an upcoming bid for a project on which Dow Corning was competing with a European-based producer. The initial bid involved the sale of two tons of a certain product with the likelihood of an additional twelve tons in the near future. The approximate value of the fourteen tons was $160,000.

The sales agent was told what the price per kilo should be, and that DCC could have the business if it gave the purchasing agent a color television set or airline tickets of comparable value. These, he said, would immediately be sold, and the money split between him and his boss. It was mentioned that if DCC was awarded the additional twelve tons, the "gift" would have to be proportionately larger. When the sales agent offered to sell the product at 8% below the stipulated price, the purchasing agent told him that this lower price would not win the bid for Dow Corning.

DCC submitted a bid for the lower price and refused to supply either the television set or the airline tickets. DCC's competitor was awarded the initial contract as well as the additional contract for twelve tons. Although Dow Corning had done business with the utility for many years before this incident without having to pay bribes, it had faced no competition in Mexico for the product in question.

The costs of refusing to make questionable payments could not always be measured in terms of lost business. In October 1983, a customs inspector at the San Miguel plant in Venezuela requested a facilitating payment from a Dow Corning manager. The request was refused. The documentation of this incident by the regional manager stated: "What we had not realized was the length and intensity of the customs investigation once the inspector had been informed that DCC would not make the requested under-the-table payment. Investigators were in the office each day for three months; the office had to be closed for normal business for five days during that period. The nature of the customs audit seemed to be harassment—a price paid for *not* paying off."

## THE MEETING

As he left for his meeting with the ASRC, Hargreaves thought of Jack Ludington's remarks during a recent conversation on business conduct: "We're going to play right, but we're going to play hard."

# Some Avenues for Ethical Analysis in General Management

The general manager inevitably confronts ethical issues, whatever his or her location in the corporate structure and whatever the size and complexity of the organization. Sometimes the demands of responsible judgment and action are obvious, e.g., when decisions involve clear, significant, and avoidable harms or indignities to persons inside or outside the organization. But often the demands of responsible judgment and action are not obvious. (One has only to consider the knot of problems surrounding the controversies over affirmative action and reverse discrimination or the debate over business operations in South Africa.) Often what the general manager seeks and needs is a more or less orderly way of thinking through the moral implications of a policy decision—a perspective and a language for appraising the alternatives available from an ethical point of view.

This note will sketch only the broadest outlines of such a perspective and such a language,

drawing upon the resources of ethics as a philosophical discipline. A fuller development of these topics is available elsewhere.[1]

## THE DUAL ROLE OF THE GENERAL MANAGER

One of the principal gods of Roman mythology was Janus, god of beginnings. His image, often appearing at the gates of cities, had two faces on one head.[2] One face looked to the city within, while the other looked outward. The Janus-faced image is a convenient one for representing the dual role of the general manager in the modern corporation.

---

[1]See especially: "Ethical Frameworks for Management," HBS Case Services No. 384—105, and "Relativism in Ethics," Case No. 381—097.
[2]Webster's *New Collegiate Dictionary* (Springfield, Mass.: G. & C. Merriam Company, 1977), p. 619, illustrates the Janus image.

---

This note was prepared by Kenneth E. Goodpaster as a basis for class discussion. Copyright © 1983 by the President and Fellows of Harvard College. Harvard Business School case 9·383·007.

Chester I. Barnard, in his classic *The Functions of the Executive,* writes:

> The survival of cooperation depends upon two interrelated and interdependent classes of processes: (a) those which relate to the system of cooperation as a whole in relation to the environment; and (b) those which relate to the creation or distribution of satisfactions among individuals.
>
> The instability and failures of cooperation arise from defects in each of these classes of processes separately, and from defects in their combination. The functions of the executive are those of securing the effective adaptation of these processes.[3]

Whether the task be policy formulation or policy implementation, Barnard goes on to argue that the executive or the general manager must attend constantly to both of these aspects of corporate life: the outward-looking and the inward-looking.

Beyond the great value of Barnard's reflections for the whole field of business policy, they also provide a gateway to the field of ethics as it relates to business policy. The study of ethics is the study of human action and its moral adequacy. Since the action of the executive has a dual aspect, we can expect the ethical responsibilities of the executive to have a dual aspect.

### Transactions and the Moral Point of View

Many people have offered elaborate definitions of the subject matter of ethics, but the most useful for our present purposes is offered by philosopher Alan Gewirth. Ethics or morality, he observes,

> is primarily concerned with interpersonal actions, that is, with actions that affect persons other than their agents. I shall refer to such actions as *transactions,* and to the persons affected by them as *recipients.* I shall also say that both

**FIGURE A**
Ethical relevance of the general manager's functions or roles.

the agent and his recipient *participate* in transactions, although the former does so actively and the latter passively, by undergoing or being affected by the agent's action toward him.[4]

Gewirth goes on to point out that there are many kinds and degrees of "one person's affecting another," but that the morally relevant transactions are those

> where what is affected is the recipient's freedom and well-being, and hence his capacity for action. . . . Such modes of affecting in transactions can be most readily recognized in their negative forms: when one person coerces another, hence preventing him from participating purposively or with well-being in the transaction.[5]

If we join Gewirth's observations about the subject matter of ethics or morality with Barnard's observations about the dual role of the executive, we have the initial contours of a framework for analysis as shown in Figure A.

In this figure, A and B represent two broad classes of transactions that are both central to the functions of the general manager and ethically important in their own right. *A-transactions* have to do primarily with managing the organization's relationship with the wider so-

---

[3]Chester I. Barnard, *The Functions of the Executive,* Thirtieth Anniversary Edition (Cambridge, Mass.: Harvard University Press, 1968), pp. 60–61.

[4]Alan Gewirth, *Reason and Morality* (Chicago, Ill.: University of Chicago Press, 1978), p. 129.
[5]Ibid.

cial and natural environment in which it operates. Examples of ethical issues that fall under this heading include product safety, environmental protection, truth in advertising and marketing, responsibilities to investors and suppliers, and various other forms of local, national, and international corporate impact.

*B-transactions* have to do primarily with managing the internal environment of the organization, including interpersonal relations, authority, incentives, and structure. Examples of ethical issues that fall under this heading include worker health and safety; fairness in hiring, firing, and promotion; civil liberties for employees; and more subtle organizational pressures that affect either the general moral climate or culture of the corporation or the character of individuals as they rise through the ranks.

In A-transactions, the general manager views the corporation as a *moral agent* in the wider society, while in B-transactions, the general manager views the corporation as itself a *moral environment* to be managed with a view to the freedom and well-being of its members. Both types of transactions involve issues of policy formulation as well as policy implementation. (See Figure B.)

From the perspective of the history of ethics or moral philosophy, the foregoing represents an acknowledgment of the (modern) fact that the corporation is in some respects a microcosm of the community in which it operates and in other respects a macrocosm of the individual citizen living and working in that wider community. Insofar as the corporation resembles the wider community, ethical issues arise that are analogous to those in classical political philosophy: legitimacy of authority; rights and responsibilities associated with entry, exit, membership, promotion, and succession; civil liberties; moral climate. Insofar as the corporation resembles an individual "person" in the community, ethical issues arise that are analogous to classical issues of personal responsibility: duties and obligations to avoid harm, to respect the law, to further justice and the common good, and to provide for the least advantaged. There will be differences in each realm, of course, since the respective analogies are imperfect, but the similarities are strong enough to help order the ethical agenda of business policy.

The general manager, then, sits at the nexus of two broad regions of judgment and action that call not only for economic intelligence but also for ethical awareness. And just as the former calls for a healthy balance of analytical skill and intuition, so does the latter. Moral reasoning, despite the aspirations of some of the great thinkers of the past, is no more reducible to a mechanical decision procedure than is economic or administrative reasoning. Ethics, though not unscientific, is not a science.

The alternative, however, need not be thought of as anarchic: "There's no disputing tastes." Ethical judgment may not manifest the same kind of objectivity that we have come to expect of the natural sciences, but few would seriously contend that reason has no place in ethics. The history of philosophical as well as theological thought about ethics reveals, amidst

| | Corporation as moral agent | Corporation as moral environment |
|---|---|---|
| Business policy formulation | | |
| Business policy implementation | | |

**FIGURE B**
Relating business policy, ethics, and the dual role of the general manager.

much disagreement, a shared conviction that moral judgment can and should be rooted in what some have called the moral point of view and that this point of view governs and disciplines what are taken to be good and bad reasons, sound and unsound arguments, principles and intuitions. For many, the moral point of view has been understood in religious terms as the point of view that reflects God's will for humanity. For others, the moral point of view has been understood in more natural terms, not dependent for its authority on religious faith. But if one sets aside questions about its ultimate *source,* one finds significant consensus as to its general character. The moral point of view is seen as a mental and emotional standpoint from which all persons have a special dignity or worth, from which the Golden Rule derives its force, from which words like *ought* and *duty* derive their meaning.

In a later section, we shall outline the main types of reasoning that have been associated with this point of view. First, however, we must locate such moral reasoning within the wider territory of philosophical ethics.

### Normative Ethics

Contemporary philosophers divide the field of ethics into three parts: descriptive ethics, normative ethics, and metaethics (see Figure C). Descriptive ethics is not, strictly speaking, a philosophical activity. It is more appropriately classified among the social sciences, since it is aimed at an empirical or neutral *description* of the values of individuals and groups. To say, for example, that a business executive or an organization approves of bribery is to make a descriptive ethical claim, one that can be supported or refuted by pointing to factual evidence.

Normative ethics, by contrast, is not aimed at neutral factual claims about the ethical characteristics of individuals or groups. Normative ethical inquiry seeks to develop and defend judgments of right and wrong, good and bad, virtue and vice. For this reason, we will examine normative ethics more closely below.

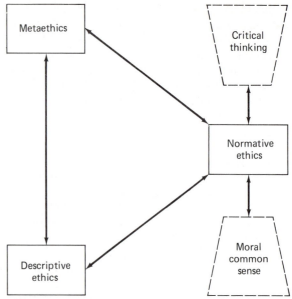

**FIGURE C**
Branches of ethical thinking.

To say that a business executive or an organization approves of bribery *and* is wrong or bad for doing so is to add a normative ethical claim to a descriptive one. If it is to be supported or refuted, some sort of criteria of "wrongness" or "badness" must be provided.

Metaethics is concerned neither with describing values nor with advancing criteria for right and wrong, but with examining questions about the meaning and provability of ethical judgments. Metaethics is therefore a level of abstraction above normative ethics. At this remove, one might explore the differences among scientific, religious, and ethical judgments; the relation of legality to morality; the implications of cultural differences for ethical objectivity, and so forth.

It is important to keep descriptive ethical, normative ethical, and metaethical issues separate, if for no other reason than that confusion results from failing to do so. To continue our example, consider a statement such as "For Americans, bribery is wrong, but for certain others it is not." On one reading, such a statement is simply a descriptive ethical remark: "Americans, as a matter of fact, generally disapprove of bribery while people in Society X do not." On another reading, however, the statement is normative: "Americans are wrong to pay bribes but people in Society X are not." On still a third reading, the implication of the statement might be metaethical: "There is no objective right or wrong about bribery, only social custom." Unless one is clear about which of these three possible interpretations of the original statement is intended, little progress will be made in any discussion of its merits.

Focusing now on normative ethics, the kind of inquiry most relevant to our present purposes, two sublevels need to be distinguished. First, and most familiar, is what we will call the level of *moral common sense*. Whether in our personal lives or in our professional or organizational lives, most of us operate with a more or less well-defined set of ethical values, principles, or rules of thumb that guide decision making. Seldom are such values or rules spelled out explicitly in a list, but if they were, the list would probably include such items as:

- Avoid harming others.
- Respect the rights of others.
- Do not lie or cheat.
- Keep promises and contracts.
- Obey the law.
- Prevent harm to others.
- Help those in need.
- Be fair.
- Reinforce these imperatives in others.

In many decision situations, such a repertoire of commonsense moral judgments is sufficient. It functions as an informal normative ethical framework, one that sometimes demands a lot from us but that we are prepared to live by both for the sake of others and for our own inner well-being.[6]

---

[6]For a fuller discussion of what is called moral common sense here and of the differences in weight among the rules, see Bernard Gert, *The Moral Rules: A New Rational Foundation for Morality* (New York: Harper & Row, 1973).

But problems arise—sometimes hypothetically, sometimes in practice. And when they arise, we seem to be forced into a second level of normative ethical thinking. The problems come from two main sources: (1) internal conflicts or unclarities about items on our own commonsense lists, and (2) interpersonal conflicts in which we find that others' lists disagree (e.g., are longer, shorter, or differently weighted). How can I keep this promise and still avoid harm to others? What does it mean to be fair? If he or she doesn't (they don't) value honesty, how can or why should I (we)? What priorities are there among items on the list?

We are driven by such questions into a level of normative ethical thinking beyond moral common sense, to what philosophers call *critical thinking*. At this level, the search is for *criteria* that will justify the inclusion or exclusion of commonsense norms, clarify their applicability in certain circumstances, and resolve conflicts among them.

### Avenues of Critical Thinking in Ethics

A full-dress review of the many ways in which philosophers, past and present, have sought to organize what we are calling critical ethical thinking is beyond the scope of this note. It is possible, however, to sketch briefly three of the more important normative views that have been proposed. These three views will provide some avenues for ethical analysis in the sense that discussions of cases often exemplify, and can even be guided by, one or more of them.

**Utilitarianism**    One of the most influential normative ethical views, at least in the modern period, is utilitarianism. There are numerous variations and refinements, but the basic utilitarian message is that moral common sense is to be governed by a single dominant *goal:* maximizing net expectable utility (or happiness or pleasure or preference or welfare) for all parties affected by a decision or action. Critical thinking, according to utilitarians, consists in testing our ethical rules of thumb against the yardstick of social costs and benefits. It is in this way that we best achieve congruence between our decisions and the moral point of view.

Adopting a purely utilitarian ethic raises many questions and problems: How does one measure utility or happiness? For whom does one measure it (oneself only, one's group, one's society, all societies)? What about the tyranny of the majority in the calculation? Defenders of the view acknowledge such problems but insist that they can be resolved. "At least," they argue, "the utilitarian approach anchors ethical thinking in something resembling a scientific, empirical method."

In the context of general management, utilitarian reasoning frequently manifests itself as a commitment to the social virtues of the market system, both inside the organization and outside. The greatest good for the greatest number comes from competitive decision making, it is argued, and market forces can be relied upon to minimize social harm.

**Contractarianism** A second influential approach to critical thinking in ethics is contractarianism. Again there are variations, but the central idea is that moral common sense is to be governed not by utility maximization, but by fairness. And fairness is explained as a condition that prevails when all individuals are accorded equal respect as participants in social arrangements. The idea of a social contract has appeal in this view because it emphasizes the *rights* of individuals to a veto in a way that utilitarianism does not.

Contractarianism in its various forms has been criticized, of course. Questions are raised about the clarity and sufficiency of its basic commitment to equality, about the practicality of its focus on rights, and about what some perceive to be its excessive emphasis on tolerance and individual liberties.

In general management settings, contractarian reasoning manifests itself in concerns about the implications of corporate policy for consumer rights, employee rights, and fair treatment of minorities. These rights-based arguments are often directly counter to utilitarian arguments on such topics.

**Pluralism** The third approach to critical thinking in ethics is perhaps the least unified and systematic, even though it is widely held. We will refer to it as pluralism. The governing ethical idea in this view is *duty*. For the pluralist, critical thinking about the first-level duties suggested by our moral common sense leads not to some single outside umpire (such as utility or fairness) but to a more reflective examination of duty itself. One must try to economize on one's list of basic duties, subordinating some to others, relying in the end on one's faculty of moral perception (or intuition or conscience) for the resolution of hard cases. The pluralist focuses on the rightness or wrongness of actions as moral qualities that are distinct from extrinsic concerns such as consequences or rights. Fidelity and honesty are obligations not because they lead to more welfare or because others have a right to expect them; they are just basic duties. Not to live by such duties is simply to be corrupt, bad-willed, to lack moral integrity.

Those unsympathetic with pluralism point to problems about securing interpersonal agreement about basic duties (either what they are or how to weight them) and claim that pluralism does not take us far enough beyond moral common sense (the point of critical thinking in the first place). Defenders acknowledge these difficulties but insist that our convictions about basic duties and obligations are more trustworthy than our convictions about avenues that try too hard to systematize them.

Pluralistic reasoning in general management is evidenced by appeals to principle. Basic obligations—such as honesty, integrity, and consistency—are cited. Rights are viewed as shorthand devices for corresponding duties to respect others and utilitarian reasoning is identified with expediency. Some actions, it is argued, are just wrong whatever the consequences. These three avenues are summarized in Figure D.

| Avenue | Type | Managing moral common sense |
|---|---|---|
| Utilitarianism | Goal-based | What action or policy maximizes benefit/cost? |
| Contractarianism | Rights-based | What action or policy most fairly respects rights? |
| Pluralism | Duty-based | What action or policy reflects the stronger duty? |

**FIGURE D**
Three avenues of critical thinking.

Each of these three isms could be pursued at great length, both conceptually and historically. For our present purposes, however, it is enough to see them as concentrations of effort at critical thinking in ethical matters. Each represents a worthwhile perspective from which specific moral issues might be addressed, if not resolved. All have in common a serious concern with improving the clarity and consistency of ethical judgment.

The debate over the moral acceptability or unacceptability of euthanasia affords a particularly striking example of how the three avenues can come into play at once. Both proponents *and* opponents of euthanasia argue on the basis of social utility (or disutility), on the basis of rights (of the living and of the dying), and on the basis of duties (to alleviate suffering or not to kill). Too often, perhaps, the parties to such arguments either fail to examine the full implications of the critical avenue they adopt or fail to appreciate that others are adopting a different avenue.

### Getting Down to Cases

What are some of the implications of the foregoing in the context of case analysis? Can the study of ethics-related management problems be improved through the use of such categories?

If these questions are interpreted as requests for decision procedures, the answers will be disappointing. But analytical *guidance* is present and accounted for. The following sets of questions offer a way to structure study and discussion:

1 Are there ethical issues involved in this case? Centrally or peripherally? Is a decision required?
2 If there are ethical issues involved, under which of the two broad roles of the general manager do they fall (A-transactions or B-transactions)? Or are both involved? How? What, precisely, are the ethical issues in each category?
3 From a descriptive ethical perspective, what appear to be the critical ethical assumptions or values shown by the persons or organizations in the case?
4 From the point of view of maximizing utility for those affected, what is the best course of action? What facts in the case support this conclusion?
5 From the point of view of fairness or concern for individual rights, what is the best course of action? Again, what facts support this conclusion?
6 From the point of view of setting priorities among duties and obligations, what should be done? Why?
7 Do the three avenues converge on a course of action or do they diverge?
8 If they diverge, which avenue should override?
9 Are there ethically relevant considerations in the case that are not captured by any of the three avenues? What are they?
10 What is the decision or action plan?

These questions are not exhaustive, but analysis based on them will almost certainly enhance the kind of learning that case discussion affords. The result may be a convergence of opinion or not; when it is not, explanations should be pursued. In either case, the moral point of view will have been sought out and joined to the administrative point of view. Sound leadership demands no more and no less.

## SELECTED BIBLIOGRAPHY

Brandt, Richard B. *A Theory of the Good and the Right.* London: Oxford University Press, 1979.

Dworkin, Ronald. *Taking Rights Seriously.* Cambridge: Harvard University Press, 1978.

Frankena, William K. *Ethics.* 2d ed., Englewood Cliffs, N.J.: Prentice-Hall, 1973.

Fried, Charles. *Right and Wrong.* Cambridge: Harvard University Press, 1978.

Hare, R. M. *Moral Thinking.* London: Oxford University Press, 1981.

Rawls, John. *A Theory of Justice.* Cambridge: Harvard University Press, 1971.

# Illustrative Case Analysis for Consolidated Foods Corporation (A)

The following discussion is offered as a guide for case analysis with "newcomers" to the case method in mind. We shall confine ourselves to "Consolidated Foods Corporation (A)" so that "Consolidated Foods Corporation (B)" and "Note on the TV Advertising and Programming Controversy, 1981" can be used as a regular classroom assignment (see pages 280–307). We begin with a brief summary of the case.

## SUMMARY OF THE CASE

John Bryan, chief executive officer of Consolidated Foods, had been receiving numerous individual consumer complaint letters as well as communications from organized groups. The most recent was an interim evaluation of the corporation's advertising and programming undertaken by the Coalition for Better Television. Lurking behind these communications was a veiled threat of boycott publicity against Hanes hosiery products (Hanes, L'eggs, L'Erin

cosmetics) as well as other Consolidated Foods consumer products (e.g., Shasta, Electrolux, Sara Lee, Kahn's meats, Monarch foods, and others). Hanes had been listed in some of the TV monitoring results as the top "user of sex in commercials."

## SALIENT FACTS AND ISSUES IMPLICIT IN THE CASE

Though not stated explicitly, the following items can be inferred from the text and exhibits in the case:

1   Bryan did not know the magnitude of the boycott threat. His staff estimated that the impact of a boycott would be small, yet the issues involved were clearly heating up in the press and the possibility existed that the company could be hurt. Perhaps more importantly, Bryan himself was conflicted over the meaning of the whole situation.

Portions of this case analysis are reprinted with permission from an essay entitled "Should Sponsors Screen for Moral Values?" by Kenneth E. Goodpaster, *The Hastings Center Report,* Volume 13, Number 6 (December 1983), pp. 17–18.

**2**   Like many of the people in the civic and religious groups forming the Coalition, Bryan was raised in the conservative Christian South. He knew of and shared many of the values of the protesters. Yet the exigencies of his corporate role demanded that he look at the issues involved with many points of view in mind.

**3**   He did not watch television much, though on occasion he had been seriously dismayed by what was passing for "entertainment" on the networks. Family values were not in evidence. Sex and violence were being depicted with increasing boldness to attract viewers and ultimately to sell consumer products. Once, when a particularly offensive program (and his company's sponsorship of it) was called to his attention by a complaint letter, he responded with an embarrassed apology and a memo to the advertising agency involved with the account in question, asking for more careful guidelines.

**4**   Bryan was probably perplexed. He felt strongly that advertisers, from self-interest if from no other motive, had to exercise care in choosing both ads and programs for sponsorship. Good taste and social awareness were essential to the marketing effectiveness of any consumer goods company. On the other hand, the products (women's hosiery) and target markets of the Hanes division seemed to demand a somewhat "sexy" image and a programming policy that reached the right customers. Nielsen ratings were important indicators of what the relevant public apparently enjoyed watching on television. The consumer was, in some sense, getting no more and no less than he or she wanted in this domain. Was it a corporation's place to do anything but "follow" the market?

**5**   Even if the "Moral Majority" and other groups thought differently, they were probably in the minority. Yet so were other important groups that challenged establishment values, including civil rights groups in the sixties. Such minorities could work through the political process for change— or they could bring their concerns to the public through protests and boycotts. In the present case, the specter of government censorship of networks and advertisers was not appealing to any of the parties. That seemed to leave the networks and the advertisers as targets. Bryan knew this, and as much as he would have liked to be rid of the problem, it persisted. Corporations were being challenged to reexamine their largely quantitative, market-following media policies in favor of more qualitative, value-sensitive policies. The marketplace was speaking, but with profoundly mixed messages.

**6**   Another complicating feature of Bryan's situation was the fact that Hanes was a recent acquisition. Its own culture, having evolved independently over many successful years, was less conservative than that of a new parent company. Hanes had methodically cultivated a "glamorous" image, a Madison Avenue appeal that was less cautious and conventional in approach than the midwestern profile of the other divisions in Consolidated Foods. Some aspects of this difference were probably welcomed, even sought; but in the present case, they might have been an unforeseen hazard. The game of mergers and acquisitions involves more than balance sheets and income statements and business unit synergies. It also involves cultures and values in subtle, but very real, ways.

Since an adequate case analysis will focus not only on the facts, analysis, and decision itself, but will often move to the more general issues raised by the decision, the following observations may help relate this case to the conceptual side of business ethics.

### CONCEPTUAL OVERVIEW OF CASE

As we reflect on the problem that faced John Bryan, we can discern most, if not all, of the central ideas discussed in the note "Some

Avenues for Ethical Analysis in General Management."

*First,* we can see that Consolidated Foods is both a "moral agent" in a wider social environment and itself a "moral environment" for its subunits, managers, and employees. John Bryan's responsibilities, therefore, extended in both outward and inward directions—like the image of Janus at the gates of ancient Roman cities.

*Second,* as a moral agent, we see the corporation in this case confronting the apparent insufficiency of two primary "substitutes" for value awareness or conscience: the visible hand of law and government intervention and the invisible hand of market competition. The problem that faced John Bryan resisted resolution through *either* of these standard channels. In fact, it was in some ways a *product* of the repugnance he felt toward the first (censorship) and the insensitivity he was noticing in the second (standard advertising practice). The corporation and its leadership seemed called upon to make value judgments without being able to rely solely upon "the system."

*Third,* as a moral environment, we see the corporation in this case having to deal with questions about its own culture. Can a highly diversified company effectively manage a nontrivial internal value system? If so, what are the responsibilities of corporate leaders for this task? Can they avoid both the Scylla of standing for nothing and the Charybdis of moral imperialism toward employees? If not, what are the implications for corporate ethics as more and more large organizations grow by a process of merger and acquisition?

*Fourth,* if corporate ethics demands, as it appears to, that managers and their organizations "institutionalize" *more* than the values implicit in law and the marketplace, *where* are these larger values to be sought and how are they to be implemented? What strategies, structures, systems, and management styles does this process require?

*Fifth,* and finally, if we seek guidance on the above issues by looking to the natural analogy between the moral life of the individual and the "moral life" of the organization, do we *gain* clarity or *lose* it? As individuals, we regularly face the fact that the imperatives of law (social sanctions) and self-interest (the "market") are insufficient for moral judgment. Can we project not only darkness but also light from this individual challenge to the level of organizational policy and governance?

John Bryan's situation as a corporate executive is paradigmatic in many ways of the situations of business leaders across the country and around the world. And the issues can be allowed to vary from advertising policies through environmental impacts of more ordinary kinds, to employee rights and international business practices. At the core of such issues are questions about the legitimacy, the authority, and the meaning of the moral point of view in the management of institutions.

## ANALYSIS AND DECISION

An adequate analysis leading to a decision in this case will include answers to the following questions:

What is John Bryan's *problem* at the end of the case?

What is the *magnitude* of the problem?

What is the *origin* of the problem?

What are his *options?*

What would you do in his place and why? ("Action Plan")

The following are some suggestions that may help in addressing these questions.

### Diagnostic Matrix

a  The first three questions invite us to construct a matrix whose column headings are "problem," "magnitude of problem," and "origin of problem." The row headings might be grouped in the two broad categories "internal" and "external."

b  For example, a row in the "internal" category might read "communication; trivial; current ad and media guidelines." A row in the "external" category might read "public relations; moderately serious; conservative revival after Reagan election."

c  For each "problem" identified in the matrix, options should be considered and some aspect of the action plan should address each option.

## Options

However the problem identification and diagnosis fall out, options can be generated with respect to each problem category. In the process, however, the total picture should be kept in mind, not just one component.

*Internally,* Bryan can:

a  Do nothing.

b  Suggest a low profile to Hanes management and perhaps modest revisions in the guidelines.

c  Suggest serious marketing policy changes, perhaps in the spirit of the recent corporate policy statement.

*Externally,* the main options appear to be:

a  Ignore Wildmon's communication and the Coalition's activities entirely.

b  Politely (or impolitely) respond but forget the whole matter or concentrate on the internal options (above).

c  Actively and openly cooperate in various ways with the Coalition.

The pros and cons of each option should be spelled out explicitly and the preferred option(s) defended. In this connection, the three "avenues" spelled out in the ethics note might be used to evaluate the options. (See the list of questions in the last section of the note.)

## Action Plan

It is not enough, in doing a case preparation, to summarize, conceptualize, diagnose, and defend broad options. Attention to *implementation* is also essential. And this means that an action plan must be developed to carry forward the preferred option(s):

- Will the preferred option(s) affect current corporate or division level policies? How? When?
- What changes, if any, in organizational structure or systems will be required? (For example, reporting relationships, monitoring of advertising copy, program sponsoring decisions, product image or "positioning," division autonomy, etc. Be specific.)
- What interpersonal considerations must be taken into account? How should Bryan relate to Elberson and Fulton internally and to Wildmon externally in carrying out his plan of action?
- How should the wider external environment be considered? (See "Note on TV Advertising and Programming Controversy, 1981.")
- How should Bryan's action be followed up in the medium and longer term? Can further decision points be anticipated?

Attention to these and other such questions may result in reconsideration of the "preferred" option(s). But it is essential to effective and responsible management and often separates "excellent" from "passing" performance in case method discussion.

If there is a "follow on" case study, as there is with "Consolidated Foods Corporation (B)," the action plan can be compared with subsequent events and further analysis of the next stage of decision making can be built on the same general pattern offered here.

# Selected Bibliography

## BUSINESS AND ETHICS

### Anthologies and Casebooks

Alexis, M., and C. Wilson: *Organizational Decision Making.* Prentice-Hall, Englewood Cliffs, NJ, 1967.

Andrews, Kenneth R., ed.: *Ethics in Practice.* Harvard Business School Press, Boston, MA, 1989. (*Harvard Business Review* articles).

Barry, Vincent: *Moral Issues in Business.* Wadsworth, Belmont, CA, 1979.

Beauchamp, Thomas L.: *Case Studies in Business, Society, and Ethics.* Prentice-Hall, Englewood Cliffs, NJ, 1983.

———, and Norman E. Bowie: *Ethical Theory and Business.* 3d ed. Prentice-Hall, Englewood Cliffs, NJ, 1988.

Bradshaw, Thornton, and David Vogel: *Corporations and Their Critics.* McGraw-Hill, New York, 1981.

Braybrooke, David: *Ethics in the World of Business.* Rowman and Allanheld, Totowa, NJ, 1983.

Brozen, Y., E. Johnson, and C. Powers: *Can the Market Sustain an Ethic?* University of Chicago Press, Chicago, IL, 1978.

Carroll, Archie B.: *Business and Society: Ethics and Stakeholder Management.* South-Western, Cincinnati, OH, 1989.

———: *Managing Corporate Social Responsibility.* Little, Brown, Boston, MA, 1977.

David, Keith, William Frederick, and Robert Blomstrom: *Business and Society: Concepts and Policy Issues.* McGraw-Hill, New York, 1980.

DeGeorge, R. T., and J. A. Pichler: *Ethics, Free Enterprise, and Public Policy.* Oxford University Press, New York, 1978.

Desjardins, J., and J. McCall: *Contemporary Issues in Business Ethics.* Wadsworth, Belmont, CA, 1984.

Donaldson, T., and P. Werhane: *Ethical Issues in Business: A Philosophical Approach.* 3d ed. Prentice-Hall, Englewood Cliffs, NJ, 1989.

Goodpaster, K.: *Ethics in Management.* Harvard Business School (9-985-001), Boston, MA, 1984.

———, and T. Piper: *Managerial Decision Making and Ethical Values.* Harvard Business School Publishing Division, Boston, MA, 1989.

———, and K. Sayre: *Ethics and Problems of the 21st Century.* University of Notre Dame Press, Notre Dame, IN, 1979.

Hahn, Frank, and Martin Hollis, eds.: *Philosophy and Economic Theory.* Oxford University Press, New York, 1979.

Hampshire, S.: *Public and Private Morality.* Cambridge University Press, Cambridge, England, 1978.

Hoffman, W. Michael: *Proceedings of the First National Conference on Business Ethics.* Bentley College, Waltham, MA, 1977.

———: *Proceedings of the Second National*

*Conference on Business Ethics.* Bentley College, Waltham, MA, 1978.

——————, and Jennifer Moore: *Business Ethics: Readings and Cases in Corporate Morality.* 2d ed. McGraw-Hill, New York, 1990.

——————, Jennifer Moore, and David Fedo: *Corporate Governance and Institutionalizing Ethics.* Lexington Books, Lexington, MA, 1984.

Jones, D., ed.: *Business, Religion, and Ethics.* Oelgeschlager, Gunn, and Hain, Cambridge, MA, 1982.

——————, ed.: *Doing Ethics in Business.* Oelgeschlager, Gunn, and Hain, Cambridge, MA, 1982.

Litschert, R., and E. Nicholson: *The Corporate Role and Ethical Behavior: Concepts and Cases.* Van Nostrand, New York, 1977.

Luthans, Fred, Richard Hodgetts, and Kenneth Thompson: *Social Issues in Business.* 3d ed. Macmillan, New York, 1976.

Missner, Marshall: *Ethics of the Business System.* Alfred, Sherman Oaks, CA, 1980.

Molander, Earl A.: *Responsive Capitalism.* McGraw-Hill, New York, 1980.

Newton, Lisa H.: *Ethics in America.* Source Reader and Study Guide to Accompany Telecourse. Prentice-Hall, Englewood Cliffs, NJ, 1989.

Partridge, Scott: *Cases in Business and Society.* Prentice-Hall, Englewood Cliffs, NJ, 1982.

Regan, Tom, ed.: *Just Business: New Introductory Essays in Business Ethics.* Random House, New York, 1984.

——————, and Donald VanDeVeer, eds.: *And Justice for All.* Rowman and Littlefield, Totowa, NJ, 1982.

Sayre, K. M.: *Values in the Electric Power Industry.* University of Notre Dame Press, Notre Dame, IN, 1977.

Serafini, Anthony: *Ethics and Social Concern.* Paragon House Publishers, New York, 1989.

Sethi, S. P.: *Up Against the Corporate Wall.* 3d ed. Prentice-Hall, Englewood Cliffs, NJ, 1977.

Walton, Clarence: *The Ethics of Corporate Conduct.* Prentice-Hall, Englewood Cliffs, NJ, 1977.

Williams, Oliver, and John Houck, eds.: *The Judeo-Christian Vision and the Modern Corporation.* University of Notre Dame Press, Notre Dame, IN, 1982.

## Books

Ackerman, Robert W.: *The Social Challenge to Business.* Harvard University Press, Cambridge, MA, 1975.

Andrews, Kenneth R.: *The Concept of Corporate Strategy.* 3d ed. Irwin, Homewood, IL, 1987.

Arrow, Kenneth R.: *The Limits of Organization.* Norton, New York, 1974.

Badaracco, Joseph L., Jr., and Richard R. Ellsworth: *Leadership and the Quest for Integrity.* Harvard Business School Press, Boston, MA, 1989.

Barnard, Chester I.: *The Functions of the Executive.* 30th anniversary ed. Harvard University Press, Cambridge, MA, 1979. (First published 1938.)

Behrman, Jack: *Discourses in Ethics and Business.* Oelgeschlager, Bunn, and Hain, Cambridge, MA, 1981.

Bell, Daniel: *The Cultural Contradictions of Capitalism.* Basic Books, New York, 1976.

Bellah, Robert N., et al.: *Habits of the Heart.* University of California Press, Berkeley, CA, 1985.

Berger, Peter: *Pyramids of Sacrifice.* Doubleday, Garden City, NY, 1976.

Bok, Sissela: *Lying: Moral Choice in Public and Private Life.* Pantheon, New York, 1978.

Bowie, Norman E.: *Making Ethical Decisions.* McGraw-Hill, New York, 1985.

——————, and Ronald F. Duska: *Business Ethics.* 2d ed. Prentice-Hall, Englewood Cliffs, NJ, 1990.

Buchanan, Allen: *Ethics, Efficiency, and the Market.* Rowman and Allenheld, Totawa, NJ, 1985.

Buono, A. F., and Larry Nichols: *Corporate Policy, Values, and Social Responsibility.* Praeger, New York, 1985.

Cavanagh, Gerald F.: *American Business Values.* 2d ed. Prentice-Hall, Englewood Cliffs, NJ, 1990.

Chandler, Alfred D.: *The Visible Hand: The Managerial Revolution in American Business.* Harvard University Press, Cambridge, MA, 1977.

Chewning, Richard C.: *Business in a Changing Culture.* Reston Publishing Company, Reston, VA, 1984.

Clinard, M., and P. Yeager: *Corporate Crime.* Free Press, New York, 1980.

Deal, T., and A. Kennedy: *Corporate Cultures.* Addison-Wesley, Reading, MA, 1982.

DeGeorge, Richard: *Business Ethics.* 2d ed. Macmillan, New York, 1986.

Donaldson, Thomas. *Corporations and Morality.* Prentice-Hall, Englewood Cliffs, NJ, 1982.

——————: *The Ethics of International Business.* Oxford University Press, New York, 1989.

——————, and A. R. Gini: *Case Studies in Business Ethics.* 2d ed. Prentice-Hall, Englewood Cliffs, NJ, 1990.

Drucker, Peter: *The Age of Discontinuity.* Harper, New York, 1968.

Dyke, C.: *Philosophy of Economics.* Prentice-Hall, Englewood Cliffs, NJ, 1981.

Estes, Ralph: *Corporate Social Accounting.* Wiley, New York, 1976.

Etzioni, Amitai: *The Moral Dimension.* Free Press, New York, 1988.

Evans, William A.: *Management Ethics: An Intercultural Perspective.* Martinus Nijhoff, Dordrecht, Netherlands, 1981.

Ewen, Stuart: *Captains of Consciousness: Advertising and the Social Roots of the Consumer Culture.* McGraw-Hill, New York, 1976.

Ewing, David: *Freedom Inside the Organization: Bringing Civil Liberties to the Workplace.* Dutton, New York, 1976.

—————: *Do It My Way or You're Fired!* Wiley, New York, 1983.

Frank, Robert H.: *Passions Within Reason.* Norton, New York, 1988.

Freeman, R. Edward, and Daniel K. Gilbert, Jr.: *Corporate Strategy and the Search for Ethics.* Prentice-Hall, Englewood Cliffs, NJ, 1988.

Friedman, Milton: *Capitalism and Freedom.* University of Chicago Press, Chicago, IL, 1962.

Fullinwider, Robert K.: *The Reverse Discrimination Controversy: A Moral and Legal Analysis.* Rowman and Littlefield, Totowa, NJ, 1980.

Garrett, Thomas M: *Business Ethics.* Prentice-Hall, Englewood Cliffs, NJ, 1966.

Gilligan, Carol: *In a Different Voice.* Harvard University Press, Cambridge, MA, 1982.

Goldman, Alan: *The Moral Foundations of Professional Ethics.* Rowman and Littlefield, Totowa, NJ, 1980.

Heilbroner, Robert L.: *Business Civilization in Decline.* Norton, New York, 1976.

—————: *The Worldly Philosophers.* 3d ed. Simon and Schuster, New York, 1967.

Hessen, Robert L.: *In Defense of the Corporation.* Hoover Institution Press, Stanford, CA, 1979.

Hovck, John W., and Oliver F. Williams: *Catholic Social Teaching and the United States Economy.* University Press of America, Lanham, MD, 1984.

Illich, Ivan: *Energy and Equity.* Harper & Row, New York, 1974.

Jackall, Robert: *Moral Mazes.* Oxford University Press, New York, 1988.

Johnson, Deborah G.: *Computer Ethics.* Prentice-Hall, Englewood Cliffs, NJ, 1985.

Kristol, Irving: *Two Cheers for Capitalism.* Basic Books, New York, 1978.

Linowes, David S.: *The Corporate Conscience.* Hawthorn, New York, 1974.

Lodge, George: *The New American Ideology.* Knopf, New York, 1979.

Maccoby, Michael. *The Gamesman.* Simon and Schuster, New York, 1976.

—————: *The Leader.* Simon and Schuster, New York, 1981.

Miles, Robert: *Coffin Nails and Corporate Strategies.* Prentice-Hall, Englewood Cliffs, NJ, 1982.

Mishan, E. J.: *Technology and Growth: The Price We Pay.* Praeger, New York, 1969. (Second printing 1971.)

Nash, L. L.: *Good Intentions Aside.* Harvard Business School Press, Boston, MA, 1990.

Novak, Michael: *The American Vision.* American Enterprise Institute, Washington, DC, 1978.

—————: *Free Persons and the Common Good.* Madison Books, Lanham, MD, 1989.

—————: *The Spirit of Democratic Capitalism.* Simon and Schuster, New York, 1982.

O'Toole, James: *Vanguard Management.* Doubleday, Garden City, NY, 1985.

O'Toole, John: *The Trouble with Advertising.* Chelsea House, New York, 1981.

Pascale, R., and A. Athos: *The Art of Japanese Management.* Simon and Schuster, New York, 1981.

Peck, M. Scott: *The Road Less Traveled.* Simon and Schuster, New York, 1978.

Peters, T., and R. Waterman: *In Search of Excellence.* Harper & Row, New York, 1982.

Petit, Thomas: *The Moral Crisis in Management.* McGraw-Hill, New York, 1967.

Powers, Charles W., and David Vogel: *Ethics in the Education of Business Managers.* Hastings Center, Hastings-on-Hudson, NY, 1980.

Sathe, Vijay: *Cultural and Related Corporate Realities.* Irwin, Homewood, IL, 1985.

Sayre, Kenneth M., et al.: *Regulation, Values, and the Public Interest.* University of Notre Dame Press, Notre Dame, IN, 1980.

Schaef, Anne Wilson, and Diane Fassel: *The Addictive Organization.* Harper & Row, New York, 1988.

Selekman, Benjamin: *A Moral Philosophy for Management.* McGraw-Hill, New York, 1959.

Selznick, Philip: *Leadership in Administration: A Sociological Interpretation.* Harper & Row, New York, 1957.

Shames, Laurence: *The Hunger for More.* Times Books, New York, 1989.

Silk, L., and D. Vogel: *Ethics and Profits: The Crisis of Confidence in American Business.* Simon and Schuster, New York, 1976.

Simon, Herbert A. *Administrative Behavior.* 3d ed. Macmillan, New York, 1976.

Smith, Craig N. *Morality and the Market.* Routledge, London, 1990.

Solomon, Robert, and Kristine Hanson: *Above the Bottom Line.* Harcourt Brace Jovanovich, New York, 1983.

Steckmest, F. W.: *Corporate Performance.* McGraw-Hill, New York, 1982.

Stevens, Edward: *Business Ethics.* Paulist Press, Ramsey, NJ, 1979.

Stone, Christopher: *Where the Law Ends: The Social Control of Corporate Behavior.* Harper & Row, New York, 1975.

Thurow, Lester C.: *The Zero-Sum Society.* Penguin, New York, 1982.

Toffler, Barbara Ley: *Tough Choices.* Wiley, New York, 1986.

Velasquez, Manual: *Business Ethics: Concepts and Cases.* 2d ed. Prentice-Hall, Englewood Cliffs, NJ, 1988.

Vietor, Richard H. K.: *Strategic Management in the Regulatory Environment.* Prentice-Hall, Englewood Cliffs, NJ, 1982.

Walton, Clarence C.: *Ethos and the Executive.* Prentice-Hall, Englewood Cliffs, NJ, 1969.

———: *The Moral Manager.* Ballinger, Cambridge, MA, 1988.

Werhane, Patricia: *Persons, Rights, and Corporations.* Prentice-Hall, Englewood Cliffs, NJ, 1985.

Westin, Alan F.: *Whistle-Blowing!* McGraw-Hill, New York, 1981.

Williams, O., and J. Houck: *Full Value.* Harper & Row, New York, 1978.

Zaleznik, Abraham, and Manfred F. R. Kets de Vries: *Power and the Corporate Mind.* Houghton Mifflin, Boston, MA, 1975.

## PHILOSOPHICAL ETHICS: GENERAL

Brandt, Richard B.: *A Theory of the Good and the Right.* Oxford University Press, New York, 1979.

Donagan, Alan: *The Theory of Morality.* University of Chicago Press, Chicago, IL, 1977.

Dworkin, Ronald: *Taking Rights Seriously.* Harvard University Press, Cambridge, MA, 1977.

Edwards, James E.: *Ethics Without Philosophy.* University Presses of Florida, Gainesville, FL, 1982.

Foot, Philippa: *Virtues and Vices and Other Essays in Moral Philosophy.* University of California Press, Berkeley, CA, 1978.

Frankena, William K.: *Ethics.* 2d ed. Prentice-Hall, Englewood Cliffs, NJ, 1973.

———: *Thinking About Morality.* University of Michigan Press, Ann Arbor, MI, 1980.

Fried, Charles: *Right and Wrong.* Harvard University Press, Cambridge, MA, 1978.

Gewirth, Alan: *Reason and Morality.* University of Chicago Press, Chicago, IL, 1978.

Goodpaster, Kenneth E., ed.: *Perspective on Morality: Essays of W. K. Frankena.* University of Notre Dame Press, Notre Dame, IN, 1976.

Hare, R. M.: *Moral Thinking.* Oxford University Press, New York, 1981.

Harman, Gilbert: *The Nature of Morality.* Oxford University Press, New York, 1977.

James, William: *Pragmatism.* New American Library, New York, 1907.

MacIntyre, Alastair: *A Short History of Ethics.* Macmillan, New York, 1966.

———: *After Virtue.* University of Notre Dame Press, Notre Dame, IN, 1981.

Mackie, John: *Ethics: Inventing Right and Wrong.* Penguin, New York, 1977.

Melden, A. I., ed.: *Ethical Theories: A Book of Readings.* Prentice-Hall, Englewood Cliffs, NJ, 1967.

Midgley, Mary: *Heart and Mind: The Varieties of Moral Experience.* St. Martin's Press, New York, 1981.

Nagel, Thomas: *The Possibility of Altruism.* Oxford University Press, New York, 1970.

Nozick, Robert: *Philosophical Explanations.* Harvard University Press, Cambridge, MA, 1981.

Rawls, John: *A Theory of Justice.* Harvard University Press, Cambridge, MA, 1971.

Regan, Donald: *Utilitarianism and Cooperation.* Oxford University Press, New York, 1980.

Singer, Peter: *Practical Ethics.* Cambridge University Press, Cambridge, England, 1979.

Smart, J. J. C., and B. Williams: *Utilitarianism: For and Against.* Cambridge University Press, Cambridge, England, 1973.

Tamari, Meir: *"With All Your Possessions"—Jewish Ethics and Economic Life.* Free Press, New York, 1987.

Williams, Bernard: *Ethics and the Limits of Philosophy.* Harvard University Press, Cambridge, MA, 1985.

———: *Morality: An Introduction to Ethics.* Harper & Row, New York, 1972.

## JOURNALS

*Applied Philosophy.* Indian River Community College, Fort Pierce, FL 33450.

*Business Ethics Quarterly.* Loyola University of Chicago, Chicago, IL 60626.

*Business and Professional Ethics Journal.* Center for Applied Philosophy, University of Florida, Gainesville, FL 32611.

*Business and Society Review.* 870 Seventh Avenue, New York, NY 10019.

*Ethics.* University of Chicago Press, 5801 S. Ellis Avenue, Chicago, IL 60637.

*ethikos.* 799 Broadway, Suite 541, New York, NY 10003.

*Harvard Business Review.* Soldiers Field Road, Boston, MA 02163.

*Hastings Center Report.* 360 Broadway, Hastings-on-Hudson, NY 10706.

*Journal of Business Ethics.* University of Guelph, Ontario, Canada.

*Philosophy and Public Affairs.* 41 William Street, Princeton, NJ 08540.

*The Public Interest.* Box 542, Old Chelsea, New York, NY 10014.

## NOTE

Additional bibliographical material is available through Professor Michael Hoffman, Center for Business Ethics, Bentley College, Waltham, MA 02154; in Donald G. Jones: *A Bibliography of Business Ethics (1976–1980),* University Press of Virginia, Charlottesville, VA, 1982; and Mary Gentile, ed.: *Business Ethics,* Harvard Business School Selective Bibliography of Case Materials, Notes, and Harvard Business Review Reprints Concerning Values, Leadership, and Corporate Responsibility, Harvard Business School Publishing Division, Boston, MA, 1990.